AMERICA'S ENERGY

AMERICA'S ENERGY

Reports from *The Nation*
On 100 Years of Struggles
For the Democratic Control
Of Our Resources

Edited by

ROBERT ENGLER

Pantheon Books · New York · A **Nation** *Book*

Articles appearing in the above work were previously published in *The Nation*: Copyright 1919, 1920, 1921, 1922, 1923, 1924, 1925, 1928, 1929, 1931, 1932, 1933, 1934, 1936, 1938, 1939, 1941, 1942, 1944, 1945, 1947, 1948, 1950, 1951, 1952, 1953, 1954, © 1955, 1956, 1958, 1964, 1965, 1966, 1967, 1969, 1971, 1972, 1973, 1974, 1975, 1976, 1977, 1979, 1980 by The Nation Associates.

Library of Congress Cataloging in Publication Data
Main entry under title:
America's energy.
Includes index.
1. Energy policy—United States—History—Ad-
dresses, essays, lectures. 2. Power resources—
United States—History—Addresses, essays, lectures.
I. Engler, Robert.   II. Nation (New York)
HD9502.U52A44   333.79′0973   80–7715
ISBN 0–394–51142–5
ISBN 0–394–73909–4 (pbk.)

Manufactured in the United States of America

FIRST EDITION

For Carey McWilliams

CONTENTS

PART III   OIL

Public Resources

Corporate Control

The Widening Reach

The Imperial Economy

"Energy Crisis"

PART IV   NUCLEAR POWER

PART V   ALTERNATIVES

PART VI   AFTERWORD

ACKNOWLEDGMENTS

VICTOR NAVASKY, editor of *The Nation* since 1978, made the initial proposal to me of an energy source book constructed from *Nation* articles. His innocent suggestion subsequently led me to go through the more than two hundred bound volumes that span the magazine's 115-year history. Naomi Kleinberg, a *Nation* intern, took responsibility for Xeroxing the countless articles that I had identified as good prospects for inclusion and which made up an original manuscript several times the size of the present collection. Karen Wilcox and *The Nation* staff were most helpful in tracking down stray issues, articles, and citations. No one at the magazine had a voice in the selection or final organization of the material. Inea Bushnaq contributed a valued critical and literary eye when reading through the progressively slimmer versions for another judgment as to whether the collection "added up." I hope it does.

ROBERT ENGLER
April 1980

INTRODUCTION

ENERGY POLICY is now recognized as central to the performance of the domestic and the global political economy. Choices about energy are intertwined with employment patterns, inflation, community survival, and war and peace. American national interest, once on the frontier of western Pennsylvania, now embraces almost every region of the earth, including the seabed.

When World War I ended, the victors hastened to dismember the defeated empires and claim the oil fields of the Middle East. It was freely predicted that "the next world war" would be over oil—the fuel displacing coal as the determinant of national power. World War II was not fought over oil. But the international arrangements made in its wake helped to integrate the great reserves of the Middle East into a corporate world order controlled from the West. The Mediterranean became an American sea, and the energy supply lines for "the American century" seemed firmly in place. In the wings was nuclear power to assure military supremacy and keep the American system "number one" should fossil fuel demand ultimately outrun supply.

The United States was soon using one third of the world's daily energy output. The consumption of more and more was celebrated as the key to individual growth and national greatness. But the assumption that this was a natural order of things received some setbacks. As the Western hold over producing areas tightened, rising nationalist movements challenged their countries' assigned role as reservoirs on tap for the "advanced" industrialized world. American faith that progress was automatic and that no balance sheet for the hazards of securing and utilizing energy need be kept was undermined as the costs of an energy-intensive economy were shifted back home and an increasing percentage of the American population became aware of their vulnerability.

As belief fades in the magic of technology and the potential of atomic power, the efficacy of the political and corporate order in defining the public interest and protecting personal well-being is now sharply questioned. Is the nation approaching the point when the unstated contemporary social contract, under which the people concede their political power over fundamental decisions in return for assurance of economic opportunity, will be abrogated?

While the United States remains blessed with more abundant energy resources than most nations, increasingly it draws its petroleum from overseas. And now American leadership claims vital national interests in the Persian Gulf. With the focus on a presumed Soviet threat, President Carter has warned that any attempt "by any outside force" to gain control of the region will be "repelled by any means necessary, including military force." Arms, food, and aid are marshalled to protect our access to oil and support the dwindling number of rulers who, despite the growing hostility of their own people, have not as of yet repudiated such hegemony. Did the prophecies err—by one war?

Two major concerns shape this collection: a sense of politics and a sense of history. An examination of the recurring struggles over the control of energy will, it is hoped, contribute to an understanding of the sources of the present "energy crisis" of the American economy. Such background may also aid in creating alternatives to the present frightening course so often portrayed as inevitable.

Looking back on the overall record on specific fuels, first coal and then each of its successors as it became important to the economy, one is struck by the sharpness of the battle lines that were frequently formed. There were critical appraisals of the performance of private ownership and challenges to the appropriateness of such power in a democratic society. There were calls for new political experiments such as regional planning. The possibility of cooperatives and of public control enjoyed the support of political movements. People believed that there were choices and that they could help make them.

Current debate, in contrast, tends to stress technological solutions. There are, of course, serious technical problems in formulating energy policy. But these are advanced at the expense of underlying political considerations. Advocates of capital-intensive programs for synthetic and nuclear fuels have their visions of the good society, as do those who favor the transition to benign renewable sources. To the former, expanded energy systems will keep the nation powerful and the citizenry independent. Solar advocates foretell the emergence of more human-scale communities where violence against nature and control over one's fellow beings caused by the drive for more energy will be minimized. Where energy options are related to politics, they are treated as though they have no base in past political experience. Where factors of political power are introduced, too often they are confined to specific conflicts, as over the pricing policy for natural gas or the location of a particular nuclear plant. These are important battles and an essential first step for creating a public aware of relationships: as between gas pricing and the oil industry's drive to command all energy forms; between nuclear plants and nuclear war; between corporate power and governmental incapacity. The tougher requirements for mobilizing the political will necessary to challenge the organized power behind the present system and to bring about effective democratic transformation remain largely unexplored.

All camps, with varying emphasis, urge the nation to conserve. Here a major burden is placed upon the "profligate" individual rather than upon the forces that dominate the political economy. Exhorting the householder to turn off the pilot light on the stove or live more simply, however beneficial, offers an easier political course than restructuring the ways the industrial society, including the energy industry itself, allocates capital, employs energy in the production of goods, and generates new wants. Meanwhile, the forces which dominate the going energy structure do everything to encourage the view that such matters are better left to the marketplace and to the presumably apolitical corporate managers. The latter, we are increasingly reminded, share with the best of us a love for science, chamber music, British drama and, incidentally, freedom from accountability for policies that determine the future of the society.

The articles in this collection were chosen from the many hundreds on the subject of energy published in *The Nation* from its inception in 1865 to the present. Never neutral, the magazine provides a unique perspective on American industrial development and the attendant political struggles for accountable policies for coal, hydroelectric power, oil and gas, nuclear energy, synthetic fuels, and renewable alternatives. While the weekly was born at the close of the Civil War in the age of wood, the country was shifting to a coal base to power the railroads, the steel industry, and then the steam turbine. Colonel Drake's discovery in Pennsylvania had occurred just six years earlier, and fortunes and empires were soon to be built upon petroleum.

The first issue reported a week "singularly barren of exciting events." But editor E.L. Godkin and his founding colleagues, who included abolitionist James Miller McKim, Harvard scholar Charles Eliot Norton, and Frederick Law Olmstead, committed themselves to the "maintenance and diffusion of true democratic principles" and the advocacy of whatever measures seemed "likely to promote a more equal distribution of the fruits of progress and civilization." National unity was imperative for a battle-torn nation, as was an abiding concern for the rights of former slaves. They pledged a critical spirit in viewing the public interest and in the arts and letters. Although it was clear that the United States was moving to the industrial stage, the scholars and literary contributors did not at the outset seem sensitive to many of the emerging tensions or to the growing power of business.

The Nation did pass stern moral judgments on corrupt political bosses, venal captains of business, and imperial ventures. But it was savage with pioneering muckrakers such as Henry Demarest Lloyd, who had documented the rise of the oil trust and the influence of monopoly power upon the political process. His *Wealth Against Commonwealth* (1894) was dismissed as "the wildest rant" which saw Standard Oil emissaries behind every institution. ". . . We doubt if Mr. Lloyd feels that the human race is altogether secure in the possession of sunlight."

Ida M. Tarbell's landmark study *The History of the Standard Oil Company* did not fare much better. And Thorstein Veblen's iconoclastic *The Theory of Business Enterprise,* seminal in dissecting the modern industrial system, was in 1905 labeled "a travesty of economics, and an unjust aspersion of our business morality." Nor did *The Nation* take much note of, let alone identify with, socialist, populist, farmer, or worker movements which were standing up to the consolidation of business power.

But it gradually shed its laissez-faire attitude toward economic matters and became absorbed in examining the premises as well as the consequences of American development. During the 1920s the magazine richly documented the conflicts in the coal fields. It drew upon distinguished scholars, activists, and writers to report the battles of miners and their communities for basic rights which would end their treatment as energy colonies. As the sections indicate, these concerns have been maintained to the present, when coal is being rediscovered as possibly the nation's most reliable bulwark against OPEC and overseas cutoffs of oil. (Now the reports come in from the mineral-rich western plains, Indian councils, and union headquarters.)

The battles for fair access to inexpensive electric energy became especially important, and *The Nation* turned to crusaders such as George Norris, Judson King, and Morris L. Cooke to interpret the fights against the utilities and for the public planning of the great river basins. A sustained critical watch was kept on oil and the efforts to bring the resources of the nation, including the public domain, and then of Latin America and the Middle East within the private planning of the corporation. Scandals such as Teapot Dome received extensive coverage as did oil-tainted interventions of the United States government in Mexico and elsewhere. There were frontier articles in the mid 1920s on the willingness of big oil to use workers as guinea pigs in hazardous refinery processes, which have a most contemporary ring. During World War II Washington correspondent I.F. Stone and other journalists kept close tabs on the corporate drive to ensure respectful government treatment and to position themselves for control of the postwar economy. Scientists and liberal political luminaries presented their high hopes and strategies for a peaceful and abundant world order. Atomic energy was hailed in the pages of *The Nation* by Leo Szilard, J.D. Bernal, J. Bronowski, and many others for the promise of unlimited power to end global want. Gradually, more sober reflections on its employment made their appearance, and discussions of the general impact of science and technology upon humanistic values became frequent. Throughout, *The Nation* scrutinized domestic and overseas reactions to American control over energy resources and conducted a continuing investigation into the "energy crisis" of the 1970s. At the same time, it reported on community and congressional fights to win acceptance of benign alternatives independent of the energy industry's timetable.

The volume is organized by energy source and each chapter has an introduction explaining its design. The articles have been chosen to provide some chronological background and suggest the political perspectives. They offer abundant, coherent data and reasoned, although not necessarily harmonious, convictions; generally they reflect the liberal and radical democratic orientation of *The Nation*. Many of the articles have been edited because of length, redundancy within the topic, or extraneous references. The cuts are indicated.

Each chapter illustrates the impact upon people's daily lives of the giant corporate and government forces dominating energy. Cumulatively there emerges a stark record of how precious and often irreplaceable resources have been manipulated and looted in the name of freedom and development. One also gains some sense of the numerous inspiring fights by individuals and regional and national movements for democratic control and of the fragmented but significant attainments toward that goal. Too often this legacy has been obscured or distorted through the pervasive power of private interests, leading to the more troubling conclusion that our history has also been plundered.

Part I
COAL

PREFACE

COAL, OUR MOST abundant fuel which now provides less than 20 percent of national energy, was until recently the dominant fuel in the economy. While the adoption of modern mining technology is vital in the history of coal, the industry has been labor-intensive. The brutal working conditions, hardship, and violence in the lives of miners and mine communities have always attracted compassionate literary, if not political, attention. Perhaps in no other energy-producing setting is the contrast between wealth and poverty, power and powerlessness as dramatically evident as in Appalachia. I have listened to coughing unemployed miners in a rickety union hall discuss ways of keeping the local school open while from the window in plain sight of all an endless train of hopper cars was slowly moving the wealth out of their hollow. It is not hard to understand why Mother Jones once said, "When I get to the other side I shall tell God Almighty about West Virginia."

James M. Cain introduces us to the mountaineer-miner and the setting of his efforts to organize. Economists George Soule, Walton Hamilton, and Colston E. Warne discuss the irrational and wasteful structure of the industry. Congressman Fiorello La Guardia indicts the unequaled barbarity of its labor practices and foresees ultimate government possession of coal and other energy resources. Cooperative League President James Peter Warbasse rejects nationalization and calls for ownership and control by consumers. The cynical disregard of health and safety in the mines is vividly described by novelist Harriette Simpson Arnow and public interest attorneys J. Davitt McAteer and L. Thomas Galloway. Harry M. Caudill, author and attorney, calls for a regional planning authority for Appalachia. Poet Wendell Berry tells of the devastation wrought by coal companies which profit from strip mining; and Duane Lockard, a political scientist from a miner family, writes about the indifference to unemployment shown in mine mechanization decisions. Curtis Seltzer, a coal writer and activist, sees the imperative for a revitalized labor movement that will organize coal as part of a larger coalition of workers to challenge an industry that has been incorporated into a global energy empire. From many of the readings we gain an appreciation of how frequently business, union, and government planning for coal fails to consult the people whose lives will be most directly affected. One is left to speculate about the limits of reform in situations where basic power relationships remain largely unchanged.

WEST VIRGINIA:
A MINE-FIELD MELODRAMA (1923)

James M. Cain

. . . COAL, COAL, COAL; everywhere coal. On one side of the creek, away up the slope, you see the blue-black streak; on the other side, the same distance up, you see the same streak. The seams run for miles, jumping across rivers and creeks, now broken by some convulsion an eternity ago, now tilted at crazy angles, but for the most part flat, thick, regular, and rich. Railroads, indispensable adjunct of mining, run beside every creek. A grimy structure of steel, a ribbon of shining rails right up the mountain side, a smudge of black dust, a monotonous grinding and clanking, and you are at a tipple. It is coal on which a third of the population depends directly for its living; it is coal on which probably another third depends indirectly. It is coal that has converted the State into one great pockwork of mines.

The coal development, however, is relatively recent. Only in the two closing decades of the last century was it of much importance; the richest fields of all are scarcely twenty years old. Before that, the State was a sort of wilderness, carved out of the backwoods of Virginia in the turmoil of the Civil War. Indigenous to it was a unique type of human being, the mountaineer. Here and there he survives today, and in spite of his baffling idiosyncrasies, is a most lovable person. If you have won his regard, he will take you into his home and seat you before his rude fireplace as the guest of honor. He will listen with respect to your discourse, and entertain you with homely comment of his own. He speaks a quaint language. It recalls an America that is fast passing, the America of the cross-roads schoolhouse and the cabin in the hills—with echoes of James Fenimore Cooper, and a forgotten generation of leather-shirted woodsmen. It uses "ary" for "nary," "cayn't" for "can't," "hayn't" for "hasn't"; "done" and "done been" with verbs, instead of "have" and "had"; it has odd words peculiar to itself: "swag" for a small marsh; and retains words long discarded in other parts of the world: "poke" for bag; a "panther" is still a "paynter." It is spoken with a plaintive drawl, gentle and unassertive. A language arresting and attractive, pathetically and insistently American. That, probably, is because this mountaineer who speaks it is one of the oldest and purest American types extant. He drifted westward with the migration of the eighteenth and nineteenth centuries, and finding habitable creek bottoms, loitered by the wayside, while his more energetic brethren pushed on to the Ohio River and the West. For a century he stayed here, and raised a few hogs, and corn for hominy, and carried on a small traffic in illicit whiskey. He was his own law, and his rifle was his last court of appeal. As time went on he and his kind interbred, the strain grew weaker and weaker, and he developed unusual ideas and customs. Personal grudges obsessed him. He nursed them for years, and prosecuted them with his rifle, until the outside world began to hear of strange feuds, such as the one between the Hatfields and the McCoys, that arose from trivial and incomprehensible causes. Whole families were exterminated in these feuds, and the rifle came forward with more and more sinister prominence in the West Virginia scheme of things.

About all this was the flavor of a queer, half-savage code, a *cavalleria montagnola* that was at least picturesque. Then came coal and the ever-advancing railroads. Mining companies bought the hillside cabin and dispossessed its lodger. The gaunt mountaineer, waiting for days, rifle on knees, eyes starry with hate, until his enemy should come up the creek bottom, was forced inevitably to enter the coal bank and toil for his living. Moreover, his new masters took leaves out of his own book and used them against him. They adopted the law of the rifle themselves. They hired armed gentry to watch him and police him and curtail his liberties. They told him where to go to church and where to send his children to school. They told him what he must take for his labor, how much he must pay for his food, and where he must buy it. Lastly, they told him what organizations he might join, and those that he must not join; prominent among the latter were labor unions. In vain he arose in his wrath. He oiled his rifle, but there was no dignity in it. He swore his vendettas against the mine guards, but the old heroic venom was gone. He killed his man, and it was a blowsy murder. He had brought all his former stage trappings, and they had become tawdry overnight. He was degraded, a serf: the Last of the Mohicans turned tourists' cook.

This was the condition of the mountaineer-miner when the United Mine Workers of America undertook to strike off his shackles. In this valiant enterprise the union was also strengthening its own position, for by the early years of the present century its pristine security in the Central Competitive Field was being threatened seriously by the growth on all sides of large non-union fields, and the largest of these was West Virginia. So it set about organizing the State. It was repulsed with medieval ferocity by the operators, who could make more money if they didn't have to pay the union scale. But it kept on, and eventually gained a membership of a few thousand. And to the occasional whisperings and shootings in the mining camp there was added a new and bigger kind of plotting. The union soon saw that the mine-guard system was the main bar to its organization; if the guards persistently ejected union organizers, there wasn't much hope of getting very far. So the mine guards quickly became anathema to all union miners; they were dubbed thugs, and took their places as permanent members of the cast, upstage, right, striding scowlishly about slapping their holsters while the trembling miner signed the open-shop agreement. . . . The first phase of the union's fight came to an end in 1912 and 1913, with strikes on Paint and Cabin Creeks, and three hundred guards imported by the companies, some of whom didn't get out alive. In all, nearly two score men lost their lives in those strikes, and people began to take gunplay and dynamiting for granted.

In 1918, the union, through a political deal, was allowed to organize the Fairmont field. By securing this territory and consolidating in the central part of the State, it pushed its membership to some fifty thousand. But ever the coal frontier receded past the horizon, and now southern West Virginia was mining enough coal to undermine the union power—to render any national strike largely ineffective. The southern part of the State was a big non-union stronghold, with the mine-guard system functioning perfectly. It embraced Mingo,

Logan, McDowell, Raleigh, Mercer, and Wyoming counties. The union tackled
Logan first—in 1919.

As usual, it met with armed resistance. Here was a mine-guard system, paid
by coal operators, its main duty to eject union organizers. Its guards were
invested with all the majesty of the law; they were deputy sheriffs of the county,
duly sworn in under the Logan high sheriff, Don Chafin, who directed their
activities and paid them out of a pool assessed against the operators. Mr.
Chafin's deputies did their work thoroughly, and soon a wail drifted down the
stage, over the Guyon Ridge: "They're a-murderin' the women an' children!"
This is a very important line in the West Virginia libretto. It is always the cue
for the big scene, of which more in a moment. So far as I know the deputies
have never murdered any women or children, but art is art, and it is a good line.
Why sacrifice it? Taking their cue, the union miners to the north assembled at
a place called Marmet, within a dozen miles of Charleston, the State capital, and
marched about a thousand strong on Logan. Then ensued the spectacle of the
Governor of the State, John J. Cornwell, hoisting the gubernatorial robes aboard
a wagon, beseeching the miners to go home, promising an investigation, and
finally threatening troops. The miners went home, and their effort was abortive.
But the West Virginian, a regular attendant at Western feature films and a
diligent student of the Pluck and Luck series, had noted the possibilities of the
scene.

So all energies were bent toward a successful staging of the great drama.
The operators hired extra guards and howled defiance at the union. The union
girded its loins, counted its money, and swore loudly that might should not
conquer right. It sent its organizers into Mingo. A number of camps were
organized. The union demanded recognition; the operators refused it. The union
called its men out on strike; the operators evicted the strikers. As fast as the
operators evicted them the union put them in tents. Guerrilla warfare broke out.
There were massacres, ten men being killed in a battle at Matewan. The operators set spies to watch the miners and the miners pot-shotted the operators'
witnesses. Plots were hatched by the dozen and card indices were needed to keep
track of vendetta oaths. Federal troops were called in twice. The new Governor,
E. F. Morgan, declared martial law, and the military commandant began clap-
ping union men in jail. Finally, two union sympathizers, Sid Hatfield and Ed
Chambers, as the result of a quasi-official feud, were shot down at Welch, and
this, with heavy mutterings and threatenings sounding to the north, rang down
the curtain on Act I—in August, 1921.

When Act II opened, two weeks later, union miners were assembling again
at Marmet for another march. They gnashed their teeth and gritted they would
redress their wrongs and stop further outrages. This time the plan was to march
through Logan, kill Don Chafin on the way, continue to Mingo, liberate prison-
ers in its jail, nullify martial law, and proclaim liberty and justice once more in
the land. For days they gathered and the press of the country screamed their
purpose far and wide. Then they started, and as they swung down the road to
Racine they sang:

> *Hang Don Chafin to the sour-apple tree,*
> *Hang Don Chafin to the sour-apple tree,*

Hang Don Chafin to the sour-apple tree,
As we go marching on!

They were halted once when their president addressed them at Madison. They threatened to hang him to a baseball grandstand, but they went home— at least, most of them did. Some of them stayed, commandeered a train and played with that—and waited. They didn't wait in vain. Down at Sharples, in Logan County, there came a clash between union miners and a party of Logan deputies and State police, coming, 250 strong, to serve warrants—at midnight *(sh! sh! sh!)*. Two miners were killed. Then came the long-delayed cue that had been holding up the show: "They're a-murderin' the women and children!" The miners reassembled, eight thousand strong. They flung out battle lines and donned red brassards. They gave out a password.

"Who's there?" whispered the sentries.

"I come creepin'," replied the miners, *misterioso*.

"Pass," said the sentries.

They drilled around the schoolhouse at Blair, while coal-company officials, powerless for the moment, snooped faithfully and took notes in memorandum books. Meanwhile the miners were bringing in truck-loads of food, rifles, machine guns, and ammunition, and presently preparations were complete for the grand offensive.

On the other side of the ridge all was buzzing action too. Don Chafin issued a call for volunteers, and several thousand sprang forward ready to die for Logan County. He imported four airplanes. Then arrived a lord defender of the realm, appointed in this emergency by the Governor. He came, he saw, he took command. He addressed his troops and told them to advance not on these misguided miners, but to retreat not a single step. In the still night he had trenches dug. He filled the airplanes with bombs. All now being in readiness, both sides entered their positions and shot at each other for three days. The airplanes zoomed and dropped bombs on the rocks. The machine guns went *put, put, put;* the rifle fire never ceased. The noise was superb. On the fourth day a regiment of Federal troops came—and everybody else went home. It was the best second act that had ever been staged, and was marred by only one unpleasant event. Three men were killed. It is true they were killed in a purely accidental encounter between scouting parties, but the incident shows that great care must be exercised in the future if this march is to become a permanent institution in West Virginia, as it now promises to be. . . .

You arise in your seat. Stay. There is another act, the great courtroom scene.

Hardly had the last miner handed his gun in than the Logan County grand jury met in special session. It indicted whole pay rolls. It indicted for murder, conspiracy, and unlawful assembly. Then it rested, met in regular session, and indicted some more. It met yet again, and to the hundreds of indictments already found, it added a score or so for treason. And so, in a few months, after a change of venue had been granted, court opened to try these cases. The court sat in the same room at Charles Town where John Brown had been convicted of treason, and oddly enough, the first case called was a treason case. Defendants and witnesses appeared by the hundreds. State police paraded in front of the courthouse carrying big pistols, and a lieutenant of State police got arrested and locked in the town hoose-gow for getting saucy with the town constable. Witnesses told gory stories for a month. Lawyers orated. Foamy spittle flew hither and yon, and flecked the coats of the jury. The first treason defendant was acquitted, but in the next month two miners were convicted of murder. Then another treason trial; the defendant was convicted and sentenced to ten years. By now the pastoral community of Charles Town was so rent with the controversy that it was impossible to get a jury. The trials were removed, once to Berkeley Springs, and yet again to Lewisburg.

Thus life in West Virginia in this year 1923. In addition to the big show there are innumerable little shows. In all the coal counties the plots, the vendettas, the murders, and the trials go on incessantly. The Federal court at Charleston is a never-ending round of restraining orders, injunctions, and citations for contempt. The sterile conflict overshadows and paralyzes everything else. Before it the State government is impotent. The State police, organized bona fide to enforce the law, are animated by no maturer ideal than to posture as moving-picture editions of the Canadian Mounted, i.e., to wear pretty uniforms, carry pistols, and growl sidewise that they always get their man. They are now quite as detested as the mine guards; the miners call them the "Governor's Cossacks," and charge openly that they are on the side of the operators.

The bustling little inner-loop-outer-loop cities are but centers where gossip is exchanged and new plots hatched. Their weekly luncheon clubs are but debating societies devoted to denying the conflict. Their newspapers are degraded win-an-auto sheets whereof every other writer is in the pay of one side or the other. The activities of the State university, with its farmers' short courses and summer camps for girls, whatever their actual merit, seem innocuous and pointless while the banging of the guns echoes and reechoes. Culture is at a standstill; the only theaters are movies that show five-reel shooting features; there are no libraries, no concerts.

The conflict mars also what might stand forth as achievement. For in these mountains industry is organized on a gigantic scale. To see it is to get the feeling of it: the great iron machinery of coal and oil, the never-ending railroads and strings of black steel cars, groaning and creaking toward destination. A plume of smoke "down the holler" and a locomotive comes stealing around the bend. You are drawn close to these big inanimate things. The locomotive ceases to be a terrifying pile of steam jets and puffing, and becomes "she"; you lean affectionately against her as you swap talk with the engineer and spit familiarly on her wheels. There is crude outdoor poetry about it. Similarly to the north. Thousands of acres of orchards grow incredible quantities of apples, which are stored in warehouses redolent of fruity perfumes and shipped to far places of the earth. But this is all enchanting for what it suggests, not for what it is. Back of it all are always the scowling and muttering that spoil it.

Futile indeed seems the $50,000,000 road program that is to civilize the State. For ever recurs the question: Is the State civilizable? The answer is not apparent yet. Possibly it would be well to remember that this new West Virginia of great enterprises is still quite young. It may have a touch of industrial indigestion. Or its malady may be more grave. Give it a century or so. Then possibly it will shoot the pianist and call for a new score.

COAL'S BLACK RECORD (1921)

George Soule

MOST PEOPLE KNOW VERY LITTLE about the coal industry except that it is the perpetual bad boy of the American industrial family. It is always getting us into outlandish trouble of some kind or other. There are shortages which nearly close down the railroads and freeze us out in zero weather. Prices mount at the most inconvenient times to prohibitive figures. There are strikes which cause both expense and wasted wrath; first we condemn the miners for their impudence in demanding a thirty-hour week, and then we discover that the miners are actually asking for longer hours than they had been permitted to work, on the average, throughout the year. We are told that some coal companies made war profits running into the thousands per cent, and yet the miners cannot be paid a subsistence income. We hear of feuds and dispossessions and murders in the war of the operators against the union in West Virginia—and such things have been going on for years.

Now, listening to the investigation of the Calder Committee, we discover that high prices have been boosted by four or five unnecessary "brokers" and middlemen between producer and consumer. We discover that the War Department appointed as its purchasing agent a large operator who bought coal from his own mines at more than twice the cost of production. We discover that as a result of a threatened bituminous shortage in some localities the Interstate Commerce Commission authorized the issuance of priority orders for coal shipments, specifying that in carrying out those orders contracts previously signed might be broken. Then we find that subordinate transportation officials forged and padded the priority orders, accepting bribes for doing so, so that coal might be diverted to speculators and contracts favorable to the purchasers might be invalidated. These measures having been taken to deal with the "shortage," we discover that up to November 6, 1920, 46,000,000 tons more coal had been mined in the United States than in the corresponding period of 1919. We read that in Scranton, Pa., the heart of the anthracite district, anthracite is so scarce that in some households there is actual suffering. And at length we get some measure of the former profiteering by seeing coal fall. Inside of a few weeks the price of export coal fell from about $14.50 at the mine to about $3.50. Whereupon the operators said that it would be *unprofitable to continue to mine coal under $3.00.* Apparently, then, they had been making a *sales profit* of some 400 per cent on every ton when the price was fourteen dollars.

After this happy and bewildering experience with the vagaries of coal, we are shocked and astonished to hear a Republican senator, Mr. Calder, threaten something very like nationalization of the industry. Does not everyone know that government ownership is a blight on enterprise, and that the present system is the ideal one because it "works"? What can the Senate Committee be thinking of when it reports: "Our investigation into the coal situation has convinced us that private interests now in control of the production and distribution of coal, in spite of the efforts of some, are actually unable to prevent a continuance or repetition of the present deplorable situation, and that it is the duty of the Government to take such reasonable and practical steps as it may to remedy the evil"?

A rough outline sketch may be helpful to understanding. Anthracite is not nearly so important as bituminous, but it comes first to our attention because most of us depend on it to keep warm. A preponderant part of the anthracite deposits in the country are owned by companies closely affiliated with a few railroads. The greater part of these fields are held out of production, but of the anthracite actually put on the market, the railroad mines account for about three quarters. The mining companies themselves make for the most part a very modest profit. In some cases their sales are handled by separate, related companies which make a large profit. But in most cases the lion's share of profit goes to the affiliated railroad carriers. The freight rates on hard coal are said by W. Jett Lauck, railroad and coal economist, to be two and one-half to three times the operating cost of transportation. The income from coal carrying comprises from six to sixty per cent of the total freight revenues of the anthracite roads. Thus immense earnings are created. In some cases they have been made the excuse for greatly increased capitalization. In some cases they are used to pay dividends on a capitalization based on the undeveloped coal deposits—as if a landlord should charge enough rent for a single occupied house to pay a profit on a hundred others which were empty. In the case of roads which have not gone the limit in possible capitalization, the surplus and dividends show the situation. The actual earnings on the capital stock between 1913 and 1918 have averaged in the case of the Lackawanna from 24 to 36 per cent, in the Lehigh Valley 29 per cent, in the Central Railroad of New Jersey 27 per cent.

The merchandising of anthracite, compared to that of bituminous, is on a fairly decent basis. There are, ordinarily, few irrelevant middlemen. But the trouble is that the anthracite market is in large measure dependent on the bituminous market, because when soft coal is scarce, hard coal is often used in its place, and its price rises. When there is a shortage of cars—as there usually is—bituminous drives anthracite off the roads and the retailers are thus given a chance to charge enormous figures for what hard coal they can get.

The mining of bituminous coal is in the hands of many companies. While the bulk of the production in Pennsylvania, for instance, comes from a small group of large operators, the marginal production is widely scattered. And there is a great difference in the cost of production of various mines, due in large part to the difference in the width of seams, and in lesser degree to differing efficiency of management and other factors. In the year 1918 the cost of production of 199 operators in the southwestern field of Pennsylvania ranged, according to the Federal Trade Commission, from $1.21 to $4.04 per net ton. Nearly 77 per cent of the total production cost $1.99 or below. Over 90 per cent cost only $2.20 or below. When there is a great demand, it is the highest-cost mine which fixes the ultimate market price. In order to get that last 10 per cent of soft coal on the market, enormous profits had to be paid on the other 90 per cent. This is an inevitable feature of widely distributed private ownership.

There is also the artificial shortage caused by insufficiency and improper distribution and use of coal cars. The operators have never devised successful ways of storing coal. If they have no cars to put it in, mining operations stop.

This causes scarcity in the market, and terrific wastage and unrest of labor. Lucky is the miner who gets a chance to work more than two-thirds of the year. Scarcity of bituminous coal is thus chronic. It creates a competitive demand, and attracts hordes of speculative middlemen. Although $3.50 a ton is a liberal estimate for the cost of production at the mine, the consumer is fortunate to get his soft coal at four times that price. This in spite of the fact that transportation rates to few industrial centers in the country are more than $3.00 a ton, and a fair overhead for the local distributor was reckoned by the Fuel Administration, under war prices, at the same figure.

In 1917 the Federal Trade Commission examined the situation and came to the obvious conclusion that "if a uniform price were fixed many mines will be shut down unless the price is high enough to make the highest mine cost profitable." It therefore suggested ascertaining scientifically the cost of production at each mine, paying the owner or operator a fair profit, and then pooling the total national supply in order to make possible its sale at an average figure. This is what Great Britain has now been doing for some years. Even then, distribution could not be effective "without similar control over all means of transportation, both rail and water, and to meet this the pooling of railroads and boat lines is clearly indicated." The Commission therefore recommended the operation of the railroads as a unit on the government account. But we have now returned the railroads to the management of private, competing owners, on account of the "superior efficiency" of that arrangement.

Mere government control of mines and railroads could eliminate enormous waste in the sale of this product which lies at the basis of our national economy. Government ownership would make possible additional savings in production. Production engineers like Walter N. Polakoff show how heat and power could be distributed at a small fraction of their present cost by a radical revision of the technique of the industry. Highly valuable chemical by-products of coal— such as dyes and fertilizer—which are now wasted, could be extracted at the mine mouth. The coal could then be transformed into electricity and much of the cost of transportation saved. In addition, the inefficient use of coal in many antiquated furnaces would be avoided. The high-cost mines could be eliminated, and labor could be continuously employed at good wages. These reforms could not be effected in a short time, of course, but they have not even been begun under private ownership.

Aside from such ambitious plans, however, there is not the slightest doubt that with no changes in technique, a merely efficient management under unitary control in the public interest would be of great value. Whether the present Congress will go so far as to adopt such a measure is doubtful in the extreme. It cannot do so much discourtesy to the god of private enterprise. We shall have to freeze and starve more than we have so far before the lesson is driven home to us. In the meantime the effort of the more daring Senators will probably be to educate us to the problem. Some form of national oversight may be established. A governmental agency may be given the power to examine the companies' books, so that publicity may be accorded to the figures. This cumbersome supervision would provide for the public a minimum of protection against conscienceless and willful profiteers, but it would leave untouched the maladjustments of the industry which, in spite of anyone's good intentions, keep us in a constant turmoil about our coal.

THE PLIGHT OF SOFT COAL (1928)

Walton Hamilton

THE STORY OF BITUMINOUS COAL is an oft-repeated history that runs from crisis to crisis. For a time the industry goes its unobtrusive way; the consumers have little trouble in filling their bins, the operators lord it over their private domains, the mine-workers do such work as they can find for such wages as they can get, and the public takes no interest in so obvious a thing as coal. Then the veil of peace is torn aside, and the industry is for the moment endowed with a grave public interest. . . .

The bituminous coal question did not emerge in a day. For a very long time bituminous coal promised to be only a minor worry to the community. As was fitting to a petty industry, coal-mining was developed under the usages of petty trade. The industry was open; anyone who could command the necessary resources was free to enter it, but no one was constrained to do so. The market was open; anyone who had the price was free to purchase, but there could be no forced sale upon an unwilling buyer. The working places were open; there was no compulsion upon the operator to hire or upon the laborer to accept a job. Each person who ran a mine, purchased coal, or became a mine-worker was free to seek his own best advantage; each was prevented from overreaching himself at the expense of others by the necessity of selling his coal, purchasing his fuel, or disposing of his services in rivalry with others who might undersell or overbid him. The competitive mechanism of petty trade was depended upon to keep the mining of coal orderly and efficient.

So long as coal remained a petty trade and consumers were supplied from nearby mines, the system at least worked. The trouble began when in the course of unintended events coal was exalted to a high place in the national economy. The series of changes called the industrial revolution introduced the machine process, dotted the landscape with factories, and quickened small businesses into great industries. The new system of production required a gigantic and continuous stream of fuel to keep it going; it found its single large and dependable source of supply in coal.

This demand for an "industrial-energies" industry raised anew the question of the control of coal. An organization which had grown up in response to the requirements of petty trade could hardly be expected to meet the larger needs of a great "key" industry. In time the various groups concerned each tried its hand at patching up the inherited scheme of order. The operators knew that the labor problem was too big for even the biggest of them and felt vaguely that other matters of concern to all were beyond the reach of any; they tried to organize trade associations. The workers found wages distressingly low, employment none too plentiful, and conditions of work far from ideal; they set out to develop a strong trade union. The State governments came to be persuaded that coal could not be left entirely alone and began to regulate the industry. Each aimed to end the unruliness of the industry by appending a new control to the ancient system of free competition.

But a lagging organization was not so easily to be adapted to the demands of a strategic industry. It was long after needs had arisen before half-hearted attempts were made to devise new instruments of control. The operators and miners worked at cross-purposes, creating a fault line through the industry, leaving it half union and half "free." The government felt it wise to walk warily in invading the domain of coal.

The net result of these protracted attempts to bring the organization of the industry up to date is easily set down. Not one of the instruments of control, whether it be trade association, labor union, legislative code, or what-not, extends over even one-half of the industry. Not one offers an agency and a procedure through which a major question can be made a matter of conscious policy. A strategic industry is still controlled by a scheme of arrangements which grew up to meet the needs of petty trade.

The demand for coal is almost the only certain thing in an industry beset with uncertainties; at present the requirement is for nearly 550,000,000 tons each year. For the most part this demand comes from industries in need of power; it rises as the index of production moves upward and falls with its decline. It depends very little upon the price of coal, for the cost of fuel is a minor item among expenses of production. It responds very indifferently to stimulation by advertising or to adroit salesmanship.

Over against this demand is to be set down a capacity to produce far too unruly to serve as a balance. The law of the land, with a true devotion to democracy, invites whosoever will to take a chance at the prizes of mining. Rich and abundant deposits, easy of access, receptive to recovery, are a lure to the adventurous. Fresh enterprises have been started to produce coal that could be had at far less expense from old workings. Every rise in the price curve has created newly manned ventures and never a sag has cleared away superfluous undertakings. The sprawling domain of coal, beginning in the East, has taken its wasteful and disorderly way toward the West and the South.

And, as if the deliberate opening of new mines were not enough, human ingenuity and initiative have helped to make the industry a jumble of enterprises. The cost-sheets tempt the alert manager to improve methods, to eliminate needless operations, to articulate processes more closely, to substitute docile machines for more vociferous units of human labor. As the new machines, the new processes, the new administration make their way underground, they accomplish a thing which was no part of the reason for their introduction. Since they enable the mine to be worked more rapidly, a given area will within a period of time yield a larger amount of coal. Thus a capacity to produce, already overdone by the opening of unneeded mines, is swollen still further by an addition which is a mere by-product of the advance in the art of mining.

Nor is there hope, under the regime of free enterprise, for an elimination of this excess capacity. The great surplus has come with the slow, the irregular, the ofttimes interrupted development of machine mining. At present, even under the wasteful conditions of operations which are usual, the mines of the country are capable of yielding very nearly one thousand millions of tons, almost double the requirements of the country. For the future an increasing excess capacity promises indefinitely to characterize the industry.

This unstable equilibrium sets the stage for an unorthodox competitive struggle without benefit of the usages of petty trade. A demand independent of price, and a capacity to produce which is lost to control, render impotent the very devices upon which competition relies to keep the industry orderly. The many coal companies engage in a scramble for a market which is too small to go around. Since the bulk of coal is mined to order, it is capacity rather than product which is peddled from factory door to factory door. The rival concerns come to secure such customs as they can command at such prices as they can get. The ordinary operator finds his market and his gross receipts alike uncertain; he gets into a hand-to-mouth habit of running his affairs, doing the best he can with the situation at the moment, and thinking none too much and none too shrewdly about the days ahead. . . .

The consumer, whose reputed role is that of innocent victim, seems to be the only beneficiary of competition. Even if on occasions he has had to give what he calls outrageous sums for such coal as he could get, his purchases have usually imposed no severe tax upon him. Nonetheless he has had his bothers. The coal which has poured into his bin has been far from uniform in quality; railroad charges have not accurately reflected carriage costs; and the operators have exacted quite different tolls from different consumers. There have been interruptions in mining and at recurrent crises at least a fear of no coal to be had at any price.

Since to the public every squire of a dinky mine is a "coal baron," the plight of the operator does not invite national mourning. Yet, in spite of lucky concerns which maintain solvency or even achieve affluence, the ordinary head of a bituminous mine has been caught in the toils of the general confusion. The inexorable pressure of the market forces him to pare his costs to the very minimum. Run-of-the-mine sort of person that he is, it is not out of sheer malice that he pays miserly earnings to his workers, overlooks the protection of life and limb, and neglects conditions of living; he would often prefer to avoid the low morale which attends industrial struggle. As recent events have shown, it is the operator who tries to live up to a union agreement who suffers most. With an evasive market in front and business failure at his heels, it is no wonder that the records abound in bankruptcies and reorganizations.

The lot of the miners reflects the chaos and depression of the industry. The operators have, as far as possible, passed their burden along to the workers. There has grown up a tangled, disorderly, and inequitable network of wage-rates. Certain rates compare favorably with those in other industries; but employment is irregular, and even a miner cannot live by wage-rates alone. The conditions of work and the protection of life and limb are alike far from uniform; a trickle of accidents day by day accumulates into statistical tables which are appalling, and an occasional disaster results in so large a number of casualties as to suggest a battle. Almost everywhere there is a dearth of opportunities for recreation, for education, for personal development—for mine-workers themselves, for their wives, and for their children.

Nor do the laborers possess an agency by which they may avoid taking up the slack of industrial disorder. At one time the United Mine Workers of America comprehended half the bituminous mines; now less than one-third of them are subject to its waning influence. From the first it was intended to be an industrial union; yet it has attempted to meet the unusual conditions of bituminous mining with the strategy usual in craft unionism. It has welcomed into the industry all the workers who have cared to come, and yet has depended for its success upon a monopoly of labor. It has resorted to the strike when the deficit of coal could all be supplied from non-union fields. The use of the strike in an industry so overdeveloped that 500,000 men are employed to do the work that half that number could accomplish attests a slavish devotion to an outworn creed. Yet the union is the only instrument whereby miners can protect their living, and the strike the only weapon the officials and men are accustomed to employ. . . .

THE COAL WAR (1928)

Colston E. Warne

CHEAP SOUTHERN COAL largely explains the tragedy which has overtaken the coal-fields of Pennsylvania and Ohio. Sixty thousand men have been on strike for a year. Thousands more are unemployed. Hundreds of mines are bankrupt. Many more are losing money. In Illinois and Indiana the situation is scarcely better. The Northern coal industry is on its back. "Conditions which exist in the strike-torn regions of the Pittsburgh district are a blotch upon American civilization" is the report of the Senate investigating committee. "It is inconceivable that such squalor, suffering, misery, and distress should be tolerated in the heart of one of the richest industrial districts of the world."

At the base of this struggle are the widely varying labor standards of the Northern and Southern fields. Thirty years of collective bargaining in the Northern States of Pennsylvania, Ohio, Indiana, and Illinois brought a steady increase in wage-rates and a marked improvement in working conditions. Neat little mining villages were built up, especially in Illinois and Indiana, where privately owned homes are the rule. The check-weighman and the pit committee became fixed institutions. Qualification laws for miners were passed in Illinois and Indiana. Miners in this Northern field felt secure. Operators came to accept the union as a desirable institution which established a standard wage scale for the industry. Both operators and miners were, in fact, lulled into a comfortable security, broken only by intermittent dickerings as to the rate of pay.

So it was that little attention was paid to the rich mining area to the south. Though freight rates were early fixed at levels which would allow Kentucky, West Virginia, and Tennessee coal to compete in the Northern markets, development in the Southern field was limited up to the time of the World War. Slowly, however, Negroes and mountaineers were trained in the art of coal-digging and company towns were established. From the beginning, unionism was everywhere resisted. With the company controlling the houses, the ground, the stores, and the government, prevailing labor standards and wages came to be very low. This, coupled with the use of modernized mining equipment and the war demand for coal, brought a speculative boom in West Virginia and Kentucky. The security of the Northern mines was challenged.

The United Mine Workers met this challenge by concerted drives to unionize the West Virginia field. Bloody battles followed between 1919 and 1923 which often amounted to civil war. Injunctions, gunmen, and the "yellow-dog" contract broke the drive of the union. Finally, in 1922, a nation-wide strike was called. This strike, though effective in limiting the production of coal, failed to unionize West Virginia. Indeed, the union through bad bungling sacrificed 100,000 newly unionized workers in the coke region of western Pennsylvania.

For the past five years the union coal-fields of the North have been paying the penalty of this defeat. Miners and operators alike have suffered. Not only have the low labor standards of the South proved disastrous, but the development of a new mining area in a period when the market for coal was stationary was suicidal to the industry. In 1913, for example, the Pittsburgh district alone produced 71 million tons of coal. This amount had by 1925 dwindled to 48 million tons, while production in Kentucky and West Virginia rose from 90 to 177 million tons. Again, since 1920, the Pittsburgh area has lost to Southern producers all of a 48-million-ton increase in the demand in Mid-Western and Lake markets.

In an ever-increasing flood, the Southern non-union coal, mined on a $3 to $4 wage scale and aided by a favorable freight-rate structure, has rolled northward into the markets, displacing the Northern competitors who had long dominated the field. With the union miners insistent upon receiving a $7.50 wage from companies whose sales and profits were rapidly declining, industrial warfare became inevitable. The greater the encroachment of the Southern fields, the more necessary the higher scale became to the union miner, since the days worked per year declined greatly.

The impending battle would have been staged in the spring of 1924 had not the Republicans thought it best to pacify the miners until after election. Under political pressure, an armistice—the Jacksonville agreement—was signed to preserve peace until April 1, 1927. This armistice was maintained in Illinois, Indiana, and Ohio despite comparative stagnation in these union fields. In Pennsylvania and northern West Virginia, however, repudiation was common. Large operators like the Consolidation Coal Company, the Pittsburgh Coal Company, the Bethlehem Mines Corporation, and the Buffalo, Rochester, and Pittsburgh mines were among those breaking their contract, in 1924 and 1925, in the endeavor to achieve lower labor costs. Most of these companies finally reduced the wage scale 33 1/3 per cent, to the 1917 level. Strikes ensued, the majority of which are still nominally continuing. The Pittsburgh Chamber of Commerce in 1925 "impartially" surveyed the mine situation with funds supplied by the Pittsburgh Coal Company. After due deliberation, the chamber sponsored a plan for the reduction of wages and the establishment of company unionism in the mines of that concern.

With a loss of 150,000 members during the three years ended December 1, 1926, and with the menace of the non-union fields greater than ever before, the United Mine Workers was forced either to accept a reduction or to fight a battle against tremendous odds. Under the slogan "No backward step," the latter course was followed. A nationwide strike which was called for April 1, 1927, brought out 120,000 miners from Illinois, Indiana, and outlying districts, together with 60,000 men from Ohio and Pennsylvania. Thus the organization which, five years before, had on its rolls 65 per cent of the bituminous miners, had only a 30 per cent grip on the industry. Even this hold was largely lost when in the summer of 1927 the union felt it expedient to sign a truce with Illinois, Indiana, and other Western operators providing for the payment of the Jacksonville scale up to April 1, 1928. Of the union fields, Pennsylvania and Ohio were alone left on strike. Production of coal at once returned to the level of market requirements. With 200,000 extra miners and a 400-million-ton extra capacity in the industry, the striking miners failed to cause a ripple in the coal market. Indeed the price of coal sagged, the greater share of purchases being made at $2 a ton or less at the tipple. Large consumers, particularly the railroads, noting the condition of the industry, encouraged a cutthroat competition among producers.

The chief hope, then, of the striking miners has been that of making operation under non-union conditions so costly to the mining companies that the attempt would be abandoned. The operators for their part have attempted to break the spirit of the strikers by the use of company police, injunctions, evictions, and the importation of strike-breakers, and thus to reestablish regular operation. At the close of a year of these bulldog tactics the issue is still deadlocked. Millions have been lost by operating companies. Bankruptcy has been most common. . . .

Still these financial losses, large as they have been, are small compared to the human costs of this struggle. With the exception of the meager $3-a-week relief irregularly granted by the United Mine Workers as strike benefit, the burden of carrying on the fight has fallen upon the shoulders of the miners, their families, and the communities in which they live. The resources of all are now almost wholly exhausted. Everywhere the food supply is inadequate. In some areas, outside relief agencies are active. The left wing Pennsylvania and Ohio Relief Committee handles labor funds. The American Friends' Service Committee has gone into central Pennsylvania; the National Guard has opened soup kitchens in Ohio; at the instance of a church appeal the social agencies of Pittsburgh have covered Allegheny County. The condition, indeed, became so bad that in February, 1928, the leading businessmen of Pittsburgh formed a relief organization which received even the support of the mine-owners. This effort has been coordinated with the administration of the Clergymen's Fund, and the result has been adequate financing for a subsistence minimum in Allegheny County.

Between employer and employee, friendly relationships growing out of years of mutual understanding have been ruthlessly severed. Not only does deep-seated antagonism arise because of the employment of strike-breakers; it has also resulted from the annoyance brought on by guerrilla warfare. Everywhere disrespect for law is being created. The miners feel, with reason, that the courts have been unfair in the issuance of injunctions. The order of Judge Langham of Indiana County, Pennsylvania, which forbade the giving of relief, the posting of strike notices, and picketing is but indicative of the trend. In western Pennsylvania and in eastern Ohio picketing and free assemblage have likewise been limited by the courts.

Miners are furthermore increasingly convinced that in the coal-fields capitalistic enterprise has utterly failed. For twenty years they have averaged but

215 days of work a year. Recently the situation has become worse rather than better. The accident rate has been appalling. In ten years there have been 535 accidents for each 1,000 men employed in coal-mining in the State of Pennsylvania. The average time lost is 40 days. During a lifetime (forty years) of work a miner stands 17.2 chances out of 1,000 of being killed in a mine accident. In this risky and unstable industry living standards at best have scarcely approached the level of a living wage. The Jacksonville scale netted the average miner between $1,200 and $1,500. Out of this amount, an average of $10 a month was paid as rent for the usual four- or five-room company house. Two out of one hundred of these houses have bath-tubs, thirteen out of a hundred have running water. The savings through inferior housing standards are largely taken up in higher food costs. The 1922 Coal Commission estimated that an expenditure for food of $800 a year was necessary to provide a healthful living for an average miner's family. If the living standards under the Jacksonville scale were already low, the miners seem justified in contending that 25 to 33 per cent wage cuts will not serve to better their condition. Indeed, wage cuts in the Pennsylvania field tend only to give impetus to greater reductions in the Southern districts.

What, then, is likely to come out of the struggle in Pennsylvania and Ohio? Just what is desired by the contending parties? Strangely enough, both the operators and the International officers of the United Mine Workers are, in general, supporting the same solution. In testimony before the Senate Committee, both request the right of coal companies to consolidate, both seem on the whole willing to have some measure of price control, or at least supervision of the industry, and both desire higher freight differentials in favor of the Northern mines. Indeed, the only discernible difference lies in the desire of the union to maintain collective bargaining and the Jacksonville scale. Most operators would willingly grant the collective bargaining if it were on a lower wage basis.

It is significant to note that the beliefs of the International officers and of the rank and file of the United Mine Workers are somewhat at variance. An insurgent "Save the Union" movement is gaining great headway, especially in the strike area. This movement is led by John Brophy, a former district president, who in 1926 contested for the International presidency of the union. For nearly a year this progressive wing of the miners was silent, feeling that at any cost a united front must be maintained. It was only when apathy and discouragement were sapping the effectiveness of the strike and when it became apparent that the fight would be long-continued that steps were taken to challenge the Lewis control of the union.

In this call Lewis is condemned in no uncertain terms. He is charged with the stealing of the election of 1926 through tactics that rival those of Philadelphia politicians. Indeed, in that election 10,000 more ballots were counted than there were taxpaying members of the union—a striking contrast to the usual 25 to 50 per cent poll. Moreover, Lewis is charged with the failure to organize West Virginia and with inactivity in resisting operators who repudiated the Jacksonville agreement. It is argued that he has failed to press the program of the union for nationalization of mines. Furthermore, he is termed a poor strategist for his action in bringing a settlement in 1922 which failed to include the coke regions; also for his withdrawal of Illinois and Indiana from the present struggle. Finally, no little attention is directed to his $12,000 salary. The slogan of "Lewis Must Go" has been adopted.

Needless to say, the Save the Union Committee and its left-wing supporter, the Pennsylvania and Ohio Miners' Relief Committee, are roundly denounced by the Lewis group as "disruptive and communistic." Delegates to the projected convention are threatened with expulsion from the union. Brophy sympathizers, however, claim that they have the solid backing of several hundred local unions and that they will be able to force the adoption of a new leadership having a more militant program. Specifically, they urge: (1) the repudiation of the Lewis leadership in the union; (2) the sending of "shock troops" into West Virginia; (3) mass-picketing among all striking groups, defying any injunctions that may be issued; (4) the pressing of an aggressive campaign for the nationalization of mines; and (5) the establishment of the Jacksonville scale, coupled with the six-hour day and the five-day week.

Whatever may be the outcome of the gathering of the Save the Union group, it seems probable that the United Mine Workers will on April 1 attempt again to make the strike nation-wide. Undoubtedly this will include another effort to capture the strongholds of West Virginia.

At this moment no solution for the coal problem is in sight. The possibility of government control seems remote both because of the political hold of West Virginia (which would be adversely affected by any national standard of wages or by any rational readjustment of freight rates) and because of the several Supreme Court decisions holding coal to be an intra-State business. Until election is past and until the court can be brought in touch with economic realities, government control holds out no possibilities. Government ownership is not mentioned in Washington, even by Senator Wheeler. It is unlikely to have a hearing on its merits. Consolidation seems likewise doomed to failure. The 7,000 mining companies do seem to be drawing together in regional groupings but only so that the competition between districts may be more bitterly contested. No substantial lowering of mine capacity through this channel is in sight. Moreover, it is improbable that mining will be specifically exempted from the provisions of the Sherman and Clayton acts.

What, then, will happen? Probably some compromise will in time be effected which will permit a certain portion of the union miners to return to work under union conditions. Several new mediation efforts have been started in recent weeks. Any probable settlement, of course, will leave unsolved the fundamental problems of the industry.

Meanwhile, as the country censures the Pennsylvania operators and miners who are locked in a death grip, the West Virginia and Kentucky mine-owners whose actions lie back of the present tragedy may count their profits from the 4,000,000 tons of coal a week which they ship into the Northern markets. They alone can afford to smile.

THE GOVERNMENT MUST ACT! (1928)

Fiorello H. La Guardia

THE PRESENT COAL STRIKE is a battle of statistics against human life. It is a test between the theories of a new school of coal economics and everyday living conditions of men and women.

I conferred with miners of the union on strike, with non-union miners, as well as with the representatives of some of the largest coal companies. Assuming that the conditions described by the coal-mine companies are exactly as they state them, still I fail to find justification for the present low rate of wages.

According to the statements made to me by the mine-owners with whom I conferred, unless the government intervenes this strike is going to be a long and bitterly drawn-out affair, costly and disastrous. The owners justify their attitude on wage reduction by what they call sound economics. I have yet to see a case where figures could not be used to prove either side of the question. Figures and mental experts are always available for both sides of a controversy.

I will concede that the soft-coal industry is unstable, that there is keen competition, and that the capacity of the mines of the country is greater than the present needs for soft coal. All that being true, what the mine-owners are seeking to do is to take the cost of an unstable industry, of cutthroat competition, and of overproduction out of the wages of the mine-workers. To illustrate the mathematics of this new school of coal economics, let me give you the formula on which the present and future wages of the mine-workers are to be fixed: Our economists take the return on capital invested, plus profit, plus all overhead expenses, plus depletion, plus depreciation, plus transportation, add them together, subtract the total from the present competitive market price of coal, and the remainder is taken as the standard to determine the rate of pay of the workers. The actual cost of living and the bare necessaries of life of a miner are entirely disregarded, and he is to bear all of the burdens of a demoralized industry and is doomed to work for starvation wages. On figuring the return on capital investment, interest is computed for 365 days of the year, while the miners are expected to live on a measly wage for only 160 out of the 365 days. When these coal economists find a way to make it unnecessary for a miner, his wife, and children to eat on the 200 days that the man does not work, they will justify their formula, but not until then.

Under the Jacksonville agreement the average earnings of a coal-miner approximate $1,200 a year. Under the present wage scale, which incidentally has been reduced three times since the breaking of the Jacksonville agreement, the highest earnings will range from $600 to $750 a year, and no family can live decently on that amount in this country.

The factors which have created the unstable conditions in the coal industry must necessarily be charged to the owners of the miners and in no way can the miners or the miners' union be held responsible. The cutthroat competition which prompts this organized and systematic campaign of wage reduction is entirely the fault of the operators themselves. The question of production is likewise due to the waste and bad business management of the coal industry.

Ninety per cent of mining coal is human labor. An industry that cannot pay its workers a decent living wage has no right to exist. Efficient operation, economic production, and stabilized prices would provide the mine-workers of this country with a proper wage scale, permitting them to live decently and happily.

Whether in Pennsylvania, Indiana, Ohio, or West Virginia the terrorism and brutality of mine-owners and their agents must cease. The custom of permitting mine-owners to uniform, equip, and arm their own police, maintain their own detention pens, and pass summary judgment on the workers is so contrary to the fundamentals of our laws that it becomes necessary for the federal Government to intervene and put a permanent stop to these outrageous conditions. The mine-owners have assumed an extraterritoriality which not even a sovereign State under our Constitution is granted. Sovereign States in our Union are subject to the limitations imposed by the Constitution. These mine-owners in their territory recognize no limitations.

Much has been said about the coal and iron police. I need not repeat it, but I simply want to state that there is nothing in the law under which they operate which gives these men the authority they assume. They wear military uniforms and Sam Brown belts, they are armed with automatic revolvers and clubs. They are paid by the mining company, they are commanded by the mining company, and they are under absolute orders from the mining company, ostensibly for the purpose of protecting property, and are responsible to no one else. I have ascertained—and it is a matter of daily and hourly occurrence—that they do not limit their activities to the protection of the mining property. They do not remain on the mining property, but they go out on the highways of the State and there they apprehend those men who have left the company and are indebted to the company. They exercise a brutality that I have never heard equaled in the United States or any other country, either now or in the past history of the world.

Ordinarily a labor dispute is so localized in one State that it is not the province of the federal government to intervene. In the case of the soft-coal strike, however, there are many compelling reasons which make either a House or Senatorial investigation imperative, to be followed by necessary governmental intervention. It is no longer a matter of adjustment between the workers and employers; it has become a national problem and must be treated accordingly.

Whether union workers or strike-breakers, it is a matter of national concern that men be enabled to live decently and enjoy the freedom which the Constitution of this country guarantees to them. It is a matter for Congressional investigation to probe the charge that strike-breakers are held in a system of peonage in the soft-coal regions in the various States. . . .

A large number of Mexicans were actually brought to these coal mines, and only through the intervention of the Mexican consul were they released and sent back home. An offense against the federal laws has been committed which justifies federal investigation and intervention.

Here is another one: The strike-breakers are kept on mine territory. If they seek to leave, they are pursued by the coal and iron police beyond mine property, taken from the public highways, arrested and brought back, all in violation of Section 444 of Title 18 of the United States Code. . . .

This is a daily occurrence in the coal districts which I visited. These private, uniformed, and armed armies of the mine-owners are daily doing this very thing, and when a local officer issues a warrant against any of these agents of the mine-owners, the mine-owners simply refuse to produce them. That, I submit, is another reason justifying federal action.

While coal may not be an absolute necessity in the future it will be so for at least a generation. In the meantime, the present disgraceful conditions should not be permitted to continue. Investigation has followed investigation. Recommendation has piled upon recommendation and nothing has been done for the simple reason that the owners of coal properties are sufficiently powerful locally and nationally to prevent action. I firmly believe that ultimately the Government will have to step in and take possession of all natural resources, coal, oil, water, and gas. These natural resources should not be owned by a favored few to be exploited at the expense of the many. The control and operation of coal along with other natural resources by the Government would permit the mining only of such quantities as industry may require, the abolition of excessive profits, and the payment of decent wages. It is not to be expected that this major operation will be performed during the present session of Congress. The very persons all through the country who are now being exploited by coal barons, monopolistic oil companies, and the power trusts would be the first to succumb to propaganda that the "Government should be kept out of business," that such a solution is "socialistic," and that it would be contrary to the Constitution. But these monopolies are becoming more powerful, more brazen, more greedy, and more defiant of constitutional law when it stands in their way. It will not be long before the American people will realize that something is fundamentally wrong and they will then be less impressed by oil favoritism, coal "economics," and power-trust "constitutionality."

COAL FOR CONSUMERS (1922)

James Peter Warbasse

. . . THE ONLY WAY by which coal can be mined solely for the service of the people is for all the people who use coal to own the mines. Coal would then be produced for use and not for profit. And this is the end that must be reached if the coal industry is to be placed on a permanently sound basis. Coal should be mined and distributed not for the purpose of making profits for owners, nor for the purpose of making wages for workers; it should be mined to be burned—to be used—for just that simple purpose.

Government ownership is supposed to be a movement in the direction of the service motive in industry. But if the government should buy the coal mines today, the political power of the owners is so great that the valuation they would impose upon the mines would be vastly beyond the equity the owners have put in and would make coal a dear commodity for the consumers for a long time to come. The credit for the purchase of the mines would be secured by the issuance of long-term interest-bearing bonds, and another burden would be added to a deeply indebted government, a more powerful bureaucracy created to gnaw at the vitals of the state. Before the government takes this step it would be well for the consumers to anticipate it. The government does not want to take over the coal mines. It will resist doing so as long as possible. Not until conditions have become intolerable will such a step be considered. The government should welcome any plan that will save it this additional complication.

There is a way by which the government may be of service to the people in helping solve this problem and at the same time save itself from a plunge into government ownership. A temporary coal commission, created by act of Congress, could provide a central machinery while the consumers are organizing to own and administer the mines. Such a commission should consist of an equal number of representatives of the consumers, the workers, and the mine owners. The chairman should be additional, and should represent the first class. In the meantime the consumers should organize locally, in state, and finally in a national federation by the well-tested and highly practical method of Rochdale cooperation. The coal commission should distribute coal to the public at a fixed percentage above net cost. The surplus saving accumulating from distribution to the consumers should be partly returned to them in proportion to their consumption and partly put in a reserve fund. This increasing surplus would serve ultimately for the purchase of local equipment for coal storage, handling and distribution, and finally for the purchase of mines. As the organized consumers come into possession of coal properties the coal commission would cease to have jurisdiction over such properties.

A survey of the coal situation is essential. We need to know: (1) the amount of coal of various kinds that is required for industrial and domestic use, (2) the distribution of these needs, (3) the locations of the most available and economically accessible coal with relation to the points of consumption, and (4) the value of the properties necessary to produce this coal. This information should be secured by the existing statistical and census agencies. It should be assembled by the coal commission and made available for the people.

The coal commission, although appointed by Congress, should be nominated by non-political bodies. An organization of mine owners representing more than half of the coal production, such as the National Coal Association, should be competent to appoint its representatives. Similarly, a national organization representing more than half of the workers, such as the United Mine Workers of America, should be competent to make the nominations for the second class. To make this plan as non-political as possible, an organization of the consumers, representing at least 1,000,000 members, such as the Cooperative League, or a combination of consumers' organizations, should be competent to make the nominations for the consumers.

It is suggested that the consumers acquire the local storing and distributing machinery before they buy mines, because it is a principle of cooperation, proved by experience, that they succeed best by first mastering the methods of distribution, by meeting the needs nearest to themselves as consumers, and then by working back step by step from retail distribution to wholesaling and then to production, rather than by reversing this order. The purchase of coal mines by the consumers should be the last step after the machinery of distribution has been perfected.

Further capital could be raised by a membership fee, or by the issuance of low-priced bonds or shares, which must be paid for, before cash savings-returns may be enjoyed. Government assistance by loans is highly undesirable, as the purpose of this plan should be to keep as far away from political subsidy as possible. Money loaned by municipal, state, and federal governments to town, state, and national consumers' associations is practiced in France, Italy, Germany, Austria, and Denmark at the present time; but it adds undesirable political control and detracts from the self-help and voluntary character of the enterprise.

The principle involved in this plan is very simple. The consumers should own and control the mines which supply them with coal, and the funds to acquire the ownership should be developed by going into the coal-distributing business. The profits in coal are not known. They are hidden away today. But if they are anything like the glimpses here and there revealed, it should not take many years to make the people owners of the mines and of the wealth that coal represents. . . .

BLOODY HARLAN REFORMS (1938)

The Nation

AFTER NEARLY three months and an expenditure of more than $300,000 the farmer jury in the Harlan conspiracy trial reported itself in hopeless deadlock, the evidence of ears and eyes apparently offset by class bias, appeals to prejudice, fear of the C. I. O., and warnings of "Rooshian" influence. However disappointing the mistrial, and however appalling the government's prospect of having to reassemble its hundreds of witnesses and to rebuild its case for a new trial, much good has been accomplished. Harlan will never be quite the same again.

In the Kentucky coal country the Roosevelt Revolution is more than journalistic hyperbole. Harlan has seen its coal barons in the prisoner's dock. Harlan in 1938 is a revelation of how far, for all the twistings and turnings, the United States has traveled under the New Deal. Bloody Harlan won its name in 1931. In February of that year a 10 per cent pay cut was ordered. Angry miners struck and marched from mine to mine "for the speakin'." The United Mine Workers sent organizers into the county. The response of the Harlan County Coal Operators' Association was swift and brutal. In May deputies fought a battle with striking miners in the streets of Evarts. There were mass meetings, publicity, and protest, but nothing came of them. A dozen miners were killed, two reporters shot, a strikers' relief kitchen blown up; a department-store owner who gave a truckload of food for hungry miners' children was forced to flee from a charge of criminal syndicalism. Seven union leaders were sentenced to life imprisonment as a result of the Battle of Evarts; four of them are still in jail.

But 1938 is not 1931. During the last few years the operators rather than the miners have been on the defensive. Since 1936 three separate governmental agencies in turn have kept the story of capital's lawlessness in Harlan County almost continuously before the public. The eleven weeks of trial in London, Kentucky, under the threat of severe penalties, with the Department of Justice and its famous Federal Bureau of Investigation laying the groundwork for a new method of enforcing the Wagner Act, were only the culmination of months of hearings by the La Follette committee and the National Labor Relations Board. The revelations have evoked so much horror that one has tended to forget the cardinal fact that this time the operators were in the prisoner's dock, a government friendly to labor in power. While the trial was under way the Circuit Court of Appeals at Cincinnati upheld the Labor Board decision ordering the Clover Fork Coal Company to reinstate sixty miners discharged for union activity and pay them $100,000 in back wages. Last month the board handed down a decision against the Harlan Fuel Company, whose president distinguished himself by personally leading the armed band which drove union organizers out of company-owned Yancey, Kentucky, some years ago. The continuous barrage of publicity and punitive action has had its effect. In Harlan County, where the coal operators own the government, where tear gas, dynamite, and guns spitting death from ambush so long kept out the union organizer, the U. M. W. A. now has an office. Ten of the forty-two mines in the county have signed contracts with the union. Its field workers travel in comparative safety. The spectacle of sixteen corporations, eighteen mine executives, and twenty-two deputies on trial is one that Harlan will not soon forget. That the charge should be conspiracy to deprive miners of their right to organize is little less than revolutionary change in Harlan.

The setting of the Harlan trial was as lawless as the deeds placed on the record. One defendant was killed, a government witness shot, the home of another witness dynamited. The deputies that went "thuggin'," the night fusillade that killed Bennett Musick, the woman who was offered $100 a head to lure union men into the woods do not seem as bizarre in Harlan as elsewhere. But the miner who might have had medical care to save his baby if he hadn't joined the union is no extraordinary figure. Conditions in Harlan can be duplicated, though perhaps in less sensational form, wherever worker or tenant in field or factory is at the mercy of great landed or industrial interests. The absentee capitalists—U. S. Steel, Mellon, Ford, International Harvester, Peabody—that provide the background of the Harlan picture are familiar obstacles to social reform. The New Deal, by reviving the 1870 Civil Rights Act, is welding a new weapon against them, and though the Supreme Court once declared the act unconstitutional, it is not likely to do so again. Like Harlan's coal operators, the justices, too, have been chastened.

HOW TO RUN COAL (1947)

McAlister Coleman

"BROPHY URGES Mines' Nationalization." This recent headline took old-timers in the labor movement back to the exciting days of 1921–22, when American coal diggers were seeking some way out of their plight other than the usual devastating strike. John Brophy, then president of District 2 of the United Mine Workers of America, with headquarters at Clearfield, Pennsylvania, was head of the Nationalization Committee created by the miners' union at its 1921 convention. For years it had been routine at conventions for the miners to pass a resolution in favor of the nationalization of the coal mines of the country. Now they decided to back their words with a plan for action.

The man they picked to work out a plan was the quiet-spoken Brophy, son of a Lancashire miner, who had gone to work in the pits in Pennsylvania at the age of twelve and who, despite his Catholic upbringing, had early come to a Fabian socialism. Brophy, aided by progressive mine leaders from Pennsylvania and Indiana, enlisted the services of two competent researchers and publicity men, Robert Bruère and Heber Blankenhorn of the Bureau of Industrial Research, and in 1922 brought out his committee's report. It was called "How to Run Coal," and its proposals started a debate which resounded far beyond the coal fields.

It is a commentary on the lack of any long-range planning by the private interests responsible for coal production that Brophy, now Director of Industrial Union Councils for the C. I. O., can make today just about the same argument for nationalization of the mines as he made a quarter of a century ago. Nothing has happened since then to affect the truth of the fundamental charge —manhandling of one of our greatest natural resources—brought against private ownership by the original Brophy report. "The coal industry," it said, "has been so disorganized and mismanaged that the situation in recent years has approached what big business men and standpat Senators describe as a 'catastrophe.' . . . Unless unification and order enter the industry, there will be a blow-up somewhere, followed by drastic, angry, and frenzied legislation. The American Kingdom of Coal is today in as chaotic and explosive condition as the states of Europe. No single, constructive suggestion has come from the operators. No large, leading idea has come from the public. The public is feeling intensely but is not yet thinking wisely. . . . The only large-scale proposal has come from the United Mine Workers of America in their demand for nationalization. It is the only proposal that grapples with slack work for the miners, higher prices, and irregular supply for the consumer." . . .

. . . Those who are at last willing, in Brophy's words, to "think wisely" about the industry will not view a sensible plan for the nationalization of the mines under democratic controls as the "opening wedge to communism," whatever the operators say. There are indications that strong popular support would be given to a plan for having coal run by a federal authority patterned after the

TVA. Purchase of the mine properties by the government after a fair valuation and through the exchange of government debentures for privately owned paper would turn a national headache into a national asset. The groups most concerned with the continuous abundant production of cheap coal—the miners, the technicians, and the consumers, small and large—would have representation on the board of directors of the authority.

The authority would operate the mines through regional boards whose decisions would not have to be made in Washington and whose concern would be the engineered production of coal for the use of all consumers. Unburdened by the present private concept of coal as "something that can be mined profitably," these boards would have an eye to the conservation of what is still our most precious natural resource. The high-cost "marginal mines" could be eliminated by a public authority, which would see to it that displaced miners received severance pay while being trained for new occupations.

The authority could integrate coal with hydroelectric power and natural gas and put an end to the present wasteful cross-hauling of competing coals by the profit-hungry railroads. And because it would be free of the domination of vested interests, it could greatly expand the underground gasification of coal, or the burning of it at the pit-mouth, with the transmission of the energy thus derived through pipe lines or power lines. Though the solid-fuels technicians in the Bureau of Mines have done a yeoman's job investigating new domestic sources of coking coal, advising federal agencies and private industries on the efficient use of fuel-burning equipment, and gathering general technical information which could save millions of tons of coal a year, the private operators have been too busy warring on their help to pay heed to such "high-brow" activities. The immediate application of such research findings and the expansion of research to the barely scratched field of coal's invaluable by-products would be a "must" for a public authority.

It is in the field of human relations, however, that the authority, under decentralized, democratic controls, would prove of the greatest value. It would bargain with the miners' union as the TVA now bargains over wages and hours with the Tennessee Valley Trades and Labor Council, which represents some 16,000 workers. Nationalization, to be sure, will not end all labor-management disputes: miners, without a contract, will walk out on government-operated mines, as was proved not long ago. But American coal diggers, despite all the recent propaganda, are good democrats; indeed, those who have lived with them have found them to be among the most likable, alert, and courageous of all our industrial workers. If they are given a voice that counts in decisions affecting their welfare and a status befitting their all-important part in the national economy, they will not be found neglectful of the public good.

Proposals now being advanced, even in some liberal quarters, that in the event of government operation no-strike clauses be written into contracts with workers in key industries are pointless, to put it mildly. It would take a large part of the standing army, to say nothing of the navy, to keep miners in the pits against their will. The public authority would look to the causes of the miners' discontent. Their present demands are not, as some . . . would have us believe, wholly a matter of wages. They have to do with living conditions in enclaves far removed from ordinary American amenities, with high prices in company stores, with inadequate educational facilities, with the deadly monotony of existence on remote cinder patches, which the younger people here as in England loathe so bitterly. They have to do, as well, with the death of 1,500 miners a year and the injuring of some 50,000 in accidents, many of which are preventable.

Under the best of circumstances the mining of coal will always be a back-breaking occupation attended by unusual hazards. However, under private operation, with a few honorable exceptions, no serious large-scale attempt has been made to better the circumstances. The general run of hard-boiled mine owners consider even the more rigid enforcement of safety codes under govern-ment operation and the setting up of health, welfare, and medical funds to be red-revolutionary activities. Of course these men and the powerful interests which they serve will scoff at the suggestion that only a public authority such as is here roughly outlined can handle these human problems. But their protests will fall on deaf ears once the public realizes that there is an alternative, and a democratic one to boot, to the recurrent coal wars which keep our power-driven economy so perilously on edge.

NO RATS IN THE MINES (1971)

Harriette Simpson Arnow

. . . MR. ATKINS TALKED of mining coal. He'd dug coal in the West Virginia mines for several years back around World War I. One of the best paying jobs he'd ever had was robbing coal. In one way of mining, he explained, coal companies had to leave big pillars of coal in the rooms to support the rock above the coal seam; that is, for the first mining. After that first mining was finished, they'd send men in to get the coal in the pillars. If the mine later caved in, it didn't matter. Taking out the coal in the pillars was called robbing.

He'd rob the coal out of any mine where he could see or hear rats, even when other miners thought the mine was too risky. Mostly he'd robbed mines with good thick seams, 6 feet, sometimes more; but every once in a while there was a low roof and he'd have to crawl. Getting out in a hurry after he'd lighted a few fuses was about the hardest part. No, he'd never stayed in any part of a mine when a charge was to go off. Foolish.

He didn't re-enter the mine to get out the coal until the next morning when he figured the dust had had time to settle and the roof to make up its mind whether or not it was going to fall. He'd never tried to rush things. Still, he did a lot of robbing and made good money; coal was selling well back then in the twenties.

I asked him if the work had not been a great deal more dangerous than ordinary mining. He considered: most miners thought it was. He guessed the only real dangerous part was shoveling up the blasted-down coal when there was nothing to hold up the rock above you. Don't forget, though, he'd had the rats.

Rats were the best safety devices a coal miner could have. They were not trying to make money out of you. A rat knew when there was about to be a rock fall a lot quicker than any seasoned miner. They could also tell bad air and stayed away from it.

First thing when he was ready to work, he put scraps of food around his dinner bucket. At noon he'd leave more scraps, and always where he was aiming to set off a blast. Whenever he'd go for his dinner or just for a drink of water, the scraps were either all eaten or had rat-teeth sign. In between he'd hear the rats squeak, or see the shine of a rat's eyes watching him out of the dark. He'd always had the rats. Except once.

That time he'd been aiming to rob a big pillar in a back room where he'd never been before; it had a lot of fine coal. He'd worked just a little while at boring holes for blasting powder, when he noticed he hadn't seen or heard a rat. He went to his dinner bucket. All the scraps were still there; not even the loud-smelling cheese and bologna he'd put out special had one sign of a rat's tooth. He ran for his tools, grabbed his dinner bucket and high-tailed it out of there.

He'd made it out of that gallery and was getting close to the mine mouth, when all at once from behind him somewhere, it sounded as though the mountain was grinding its teeth. The awfulest racket a man ever listened to. Next morning he'd gone back to the room he'd been scared out of; it wasn't there any more. The rats had told him.

My friend said something about being glad modern mines were safer than they used to be. There were also, he pointed out, more state and federal mine safety laws, and inspectors to see that the laws were enforced. He reminded Mr. Atkins of the then new 1952 safety mining law.

Mr. Atkins shook his head. Laws? Inspectors? No, he'd take the rats. Miners still got killed. They've got no rats. In a big mine there's an awful lot can go wrong. But no matter how many miners get killed in one accident now, not all the dead men and maybe no one can be blamed for the accident. But listen to the higher-ups. They blame all the accidents on the miners and God. If you read the papers you'll know.

Yes, I read the papers, and continue to read them. I also, for several years, lived close enough to Kentucky's eastern coal country to hear a good deal. . . .

In late April, about four months after the Federal Mine Safety and Health Act became law, a group of operators representing the National Independent Coal Operators filed suit in a federal district court in Abington, Va. They asked for a restraining order against the more stringent demands of the new law—specifically, many of the safety regulations; nor did they want to pay the heavy fines. The federal judge granted an injunction against the federal law. An Under Secretary of the Department of the Interior forbade any representative of the Bureau of Mines to attend the hearing. The temporary injunction, with no opposition coming from any source, became permanent and trial was set for November.

Word was next handed down from Washington to the federal inspectors in the coal fields that, since some operators now had the legal right not to pay fines, it would be unfair to fine any mine operators for a safety violation. Later, a list of fines was handed down from Washington. These were so low and so hedged about for the protection of the operators, that they could have been called laughable—except that miners were being killed at a faster rate than during the preceding year.

The power of an inspector to close at once a mine he deemed a deathtrap was also taken away, but not by the injunction. Washington ordered inspectors to telephone Washington for approval—or disapproval.

The law as passed by Congress had stipulated that each mine should have four "thorough" inspections a year. This was changed by Henry Wheeler, a deputy director of the Bureau of Mines, into "Partial but Representative Inspections." This meant an inspector was to go over only part of each mine, which could be the part the owner wanted him to see.

In spite of sabotage from above, inspectors continued to crawl into mines and make inspections. Heavy demand for coal and high prices had increased the number of mines; during 1970 there were about 2,000 in Kentucky alone. Some half of these were small mines in out-of-the-way places serviced only by trucks.

Such were mines number 15 and 16 of the Finley Coal Company. Located in Leslie County, Kentucky, on land leased from the Ford Motor Company, they were adjoining and served by one coal-conveyor belt. The average height of the mines was only 32 inches, but despite the thin seam, profits were high enough to warrant two shifts of miners, a maintenance shift, and a few workers above ground—a total of eighty-five men.

Mine number 15 was first visited by Federal Mine Inspector C. E. Hyde in June of 1970. He found fourteen safety and health violations in the one mine; two or three of these concerned the general health and comfort of the miners; there was no drinking water in the mine, and no toilet facilities either below or above ground.

More violations jeopardized the lives of the miners, the most serious being the heavy accumulations of coal dust and coal along the roadways. Multiplying the danger from the highly explosive coal dust was the careless handling of electric cables: several splices were uninsulated, fuses had been removed in many places, there was evidence of cigarette smoking, and no one had tested for gas. Also, only nine of the mandatory self-rescue masks had been provided for the thirty-nine men on the first shift in both mines.

Inspector Hyde's power to levy the legal fines had been taken from him; but he could still order the mine closed on the ground that the lives of the miners were in danger. The mine was closed over a weekend; it was supposedly cleaned up; the Finley brothers lost no production, as the miners worked a five-day week.

State inspectors also visited the mine at intervals and found twenty-four violations of the state law; many of those classified as "potentially disastrous" were the same as those noted by federal inspectors: dangerous accumulations of coal dust, explosives improperly handled, insufficient roof bolts, and the usual poor maintenance and dangerous handling of electrical equipment. Charles Finley, operator, received letters from the Kentucky Department of Mines and Minerals politely insisting that the violations be corrected.

During 1970 federal inspectors made six partial inspections of Finley mines 15 and 16, during which they found thirty-eight violations, most of them potentially dangerous. There were still no self-rescue masks, and in one section of the mine a sampling of the air showed eleven times the legal limit of coal dust.

An inspector also came to investigate an accident that had injured one miner and blinded another. Another accident that killed a miner required a later trip. The inspector found management at fault in the death of the miner. No fines were levied against the Finley Coal Company. All power of an inspector to do anything but note violations had been taken from him by Washington.

On the morning of December 30, 1970, thirty-nine miners were underground in Finley mines 15 and 16. The foreman and his explosives expert were getting ready to blow out a section of the low roof, to make room for the loading boom on the end of a conveyor belt that Finley wanted to connect with the main belt in mine number 15. The other men were at their usual jobs. Shortly after twelve o'clock an explosion ripped through the mine. One miner near the entrance was flung about 60 feet from the mine mouth. The other thirty-eight miners were killed. Charles Finley, outside in his trailer, was unhurt. Dr. William Beasley, the closest doctor, was the first to examine the bodies.

Back in Washington, Elburt Osborn, director of the Bureau of Mines, was soon wondering what, if anything, the bureau should do. That was decided for him. Sen. Henry Jackson, chairman of the Senate Committee on Interior and Insular Affairs, and Sen. Harrison Williams, chairman of the Senate Committee on Labor and Public Welfare, telegraphed the acting Secretary of the Interior, Fred Russell. He was told that his Bureau of Mines must hold a public hearing on the disaster.

Rep. Ken Hechler demanded, and got, copies of inspectors' reports on Finley mines 15 and 16. He, too, demanded a hearing that would cover "all aspects of the operator's actions since the mines were opened, and the degree to which the operator failed to comply with the law." He also secured a copy of the 25,000-word report on the Finley Coal Company disaster made by researcher Thomas N. Bethell for the Coal Miners Legal Defense Fund. Representative Hechler had the report inserted in the "Extension of Remarks" of the *Congressional Record.* Most of the facts given here are taken from the "Extensions."

President Nixon was so aroused by the disaster that he said he would do everything possible for the widows. He, or somebody, did. Social Security bureaucratic red tape was untangled with such speed that the widows with their ninety-seven children received the usual death payment only thirteen days after the disaster.

The Kentucky State Workmen's Compensation Fund was even faster. The widows were called together on January 4 to sign papers and then received a death payment of $500 each. Since the Compensation Fund valued each married dead miner, regardless of age, at $19,700, the widows would further receive 400 weekly payments of $48 each. The five bachelors were worth only the death payment to the undertaker.

Several dignitaries, including William Boleyn, sent to represent the White House, watched the widows sign. Not one of these men bothered to tell the widows of a clause in the Workmen's Compensation Act that would allow them a 15 per cent increase in payments if the employer of their dead husbands was found to have been negligent. By signing the papers given them, the widows forfeited their right to apply.

The public hearing was held on January 6, jointly by the Bureau of Mines and the Kentucky Department of Mines and Minerals. The two had already issued a joint statement saying that they believed the explosion had been caused by the blasting of a boom hole and had been *propagated by coal dust.* The huge amounts of coal dust found in the mine by inspectors had no part in the hearing, though it was said that at least two federal inspectors believed the Bureau of Mines would accuse the Finleys of criminal negligence.

However, shortly after hearing of the disaster, Bureau of Mines Director Osborn let the world know how the winds should blow when he said: "This disaster was not unexpected. We've had two good years since Farmington, and we can expect one of these a year." The "two good years" were 1969 and 1970, during which 458 miners were killed, 255 of them in 1970 under Osborn's "administration" of the new law.

The public hearing could not be called a whitewash or a farce. Nobody took that much trouble. No mine inspector was called to testify, nor any of the widows, who had doubtless heard their men talk of conditions in the mine, nor the mine superintendent, a cousin of the Finleys; and no victim of previous accidents was questioned. It was not the purpose of the hearing, Osborn explained, "to levy criminal penalties against the mine operators."

However, several witnesses were called, and several hours were spent in questioning them. Finley was allowed to talk with the second shift miners before they were questioned. A few did testify that they had seen illegal explosives in the mine, but most said they had not. Investigators of the accident could have told them that they had seen pieces of Primacord, an explosive fuse that burns with a flame and is thus illegal for use in underground mines; the inspectors found evidence that Primacord had been used to connect 100 sticks of dynamite to blow out the boom hole.

Charles Finley, gently questioned on this point, didn't remember buying illegal explosives and said he knew nothing of the matter. He wasn't pressed, nor was he or anyone else questioned about past violations. Osborn said he wasn't interested in the past record of the mine.

The most important witness on the cause of the miners' deaths was not called to testify. He was Dr. Beasley, the first and only physician to see the bodies. Of the thirty-eight, he was certain that at least five had not died at once from the explosion. Their skins had the color of men dead of carbon monoxide. Men who went into the mine after the explosion found signs that miners had crawled 50 to 100 feet after the blast. They would have been breathing for at least a part of the time they crawled, but whatever air remained in the mine was quickly displaced by carbon monoxide. The five miners dead of it might have been saved had self-rescue masks been within easy reach; these masks give a man thirty minutes of breathing. Finley, though he had repeatedly been cited for not having the required masks, had none in the mine at the time of the explosion.

Charles Finley must have known from inspectors' visits that mines number 15 and 16 were deathtraps. One wonders why the blowing of the boom hole, to be done with illegal blasting materials, couldn't at least have been carried out during a weekend, when the miners were at home.

However, wonder could lead to criticism. Elbert Osborn, director of the Bureau of Mines, and thus an important cog in an Administration whose theme is "law and order," said a few days after the hearing: "I'll bet many mines have just as bad records as the Finley mines. Don't criticize the Finleys."

It looks as if Mr. Atkins was right all the way.

APPALACHIA:
THE PATH FROM DISASTER (1964)

Harry Caudill

AMERICA HAS RECENTLY discovered that a sub-nation of paupers is hidden within its opulent structure. During the past year television commentators, newspaper reporters and photographers, sociologists and assorted government agents have swarmed through the Kentucky mountains, and have beamed a panorama of misery into practically every living room in the country. To a man, the invaders have been baffled by the huddled ugliness and want that scar the landscape.

The Cumberland Plateau of Eastern Kentucky is the hard, bleak core of Appalachia, and Appalachia is a huge region of stagnation that extends through parts of nine states from Pennsylvania to Alabama. It is the largest and the best known of the islands of poverty that endure, and grow, in the United States.

In the Kentucky hills, dozens of drab little towns and mining camps and thousands of dilapidated shacks stretch up a maze of creeks and hollows. Heaps of junked automobiles clutter the roadsides and incredible quantities of trash and garbage clog the silted streams.

The roads are little more than ribbons of mud which wind through countless communities that travelers on the main highways never see. The schools fall so far short of national standards that the high school graduate generally possesses little more learning than an eighth grader in more fortunate parts of the country. The housing, if the word can be applied without irony to many of the shacks, is so poor that in November, President Kennedy ordered an emergency program to preserve the health of the people until spring. Grants of up to $1,000 per family were extended for flooring, roofing, shingles and other essential repairs.

Amid this squalor dwells a people so thoroughly pauperized that at least 50 per cent of them are dependent upon the dole and public-assistance grants for their daily bread. The reduction of this land, once so rich in natural resources, to such shabby dejection is one of the tragedies of history. The region never had good schools because the frontiersmen who settled it six generations ago were almost entirely out of contact with formal education, and the state government never required that good schools be built. Industrialists were able to buy up the mineral wealth for a pittance long before its value was recognized by the mountaineers, and, in effect, the region was placed at the mercy of a few score absentee corporations. For more than half a century the land has been systematically looted of every valuable thing within or upon it. Its timber has been converted into lumber, furniture, railroad ties and whiskey barrels. What wood escaped "development" for these purposes was sawed into props for the coal mines. Hundreds of millions of tons of coal were hauled away to distant factories. During all this orgy of extraction only the most minimal investment was made in schools and other regional facilities.

Until after the Second World War the coal industry was a mass employer of men. Abundant investment capital and advancing technology threw 100,000 American coal miners into abrupt obsolescence at almost the same moment in history as the Kentucky log forests played out and the worn mountain farms became so exhausted that crops were no longer worth the planting. The mountaineer's agricultural methods have always been extremely primitive, and his continual search for "new grounds" brought the soil to almost total ruin.

When this alarming situation was reached fifteen years ago, the nation made a grave decision, though not a conscious one. It determined that the mountaineer, though scarcely worth rehabilitating, was nonetheless an American and could not be permitted to starve to death. Half the population was put on the dole, receiving monthly issues of rations out of the scandalously large national stores of agricultural commodities. After fifteen years of "molly-grub," idleness, frustration and bewilderment the mountaineer is so demoralized that outsiders who see him almost invariably throw up their hands and flee back to the cities to tell the awful story. No one in this ingenious age has offered a real solution for his difficulties and at least one gentleman, long an adviser to Kentucky's governors, has remarked that the problems of the Kentucky mountains are past solution.

This attitude is ridiculous. If we would help the Kentucky mountaineer, we must look at him frankly, disabuse our minds of old and erroneous notions, and start a rehabilitation program geared to the needs of the man and his land.

Government programs thus far have been geared to teaching the mountaineer to farm, and year after year they have come to naught. The mountaineer is not a farmer. Few of these highlanders have farmed for a living in the last generation and most of them have been out of touch with the soil for more than half a century. They are in the main industrial workers and to them the earth is scarcely more than an expanse of dirt covering quantities of coal. Historically, it has been practically impossible to convert industrialized or urbanized people back to the land, and the Kentucky mountaineer has been no exception to this rule.

If he is to work again, it must be for industry. The immediate question is: "What can the mountaineer produce that the nation needs in large quantities?" When the nature of his land is considered, the answer is inescapable: electricity.

The Appalachian coal field is within less than a thousand miles of practically all the nation's great population centers, with the exception of Los Angeles. For more than half a century the electric power demands of the nation have doubled every eight years and experts foresee a quadrupling of electric power needs by 1980. The Edison Electric Institute has estimated that the staggering total of $175 billion will have to be invested in new generating facilities in the next twenty years if an electric-power famine is to be avoided. Thus the Appalachian coal field sits in the middle of a great and rapidly growing power market.

The corrugated landscape is streaked by swift-flowing and filthy creeks. Thousands of acres of mountainous terrain have been turned upside down by strip miners gouging out the coal. Forty-five to fifty inches of rainfall strike this tortured earth each year, lashing the region's towns and scattered hamlets with ferocious flash floods. In eastern Kentucky alone, more than 3 billion tons of coal lie unmined.

The land and people cry out for a Regional Authority comparable to the TVA and charged with a mandate to develop the total resources of the region for the nation's benefit. A modernized version of the TVA could restore the region to beauty and usefulness without any ultimate cost to the taxpayers. As in the valley of the Tennessee it should invoke that mighty trinity: water, electric power and fertilizer. An investment of approximately $1 billion could restore eastern Kentucky to productivity and, by present standards, to prosperity.

On the experience of the Tennessee Valley Authority such an agency could repay its investment with interest within thirty or thirty-five years, thus enabling the nation to retrieve this lost land and people while assuring recovery of its entire investment.

The authority should be established by Congress as a corporate body. The region's turbulent rivers and creeks should be restrained by strings of dams which would simultaneously provide substantial reservoirs for both recreational and industrial uses. Of more immediate importance, the lakes could supply cooling water for immense coal-burning electric generators. The development of mine-mouth power plants, plus construction of rather small peaking-period hydro plants, is the most likely solution to the area's troubles. The availability of an abundance of low-cost power would attract light manufacturing industries —particularly those using wood or coal derivatives—and commence a cycle of economic diversification. Five plants similar in size to those operated by TVA and situated on the fringes of the plateau would consume nearly 500 carloads of fuel per day. The surplus power could be conveyed by new high-voltage systems to any load center in the nation. This immense market could restore the moribund coal industry to prosperity and send at least 3,500 mountaineers back into the pits.

The region is presently dying for lack of revenue for investment in schools and other public facilities. Congress should charge the corporation with the stern duty to plow back into regional development in the impoverished counties at least one mill per kilowatt-hour produced. Such an investment in schools, roads, libraries, health facilities, reforestation and land reclamation could work a genuine miracle in transforming the whole face of the land. Most of the expenses of the authority could be paid out of the proceeds of power sales. However, it should not be expected to pay the entire cost of regional renaissance from income. The population of the United States is mushrooming at such a fantastic rate that current estimates envision one billion Americans by 2065. An unavoidable duty to our posterity should impel us to set many of the idle mountaineers to work reforesting the hillsides so that the multitudes who will crowd into the country on our own departing footsteps will find this tattered region in a state fit for their occupancy.

Obviously this scheme cannot work unless it is hedged with certain safe-guards. Most urgently needed is an act of Congress to prohibit the strip mining of coal in the steep Appalachian Mountains. This atrocious practice is transforming vast areas of forest land into desert, silting up countless miles of public waterways, rendering the countryside hideous to look at, and wasting immense quantities of coal—coal that can never be mined by any presently known method of recovery.

A national agency is the appropriate device. The water and mud pouring down from the highlands cross state lines, as do the coal shipments. Similarly the region's problems are being transmitted at a quickening tempo to the nation's cities, so that the tragedy of Appalachian deterioration forces itself upon the mind and conscience of the entire country. Unless national solutions for its ills are found, Appalachia will become a rotting corpse nauseating our national system.

The authority must be vested with power to discipline the inhabitants into acceptance of normal social standards. The dumping of trash and garbage into waterways ought to be sternly suppressed. Sanitary trash disposal centers should be established and the unsightly junkyards should be swept away from the roadsides.

There is nothing radical or visionary about this scheme. The mechanics have been tested and proved in the Tennessee Valley and the Columbia River Basin. The risk of financial loss is minimal, since the growth of the nation will virtually guarantee a reliable market for the region's product. Spokesmen for the Southeastern Power Administration have repeatedly asserted that it could market the area's entire power output—both hydro and steam—without any foreseeable difficulty. As the coal reserves decline, cleaned-up countryside, glistening with lakes and green with new forests, would make possible the adaptation of the land to other uses. Thus a 10,000-square-mile territory presently reverting to wasteland could find a stable place within the national framework.

In April, 1963, President Kennedy appointed a committee—the President's Appalachian Regional Commission—to make a careful study of the woes of Appalachia and recommend remedial legislation for submission to the Congress. Under the chairmanship of Franklin D. Roosevelt, Jr., the group conscientiously and zealously tackled its task. In protracted tours of the Appalachian backlands its members acquired an excellent grasp of the problem. As might have been expected, they found a monumental lack of interest in several state houses. In some states effective political machines have been constructed on the servile support of a "kept" population of "welfare voters." Local political pressures thus enforce the *status quo* and are exerted strongly upon state officials.

The commission's report to President Johnson was released on February 25. It recognizes the essential difference between foreign aid and domestic welfare programs, and sees the fallacy of the latter:

> By Congressional directive, our foreign aid funds are spent to build institutions and provide the structure for self-generative growth; by tradition we spend welfare funds in Appalachia to sustain over a million American families in unproductive destitution.

The commission's recommendations are excellent—as far as they go. They contemplate an investment of about $1 billion in eastern Kentucky in an effort to lift it to the threshold of a self-supporting economy. Principally, this capital investment would go for education, highways, airports, recreational and flood-control lakes, reforestation of private lands and the establishment of a huge new national forest. All these are essential objectives.

The difficulty with the report is threefold: it contemplates a weak state-federal agency to sponsor regional renaissance, it omits any provision for utilization of the immense coal beds, and it does not contemplate any effective effort to upgrade the schools to normal national standards. The suggested development corporation would divide responsibility between Washington and the state capitals. It would thereby place in the hands of dozens of potent county political machines the indirect power to veto or cripple any undertaking deemed too disturbing to the ultraconservative courthouse cliques.

In many areas—and in eastern Kentucky particularly—the sole industrial resource of any real consequence is coal. To undertake the rehabilitation of an idled mass of industrial workmen without resort to their principal industrial resource would appear to be as difficult as dipping water with a sieve. As one jobless coal miner remarked, "It looks like they're going to make a wrecked car run without fixin' its engine!" . . .

THE LANDSCAPING OF HELL (1966)

Wendell Berry

AT FRANKFORT, KY., last August 25 and October 4 and 5, there was a hearing on three new strip-mine regulations proposed by the Strip Mining and Reclamation Division of the Kentucky Department of Natural Resources. These new regulations were later adopted and put into effect, and now even stricter measures are pending before the present session of the state legislature. And so there begins to be some evidence that the state government has at last undertaken a serious interest in one of the state's most urgent problems. But since they face a powerful and determined opposition, the supporters of Governor Breathitt's new legislation might do well to consider the attitude and the morality displayed by the mining companies at the hearings of last August and October.

The proposed rules, as was made clear, were based on the careful research of trained men. Their purpose was to control—if not stop, then at least reduce—the erosion and water pollution that have so far been the inevitable by-products of strip mining. The gist of much of the testimony of the division's expert witnesses was that the authors of the regulations had striven toward a maximum leniency. For instance, the table of standards that would regulate contour stripping of the steep slopes of East Kentucky was based upon a safety factor of one which would assure control only under ideal conditions—the lowest possible safety factor. "To recommend a factor lower than one," a University of Kentucky professor of Civil Engineering testified, "is to recommend failure." It was also stated without contradiction by the coal companies, that of the 112 coal operations in East Kentucky all but twenty-two were at present working within the proposed limits as to extent of cut and degree of slope—which suggests that the regulations are lenient indeed.

But in spite of the minimal nature of the proposals, the opposition of the coal companies was inflexible and absolute. The company lawyers in their rebuttal made it clear that they would not be satisfied except by the defeat of even the least attempt to establish not only stricter controls but *any* controls whatsoever. They displayed no disposition to compromise, and no interest in discovering less destructive ways of mining. (Their witnesses indicated that the companies spend little or nothing on experimentation which might lead to less wasteful methods of extraction and reclamation.) The testimony of the expert witnesses who appeared in behalf of the companies was peculiarly clouded and disordered by the assumptions and intentions of the company lawyers, and by the testimony of several coal operators who also appeared as witnesses. There was a very obvious intent to use scientific evidence to prove that the best method of mining is the one that is most profitable, and that the best method of reclamation is the one that is cheapest. There was much yielding to the temptation to present theory and opinion as fact, and to look upon the failure to discover a remedy as proof that there is no remedy. . . .

There was in the statements and questions of the coal company attorneys, and in the testimony of the operators, the unmistakable implication that anything can be justified by profit; that a man may own the land in the same sense in which he would own a piece of furniture or a suit of clothes; it is his to exploit, misuse or destroy altogether should he decide that to do so would be economically feasible. The question of the morality of any practice, for these men, has been completely replaced by the question of its profitability: if it makes money it is good; if it makes money for *them* they are doomed and eager to defend it. Evident in the testimony of some was the assumption that the steep mountainsides, now being ruined on an almost unbelievable scale and at great speed, are good for nothing else.

In short, the strategy of the coal companies was simply to ignore or redefine the issue. The issue, so far as the division was concerned, was to determine how much control there should be. The coal companies hardly bothered to deal with that question. The issue they persisted in raising and speaking to was whether or not there should be any control at all.

At the close of the hearing one of the company lawyers rose to offer the "assurance" that, though the operators are working for profit, they do not wish to do so at the expense of the public welfare, or the welfare of their neighbors. They're concerned about the economic factor, he said, because they operate on a narrow margin of profit. There are a lot of irresponsible people in the coal business, he admitted, but he predicted reassuringly that those irresponsibles will bring about their own failure. He did not explain this process; presumably they will be dealt with by the same just and unerring Fate that so effectively deletes irresponsibility from the legal profession. . . .

The mining companies, then, have made it abundantly clear that they will destroy anything, they will stop at nothing, so long as the result can be inked in black on their accounting sheets. They have been abetted by the mischief and greed of local officials, by public indifference, by state paralysis, by federal cross-purposes and confusion. Against them there has been only a local organization of small land-owners: The Appalachian Group to Save the Land and the People, headed by Leroy Martin of Hazard.

It has become plain that if there is to remain any hope at all for the region, strip mining, at least in its present methods, will have to be stopped. Otherwise, all the federal dollars devoted to the region's poor will have the same effect as rain pouring on an uprooted plant. To recover good hope and economic health the people need to have their land whole under their feet. And much of their land, seemingly beyond the reach of the bemused and fumbling powers that might have saved it, has already been destroyed.

To destroy a forest or an ecology or a species is an act of greater seriousness than we have perhaps yet grasped, and it is perhaps of graver consequence. But given even a comparatively short time, these destructions will mend. The forest will grow back, the natural balances will be restored, the ecological gap left by the destroyed species will be filled by another species. But to destroy the earth itself is to destroy all the possibilities of the earth, among them the possibility of recovery. The land destroyed by strip mining is destroyed forever; it will never again be what it was; it will never be what it would have become if let alone. Such destruction—which can now be accomplished on a vast scale by a few men in a short time—makes man a parasite upon the source of his life; it implicates him in the death of the earth, the destruction of his meanings. Those men who send the bulldozer blades into the mountainsides bear the awesome burden of responsibility for an act that no one can fully comprehend, much less justify.

And though violence to the earth must seem in the long view to be the gravest of their offenses, one is no less troubled by their violence to justice. For do not all our rights have as their ultimate expression and meaning the right of a man to be secure in his own home? When this right is no longer defended by any power greater than himself, his days begin to come to him by accident, in default of whatever caprice of power may next require his life. When the possessions and households of citizens are no longer honored by the acts, as well as the principles of their government, then the concentration camp ceases to be one of the possibilities of human nature and becomes one of its likelihoods. . . .

MINE SAFETY AND STRIP MINING (1974)

Duane Lockard

. . . THE SHARPEST CONTRAST of all between American and British miners is . . . the little known story of the varying ways the two countries faced the issue of technological unemployment. Typically, the American way was simply to automate—and let the consequences fall on the worker who inevitably was unable to protect himself without support of his union. In Britain, with a stronger union movement and nationalized mines, the issue of "redundancy" of workers idled by ever higher productivity was resolved in such a way as to give the miners full consideration.

The coal industry is one of the most outstanding examples of greatly increased industrial productivity in the last thirty years. The output of coal in

America is now roughly what it was at the end of World War II (British production is somewhat lower), but the work force required for that production in both countries has been reduced by about 400,000 men. (In Britain it dropped from 700,000 to 260,000 and in the United States from 500,000 to 125,000.) Some mechanization began earlier, but at the close of World War II, most coal was still mined underground with pick and shovel. Now half of all American coal comes from surface mining, and underground mining technology bears little resemblance to the crude methods of the 1940s. As a result, British production per man-shift doubled and in the United States the increase has been even greater.

In Britain it is the proud claim of the National Coal Board that, by making adjustments, this enormous reduction in work force did not result in dismissal of superfluous workers. Staff experts of the National Union of Miners and their counterparts in the National Coal Board agreed: no one was to be left to fend for himself because of job setbacks or when collieries were closed. Four alternatives were open to redundant miners. First, the retirement age was lowered and early retirement benefits took care of a considerable proportion; the average age of British miners is much higher than in other industries. Second, relocation at other mines was an option for many workers. And that was a real offer, for the miner and his wife could visit, at NCB expense, any mine with job openings, to size up the mine, housing and community. Many took that option, remaining if possible in their own regions. Another option was to accept a tiding-over severance pay to sustain the worker while he sought other employment. (This supplemented unemployment compensation benefits.) Finally, retraining for another line of work was provided for, but like manpower retraining programs here it appears to have had little success.

One sociological study of the impact of closing a mine near Durham gives an indication of how the alternatives worked out in practice. When the Ryhope mine closed down after more than 100 years, 844 workers were jobless. More than 60 per cent of them were relocated in mines within the Durham region. Only 3 per cent went to mines in other regions. Some 100 workers stayed on for salvage work or left voluntarily for other employment, leaving 182 officially declared redundant. Of these, forty-three were retrained for other jobs, the majority of them ending in unskilled occupations where they earned less than they had as miners. Another eighty-four registered as disabled and got benefits, and the remainder either retired early or received redundancy payments, based upon the length of time they had been miners. The median sum was about £350, but a sizable minority got in excess of £500. Admittedly these are not princely sums, and miners complain of the inadequacy of their compensation, but *something* was indeed done for every man thrown out of work.

It is an indication of the American attitude that we do not know how many miners were cast aside by the automation process. In Britain the annual reports of the Coal Board reflect these figures, but in the United States one can only find rough estimates, the best of them being that about 10,000 to 15,000 lost their jobs each year during the 1950s and 1960s. There is even less hard information about what became of the surplus miners. Only workers old enough to retire got any kind of amelioration and that was minimal—$100 a month, which was reduced to $75 for a period in the early 1960s—until as a campaign ploy by Tony Boyle in his contest with Jock Yablonski it was raised to $150. To aid somewhat, in 1965 the age of eligibility was lowered to 55, but to a pensioner of that age, not yet able to get Social Security, $100 or even $150 a month was not much help.

The essence of it is that John L. Lewis sold out the mass of miners in 1951 when he decided that automation was necessary for the survival of coal in its competition with oil and gas. As a result he reached an accommodation with the industry that was to last during the remainder of his tenure and that of his successor, W.A. (Tony) Boyle. Nor was it necessarily wrong to support automation. Cutting manpower is one thing, but the question of who pays for it is another. Lewis and the coal companies he once scourged with abusive rhetoric decided to let the miner bear the cost alone. The union refused to incorporate any benefits that the British miner received except for the retirement benefits. Even so the eligibility rules for retirement and health benefits were juggled about so much that many miners who had worked as long as forty years were declared ineligible for retirement benefits—because they had not spent twenty of their last thirty years in mines covered by the royalty agreement. In 1973 in the *Blankenship* case a court ordered 17,000 former ineligibles returned to the rolls, and the judge spoke of the capriciousness in manipulating rules for eligibility.

The results in Appalachian coal fields were inevitable: unemployment was widespread and poverty was so extensive that it moved John F. Kennedy to voice his concern about West Virginia during his campaign for the Presidency. And laying off these tens of thousands of men helped bring the special legislation aimed at relieving Appalachian poverty. That at least was its ostensible purpose, although it achieved little. The ultimate degradation came late in the Lyndon Johnson era when the make-work "happy-pappy" program was inaugurated. It soon was allowed to expire.

If what the government did was little and sometimes demeaning, union and industry did nothing. So the squalor grew in half-abandoned mine towns, where former miners living in shacks saw their children go hungry, deprived of a good education and denied opportunities for a career. Congressional committees investigated the issue again and again, and both the union and company spokesmen emphasized that the difficulty was competition with imported oil. Little was said of the impact of automation. Indeed union spokesmen showed so little interest in the subject that their presentations varied only slightly from year to year. . . .

The coal industry is highly concentrated, like most of American industry, and the coal companies therefore command sizable economic resources. At present fifteen companies produce more than half of America's coal output, and the fifty largest produce two-thirds of it. Of the fifteen largest producers only one is an independent coal company, and it has other mining interests scattered around the world. Six of the fifteen are directly owned by oil corporations, resulting in a classic conflict of interest. In fact, one reason for the recent worldwide oil crisis was the oil industry's refusal to develop the technology to produce petroleum from bituminous coal. It preferred, instead, to exploit the cheap Middle East oil, thus escaping American taxes and reserving American oil holdings and all coal reserves (comprising 87 per cent of the available fuel in the United States) for future exploitation. The Germans developed methods to convert coal into oil during World War II, but Jersey Standard acquired exclusive American rights to this process as a way of reducing competition. Now the oil companies that own coal firms have better ways of dealing with the problem: they can manipulate coal operations to suit their larger interests in oil. While oil and natural gas represent our scarcest fuel reserves, they also represent 77 per cent of our national energy consumption, a strangely skewed allocation of scarce resources. But of course we have no national fuel policy, just a national profits policy.

The coal industry has the resources and an economic interest to manipulate coal production to its own ends. And now with the unprecedented demand for coal, and with the price high, the industry wants to go where the cheapest low-sulfur coal is. That is not under the hills of Appalachia but in the strip mines of the upper Plains States, where there is good quality coal which can be extracted at relatively low cost.

The prospect of exploiting Western coal, along with the drive for mine safety, has put Miller in a dilemma. When he was campaigning for the union's presidency Miller was anti-strip mining, but after he took office he was more reticent on the issue and for a long time the union took no position on the bill before Congress to set a national policy of control of strip mining. The problem is that strip mining now produces one-half of all coal and that means it pays half the royalties into the welfare fund, royalties that are essential to the well-being of Eastern underground miners. Moreover, Miller wants to organize the Western strip miners and an anti-stripping position might jeopardize that task. However, in spite of pressure from some union officials against that stand, Miller announced his support of the strongest version of the bill.

Whatever this does to the UMW's prospects for organizing Western strip mining, a problem remains. The industry wants to move toward stripping because it is concerned about the costs of the "safety or else" campaign, which will boost the price of coal. As the recent history of European mining indicates, mining death and accident rates can be sharply reduced, but admittedly not without paying for safety. In Europe, governments subsidize safety; here the miner subsidizes the cost of coal—in blood. Thus the new militancy of the union on safety may be another reason for pushing the coal companies westward. That is why the current controversy in Congress over the strip-mining bill is being fought so intensely: the issues at stake greatly transcend the conservation issue that always arises. The prime question is in fact the future of coal and coal miners for decades to come.

COAL: STILL A DISASTER AREA (1977)

J. Davitt McAteer and L. Thomas Galloway

IN 1969 CONGRESS enacted the Federal Coal Mine Health and Safety Act, the toughest safety and health law in the country's history. In the years since the Act has been in effect, the hopes it raised have been dashed, the promise of improved health and safety remaining largely unfulfilled. Coal mines are still America's most dangerous work places.

The reasons for the failures are many, but a major factor has been the people selected during the Nixon-Ford years to administer, interpret and enforce the law. The Carter administration could have changed that situation by now, but it has done little, leaving the high-level positions in the hands of "acting" personnel.

Like most other safety legislation, the 1969 Act followed a major disaster —the explosion of the Consol No. 9 Mine in Farmington, W. Va. Even so, the legislation ran into stiff White House opposition, and Nixon signed the bill only after miners threatened a nationwide strike. His administration's lack of enthusiasm for mine safety, as shown by his threatened veto, continued into the implementation of the legislation. A month after the Act became effective, the able, tough Bureau of Mines director who was to have overseen its enforcement was dismissed by the White House on twenty-four hours' notice.

After six months during which one nominee for the vacant post was withdrawn because of Congressional protest that he was unqualified, Nixon appointed an engineer with little interest in health and safety. This new chief safety-enforcement officer publicly assured the industry that he did not think various sections of the tough new law called for vigorous enforcement. The tone was thus set for lax administration and enforcement of the new law.

Industry was pleased, but men continued to suffer injury and to die at an appalling rate, and Congress became increasingly disturbed by the failure to enforce mine health and safety regulations. On December 30, 1970, the Finley Mine in Hyden, Ky., exploded, killing thirty-eight men. As a result of this disaster and the continuing clamor by various Senators and Congressmen about the lack of inspections and the low civil penalties, safety and health enforcement matters were separated from the Bureau of Mines. A new agency, the Mining Enforcement and Safety Administration (MESA), was created within Interior.

The agency's name changed, but Nixon saw to it that the lax enforcement would continue. He chose as the first administrator of MESA James M. Day, a former Republican county chairman of Arlington, Va., who had little experience in coal mine safety. Under pressure from the United Mine Workers the Senate balked at the nomination. The White House refused to withdraw Day's name, and he served one year as a virtual lame-duck acting administrator. Enforcement of the Act continued to drift; for all practical purposes the agency was leaderless.

Political cronyism was not restricted to the top position in the mine safety bureaucracy. Ed Failor took over as head of the office charged with collecting fines for violations of the Act. He had no experience in mining, and was apparently appointed in return for his work as campaign director for the GOP stalwart Clark MacGregor. His previous employment included one term as a municipal judge in Dubuque, Iowa, and lobbyist for the Iowa Association for Coin-Operated Laundries.

The fines assessed by Failor's office would not have financed a week's wash. They amounted to less than 3¢ per ton of coal mined. In fact, the program was so carelessly designed and administered that a federal court struck down even these small fines as being arbitrary and capricious.

The Interior Department and mine safety were popular resting places for other Nixon campaign supporters. John Ehrlichman attempted to place a political protégé as head of the Office of Hearings and Appeals (OHA) to replace a previous political appointee who had fallen from favor. However, this move was so crass that the usually somnolent Civil Service Commission rejected the appointee. James P. Richards, formerly a Nixon campaign official in Colorado, ultimately filled the position, a key office in interpreting the new law.

While director of OHA, Richards also sat as an ex officio member of the Board of Mine Operations Appeals, the Secretary of the Interior's final voice in mine safety matters. During its six years of operation, the board became a political dumping ground. The chief judge of the board had been the legislative assistant to Republican Sen. Len B. Jordan of Idaho, and before that a two-term member of the Idaho House of Representatives. He had no connection with coal mining or any known commitment to coal mine safety.

No board member had any previous experience in coal mine safety law or in coal mining, notwithstanding the fact that the board must constantly decide complicated technical issues of mine safety. Nor were any of the members outstanding in administrative law or procedure. By and large, they were simply politically active Republicans who were being rewarded for their efforts and connections with well-paying sinecures for life.

The board has continually ruled against the miners' interests, opting for crabbed and often illogical interpretations of the Act. For example, in one of its most shortsighted rulings, the board has refused to allow federal inspectors to close a mine unless there is a 50 percent chance that a man will die or suffer serious injury—hardly the criterion Congress had intended in 1969.

In addition to the political cronies, appointments have gone to persons with long-standing ties to industry or a strong industry bias. Secretaries of Interior have historically been pro-industry, possibly the most extreme example being Rogers C.B. Morton, Nixon's second Secretary of the Interior, whose brother sat on the board of the Pittston Coal Co., one of the nation's largest producers.

Kent Frizzel, a Kansas Republican who lost his gubernatorial race in 1970, was in the number-two spot at Interior for a substantial time. Known to be one of the coal industry's strongest supporters, he improperly censured an administrative law judge for raising penalties against an operator, and reversed a decision imposing liability on independent contractors who break the law at coal mines. Frizzel appointed Fred Karem, a lawyer with no mining experience, as political watchdog on the Scotia Mine Disaster investigation panel. Karem, formerly a staff aide in the Nixon White House and an assistant to former Kentucky Gov. Louis Nunn, was reported by the *Mountain Eagle* (Whitesburg, Ky.) to have ties to Kentucky coal operators, mainly through soliciting campaign contributions for Governor Nunn.

Another appointee, the assistant secretary for Energy and Minerals, who supervised mine safety enforcement, was criticized as follows by the Carter transition team for hindering mine safety efforts: "In the past four years, the assistant secretary has not supported the [MESA] program and has delayed or obstructed efforts to improve mine safety programs. . . ."

The revolving door between government and industry has not been used exclusively by those in high-policy positions; it has been open also to the middle and lower echelons of the mine safety bureaucracy. Common Cause, in a recent study of conflict of interest in the executive branch, "Serving Two Masters," points out that "three Assistant Administrators in the Mining Enforcement and Safety Administration came from copper or coal mining companies, one of which has received a special subsidy from the Bureau of Mines." In January, one of these three left government employment to become a vice president for Pittston Coal Co.

The same pattern has developed for lawyers charged with representing MESA in the courts and before the board. The top safety lawyer recently resigned to accept a position with the American Mining Congress, an industry lobbying organization. Rank and file lawyers come to the office for a few years, learn the trade, and then depart to the coal companies. After one year, the law permits them to handle health and safety matters for the companies with their old friends at the solicitor's office. Recently, two lawyers left the office to take employment with Old Ben Coal Co., one of the most litigious companies and with one of the worst records for compliance with the federal law. Another former MESA lawyer currently represents the National Independent Coal Operators Association, a bitter if not fanatical opponent of the 1969 Act and its requirements. Yet another MESA lawyer left to monitor the surface mining works for the American Mining Congress.

While all this political maneuvering and job-hunting was taking place, more than 1,000 coal miners died of work-related causes. Since 1970, an estimated 125,000 miners have been injured. And, according to the UMWA, 2,500 miners have died of black lung, and seventeen out of every 100 working miners have contracted the disease. Each year a working miner faces a one-in-eight chance that he will suffer an injury.

And the major disasters continue:

Hyden, Ky.		
Finley Coal Co.	Dec. 30, 1970	38 killed
Buffalo Creek, W.Va.		
The Pittston Group	Feb. 26, 1972	125 killed
Blacksville, W.Va.		
Consolidation Coal Co.	July 22, 1972	9 killed
Itmann, W.Va.		
Consolidation Coal Co.	Dec. 16, 1972	5 killed
Scotia, Ky.		
Blue Diamond Coal Co.	Mar. 9–11, 1976	28 killed
Tower City, Pa.		
Kocher Coal Co.	Feb. 27, 1977	7 killed
St. Charles, Va.		
P. & P. Coal Co.	July 7, 1977	4 killed

Meanwhile, the penalties paid for violations of the Act have remained less than 3¢ a ton, and American coal mines continue to be among the most dangerous work places in the Western world.

The Carter administration came to power with an opportunity to effect radical changes in coal mining safety. The President and his Secretary of the Interior, Cecil Andrus, must fill a number of positions that will have a direct bearing on safety in the mines. Many of these positions are in the hands of lame-duck holdovers. The top job, administrator of MESA, awaits a final appointment; the number-one safety lawyer job is still vacant. Until these and other key positions are filled—with qualified and dedicated persons—the administration is vulnerable to the charge of indifference to the miner's lot.

THE UMW:
NEED PAST BE PROLOGUE? (1980)

Curtis Seltzer

A DECADE AGO, dying was a way of life in the Appalachian coal fields. Newspapers across the country headlined a grisly murder out of southwestern Pennsylvania. Joseph Yablonski, a maverick senior staffer of the United Mine Workers of America (UMWA), had been shot to death along with his wife and daughter. To many coal miners, it looked like a political assassination. Yablonski had made a respectable showing as an insurgent, reform-minded candidate in the union's presidential election only three weeks earlier. After several years of investigation and two trials, W. A. (Tony) Boyle, UMWA president until December 1972, was imprisoned for masterminding the murders which he financed with union cash.

Ten years ago Richard Nixon, who was courting blue-collar constituents at the time, reluctantly signed the most substantial occupational health and safety bill Congress had ever passed. The 1969 Federal Coal Mine Health and Safety Act responded to political pressure created by two tragic events in 1968–1969 that wheeled national media into the stark hollows of wintertime West Virginia.

First, methane blew up an underground mine in Mannington, West Virginia, operated by Consolidation Coal Company, a subsidiary of Continental Oil. Seventy-eight miners were entombed. Had there been adequate federal regulation or had Consol taken common sense precautions, the methane would not have been ignited. But the law was a "sham," as President Truman had said when he signed it. A lot of straight-thinking folks throughout the coal industry thought that Consolidation had assassinated those seventy-eight miners just as surely as if its chief executive officer had sparked the gas himself. The 1969 Act, therefore, spelled out strict mine ventilation standards and gas control procedures. Over the last decade these regulations have almost eliminated methane explosions from coal mining, which had lost more than 7,500 lives to them since 1906.

Second, about eleven years ago 40,000 West Virginia miners quit work for three weeks over some invisible dust. After twenty or thirty years, thousands of veteran miners had each sucked in a couple of ounces of mine dust. By the late 1960s, these specks, which billowed from the cutting heads of the mining machines introduced in the late 1940s, had blackened their lungs and darkened their future. Miners wheezed; they choked; they died. Coal dust won't hurt you, the company doctors told them, it's cigarettes; why some even said the dust kept down tuberculosis.

But observable facts, thousands of disabled miners and a handful of hell-raisers, three MDs, a spunky congressman, some VISTAs and a few dozen angry miners and their wives, crashed through this scientific stonewall, inserting "coal workers' pneumoconiosis" into coal-field vernacular. The critics demanded disability compensation from the West Virginia legislature in early 1969. And it took a statewide strike and several thousand miners threatening to take the state capitol apart "brick by brick" to thread a modest bill through the legislature. UMWA president Boyle didn't help much. Although some union-related medical professionals had battled the medical community for years over recognizing coal workers' pneumoconiosis as a disabling disease, Boyle ridiculed the black lung insurgents. He correctly saw that the prevalence of the disease was as much an indictment of UMWA policy since 1950 as it was of the operators' negligence.

Ten months later, Congress mandated a comprehensive dust-reduction program—the strictest standard in the world, mine-by-mine dust-control plans and an unprecedented monitoring program—as well as federal compensation for the disabled. The results are clear. An industry that never thought to suppress the dust that killed its workers, now does. Today many fewer miners are contracting occupational respiratory disease than a decade ago.

A shaky but determined rank-and-file reform movement emerged from these episodes. It sought to alter the industry's most important power balances —between miner and operator, between miner and union leader, between miner and politician. For a while in the mid-1970s the reformers, who ousted Boyle in a court-ordered election in December 1972, struck tentative new balances. But the insurgent spirit flagged. Reform leader Arnold Miller lost his rank-and-file bearings after three or four years. When he retired in November 1979, Sam Church, Jr., took over.

To understand how the UMWA spent eight turbulent years completing a 360-degree political circle requires understanding why death was a way of life in the union coal fields in the late 1960s. Those answers are deeply embedded in the "sweetheart" relationship John L. Lewis arranged with the major coal companies in the last decade—the 1950s—of his forty-year tenure as UMWA president.

In the late 1940s demand for Appalachian coal dropped out of sight, much as it has for the last three years. Oil and gas had infiltrated coal's traditional markets in locomotive fuel and residential heating because of their cheapness, reliability, and convenience. The coal industry had too many mine operators, too much coal, too much competition, and too little labor peace. Too much coal meant falling prices and falling profits. It also meant a lot of unemployment.

After several unsuccessful experiments, Lewis concluded that the UMWA's interest lay in helping the major companies weather the extended drought. So he aligned the union with these companies, who had organized the Bituminous Coal Operators' Association (BCOA). His end of the bargain involved: 1) reducing the labor cost of mining for unionized companies by helping them mechanize and hold down wages and benefits; 2) reducing output and price competition from small companies; 3) combining with the industry to promote coal use and preventing public regulation; and 4) keeping his members in line when working conditions, safety and employment deteriorated. In return, he made the UMWA into one of the richest unions in the country, financed cradle-to-grave medical coverage for employed miners, and made sure that an industry crunch would not lead to nationalization as it had in Britain.

The operators dovetailed a four-part survival strategy of their own which they coordinated with Lewis.

Part one involved the workplace. Labor productivity was tripled through the new "labor-saving" underground machines; strip mining, which was two or three times more efficient than deep mining, doubled its share of output; working conditions improved only as a by-product of mining technology; mining jobs were cut by 70 percent between 1950 and 1969 with no drop in output; miners, thankful to be working during an industry-wide depression, swallowed their grievances rather than file them.

Part two involved the industry itself. Small companies, which could underprice the majors, were cut out of their markets; the big companies reduced competition among themselves through a kind of industrial conference of Versailles in 1954 when the victors—the big companies—decided which smaller companies each was to get (mergers, they called them); the big companies negotiated long-term contracts with electric utilities that guaranteed a market at predictable prices; and, finally, once the big coal companies had plumped themselves sufficiently oil companies and conglomerates scooped them up like so many fat hens.

Part three involved the UMWA. Lewis prompted productivity gains even to the point of loaning mechanization capital from the union or the UMWA-owned National Bank of Washington; the UMWA never called a contract strike against the industry from 1950 to 1972; and Lewis and Boyle snuffed out wildcat strikes.

This UMWA-BCOA strategy in the 1950s produced conditions of life and work that created the rank-and-file rebellion in the late 1960s. Pneumoconiosis, for example, was a direct product of the lack of dust controls on the new underground machines, industry's disregard for the health implications of its new technology, the UMWA's inattention to occupational health protection, and Congressional and administration disinterest in imposing dust standards or providing disability benefits. Mine safety problems which the Mannington disaster illuminated were products of the same factors. Finally, the 1969 Yablonski challenge to Boyle, which the black lung revolt and the Mannington explosion precipitated, was a reaction to Lewis and Boyle's ham-handed management of union miners. Stripped of their right to elect district officials and ratify contracts, cut off arbitrarily from medical and pension benefits, intimidated at union conventions and fearful of workplace retribution for union militancy, miners began to strike and organize against the union in the mid-1960s to protest the anti-labor terms of the UMWA-BCOA alliance. Eventually, things got so bad that Yablonski jumped ship.

When the reformers—Miners for Democracy (MFD)—dumped Boyle in a December 1972 rerun of the disputed 1969 election, observers thought the slate had been wiped clean. New faces appeared at the union's Washington headquarters. Miller, a disabled mine electrician and black lung victim who had never been a UMWA employee, was now president of 150,000 working miners. Gutsy, pro-worker language sparkled in union publications and press statements. New programs were whipped into being. A cadre of smart, young lawyers and journalists whose political ideas were shaped by the 1960s and their organizing experiences in the coal fields took on important staff jobs. As promised, the MFD democraticized the union's constitution and its internal procedures. The 1974 contract made up a lot of ground that Lewis and Boyle had deliberately lost. Doubled coal prices and talk of a new coal boom gave industry negotiators enough flexibility to try to "buy" labor peace after the Lewis-Boyle "sweetheart" appeared canceled.

The comparative ease of instituting these first-step reforms generated enthusiasm and momentum. But it had the effect of papering over the reformers' weaknesses. MFD had no program or ideology to help its leaders frame goals and link them to a process of achieving them. As administrators, MFD people were further impeded by their own lack of union management experience. Consequently, they either shied from or were unable to effect the changes needed to institutionalize and depersonalize their victory. For these reasons and others, the reform base in the union's membership never grew.

By December 1977, when Miller's second term began, the reform movement had ended. The spirit that had mobilized miners in the early 1970s had run its course. Expectations were still high but nothing much seemed possible any more. Many miners had turned either left or right during the last years of Miller's first term. More often than not they had become cynical and disgusted with their leaders.

Collective bargaining in the winter of 1977–1978 brought the failures of Miller and the UMWA into focus. Although the UMWA's convention had developed a strong set of bargaining objectives, union negotiators ignored almost all of them.

The operators, while having divisions of their own, were generally of one mind about the need to use deteriorating markets as a means to establish contractual power over their workers. "Labor stability" was the industry's term, and reporters usually wrote it without attribution. It thus became a "public-interest" objective. The BCOA also wanted to refinance the jointly administered welfare and retirement fund and to increase worker productivity through bonus-for-output plans. A long strike would not necessarily hurt many big coal companies because their customers—electric utilities and steel mills—had built mammoth stockpiles. Further, since many of the major operators were themselves subsidiaries of energy companies, a long shutdown in coal would not have disastrous financial impacts.

The BCOA demanded a labor pacification program to create "labor stability" that was a page out of the industry's nineteenth century. Strikers and absentees could be fined and fired without appeal. With the help of the Carter Administration the BCOA forced Miller to accept contract language so repressive that it was twice rejected by the union membership, once through a formal vote. A third contract was approved only after the BCOA moderated the tone, though not much of the substance, of their demands. Miners resigned themselves to Miller's inability to battle the companies. They ratified after striking for 110 days when they saw few choices left. The strike showed the union's loss of power. Utilities wheeled power from unaffected plants to coal-dependent ones. Non-union coal moved out of Kentucky and Virginia and over from the West. Stockpiles fell but never vanished. The Carter Administration's Taft-

Hartley injunction was voided by a federal judge who found no evidence of a national emergency.

When the strike ended, both sides licked their wounds. Things moved quickly. Eastern coal markets worsened, laying off miners already punched out by the long strike. Wildcat strikes declined in proportion to rising unemployment. Miller and Church joined the BCOA in calling for cooperation and labor peace. Miller's health deteriorated and he spent much time away from Washington. Church assumed a good deal of day-to-day management of union affairs. Miller directed Church to take responsibility for safety and organizing soon after the strike. West Virginia Governor John D. Rockefeller IV, who chaired Carter's Commission on Coal, used that platform to effect a cuddly reunion between union and management. Differences between them were not as important as the common interest in mining more coal, the Commission's line went. For two years they would be heard chanting a three-line mantra to the press and federal officials: mine more coal, burn more coal, relax "unnecessary" regulations.

These ins and outs of coal-operator politics reflect much more profound changes that are recasting the energy industry. Coal is the only important fuel whose price has not been federally regulated or fixed by a producer cartel in the last three decades. To avoid the kind of market competition that nearly bankrupted the coal industry in the 1920s, the big operators established production and marketing mechanisms in the 1950s that adjusted supply and demand, regulated competition, and concentrated production in larger and larger units. Oil companies and a few conglomerates took over in the mid-1960s and 1970s as doubts grew over oil, gas, and uranium supplies. A second motive behind the takeover was even more obvious: coal was a moneymaker. Changes in mining methods and industry structure, labor stability, and the absence of environmental and occupational regulations had turned the big coal companies into inviting prospects by the late 1960s.

As the oil companies moved in, new coal industry policies emerged. The oil companies did not invest in new coal capacity at the same rate as independent coal producers. Most of the oil company investment in coal was in the West where the UMWA is an insignificant factor and mining is more profitable. Another large part of the oil company investments went into non-energy business as part of a diversification strategy for the coming non-fossil fuel future. With OPEC driving energy prices up, the oil companies dragged their feet on shifting much of their business to coal. Oil was simply too profitable. High oil prices, in addition, allowed the coal companies to push their prices higher than cost increases would justify. (Coal's return on equity exceeds the five-year median for the top eight international oil companies, although it's not as high as some of the independent oil producers, *Forbes* reported in January 1980.) The coal industry lined up behind the oil lobby on synthetic fuel legislation, opposing federal synthetic fuel plants even when they would burn private-sector coal.

The coal-owning oil companies also began to smarten up coal's smudgy image. The companies had their scientists challenge federal air-pollution models that estimated almost 50,000 premature deaths annually from coal-fired pollutants. Acid rain and carbon dioxide buildup in the atmosphere were said to be exaggerated. Social problems in coal-field communities experiencing increased production were overblown and not really a private responsibility. Oil management began infusing fresh blood into coal's veins—even some Ivy Leaguers and a handful of hip-talking bearded types. The board rooms targeted a new "enemy" as part of the media campaign. Coal producers became the patriots of America's energy world, while federal regulations, which allegedly hampered the growth of coal, became the whipping boy. Washington bureaucrats replaced the industry's old stalwarts—wildcat strikers, do-gooders and Communists. Cleverly, the companies aligned themselves with obstreperous union miners by creating a common foe, the environmental regulators. Sam Church calls them "the EPA lobby." To its discredit, the UMWA lined up behind the industry without independently ascertaining the actual degree to which federal regulations were responsible for weak coal markets.

The outline of UMWA policy has begun to take shape. Following the December 1978 union convention, *Business Week* reported that the union ". . . now appears ready to make peace with the coal industry and itself . . ." and that Church ". . . will exercise more control over rambunctious miners." The union-BCOA partnership that Lewis arranged in the 1950s seems to be resurfacing. "Labor stability," as the industry defines it, will probably follow. That means suppression of dissenters, expulsion of mavericks and wildcat strikers, pruning of independent local leaders, and deemphasis of contract strikes as a tool in collective bargaining. Some observers guess that miners might ultimately lose the right to ratify contracts somewhere down this road.

Coal miners will be the most important labor factor in America's energy future for the next two decades. If a nuclear moratorium or construction slowdown occurs; if utilities convert boilers from oil to coal; if coal-based synthetic fuels are commercialized, then miners will be a key component in energy politics and in any consumer-labor-environmentalist coalition that materializes to oppose the energy industry.

The energy companies have all but decoupled their business from any home nation-state. Competition, as it was known earlier in this century, does not occur among energy producers or distributors. Taken as a group, they are an emerging political sovereign. Almost every one of the major energy companies has evolved in more or less similar fashion since the mid-1960s. Each has established a "position" in every fuel system (oil, gas, coal, nuclear, and solar); locked up production, transportation, and distribution facilities in each fuel system whenever possible; pegged the price of all fuels to OPEC oil; and sopped up surplus oil profits by acquiring non-energy subsidiaries.

Today, American unions—especially energy-related unions—are still applying a nineteenth-century model of industrial relations to their employers. That model won't work in the 1980s. Single-fuel unions are as outmoded as single-fuel companies. A union of coal miners cannot bargain effectively with coal executives who are fronting for international energy conglomerates. The same is true of oil and gas workers, as well as utility and transportation workers. The pressure to form a single union of U.S. energy workers would logically involve bargaining coordination and institutional links with energy workers in energy-producing countries. Such a path is nothing more or less than that already traveled by the industry. A single-energy union would provide labor with a new kind of bargaining leverage, increase labor's political influence, and allow workers to shape environmental and economic decisions that management now makes on its own.

Part II
HYDRO-ELECTRIC AND ELECTRIC POWER

PREFACE

HYDRO PRODUCTION is relatively modest in the overall energy picture of the United States, providing about 4 percent of the national total. But it is significant in terms of the underlying political issues it has raised and the political forces it has stimulated. The chapter opens with Senator George W. Norris, "father" of the Tennessee Valley Authority, explaining in 1923 why he opposed the turning over of a major water-power site to industrialist Henry Ford, who wished to build dams for cheap power on the Tennessee River: "I would not give away the heritage of a people even to a saint." Successive readings trace the fights for public development of water power and the militant opposition of the electric utility industry and its allies to public regulation or ownership. The buying of professors and educators and the manipulation of the press as part of a massive public relations campaign to convince the public are summarized, drawing upon such landmark documents as the 1934 report of the Federal Trade Commission.

The call of Morris L. Cooke, pioneering engineer and conservationist, for public planning and yardstick public ownership expresses the progressive sentiment that was to guide future fights throughout the nation. Writers Raymond Gram Swing, Stuart Chase, and Ernest Kirschten highlight the achievements of the TVA and Judson King, reformer and planner, recounts the triumphs of the Rural Electrification Administration. Author Carey McWilliams's careful discussion of the bitter fights over the proposals for organic development of the Columbia River under a Columbia Valley Authority provides basic clues as to why a Missouri Valley Authority never came into being and why the TVA, the highpoint of American experimentation and internationally perhaps the most admired of its development efforts, has never been repeated. *Nation* correspondent Bruce Catton and TVA head Gordon R. Clapp report on specific legislative assaults under the Eisenhower administration to undo the public power accomplishments. This was the period when the TVA was fighting for its life. One recalls congressional proposals to remove from the Norris and other dams the inscription "Built for the People of the United States" lest it encourage favorable attitudes toward public ownership.

About 30 percent of the nation's total fossil fuel use goes to the production of electricity. Populist Senator Lee Metcalf explains some of the devices used by utilities to pad their rates, and law professor William H. Rodgers, Jr., reports on the national planning of a major holding company. Attorney Irving Like demystifies the rate-making of the private utilities and provides groundwork for opposing nuclear development by these companies and for linking alternative renewable energy with public ownership. And a cluster of articles offers glimpses of current battles in New England, the Great Plains, and California for responsible electric power and conservation. One could add many other regional illustrations, if space permitted, but these selections offer some evidence that those who are fighting the planning of private utilities are not as isolated as they are often led to feel.

WHY HENRY FORD
WANTS MUSCLE SHOALS (1923)

George W. Norris

I READ WITH interest *The Nation*'s challenge to Henry Ford to operate Muscle Shoals to make cheap fertilizer for the people, without profit. It is a novel plan. There is no danger, however, of Mr. Ford accepting it. If we were to give Muscle Shoals to anybody, I would just as soon give it to Henry Ford as anyone else. I have never made any personal attack upon him, and I am not moved in my opposition regarding Muscle Shoals by any feeling of animosity or ill-will. He is a man whom in many respects I greatly admire, but I would not give away the heritage of the people even to a saint. I would not be willing to do it even if Mr. Ford could give us a guaranty that he would live for one hundred years—the lifetime of his corporation, which, under his plan, would have the ownership and control of the property. If it were not for his popularity in the country, his proposition would not receive favorable consideration from the hands of anyone.

If Mr. Ford is able to produce nitrates as cheaply as it is claimed he can, there is no reason in the world why he should not at once proceed to do it. It is not necessary that the Government should donate to him millions of dollars' worth of public property in order to have him perform this very much desired thing. If he were a poor man and claimed to have some knowledge that no one else possessed, which he could not transmit to anyone else, and was thus moved by the philanthropic desire to help his fellow-men, there would be some justification for him to come to the Treasury of the United States for funds. But no one can offer in his behalf the claim that he lacks funds to produce nitrates. Muscle Shoals is not the only place in the world where this can be done. There are many other places where there are even better water-power opportunities than at Muscle Shoals. . . .

The facts are that nowhere or at any time has Mr. Ford ever agreed to make any guaranty, either that nitrates could be produced cheap enough at Muscle Shoals to become valuable as a fertilizer proposition or that the corporation which he organizes will not be under the control of Rockefeller or some other Wall Street interest within a very few years after it is turned over to him by the Government.

Mr. Ford's criticism of Secretary Weeks for the sale of the Gorgas plant is without any foundation, without any logic or reason. Anyone who has studied the Muscle Shoals proposition must agree that the Gorgas plant has no more connection with Muscle Shoals than the fifth wheel of a wagon. The reason why the Government put its money into Gorgas and doubled the capacity of that plant, owned by the Alabama Power Company, was to enable it to have power for building operations at Muscle Shoals. It was the nearest place where cheap power could be had. The only object of it all was to secure this power until they obtained power at Muscle Shoals. . . .

MUSCLE SHOALS—OURS (1924)

The Nation

"IF I WERE greedy for power over my fellow-men I would rather control Muscle Shoals than to be continuously elected President of the United States." So Newton D. Baker, the Secretary of War under whom the power project was begun, wrote last spring to the Committee on Agriculture of the Senate. This enormous power was nearly sold for a song to Henry Ford at the last session of Congress. The House passed a bill to that end, and there was strong sentiment in the Senate for similar action. Fortunately Senator Norris induced the Committee on Agriculture to favor instead a continuance of government control, but the danger of selling a national birthright for a mess of nitrate was not averted until Ford himself withdrew his offer.

Nor was it more than temporarily averted then. There were three detailed offers before Congress last winter besides that of Ford. Ford's offer was, in fact, the poorest of the lot, although it carried the most prestige because of the myth which had set up the auto-maker not only as an industrial superman but as a philanthropist to whom almost any power might safely be intrusted. The three other offers have not been withdrawn, and an effort is being made to induce the present session of Congress to turn over to private control the great power development in northern Alabama. But it is predicted in Washington that the offers will not again be pressed in competition with one another but will be superseded by an amalgamated plan having certain definite farmer support and strong business backing.

We are not especially interested in the details of this possible new plan or in the features of any of the old ones. We think it beside the point to contrast them, for one can be better than another only in that it offers a little more money —soon spent and forgotten—or a little more possibility of regulating a power so vast and vital that its complete control ought always and indisputably to be vested in the public. Let it not be forgotten that such control *is* vested in the public now. The problem is not like that of the railroads. There is no proposal that the nation buy at a huge outlay and plunge into the operation of a great privately owned industry. The nation *owns* Muscle Shoals. The question that it faces is the maintenance of that ownership and the gradual conversion and transmission of power, with plenty of time to work out a policy and a personnel as the size and importance of the project increases. It can sell out at any future date if it wants to, but it is safe to say that if it waits twenty years it would no sooner think of selling something of such paramount national interest than it

would think today of selling the Panama Canal. On the other hand, if it sells
Muscle Shoals now, Congress will within twenty years have to meet an insistent
demand to buy it back at enormous expense and difficulty. Let us remember that
we are now trying to recover two great oil basins that were too lightly disposed
of.

The comparison with the Panama Canal is a good one. The public is still
too little informed as to what Muscle Shoals actually is and can be. The power
development there was begun in war time to furnish nitrates for making muni-
tions. After the armistice the notion was spread that Muscle Shoals had lost its
value and should be sold like our wooden ships for whatever it would bring.
Ford's offer cleared away a little of that mist, for the public knows that Henry
Ford is not collecting a menagerie of white elephants. But Ford put his emphasis
entirely on producing cheap fertilizer for the farmer and so obscured the immensely more important facts about Muscle Shoals as a source of electric power
for half of the United States.

Muscle Shoals is probably our greatest single water power. There is a drop
in the Tennessee River at that point of 130 feet in thirty miles. The dam is 5,000
feet in length, or nearly a mile, impounding an estimated horse power of
850,000. Less than an eighth of this is needed to manufacture the amount of
fertilizer promised by Ford.

The power has a transmission radius of 500 miles and an incalculable
bearing not only upon the future evolution of all of the Southeastern section of
the United States but upon virtually all of the country east of the Mississippi
River except New England. The power at Muscle Shoals is far too great for any
one State to use or control. It is the king-pin in the forthcoming development
of electrified industry. It is fully comparable to the Panama Canal in its national
significance and its possibilities of commercial revolution. To quote Newton D.
Baker again:

> To grant Muscle Shoals to any individual or company for a hundred years, or even
> fifty years, grants to such company or individual industrial dominance for that
> period of the whole Southeastern portion of our country. . . . All the figures one
> sees about the gifts in present values in money to Mr. Ford or other proposed lessees
> are trifling as compared with the growing value of the industrial power that any
> such lease necessarily entails. . . . I am therefore clearly of the belief that Congress
> should retain Muscle Shoals, provide for its operation directly by the corps of
> engineers of the army or by a public corporation analogous to the Panama Railroad
> Company, and through such operation deal with the power produced in the mass,
> without entering into retail operation. By so doing the public interest, which we now
> see to be large, will be continuously served, and as the importance of this power
> source grows the hand of the Government will be free to make it continuously
> serviceable in the highest degree as the changing public interest demands.

The chief of engineers of the army has just reported that current expenditures at Muscle Shoals are at the rate of about $800,000 a month and that the
electric-power and nitrate plants will be completed by next October but could
be hurried through so as to be ready by July 1. More than $150,000,000 will
probably have been expended upon Muscle Shoals by the time the work is done.
There will be a tremendous drive upon the present Congress to turn this enormous undertaking, with its still greater potentialities, over to some private
financial group to exploit for its own profit. Only a determined show of popular

opposition can prevent this tragedy and this betrayal. *The Nation* has pointed out several times within recent months the striking economies and benefits that have been obtained in the province of Ontario through the public development and sale of power from Niagara Falls. Mr. Underwood's bill—supported by President Coolidge—to deliver Muscle Shoals into private hands under a fifty-year lease would tie it up for too long a period. Senator Norris has a better plan for continued government ownership, with the option of operation by the government or by private agency under government control.

THE MILLION-DOLLAR LOBBY (1928)

The Nation

WE HAVE occasionally shied bricks in the direction of the reorganized Federal Trade Commission, and we feared that its investigation of the power interests' lobby would amount to little. The gentlemen of the lobby evidently agreed with us, for they toiled manfully to keep the investigation out of the hands of a Senate committee and forced the job on the Commission. They expected to control it there. But the investigation personnel of the Federal Trade Commission went out and got the facts and the documents. They did a good job. They uncovered important facts. Despite the best efforts of a sleepy and incompetent press, they are making news.

Readers of the Hearst newspapers—another organization which we have often dispraised—know what is being uncovered by the investigation. The Hearst newspapers have told them. Readers of few other papers know, for with amazingly few exceptions the other papers have slurred the story. We suggest that if our readers think it news, as we do, and have not seen it reported, they ask the editors of their local newspapers why.

The Joint Committee of the National Utilities Association, composed of the National Electric Light Association, the American Gas Association, and the American Electric Railway Association, maintains in Washington a gigantic lobby which in each of the past three years has spent in excess of $1,000,000 to oppose government ownership—"to represent the utilities companies . . . on all matters of pending legislation before Congress" was the polite phrase used by the Joint Committee's general counsel. This million-dollar committee has been the heart and soul of the opposition to federal development of Muscle Shoals and Boulder Dam; and it has ex-Senators, ex-ambassadors, ex-governors, newspapermen, and universities on its pay roll.

The lobby paid $7,500 to Richard Washburn Child, former United States Ambassador to Italy, to prepare an unsigned "booklet" opposing federal development of Boulder Dam. It paid Ernest Greenwood, former American agent of the League of Nations Labor Office, an "initial fee" of $5,000 to write a propaganda book, *Aladdin, U. S. A.*, published by Harpers. It paid ex-Senator Lenroot of Wisconsin at least two fees of $10,000 each to lobby for it among his former colleagues. It paid the law firm of Meechem and Vellacott of Albuquerque, New Mexico, $5,299.66 to "report" the Governors' Conference on Boulder Dam at a time when Merritt Meechem, former Governor of New Mexico, was supposed to be representing the State of New Mexico at that conference. It paid the General Federation of Women's Clubs $30,000 for an "urban and rural home survey." It paid the Harvard Graduate School, in three years, $62,000 for "research" which, after study of the views of the responsible professors, it felt safe; and after equally careful study of the professorial field it contributed at least $62,500 (perhaps $95,000) to Northwestern University, $12,249.37 to the University of Michigan, $3,000 to the Massachusetts Institute of Technology, $5,000 to Johns Hopkins University, and $33,000 to Howard University. It has twenty-eight committees working in thirty-eight States, teaching that "government ownership is the masked advance agent of communism."

Samuel Insull—the same Insull who tried to buy a seat in the United States Senate for Frank L. Smith of Illinois—is the largest individual contributor to the million-dollar fund, but one-quarter of all the utility companies in the United States contribute to it.

This national committee is only the capstone of the enormous propaganda structure maintained by the public-utility companies. The Illinois Committee on Public Utility Information, founded by Mr. Insull, was one of the pioneers in the field, and it is admitted to have served as a model for the work in more than a score of other States. It was Rob Roy MacGregor of this committee who, when asked how to campaign against a Senator who believed in public ownership, penned the famous memorandum explaining: "My idea would be not to try reason, or logic, but to try to pin the Bolshevik idea on my opponent."

Mr. MacGregor's committee was the pathfinder in work in the public schools. It began with a thorough study of textbooks dealing with public-utility questions. It circularized local companies urging them to set to work on local school boards and through personal friendships to have "bad" books removed. This, it reported, "is a very slow process but has to be gone through with." Then it sought to prevent the publication of more "bad" books. It urged its members to work through "personal friends in publishing houses." It wrote letters to the universities and discovered just which professors were writing on the subject. It offered these budding authors the honeyed bait of "reliable statistics" together with aid in getting their books marketed. "We have located," the industrious committee reported, "practically every textbook and also have found the textbooks in course of preparation, and have been able to be of considerable assistance to the writers of these books in providing them with reliable data." Finally, as a result of persistent effort, B. J. Mullaney, of the Illinois committee, was able to report that it had got to the point where *"635 Illinois high schools, more than three-quarters of the total number, use specially prepared utility-industries literature in the classrooms."*

In Connecticut a similar committee planted more than 10,000 grossly false public-utilities "catechisms" in seventy-six high schools; and in Pennsylvania 30,000 sets of pamphlets, four to a set, were distributed among county superintendents for use in the schools. Presumably similar practices have been followed in other States, but the witnesses have not yet appeared on the stand.

The energetic Illinois committee not only arranged for its own selected speakers (1,137 speeches in eighteen months) and distributed its tons of literature (5,000,000 pieces of literature before it was two years old); it circulated blacklists similar to those used by the D. A. R. in the hope, apparently, of keeping the public-ownership point of view from any expression whatever. It even prepared pamphlets for its agents on How to Talk to Grade School Pupils.

"Is there any method of publicity not used by your organization?" Judge Healy asked one of the propagandists.

"Only one that I know of," he replied, "and that's skywriting."

Of course, the newspapers were a rich field for cultivation. Perhaps that explains their lack of interest in the investigation. The Illinois committee mails a weekly news service to 900 newspapers in Illinois. Keeping tab on its utilization has become expensive, but in its first year an average of 5,000 column-inches of material prepared by the utilities committee lobby was printed every month in the Illinois newspapers, and the second year, when the clipping service was discontinued, the rate was running higher still. The New England lobby reported that in 1927 7,203 1/2 column-inches of its material—enough to fill 56 1/2 eight-column pages of solid reading matter—had appeared in the news columns of New England papers, and 1,584 column-inches in the editorial columns!

Mr. Mullaney estimated that the utilities companies spend from $25,000,000 to $30,000,000 annually in direct advertising, and all the committees showed themselves insistent that local-utilities advertisers should maintain their contacts with local editors. One of the most disheartening revelations of the investigation was the letter written by the advertising manager of David Lawrence's *United States Daily* suggesting a $200,000 advertising campaign in that paper, and outlining a program by which the bills could be charged to fifty-two local companies, "so that there could be no possible ground for criticism on the ground that one organization or institution was conducting a general campaign." It is fair to Mr. Lawrence to add that his paper, although somewhat belatedly, has been printing the verbatim testimony before the Federal Trade Commission. Furthermore, it did not get the $200,000 advertising contract.

It has been charged that whole strings of newspapers were to have been bought in the interest of the public utilities. This charge has not been definitely proved. One of the chief buttresses of this charge is the history of Ira C. Copley, an Illinois public-utilities magnate who in 1926 sold out most of his utilities interests to Samuel Insull and went into the newspaper business. After purchasing one string of newspapers in Illinois he invaded California, buying three papers in San Diego and immediately killing that one of them which had supported government ownership. When the charge was made, Mr. Copley published in his papers the statement that "I have no connection with any public utilities anywhere, and no connection with any companies [other] than the newspaper business anywhere." One month before making that statement Mr. Copley had resigned as president of the Western United Gas and Electric Company and of the Southern Illinois Gas Company, and at the time of making it he still held preferred stock of the company to a value of $2,400,000, bonds to a value of $1,000,000, $70,600 in preferred stock of its holding company, and 50,000 shares of no-par-value Class A common stock—enough to assure himself of a directorship at any time he wanted it. Mr. Copley's editors, however, insisted that while they agreed with him in opposition to government ownership, he had never given them any instructions on the subject and they had written little about it.

The legislatures and the politicians appear in the picture, too. A letter found in the files of Robert V. Prather, secretary-treasurer of various Illinois public-utilities associations, read:

> The legislature is in session here, and it looks like a very stormy session and I could use handily a little "J. Walker" to very good advantage and it occurs to me that you could do me a very great favor if the first time you are coming West you would call on a friend of mine in New York and bring me half a dozen.

That was in 1921. In 1925 Mr. Prather wrote another letter suggesting that he needed "something to sweeten up the palates of the legislature." He did not explain whether he wanted "J. Walker," or what.

The gentleman who placed the public-utility catechisms in the Connecticut public schools, the commission discovered, is also the publicity agent of the Republican State Committee. J. H. Bigelow, chairman of the Pennsylvania Democratic State Committee, got $1,000 from the lobby; John P. Connelly, of Vare's Republican machine in Philadelphia, got $14,103. Walter H. Johnson, chairman of the Public Policy Committee of the Pennsylvania Electric Association, an avowed lobbyist at the State capital, could not account for $20,225 which had recently passed through his hands. He thought he might have used some of it to watch "pinch bills"—bills introduced by legislators in order to make the utilities "come across."

"Across with what?" he was asked.

"With cash," he replied; but he insisted that he had "fallen for no pincher yet." He explained, however, that he had kept no accounts because he did not want it known who got his money.

Schools, press, legislatures—the power and utilities gentlemen have flooded the country with money and lies. The government's investment in Muscle Shoals has been hamstrung and the water still pours idly through Boulder Canyon— tributes to the success of the million-dollar lobby in fighting public development of natural resources.

THE TRIUMPH OF
THE POWER COMPANIES (1929)

H. S. Raushenbush

LIGHT AND POWER are governmental services, so necessary and monopolistic in their character that they must be controlled, in some form, by the government. This is a Supreme Court dictum. They are services which we have a right to ask be furnished as cheaply and abundantly as possible. We might perform them ourselves. We can turn them over to private enterprise to perform, and then try to regulate the performance. Except in those cases where cities insisted on having these services before the companies were willing to give them, or where the companies got too stubborn about their rights to charge more than the traffic would bear, we have let the privately owned companies furnish the service. We tried at first to control them by cities. The granting of franchises turned into a pollution area. The companies also expanded. It was hard for a single city to regulate a company that extended throughout a State. The States then began to regulate, setting up commissions. The question of the day is: How well does that regulation work, and how can it be made to work better? With this goes the further question which all friends of the system have to meet: What chance is there of making it work better when every attempt to do so is defeated by the utilities?

The essence of regulation is the ability to fix rates, and when you lose that ability you regulate no longer. That is exactly what, to a large extent, the commissions have lost. They can no longer say: "You have put a certain amount of money into the business, you must be content with a fair return on that money." What they say now is: "You can earn a return on a large amount of money you never invested, you can cash in on the growth of the cities you serve, on the increased values of land, and we cannot stop you. We can try, however, to limit the flights of your imagination." These are two somewhat different things.

What the commissions have lost here is control of the rate base. The Indianapolis Water Company case and the O'Fallon case this year have toppled over the attempt to get service at cost. In its place is being put a system of guesswork which triples and quadruples the equity of the common stockholders and loads the rates to the gunwales. The Interstate Commerce Commission showed that if this new system were also applied to the railroads, they would in 1923 have added 12 billion dollars to the 19 billion invested. In the Indianapolis case the money put into the utility was $10,434,000. The new rate base was fixed at $19,000,000, an increase of 82 per cent. The book costs of the New York Telephone Company were $542,693,000 in 1925, the company asked for $240,000,000 more. A large part of this invoked the appropriation of consumers' money. The power company in Cambridge did not want to lower its rates. The commission found a fair value of $2,500,000. The company wanted $1,175,000, or 47 per cent, more. In the proceedings in which San Francisco took over the private-power systems, the city claimed that the actual cost of the properties plus severance damages was $31,223,000. The companies claimed $90,000,000, almost three times as much. The commission fixed $38,500,000 as a fair price, and has been informed by the companies that the case will be taken into court. Here obviously is a system of regulation where the essential control has been lost, where service at cost is no longer possible, and where favorable commissions are very important to the utilities.

In some States, notably California, Wisconsin, and Massachusetts, the public-service commissions try to keep as close to actual cost of service as they can, but they, too, feel obligated to make something of a bow toward the new uncertainty. On this very important matter of securing a stable rate base two bills were introduced this year, both of which failed to pass. In Massachusetts the board favored a State contract with the utilities, evening up any past deficits in dividends and guaranteeing that their stock should not be allowed to go below par, in return for the uncontested right of regulating the companies on the basis of their adjusted capital. In Indiana Senator Moorhead proposed that the commission should not allow securities to be issued above a fair value of the property, and that rates should be fixed on the basis of actual cost. No other States tackled this problem in a serious way. Several minor attempts, in Missouri and elsewhere, were defeated also.

Another control the commissions have to a large extent lost is that over operating expenses. The advent of holding companies means that the operating utilities let the holding companies do many services of engineering and financing for them. Over these the commissions have small power. The case for interstate control lies less in the fact that some power is shipped across State lines in a way to dodge regulation than in the fact that the holding company charges can not now be controlled, although the two companies have common ownership. Only in one State, Indiana, was a bill for holding-company control introduced, and that was defeated by adjournment of the House. The New York bill, once supported by the commission in that State, was not introduced.

Twenty-nine States do not even have nominal control over the purchase price paid for all operating utilities under their jurisdiction, and there is a danger that the excess prices now being paid by holding companies will, within a few years, become part of the base on which we will have to pay rates. But even States like New York which have a nominal control permit excess prices. In four years the New York commission let an excess over costs of $202,000,000 be paid and then began opening the way for it to become part of the rate base. A little more delay and the holding companies will not be afraid of control.

Bills for investigation of the regulatory system of the water-power situation were defeated in Kansas, Missouri, North Carolina, Minnesota, Pennsylvania, and Georgia. In New York several similar bills were offered, and one which gives the majority political leaders six places on a commission of nine was passed. Colonel William Donovan has been appointed counsel for the investigating body. Massachusetts voted to investigate the financial holdings of its utilities.

There are eight States without commissions to control the power industry. In Texas, Florida, Kentucky, and Delaware bills for such commissions were introduced and defeated. In Kentucky the utility men appeared in favor of the proposal. In West Virginia the water-powers were put under a commission on about the easiest licensing terms allowed in any State in the country, and an amendment that power could not be sold outside the State cheaper than inside was defeated. Similar proposals concerning the export of hydro-electric power were shelved in other States. Maine voted to export its power, subject to a referendum and an excise tax on all export, of which a quarter million dollars annually is to be devoted to rural service. No guaranty as to lower rates accompanies the proposal.

The only improvement in the system which passed this year was a relatively small one in Ohio. A legal and engineering staff is to be set up inside the commission to hear and submit cases to that body. This is a small recognition that the commissions have gone judicial. Otherwise the record of nibbling toward improvement of the regulatory system is a consistent one of defeat. In Indiana and Pennsylvania bills allowing the commissions a few more months to consider rates before they go into effect were lost. In Illinois, a proposal to allow the commission to collect reparations for over-charges was lost. Bills in Texas, Missouri, and New York to reduce the rate of return were lost.

In addition to these attempted changes in regulation several efforts were made to supplement the breaking system by a program of government or municipal ownership. In New York Governor Roosevelt got nowhere with his proposal for a board of trustees to develop the St. Lawrence water-powers. In Minnesota the proposed $50,000,000 bond issue for State water-power development was lost. In Wisconsin the Senator defeated the constitutional amendment to allow the State to recapture and develop its water-powers. In Texas a bill to revoke all permits for dams on public streams which had not been started to date was lost. In Nebraska a bill to establish a bureau of water conservation and utilization was lost. Bills for power districts in Iowa, Illinois, Wisconsin, and Washington were either voted on adversely or shelved. In Nebraska, however, the power district bill of 1927 was amended to meet constitutional objections and repassed.

The municipalities of the country have long been suffering from limitations put upon them which prevent them from raising money for power and light plants in the same way as the companies do, on the strength of the expected earnings of their proposed plants. They have, for the most part, to stay within debt limits which in thirteen States are below 5 per cent of their assessed valuation and in thirteen others below 10 per cent of it. These limits they use up quickly enough for schools, sewers, and other public necessities. They are also held down by law in most States from expanding beyond the city as private companies may do. These two limitations, far more than the tall talk of the utilities about "governmental inefficiency," explain the lack of growth of municipally owned plants in this country. A great number of bills to give them more freedom to grow on an equal plane were introduced, notably by some of the Western leagues of municipalities. With one exception in Nebraska, one in Wisconsin, and another in North Dakota, those of major importance were all defeated.

There is no reason to believe that this record of power company victories will be changed next year under a similar scattering and random attack. Any changes to be made in the interests of the consumers will come only through heavy mobilization. There is little nourishment to be had in nibbling the insiders in the power industry out of the favorable positions they have captured inside the lines of regulation. They profit far too heavily where they are to yield lightly. They have concentrated enough wealth to control the country and apparently that is exactly what they propose to continue to do.

PLANNING FOR POWER (1932)

Morris Llewellyn Cooke

THE COLLAPSE OF the valuation and holding-company rackets and the emergence of the small consumer as the arbiter of power policy are the high points in the current utility situation. Transportation rates are less and less affected either by the cost or by the present value of property used and useful in rendering the service, while the electric, gas, and telephone industries consider unfair the basing of rates on the reproduction-cost basis which until the 1929 debacle was touted as the equitable "law of the land." Most of the important arguments heretofore advanced in favor of the holding companies have been exploded, and these companies are at grips with seemingly insuperable difficulties.

If electric rates, at present highly discriminatory against the small user, can be regulated so as to approach the standard of cost plus a fair profit, consumption can be so increased as not only to eliminate the drudgery of housework but to pave the way for a new artistry in living for even modest homes. Through low-priced current for the farms, agriculture can be energized and the cultural level of our rural population radically improved.

In this atmosphere of change, planning offers great possibilities for a public conscious of its power and responding to competent leadership. Governor Roosevelt has given constant testimony to his realization of the importance of the power issue as it affects the social and economic well-being of the people and has moved effectively to clean up abuses and open the way for the new day. He initiated an illuminating investigation into State regulation by a legislative commission, has advocated prudent investment as the basis for valuation, and insists that public-service commissions are more administrative than judicial bodies. Through the St. Lawrence River Power Authority Act Governor Roosevelt secured for domestic and rural consumers the benefits of the low-priced electricity there to be generated. He contends that if the private companies are allowed to market St. Lawrence power, it must be on the basis of cost plus only a fair and recognized profit; otherwise the State may have to build its own transmission lines. As facilitating a balanced State power development Governor Roosevelt has proposed legislation permitting the voters of any area to provide publicly owned power facilities if they so desire. He advocates the federal regulation of interstate electric traffic.

Special interest attaches to public planning for the utilities because their activities can now legally be regulated by public authority. In this field many of the constitutional prohibitions against interference by public authority with private business do not hold. The most important appeals from commission and court findings in utility cases have been based on claims of confiscation sought to be resisted under the Fourteenth, or "due process," Amendment to the Constitution. Only those private undertakings invested—or as one typesetter put it, "infested"—with a public interest may be regulated by public authority.

Possibly as much as one-fifth of the productive and transportation capacity of the country is now included in the utility or "regulated" classification. . . .

However, it is electricity which dominates the utility scene. While its claimed invested capital is only half that of steam railroads it is still in its youth. The electrical industry has achieved a solidarity of purpose and action as between its functional units, such as financing, operating, manufacturing, engineering, construction, and contracting; a representation in the major political party organizations; and a control of the means of mass propaganda and ballyhoo which set an all-time record. Its operating companies are as a rule in healthy financial condition, and everything suggests that in times anything like normal the saturation-point in the use of electricity would not be in sight. It is in coping with the electrical industry and planning for it that the case of the People *vs.* the Utilities will be won or lost. Obviously, also, if we cannot plan effectively for electricity, it is unlikely that as a people we shall be equal to the task of broader social economic planning.

The enhanced position of electricity in American life is shown by the increase in its use from 110,000,000 K.W.H. a day in 1921 to 265,000,000 K.W.H. a day in 1929. During 1926–31 small consumers used 30 per cent of the current but contributed 61 per cent of the revenues. On the other hand, the wholesale consumers, that is, the larger industries, the street railways, and the electrified steam railroads, have required 70 per cent of all current sold and yet have yielded only 39 per cent of the industry's total revenues. American industry is 70 per cent electrified. That the net revenues of the industry have held up well in the face of a heavy decrease in the use of industrial power tends to prove that the small user is the profitable and reliable consumer.

Practically the whole cost of service to a large consumer lies first in generating the electricity and then in transmitting it on high-voltage lines to the point of use. The cost of this "transmitted current" is of course the same whether delivered to a large industrial establishment or to one of the substations from which the current is distributed over wires of lower voltage to homes and farms. In order to get the entire cost of service to these small-scale users, we must add to the cost of the "transmitted current" the capital charges and operating expenses required to put it through the distribution substation and the low-voltage distribution lines to the far side of the customers' meters. Thus the whole cost of domestic service will be the cost of transmitted current plus the distribution charges.

There are three classes of electric service into which distribution enters as an important cost factor, that is, domestic; commercial light and power, retail; and municipal, largely street lighting. The current consumed by each class and the revenue derived therefrom in 1931 were as follows:

	K.W.H.	Revenue
Domestic	11,785,000,000	$686,000,000
Commercial light and power	13,837,000,000	569,000,000
Municipal and street lighting	2,793,000,000	108,000,000
	28,415,000,000	$1,363,000,000

We may assume that the "transmitted current" used in these services costs on the average 1 1/2 cents per K.W.H., including return on invested capital. The national average rate for wholesale transmitted power is 1.42 cents per K.W.H. The part of the sales price, therefore, attributable to 28,415,000,000 K.W.H. of current would total $426,225,000. Subtracting this from the $1,363,000,000 charged for these services, there remains $936,775,000 to be justified as the cost, including profit, of distribution, or nearly one-half of the total revenues of the industry. If, as suggested by my own studies carried on continuously for nearly twenty years and outlined in "On the Cost of Distribution of Electricity" and elsewhere, this public outlay for distribution is about twice what it should be, we are confronted with an annual overcharge against the small consumer of between $400,000,000 and $500,000,000 a year.

Certainly $900,000,000 a year is far too large a tax to be levied without reasonable proof of its approximate justice. And yet there is an almost complete absence of anything approximating cost control or even of cost knowledge concerning electrical distribution, and not one generally recognized cost standard. Practices and results obtained in different areas cannot be compared. The usual process of improving methods by setting one up against another is therefore generally missing. Waste necessarily results.

Engineering literature teems with meticulous data on generating costs. We know within narrow limits the cost of transmitting current. But we have no information about an item which would come near to balancing the national budget and which is certainly much more important to the small consumer than the costs of generation and transmission combined. The cost of the distribution of electricity is taboo before every engineering society in the United States. This lack of definite data in regard to distribution costs accounts for the present meaningless multiplicity of rate schedules. Before many years a single rate schedule will cover vast areas.

Through propaganda fostered by the electrical industry the public has been led to believe that domestic electric rates have been "steadily going down." The nation-wide average price fell from 7 cents per K.W.H. in 1926 to 6 cents in 1931. This drop in the national average chiefly affects, however, only that very small percentage of customers whose exceptionally large consumption gives them the benefit of low promotional rates. Such lowering of the national average has very little bearing on the trend of rates paid in the majority—possibly 90 per cent —of American homes.

The revenue derived from the average domestic user increases yearly. It was $29.70 in 1926 and $33.70 in 1931. It is highly probable that the industry has secured a greater profit per domestic customer, and per K.W.H. used in domestic service, with each drop in the national average. For in serving the average domestic customer with the small annual increments in the quantity of current indicated in recent years, practically the only added expense is for the current itself. Computing this at 1 1/2 cents per K.W.H. we find that in each of the last five years the amount required to cover the additional current averages only about half the added revenue received.

Until within the last two or three years, except for the supervision of the Interstate Commerce Commission over the railroads, public authority has hardly been felt in the utility world. Barring a few sporadic instances of gentle discipline, and these confined to a few States, the utilities have been allowed to work out their own salvation, if you can call it that. Electrically speaking, Sidney Z. Mitchell was Alpha and Samuel Insull was Omega. An occasional Hopson was the only fly in the ointment. But the substitution by Governor Roosevelt of Maltbie for Prendergast as chairman of the New York Commission, the recent appointment of Lilienthal in Wisconsin, the activities of Seavey in California and of Morse in New Hampshire, and the refusal of the Massachusetts Commission to allow the Boston Edison split-up are happenings which serve to remind the general public of what was originally expected of regulation.

Things have also been occurring in the public-ownership field. When gas and electricity supplies and telephone services were confined to single localities, thousands of such plants were publicly owned. Coincident with the interconnection of these utilities over wide areas, the private interests initiated a process of eliminating the competition of the public plant. More than forty years ago Edison advised the electrical industry to insure the permanency of its investment "by keeping prices so low that there is no inducement to others to come in and ruin it." Because this advice has not been heeded, strong and apparently effective public-ownership currents have been set up in various parts of the country. There are well-managed publicly owned electric plants of considerable size in Seattle and Tacoma, Washington; Los Angeles and Pasadena, California; Springfield, Illinois; Jamestown, New York; Holyoke, Massachusetts; and Jacksonville, Florida. There are at present more than 2,000 such municipal electric plants—most of them quite small.

But far more significant is the legislation already passed in Nebraska, Wisconsin, Washington, and Oregon, and proposed in New York by Governor Roosevelt, to facilitate the tying together of individual municipal gas and electric plants into power districts technically and otherwise able to compete with privately owned superpower systems. All legal barriers against providing a public plant, once the people have voted for it, should be removed. Nothing has proved so effective in securing reasonable rates from the private companies as the realization that the public has this remedy at hand.

Except as to water supplies, public ownership in this country is of the "yardstick" variety. While in any one industry the percentage of public as compared with private plants is low, such public installations as there are exert an important influence in providing the public with the standards by which performance of the private plants can be measured. I am convinced that it would be a mistake to plan now for widespread public ownership in this country. Rather we should concentrate on the effective operation of a few favorably located installations, large enough to fire the public imagination and to exclude petty politics. The water-power projects at Boulder Dam, on the St. Lawrence, and at Muscle Shoals should be pushed, and experiments should be made in extended but intrastate power districts; these are already under way in western Washington and are being actively planned in Wisconsin.

On the other hand, in the light of the experience during two generations, it would be a mistake to place too much reliance on either federal or State regulation. The Interstate Commerce Commission has on the whole done a remarkably good job in its piloting of the difficult railroad situation. The early adoption of standardized and revealing accounting, reasonable success in keeping politics at a distance, and the presence on the commission almost from the start of some unusually able men are among the contributing causes. But the end seems not far off. Especially in case the depression continues, it appears to be only a question of how long most of the steam roads can hold out. Bonded as they are to the hilt and with no market for their stocks, the solution will inevitably be public ownership, not because it is desirable in itself, but because it has become inevitable. Public ownership the world over has usually come by this route.

But "yardstick" public ownership and regulation will have to be supplemented by fundamental and extensive research conducted under public auspices as a guide to future public planning. There is no such thing as scientific management without unprejudiced research. To meet this need Governor Pinchot suggested a giant power board instructed to study out Pennsylvania's electrical future. This idea has since been carried out in Great Britain by the appointment of the Central Electricity Board. It has been effectively active in executing projects looking toward a better planning of Britain's electrical economy—its duties are wholly outside regulation as we know it. The Wisconsin legislature at its last session followed the suggestion of Governor La Follette and provided for a similar board to study the future power needs of the State, to plan the facilities and agencies found to be necessary, and to plot the method for coordinating all public and private power and light activities.

A federal utilities planning board, unhampered by the routine regulatory responsibilities which harass the Interstate Commerce Commission and the Federal Power Commission, and supplemented by similar agencies in a half-dozen States, might in time clarify the questions which keep regulation relatively ineffective. . . .

SO THIS IS BUREAUCRACY! (1934)

Raymond Gram Swing

. . . THE TVA IS A bureaucracy. The common supposition is that bureaucracies are slow to move, awkward in action, uninspired by inventiveness. The construction of the Norris and Joe Wheeler dams of the TVA are well ahead of schedule, and will be finished in 1936. They are already one-third completed, a little over a year after the creation of the Authority. The model town of Norris, near the Norris Dam, is more than three-fourths built, after careful attention to architecture, town planning, and other requirements of permanence. Cheap electricity is already being sold in the Tennessee Valley; what is more, a subsidiary of the TVA has induced manufacturers of electric appliances to make simple, cheap, standardized models for use in the district, so that these cost less to the consumer, yet greatly increase the volume of sales. A useful electric refrigerator, shorn of some of its gadgets, is to be bought for $79. It can be bought on the installment plan, financed by this subsidiary at just over 5 per cent interest. The subsidiary is the EHFA (Electric Home and Farm Authority), and it is making business for private electrical manufacturers. At the same time cheap rates make it possible in Tupelo to operate an electric refrigerator, electric range, and electric hot-water heater on about $7 a month for current.

The bureaucracy known as the TVA is manned by a staff with a spirit not to be found in any private enterprise I ever heard of. Relations between employer and employee produce a team spirit which would be the envy of any corporation. More than that, employment includes the opportunity for education and training, so that men now working, for instance, on the Norris Dam are being fitted for permanent usefulness and economic value when the dam is finished.

Those who visit Tennessee and those who visit the great construction centers in Russia remark the same thing—the astonishing enthusiasm of the people on the job. What creates this enthusiasm in both communities is the same. It is the sense of doing something constructive and creative, for the common good. This is not the profit motive, supposed to be the only one which can keep the world going. It is the service motive, and in the Tennessee Valley it is already producing results better in every way than those to be had from the profit motive.

The TVA, admittedly, is no ordinary bureaucracy. Its functions are not simply defined. It can be taken as being merely a federal power project, utilizing the Muscle Shoals Dam and building other dams with the immediate objective of supplying electric current in the valley at rates unobtainable from private enterprise. In this perspective it links up with the five other major federal projects in other parts of the country. These are the Grand Coulee and Bonneville dams of the Columbia River Basin, Boulder Dam on the Colorado River, Fort Peck Dam on the Missouri River in Montana, and the Casper-Alcova Dam in Wyoming. The total cost of the six has already been allocated and will be $230,000,000. Looking still further, these six projects will be fitted into a still greater picture to include the St. Lawrence power project. Congress will be asked this winter once more to ratify the treaty which makes the public exploitation of the St. Lawrence River more possible. This time the issue should be clear enough for Congress to respond. When these projects are finished, the supply of cheap electricity to the homes of America, whether urban or rural, will be assured, and America will be on the way to an all-electrified material life. (I shun the word "civilization," not wishing to describe civilization in terms of refrigerators and hot water.)

Within the bounds of its immediate objective the TVA looms impressively. It is sure to accomplish much in its own district, and as the valley has an area two-thirds the size of Great Britain, the project is a major one, by any measure. It becomes an intrinsic part of something still greater and more fundamental as part of a vast continental scheme.

The TVA is also an experiment in planned economy. The Tennessee Valley is to be transformed not by a cheap power rate but by human schemes in which cheap power plays a part. The valley one day is to be a vast community of decentralized industries. Workers will live a divided life between the factory and the small farm. After the building of Norris, one imagines scores of such villages coming to life, laid out for loveliness as well as cheap rents, supplied with comforts, with farm gardens where vegetables will be grown which the hapless Tennessee farmer now does not know. The farm gardeners will work in factories for their cash, or, put the other way, factory workers will farm part of each day for some of their daily food.

If it were not for the present low standard of life in the Tennessee Valley, such a final development might warrant closer examination to make sure it is not part of a device to give private industry contented cheap labor. But in a district where most farm families do not see more than $85 in cash a year, the outlook of a fair industrial wage supplemented by profuse kitchen gardens, and of a life in electrified communities with organized social activity and improved educational facilities, is above suspicion. . . .

TVA: THE NEW DEAL'S
BEST ASSET (1936)

Stuart Chase

. . . THE TENNESSEE VALLEY has little in the way of manufacturing and less in the way of services to offer the world beyond its hills. Its exchange base must be primarily natural resources—foodstuffs, raw materials, water-power. What is the TVA doing specifically to increase these resources?

The Constitution of the United States knows nothing of regional planning, for the conception would have been fantastic in 1787, when a specialized exchange economy was still in the womb of time. The Supreme Court knows nothing of regional planning except in the negative sense that a watershed comprising portions of seven states is suspect in the light of the commerce clause, and probably unlawful. Congress has never heard of regional planning officially, and would be seriously confused as to the patronage involved, if it had. The President first had a definite idea as to the functions and scope of the TVA. He saw the watershed as a geographic and hydrologic unit; he wanted to make the people in that watershed more comfortable, and he wanted to set up a series of yardsticks to measure power facilities, rural electrification, flood control, erosion control, progressive agriculture; yardsticks hopefully to be applied in other regions and to make people more comfortable there. Many members of Congress undoubtedly shared these desires with the President, especially Senator Norris.

But under the American system one cannot go straight to one's desire. One must adopt a crab-like course which defers to established taboos and symbols. To control the watershed of the Tennessee in the interests of the people living within that watershed is legally an outrageous procedure, as Professor Arnold of the Yale Law School ironically suggests, and not to be tolerated by right-thinking citizens. But both navigation and flood control have sidled past the taboos in times gone by, and are now admitted as right and necessary functions even by the lawyers of the American Liberty League. Federal production and sale of power, however, was on the fence—until the United States Supreme Court settled it in the affirmative by eight votes to one.

The TVA act was framed with these taboos in mind. It provides for:

1. A maximum development of the Tennessee River for navigation.
2. A maximum amount of flood control.
3. A maximum generation of electric power consistent with flood and navigation control.
4. The investigation of a proper use of marginal lands.
5. Studies on a proper method of reforestation.
6. Recommendations for "the economic and social well-being of the people living in said river basin."

This last provision was perhaps too frank. It may yet prove the undoing of the whole experiment. It comes perilously close to stating what the act was really designed for. It is bad form and bad law to consider the social well-being of two million people scattered over seven states. Such frankness was not really necessary. All that needed to be stipulated in the act was navigation, and nature would do the rest, even including the welfare clause. Why? Because you cannot tinker with nine-foot channels from Paducah to Knoxville without tinkering with the whole flow of water down the basin, which involves the hydrologic cycle, which dominates and controls the ecology of the region, and thus lets in the whole program—animal, vegetable, human, and divine, if you please. Of course, you can dig a nine-foot channel at fabulous expense without considering any of the related factors, but the first spring flood will damage it, and silt rushing down from the eroded fields will complete the ruin. Various "navigable" channels have been so constructed in the past, but they have fallen under the general title of the Congressional pork barrel. There is no pork to be had in the TVA, as any member of Congress will sadly tell you, but instead rather a strict interpretation of a permanent nine-foot channel.

You may or may not respect men and their taboos, but you must respect the laws of nature. You put a nine-foot channel up to nature, and ask that it be made permanent. What does she stipulate? She first makes it very clear that what goes up must come down. Water is drawn to the clouds from the Atlantic and the Gulf and precipitated in rain and snow over the Valley, especially on the Eastern mountains. This water feeds plants and is transpired by them, runs into lakes and underground reservoirs for slow seepage seaward, and runs off on the surface through rivulets, creeks, and rivers. Ultimately it finds the sea, and the cycle repeats itself—so long as this planet endures. *The water will come down.* The people of Hartford, the people of Pittsburgh, the people of Johnstown, have no illusions on this score.

Dependable navigation calls for flood control; flood control calls for dams and reservoirs; reservoirs must not fill with silt or their function vanishes; Hales Bar Dam in the big river is 33 per cent silted in twenty-three years. Silt can be prevented only by the control of erosion on agricultural lands and little waters. Erosion control calls for cover crops, both forest and grass, and scientific methods in tillage and crop rotation; cover crops call for cheap fertilizer, otherwise they will not take root on the exhausted soils; cheap fertilizer, especially phosphate, which is the major requirement in the Valley, can best be made with the help of electric furnaces and cheap power. So the cycle returns on itself, a house-that-Jack-built. If you really mean navigation, all these things will be added unto you. Similarly if the national taboos frowned on navigation and smiled on fertilizer, let us say, the cycle would be almost identical. Nor does it stop here. Large reservoirs demand the removal of many houses, which calls for an intelligent resettlement program. Large reservoirs demand an extensive re-planning of railways, highways, schools, and recreation areas. The forest cover which is to check erosion calls for permanent management and many jobs for fire patrollers and forest workers. Large reservoirs often produce trillions of mosquitoes—probably in these latitudes mosquitoes which spread malaria; ma-laria calls for a medical-engineering control as rigorous as the methods of Colonel Gorgas when the Panama Canal was built. Malaria is less lethal than yellow fever, but it is at least as hard to eradicate. Water control ties in with fish and wild-life preservation, with purification of streams polluted by city sewers and industrial wastes.

Such are nature's demands. In writing them down, I have automatically listed the functions of the TVA. To the list may be added certain collateral functions which appear to fit the cycle logically enough: a labor program for the very extensive engineering operations involved, primarily dams and reservoirs; the conservation of the Valley's mineral resources, especially phosphate rock; the development of the hydroelectric power resources of the Valley as one integrated, low-cost system; and the discovery of ways and means, such as rural electrification, to put the power to useful employment. There are other functions which are somewhat more indirect, such as land classification, including aerial mapping, a program for the use of marginal lands, and the development of domestic industries to supplement agriculture and provide employment.

We start with navigation and end with a pretty comprehensive program of regional planning. We could start with flood control or with power and arrive at substantially the same program. As a matter of fact—and I trust the Supreme Court is safely asleep as I whisper it—navigation is probably the least important aspect of the cycle, from the point of view of the well-being of the people of the Valley. Army engineers anticipate a very substantial traffic by 1950—some eighteen million tons in fact—but it is safe to say that they have not anticipated all the technological developments which may occur in transport within the next fifteen years.

As one drives down the Valley, its appearance is probably not very much changed from ten years ago—with a few exceptions shortly to be noted. This experiment which so agitates the nation is rather hard to find, unless one knows where to look. Ten years ago there was a great dam at Muscle Shoals, now called the Wilson Dam. It was equipped with generators for producing power and with two nitrate plants. These assets the TVA, a corporation outside any government department, took over. The generators were put to work and power was sold to various private companies and to a few towns. One of the nitrate plants was converted into a laboratory for experiments on a cheap phosphate fertilizer. Headquarters were established in Knoxville, three hundred miles from the original assets, and work begun on a dam in the Clinch River, a tributary of the

Tennessee, twenty-five miles from Knoxville. To house the dam workers and part of the headquarters' staff, the town of Norris was built. The Norris Dam is now completed, generators are being installed and power will flow early in the summer. As the reservoir fills behind the dam, it will back upstream at least forty miles, and then the TVA will begin to make a very tangible impression on the landscape. . . .

Nine dams in the main river, including Hales Bar, built and leased by a private power company, and three in tributary rivers. With these twelve dams in place, the nine-foot channel running 650 miles from Knoxville to Paducah is assured and protected; no conceivable flood can seriously damage the Valley, for the plans are based on a flow of water 50 per cent greater than the historic flood of 1867. The power load will be integrated from dam to dam, so that the resources of those where the water is low will be supplemented by those where the water is high. Any power engineer can tell you what this means in dependability and low cost. Great transmission lines will link generator to generator. To take a specific instance: Wilson Dam is a run-of-the-river plant. Its reservoir does not provide much storage, and in the summer and fall, when the river is normally low, its power output is at a minimum. Norris Dam, on the other hand, is designed primarily for storing flood waters, and has a huge capacity. While Wilson is well supplied by the high river in the spring, the Norris gates will be closed; flood waters will fill the great reservoir. As Wilson declines, Norris comes in. The gates are opened. Power is generated once at the Norris turbines, and as the released water goes down the river, generated again at Wilson. Norris and Wilson together can generate three or four times as much dependable power as either could produce alone.

With nine run-of-the-river dams, it is conceivable that every bucket of water released from Norris, or other tributary reservoirs, will be used ten times. Within a year from today every bucketful will be used three times, once at Norris, once at Wheeler, once at Wilson. This is the engineering ideal of balancing the load, and makes for cheap power. No private company can hope to rival such watershed control.

By the end of 1936 about $85,000,000 will have been spent on six dams— Wheeler, Norris, Pickwick Landing, Guntersville, Chickamauga, and Fowler Bend. By the end of 1940 all six will be completed—Congress permitting—at a total cost of about $185,000,000. By 1944 another $144,000,000 can be expended to advantage in constructing four more dams to make the system complete— Gilbertsville, Watts Bar, Coulter Shoals, and Fontana. The total outlay is thus estimated at about a third of a billion—say the cost of half a dozen battleships. The work has been planned, furthermore, to keep the skilled labor force steadily employed for the next eight years, thus preserving the human balance as well as the hydrologic. . . .

TVA—THE FIRST FIFTEEN YEARS (1948)

Ernest Kirschten

THE RECORD [of the TVA] . . . is one of the thrilling chapters of American history. The more men got to know the Tennessee, the more they became convinced that they ought to be doing something with it. Andrew Jackson dreamed of its development, and Theodore Roosevelt had enough of the vision in 1903 to veto a bill for its private exploitation. The First World War started the Muscle Shoals development. Then came Henry Ford with his offer to take it off the government's hands. Nebraska's George Norris, however, was on the scene. And the story really begins in 1933 with Franklin D. Roosevelt's arrival in the White House. Norris at last had a partner in the project of turning a dream into concrete.

The dream was to handle all the problems and possibilities of the river and valley as one. . . . TVA . . . has been remarkably faithful to its mandate. A score of dams have been built between Gilbertsville in Kentucky and Fontana in North Carolina. They have turned a once shoal-dotted and troublesome stream into a succession of beautiful inland lakes which in 1947 carried an estimated 341,000,000 ton-miles of freight, exclusive of sand and gravel. This was more than ten times the traffic in 1933.

As for flood control, TVA reduced by ten feet the crest of last February's flood and saved Chattanooga alone about $6,000,000 in flood losses. It is estimated that $27,500,000 in flood losses has been saved since Norris Dam went into operation in 1936. Nor can it be overlooked that control of the Tennessee has lowered flood crests on the Ohio and the Mississippi.

TVA has always been well aware that flood control begins on the land. Again faithful to the act, it has planted thousands of trees and fostered contour plowing. To reclaim marginal land it has made progress in breaking the one-crop habit. It has demonstrated that grass—in the form of meat and dairy products—is more profitable than cotton. It has shown that fertilizers, especially phosphates, can make well-nigh barren land fertile. Thus, while tobacco acreage is down 8 per cent, the yield is up 48 per cent. Corn acreage is down 19.7 per cent, but the yield is up almost 20 per cent. Between 1939 and 1944 farm prices rose 105 per cent, but the value of Tennessee Valley farm products went up 147 per cent—from $110,803,000 to $274,466,000.

The once backward valley has been transformed into an industrial region of increasing importance. Between 1933 and 1945 employment opportunities in factories went up 161 per cent, or 30 per cent more than in the rest of the country. Since 1933 more than 1,800 new plants have been opened in the area. And as Mr. Clapp said in a recent speech, "so far as is known, only four of these new plants were moved in from other regions."

Per capita income in the valley is rising more rapidly than in the United States as a whole. In 1933 it was only 40 per cent of the national average. By 1945 it had risen to 58 per cent. The dollar figure for 1945 was a round 2.1 billion

—or $680,000,000 more than it would have been had it increased only at the national rate. Income-tax figures show how this has benefited the nation. In 1933 collections in the valley represented 3.4 per cent of the total. By 1946 the figure was up to 6 per cent. Also, of that extra $680,000,000, no less than $450,000,000 was used to buy products of other sections of the United States.

The big chapter in TVA's story, of course, is power. Increased incomes in industry and agriculture alike are based on it. It also has enabled TVA to make its prescribed contribution to the national defense. TVA electricity made the aluminum that filled the air with American planes. TVA electricity runs Oak Ridge.

TVA produced 14,797,000,000 kilowatt-hours in 1947 compared with 12,314,000,000 in the previous year. (Incidentally 92 per cent of the 1947 output came from hydroelectric plants.) But the demand still is rising. Between June 30 of last year and the end of February, 1948, the number of consumers increased from 743,000 to 810,400. And the use per consumer is mounting. The average for 1947 was 2,197 kilowatt-hours; by the end of last February it was up to 2,446.

Surely this is proof of the theory that low costs will promote widespread use of power. And TVA power is cheap. The average price at the end of February was 1.59 cents per kilowatt-hour compared with a national average of 3.08 cents. For 100 kilowatt-hours the residential rate in the TVA area is $2.50. In New York it is $4.86; in Chicago, $3.35; in St. Louis, $2.85; in San Francisco, $2.82. In McMinnville, Oregon, served by Bonneville, it is $2.50, as in the TVA area.

And now the storm breaks! Sure TVA rates are low, but they are subsidized, runs the charge. Well, at least Congress is satisfied that TVA is not allocating to navigation and other activities expenses properly chargeable to the power account. Of TVA's bookkeeping the General Accounting Office has said that it probably is "the finest accounting system in the entire government and probably one of the best accounting systems in the world." So no facts are concealed. But known facts can be variously interpreted.

TVA does not pay interest on the sums appropriated by the federal government for the construction of its facilities. It regards this money as an investment rather than as a loan. And TVA does not pay federal taxes. Certainly, these factors should be considered in comparisons with private power rates. Privately owned utilities cannot raise money in quite the same way. On this point Mr. Clapp says:

The charge of subsidy can best be answered by examining what the books show for the fiscal year ending June 30, 1947. In that year TVA showed a net operating revenue of $21,800,000, representing a 5 1/2 per cent return on all the money—$400,000,000—invested in the power system. This is the sum remaining after state and local ad valorem tax payments, straight-line depreciation, and all operating expenses incurred in generating and transmitting power. The $21,800,000, therefore, corresponds to the sum which a private corporation, utility or otherwise, has to divide among those who have invested money in the business and to pay federal income taxes. It is the significant figure in determining the financial soundness of the enterprise.

All of this $21,800,000, or 5 1/2 per cent return, is the property of the federal government. It can be divided up according to any theory you care to use. For example, if interest were charged at 2 per cent, the average cost of money to the government during the period, on the entire TVA average net power investment of $400,000,000, there would still remain $13,800,000. If income taxes were calculated at the rate charged large corporations, 38 per cent on net income after interest, or roughly and generously $5,300,000, there still remains a surplus of $8,500,000.

A return of $13,800,000 or even of only $8,500,000 a year to the government is certainly enough to prove that TVA is a going concern. Understandably, Mr. Clapp and his associates want to make their record look as good as possible, and so they use the $21,800,000 figure. They do not even make a bookkeeping allowance for interest, arguing that the taxpayers have invested in TVA rather than made a loan to it. But is it absolutely fair to use this figure in comparisons with privately operated utilities? Is this really living up to the yardstick idea? Would it not be wiser to make an allowance for interest in such comparative statements? Would this not deprive the opposition of some of its ammunition? And what difference would it make? All the money belongs to the people of the United States.

And the last word: In the 1948 appropriation bill Congress provided a formula whereby the government's investment in TVA power facilities—set at $348,249,000 rather than the round figure of $400,000,000 used by Mr. Clapp—is to be paid back into the Treasury in forty annual instalments. After that, TVA power earnings will be virtually a windfall for the American taxpayer. . . .

THE RECORD OF THE REA (1944)

Judson King

. . . A GENERATION AGO the idea of "area service"—that is, of making electricity as available in rural regions as in cities and towns—was scoffed at as a dream of impractical idealists. Today the REA, by making the dream come true, has captured the imagination of the American people and become universally popular. What is not understood in urban circles, however, and what needs sharp emphasis, is the fact that cheap electric *motor power* in barn and field, as well as lights, running water, and refrigerators in the farm home, is necessary for the rehabilitation of agriculture in this country. By "cheap" is meant an average cost of around 1 cent per kilowatt-hour instead of the 3 to 10 cents now charged. Such a price would bring current within the reach of the pocket-books of the middle- and lower-income farmers, including share-croppers, who constitute over 80 per cent of our rural population. And it is not a pipe dream. Already some of the older cooperatives in the TVA region, as well as around Tacoma and in the Bonneville area in Washington and Oregon, are selling current at 1.5 cents or less. How can they do it? Their lines are being amortized, and they benefit from the very cheap wholesale rates of public-power dams.

Five years after the close of World War I only 177,000 American farms—2.6 per cent—were electrified. Thousands of progressive farmers were growing restless, and private industry moved to meet the demand. In 1923 the National Electric Light Association, representing 90 per cent of the nation's electric utilities, formed a "Committee on the Relation of Electricity to Agriculture," and started an impressive campaign to "electrify rural America." It invited and obtained the active cooperation of the national farm organizations, the agricultural colleges, the appliance manufacturers, the American Society of Agricultural Engineers, the General Federation of Women's Clubs, and the United States Departments of Agriculture, of Commerce, and of the Interior.

During the next eleven years some $2,400,000 was spent on research, experimentation, and an intensive advertising campaign to "sell" electricity to our farmers. By 1935 the industry's own statistics showed that 743,954 farms were being served. That meant only 11 per cent; some 6,000,000 farms were as yet without current—this at a time when from 50 to 80 per cent of the farms in the advanced countries of Europe, in New Zealand, and even in Japan were electrified. In the winter of 1934 the national farm organizations, discouraged and disgusted, withdrew from the Committee on the Relation of Electricity to Agriculture. The grand effort of free enterprise to solve this great socioeconomic problem had failed.

It had failed because of the rates charged, which were so high that only the rich farmers could afford to pay them. At the start of the campaign the utilities asserted that rates were not an essential factor, and the cooperating agencies were silent on this point. Rate schedules were kept high in order to yield customary profits on alleged "fair values." When the campaign died down, the utilities, under stinging criticism from farm leaders, replied bluntly that the companies were "not eleemosynary institutions . . . ; therefore, conspicuous advances in farm electrification must wait"—until farmers could afford it.

In the winter of 1934 the National Grange and the American Farm Bureau Federation applied to the national government for help. The Natural Resources Board and the Civil Works Administration investigated and strongly recommended federal aid. Progressives without regard to party affiliations supported the movement. Senator Shipstead, for example, promoted an electric cooperative in his own county in Minnesota in 1934, and declared that without federal-government leadership the task of farm electrification could not be accomplished within any reasonable time. In April the Emergency Relief Appropriation Act earmarked $100,000,000 for rural electrification, and on May 11, 1935, President Roosevelt by executive order created the REA. In 1936 its life was extended for ten years by the Norris-Rayburn Act.

The principal function of the REA was to make twenty-five-year loans to rural cooperative groups or public-power districts at low interest rates to enable them to serve themselves electrically. The present Congress has extended the term of the loans to thirty-five years. To date $382,600,000 has been lent out, at an average interest rate of 2.5 per cent. "Area service" is a different thing from the company practice of running a few lines into thickly settled neighborhoods, and to protect the government loans the REA set up legal, finance, engineering, research, utilization, and other divisions at headquarters. The job of the technical staffs of the REA was to make cheap current possible, and they did it.

A "co-op" comes into being about as follows. Farmers and others in an unserved area organize a non-profit cooperative under state law, with the aid usually of an REA field man. They hire an engineer, draw up plans, and apply for a loan. If investigation shows the project will pay and the engineering plans are sound, a loan is made by the REA. The co-op proceeds with construction, and presently the area has light and power, distributed by itself. Power is purchased wholesale from private utilities. If the price is too high, the co-op builds its own generating plant. Some co-ops cover a relatively small area with a few hundred members; others serve four or five counties with from 5,000 to 8,000 members.

Rural America eagerly embraced the opportunity offered by the REA. Though construction was abruptly halted by the war, there are now 812 cooperatives in 45 states serving 1,115,056 rural consumers. The essential test for the conservative mind is, are these co-ops paying? The answer is that on April 1 the total amount due on all REA loans, principal and interest, was $50,252,000 and that the government had been repaid $16,131,794 in excess of that amount in advance payments. Only 9 of the 812 co-ops, whose average age is four and a half years, were in real financial trouble. Social benefits are well and good, but it is this evidence of financial success that has brought the REA almost universal approval.

The continued hostility of the private utilities, which is intensifying as peace approaches, has puzzled many people. Why, they ask, should the utilities fight against the accomplishment of a needed task which they declined to undertake, especially when the REA Act of 1936 prohibits loans to farm co-ops in territory already served by private companies? The reasons are simple. The power trust knows that co-op rates are lower than company city rates and that this is bound to have a powerful effect upon public opinion. Like all big business men, utility leaders fear the spread of the cooperative idea. When the REA challenged the supremacy of the private utilities, their executives suddenly began doing what they had declared was impossible. *Since 1935 they have electrified as many farms as the cooperatives.*

The total effect, then, of the establishment of the REA is that today some 42 per cent of American farms are electrified as against 11 per cent in 1935. However, the job is not yet one-half done, and the rest cannot wait indefinitely. Medium and small farmers are threatened by large-scale mechanized farming today just as small business is threatened by big business, and competitive enterprise by monopoly. To meet this threat they must have adequate modern machinery and electric power.

If we take a broad view of it, the farm problem is the same that faces our people in every field of endeavor. The crux of it is whether dollars shall be placed above human welfare. All intelligent men and women are aware of the approaching crisis. Hence the encouraging multiplicity of post-war planning. The REA has something constructive to offer. When nineteenth-century banker-utility practices failed them, American farmers, with the aid of their government, started doing the rural-electrification job themselves. . . .

RANK-AND-FILE KILOWATTS (1944)

McAlister Coleman

. . . UNDER THE BANNERS of "free enterprise," the privateers are launching a nation-wide assault upon the people's ownership and use of their own resources. In the Northwest two related campaigns are under way in the free enterprisers' current attempt at a glorious comeback. In one, private ownership is fighting public ownership in the field of electric light and power; in the other, private ownership is fighting public ownership over the disposition of the new war plants that have sprung up around the great dams.

The fight on the power front is at its hottest right now in Washington, where the public-power people are working for a referendum permitting the fast-growing Public-Utility Districts in the state to acquire and operate entire electrical systems, instead of being compelled as at present to operate only small portions of systems using Bonneville-Coulee power. A statement of Pacific Northwest labor men—C. I. O., A. F. of L., and railroaders—urging the passage of the Public-Utility District measure reads as follows: "The huge Alcoa plant at Vancouver, the Reynolds plant at Longview, the Olin Aluminum plant at Wenatchee—all of these are accomplishments of public power. Without public power, shipbuilding and airplane manufacture would still be bawling infants instead of the young giants they now are." These labor men are looking forward with lively apprehension to the situation which the Northwest must face immediately after the war, and at the same time they are combating the propaganda of what Amos Pinchot once called "the kilowatt klan."

A recent example of such propaganda was the sprawling advertisement of the Puget Sound Power and Light Company in the Seattle papers. This privately owned concern has long been a thorn in the side of City Light, Seattle's great publicly owned hydroelectric development, which has given the town its reputation as "America's best-lighted city." By order of the SEC and a Massachusetts court the Puget Sound Company was compelled the other day to hold an election for a new board of directors—one on which Eastern financial interests would not be so conspicuous as formerly. In the advertisement a picture of a number of substantial-looking citizens sitting chummily around a directors' table was accompanied by this blurb: "This is free enterprise in action . . . chance for progress in the American Way. This is public ownership, honest-to-goodness American style, with business management under government regulation. With Puget Power it is a case of pooling the money and talents of a lot of people for mutual benefit in the rendering of a valuable public service. We are working and will be working with you as partners in the building of an ever-greater state of Washington—which, it can be truly said, has a future bright with promise."

Old-time battlers for City Light smiled sardonically when they read this, remembering how desperately and with what dubious tactics Puget Power had fought to destroy both the municipally owned plant and its fearless superintendent, the late James Delmage Ross, the Northwest's beloved "J.D." With a certain pride they pointed out that only in such a strongly held public domain as theirs would a private company attempt to sell itself as an "honest-to-goodness" public-ownership enterprise.

A more familiar argument along the old lines of "Pin the Bolshevik label on 'em" was used in this "stuffer" enclosed in the bills of a privately owned company: "Let's fight and work to keep our business system in the hands of free men. Let us turn a deaf ear to those who, under cover of war emergency, would lead us into a system of national socialism, which is the slavery typified by NAZI."

In Seattle at any rate, where residential consumers are enjoying the use of three times the national average of light and power at a cost of around one cent a kilowatt-hour, the outcries of the private companies fall on deaf ears. When the Seattle owner of an "all-electric home" receives from City Light a monthly bill of only $5 for juice that runs an electric range and an automatic hot-water tank, in addition to his lighting and a number of electrical gadgets, he is not likely to be impressed with the "American Way" of free enterprise. Nor is the citizen of neighboring Tacoma, where the publicly owned plant charges the lowest rates in the country, or of the twenty or so other towns throughout the state that own their plants. Not long ago the Seattle City Council, by no stretch of the imagination a radical body, voted unanimously not to grant a franchise to Puget Power after its present franchise expires in 1952, thereby setting a precedent which future councils will find it difficult to ignore.

Outside the cities, out in the grass roots and tall timber of the Northwest, the struggle continues. Here it is the rapid growth of Washington's "Public-Utility Districts" and Oregon's "People's Utility Districts" which the private interests are seeking to strangle. In Washington, which has one-fifth of the nation's hydroelectric power, with an aggregate potential of more than ten million horse-power, the Public-Utility Districts came into being as the result of an initiative enacted in 1930. The districts may buy and sell power inside and outside their limits, which are usually those of the county, and have the right of eminent domain—they may buy, condemn, or lease properties. Three commissioners elected by the district's voters run its affairs. Washington now has fifteen Public-Utility Districts in highly successful operation, saving customers huge sums in rates and making cheap and abundant power easily accessible to thousands of farmers and small home-owners. These P. U. D.'s are developing new types of public servants, who understand the problems of our future industrial and agricultural civilization. Instead of being high-pressure salesmen for Eastern holding companies, like the officials of privately owned utilities, the P. U. D. commissioners are farmers, workingmen, and small-business men, responsive to the needs of the community.

Commissioner J. N. Erlandsen of Everett, Washington, for example, is an active unionist who has just announced that the Public-Utility District of Snohomish County will now proceed to construct its own system. He explains that this step is necessary in order to derive full benefit from cheap Bonneville power rates. The privately owned power company in the county wanted $13,500,000 for the properties involved in the condemnation suit, whereas the P. U. D.'s engineers valued them at no more than $4,000,000. Incidentally, the assessed value of the properties, on which the private company pays taxes, is but $900,000. Commissioner Doyle, of the militant Cowlitz County district, is a member of the Machinists' Union and former president of his local. Commissioner Marshall of Thurston County is a member of the United Mine Workers of America. It is significant that one of the first acts of the Washington Commissioners' Association was to insist that all Public-Utility Districts bargain collectively with unions.

While farmers are naturally more interested in the irrigation than in the power possibilities of the big dams, they too are strong for public power. The usually conservative Grange in both Oregon and Washington supports it wholeheartedly.

It was good to talk to those rugged men of the rank and file after a session with the watered-down descendants of the pioneers, city slickers calling themselves "free enterprisers." One district commissioner, a member of the C. I. O. Woodworkers' Union, said: "These private fellers can't get up enough enterprise, free or otherwise, to bring cheap juice from Bonneville right down the line. So we've got to get it for ourselves. We figure that's enterprising for everybody's good, the way it was out here in the early days. And we are appeasing nobody." This last was a reference to what many of the rank-and-file public-power men believe to be the over-cautious policies of some top men in the Bonneville administration. The commissioners don't accept the idea that we are heading for a reactionary regime after the war and so what's the use of fighting the privateers? Some would welcome the organization of a militant farmer-labor alliance for independent political action.

Some sort of effective action in the political as well as the economic field must be taken—and soon—if there is not to be that mass exodus from the Northwest which forward-looking citizens fear when the curtain finally drops on the war. The plans of the capitalists in both old parties are plain enough, and the Northwestern delegation in Congress—which includes the progressive Homer T. Bone in the Senate and Representative John Coffee in the House—is now girding its loins against their political maneuverings. Evidently they hope to reduce the Northwest to its former subordinate position in the national economy, with shipping, lumber, and fishing its main enterprises. Indeed, S. W. Murphy, president of the Electric Bond and Share Company, has gone so far as to suggest that after the war Bonneville and Grand Coulee, together with the TVA, be sold to private interests for the purpose of "reducing the public debt." At a public meeting in December Henry Kaiser said that within a year after the war there would not be employment for more than 5 per cent of the workers now employed in his Portland shipyards. Behind the scenes there are moves to nip in the bud the hopeful start of a steel industry near the dams; though the coal in the region is mostly sub-bituminous or lowly lignite, geologists and engineers say that it could be put to productive use. Naturally the Alcoa crowd discourages the project of making aluminum from native clays in Oregon.

Already, through Jesse Jones's Defense Plant Corporation, the government has invested more than $170,000,000 in the plants at the big dams, as compared with private industry's $27,000,000. The two chief products are aluminum and magnesium, the light metals of which tomorrow's world, according to the advertisements, will be fabricated. Nothing, of course, would please the ineffable Jones more than to give back the government-subsidized plants to the indicted Indians of Alcoa and Dow Chemical the minute the guns cease firing overseas. The erstwhile aluminum and magnesium monopolists are anguished to see

Uncle Sam owning 70 per cent of the nation's aluminum-production facilities and 94 per cent of the magnesium facilities, and obtaining the power which is so large a factor in the production of both metals from publicly owned dams at $17.50 a kilowatt year—Bonneville's wholesale industrial rate.

The labor men whom I quoted above say that "thanks to public power the future of the Northwest is brighter than it has ever been before. Public power is cheap power, and cheap power is a strong industrial magnet." Hope for a continued high level of employment, they say, must be based on "the full utilization of the resources of the region. The most vital of these resources and the peculiar advantage of the Northwest is its hydroelectric energy, which exceeds that of any area of similar size on the continent." Here, they believe, "is the foundation for a post-war expansion unrivaled elsewhere on earth."

. . . If the present drive for a return to free enterprise succeeds in destroying the publicly owned projects in the Northwest, it will destroy the most hopeful opportunity in the United States for achieving full employment, production for use, and genuine industrial democracy.

THE NORTHWEST NEEDS A CVA (1945)

Carey McWilliams

I

AT THE END OF THE WAR the people of the Pacific Northwest face not a problem but an emergency of major proportions. In this region "post-war adjustment" will require a redistribution of population, a rapid development of resources, and a general reorganization of the economy. Other war-industry centers are concerned with shifting war workers to peace-time jobs; in the Northwest the problem is to create the jobs. The talk here is not of "reconversion" but of possible "new industries," not of "adjustment" but of "regional development."

Before the war the Northwest was one of our newest and brightest domestic colonies. Since it was a new colony, it did not show the outward evidences of exploitation. The average per capita income was relatively high. The inventory of untapped resources was impressive. The signs of blight were negligible. Yet to a large extent the region was living on its capital. The basic resources from which much of its income was derived were in some cases being rapidly depleted. It was not a "problem area," but it had many serious problems. It lacked balance. It had too much water in some sections and not enough in others, power going to waste in some places and a lack of power in others. Its industries lacked diversity, its pay rolls stability. The situation was made worse by the fact that powerful interests, profiting from the region's undeveloped colonial status, were opposed to industrial expansion. Only after a bitter fight with these interests was the expansion obtained that the war emergency demanded.

Since the beginning of the war the labor force of the region has increased 50 per cent, its income 100 per cent, and its population 10 per cent—the interior areas have been drained of man-power by the war industries on the coast. The chief war industries are shipbuilding, aircraft manufacture, and light metals, in all of which severe cut-backs are clearly foreseeable. New jobs must somehow be found for 500,000 war workers and veterans. That means that the region will have to produce goods and services worth $8 billion a year and provide around 2,300,000 jobs of one kind or another. Since its resources are largely undeveloped, an enormous investment program will be required. And since the economy is already out of balance, there must be unified regional development. Both requirements demand a plan and a planning agency.

The immediate problem, of course, is to cushion the effects of the cut-back period. Plans for this transitional period already exist. The governors of the Northwest states, through the Northwest States Development Association, have approved blueprints for fifty large-scale post-war projects requiring an investment of $600,000,000 and providing employment for perhaps 100,000 workers. Fortunately these plans are all related, directly or indirectly, to the development of the Columbia River basin. If the projects can be constructed quickly and as a single planned development, they will greatly accelerate the general industrial and agricultural expansion needed to provide permanent jobs. For example, developments and installations necessary to open up 1,000,000 acres of Columbia Basin lands for the settlement of an estimated 50,000 farm families, previously projected over a period of fifteen or twenty years, might be completed in half the time if intelligently planned and efficiently carried out by a regional development corporation. Such a project cannot be accomplished through the cumbersome device of interstate compacts or by agencies directed from 3,000 miles away.

Plans for the larger task are also in existence—on paper and in broad outline. The seven-point program calls for (1) preparing some two and a half million acres of land for development; (2) developing a river transportation system to provide the Inland Empire with cheap and easy access to the sea; (3) harnessing the region's vast sources of hydroelectric power; (4) exploring its untapped mineral wealth; (5) creating, in the Northwest, a power technology region in which the electro-chemical and electro-metallurgical industries of the West would be concentrated; (6) protecting and stabilizing the fishing and lumbering industries; and (7) exploiting the unlimited possibilities of the region as a tourist and recreational area. Each and every phase of this plan depends upon the unified development of the Columbia River and its tributaries; power is the key to the entire accomplishment. As Dr. Paul J. Raver, administrator of the Bonneville Power Administration, has said, the task is "one of unification—involving the unified, balanced development of a river basin and its resources, envisioned in their entirety."

Plans and planners are not lacking in the Northwest, but at the present time there is no organization responsible for the prompt and efficient execution of either the transitional or the long-range part of this program. Existing agencies cannot undertake the task; it requires a single regional authority with broad powers and a high degree of autonomy. The Bonneville Power Administration is not such an authority. It is an administration and a power-marketing agency, not a development corporation. It was created by Congress in 1937, within the Department of Interior, for the sole purpose of transmitting and wholesaling power generated at Bonneville. Three years later it was given, by executive order, the function of selling the power generated at Grand Coulee. While it is empowered to construct and operate a transmission system, it has no authority over unified stream development or control. Even as a power marketing agency it lacks authority to acquire existing private generating and distributing facilities. Nor are its functions in any way related to industrial research or economic progress.

As a great river system, the Columbia calls for unified, organic development. All of the uses to which the river can be put should be considered in relation to the development of the region as a whole. A planning function of this kind cannot be ladled out, a little to this agency, a little to that. Yet the federal agencies that are interested in some phase of the Columbia River are too numerous to mention. The aims of these agencies are not identical; their functions overlap; and with the exception of the BPA they are operated from Washington as straight-line government agencies. It is fantastic to assume that these various agencies, with a little gentle compulsion, can prepare a master-plan for the region or that they could jointly execute a plan if one were prepared. The matter of soils, for example, is of interest to several agencies within the Department of Agriculture; but it is also of interest to the Bureau of Reclamation, the General Land Office, the Geological Survey, the Grazing Service, the National Park Service, the Bureau of Indian Affairs. River development concerns the Bureau of Reclamation, the Geological Survey, the Bonneville Power Administration, the Army Engineers, the Fish and Wildlife Service. Water and minerals concern a host of agencies. Underlying the whole problem, moreover, is the important question of enlisting the cooperation of state and local agencies. With whom are these agencies to cooperate?

To meet this general situation, Senator Hugh Mitchell of Washington, on February 4, 1945, introduced Senate Bill No. 460 to create a public corporation to be known as the Columbia Valley Authority. The corporation would be governed by a board of three directors to be appointed by the President with the advice and consent of the Senate. Within two years after its establishment the authority would be required to submit a master-plan for the development of the region within certain policy objectives set forth in the act. The functions, facilities, and personnel of the Bonneville Power Administration would be completely absorbed in the new organization, and other federal agencies would be authorized to participate in CVA activities on mutually agreeable terms. The CVA would have the right to acquire private power facilities, but it would be obliged to sell the distribution facilities so acquired as rapidly as possible to local public agencies. It could obtain the transfer, upon request, of other water-controlled projects. It would be authorized to dispose of surplus electric energy in accordance with established federal policies. It would have broad powers in relation to power development, flood control, reclamation, and navigation. Whether Senator Mitchell's bill is preferable to the Murray bill or the Rankin bill may be debatable; that it can be improved and clarified is altogether probable; but that some such authority is needed is indisputable. It is needed not only to ease the shocks of the cut-back period and to unlock the resources of the Northwest but to protect the more than $325,000,000 which the federal government has already invested in public projects on the Columbia and the $110,000,000 it has invested in war plants in the region. . . .

II

. . . With the exception of the Yangtze, the Columbia River is the greatest potential source of hydroelectric power in the world. The flow of the river is rapid and continuous; no stand-by steam plants are necessary. Fed by vast glaciers in Canada, the flow of the river actually increases in late summer when that of some of its competing systems has greatly diminished. The power of the Columbia is certainly one of the most valuable and durable assets of the nation.

The crucial question today is who is to control the distribution and utilization of the staggering power potential of the Columbia River system. At the present time Grand Coulee and Bonneville generate 1,350,000 kilowatts of power at the lowest wholesale rate in America—$17.50 per kilowatt-year. With the construction of the additional dams planned, this output will be increased by more than 1,000,000 kilowatts, and the Northwest will then have more hydroelectric power than was produced in the rest of the United States before the war. Whoever controls this power can dictate the economic and industrial future of this great section.

Since the completion of the Bonneville and Grand Coulee dams the private power companies in the Northwest have largely abandoned their quarter-century fight to prevent the development of Columbia River power. What they are fighting for today is the special privilege of purchasing power "at the bus bar," that is, at the dam sites. They would probably not oppose the construction of even more dams on the river, if they were granted this privilege. They are quite willing for the government to produce the power if they can control its distribution. If they should win out, the social potential of Grand Coulee, Bonneville, and the other dams which the government intends to construct on the Columbia would be largely neutralized. As a result of the war the situation in the Northwest is such that they believe they can attain their objective.

Since the availability of Grand Coulee and Bonneville power coincided with the expansion of the defense program, the problem of utilizing this power, the problem of markets, was temporarily solved. Today almost 90 per cent of the power distributed by the Bonneville Power Administration goes directly or indirectly to war industries in the region. Once the war is over, it will be necessary to find other markets. Of 1,300,000 kilowatts of power now being distributed by the Bonneville Power Administration to some eighty customers throughout the region, more than 750,000 kilowatts are subject to cancellation in the immediate post-war period. The cancellation of these contracts will mean that the $24,000,000 of annual revenue now being collected by the BPA will be reduced by $13,000,000. If new markets cannot be found, the private utility companies will contend that the government is "spilling millions of dollars of power over the dams." At the same time they will wave before the eyes of every Congressman photostats of the handsome checks they are willing—and even anxious—to pay for this power. They will want, of course, long-term contracts. In order to confront the BPA with this dilemma, the private utilities are now trying to capture existing markets.

How far they have already gone may be illustrated by a brief account of their dealings with the Vera irrigation district on the outskirts of Spokane. The farms in this district are small. Most of the owners are part-time farmers—teachers, clerks, and industrial workers employed in Spokane. The district's contract for power with the Washington Water Power Company expired in December, 1944. When the company failed to meet the rate offered by the Bonneville Power Administration, the district signed up for Bonneville power. The Bonneville rate is about 57 per cent less than the rate offered by the private utility, and when the power is available, the consumers to whom the district distributes the power will benefit from a 30 per cent net reduction. Under the regulations of the WPB, however, the Bonneville Power Administration cannot obtain priorities for materials to build a substation and connecting lines to the district, although its existing lines are only a short distance away.

Faced with Bonneville competition, the private utility offered every inducement to the district to sign a five-year contract, but since the rate offered failed to meet the Bonneville rate, the district refused. The private utility then notified the district that it would not provide power during the interval that Bonneville was unable to serve the district. In effect, this was a threat of death to a prosperous farming community. Finally local public-health officials intervened to protect the district, and the company backed down.

That cheap Bonneville power will be attractive to municipally operated systems in the Northwest is illustrated by the experience of McMinnville, Oregon, a town of some four thousand people, the center of a prosperous farming community. McMinnville has one of the oldest municipal power systems in Oregon. Since 1924, by using diesel engines, it has been able to produce power more cheaply than it could buy it from the private utilities. It was compelled, however, to set aside 24 cents out of every revenue dollar for new equipment and repairs. When it obtains Bonneville power, the city will not only be relieved of this necessity but will be able to effect a 40 per cent reduction in rates to commercial and a 20 per cent reduction to residential consumers.

For a number of reasons the Bonneville Power Administration is not in a position to organize the municipal markets. Legally it can sell power only to large industrial consumers and public distributing agencies. To meet war demands, a power pool has been formed of all the available power, private and public, in the Northwest. With most of its power being distributed to industrial plants or, under the pool arrangement, to private utilities, Bonneville cannot undertake an immediate campaign for municipal contracts. During the war it is placing no ceiling on the resale rates charged by private utilities, but after the war it will insist on such ceilings. The moment this is done, the power fight will really get under way. The Northwest will then see considerable activity in the promotion of public distributing systems—at the end of 1943 Bonneville had only fifty-two "public-agency" contracts. But this is a slow process under the most favorable circumstances, and it will be bitterly opposed, at every step, by the private utilities. If the Bonneville Power Administration were reorganized along the lines of the TVA, it could buy out the private systems, lock, stock, and barrel. At present it lacks authority to take over existing generating, transmission, and distributing systems.

Other markets exist, however, and can unquestionably be developed. The

Northwest has long suffered from a lack of fuel. The development of space heating would find a large market and would greatly stimulate the service industries. Irrigation pumping, the use of electricity to generate steam for industrial processes, railroad electrification, the increased use of electricity in manufacturing and service industries, and the great possibilities of power on the farm all promise to provide expanding markets. But the prompt and full development of these markets presupposes the existence of an agency equipped with more than the marketing function which is the only one that has been assigned to the BPA.

A rapid development of these markets must be forced, not only to prevent the waste of public power, but to stimulate industrial expansion in the Northwest. The vast supply of cheap government power must be used dynamically, as the key to unlocking the resources of the area. Power can be made to pay the bill for improved navigation, for reclamation, for the stimulation of new industries (through pilot-plant operations), for the exploitation of mineral resources. The development of 1,029,000 acres of irrigable land in the Columbia Basin would have involved a prohibitive expense if the full costs properly allocated to irrigation had been actually imposed upon the land. With the exception of $1,000,000 charged off to navigation, however, power is expected to pay three-fourths of the cost of the entire project. In an undeveloped region like the Northwest "power is the banker." But if power is to be used in this manner, it must be controlled by an agency with authority commensurate to the task, such an agency, for example, as that proposed in Senator Hugh Mitchell's bill (Senate Bill No. 460) to create a Columbia Valley Authority.

Since they know that their fight to buy power at the dam sites will be lost if the Bonneville Power Administration is merged in a Columbia Valley Authority, the private utilities can be relied on to make every effort to prevent the establishment of a regional authority. If they succeed they stand a chance of winning the power struggle in the Northwest. For if the BPA is unable to develop new markets rapidly enough to offset the post-war contract cancellations, the bids of the private utilities can be made to appear very attractive to a reactionary Congress.

In support of their "economy argument" the private utility companies will contend that since the rates they charge for power are subject to regulation, it is really immaterial who distributes the power. There are many fallacies in this argument, but it will suffice here to point out that, given their present stock structure and bonded indebtedness, even the most efficiently operated private utilities cannot pass on to the public the benefits arising from an abundance of cheap public power. Nor are cheap rates the only issue. In a region like the Northwest the way in which power is used is probably as important as the rates charged: if properly used, power will act as a magnet to attract a healthy distribution of population and industry. The private utilities will also contend, of course, that lower government rates merely reflect the fact that government agencies enjoy tax exemption. But if the Bonneville Power Administration enjoys tax exemption, the concerns which its power has attracted to the Northwest do not. One site in the Spokane area on which an aluminum plant has been built paid only $42.05 in taxes in 1943; in 1944, with the plant installed, it paid $88,435.21. . . .

III

The novel aspect of the fight now gathering strength in the Northwest over the Columbia Valley Authority is found in the fact that two government agencies are playing an active role in organizing the opposition. Though they are traditionally rival agencies, the Army Engineers and the Bureau of Reclamation have formed an agreement to oppose the creation of river-valley authorities. Their chief purpose is to forestall a Missouri Valley Authority, but their opposition extends to one for the Columbia.

Both the Army Engineers and the Bureau of Reclamation are old-established, highly centralized agencies, with powerful political connections formed over a period of years. Both regard their traditional policies and procedures with a semi-religious veneration. Within the limitations of this attitude, both agencies are efficiently operated and can be credited with truly impressive accomplishments. Enduring examples of the great work they have done may be found throughout the West. In the past they have frequently clashed over matters of policy, but the opposition which they share to integrated regional authorities has effected a reconciliation. Both organizations are today conducting an under-cover campaign against the various proposals to create a Columbia Valley Authority, particularly Senator Hugh Mitchell's Senate Bill No. 460. The Bureau of Reclamation has always regarded power development as incidental to reclamation; the Army Engineers have always thought of it as incidental to navigation and flood control. It is quite natural that the two agencies should be critical of proposals fundamentally at variance with their respective philosophies. But their clandestine alliance with various special-interest groups constitutes a major public scandal.

The link between these agencies and the private interests that oppose a CVA is the National Reclamation Association and its state and regional affiliates. Since "reclamation" is a magic word in the West, the association provides the perfect front for the forces fighting river authorities. For many years the National Reclamation Association has been an arm—more accurately the "private lobby"—of the Bureau of Reclamation. Its officials have always worked in close collaboration with the Commissioner of Reclamation. Like the bureau, the association is interested not in power development but in old-style, single-purpose reclamation projects. It was once a vital and progressive force, but the dirt farmers of the West have gradually withdrawn from membership, and today both the national association and its affiliates are dominated by the railroads and the private power interests.

The campaign against the CVA was launched at the convention of the National Reclamation Association held at Denver in November, 1944. It was apparent to the genuine reclamationists at this meeting that the private power interests were in control. Two basic themes were emphasized—opposition to regional authorities, including a CVA, and praise for the concordat between the Army Engineers and the Bureau of Reclamation. Adoption at this meeting of a resolution opposing valley authorities and recommending river development by existing agencies was followed by the adoption of similar resolutions at meetings of the branch organizations.

At these state and regional meetings "the private power boys" were again much in evidence. The chairman of the resolutions committee at the Oregon

Reclamation Congress, for example, was the attorney and principal lobbyist for the Pacific Power and Light Company. At a regional meeting held in Spokane a representative of the Washington Water Power Company acted as page and doorkeeper, and the company supplied the stenographic service.

High-ranking officials of the Army Engineers and the Bureau of Reclamation also attended the meetings. When called upon to present the point of view of the Bureau of Reclamation on river-valley authorities, one prominent official declined to speak on the ground that the issue was "too hot." The Army Engineers, however, unhampered by any connection with the Department of the Interior, have not hesitated to make known their views. At a recent meeting of the Montana Reclamation Association, Colonel Conrad P. Hardy, district engineer, exclaimed: "While our young men are giving their lives in this war, are we going to let fascism be set up right in this country? Although river authorities are not fascist in name, they are fascist in character." The general strategy of the fight against a CVA was prepared at these meetings, and the delegates were repeatedly assured that "ample funds" would be "forthcoming" to finance the campaign. At the Oregon meeting speakers suggested that the Power Division of the Department of the Interior be abolished and its functions returned to the Bureau of Reclamation.

Next the various state legislatures were urged to go on record against a CVA. A memorial asking Congress to defeat "any bill to establish a Columbia Valley Authority" was approved by the Oregon legislature after it had "studied" Senator Hugh Mitchell's bill for exactly ten minutes. This memorial was introduced at the request of the Oregon Reclamation Association. . . . A regional meeting of the reclamation association was held in Spokane . . . for the specific purpose of organizing a grass-roots campaign against a CVA. As a result, resolutions and petitions against Senator Mitchell's bill were adopted by civic groups, chambers of commerce, and similar organizations throughout the Northwest.

Thus a number of interests are lined up against the CVA: two old-line government agencies, with many "friends" throughout the West; the private power interests and the railroads, working through the various reclamation associations; the reclamation associations themselves; the chambers of commerce; and many absentee-owned or -controlled industries. In addition, organized labor is to some extent opposed. In the Northwest the private power interests have shrewdly cultivated the political support of organized labor by working out satisfactory agreements with such unions as the electrical workers. Dave Beck, the dominant labor leader in the region, is reported to be unfriendly, if not actively hostile, to the idea of a CVA. Lined up in support of a CVA are the various Public-Utility Districts, the Oregon Grange and the Washington Grange, the C. I. O., and the unnumbered but also unorganized friends of public power throughout the Northwest. Not a single metropolitan newspaper in the area supports the proposed CVA, nor does the rural press, with a few notable exceptions. The fact that the public-power fight cuts across party lines in the Northwest makes it difficult to present the proposal as a clear-cut political issue.

Other federal agencies in the region, while not as actively hostile to a CVA as the Bureau of Reclamation and the Army Engineers, give it only lukewarm support. Some of their officials like to quote Mr. Ickes's remark that the problems of the world cannot be solved "by lighting a candle and intoning 'TVA,

TVA, TVA!' " And they stress the differences between the Tennessee Valley and the Columbia Valley. Admittedly such differences exist. Soil-erosion and flood control were important considerations in the Tennessee Valley; neither is a major problem in the Northwest. Irrigation was not greatly needed in the Tennessee Valley; it is of paramount importance in the Columbia Basin. The development of domestic water supplies was a need in the Tennessee Valley; it is not particularly urgent in the Columbia Valley. Fishing and lumbering, minor factors in the Tennessee Valley, are major industries in the Northwest. There were no pre-existing reclamation projects in the Tennessee as there are in the Columbia Valley, and the problem of government lands was not involved. In considering the powers to be granted to a Columbia Valley Authority these differences should be carefully examined, but they should not be permitted to obscure the necessity for regional planning. It was required in the Tennessee Valley to rehabilitate an area; it is required in the Northwest to develop an area.

The really important difference between the two regions lies in the fact that existing government agencies had confessed their inability to solve the problems of the Tennessee Valley. The TVA did not have to cope with the opposition of such powerful agencies as the Bureau of Reclamation and the Forestry Service. While Mr. Ickes, by his support of river-valley authorities, has indicated a commendable willingness to permit the reorganization of the Department of the Interior, his subordinates will stubbornly resist such proposals.

A major reorganization of all federal agencies concerned with the protection and utilization of natural resources is implicitly involved in the idea of river-valley authorities. In the past such agencies have functioned nationally in their specific separate fields—wild life, parks, forests, soils, or mineral resources; the success of the TVA shows the value of a different approach—of an integrated development of natural resources on a regional basis. For this the most efficient tool is the public corporation. . . .

THE ATTACK ON PUBLIC POWER (1953)

Bruce Catton

I

THEY ARE COMING in hungry, and they are not hungry for peanuts. The vast public-utility, oil, mining, and lumber interests that supported the Republican campaign are getting ready to move in on America's natural resources, and what they want is all the country has got. The new Administration is prepared to make things easy for them, and the program is beginning to be clear. It adds up to what is probably the greatest raid on the national wealth ever contemplated.

First, of course, will come the off-shore-oil grab. . . . Next will come the grab for public power. Here the general idea is to go on building big power plants with public funds but to make sure that they are run for the benefit of the power companies rather than for the people. The third step, which is still in the formative stage, is in some ways the most appalling. It is proposed that the tremendously valuable public domain be handed over to the states for parceling out to such private interests as can make the most lucrative use of them.

Altogether, the program represents an attempt to get back not only to the days of Herbert Hoover but all the way back to the era before Teddy Roosevelt. It is spelled out quite clearly in the record of the Senate hearings on the confirmation of Douglas McKay as Secretary of the Interior. The Department of the Interior is the official custodian of America's publicly owned wealth. When the hungry special interests moved in after the election of Harding, this department was one of the first things they looked at. It is even more attractive to them today, for on top of everything else it now contains, in the Bureau of Reclamation, the largest single generator and transmitter of electricity in the world. In other words, the stakes are immense. The attitude of the Secretary of the Interior is vitally important.

Bear in mind that everyone who attacks the public-power program attacks it by indirection. The first target is the famous preference clause, which simply provides that the co-ops of the Rural Electrification Administration, cities, public-utility districts, and other public bodies get first rights to the purchase of power from federal dams. If the preference clause can be knocked out, if the federal government can be kept from building its own transmission lines, and if—these things having been done—the utility companies are then allowed to make long-term contracts with the agencies that sell federal electric power, the public-power program is done for, and the government's power facilities exist solely for the benefit of the private companies.

When he appeared before the Senate Interior Committee, Secretary McKay declared that he believes in the preference clause—"if the people want it." But he also said that "private enterprise has a right to pursue their business," that public power should not be given an advantage, and that the power companies ought not to be throttled. He thought that long-term contracts ought to be made with the power companies and that at the present time, in the Pacific Northwest, public power was getting most of the breaks.

Senator Jackson of Washington, a staunch public-power man, pressed the new Secretary: Isn't it sound policy to have power from government dams sold first to public bodies? "Not necessarily," replied McKay. "It is a sound public policy that all citizens be treated alike. . . . If that preference [clause] is in there, you are unfair to some of the people of the states, because they might want to buy from a publicly owned place and they can't."

There is nothing mystifying about any of this if you understand the jargon. You never attack the preference clause openly; you simply say that everybody ought to get equal treatment and that private utilities ought to be free of handicaps. You agree that the government ought to build the great multi-purpose dams, but you object, as McKay did before the Senate committee, to "the part of the federal government in imposing themselves in authority," because you feel that the people of the state ought to have control over their own resources. . . .

Long-term contracts for government power executed with private power companies in the absence of a preference clause and also in the absence of government transmission lines would, as Senator Jackson pointed out, "simply dedicate the federal dams to the utilities." And as the retiring Commissioner of Reclamation, Michael Straus, remarked, in practice such contracts would tend to become perpetual. Each one would become an inalienable right, with money invested, territory developed, markets arranged; to try to change or cancel one would be to raise a storm of protest about loss to customers, economic upheaval, and so on. All this is the more disturbing since Congress is definitely to be asked to change the preference clause and a determined fight will be made to keep the government from building any more transmission lines. In the face of these attacks it is hard to imagine a winning fight for public power being put up by a Secretary of the Interior who talks as McKay talked before the Senate committee. . . .

II

The forced resignation of Claude R. Wickard as head of the Rural Electrification Administration does not stand by itself. It is part of the present Administration's relentless attack on the whole public-power program. . . .

The job of administrator of the R. E. A. is supposed to be non-political and for a fixed number of years. Mr. Wickard's term had approximately three years to run. He resigned because the high command in the Department of Agriculture, of which the R. E. A. is a part, made it clear that if he did not jump he would be pushed. Oddly enough, this marked the coming home to roost of a rather clumsily begotten chicken which first took flight in the regime of Franklin D. Roosevelt.

Roosevelt dismissed Arthur E. Morgan from the chairmanship of the Tennessee Valley Authority after a public disagreement between Morgan and David Lilienthal, a T. V. A. director, over negotiations to buy the Tennessee Electric Power Company. Morgan fought his dismissal in the courts—like Wickard, he held a non-political job for a stated term of years—and the courts finally ruled in effect that the President had the power to say whether the occupant of such a job had conducted himself in a way to warrant his dismissal.

In the act creating the R. E. A., tenure of office was defined in roughly the same language as in the act creating the T. V. A. This fact and the court decision in the Morgan case were cited to Wickard to indicate that the President could summarily remove him if he chose. When Wickard protested that there was no proper ground for his removal, he was informed that inasmuch as he had been a Cabinet member under a Democratic President he was a political character and consequently did not belong in a non-political job.

So Wickard resigned. Behind his resignation is the big argument now going on over one of the fundamental features of the public-power program—the R. E. A.'s authority to lend money to cooperatives and groups of cooperatives which wish to build electric transmission and generating facilities. With such loans the rural-electrification co-ops are out from under the dominance of the public utilities. Without them they are at the utilities' mercy.

The R. E. A. makes its loans only in areas where insufficient power is available at reasonable rates to meet the needs of the members of the rural co-ops. In the past the utilities have sometimes taken over co-ops that were not able to get an adequate power supply. Proponents of the R. E. A.'s loan program believe that if it is sufficiently weakened, there will be many more such cases. A co-op unable to build transmission lines or generating facilities would be easy prey for the nearest utility.

Wickard's forced resignation is taken as a strong indication that the R. E. A. is to be directed by someone much less anxious to push the electrification program. . . .

Before Wickard's resignation the R. E. A. program had already taken a couple of serious blows in the sacred name of economy. Just after President Eisenhower took office, he ordered all departments and agencies to review their construction programs and halt nonessential projects. . . .

Meanwhile under the White House order the army has stopped construction of Table Rock Dam in Missouri, which was to have provided extensive generating capacity for R. E. A. co-ops. Originally, the government had built Bull Shoals Dam to meet the co-ops' needs, but construction of a defense aluminum plant in Arkansas diverted that power. Now there will not be enough electricity generated to meet the needs of co-ops in Missouri, Arkansas, Oklahoma, and Kansas. . . .

DIXON-YATES (1954)

Gordon R. Clapp

WHEN T. V. A. BEGAN its work in 1933, the valley's private enterprise was mostly farming and mining. The private electric utilities supplied one and one-half billion kilowatt hours of electricity for the whole region of 80,000 square miles. They said the flood-control, navigation, and hydroelectric dams T. V. A. was starting to build would create a surplus of power no one would use; a waste of the taxpayers' money, they said.

Today the Tennessee Valley is one of the fastest-growing industrial areas in the country. It is one of the fastest-growing private-enterprise areas in the country. More than thirty-five billion kilowatt hours of electric energy are generated by T. V. A. dams and modern steam plants and distributed by 150 locally owned and operated municipal and rural cooperative electric systems. Even this amount of power is not enough to meet growing demands from aluminum, chemical, and processing industries, from farms, homes, and hundreds of new private enterprises. Low-cost electricity has had a lot to do with this truly enterprising performance.

Now comes the Dixon-Yates deal, hawked by its architects, the United States Bureau of the Budget, and the Atomic Energy Commission, with the blessing of the President, as a return to the "free-enterprise" system. Under the proposed Dixon-Yates deal the government would financially and politically underwrite the construction and operation of a 650,000-kilowatt steam electric plant to be built by Messrs. Dixon and Yates—officials of two Southern utility companies not accustomed to building plants of this size. The government would contract to buy the power at rates that total almost twice the cost of the plant during the life of the power contract. Dixon and Yates will put up very little capital but will own the plant even after the government pays for it twice. The government will pay, through the power rate, the state and federal taxes Messrs. Dixon and Yates incur.

What is free or enterprising about this deal? The only "enterprise" involved was that displayed by high officials of the federal government in devising specifications attractive to Dixon and Yates and in the tactics used to block T. V. A.'s better and cheaper solution to the problem—the proposed new Fulton T. V. A. steam plant.

The only "risk" in this "private" development is borne by the federal government and the taxpayers. There is real risk from severe floods on the site hurriedly selected to checkmate T. V. A.'s plan. And there is risk in relying upon Dixon-Yates to meet schedules or estimates. The A. E. C. and the Budget Bureau are backing again some of the same utility interests which perpetrated the Ebasco fiasco, the slow-motion, high-cost, cost-plus Joppa steam plant on the beautiful Ohio near Paducah, sponsored by the A. E. C. This plant was supposed to demonstrate that T. V. A. didn't know how to build steam plants as fast, as well, or as economically as the private utilities. The Joppa builders, of which Dixon was one, did not meet their schedule or their cost estimates, and Ebasco, the promoter-contractor, was fired from the job. T. V. A.'s Shawnee steam plant, just across the river, started construction at the same time as Joppa and finished its first four units before Joppa was halfway. T. V. A. built within its estimates, paying about the same wages as at Joppa. T. V. A.'s superior performance is saving money for the taxpayer on actual cost of power to the A. E. C.

The only thing "free" about the Dixon-Yates deal is the gift of a huge steam plant to Messrs. Dixon and Yates. And it looks as if the Budget Boys will try to force consumers of T. V. A. power to absorb the extra costs of this gift to T. V. A.'s competitors. When the provisions of the contract are revealed, it will be interesting to discover whether the United States government has also agreed to reimburse Dixon-Yates for the costs of litigation which will probably bedevil this deal.

The stakes here go far beyond the gift of a single large steam plant to a pair of private citizens. The power load of the A. E. C. served by T. V. A. represents five such steam plants. If the Dixon-Yates deal goes through, it may well be the beginning of a program to circle the T. V. A. with cost-plus "gift" plants paid for by T. V. A. consumers under the terms of a federal fiat. If the utilities and the Bureau of the Budget can force T. V. A. to raise its rates by loading on to T. V. A. the excessive costs of these gifts, the yardstick will be gone. Millions of power consumers outside the Tennessee Valley will feel the effect in higher electric rates.

UTILITY STOCK OPTIONS v. PUBLIC INTEREST (1964)

Lee Metcalf

ON OCTOBER 5, 1959, the president of a private utility company supplemented his $75,000-a-year salary in a one-day transaction which netted him $370,000—or more than the average American will make in his lifetime.

More important, however, are the facts that this one-day windfall will come out of the pocket of the average American, and that the utility executive may pay less federal income tax on it than the average American will pay on his much-lower lifetime earnings.

Illegal? Not a bit. The utility president's profit and tax advantage are part of a perfectly legitimate modern business "incentive"—the restricted stock option device—which is supposed to help highly competitive businesses attract and hold competent executives.

Under this deceptively simple scheme, a certain amount of stock is set aside for sale to company insiders (mostly top executives) at some later date when, it is hoped, the market value of the stock will have risen. When the time comes for the executive to exercise his option, he does not buy the stock at its current price, but at the price as of the day his option was granted. Thus he makes an automatic profit—and without risking a hair, since he has no obligation to buy the stock. If its value rises, he buys; if it doesn't, he doesn't.

There are those who contend that the stock option is perhaps a superfluous incentive for people making $75,000 a year, and I tend to agree with them. However, my concern here is not with the option in general but with its use in one of the most stable, least competitive, most profitable enterprises in America —the electric light and power industry.

In spite of the enormous sums they spend to advertise themselves as such, the privately owned companies that provide 75 per cent of the nation's electricity are not "just another business." There is a significant difference between an electric light and power company (or any private utility, for that matter) and an electronics, plastics or space-age company or any non-utility businesses for that matter. The latter compete, more or less, with other firms in the same field and run the risk of being forced to close up shop if they fail to offer a desirable product at a competitive price.

The electric light and power companies—the nation's largest industry, with about 12 per cent of the capital invested in *all* American business—have little normal competition. As "public service" companies, they operate under government franchises and enjoy the power of eminent domain and other special privileges. But most of all, they are monopolies in their communities, and therefore above the everyday fight for economic survival. Each year some 15,000 businesses go on the rocks; not a single private power company has failed in more than a generation.

Instead, the industry annually chalks up record profits—partly because of technological advances, but mainly because it is a monopoly selling a necessity for which demand is constantly increasing.

Since the industry is not competitive, and since the consumer is forced to foot the bill for company operating costs and profit, the question should be asked whether the investor-owned utilities (as they like to call themselves) or IOUs (as I prefer to call them) should be allowed to use the restricted stock option.

Option plans are increasing in the utilities. They began spreading quietly through the industry during the complacent fifties, and at last count some twenty-nine private electric companies had option plans for executives. Even had it wanted to—which it didn't during the Eisenhower administration—the Federal Power Commission could neither herald nor halt this invasion. FPC jurisdiction over security issues is severely limited to the few independent operating companies that are organized outside the states in which they operate, or that are organized and operating in states which lack a state agency authorized to police issuance of securities.

As a result, only one of the twenty-nine plans was approved by the FPC. Of the remainder, ten are part of holding-company option plans approved by the Securities and Exchange Commission, and eighteen were presumably approved by state regulatory agencies which are even more susceptible to "taming" than federal agencies and which, in some states, are little more than industry lap dogs. Only three state regulatory agencies (Maryland, Georgia and New York) have taken stands against the stock option for public utilities.

On the federal level, the SEC has considered three cases involving utility use of stock options and the FPC has considered two. Both agencies have consistently held that option plans for utilities are not prohibited by law. But although both are also specifically authorized to reject such plans on the ground that they are detrimental to the interests of stockholders and consumers, only the FPC has found any merit in this position.

The first option plan to come before the SEC was opposed by the SEC staff on this basis, among others. However, the Eisenhower-appointed commission rejected the staff position and the two subsequent plans were approved without hearings.

The precedent set by the Eisenhower commission was also followed by the New Frontier commission (four Kennedy appointees and one Eisenhower holdover) which approved the third holding-company plan.

Kennedy appointments did make a difference at the FPC, however, as was demonstrated in the Black Hills Power and Light Company case early this summer. By a 3-2 vote, the present commission rejected the company's application to set up an option plan for top executives on the ground that the plan "is not compatible with the public interest." (One hopes this decision will encourage the SEC to re-examine its position when next it considers a utility application for stock options.)

The Black Hills decision reversed the position taken by the FPC under the Eisenhower administration, which, after it had shed even the pretense of regulating electric utilities, approved—with neither hearing nor dissent—the application of Montana Power Company to issue options on 100,000 shares of stock.

That was in 1956, when the company was a New Jersey corporation operating in Montana. The authority for that issuance was to expire in June, 1959, but on May 27, 1959, the cooperative Eisenhower commission authorized the company to issue 5,693,382 additional shares to cover a three-for-one split of all the firm's stock. Neither the company's application nor the commission's approval mentioned anything about stock under option or the June expiration date, so the 100,000 shares under option were also multiplied by three.

In addition, the company boosted the total number of shares subject to option to 750,000, or 10 per cent of its total common stock issuance—without official approval insofar as can now be determined. When the honeymoon ended with the advent of the Kennedy administration in 1961, the company escaped FPC jurisdiction over security issues by moving "home" to Montana.

The FPC now estimates that the 750,000 shares the company has under option will eventually cost $9 million in capital foregone—$9 million which will come out of the pockets of the ordinary stockholders and the company's customers.

It comes out of the ordinary stockholder's pocket because issuance of cut-rate stock to company insiders dilutes the equity of ordinary stockholders and thereby reduces their earnings per share. And it comes out of the consumer's pocket because the capital loss resulting from the sale of stock at prices far under market value tends to discourage rate reductions and encourage rate increases.

But for the favored few, the stock option is a virtual guarantee of additional riches to pile atop their already fat incomes. . . .

The FPC noted in the Black Hills case that not only are the actual costs "hidden from shareholders and consumers," but stock options "distort the real cost of electric utility service" because there is no practical way of including their cost in the rate formula.

Furthermore, the secrecy surrounding utility use of restricted stock options, the lack of adequate reporting on option windfalls by utility executives, and the shortage of staff in most regulatory agencies, both state and federal, cripple any attempt to determine the precise use and consequences of restricted stock-option plans.

The staff shortage is especially significant in the federal regulatory commissions. For example, during the Eisenhower years the staff of the SEC Ownership Reports Section was slashed from fourteen to seven. This section reviews ownership reports of many companies, including the power utilities.

The staff has since been upped to nine, but because of the increased number of businesses the section now has twice as many ownership reports to review as when there were fourteen on its staff. Yet this section is one of the few places where prospective investors, stockholders and rate payers can get some idea of the extent to which company insiders have utilized restricted stock options.

Similarly, the staff of the FPC is still suffering from its reduction to skeleton force during the 1950s and the Eisenhower de-emphasis of electric utility regulation. Consider, for example, the comments of the present chairman, Joseph C. Swidler, a Kennedy appointee:

> There is small wonder that knowledge of the FPC's rate jurisdiction has not been widespread. When I became a member of the Commission it took me some time to find the Commission's electric rate staff. It turned out that it was hidden away in the Bureau of Natural Gas.

Expansion of the FPC staff, to provide a degree of protection and information for investors and consumers, is now imperative in view of this year's Supreme Court decision in the Colton (California) case, which gives the FPC jurisdiction over wholesale power rates.

Fifty-year licenses for hydroelectric projects, granted to private power companies under the Water Power Act of 1920, will begin expiring in 1970, and Congress must have, well in advance, information to determine whether these licenses should be renewed.

The industry will do all it can to prevent appointment of consumer-oriented commissioners or additional staff at either agency. And the industry will continue to cry that it is the body and soul of competitive American free enterprise, and that all businesses pass taxes and operating costs on to the consumer. However, it must be repeated that competition limits what other businesses can pass on.

No one denies that the electric light and power industry faces competition of a sort. For example, it faces limited competition from the gas utilities (also monopolies, and in many instances incorporated in the same firm as the electric monopoly) which offer a product that is just as good as electricity for some purposes, such as cooking. But there is little danger that gas will replace electricity as the means of lighting the nation's homes and streets or powering its industry.

Further, the few public-owned municipal power systems, the rural cooperatives and the federal power program also might be considered competitors in that they serve as yardsticks against which private power operations and rates can be measured.

But even such remote competition as this is obnoxious to the private-power industry. It has mounted a multimillion-dollar propaganda campaign—paid for in part by electric consumers—against these other suppliers of electric power, and it regularly contributes money and executive leadership to a host of right-wing organizations which attack public power—as well as the income tax, aid to education, civil rights and the United Nations—as part of the Communist conspiracy.

Yet despite these quasi-competitors, the fact remains that the electric light and power industry is delightfully different as it perches on a luxurious tax shelter far above the battle for economic survival in which ordinary businesses engage.

THE VISIONARY OCTOPUS (1973)

William H. Rodgers, Jr.

DONALD COOK, president and chief executive officer of the American Electric Power Co. (AEP), has a vision, and it is not unlike the visions of the Guggenheims, Rockefellers and Carnegies before him. Mr. Cook proposes to transform the hundreds of electrical companies in the United States into a dozen or so giant regional monopolies.

Of course there will be victims in this march toward economic efficiency, as there were in the earlier campaigns to monopolize the copper, steel and petroleum industries. The obvious victims are the smaller electrical systems, many of them municipally owned; and as they disappear the accountability to which they are held will disappear with them. For the move to electrical monopoly promises to visit on the public the usual costs of concentrated corporate power: stagnation in research and development, further undermining of a shaky regulatory apparatus, perpetuation of injustices in rate structures, in pollution control, minority employment and plant-siting policies.

Cook's vision is now being acted upon by the giant investor-owned electrical utilities across the nation: between 1955 and 1965 more than 100 of the smaller private systems, along with 150 municipals, were gobbled up through mergers. The trend continues and tactics that have proven successful are continually polished: Southern California Edison trains a cadre of experts to take over municipals and makes contributions to sympathetic politicians; Pacific Gas & Electric Company uses political pull to frustrate the development of generating capacity by municipalities, and sites its plants to perpetuate the company's monopoly position; a group of investor-owned heavyweights in New England conspires to head off regional public power development; the Duke Power Co. resists the construction of federally owned transmission lines that would bring energy to small wholesalers on other than the corporation's terms; the Florida Power Corporation hires a New York public relations firm to assist in takeover campaigns and grooms friendly candidates to run for local public office. The electric monopolists resist proposals for joint ventures, power pools and other such cooperative endeavors that would bring the economies of scale to the smaller, more local systems without eliminating them. Total control is the preferred dogma.

Every electrical giant in the country could learn a few tricks from Donald Cook's own American Electric Power Company, a $2-billion-plus holding company owning virtually all of the common stock of several utilities serving parts of Michigan, Indiana, Ohio, Kentucky, West Virginia, Virginia and Tennessee. AEP has more generating capacity, sells more power and creates more pollution than does any other privately owned utility in the country. Over the last several years, it has absorbed many electrical systems in its service area, and more are marked for extinction.

In recent times, while one tentacle of the AEP octopus reached out to strangle the smaller systems, another reached for bigger game—the Securities and Exchange Commission. The SEC is a theoretical obstacle to Donald Cook's theories about electrical monopoly by reason of the Public Utility Holding Company Act of 1935, which requires commission approval of the acquisition of any utility by a registered company. Now pending before the commission is an AEP application to acquire 100 per cent of the stock of Columbus & Southern Ohio Electric Co. (C&S), whose system in south-central Ohio adjoins the AEP system, is interconnected with it and is an obvious candidate for merger. This would be no small-town takeover, for C&S serves more than one-third of a million customers in about 170 communities, and earns annual electric revenues in excess of $60 million.

The AEP-C&S merger proceedings have supplied vivid but little noticed documentation of the vicious politics on which electrical monopolies are built. The experiences of the city of Danville, Va., are typical. In 1968, the city council voted to build additional generating capacity and to submit a proposed $11 million bond issue for voter approval in 1969. Responding predictably, the local AEP subsidiary (Appalachian Power Co.) invested $4,200 to survey initial reaction to the proposed bond issue, in the process accounting improperly for the expenditures. Upon discovering that the people of Danville favored the proposal by a 3-to-1 margin, the company set about to change their minds with a front group, strategic expenditures and heavy propaganda. The front group was called the New Day for Danville Committee, the expenditures went into the thousands (not all contributed by AEP), the propaganda hit a high point with an ad displaying a hole in the street, coupled with the message: "We need an $11 million generator like we need another hole in Main Street." AEP displayed consistency by accounting for some of its 1969 political expenditures as it did for its 1968 political survey—charging political expenditures as operating expenses means they are paid for by the consumers instead of the utility stockholders.

Danville was forced to drop its expansion plans. The manager of the municipal system reminisces: "This was a carefully planned, well-executed campaign of untruths which achieved the desired effect—namely, to cripple the Danville system so as to make it less competitive and more dependent upon the power companies." A complete takeover by AEP should be only a matter of time.

Internal AEP documents disclose how the will of the people is to be bent to the needs of the corporation elsewhere on the company's system. The South Haven, Ind., election plan anticipates the use of volunteers: "Gather a group of capable, loyal women willing to work part-time and be reimbursed if necessary." Taking over the system in Willard, Ohio, requires making friends: "We should consider the free installation of a lighting system for a Little League baseball field in Willard."

AEP's planned "Acquisition of [the] Dover [Ohio] Municipal Electric System" goes into details: "Develop a list of prominent and influential people 'and set them up as a' citizens' committee. The committee would be fed information which they and we mutually feel would be beneficial in selling the citizens on the need for being customers of [AEP]. . . . Throughout the entire plan, develop a special series of public relations ads to imprint an image of [AEP] on the minds of Dover citizens well in advance of actually trying to acquire the system by vote." Another memo advises: "Feed weaknesses . . . to malcontents. . . . Permit this group to present the problems of the system to the Dover Public, undermining present leadership and stirring up general discontent."

AEP soon forgets that the reason for taking over the municipals is to benefit the people. Another company memo on the Dover system discloses that it is in "fairly good condition," pride of ownership is "high," the financial picture "far from poor." The only weakness is a need for more generating capacity. "Unless we prevent the installation," the memo reports, it may be the late 1970s "before we will have another opportunity to obtain additional load" from the city.

The long-run aim is unmistakable: "We believe that by getting our foot in the door at this time through the wholesale of electric energy, we will permit [AEP] to make friends with Dover officials, customers and the public and permit a gradual public relations program that could eventually result in the municipal generating plant being acquired" by AEP. All for the good of the people? AEP acknowledges that the Dover takeover has run into obstacles because the city's domestic rate is "considerably lower than ours." Turning around rate structures that favor small users is one of the "benefits" that accrue from expanding a monopoly.

The C&S merger proceeding before the Securities and Exchange Commission is but a bigger version of the takeover tactics which AEP has refined impressively. Donald Cook used to be chairman of the SEC and he counts on his influence to weather any storms within the agency. But just to make sure, AEP has put the commission through the political wringer reserved for any decision maker standing in the way of the company's idea of technological fulfillment.

The SEC reports that not since the passage of the 1935 act has a holding company system "brought to bear such a massive and concentrated effort to influence and pressure the outcome of an adjudicatory proceeding through means other than on-the-record evidence and cross-examination." The commission has received hundreds of inspired letters and form protests, supporting the merger and submitted in violation of SEC rules designed to protect the administrative process from political sniping. When Louis Roddis, president of New York's Consolidated Edison Co., broke ranks to testify in response to a government subpoena, AEP retaliated directly. Before Roddis' testimony, an irate Donald Cook called two bank-connected directors of Consolidated Edison, asking them to let Roddis know how much Cook resented his testimony. When Roddis nonetheless showed up to testify, he was greeted at the morning recess with a massive subpoena directed at Con Ed and calling for the production of thousands of documents from its files covering a five-year period, including Roddis' unpublished M.I.T. Master's thesis on "Modern Airfoil Theory as Applied to the Design of Wide-Bladed Marine Propellers." (The hearing examiner subsequently quashed most of the subpoena on the ground that it was designed to intimidate and harass.)

As the record before the SEC climbed past 20,000 pages, 100 volumes and 1,000 exhibits, it was clear the commission's forum had become the center ring for testing Donald Cook's theories about electrical monopoly. Years of administrative and judicial appeals lie ahead. Mr. Cook will be working every step of the way to assure that his theories become the law. Public awareness of this planned predation does not guarantee that it won't happen, but the company's planning is that much easier if the victim is unaware of the assassin's intentions.

THE EMERGING CASE
FOR PUBLIC POWER (1980)

Irving Like

SHOULD THE UTILITIES which provide the bulk of America's electric and gas power be owned and operated by private stockholder investors, or by municipalities or other forms of public or cooperative ownership?

This question has been debated for many years, most recently in 1979 when a voter referendum in Westchester County, New York, rejected a proposal to study the feasibility of County acquisition of Con Edison's generating and transmission facilities located in that County.

The arguments are familiar and generally economic in nature. Supporters of the public power alternative say it is cheaper because there are no stockholders' dividends to pay, municipalities pay no income taxes, the cost of loan capital is lower to tax exempt municipalities, and they can purchase wholesale power for resale to their customers from state power authorities, such as the Power Authority of the State of New York (PASNY, which owns hydroelectric and nuclear power plant facilities) at a preferential price mandated by federal law.

The opponents of public power recite the familiar litany of free enterprise marketers. Private investor-owned utilities (I.O.U.s) are more efficient. Government bureaucracy is wasteful, more susceptible to corruption and scandal, and any cost differential favoring public power is really a hidden subsidy borne by the taxpayers. Moreover, they allege the huge cost of acquisition of a utility system, either through negotiated purchase, or more likely, condemnation, will saddle rate-payers with higher energy costs than continuance of the system in private ownership. And so it goes, with the utilities winning through massive advertising and lobbying aided by growing voter distrust of government and its office holders, fueled by a succession of scandals in high places.

The history of corporate bribery, and "lemon" socialism, has apparently made no dent in conventional voter perceptions that private enterprise is more honest and efficient than government in running anything.

Traditionally, the public power vs. private power controversy focused on who should own and operate the means of producing and distributing electricity and gas. The terms of the discourse did not question whether fuels for power generation would continue to be available in sufficient quantity. The contestants were indifferent to the issue of whether the mode of power generation should be fossil fuel, nuclear, or some other alternative. They also took as given the need for more and more baseload generating capacity without questioning the conventional methods of forecasting demand, and with little interest in inquiry into the factors which affected the power supply/demand equation, rate making and rate structure design, and the pricing of power. In short, the argument was simply whether it was cheaper for a public or private entity to control and market the ever increasing generation and supply of power per se.

The 1973 oil embargo and the rise of the anti-nuclear movement have profoundly changed the terms of the debate and in doing so, illuminated a fertile new terrain for the public vs. private power controversy. New questions are now being asked which stem from a new public awareness of the finite nature of depletable fossil and uranium resources, growing concern over the grave safety, health, environmental, and economic risks and costs of the nuclear and coal options, and increasing interest in the so-called soft energy alternative paths (energy conservation, improved energy efficiency and productivity, solar energy, wind power, and other renewable energy sources). These enlightened concerns go beyond the incompletely formulated questions of who should own and operate utility systems, and which is cheaper, and demand answers concerning fuel resource policy, preferred type of power generation, and power supply and demand management. These are questions which require an investigation into the traditional management decision-making areas of investment, production, distribution, and pricing, and are embraced in the supply side of the equation.

The critics also began to ask questions concerning the means of managing consumption patterns—the demand side of the equation. As the questions became more pointed and rigorous, they inevitably penetrated to the inner provinces of the utility business—the engineering, legal, financial, accounting, economic, and statistical aspects of rate making and rate design. By intervening in power plant licensing proceedings, and rate cases, municipalities and citizen groups began the process of demystifying the private I.O.U. business, and gained new and powerful insights and arguments with which to strengthen the case for public power.

Intervenors learned the basic mathematics and financial facts underlying rate making, and exposed the profit maximizing dynamics which drive the private I.O.U. Two equations were particularly revealing. The first is that a utility's revenue requirements are determined by multiplying its rate base by its cost of capital and adding its operating costs for the rate year in question. The rate base represents that portion of the utility's plant and equipment (used and useful in rendering utility service), and other asset requirements (i.e., allowance for working capital) which have been supplied by investors (bondholders and stockholders), and upon which they are entitled to a fair rate of return. A fair rate of return is determined by the Public Service Commission or agency which regulates the utility. The operating costs include operations and maintenance expenses, depreciation expenses, and taxes. Obviously, any increase in rate base, rate of return, or operating costs means an increase in the revenues the utility is allowed to earn, and thus an increase in the rates it can charge its customers.

An example will illustrate how sensitive utility rates are to increases in the rate base. If a utility's rate base is $1 billion, and the weighted rate of return paid to its investors (bondholders and stockholders) is 10 percent, the utility is entitled to a return of $1 billion × 10 percent, or $100 million (not including revenues needed to recoup its other operating costs). Since the utility is likely to be in a 50 percent federal income tax bracket, in order to earn $100 million in income, it must charge its customers revenues of $200 million. If the rate base is increased by inclusion of a new nuclear plant, costing $2 billion, the rate base increases from $1 billion to $3 billion, and the revenues the utility is entitled to receive rise from $100 million to $600 million. The difference of $500 million is arrived at by multiplying the $2 billion addition to rate base by the 10 percent cost of capital, and grossing it up for income tax purposes. No wonder utilities are biased toward capital intensive construction projects, like nuclear plants and anxious to get them into rate base as soon as possible.

It follows that ownership of the utility carries with it control of the investment decisions which determine the impact on ratepayers of the rate base equation. Since private I.O.U.s are in business to make profit, and publicly owned utilities are not similarly motivated, the latter are in a position to view the rate base equation with an entirely different set of motives—a key one, for example, being what energy conservation measures can be implemented to keep the rate base from growing unnecessarily.

The profit logic of the rate base equation drives the utility to seek inclusion in rate base, at the earliest point it can, the cost of any construction work in progress (CWIP), because the sooner it succeeds, the sooner it can earn a return on such CWIP. The utility, expecting favorable CWIP rate base consideration, has an incentive to build, and to place its plant in service as soon as possible so that the total plant cost can be included in rate base upon completion. The financial bias favoring early inclusion of a plant in rate base can be dangerous to public safety if the plant is prematurely placed in service with defective equipment or safety systems as occurred in the case of the utility operator of the Three Mile Island #2 nuclear plant, which succeeded in getting such plant into service and rate base at the end of 1978.

The pro-CWIP bias is compounded by federal investment tax credit, tax, and depreciation policies, which may give the utility with a heavy capital construction program opportunities to improve its cash flow without always passing such benefits through to its ratepayers.

The public utility, on the other hand, has no profit motive impelling it to pursue similar CWIP policies. The pro-CWIP bias weakens the private utility's incentive to accurately forecast future peak demand, and results in overcapacity, while its anti-energy conservation bias results in higher energy prices and under-consumption. These contradictions resulting from clashing institutional biases are absent in the publicly owned utility.

The growth of rate base results from the utility's capital construction program which in turn is determined by its estimate of future peak demand on its system, which in part may be influenced by the company's rate design structure, pricing, and demand and load management policies. Since the life-blood of the profit-oriented private I.O.U. is to sell as much electricity and gas as possible, it is less likely to pursue serious energy conservation measures than a utility owned cooperatively by its ratepayers, whose motive is to minimize increases in their rates, and therefore have an incentive to conserve.

In a private I.O.U. system, energy conservation may reduce sales of electricity, and hence force the utility to charge higher prices in order to realize its allowed rate of return. This perverse result can be more easily avoided in the public not-for-profit utility, where there are no stockholders to feed and where the benefits of conservation are captured by the ratepayers in lower operating and capital construction costs. In short, energy conservation and alternatives to costly central station generating facilities are less likely to be realized in the stockholder-owned utility, because its institutional biases favoring growth and demanding profits are shackles which need not bind the public utility, conscious of the economic benefits of energy conservation.

Once the revenue requirements of a utility are determined, it allocates the prices which will be charged to ratepayers for the service supplied, over its various classes of customers—residential, commercial industrial, municipal, institutional, etc. In the past, the private I.O.U., through its rate design or pricing policies, has favored large energy users through discounts and preferential rates thus increasing consumption and peak demand, and contributing to the upward spiral of more capital construction, increased rate base, increased allowable return on investment, and increased rates.

The public utility, by controlling rate structure, is free to pursue pricing policies which will reward energy conservation and stimulate solar installation, because its orientation will be changed from that of profit to service of its ratepayers.

On the supply side, the private I.O.U. fears any alternative competitive source of power, such as solar energy, wind power, co-generation, etc., which it doesn't control, and the cost of which it may not be able to include in its rate base so as to earn its allowed return on investment. It has no incentive to invest in, or engage in any serious research and development that would favor any alternatives that might lower its profitability. Thus the R&D programs of such utilities will spend millions of dollars in furtherance of breeder reactor programs, and other fission reactor and hard energy technologies, with only a pittance by comparison for the soft energy alternatives such as solar, wind power, biomass, and other renewable sources of energy. Not so the public utility whose ratepayers stand to benefit by any new or improved energy supply technology, which is safer from a health or environmental standpoint, or which is more economical or reliable, irrespective of whether it can be added to rate base. A recent study by the non-profit Council on Economic Priorities concluded that investment on Long Island in energy conservation and solar energy of an equivalent sum as the Long Island Lighting Company, a private I.O.U., was proposing to spend to build two nuclear plants at Jamesport, New York, would save more oil, at less cost and risk to health, safety, and the environment and would create far more jobs and economic benefits than if the nuclear plants were built. The Council's findings dramatize the important advantage possessed by the public utility. It can plan its investments in a way that keeps down ratepayer costs, while stimulating the economy of its service area through financing job-generating energy conservation and solar energy programs.

The second important equation is the cost of capital. The capital structure of the private I.O.U. for rate making purposes consists of its long- and short-term debt, and preferred and common equity stockholders. The bulk of its financing is long-term debt held by institutional bondholders to whom it pays interest, the rate of which is determined through negotiation or bid through underwriters' placement in the Wall Street capital markets.

The cost of common equity stock is harder to determine because it is arrived at through use of a mathematical formula which uses subjective variables and purports to yield an appropriate return on equity based on the expectations of actual common equity investors about the utility's future financial performance. The usual formula used is known as the Discounted Cash Flow (DCF) study:

$K = D/P + g$, where $K =$ return (or cost of equity capital), $D =$ current divided rate paid by the company, $P =$ current market price of the company's stock and $g =$ anticipated growth rate in dividends paid by the company. The rationale for the DCF method is that investors are assumed to bid the price of the utility's stock to a level commensurate with the risks they perceive given the current dividend level and their expectations about future growth in dividends. The name of the game every utility plays when it seeks a rate increase is to try to persuade its regulatory agency that the utility's cost of capital—i.e., its rate of return on equity (K)—should be higher than the rate of return it is currently allowed to receive. Thus it is customary in a rate case for the utility and the regulatory staff to present conflicting estimates as to all the factors which influence the cost of capital equation—i.e., data on dividend rates, earnings and book value, market price, growth rates in dividends, flotation costs and market pressure associated with the issuance of common stock, market to book ratios and trends, dividends' payout ratios and yields, common equity ratios, investment ratings, and a mass of other financial information, all designed to prove that the utility should be allowed to earn a greater profit. In jurisdictions where the regulatory climate is favorable to utilities, they often get the rate of return they ask for. In stricter states, they will likely receive something less than they ask for, but more than the regulatory agency's staff recommends as an appropriate rate of return.

The vice of this DCF process, aside from its speculative nature, is that it lends itself to self-serving utility manipulation of its financial policies in a way that biases the equation in its favor. And since the DCF equation is designed to plug in the financial data of comparable private I.O.U.s, also engaging in financial policies designed to make their securities attractive to investors and also striving to persuade their regulators to increase their allowed rate of return, the cumulative impact of the private I.O.U. industry is incestuous and exerts a constantly upward pressure on the rate of return.

The heavy price paid for supporting a stockholder class is discernible in the following example. If a utility has a rate base of $1 billion, of which $250 million represents common equity stockholders, and if they are allowed a 14 percent annual rate of return, it is entitled to earn income of 14 percent $\times$ $250 million, or $35 million annually, and thus must charge its ratepayers $70 million to yield a net of $35 million after income taxes.

A small upward swing in the authorized rate of return on equity has a large impact on the ratepayers. For example, on a rate base of $1 billion, of which $250 million represents common equity stock, an increase in the return on equity of 1 percent results in allowed income of $2.5 million, and a rate increase of $5 million. Thus doing without the stockholder class, in a public utility, removes a burden from the backs of the ratepayers and the constant pressure by the stockholders to increase their profit returns.

The existence of a stockholder class presents other more subtle disadvantages. One of these is the possibility of anti-competitive conduct resulting from corporate stockholder and director interlocks between such utilities and the financial institutions which supply their capital, and the vendors and fuel suppliers. The nature and extent of such linkages were exhaustively documented by studies of the House Banking Committee (Concentration in Banking, 1968) and by Arthur D. Little, Inc. (Competition in the Nuclear Supply Industry). Whether such relationships exist now is not the point. The stock forms of ownership lend themselves to such interlocks, which present the risk of sweetheart transactions driving up the cost of capital to the utility and the cost of the commodities and services it purchases.

A second disadvantage is more serious. Since private I.O.U.s comprise the bulk of the electric and gas utility industry, their negative characteristics are magnified nationwide and prevent a rational energy policy. The combined economic and political power of these utilities, their trade associations, vendors, fuel cycle industries and suppliers, and academic retainers, create a national energy policy distorted by the forces at work in each individual utility, which pursue irrational aims leading to waste of energy resources and creation of dangerous, life-threatening energy forms.

The public power alternative devoted to the soft energy path can, if it grows to command a significant share of the nation's utility industry, lay the foundation for a sane energy policy.

There is no doubt that public power can be inefficient, wasteful, bureaucratically insensitive, and vulnerable to political manipulation. Municipal governments have experienced their share of public works failures. It doesn't follow automatically that municipal acquisition of a private utility will lead to all the benefits previously described. It is even possible that in some cases, municipal purchase of a private utility system would not be in the public interest. This, however, doesn't gainsay the institutional advantages of public ownership which have been described principally in terms of the opportunity to control decision making in investment, production, consumption and pricing policies. New approaches to the form of ownership need to be studied.

One example is the mutual form of ownership, long established in the United States and used in the savings and loan industry, insurance industry, and credit unions. Institutions of the mutual form have no stockholders. They operate under corporate charters and are legally owned by their members (who can be depositors, account holders, or borrowers), and managed by a salaried board of directors, elected by the voting members. A second example is the cooperative form of ownership, a familiar institution in rural America and used by agricultural producers engaged in cooperative production and marketing activities. A third example is the public district, of one form or another, generally created in municipalities to construct and operate water or drainage works, sewage systems and park districts, utilities, and a myriad of other services. A fourth example is the public benefit corporation, organized to construct and operate transportation, water supply, or port facilities.

Much of the nation's vital business is carried on effectively by these nonprivate I.O.U.s operating under well-considered charters by responsible salaried management. It is time now to reexamine the private I.O.U. concept to determine if it is equal to the task of coping with the imperatives of the energy crisis, and whether it is prudent to replace it with proven self-governing institutions devoted not to profit but to service.

HIGH TENSION
ON THE PRAIRIE (1976)

Mark McKeon

THREE TIMES LAST JUNE groups of angry dairy farmers chased electric power association surveyors from fields and county roads in central Minnesota's Stearns County. The confrontations between farmers and surveyors put a halt to work on a 400-kilovolt direct-current transmission line being constructed by two rural electric generating and transmitting cooperatives—Cooperative Power Association, Edina, Minn., and United Power Association, Elk River, Minn. Through a combination of voluntary and court-ordered stays, the suspension lasted through the summer. The transmission line, along with a generating plant in Underwood, N. Dak., and a distributing terminal near Minneapolis, is known as the CU project, and has been in the planning and development stage since 1973.

If and when it is built, the line will be the biggest of its kind in the country. A number of 750-kilovolt alternating-current lines are already in operation, even though some of them were also opposed by farm and environmental groups, but only one other extra-high voltage direct-current line is in operation, and it is fairly new. It belongs to the Bonneville Power Authority (BPA) in Oregon, and transmits power from Oregon to Los Angeles. BPA is a federal power authority like TVA.

No farmer wants a high-voltage transmission line to cross his land. Even the old generation of now relatively small lines are more than eyesores; their presence on farm land modifies field work and irrigation patterns, limits future land use, and sometimes reduces the value of the land. The CU line, however, belongs to a new generation of high-voltage transmission lines. Its 160-foot towers will dwarf everything on the open prairie landscape, and with their long, outstretched arms will look like a file of gigantic robots immobilized on the horizon. In addition, the line's extra high direct-current voltage may involve health and environmental problems not previously encountered.

Organized as Counties United for Rural Environment (CURE), farmers opposed the transmission segment of the CU project during two years of public hearings. Their opposition failed to achieve more than minor changes and drew little public attention. The dramatic physical confrontations were more effective. One farmer allegedly drove his tractor over surveying equipment, and then battered the surveyors' pickup truck with his big machine. Such events finally made the farmers' opposition newsworthy, and local media covered the ensuing flurry of meetings and news conferences held by both sides. Disturbingly, however, local news facilities have not reported adequately the reasons for the farmers' opposition nor the public issues which that opposition has brought to light.

The farmers object that, in effect, they and their crops and livestock will be used as guinea pigs in a technological experiment. The proposed line entails two potential hazards. It will create an intense electrostatic field and, through discharges into the atmosphere all along its length, will create two of the most toxic of known air pollutants, ozone and nitrogen oxide. No one denies that the line will have these effects, but there is great controversy over the amount of pollution the line will create and over the biological effects of the electric field.

At public hearings held by the Minnesota Environmental Quality Council (EQC), spokesmen for the power associations testified that concentrations of air pollutants will not exceed Minnesota air quality standards. They also testified that the electric field, while something of a nuisance, will not present problems that cannot be offset by simple precautions and that its intensity will not be great enough to make it a health hazard.

But outside experts told the council that association testimony may be faulty and misleading. They pointed out, first, that the association testimony refers to ground level, edge-of-the-easement intensity and concentrations. They said further that in the case of the air pollutants the testimony is based on theoretically derived computations rather than on experimental measurements, and that other theoretical computations predict yields of ozone and nitrogen oxide at or well above levels allowed in Minnesota.

Dr. Merle Hirsh, physicist at the University of Minnesota at Morris, said that, using a U.S. Army developed model, he had computed ozone concentrations sixty times as great as those predicted by the power associations. Hirsh also pointed out that experimental measurements from the electrochemical industry lead to predictions of pollutant concentrations "dangerously close to the Minnesota maximum level."

Dr. Hirsh's testimony was reinforced by Gary Eckhardt, a Services Section chief with the Minnesota Pollution Control Agency. Mr. Eckhardt pointed out that power association testimony was based on theoretical computer models, and said that "more substantive field data should be taken to verify 'real' transmission-line conditions." He said that generally the highest concentrations of air pollutants are determined by measuring the worst possible pollution situations rather than by calculating average situations. Eckhardt also outlined the reasons for the farmers' fear of ozone by noting that broad leaf plants, such as soy beans, and crops like corn are severely harmed by even small concentrations of ozone.

Harold Josephs, an electrical engineer with extensive research experience on the production of ozone and electric fields, said that human beings and tall crops would be exposed to the line's hazards at well above ground level—as in the case of 8-foot corn or of a man driving a 15-foot-tall combine, and often right under the line. He, too, noted that association testimony on air pollutants doesn't take account of worst case conditions—no wind or very low wind—and said that ozone concentrations at ground level could greatly exceed Minnesota standards "for a considerable distance beyond the right of way."

When it speaks of the line's electric field, association testimony tends to dismiss it as no more than a nuisance. Fences and buildings near the line will have to be well grounded; machinery stalled or left under the line will have to be grounded; irrigation under the line, if indeed possible, will entail caution. Moreover, association testimony is that an electric field such as created by the proposed line produces no ill effects on human beings. For evidence, it cites the power industry's general experience and a Johns Hopkins University research project, performed by a team of doctors who monitored the health of ten linemen doing repair work on 345-kilovolt lines. The study lasted nine years, and at the end none of the linemen exhibited ill health.

In an article in the December 1974 issue of *The Bulletin of Atomic Scientists,* Louise Young points out that "studies of this type should examine a larger number of people over a longer period of time." Significant research into the biological effects of electric fields has just begun, and early results are not reassuring. . . .

The potential health hazards of the CU line are worrisome enough. What is also troubling, however, is that the line is only the first new link planned between the Western coal fields and the energy-needy Midwest and East. It appears that, at least in some cases, it is now cheaper and politically less abrasive to build mine-site generating plants and long-distance transmission lines than to ship coal by rail and build urban area generating plants.

The near certainty that other extra-high voltage transmission projects are soon to come raises an intertwined series of environmental, political and financial issues. They arise out of the planning processes within the power industry, out of the interstate nature of the long-distance lines, and out of the phenomenal costs of such projects. . . .

To maintain what it calls its "reliability" the industry operates on a regional, interstate basis, but regulation remains bound to a state level of organization aimed at individual utilities. Obviously, the situation calls for interstate cooperation among the regulatory agencies. . . . Unless they coordinate their efforts, and unless they are involved at the planning stages of generating and transmitting projects, the state agencies are more likely to become allies than regulators of the power industry in its conflict with public, private and environmental interests.

SMOG OVER THE GREAT PLAINS (1971)

Jack Waugh

. . . BY SEPTEMBER 1964, conservationists in the West had gone complacently asleep. They had beaten back a network of hydroelectric plants which the public power industry had tried to build along the Colorado River in the 1950s and which would have backed water up fathoms deep into some of the West's most majestic canyons.

But even as conservationists sat back that September with arms folded in self-satisfaction, ten investor-owned public power companies met and formed an association called WEST (Western Energy Supply Transmission Associates). Under the guise of being the benevolent suppliers of a galloping demand for electric power, WEST members, without fanfare, started to draw contracts for a network of coal-fired plants on the Colorado Plateau.

By the time environmentalists realized what was happening, WEST had grown to twenty-four member companies and into one of the biggest electric-power combines in the country. Its members had either built, were building, or had on the drawing boards six of the largest fossil fuel power plants in the world, with the potential to turn the crisp air of the West into a major pollution problem.

Now, despite a national alert that has finally attracted the attention of the federal government, it appears too late to stop the plants. The best environmentalists can hope for is to dull the impact of the inevitable pollution.

WEST, not a company on its own, but an umbrella under which companies combine to build plants beyond the financial reach of any one of them, moved first into the Four Corners region where Utah, New Mexico, Arizona and Colorado meet. The Arizona Public Service Company, a WEST member, has maintained a 575,000 kilowatt capacity plant near Farmington on the New Mexico side since 1963. A phalanx of six companies, led by Southern California Edison, has now moved in, added two more units to the Farmington plant, and tripled its kilowatt output.

Another combine of six companies has built a 1.5 million kilowatt giant in the Nevada desert outside Mohave. Now four more huge plants are either rising on the plateau or are on the drawing boards, with operational target dates of no later than 1977. One, the Navajo plant, a 2.3 million kilowatt facility, is now building outside Page, Ariz., on the banks of Lake Powell. Another big plant, called the San Juan, is projected for a site near Farmington; another is planned for outside Price, Utah. And the last and most massive of all—a facility with a 5 to 6 million kilowatt capacity—is projected for the Plains of Kaiparowits, a coal-rich plateau on the Utah side of Lake Powell. It will be the biggest coal-fired generating plant in the world, capable of producing enough power to run a city the size of New York.

The prodigal at Kaiparowits and its five companion plants will generate together 14 million kilowatts of electric power. With that, the pollution of the Western air will be massive, but the WEST master plan does not stop there. Other plants, scheduled for a post-Kaiparowits phase running through 1985, will bring the capacity for power generation on the Colorado Plateau to 36 million kilowatts—three times the power of the Tennessee Valley Authority (TVA) and seventeen times more than the Aswan Dam in Egypt.

Already the single 2.1 million kilowatt plant at Farmington, the first venture under the WEST umbrella, throws out as much particulate matter (fly ash and smoke) each day—250 tons—as New York (140 tons) and Los Angeles (110 tons) combined. The plume of smoke and ash drifts across more than 200 miles of Indian reservation. It was the only man-made landmark that the astronauts on the Apollo 8 flight could consistently see and photograph from cislunar space.

Because of the opposition that boiled up when this new generation of plants was discovered, the power companies are finally moving to clean up the fly ash. New Mexico has ordered the Arizona Public Service Company to make the stacks at Farmington 99.2 per cent pure by the end of 1971 or shut down. The

APS is installing wet scrubbers, at a cost of $7 million, that will reduce the ash to 15 tons a day. But when all six of the goliaths of the desert are operating in the late 1970s, and even if they are all equipped with wet scrubbers, they will still belch 350 tons of fly ash a day into the air across the plateau.

If not forced to clean up, they will also put out 2,160 tons of sulfur oxides a day—more than Chicago (1,920 tons) or New York City (1,077 tons), and many times more than Los Angeles (225 tons). Los Angeles considers even its 225 tons, that low because of a strict enforcement code, intolerable. Los Angeles —and other cities follow a similar policy—no longer permits an electric-power plant to build in its urban interior. That is why suddenly the once big-sky West is getting them.

The power plants of the plateau by the end of the 1970s will also be dumping 850 tons of nitrogen oxides into the sky each day. Nitrogen oxide is a co-producer of the infamous Los Angeles-type photochemical smog, of which that city, with its millions of automobile exhausts, in 1968 never produced more than 950 tons a day.

The power companies showed a near-total disinterest in developing any anti-pollution safeguards—until forced to do so. Not until New Mexico demanded it did the Arizona Public Service Company install wet scrubbers at Farmington. When the Salt River project in Phoenix was drawing plans for the WEST-inspired 2.3 million kilowatt installation at Page, little of its $309 million budget went to pollution abatement. Only after environmentalists demanded safeguards did the Salt designers add $90 million for pollution abatement.

By negotiating contracts largely with Indian tribal councils, both for the land on which to build the plants and for the rights to the coal which powers them, the electric companies attracted almost no attention until late 1969 and early 1970. . . . The contract signed with the Navajo and Hopi tribal councils for the rights to coal from Black Mesa, a coal-rich mountain deep within the reservation and long held sacred by the Indians, is typical. . . . The tribal councils of both tribes liked the deal; the Department of the Interior smiled approval. But from the beginning, some Indians first frowned and then vigorously objected. Enormous cranes and shovels began biting into shoulders of the mesa, long considered essential to the harmony of Navajo life. . . . Roads are slicing across the mesa and giant flatbed trucks shatter the traditional quiet. The Hopis fear that the gulping slurry pipeline that carries coal 275 miles to the Mohave plant will deprive them of water that has sustained their farms and villages for a thousand years. . . .

For the past year and a half, environmentalists, led by the Central Clearing House in Santa Fe, have been mounting a sometimes limping attack on the unbridled growth of electric-power plants existing, building, and projected. They have found it hard, until the last six months, to get adequate publicity and almost impossible to get the federal ear. Finally they are being heard. . . .

Interior Secretary Morton, backed by the President's Council on Environmental Quality, . . . ordered a moratorium on new plants until an Interior task force named by him can make a report. That will take about a year. The moratorium will not stop plants now in progress. Indeed, it will halt only one —the one at Kaiparowits. But for the environmentalists, outmaneuvered for so long, it is at least a mini-victory.

THE GASLIGHT INDUSTRY (1967)

Wallace I. Roberts

SINCE THE GASLIGHT ERA, power in New England has been controlled by the private companies, but recent developments initiated by public-power advocates suggest that the Yankee capitalists, who have administered the industry with an amazing lack of their traditional ingenuity, may be forced to change their ways. Except for a transmission system half owned by Vermont and providing about a quarter of the state's electric needs, there are no large publicly owned generating or transmission systems in the six states, so they have escaped until now the passionate, flag-waving defenses of free enterprise that have previously been exhibited in private vs. public power battles in nearly every other section of the country. The controversy in New England has taken the form of a series of complicated legal and financial maneuvers, a somewhat misleading public relations and advertising campaign, and intensive political lobbying. It has all been most decorous, but with the April announcement by the Justice Department that it is making preliminary investigations of possible antitrust violations by the private New England utilities, and with the threat of similar action by the Federal Power Commission, things may become less restrained.

Beginning two years ago with a request for money to finance engineering studies for a federal hydroelectric project on the St. John River near the town of Dickey in northern Maine, the conflict has grown and developed on several additional fronts. It promises not to be over for some time, given the determination and recent successes of the public-power groups and the distaste for change exhibited by most private company officials.

If there is no agreement about what kind of power projects to build, there is absolute agreement as to why they are necessary—New England's electric rates are the highest of any region in the country. There are many ways to compare the cost of electricity, and by any of them the New England states, except Vermont with its public power, are at the top of the list. Federal Power Commission figures for 1963 show that the average price per kilowatt-hour sold by the private utilities in New England was 2.48c compared to 1.77c for the private utilities of the country, a difference of 40 per cent. Similar comparison reveals that fewer kilowatt-hours per customer are sold in New England. Higher prices inhibit sales, and lower sales force the prices even higher because a smaller total revenue must be spread over the fixed charges.

Private company executives acknowledge the region's high rates, but their reply has become as automatic as an echo: "Yes, but our fuel and labor costs and taxes are so high." There is some substance to that explanation, though Joseph C. Swidler, former FPC chairman, said several years ago that if New England utilities had to pay only average fuel costs, the region's electric bills would be lowered by less than 5 per cent.

An equally substantive explanation, however, is the fact that administrative expenses range, depending on how they are measured, from 33 to 100 per cent above the national average, and, according to William D. Shipman, professor of economics at Bowdoin College, account for one-quarter to one-half of the difference between the average price for electricity in New England and in the rest of the country. Local taxes, which are one-third higher for New England utilities, are the only significant inequity that is apparently beyond much control.

The most important factor in rate reductions is increased per capita use. Because New England is an "old" region in demographic terms, neither its industry nor its population, and hence its per capita use of electricity, has kept pace with the rest of the country. A slow growth rate in per capita use is almost a built-in barrier to lowering prices, but reductions can be encouraged by cutting costs through efficiencies.

Compounding the high fuel costs, the coal or oil is burned in plants that for the most part are little old teakettles, barely able to get up enough steam to whistle, when compared to the giant and efficient boiler-turbine-generator combinations that have been available for years. The region does have one showpiece, the Brayton Point, Mass., plant of the New England Power Co. It opened in 1964 and was rated by the FPC as the most efficient in the country, but for thirteen years before that New England had no entry on the commission's list of the top ten most efficient plants.

Mechanical inefficiency cannot be blamed on the region's age or geographical deficiencies; it is the result of administrative decisions. Two generations ago, Samuel Insull, the man who did for electricity what Henry Ford did for the automobile, showed the power industry that it was much more efficient to use large generating plants serving as many people as possible. No one believed him at first, and it might appear that many private company executives in New England still don't. On average, the public utilities companies of the country serve three times as many people as do the companies of New England, and there are more than one and a half times as many people for every generating plant. This means for New England more executives, more plants and lines to maintain, more secretaries, more maintenance workers, more pensions and insurance, and higher labor costs per customer. New Englanders are paying to perpetuate a quaint private industry organization that is not nearly as charming as a covered bridge and much more expensive.

Attempts at consolidation have been made, but the pace is slow. In some places in New England, covered bridges have rotted away before the public realized what was happening. It is unlikely, however, that any private utility in the region will collapse, for they are protected by the state regulatory agencies and an apathetic public. Almost all of the region's utilities make the maximum profit allowed by law, and a few are considerably above the prescribed limit. Blackstone Valley Electric Co. of Rhode Island earned in 1965 a return of 9.34 per cent, almost twice the limit.

Only Vermont's Public Service Board seems to take seriously its obligation to set reasonable rates. New Hampshire and Connecticut appear indifferent at best, and the regulatory agencies in Maine, Massachusetts and Rhode Island have exhibited what can only be called an affection for the private companies.

The Maine and Massachusetts agencies have been hostile, almost insulting, to recent appearances by public-power groups.

Part of this situation results from the fact that none of the agencies has money or staff to do an adequate job. Most are so short of skilled help that they are forced to accept company operating statistics as a basis for determining rates. Unless the public demands it, the regulatory agencies are not likely to hire qualified accountants or engineers, and the prevailing public attitude is that the cost of electricity has formed a triumvirate with death and taxes. The result is that the regulatory agencies are permitting monopolies to earn good profits with equipment and organizational structures that would drive them to the wall if they were faced with even moderately aggressive competition. Allowing each utility exclusive control of its sales territory prevents wasteful duplication of plants and lines, but it also creates an attitude of *status quo* complacency. Creative regulatory policies could impose penalties for continued use of outmoded steam plants, instead of allowing them to be included in the rate base.

However, conventional steam plants have had their day in New England. After 1969, the region's power industry will most likely build only lower-cost nuclear plants. It already has an experimental nuclear plant, Yankee, at Rowe, Mass., and five others are either under construction or committed. These five are part of what the private companies have dubbed their "Big 11 Power Loop"; the other six installations consist of five conventional steam plants and a pumped storage plant. All eleven are scheduled to be finished by the end of 1972 and will be connected by 900 miles of 345-kilovolt transmission lines. The cost of the project is about $900 million, and the plants will provide about 6.3 million kilowatts of power.

The name "Big 11 Power Loop"—but not the plants or transmission lines —is a gimmick, pure and simple. No engineering plan or study supports the location, type or design of the plants on a system-wide basis. It all started with a full-page newspaper advertisement announcing the "Loop" and implying that the whole thing was thought out well in advance. The campaign, carried on with television commercials costing about $200,000 a year, was devised by the private companies' trade organization, the Electric Coordinating Council of New England (ECCNE), in response to the threat of the federal government's Dickey-Lincoln School hydroelectric project. . . .

The dam at Dickey is the practical reality left over from the dream of harnessing the tides in Passamaquoddy Bay at the eastern tip of Maine. . . . By 1980 it will provide only 1 per cent of the area's electrical requirements. But it will probably bring with it a Northeast Power Commission to market the power. It is expected that the cheaper power of Dickey, combined with the prodding effect of the power administration on state regulatory agencies, will be to force lower electrical rates. . . .

THE SQUEEZE IN CALIFORNIA (1974)

Thomas Brom

FOR SIXTY YEARS, the Los Angeles basin has been a battleground for public and private electric utilities. City-owned systems of two types exist side by side with the huge Southern California Edison Company, vying for fuel supplies, refinery service, customers and ultimate supremacy in Southern California. They've had territory battles before—refereed by the state Public Utilities Commission, the Federal Power Commission, the legislature and the courts —but none to compare with the scramble for scarce low-sulfur oil that began early this winter.

The municipal power utilities of the Los Angeles basin are anomalies in Southern California, being surrounded by the vast service territory of the Southern California Edison Company. SCE consolidated most of the lower third of California when it purchased the holdings of thirteen private utilities in 1909, but several of the existing municipal systems refused to sell their distribution systems, built with public money and even then were able to deliver power at lower cost than the private companies.

As the population of Southern California grew, however, power demand rose to the point where some of the municipal systems had to buy power wholesale from Edison. Colton, Riverside, Anaheim and Azusa—all with city utilities built in the 1890s—became wholly dependent on privately generated power.

Water was the key to electric utility independence in the central Los Angeles basin. The city of Los Angeles bought the local water company in 1902, built an aqueduct to the Sierra Nevada and developed an electric power system with dams along the route. The smaller power systems of Pasadena, Glendale and Burbank were all able to acquire federal hydro power from the Hoover Dam project in 1937. Subsequently, they built their own steam generation plants. These four greater Los Angeles cities are the only Southern California public systems with power generation capability.

Both the generating and the purchasing municipal systems were caught in this winter's power shortage. Cities that generate their own power had the immediate problem of disappearing fuel supplies. But the cities that bought power wholesale from Edison for retail distribution were even more desperate, trapped by Edison's pricing and with no other source.

A year ago, no one in Los Angeles thought much about a power crisis. Then a series of disasters struck first at the power-generating utilities—and at the municipal systems hardest of all. In August, the Federal Power Commission drastically curtailed deliveries of natural gas to Southern California for purposes of power generation. It ordered El Paso Natural Gas, instead of piping supplies to the Southern California Gas Co. for resale to the utilities, to give preference to residential customers in Arizona—an order that El Paso was only too happy to obey.

Thereupon, the Los Angeles Board of Water and Power Commissioners contracted for low-sulfur oil to burn in the city's generators. The only oil then available came from the Mideast, so the commissioners took that. The Arab oil embargo in October knocked out 48 per cent of the city's fuel supply overnight, and its only firm source of electricity was the federal Bonneville Dam Project along the Columbia River, which sent power south via the Pacific Intertie to supply 10 per cent of the city's needs. But long periods of drought in the Northwest had been followed by an early and massive cold wave. Streams that fed the Columbia froze, drastically reducing the runoff that supplied the Bonneville reservoirs. Coming at a time when its customers in the Northwest were drawing heavily on Bonneville for additional heat, the reduction in power forced it to cut all service to the Southland.

In mid-November, the Los Angeles commissioners convened in panic. They had been told by Department of Water and Power engineers that the city had fuel for its steam generators only until March 1. Faced with energy starvation for the city's 1.1 million customers, the officials produced a sweeping, five-phase Emergency Energy Curtailment Program in less than three days.

First step provisions, which went into effect immediately, included mandatory power cutbacks of 10 per cent for residential and industrial users, and 20 per cent for commercial users. Penalties for violations ranged from a 50 per cent surcharge on customer bills and short-term blackouts to service discontinuance for a month.

Phases two through five would raise mandatory curtailments as high as 33 per cent, cut business hours, sanction the burning of high-sulfur oil, and finally resort to rolling blackouts.

The nearby cities of Burbank, Glendale and Pasadena—all of which generate their own power—enacted similar ordinances. Burbank raised the immediate mandatory cutback to 30 per cent for industrial and commercial users, including Lockheed Aircraft and NBC Studios. Glendale and Pasadena added $500 fines and jail sentences for offenders.

Glendale, assured of low-sulfur oil deliveries only through January 10, applied for and received a variance from the L.A. Air Pollution Control District to burn conventional high-sulfur oil. Pasadena, Burbank and Los Angeles followed, with APCD approval awaiting the result of a desperate attempt to find low-sulfur supplies.

Meanwhile, Southern California Edison, whose territory extends from San Diego north to Santa Barbara and east to the Nevada border, laid low. Edison had long-term contracts extending through 1976 for Indonesian oil—low in sulfur and at bargain prices on the world market. Along with Pacific Gas and Electric, Edison had a near monopoly of Indonesian supplies. Edison has been building massive storage facilities for the past five years. By the end of 1974, the company will be able to store 25 million barrels, a four-to-five-month supply. Half of that capacity has been built since 1972.

Although Edison has sold the Los Angeles DWP modest amounts of its excess power, the company preferred not to get involved. It was in a position to watch the four Los Angeles basin municipals squirm. Edison had made repeated attempts to buy the smaller systems, and took no small satisfaction from seeing Los Angeles DWP, largest of the nation's 2,000 public power systems, scramble for oil shipments on the world market.

"It's been difficult for us to do business," says Los Angeles Chief Engineer William Sells. "We have a harder time obtaining oil because of the traditional relationships between the privately owned power companies and the privately owned oil companies. We're just not part of the team."

The cities that bought from Edison at wholesale fared even worse. On January 2, Edison filed a petition with the FPC asking for a 20.1 per cent base rate increase, and a 15.5 per cent fuel cost adjustment. Anaheim utilities director Gordon Hoyt says: "When this is coupled with the increase of 52.5 per cent which became effective last September, and the 12 per cent increase of November 1971, it means we'll be paying 300 per cent of what we were paying in October of 1971."

To protect the city from takeover attempts by a private utility, Anaheim's city charter reads that utility rates within the city cannot be higher than Edison rates in the surrounding areas. Hoyt plans to abide by that clause, but it means that his system must absorb the costs it cannot pass on. "That's going to cost this city revenue," he says. "We contributed 18 per cent of our gross revenues to the city in 1972–73. Now, our support will be reduced by about $230,000 a month.

"What really burns me is that if we were an industrial customer of Edison, instead of a wholesale municipal buyer, we would pay considerably less for our power. I haven't done the statistics for Anaheim, but Riverside estimates in their case they would pay 16 per cent less if they were an industry.

"The effect is that Edison puts a price squeeze on us. With our rates higher than [those for] their industrial customers, Anaheim will be unable to compete for very large industries. We can't sell power to them for less than we pay for it. Sure, Edison's screwing us. I have accused their vice presidents of doing exactly that."

So the public power cities in Southern California are caught in a whipsaw —scarce oil supplies at outrageous prices for those that generate power, and rapidly escalating rates for those that buy power wholesale. Either way, Edison comes up the winner.

But it isn't just because of Edison that the public utilities are in trouble. Some of the difficulties were of their own making, and some were forced by competing energy industries. The municipals have learned a lot in the past year, and with any luck they will emerge stronger and more united for all their problems.

Public power cities have a ninety-year history of surviving adversity. Born of Populist, reform and progressive reaction to the excesses of private utilities, they have grown used to corporate collusion with government and the courts.

As a group of nearly 3,000, they weathered the onslaught of Samuel Insull's power trust in the 1920s, when the industry-backed National Electric Light Association (NELA) sponsored a massive propaganda campaign against "Socialist" electric utilities, coordinated takeover moves and blocked public agencies from all access to capital. By the time Federal Trade Commission hearings could expose these practices in the late 1920s, the number of public power systems had declined to less than 1,900. [Although] the public power movement enjoyed a renaissance with the coming of the New Deal . . . the private utilities quickly regrouped to contain the municipal systems. The Edison Electric Institute replaced the discredited NELA, and formal lobbying groups were organized in Washington. For the next forty years, public and private utilities held their ground in an uneasy stand-off.

The benefits of municipal, county or district power companies have been trumpeted for decades, and they are no less pertinent today. Public power systems are built with low-interest, tax-exempt bonds. The agencies are not required to pay federal, state or local taxes, although virtually all make substantial payments in lieu of taxes. Over the years, public systems have consistently paid less than the private utility for advertising, less for public relations, less for lobbying, less for political donations, less for accounting and collections, less for executive salaries and less for internal bureaucracy. The result, year in and year out for the past ninety years, has been lower rates and a high degree of public accountability.

Public power cities do have their problems. Most of them have to fight continuously for bond measures to enable capital improvement and the development of new power sources. Management has a tendency to become entrenched in city bureaucracy, and lack of size keeps the public agencies in a weaker political position vis-à-vis the investor-owned utilities.

All of these problems came to haunt the Los Angeles basin municipal power departments this winter. Their lack of national political influence allowed El Paso Natural Gas to curtail supplies just as winter approached. The natural gas industry has been trying to force deregulation of its prices for years. At present those prices can range higher for gas welled, piped and burned within one state than for gas transported across state boundaries. The Federal Power Commission takes jurisdiction on interstate shipments. Thus El Paso would much rather sell its gas where it is found in Texas and Arizona than pipe it into Southern California. "It's a safe assumption to make that this cutoff is an attempt to make us allies in the move to de-regulate natural gas," says Richard Young of the Glendale Public Service Department.

Natural gas curtailment for power generation was also a boon to the oil companies that were the obvious alternative sources of fuel. General Motors, Shell Oil and the Southwest Gas Corporation were among those who opposed the DWP petition for relief from the FPC ruling.

Utility size immediately became a factor in the scramble to buy and store oil. Before the natural gas curtailment, the four power generating cities in the Los Angeles basin relied on oil as a backup fuel. They maintained small storage capacities, bought small quantities of oil on public bid and specification, and dealt almost exclusively with small, local oil companies. The international oil giants weren't interested in these markets; the quantities were trivial, and they didn't like the public bid process.

With the Arab oil embargo, both the oil supplies and the small suppliers dried up. "Our supplier was Carson Oil," says Pasadena Power Department engineer Jerry Lohr. "But they went out of business in October. We have a contract now with the company that absorbed them, Golden Eagle Refinery, for conventional high-sulfur oil. The contract's got a cancellation clause in it in case the Air Pollution Control District won't let us burn it."

All four of the public systems had to secure special powers from their city councils to suspend public bidding and to negotiate on the world market for oil. "When you get out into the world market," comments William Sells of the Los Angeles DWP, "you're bidding against Japan and Western Europe as well as the other utilities in the United States. We're dealing through brokers on the world market for the first time."

Buyers for the Los Angeles system have contracted small shipments of oil from Peru, Venezuela, Italy and Indonesia, with price tags from $18 to $25 per barrel. That's five times what the department paid a year ago, and has forced the issuance of $100 million in short-term bonds. The bond sale was the largest in the sixty-year history of the DWP.

Probably the most damaging effect of being both small and a public utility is the difficulty encountered in the development of alternative power sources. Both municipal systems, those that generate their own power and those that buy from Edison, desperately want to build generating and transmission facilities. Edison and Pacific Gas and Electric, among the top ten utilities in the nation, are not eager to help them.

The Los Angeles DWP has tried four times to build a nuclear plant, but has yet to begin construction. The Malibu plant was opposed by the Marblehead Land Company. Bolsa Island Nuclear Power and Desalting Plant was dropped due to cost when the AEC demanded additional safety devices. The site of the Tulare County plant was unsatisfactory because of unstable geological conditions. Finally, the DWP entered into joint-venture agreements with Edison and PG&E for a nuclear plant in the southern San Joaquin Valley, in PG&E's service territory. The most optimistic date for its completion is 1982.

Meanwhile, the DWP has been building joint-venture, coal-fired plants in Nevada and Arizona. Both the Mojave Power Project near the Colorado River and the Navajo Power Project at Page, Ariz., are fueled with strip-mined coal from Black Mesa. Two new coal-fired plants, the Arrow Project near Las Vegas and the Intermountain Project in southern Utah, are planned for the late 1970s.

Edison has been drawing huge quantities of power from its own coal plants at Four Corners, N.M., and from its 50 per cent share of the Mojave plant. But the embarrassments are especially acute for public agencies—supposedly more responsive to the public welfare—that excavate the Navajo and Hopi land at Black Mesa along with the private corporations.

The wholesale power buyers have found it even more difficult to enter the power generation field. Until a settlement agreement was signed last year, Anaheim and other wholesale buyers were Edison's captive customers. Because Edison refused to provide transmission service across its lines, the cities could not seek alternative power sources, and were held to ten-year service contracts.

Gordon Hoyt of Anaheim led the fight for emancipation. Anaheim intervened in two Edison hydroelectric relicensing projects, alleging that until the company stopped its anti-competitive activities it wasn't entitled to another fifty-year license to develop the resources of the United States. The city also intervened in a proceeding before the California Public Utilities Commission that involved construction of an Edison 500-kv transmission line. Anaheim asked that approval of the line be conditioned upon Edison providing transmission service to the city.

Anaheim also intervened in the license proceeding of the San Onofre nuclear power plant, demanding rights to participate in the construction and power resources of the Edison plant. Finally, Anaheim alleged before the PUC that because Edison prevented the city from obtaining transmission service, it was engaged in regional monopolistic practices in violation of the antitrust laws.

Edison was limited in the ways it could retaliate, because it was bound by the state PUC to supply Anaheim with power. The settlement agreement reached in 1973 not only granted a broad bill of rights to all wholesale buyers but included a cash payment as well. Anaheim, Riverside, Colton, Banning, Azusa and the others now have the right to wheel in power across Edison lines, the right to buy power from alternative sources, the right to participate in generation at the San Onofre plant, the Kaiparowits Coal plant in Utah and subsequent Edison projects, and the right to interconnection operations with Edison.

"Unfortunately," says Hoyt, "now that we have the rights, we don't have the power sources. We'll be involved in the Intermountain project eventually, but in the meantime, all the available power comes from Edison." . . .

The Los Angeles DWP will probably be able to compete with Edison in the near future because of its size, and the preferential treatment it receives from the government in the construction of hydro projects. Federal control of dams on the nation's waterways is one of the legacies of the New Deal that still directly benefits many municipal systems. The Los Angeles DWP plans to receive 2.5 million kilowatts from the Castaic, Piru and Terminal Power Projects now under construction. All three are on the West Branch of the California Aqueduct, with most of the power to be shared equally by the State Water Resources Board.

The others, the small generating municipals and the newly emancipated wholesale buyers, will be left to sort out the energy squeeze on their own. Virtually all of the public power cities support the creation of a state energy office in California, and federal allocation of low-sulfur oil. Both moves have so far been blocked by Edison, Pacific Gas and Electric, five major oil companies and the Southern California Gas Company.

Burbank, Glendale and Pasadena have created an informal consortium to buy and store oil. The agreement allows the three to buy in ship lots for the first time. In late January, Burbank surprised the Edison company when it bid more than $700,000 for geothermal leases of its own in the Imperial Valley. The Public Service Department entered into a cooperative arrangement with Republic Geothermal to negotiate the leases.

Hoyt and the other wholesale buyers realize the necessity of collective action. "The answer for all of us is a system of regional generation and transmission," Hoyt says. "If the Edison company would sell us power at the same rates that we could develop it ourselves, we would never go looking for power. But they won't do that. So we are trying to force our involvement in every announced power project planned anywhere in the West.

"Sure, we're a thorn in the side of the Edison company. We're buying power from a very large supplier who doesn't really want us to be in business, and apparently continually works both in the legislature and at the local level to make life more difficult for us. We have to keep pushing if we're going to survive."

Purchase by the Edison company is the specter facing those municipal systems that can't move quickly enough to secure power needs. Pasadena, Anaheim and Riverside have weathered takeover attempts in the past, and are the most likely targets of forced consolidation.

"Edison got the city of Vernon to go for a lease arrangement," says Anaheim's Hoyt. "Technically, the city owns the system, but it is under contract to Edison. The company tried to get the same arrangement in Azusa a few years ago but failed. Edison took over the desert cooperative out in Twenty-Nine Palms a while ago, and tried to buy the Anza Cooperative, too. Edison says that it's just a question of the will of the people, but I know that the company was involved backstage."

"The reality of the situation is that we are the only buyers," smiles Edison vice president Edward Myers. "When the people indicate to their elected representatives that they are interested in selling a system, we are the logical ones to step in."

So the battle between public and private power in the Los Angeles basin continues. The struggle has shifted temporarily to the world oil market, where the municipals gamble for scarce supplies at prices they cannot afford. But ultimately, the success or failure of public systems will rest on their ability to develop alternative fuel supplies. If they can combine their resources, ingenuity and generating capacity, most can survive the crisis.

"The people themselves should have control of something as important to their lives as the utility system," says Richard Young. "They can't be put in the position of having anybody with a stranglehold on them. In Glendale, the people banded together and formed their own company almost seventy-five years ago. It's still the choice of the people. With their support, we can make it."

Part III
OIL

PREFACE

THE CONTEMPORARY CRIES of "energy crisis" are most immediately concerns about the supply of oil and gas, for these fuels account for 75 percent of total consumption. The United States was once the world's largest exporter as well as producer. Now there is the fear that it is producing at a faster rate than that of discoveries of new reserves and that the dependence upon imported oil, now almost 50 percent, is increasing.

In American history oil policy has largely been corporate policy. The United States has accepted subsurface mineral rights as belonging to the land-owner and has encouraged private development on private lands as well as on the public domain which is one-third of the area of the United States and which is believed to contain perhaps 50 percent of the remaining fossil fuels of the country. It subsequently supported overseas expansion to stake out more re-serves and backstopped corporate leaders in their negotiations with foreign powers. Few questions have been asked about the allocation of investment capital in energy or about the uses of energy in the various sectors of the economy. It was generally accepted that high energy consumption meant a higher gross national product and hence a stronger society. What subsequently emerged was a cluster of private governments, prototypes of the modern trans-national corporations, which together formed what I described in 1961 (in *The Politics of Oil*) as the first world government. Their community of interests led the oilmen to plan to keep supply and effective market demand in as close a balance as possible so as to minimize the threats to price structure and private control. While not always completely successful, their efforts to maintain a tightly wound mechanism in oil help account for the immediate impact of relatively modest disruptions in supply, such as the Iranian cutoff in 1979.

To help the reader trace this complexity and the resulting dependency, the articles in this chapter are divided into five sections. The first group illustrates the reaching out of private industry to the public domain, the naval reserves, Alaska, and ultimately the sea and its shipping lanes. One notes quite early the political corruption attendant upon this expansion. The section on corporate control explains the quest for order within the industry—the growth of integra-tion of production, pipelines, refining and marketing, and the ultimate turning to government to curtail competition and sustain private planning. Of special significance here are efforts for "conservation" in production, the role of the NRA codes under the New Deal, and the struggles in Washington during World War II, especially as reported by I.F. Stone, to maintain corporate prerogatives. "The Widening Reach" and then "The Imperial Economy" sketch the expan-sion of the industry, first into Latin America and then the Middle East. The cases of Mexico and Iran are particularly instructive for understanding the economic consequences of such penetration and the political reactions of the people of the producing countries. The emerging role of OPEC and the relation-ship to the corporate cartels are explored, including some of the ways in which they have collaborated to sustain one another's power. And finally the chapter returns to the "Energy Crisis" in the United States and to the efforts of the corporations, as extraordinarily successful profit-gatherers, to assure an angry public that while the supply-price pressures were beyond corporate control, they remained the best instruments for national energy policy. One also notes the trained incapacity of American political leaders to break out from the conventional bounds of treating energy as a private matter. For their policy actions, rhetoric notwithstanding, appear to reinforce the corporate fear that the "wicked" OPEC might undercut corporate wealth and power by lowering the price of oil.

Public Resources

OIL (1920)

The Nation

THE WAR WAS NOT fought because of oil. But the dividing up of the swag among the victors was in part determined by oil, and certain protectorates were nicely adjusted to the presence of it. If the white western world is able to achieve another war in a few years, the causes and objects will probably center around potential oil territory. A good many people are stacking the materials for such a bonfire. The stakes of diplomacy used to be coal, iron ore, rubber, and copper. But the most inflammable recent addition to international poker is oil.

"Lloyd George Uses Oil on Diplomats in San Remo," said a headline of the New York *Sun* on April 26. Thus, oil becomes an instrument of policy. The *Sun* article describes in the orthodox terms of economic determinism how the world of politics is the pasteboard façade for the silent concealed economic forces, and how politicians are the puppets and showmen of the business interests. This new organ of Marxism makes such comment as: "To the effective use by British diplomats of the great economic weapons, coal and oil, is largely attributable the accord which seems to have been reached rather suddenly at the San Remo conference. It is the new diplomacy into which oil is entering more and more as a factor as the British diplomats play the game." Lloyd George, in his talk to the Commons on April 29, tucked away in one sentence the vital decision. He said "There has been an agreement arrived at with the French with respect to oil distribution in Mosul."

When Bolshevik and British troops march into the new free state of Azerbaidjan, it is not alone to preserve the liberties of the happy little republic. They also come because Baku, on which they concentrate their regard, is the center of one of the largest oil fields in the world. The strange Caucasian deploys of

British troops during the recent war puzzled simple-hearted military men, like General Maurice, who wished to defeat the German Army. But even in the midst of alarms, British policy saw a vaster struggle in the years to come, and obeyed the imperial instinct, so much stronger than mere blood-lust. When Admiral Fisher, one of the greatest sea dogs since Nelson, first said "Oil," men thought him mad. Was not England built on her bed of coal? Her commerce sailed to it; her world markets had been captured by it. Like most men of genius in action, Fisher has a style. He throws his full weight into words. He preached oil in his famous terse letters, fifty words long, till that rock of reaction, the Admiralty, smitten, flowed. Fisher says:

> The oil engine . . . will revolutionize commerce and alter the whole art of sea war. I was dubbed an oil maniac when I was at the Admiralty in 1885. The internal combustion engine is as imperative for commerce as for war. I should build tramps to carry oil, with ever-improving combustion engines fitted in them . . . inexpensive vessels, more or less hulls to carry these experimental internal combustion engines. A few years hence we shall require a species of hippopotami, both for sea war and sea commerce.

Said Earl Curzon, "The Allies floated to victory on a sea of oil." Walter Hume Long, First Lord of the British Admiralty, has said, "If we secure the supplies of oil now available in the world we can do what we like." He warned the Institution of Petroleum Technologists that the Government would be blamed "for inaction at this moment of great national importance. We are on the threshold of tremendous opportunities, and the nation must take care to occupy the house, or others will take it and with it the key to all future success." An even franker statement is that of Sir E. MacKay Edgar, head of Spaling & Company, quoted in the Manchester *Guardian* of September, 1919:

> We hold in our hands the secure control of the future of the world's oil supply. We are sitting tight on what must soon become the lion's share of a raw material indispensable to every manufacturing country, intimately bound up with maritime power, and unobtainable in sufficient quantities outside the sphere of British influence. Before very long America will have to purchase from British companies. If the fall in the pound on the New York money market has not been stayed long before then, the British control of the greater part of the world's oil will not only suffice to arrest it, but will go a long way towards reestablishing the old exchange equilibrium.

At some points these words are the substance of things hoped for rather than things sat upon tightly.

A representative American oil man summed up at the beginning of May the situation as he saw it. He said he admired the British; anybody would who watched them at work. Their political policy backed up their commercial policy—together, the two policies made their imperialism. Their fleet froze out any little nation that interfered with British investors. By a bloodless, friendly, but thorough blockade of necessary raw materials, they softened the governmental policy of the lesser breeds till British business men had established themselves and were respected. The present Government of the United States, this business man lamented, did not back up its investors in other countries, and it was impossible to get a clear-cut policy from the State Department. The pressing need of expanding American business (particularly in oil) was, therefore, to come to a working basis with the State Department. . . .

OIL-BURNING POLITICS (1923)

William Hard

WHAT OTHER COMMODITY gives us so many nice large events at Washington? I dedicate these few admiring paragraphs to oil.

Senator La Follette—day after day—at the end of a long table in a committee room on the gallery floor of the Senate—his fighting face turned inquisitorially upon rows of citizens who humbly offer him whole suit-cases and whole trunks of documents—is investigating oil and the prices of oil. Senator Walsh of Montana—great constitutional lawyer—is addressing his mighty mind to the mysteries of geology in order that he may be fully prepared to interrogate all comers in the course of the inquiry which presently the Committee on Public Lands will conduct into the matter of Mr. Harry Sinclair's lease from Mr. Secretary Fall of the vast oil resources of the Wyoming Teapot Dome naval land reserve. Mexico is languishing without diplomatic recognition from the United States because President Obregon cannot politically see his way to producing a piece of paper with formal words on it satisfying Mr. Secretary Hughes's anxiety for the legal and physical safety of American corporations in Mexico engaged in producing oil. The United States of Colombia in South America is gradually consuming $25,000,000 of American public governmental money as a tribute from the American Treasury to the Colombian Treasury, explicitly in order that American private business men may be well treated by the Colombian Government in the matter of explorations in Colombia for oil. Palestine and Mesopotamia—the lower valley of the Jordan and the upper reaches of the Tigris—the water with which John the Baptist baptized and the garden which Adam tended—are stirred with the high winds of our American diplomatic crusade for the open door in the international search for oil. The patient and unobtrusive Dutch—getting quietly fatter and fatter in the isles of the South Seas off Singapore—are haled into the arena of international controversy by our exigent notes demanding that we Americans be allowed to "assist"—such is the elegance of the language of diplomacy—"assist"—in the development of a certain resource of the Dutch East Indies—namely, oil. Coal is by comparison local. Cotton is by comparison tame. Oil is really international and quite considerably belligerent.

In the year 1906 the oil industry of America had for its principal purpose and achievement the production of some 33,000,000 barrels of kerosene. In the year 1921, besides producing some 46,000,000 barrels of kerosene, it had a totally new principal purpose and achievement—namely, the production of 150,000,000 barrels of gasoline. Motor cars have necessitated the struggle for more and more oil, and Mr. Ford, our great lover of peace, is one of the chief causes—unconscious but compelling—of the world's present belligerent oil diplomacy.

In the year 1919 our imports of crude oil into the United States were 14 per cent of the volume of our domestic production of it. In the year 1920 they were 24 per cent of our domestic production. In the year 1921 they were 27 per cent. Washington needs no oil lobby to tell it that if we are going to joy-ride and truck-ride and plow with oil, we shall have to look overseas for the means with which to do it.

The very first act of this Administration was to come into the Senate with an outright—though unintentional—canard about British governmental ownership of British international oil companies. By means of this canard it induced the Senate to give the United States of Colombia $25,000,000 in alleged compensation for an alleged wrong which both of the Administration's principal spokesmen had previously declared did not exist. Mr. Secretary Fall and Senator Lodge had previously signed their names to a report in which they said, "The Colombian Government has no just or equitable claim against this nation." Nevertheless, on April 12, 1921, Mr. Lodge laid on the desk of each of his fellow-Senators a document containing the names of some one hundred and twenty-three oil companies associated with the Royal Dutch-Shell interests, and asserted that these interests were British governmental interests, and exclaimed, "It would be a very serious matter if we were cut off by the governmental competition of other nations from an increasing oil supply." He added, "England is taking possession of the oil supply of the world." This idea and the document maintaining it came from Mr. Secretary Fall. Britain, as a nation, as a government, was seen flinging the Union Jacket over the oil lands of Colombia. Against it we hurled the Stars and Stripes in a gesture which previously a majority of the Senate had declared to be striking the flag to blackmail. We voted $25,000,000 of apology to Colombia for Theodore Roosevelt's "taking" of Panama; and in the succeeding months of the year 1921 the Petroleum Company, Ltd., an American "Standard" company, acquired large exploratory rights in Colombian territory. . . . The British Government in fact does not own the Royal Dutch-Shell Company. The British Government has no investment in it. The only known and proved oil investment of the British Government is in the Anglo-Persian Oil Company. In that company the British Government has an interest without having a control. The idea that the British Government owns and controls the British world adventures in oil is pure myth.

So is the idea that these adventures have given Britain "the oil supply of the world." Last week the Standard Oil Company of California was here in Washington testifying before Senator La Follette. It had spent several weeks accumulating data which it brought to Washington in a trunk of admirable size. It felt lost when Senator La Follette was content with investigating it for the space of just one day. It had looked forward to being investigated to the bottom of the trunk and had packed the trunk with some wonderful proofs of its virtues. It felt frustrated. Finding it in that state of mind, I addressed to it a few companionable, reviving questions on British oil diplomacy. I got the sort of answer which on that point I usually—not always, but usually—get from American oil men of genuinely broad experience. The Standard Oil Company of California is doing explorations for oil in Colombia, in Ecuador, in the Argentine, and in various other places. It encounters no British monopoly. It is not crushed by British intrigue. It does not get ousted from anywhere by the British Foreign Office. It is putting many millions of its silver dollars into holes in foreign territory, and it gets all the chances it can use for drilling those holes and for dropping those dollars into them.

The ultimate proof of the ridiculousness of the idea of any attempted British world oil monopoly is in Persia. If any non-British country might well be regarded as a British oil preserve, it is Persia, where Mr. W. K. D. Arcy, a Briton, got a concession for the Anglo-Persian Oil Company more than twenty years ago, and where the British Government on behalf of an oil supply for its naval ships has become a shareholder in that company to the extent of £4,250,000, and where—finally—the passion of Mr. Winston Churchill for marching up hills and down again put temporarily a thin red line of occupying heroic—or at any rate fatigued—Tommies. Yet in Persia itself the Standard Oil Company of New Jersey and the Sinclair Consolidated Oil Corporation are reported by the British press to be vigorously pushing the oil door open for American entrance.

A line is to be drawn between the sort of thing that we did in the Colombian treaty and the sort of thing that we are doing to back our oil companies in Persia, in Mesopotamia, in Palestine, in the Dutch East Indies, and elsewhere. In the Colombian treaty we put American public governmental money into the international private scramble for oil lands. Elsewhere we are simply trying to see to it that by our governmental influence our oil adventurers shall suffer no artificial disadvantages in their adventuring.

In the Dutch East Indies we have failed. The beautiful Djambi fields were committed to a company which the Dutch Government liked but which was "assisted" by no American oil company, although two American oil companies were palpitating with the emotion of "assistance." In the case of the Dutch East Indies we were handicapped by the case of the Philippines. We do not grant equality of opportunity to foreigners on public lands in the Philippines. The Dutch were stolidly unmoved by our rhetoric regarding the charms of equality of opportunity in the Dutch East Indies.

In Mesopotamia, in Palestine, in all other "mandated" territories, our diplomacy has been on a firmer argumentative ground and has achieved a high degree of actual success. We helped to defeat Germany and therefore helped to hand over the ex-German "mandated" territories in Asia and in Africa to the British and the French. They point out to us that we do not now help them carry the cost of shooting Arabs and others who object to being "mandated." They nevertheless, in spite of our drawing back from a comradeship in the expense of "mandated" military campaigns, profess themselves completely willing now to admit us to a comradeship in the exploitation of "mandated" natural resources. Mr. Hughes has brought them firmly to that point; and—considering the great natural difficulty after all of persuading people who have to do all of the shooting of the natives that they ought to share the shooting of the oil wells —he would seem to deserve credit.

It is an achievement which is not without its bearing upon the negotiations at Lausanne. If our Mr. Child at Lausanne seems sometimes to be quite severe toward the Turks, he doubtless is moved by the esteem which I often have noticed in him for missionaries, but he doubtless also—if he is in touch with the State Department at Washington—is not unmindful of the fact that with the

British established in the Mosul district we now are certain of the open door, whereas with the Turks established there we could not be certain of it. The lion and the eagle are at peace in the regions where the Hebrew prophet saw them in his vision. All that remains now to do is to find the oil and get it out—which has not yet at all been done.

With no oil coming from Palestine and Mesopotamia and with only a greatly reduced amount of oil coming from Russia, the importance of Mexico remains undiminished and even enhanced. Because of Mexican oil we violate the principle announced over and over again by the founders of this Republic, to the effect that it is and ought to be our policy to recognize all *de facto* governments. The State Department is accordingly suspected of being in a sinister sense under the influence of an "oil lobby." My best endeavors reveal no such influence there in that sense. The State Department—so far as I can see —is influenced in the first place by the currently accepted notion that just as every American citizen is nowadays under a moral obligation to reform the habits of every other American citizen, so the American nation is under a moral obligation to reform the habits of all other nations and peoples. Mr. Hughes is just as much under the influence of this notion as the mass of the rest of us. We reformed the Pueblos to within an inch of their lives, and unless the Mexicans continue to have enough military strength to make it difficult for us we shall reform them similarly. In the second place our State Department—without consulting any oil lobby whatsoever—knows that for our ships at sea as well as for our vehicles on land we need increasingly more oil than we seem likely to be able to produce out of our own soil. Patriotically, therefore, Mr. Hughes insists that there shall be no shadow of doubt that a recognized Mexican Government will give American oil companies an assured exercise of their acquired rights in Mexican soil. Meanwhile, in order to use up our local supplies of oil as rapidly as possible, we have broken into all our naval-oil public-land reserves in California and in Wyoming. Mr. Fall, who was so eager in 1921 to use American governmental resources to assist American private capital in Colombia, was equally eager in 1922 to use American governmental resources to assist American private capital to produce oil for the American market out of the Teapot Dome naval oil reserve in Wyoming. Senator Walsh, who has no superior in the Senate as a legal analyzer of principles and of facts, will presently take Mr. Fall in hand and will then proceed to analyze three things. One: The negotiations between Mr. Fall and Mr. Sinclair for the leasing of Teapot Dome to Mr. Sinclair were secret and gave Mr. Sinclair's competitors no opportunity to compete. Two: There was no geological necessity for exploiting the whole of the Teapot Dome at present. Three: Mr. Sinclair's competitors profess to be scandalized by Mr. Sinclair's prospective profits and they support their professions by many calculations which they are eager to paint on the sky. It will be Washington's *cause célèbre* in this quadrennium.

It is oil.

Oil also—ultimately—is the opening of Russia. Oil men in New York, on behalf of a company bearing the name of Standard, have invested in the securities of Russian oil companies of the old regime and may seem to be gambling on a return of the old regime. Oil men in San Francisco, however, on behalf of a company also bearing the name of Standard, have invested in the Vanderlip Russian oil concession, which is a concession from the new Bolshevik regime.

Sinclair interests have likewise invested in a concession from the new Bolshevik regime—in the island of Sakhalin. The Barnsdall Oil Corporation also has invested in a Bolshevik oil concession—in the Baku district—and is on its way physically to working it. A gentleman intimately known to Mr. Hoover—it is thought not by Mr. Hoover's suggestion or counsel—has undertaken to supply a large amount of oil machinery to the Russian Government for use in the Baku district. If Mr. Hughes could be controlled by the pressures of "lobbies," he long ago would have recognized the Soviet Republic. The commercial pressure toward the Soviet Republic at Washington is stronger than the commercial pressure against it. The pressure against it is very largely legal, moral, sentimental, social. In time this resisting negative pressure is certain to be overcome. In overcoming it the chief influence is not Senator Borah or Senator Johnson. It is oil, oil, the need of oil.

THE TALE OF THE TEAPOT (1923)

William Hard

Now that the first senatorial hearings on the Teapot Dome Naval Oil Reserve affair have been completed, and now that all the star witnesses have shed their full if not their final rays upon the subject, it becomes possible for the first time to tell in assured detail and in coherent sequence the total story of the policy and behavior of the United States Government in the management of its naval oil estate, called the Teapot Dome, in Wyoming.

The first character in the story is President Roosevelt. He gave support and prestige to the policy of the conservation of oil in the ground for the use of the government at some future time when the customary commercial supplies of oil might be insufficient and when some great impending national emergency might demand a governmentally reserved and controlled abundant source of fuel for our fighting ships.

The second character in the story is President Wilson. Out of the Federal public domain in Wyoming he set aside for exclusively naval purposes a reserve called commonly the Teapot Dome and called technically Naval Oil Reserve Number Three.

The third character is Secretary of the Navy Josephus Daniels. He stood resolutely on the rights of the United States Government in Naval Oil Reserve Number Three and also in all of our other naval oil reserves, totaling five; and he refused to budge from those rights, when attacked by private citizens urging private claims upon naval oil-reserve lands. Under him the policy of the Navy Department was to resist private claims by every possible resource of administrative action in the government departments and by every possible resource of legal defense in the courts. Under him, at one time, when a certain other member of the Cabinet proposed to make a surrender of naval oil land to a private claimant without a fight, President Wilson told that other Cabinet member that any such behavior on his part would mean his resignation.

The stage thus having been set and the preliminary dialogue having thus been delivered, the fourth and final great character of the play was ready to make his entrance. This character is Albert B. Fall. Mr. Fall, as a Senator of the United States, had evidenced a great interest in conservation. His interest in it was that he disapproved of it. It was his view that the public domain of the United States should go as rapidly as possible into private hands.

Mr. Fall's first feat as Secretary of the Interior was to provide the State Department and the chairman of the Foreign Relations Committee of the United States Senate with the oil-exploitation motives and arguments which led to the ratification of our $25,000,000 treaty with Colombia. Mr. Fall, as a Senator of the United States, had taken the position that the United States owed nothing to Colombia for any alleged violation of the national rights of Colombia in the matter of the setting up of the Republic of Panama in the days of President Roosevelt. Mr. Fall, as a Senator of the United States, had sided with the memory of Theodore Roosevelt against the claim of Colombia. As Secretary of the Interior, however, he perceived before him a divided duty. On the one hand there was the memory of Theodore Roosevelt which he had defended. On the other hand there was the opportunity on behalf of American oil interests to get from Colombia a new and open era of oil concessions. Mr. Fall chose oil.

He sent to the United States Senate a document in which the oil holdings of British oil companies in Colombia were listed; and in this document it was erroneously alleged that these holdings were holdings of the British Government; and on that argument, and in the openly admitted hope that for $25,000,000 out of the public treasury of the United States the Colombian Government would give oil concessions to the oil companies of the United States, the Colombia Treaty was passed.

Having thus demonstrated his willingness, at any cost to what he had once regarded as national honor, to secure oil concessions for oil companies, Mr. Fall was then picked out by Secretary of the Navy Denby to be made the managing master of the navy's oil reserves with this country. Known to be an anti-conservationist, and known to have been willing to take $25,000,000 out of the United States treasury to buy an entrance for American oil companies into the public domain of Colombia, he was made the supervisor of the navy's public domain in the United States.

This honor, however, was not heaped upon him by its own spontaneous gravitation toward him. He sought it. He wrote the order transferring the control of the naval oil reserves from the Navy Department to the Department of the Interior. He composed a letter for the Secretary of the Navy to sign, transmitting that order to the President to be signed.

Admiral Griffin, chief of the Navy Department's Bureau of Engineering, in charge of the naval oil reserves, objected to the transfer. Commander Stewart, in immediate management of the reserves, objected. No naval officer technically familiar with the naval oil-reserve situation is reported to have concurred in the transfer. Nevertheless Mr. Denby, choosing between the proved advice of his technically experienced officers and the proved passion of Mr. Fall for getting public lands into private hands, transmitted the order for the transfer on Mr. Fall's behalf to President Harding, who signed it on May 3, 1921.

Approximately one year later, on April 7, 1922, Mr. Fall leased the Teapot Dome Naval Oil Reserve to Mr. Harry Sinclair. For two weeks thereafter he made no announcement of his action. He then announced it only in reply to an urgent communication to him from Senator Kendrick of Wyoming who had heard rumors of such an action and who wished to know if those rumors were correct.

Mr. Fall, admitting that they were correct, lifted for the first time the curtain of secrecy behind which his action had been consummated. It then simultaneously appeared that the lease, besides being secret, had been non-competitive. No bids by others than Mr. Sinclair were disclosed. *Mr. Sinclair, by himself, and in the dark, on his merits as oil man, as campaign contributor, as friend, and as hospitable owner of a private car suitable for personal conferences, had become the sudden owner of the total right to drill oil wells over the whole of the Teapot Dome.*

Then, after the event, came the setting forward of the alleged reason for it. This reason was, and is, that oil is said to be leaking out of the Teapot Dome Naval Oil Reserve into wells located on other federally owned public land just outside the Reserve. The Department of the Interior had granted the permits for the drilling of those wells. It itself had permitted and procured the activities responsible for the draining of oil out of the navy's reserved oil supply. It itself had authorized this indirect and partial loss of that supply. Its contention thereupon was, and is, that the loss should become direct and total.

Geological testimony adduced before the Public Lands Committee of the Senate in the course of its Teapot Dome hearings has been strongly to the effect that straight across the Teapot Dome there is a "fault" which protects a certain considerable part of it from leakage. The leakage from the remaining part of it was alleged by geological testimony to be likely to be perhaps not more than 25 per cent. It was convincingly demonstrated that there was a strong technical possibility that if the total oil content of the Teapot Dome is 25,000,000 barrels, then not more than 4,000,000 barrels of it was in danger of flowing away into the private wells on the adjoining public domain.

It now appears that from the wells which on adjacent public domain are draining oil out of the Teapot Dome the government gets royalties averaging from 25 to 50 per cent of the flow, whereas from the wells which Mr. Sinclair has sunk in the Teapot Dome itself the government is getting royalties averaging less than 20 per cent. From the standpoint of income in oil for the government it thus appears that the government was better off when the oil was coming to the surface in the wells which were called a "menace" to the Teapot Dome than it is now when the oil is coming to the surface within the Teapot Dome in Mr. Sinclair's wells.

It further appears that perhaps two-thirds of the oil which Mr. Sinclair will pay to the government in royalties will not remain in the possession of the navy in the form of oil. Perhaps two-thirds of it will be paid back to Mr. Sinclair by the navy for some tanks in which to keep the remaining one-third of it.

It has been customary for the Navy Department, when it feels in need of tanks or of guns or of battleships or of money with which to pay its employees, to ask Congress for it. It has also been customary to believe that when the people of the United States gave the Navy Department a lot of oil in the ground of the public domain, it gave it to the Navy Department to be a supply of oil and not to be a means by which it could purchase other supplies without going to Congress for authorization.

Under Mr. Fall's influence, however, the Navy Department proceeded to sign contracts for the building not only of tanks but also of docks and of channels leading to the docks on the basis of paying for these things with oil out of naval oil reserves. Thus not only was this oil taken out of the ground, where President Roosevelt had wished it to be left, but, having been taken out, a large part of it was spent, or will be spent, in acquiring things other than oil and in escaping the customary legalistic squeamish necessity of going to Congress for the people's consent to naval expenditures.

If in the Teapot Dome there were originally 25,000,000 barrels of oil, and if Mr. Sinclair now gets all of it out, the government, at the present running rate of royalties, will get—at the most—5,000,000 barrels. Of this 5,000,000 barrels, at the present running cost of materials, it will pay back to Mr. Sinclair some 3,333,000 barrels for tanks. It then in those tanks will have the residuum of its Teapot Dome inheritance—namely, some 1,666,000 barrels of oil out of an original total of 25,000,000; and it will have it not in the ground, where it would be totally safe to be used at some future time in the forms which that future time with new technical developments might unfold and require, but in metal containers in seashore positions and in manufactured forms and qualities which the technique of this passing and changing moment has fixed.

Either this result is an absurdity or else President Roosevelt, with his policy of naval oil conservation, was an idiot.

Theodore Roosevelt, Jr., Assistant Secretary of the Navy, did not make the decisions which have brought his father's naval oil policy to frustration, nor did he have knowledge of them while they were being made.

The Roosevelt naval oil conservation policy is dead, and the final stab given to it was by the same man who stabbed the Roosevelt justification of the Roosevelt Panama policy to the heart in the Colombian Treaty.

Senator Walsh of Montana, a member of the Senate's Public Lands Committee, a man of the deepest learning, a man of the highest personal probity, a man who morally is not capable of deception and who mentally is not capable of self-deception, has taken the leading part in the toilsome task of eliciting the pivotal facts from the chaos of the bewildering situation presented in testimony to the committee; and he has seemed to be moved toward entertaining the belief that possibly the contract leasing the Teapot Dome to Mr. Sinclair is illegal in that there was no competitive bidding for it and in that it includes provisions for the purchase of naval supplies—namely, tanks—not with money from Congress but with oil which already was naval property and which was not negotiable.

Meanwhile, however, Mr. Sinclair has long been at work drilling the Teapot Dome and draining oil from it; and Mr. Fall, having retired from office, has entered the employ of Mr. Sinclair and has visited Russia to induce the Russian Government to allow Mr. Sinclair to drain oil from the Russian public domain in Sakhalin.

Thus Mr. Fall departs from the story, carrying with him his well-known fear of a British world-wide monopoly in oil and having done something to exhaust our government's reserved supply of oil in its own country and having done nothing to acquire for it any other reserved supply; and if ever this country comes to be without oil while in Latin America north or south of Panama there still are undrained reservoirs of it, the ultimate chapter of our abandonment of our naval oil conservation policy will be written.

It will be written in intrigues and aggressions, diplomatic or military or both, to acquire abroad the naval fuel security which was ours for the keeping at home.

THE NAVY'S OIL (1974)

George L. Baker

A FIERCE STRUGGLE, waged largely out of public sight, is taking place over the disposition of the nation's largest oil reserves. Improbably, the oil belongs not to Exxon, Shell or any other oil company but to the United States Navy. What, you ask, is the Navy doing with 24 million acres of California, Alaska and Wyoming land, containing nearly 35 billion barrels of oil (a figure equal to the nation's current recoverable reserves) and worth, at current prices, up to $350 billion?

Right now it is holding the oil for national defense purposes, according to Presidential directives which set the land aside in the years from 1912 to 1923. But a lot of people, including President Nixon, members of Congress and the oil companies, believe the Naval Petroleum Reserves (NPRs) should not be held solely for a national emergency as yet unforeseen. Rather, they say, the fields should be opened to private exploitation now.

Whether the land should be put in trust for another time, opened to exploitation or disposed of in some other manner are multibillion-dollar questions that deserve a better public airing than they have received. Congress has looked only superficially at one aspect of the reserves in a not untypically near-hysterical fashion. The Administration's bureaucracy is rolling along with the tide, tilting ever so gradually toward handing the reserves to the oil industry. And, except for *The Washington Post* and *St. Louis Post-Dispatch,* no prestigious newspaper has given the public much insight into the issues and amounts of money involved. The end of the oil embargo has for now dashed hopes that the reserves can be opened immediately, but there is still great pressure within Congress to turn the oil over to private oil companies.

For more than fifty years, the oil industry, regardless of the party in power, has used every available scheme, device and rationale to get its hands on the reserves. With the current oil shortage, its well-orchestrated efforts appear to be gaining ground. The wellhead of the current controversy is a proposal to tap one of the reserves for a year—Elk Hills near Bakersfield, Calif. With estimated reserves of 1.3 billion barrels, Elk Hills is the second largest oil field in the continental United States, trailing only the East Texas field. The Elk Hills scheme is intended to relieve, at least temporarily, the West Coast oil shortage by permitting production of 160,000 barrels a day, 58 million barrels in a year.

While Elk Hills is a huge field, it is almost a stripper well compared to the NPR in Alaska, dubbed Pet 4. It embraces 24 million largely unexplored acres and has reserves conservatively estimated at 33 billion barrels. Pet 4 lies on the Alaskan North Slope, just west of the major new oil discovery at Prudhoe Bay. Several companies, with the help of the Department of the Interior, have already encroached with wells onto the Navy's 2-mile buffer zone, thus siphoning oil that belongs to the reserve. So far the oil industry has expressed little interest in two other NPRs—Buena Vista Hills in California and Teapot Dome in Wyoming, after which the scandal was named—primarily because, according to the General Accounting Office and the Navy, much of the oil has already been drained by the kind of poaching going on at Pet 4.

Because of the NPRs' checkered political history, the plan to drill at Elk Hills has raised the eyebrows of a few Congressmen and Senators who recall how the reserves were handled in the days of Albert Fall and the Harding Administration. When the Nixon Administration presented the proposal to Congress last fall, with the concurrence of browbeaten Navy officials, it seemed reasonable, and the authorization measure easily slipped through the Senate and was shunted to the House. But there it has remained in the lair of the House Armed Services Committee, whose chairman, F. Edward Hébert (D., La.), is adamantly opposed to opening any of the reserves. As time went on, Rep. John E. Moss (D., Calif.), a self-styled guardian of the public trust, began asking more and more embarrassing questions. For instance, he asked, wouldn't the plan allow Standard Oil of California to reap what would appear to be enormous windfall profits? Standard owns 20 per cent of the oil within the reserve and as a consequence could extract oil that it otherwise would be unable to get under the unit plan contract by which the reserve is run with the Navy. If Standard were allowed to produce freely on its land, which is interspersed in a checkerboard pattern with the Navy's, that would force the Navy to produce as well (otherwise, its oil would be drained), and the reserve would be seriously depleted.

In normal times, Elk Hills is producing only at the rate needed to test, conserve and maintain the 1,000 wells already sunk. Tough as it sounds for Standard, the oil company has not suffered unduly. It has been allowed to extract $10 million worth of oil in return for signing the contract and enough additional oil to cover property taxes on the reserve land. Standard has not been pressed to pay its bills, and in all owes the government $24 million.

Moss asked this question: Since the contract specifies that the reserves can be opened only for national defense purposes, what is to prevent Standard from using the Navy, claiming that the reserve was opened in breach of contract; and then, if successful, freely producing on its land and ridding itself of the $24 million obligation? Officials of the Department of Navy and the Department of the Interior acknowledged publicly and before a Senate subcommittee that this could happen. The fact that Standard later said in a letter that it would not attempt to subvert the contract in this manner doesn't mean it couldn't be done.

Who would be the beneficiaries if Elk Hills were opened? Full production could supply 5.6 per cent of California's yearly consumption of oil products, hardly a solid contribution to meeting the oil shortage. That is assuming the oil, once produced, remains in California. Representatives of Standard could give

Congress no assurances that the oil would not be traded away to another oil company, exchanged, or even exported.

At the same time, Standard would gross $116 million, at current oil prices, from the sale alone of its share of the oil. And since it already has the contract to operate the reserve, it would receive most of the $64 million Congress has appropriated to gear up for full production. Moreover, even temporary production at Elk Hills might be the wedge the oil companies have been seeking to get control of all the reserve oil. The capacity of pipelines to carry oil off the reserve is only 90,000 barrels. New storage tanks and pipelines would have to be built and new wells drilled to protect the integrity of deeper pools for future use. With such an investment, Standard and its cohorts could press a vigorous claim that its investment and that of the United States are lying idle and wasted. If Elk Hills could be opened "temporarily" for one year, why not for two, five or ten years?

To Sen. Adlai Stevenson (D., Ill.), the scent of corruption is in the air: "History is repeating itself, except that the stakes could make the raid on Teapot Dome a petty misdemeanor by comparison," he told a Senate hearing. While the issue may be less clear-cut than that, it is obvious that the government has made it as easy as possible for the oil industry giants to reap special benefits from the oil already taken out of the NPRs. Consider:

¶In 1970 the Navy advertised for bidders to buy its share of the oil produced at Elk Hills. Having thrown out the bid of an independent refiner, the Pima Refining Co., it was left with two serious bidders, Shell and Standard. And by the strangest coincidence, Shell and Standard had submitted identical bids. Not concerned with the possibility of collusion, Navy flipped a coin and awarded the bid to Shell.

¶A year later, the Navy was seeking bidders on a five-year contract to operate the reserve. When sealed bids were opened in the fall of 1971, a consortium of petroleum engineers and oil well maintenance executives, called the Coastal Engineering Co., had underbid Standard. Yet, despite the recommendation of the Navy's Elk Hills staff, the bid went to Standard.

¶When Standard began drilling on a field adjacent to Elk Hills in 1967, it took the Navy four years to convince the Justice Department that it should bring the oil company into court. Justice lost in its attempt to have the field annexed to the reserve, as the amended unit contract permits, according to the Navy. The case is now on appeal, but in the meantime, Standard extracted most of the oil from the pool.

Elk Hills by itself is bad enough, but when it is viewed in concert with the subtle pecking at the fringes of Pet 4, one sees that an all-out attempt is being made to take what belongs to the government (i.e., the public) and give it to a handful of companies. If this prevails, the oil companies will have invested a nickel's worth of exploration and gotten a dollar's worth of oil in return. It would be akin to giving away or selling at a nominal price the Tennessee Valley Authority.

For a change why shouldn't the taxpayers recoup the benefits of the public domain? All too often public land—which these reserves were before they were withdrawn from settlement—has been turned over to the railroads, lumber companies, speculators, agricultural corporations and, yes, even oil companies. Lacking is a clear shape of what should be done, a national purpose. The House

Armed Services Committee noted this in a subcommittee report: "Tapping Elk Hills would contribute virtually nothing to the solution of the nation's basic energy problem. At best it would only be a temporizing palliative which could delay the pursuit of effective remedies by making them appear less urgent."

Navy, which by an act of Congress has ultimate authority over the reserves, has been well-intentioned but unable to hold back the various interests intent on getting at the NPRs. The deputy director of the reserves, Lt. Comdr. Kirby Brant, turned in his commission in early January, declaring he was tired of writing lies about the need to produce from the reserves. He remarked dryly to a reporter that somebody between "me and God wants the reserves opened up." Interior and Defense, he told the Senators, have combined to heist control of the reserves from the Navy. But while Interior is in open opposition to the Navy, the Defense Department "keeps its tracks hidden," Brant said. "In short there are two wolves in this particular sheepfold and one across the river [the Pentagon] wears sheep's clothing."

There is good reason for the Pentagon to play shy. One of the sheepherders is Under Secretary of Defense William D. Clements, Jr., who before he joined the Administration was chairman of the board of the Southeastern Drilling Co., a Dallas-based outfit that does work for major oil companies throughout the world.

Clements, who has refused to put his $102 million of SEDCO stock in trust and who retains a vested interest in the company's profit-sharing plan, took energy matters at the Pentagon into his own hands last fall by creating an energy policy council that reports directly to him. A few days later he wrote an internal memorandum, since uncovered by Moss's investigators, calling for a plan to permit oil companies to produce the reserves. Perhaps it was only coincidental, but one of the companies involved with several of the majors in developing the North Slope, and the one most likely to join them in developing Pet 4, is Clements' SEDCO. It all amounts to a clear-cut conflict of interest. Clements later told a Senate subcommittee that he had removed himself from direct involvement in energy matters. But Defense Secretary James Schlesinger said he would still be available to offer something called "technical advice."

The attitude of Interior's Bureau of Land Management is equally curious. In clear violation of a 1938 Act restricting the leasing of mineral rights on federal land adjoining the reserves, BLM has issued permits for wells to be drilled as close as 50 feet to the reserves' boundaries. Because the drilling has often hit pools which lay within the NPRs, the Navy has had to produce offset wells to protect its interest. No one knows how much oil has been taken because of this leasing policy that has gone on uninterrupted since 1954; but it is at least several million barrels. For instance, BLM ignored Navy protests and allowed operators to drain nearly a million barrels on the periphery of Teapot Dome. From 1958 until late last year, the Navy was forced to produce 3.7 million barrels that otherwise would have been captured by these exploiters.

More recently, Standard began pumping oil from a field next to Elk Hills. The pool was connected to the reserve, but Standard vigorously denied this for months. Before the Navy could get a court order to stop the pumping, Standard produced more than 1.5 million barrels from the 72-million-barrel pool. A Standard document, uncovered in the proceedings, showed that it ignored Navy requests to cease the drilling because it wanted to extract as much oil as possible before an issue was made of it.

BLM has continued its generous leasing policies at Pet 4. Again over the objections of the Navy, it permitted Alaska to select land ripe for oil development within a 2-mile buffer zone when the territory gained statehood in 1958. After selecting the land, the state naturally leased it to oil prospectors. Now the BLM is trying to rewrite the boundaries of the reserve so that potential oil-bearing land along the Coleville River lies outside Pet 4.

Understandably, the Navy has been outflanked: after all, if it has trouble mustering support for aircraft carriers or submarines, how much muscle can it exert to protect the reserves? At every turn in its struggle, it has been outgunned and it's not too hard to understand why—not many admirals contribute to Presidential campaigns.

Such isn't the case elsewhere. The list of oil industry contributions to Nixon's re-election, compiled by Rep. Les Aspin (D., Wis.), comes to $5.7 million—more than 10 per cent of all the money raised by CREEP.

For example, officers and directors of Standard plunked down the attention-getting sum of $165,000. Board Chairman Otto N. Miller (since retired) chipped in $50,000, and director David Packard, Clements' predecessor at Defense, contributed $87,000.

One of the most vociferous proponents of the scheme to tap Elk Hills has been the Pacific Gas & Electric Co., the monopolistic California utility. Board member Walter Haas weighed in with $48,447 and board Chairman Robert Geerdes gave $1,000.

The Shell Oil Co., which, under a 1970 contract, has the exclusive right to purchase all of Navy's share of Elk Hills production, is listed for a $24,500 contribution. The only other company besides Standard with facilities to transport oil off the Elk Hills Reserve is Atlantic Richfield, and its officers and directors contributed $62,518. One of those directors, Donald M. Kendall, head of Pepsi-Cola and personal friend of Nixon, gave $30,000.

SEDCO, the company that most likely would benefit from "industry participation" at Pet 4, was also generous. Its officers and directors contributed $68,225, including $26,000 by Clements himself.

While no one can draw a direct link between the contributions and Administration oil policies, it would be, as Aspin said, exceedingly difficult for the Administration to turn its back on an industry which supplied so much of its political war chest. "What emerges," said Moss, "is a cumulative attempt by several major oil companies to loot a government oil reserve with the connivance or incompetence of government authorities."

Why the panic to open the reserves? It makes good sense to leave some oil in the ground, in the event of a real national emergency. Perhaps the oil should not be in the entire province of the Navy, but the headlong rush to tap the reserves in an atmosphere of crisis does little to further the public interest. There is a great deal of undiscovered oil elsewhere and the oil companies ought to invest their own money to find it rather than ride piggyback on the government to take over the NPRs.

And one wonders, if the government is going to be in the business of selling oil (as it would be at Elk Hills), why shouldn't it take an even more active role? What would be wrong with eventually turning the reserves over to the Federal

Oil and Gas Corporation envisioned by Senator Stevenson and others? It would provide the base such a corporation needs to serve as both a yardstick and foil to the integrated oil companies whose earnings continue to pile up at record levels.

THE RUSH TO THE SEA (1975)

Ernest F. Hollings

JUST ABOUT A year ago, the United States pulled its head out of the sand far enough to open one eye. What we saw was the hazard in a domestic energy policy based upon an insecure source of high-priced fuel—the Middle East. If only we had dusted the sand from the other eye, we might have perceived other hazards right here at home, hazards associated with a do-nothing national energy policy shaped to confer special favors on Big Oil. The dangers of such a policy are now only too clear, with the nation running out of money, running out of oil, running out of clout and running out of time. . . .

Who would have supposed that the Arab countries could have thrown the United States into such a tailspin? In fact, they have not done it alone. The Arabs could never have succeeded without very substantial help from the folks in charge in Houston and Washington—the multinational major oil companies, with Secretary of the Interior Rogers C.B. Morton and Treasury Secretary William E. Simon following the time-honored tradition of giving the oil companies everything they want, and making the American people pay through the nose.

It's easy to point the finger at the OPEC nations as a scapegoat for our own domestic failures. But the Arabs are only using their economic wealth in a logical and powerful manner. It's the one weapon they have, and the multinational corporations which deal directly with them respect it. By contrast, our own so-called energy leaders have been pushovers for Big Oil. Rogers Morton hasn't kept secret his feelings about the oil companies. In August 1973, while briefing oil executives in the White House, Morton said: "Our mission is to serve you, not regulate you. We try to avoid it. I have tried to avoid regulation to the degree that I possibly can."

We can look not only at what the Administration says but at what it does. The closest thing we have to a national energy policy is a bag of tricks designed to preserve the vested interests of the energy industries. For example, Nixon, Ford and a succession of energy "czars" have given lip service to energy conservation, but as soon as the Arab oil embargo ended they took care to avoid using the tools which could make conservation work. We're supposed to reduce oil imports by a million barrels a day, but without a gas tax, without rationing, and without mandatory fuel economy standards for new cars.

We're supposed to fight inflation with WIN buttons, and we're reminded that fuel costs are the single largest factor in rising prices. But we're also supposed to sit back while the Administration works to de-regulate the price of natural gas, an act which by itself would add as much as $10 billion annually to inflation and the nation's energy bill, mostly in windfall profits for the oil companies. We're supposed to balance our need for energy with our desire to protect the environment, and this energy/environment balance is supposed to be achieved preeminently in the new proposals to tap the nation's greatest single energy treasure: the outer continental shelf. That energy boondoggle demands the closest scrutiny of all, because it is the best present example of the determination of the Department of the Interior (with apparent White House blessings) to give away public resources.

The outer continental shelf and its storehouse of resources have been a subject of legal controversy for many years. After much bickering between the states and the federal government, President Truman issued in 1945 a proclamation declaring that the United States regarded as federal property all the "resources of the subsoil and seabed of the continental shelf." Congress modified this position in 1953 by passing the Submerged Lands Act, which granted to the states jurisdiction over offshore lands out to the 3-mile limit. Congress then established federal control for everything beyond 3 miles through the Outer Continental Shelf Lands Act.

Today, government experts believe U.S. offshore undiscovered oil and natural gas liquids to be between 64 billion and 130 billion barrels and undiscovered offshore natural gas to be from 395 trillion to 700 trillion cubic feet. In terms of present domestic consumption, the riches of the outer continental shelf are truly beyond measure.

The Department of the Interior now proposes a mammoth increase in leasing these offshore lands to the multinational oil corporations in one of the biggest potential giveaways of all time—without environmental protection, without a fair return to the public for a publicly owned resource, without concern for the potential oil pollution to our beaches, without regard for the feelings of the coastal states, and without any requirement that the oil companies share with the government and the American people the information they have about these resources.

The Administration and the oil companies claim they must go pell-mell this year into the Gulf of Alaska, the Atlantic and the Pacific to increase domestic oil supplies. These are the areas we know the least about, and they are among the toughest of offshore areas to exploit—even tougher under some conditions than the stormy and turbulent North Sea. And the sites chosen by Interior also lie off some of the most heavily used beaches in the United States: for example, Southern California; Long Island, N.Y.; Rehoboth Beach, Del.

The Interior Department grudgingly admitted in November discussions with coastal state Governors that the 10-million-acre leasing program targeted for 1975 just might not be attainable. But Interior dismissed the oil industry's own admission that it couldn't handle that much because it doesn't have the drilling rigs or the men to work them. The industry also lacks the capital to bid on 10 million acres at the prices these leases have been bringing lately. But there remained the big question of whether Interior would take whatever the companies offered—even if the price per acre were substantially below previous bids.

It is now obvious that the U.S. Geological Survey, which regulates the oil companies on the tracts after they are sold, also could not supervise an additional 10 million acres. The safety inspections and the oil spill prevention regulations may have tightened up since the disastrous Santa Barbara blowout of 1969, but recent reports by the National Academy of Engineering and the General Accounting Office indicate that the Geological Survey still has a long way to go before it can assure the American people that offshore oil operations are using the best available technology and the best safety practices. (During the second session of the 93rd Congress, the Interior Department lobbied long and hard to defeat a bill, S. 3221, imposing tough new standards for offshore oil development which passed the Senate anyway.)

The coastal states, which recognize that theirs is the responsibility to cope with the onshore consequences of federal leasing, aren't prepared to handle 10 million acres worth of offshore development. Texas has estimated that expanded federal leasing of that state's coast will cost state and local governments each year $62.1 million more to provide public services and facilities than the oil industry will pay to the economy in increased taxes and other revenues. A 1973 Louisiana study found that federal offshore oil had cost that state $38 million the preceding year.

Texas and Louisiana don't oppose offshore oil development, nor do many of the states bordering the so-called "frontier" leasing areas. But they do know that they will need to plan ahead in order to absorb these costs without sacrificing other values. All the coastal states are developing programs to manage their coastal zones under the Coastal Zone Management Act of 1972. Once they are completed and approved by the Secretary of Commerce, these programs will be the guiding force for all coastal development, including any development spurred by offshore oil. The federal leasing program will have to be consistent with the state plans. The Interior Department obviously doesn't wish to wait for the states to finish the coastal zone management programs; Mr. Morton says the nation's hunger for oil prohibits delay. Yet ironically, or perhaps knowingly, the Nixon Administration held up the funding of the Coastal Zone Management Act for a full year, causing that much delay and more in the states' efforts to get set.

If the Department can't sell 10 million acres, it will nevertheless hold six lease sales this year, including four in the "frontier" areas of the Atlantic off New Jersey and Delaware, the Gulf of Alaska, and off Southern California. Secretary Morton says we must have more wells offshore, despite the fact that already some 4,000-odd wells in the Gulf of Mexico are shut-in and nonproducing. Many of them could produce oil in paying quantities. The Department says the number of shut-in wells jumped in the last few years only because the Geological Survey changed its definition of shut-in wells. That explanation recalls the refinery situation a few years ago, when there was a lot of public concern about whether or not the oil refineries were doing all they could to turn out needed oil products. The American Petroleum Institute suddenly changed its definition of refinery capacity, and just as suddenly all the refineries were operating at 102 per cent of capacity! Apparently the rule of thumb is, when the definition doesn't fit the real situation, change the definition.

One of the major oil companies used to have a public relations advertising campaign consisting of a series of ads built around the phrase, "We'd like you to know. . . ." But the problem is, there's so much they *don't* want us to know, so much we *need* to know. And what we already know is enough to convince me that a successful energy policy for this country must begin by decoupling the oil interests from the policy makers. The companies apparently take their text from Lord Palmerston: "We have no permanent friends, we have no permanent enemies. We have only permanent interests." But the nation also has permanent interests.

The national interest in energy policy can best be determined by an Energy Policy Council, which would be set up in the White House under legislation which has passed the Senate no fewer than four times. Each time, lobbying by the oil companies and the Administration successfully blocked the bill in the House. This council would correlate all data that are necessary to an energy policy, and then oversee the implementation of a national strategy. . . . We should proclaim the oil of Teapot Dome and Elk Hills reserved for national defense needs, but state candidly that the present emergency warrants drilling in Naval Petroleum Reserve Number 4 in Alaska right now. That oil, along with oil in fields in the Gulf of Mexico, can be brought to the consumer a good two years earlier than anything along the Atlantic seaboard.

And finally, we should delay Atlantic and Pacific and Gulf of Alaska frontier area leasing as a matter of good business judgment. Before we lease those areas to oil companies, we should consider an experimental pilot project of government-sponsored exploratory drilling—perhaps in the Atlantic off New Jersey and in the areas off Southern California. Our government and our citizens deserve to know what we have before we lease it away to Big Oil. The oil companies are pleased by the prospect of acquiring so much leased land: buy low, sell high; postpone production and watch the price go higher. Stretch out the timetable for drilling, but send the available equipment overseas. Thus, the 10-million-acre leasing program is a fraud on the American public. It will produce no energy in the next few years when we need it. It will only divert our attention from the sources which have already been found and which could be developed immediately.

Clearly, the problems of offshore drilling and energy supply demand a national ocean policy. If we accept the predictions of the experts, the oceans, not the land, will provide the United States with the great bulk of its petroleum energy supply between now and the year 2000. As land reserves are slowly exhausted, the oceans' untapped oil and gas will help fire the world's economy. At the same time, the oceans' other resources, particularly the living resources, must be preserved. But today, with short-sighted leadership, the oceans of the world are a mammoth chessboard in our international game of détente. What happens today when a productive oil field is found beneath lucrative fishing grounds which could help feed the world's starving? What happens when drilling rigs must be built in the center of busy shipping lanes, or when pipelines carrying oil pass through an estuary vital to the life cycle of fish and shellfish? What if a prime piece of coastal land is the target of competing development plans by both refinery builders and recreational interests? Who plays traffic cop for all these interests? Who mediates the public interest and the special interest? The answer is nobody.

The oceans will make or break life on this planet. They are the ultimate life support system. And yet the United States is as blind as the rest of the world to the importance of the oceans. While we play a game of international cat and mouse in attempting to establish a new body of sea law at the United Nations, our own national interests are being ignored. The time has come to protect these interests by establishing a strong, independent ocean agency or department within the federal government. The need for such an agency has been widely recognized by ocean experts for many years. The National Oceanic and Atmospheric Administration (NOAA), now part of the Commerce Department, is the logical nucleus for the new entity.

The oceans show signs of growing weary under the burden of man's assaults. The Mediterranean is dying; the Black Sea is dead. And throughout the world, prolific fisheries no longer produce the tonnage they once did because of blatant overfishing by huge factory ships which sweep the seas like vacuum cleaners.

Outer continental shelf oil is an important crop, but it is a one-time crop. Our offshore oil must be harvested, but with care and concern about the future and about the world our children will inherit. Life was born in the ocean and evolved in the ocean. The ocean offers life and energy. Men of good will and wisdom now recognize that our future path leads to the ocean. The Age of Environment and the Age of Energy meet at the sea. They can live together, or they can end there. A reconciliation seems indicated.

OIL ON THE WATERS (1969)

Edward Cowan

THE ESCAPE OF oil from Union Oil's offshore well opposite Santa Barbara, Calif., and the subsequent chain of events, political and natural, should be read as an object lesson in humility. The leak, the difficulties in plugging it, and the quick dashing of hopes that the shoreline would be spared serious pollution, are all reminders that man has repeatedly and injuriously lost control of his own inventions, usually when he least expected to.

Fred J. Hartley, the aggressive marketing man who is president of Union Oil Company of California (record 1968 profits of $151.2 million on $1.9 billion of sales), argued that the eruption that produced the leak could not reasonably have been anticipated. Perhaps not. Nor could the loss of a hydrogen bomb over Spain. Nor the 1965 Northeast power failure. Nor the stranding two years ago of the supertanker *Torrey Canyon,* whose captain ran her onto a well-marked granite reef off England in broad daylight, causing the biggest shipwreck and oil pollution ever. Nor, just a year after that, the stranding and breakup of another Liberian flag tanker, the *Ocean Eagle,* at the entrance to San Juan harbor—hardly an uncharted shoal.

Surely no one could reasonably have expected in November, 1968, that an oil barge carrying more than 1 million gallons of heavy fuel oil would be torn loose from its tow by rough weather and grounded on Rehoboth Beach, Del., where Washingtonians soak up the summer sun. Or that, also last November, a Standard Oil of California hose would rupture and let 60,000 gallons of diesel oil pour into Humboldt Bay, not far from Eureka, Calif.

Who could reasonably be called on to anticipate that a 365-foot tanker would break in two in the Panama Canal in December, 1968, losing some of its cargo of fuel oil? Or that two days before Christmas, the little tanker *Mary A. Whalen* would run aground off Rockaway Point, N.Y., on the south shore of Long Island, hard by New York City's most heavily used stretch of beaches? Or that on Christmas Day Japanese authorities would have to close the Naruto Strait because of the danger to ships from gasoline that had escaped from a grounded tanker?

Who might reasonably be expected to warn the Coast Guard that quantities of what appeared to be heavy fuel oil would wash up onto the Rhode Island coast on Inauguration Day, 1969—but that there would be no clue to the ship or shore plant from which it escaped?

As any lawyer can quickly point out, there are differences in the origins of these several disasters which are worth defining if one is concerned about writing useful public policy. There are acts of God, such as violent storms; there is human error, such as putting a tanker on a known reef; there is the inevitable breakdown in any man-made mechanical system, such as the tendency of tankers with riveted sides (a construction technique largely discontinued about six years ago, according to one expert) to ooze oil around the rivets. That leakage may be only a barrel a day, but a barrel of crude oil, thick and persistent stuff, may be more than a drop in the ocean. In the Rehoboth Beach incident, the barge that was washed ashore lost, from a pipe that broke, a quantity of oil described by Interior Department officials as "very small," somewhere from 5 to 30 barrels. That "very small" dose of heavy oil, according to the officials, "marked" 2 to 3 miles of beach and caused substantial pollution to about three blocks of beach front.

Looking back over the two years since the *Torrey Canyon* disaster alerted the public and governments to the dangers inherent in the transportation of vast quantities of crude oil, it is startling to observe how many pollution incidents and near misses there have been; the list just recited is far from exhaustive.

It was instructive, for example, to learn from a trade publication this winter of two tanker casualties off southern Africa in the spring of 1968. On April 29, about 3 miles off the Cape of Good Hope, the *Esso Essen* struck an underwater obstruction and cut herself open at three points. She lost about 30,000 barrels of Arabian heavy crude oil. ESSO said it applied its new dispersant, Corexit, "with great success." In the other reported casualty, the tanker *Andron,* whose owner is listed as a Greek company, split a seam in heavy seas. After discharging her cargo of Kuwait crude, she underwent temporary repairs at Durban, reloaded the oil, resumed her voyage for Venice, and sank about 10 miles off Southwest Africa. Exactly what happened to her cargo of about 16,000 tons (117,000 barrels) is not fully known but there are only two possibilities: immediate or gradual pollution of the sea.

In short, with the world's consumption of petroleum products—in homes, factories, office buildings, schools, chemical plants, aircraft, ships, motor vehicles and electric generating stations—increasing by 7.5 per cent a year (it is now seven times what it was in 1938), the waterborne shipment of oil has become an industry in itself. Twenty-five years ago, the *T-2,* workhorse tanker of World War II, carried about 16,000 tons. By the early 1960s, Japanese shipyards, emerging as the world's busiest, were building ships to carry more than 100,000 tons and were "stretching" smaller ships. The *Torrey Canyon,* for example, built at Newport News, Va., to carry 67,000 tons, was jumboized in Japan to carry 118,000 tons. By keeping her original power plant and propulsion system, the most expensive part of a tanker, the *Torrey Canyon,* at only a slight sacrifice of speed, nearly doubled her delivery capacity. The saving worked out to roughly a penny a barrel. Show any international oil company how to add a penny a barrel to profits and it can make you very rich by cutting you in for only a few daubs of the extra icing.

The same economic logic lifted tanker size to 312,000 tons by 1968 with the launching of the *Universe Ireland,* first of six such ships to be operated by Gulf. Last November the Japanese yard that built her, Ishikawajima-Harima Heavy Industries Co., got an order for a 370,000-tonner, to cost between $22 million and $25 million. Disputing some industry experts, the buyer, Tokyo Tanker Co., said it thought that economies of scale would persist as capacity approached 500,000 tons.

The 370,000-ton tanker will carry three times as much oil as did the *Torrey Canyon.* The 50,000 tons or more of oil that she spilled contaminated 140 miles of English coast and a considerable stretch of Brittany's northern shore, 110 miles from the wreck.

Could a *Torrey Canyon* disaster occur again? Like today's new supertankers, she was well made and equipped with modern navigational aids. She stranded solely as the result of her captain's bad seamanship—an "aberration," one expert mariner called the performance. If it seemed too incredible to happen more than once in a lifetime, one had only to wait a year for the captain of the *Ocean Eagle,* which split in two, to fracture her bottom on the ocean floor in front of San Juan harbor.

Britain's aerial bombing of the *Torrey Canyon* (an attempt, successful said Whitehall, to burn the oil remaining in her tanks) and the struggle by troops and civilians to remove inches of oil from beaches and harbors attracted hundreds of newsmen. Overnight, governments, editors and the public discovered how much oil a single ship can carry; how persistent, noxious and, for waterfowl, lethal, crude oil can be; how emotional can be the argument about how to clean it up, with tourism-minded merchants advocating chemicals for a quick, thorough wash, and fishermen and naturalists preferring mechanical methods; how unprepared, in law and in practical arrangements, national states are to cope with, much less put an end to, oil pollution.

In the United States, the *Torrey Canyon* episode and unrelated instances of pollution to the New Jersey and Cape Cod shores a few weeks later dramatized not only the enormity of the (infrequent) major disaster but the fact that coastal oil pollution is an everyday problem. Despite efforts of the big tanker fleets to dispose of their residues innocuously, there is a lot of clandestine bilge washing by countless freighters, trawlers and tankers.

These events fired up a mood of reform in Washington. President Johnson directed the Secretaries of Transportation and Interior to make a study of oil pollution and recommend legislation. A number of Congressmen—and lobbyists—began to gird themselves for another round in the continuing conflict between public and private interest. In London, meanwhile, an emergency session of the Inter-Governmental Maritime Consultative Organization (IMCO), a UN body, had been convened at Britain's request. It began deliberations on two conventions to supplement existing international law. One would establish the right of a state to take action against a foreign-owned ship lying offshore, but in international waters, to protect the state's coast from pollution. (Britain, despite the readiness of the Royal Navy to try to fire the leaking *Torrey Canyon* immediately, stood aside for ten days of fruitless salvage attempts, in part because there was no legal authority or precedent for destroying someone else's property on the high seas.) The other convention would establish liability of ship owners for pollution damage. With uncommon dispatch, IMCO also adopted a package of recommendations to national states on technical safety matters and on tougher enforcement of anti-pollution law.

Another aspect of the tanker business that was illuminated by the *Torrey Canyon* and *Ocean Eagle* casualties is the role of the Republic of Liberia as the world's leading country in registered merchant marine tonnage. In 1947, because of difficulties with Panamanian consuls who, owners said, sought to collect "fees" every time a Panamanian-flag ship cleared their ports, United States shipping interests were looking for a new flag of convenience (or flag of necessity, depending on how one chooses to approach the wage and tax argument). That need coincided with the engagement of the late Edward R. Stettinius, Jr., to assist Liberia's economic development. The result was the drafting by three Wall Street law firms of legislation, duly enacted in Monrovia, that put Liberia in the business of registering ships.

In the ensuing twenty years, Liberia has taken great pains to rebut trade union accusations that hers is a "run-away flag," flown by unsafe, leaky old tubs whose crews are virtually galley slaves and incompetent, too. Without getting into that argument, it can be said that the jumbo tankers which today fly the Liberian flag are well-made vessels. The African state has what seem to be exacting regulations governing seaworthiness, loading and safety equipment. It issues officers' papers either reciprocally or after an applicant passes examinations which Liberia says are tougher than those of other countries. Liberia, says Albert J. Rudick, an American lawyer who is employed full time in New York with a staff of forty as Liberian Deputy Commissioner of Maritime Affairs, tries to make a ship owner's responsibilities commensurate with the benefits (no corporate income tax) of the Liberian flag.

Nevertheless, the Liberian maritime program remains very much as it was conceived—an affair for the benefit of American ship owners and quietly managed by them and their lawyers who decide, without "benefit" of public scrutiny or debate, how to balance private and public interest. (Mr. Rudick argued that there is meaningful debate in Liberia's Congress but he was unable to name the relevant committees or their chairmen.)

When the *Torrey Canyon*'s board of investigation met, it had no rules of procedure to follow. Its mandate was a regulation for inquiries which stresses the possible negligence of the crew and thereby underplays the possible role in a casualty of the ship's mechanical condition or of acts or omissions by its owners. . . .

The overriding issue posed by the *Torrey Canyon* disaster, the *Ocean Eagle* episode, the eruption of the well opposite Santa Barbara, and lesser instances of pollution is that of responsibility. Shall a tanker, drilling rig, shore installation (e.g., refinery, trans-shipment terminal, depot, etc.) or other oil facility be responsible for damage done by its oil? Shall it be responsible absolutely, that is, regardless of whether or not it is at fault, or only if negligent? And if liable shall it pay the full damages, or only up to a limited amount?

The questions are being debated in London at IMCO meetings of legal experts and in Washington in hearings before the subcommittee on air and water pollution of the Senate Public Works Committee. One of the conventions that IMCO experts hope will be completed at Brussels next November would deal with the liability of tankers for oil damage. . . .

The United States has proposed two to four times the 1957 liability convention limit of $67 a gross registered ton, with a maximum of $5 million. (Washington has never signed that convention.) The International Maritime Committee, a small, little-known, powerful Antwerp-based network of lawyers, which has drafted several important maritime conventions, is expected to press for its 1957 formula or not much more. . . . The issue may be argued as one of how much damage can be reasonably expected, with cleanup costs from various spills offered in evidence. At bottom, it is a matter of tanker owners and operators trying to minimize their extra insurance costs. Washington estimates the convention may add 10 per cent to a tanker's normal insurance costs, or about 2 per cent to operating costs. A 2 per cent rise in operating costs in any business is not trivial.

The same question has arisen before the Senate subcommittee, which is considering legislation (S.7) sponsored by its chairman, Senator Muskie. It would, among other things, authorize the government to clean up oil spills in inland and territorial waters and require the tanker to pay the costs. The legislation proposes a limit of $450 a ton up to $15 million. Asserting that these levels would "amount to a denial of ship owners' right to limitation of liability," the Maritime Law Association of the United States, representing some 2,000 admiralty lawyers (who generally work for ship owners), urged the Congress to return to the $67 a ton and $5 million limits written in legislation passed by the Senate and weakened by the House Public Works Committee (where an oil man and a shipping man held sway) in 1968. The American Petroleum Institute proposed $100 a ton up to $10 million. Last year it proposed $250 a ton up to $8 million. It changed its mind, it said, to go along with the limits adopted by seven major oil companies which have established a voluntary cleanup plan (which will come into effect only if a lot more tanker owners adhere). An API tabulation showed that the most expensive cleanup on record—for the tanker *General Colocotronis* in the Bahamas a year ago—was $800,000. Conveniently, the API explicitly excluded the *Torrey Canyon,* whose cleanup expenses it put at $8 million (half the claims of Britain and France), because of "technological progress over the past two years and many of the mistakes made in the *Torrey Canyon* incident would not be repeated, and, of course, research on cleanup methods is continuing." Those few words hardly justify ignoring $7.2 million of an $8 million cleanup bill.

The Maritime Law Association, seeking to establish limitation as something close to divine right, argued that it "is rooted in the universally recognized principle that it is of paramount consideration for maritime nations to preserve the continuity of maritime commerce as a matter of vital national interest." The association, noting that Congress granted limitation in 1851 (the legislation has not been significantly altered since then), went on to cite an 1871 Supreme Court decision which recognized that the law's object was "to induce capitalists to invest" in ships. . . .

THE TRANS-ALASKA PIPELINE (1973)

Robert Sherrill

A LINE OF frontier terrain 92 feet wide and nearly 800 miles long stands between the United States and what could be its biggest ecological blunder. This strip of land is what the oil companies, eager to exploit the remote Alaskan oil fields, do *not* have and it is what the courts have ruled they must have (in addition to the 54 feet of right of way already under their control) if they are to build their pipeline from Prudhoe Bay, on the Arctic Ocean, to the port of Valdez, on the Gulf of Alaska. At peak production, 2 million barrels of oil would pass through the pipeline each day, to be picked up at Valdez by tankers and taken to market on the U.S. West Coast. (At least that's where the oil companies say they will market it, but there's reason to think they may be lying.)

The pipeline would be the largest private construction project ever undertaken, but well worth it to the companies which have already sunk $5 billion into their Alaskan ambitions; for the oil at the source of the line—the three enormous pools in the Prudhoe Bay area, an underground petroleum ocean as large as Massachusetts—is thought to be the largest such discovery on this continent. Conservative estimates put it at 10 billion barrels; moderately optimistic estimates increase that to 40 billion barrels. Even at the lowest estimate, it would be 25 per cent of the proved reserves of oil within the fifty states.

If one looked at it merely as a big bowl of energy sitting there ready to help feed an energy-hungry nation, there would be no reason to debate the method or route for bringing it out. But the geography of this oil is very special.

The pipeline would cross the entire state, north to south, and would roughly parallel the border between Alaska and Canada. By splitting Alaska according to the oil companies' plan, the pipeline would for all practical purposes stake out America's forty-ninth state as the private domain of the companies and would also be the first giant step toward destroying the last authentic wilderness available to those living under the U.S. flag. Only about a tenth of U.S. lands are still in a wilderness condition, and virtually all of this wilderness is in Alaska—more priceless in a sense than the oil itself; once it is gone, it will be gone forever, whereas the oil is only another form of expendable energy, which in any case must eventually be supplanted by nuclear or other fuels. Moreover, the wilderness is still in public hands, most of it owned by the federal government and the rest by the state of Alaska, and its future is still fortunately protectable by the pressures of public opinion. So the debate over how the oil should be handled is not a futile debate at all.

At the moment, the oil companies are being held at bay by an old, mildewed law, the Mineral Leasing Act of 1920, which the companies had assumed was defunct because they had successfully violated it many times in the past, and by the almost miraculously successful court battle waged by The Wilderness Society, Friends of the Earth and the Environmental Defense Fund.

If it had not been for these groups, the oilmen would have carried away Alaska four years ago. The cocky petroleum moguls were so certain that they had the whole deal sewed up that they bought $100 million worth of pipe from Japan (probably through barter for future oil delivery) and laid out the pipe along several portions of the chosen route—a bit of arrogance that is reportedly costing them $5 million a month just to fight the rust. They had good reason to be confident—the Nixon crowd was eager to turn over the oil-rich wilderness to them. But unfortunately for their plans, the great environmentalist movement of the 1960s had culminated in the National Environmental Policy Act of 1969, which requires the federal government to justify the exploitation of federal lands with an "environmental impact" statement showing that a project balances out on the side of public good. Court battles built around the NEP Act destroyed the oil companies' timetable. . . .

The discovery leases to the Prudhoe Bay oil fields were granted by Interior Secretary Stewart Udall in June 1964—well timed, if such was the intent, for a *quid pro quo* for oil company contributions to Lyndon Johnson's campaign that year. . . . The search for oil on the North Slope (the northern slope of the Brooks mountain range at the top of Alaska) had been going on without much luck for two decades, mostly conducted at taxpayers' expense by federal geologists. Despite this record, oilmen were certain that a rich field awaited the lucky driller. . . .

Atlantic Richfield and British Petroleum are the kingpins of the Prudhoe Bay adventure. In January 1967 the discovery well came in for ARCO. The previous year, ARCO had been created without a particle of trouble, even though a number of antitrust principles seem to have been violated in the merger of the Atlantic Refining Co., one of the largest distributors in the East, with Richfield Oil Co., one of the largest distributors on the West Coast. This merger, creating a company with combined assets of $1.4 billion, was the largest on record, and to say that it suppressed competition is putting it mildly—but the Justice Department did no more than grump a bit. Moreover, in 1969 Atlantic Richfield gobbled up Sinclair, worth $1.81 billion, and once again the Justice Department did nothing, except force Atlantic Richfield to divest itself of $400 million worth of Sinclair's retail distributorships—that is, ARCO had to sell most of Sinclair's 10,500 filling stations in the Midwest and the East. . . . And guess who bought the stations—British Petroleum, which by 1969 was ARCO's partner in the Alaskan venture.

One reason why ARCO had plenty of money to bid on the Alaskan leases was that the company had been receiving some striking favors from the Internal Revenue Service. From 1962 to 1968, ARCO earned a net income of $797 million but paid not one penny in income tax. . . .

As for British Petroleum, it parlayed its holdings in Alaska into fulfilling a long-time dream. For twelve years B.P. had wanted to penetrate the United States market, but it had consistently failed to find a crack to slip through. It was handicapped, for one thing, by British restrictions on taking much money out of the country. With its oil discovery in Alaska, however, B.P. was in a position to strike. By cleverly bartering oil from future production in Alaska, B.P. was able not only to swing the purchase of the Sinclair service stations from ARCO but also bought Standard Oil of Ohio (the first company founded in the Rockefeller oil empire), thus giving B.P. nearly 4 per cent of the U.S. market. . . .

The move also tightens the ties of the international oil giants. Standard of Ohio gives B.P. an excellent marketing and refining operation in this country; B.P. gives Sohio one of the world's great supplies of crude oil to draw on. Even without being able to tap its new Alaskan possessions B.P. regularly produces more crude oil than any other company. For years B.P. has been a major partner with U.S. oil firms in the exploitation of the Mideast and African fields and has accounted for its share of violence. . . .

In 1969, in a lease auction that brought Alaska nearly a billion dollars—$900,220,590 to be exact, which was nearly 50 per cent more than had ever been obtained via an oil lease auction before—four other companies joined the consortium: Mobil, Phillips, Union and Amerada Hess. These, along with the original three leaseholders (who controlled more than 80 per cent of the leased land), called themselves the Alyeska Pipeline Service Co.

Actually the big three (ARCO, B.P. and Humble) had preferred their old alliance, known as the Trans-Alaska Pipeline System (TAPS), for TAPS had no formal corporate structure at all and therefore was almost immune from government regulation. . . . But to let their allies in the Interior Department save face, they agreed to enter into the formal corporate arrangement with the other four companies under the Alyeska Pipeline Service Co. umbrella.

With only seven companies involved in the biggest pool of oil on the continent, and with only three companies dominating the pool, the concentration of ownership was obviously so intense that the staff of the Justice Department's antitrust division recommended that Alyeska be investigated to see if its control of the proposed pipeline violated federal laws. That was in 1971 and John Mitchell, who was still Attorney General at the time, overruled the recommendation for an investigation. His veto memo read in part: "In view of what's going on this is not the time." Among the things going on at that time was the gathering together of the largest political slush fund in history—with a major share of it coming from the oil companies. . . .

Before coming to Washington [as Nixon's Secretary of the Interior, Walter] Hickel was governor of Alaska, and he was so eager to help the oil companies open up the North Slope that he had built a highway from Fairbanks to the Arctic Ocean, a distance of about 400 miles, so that trucks could carry equipment to the drilling site. (Up to then, all equipment was flown in.) The highway was a budgetary, engineering and ecological disaster. It was supposed to cost $125,000 but ran to $1 million; it was so poorly constructed that after the first winter it resembled a drainage ditch more than a road, and was impassable. Ecologically, because of the destruction it caused to the tender frozen soil of that region, it was what one University of Alaska professor called . . . "the first violent change, the first major intrusion of the modern industrial world" into the last great wilderness in North America, and all the more shocking because "the great Range [Brooks Range] had been split and its unity with past ages destroyed—destroyed without a public decision, destroyed without the knowledge of most Americans."

Once in the Interior Department, the unrepentant Hickel was ready to try again to build roads or pipelines or anything else that the oil companies wanted. Only three days after the Interior Department published a scientist's warning that burying the 48-inch pipeline carrying oil at 140 degrees would create serious problems by thawing frozen ground along its route and causing the pipeline to buckle and rupture, Hickel met with oil company officials and assured them that such criticisms would not interfere and "the pipeline will be built." Publicly he conceded that he and oil officials had reached a "full understanding" that the Interior Department would not stand in their way. Pressure to build the pipeline was coming also from the Department of Commerce, where Maurice Stans was then Secretary. He, too, overruled environmental scientists in his department. Stans's pro-oil position paid off royally when he later became chief fund raiser for Nixon's 1972 campaign.

Even though then Under Secretary of the Interior Russell E. Train admitted that government officials did not know the answers to all the environmental problems raised by the proposed pipeline, he said, in October 1969, that he was recommending that Hickel go ahead and approve the construction permit. As Hickel later admitted in his book, *Who Owns America?,* the oil companies at that time had made no environmental safety plans at all and didn't care to make any. That didn't seem to bother either Hickel or Train. Later Nixon would make Train head of his Environmental Council, a responsibility that did not change Train's opinion that building the pipeline was a swell idea.

Other pressures to build the line came from Alaska officials, whose greed for money had become extravagant after they got the $900 million lease money in 1969. For a state whose entire budget came to only $154 million that same year, it was heady stuff, promising all sorts of delicious rake-offs and fringe benefits. And Alaska still controlled 800,000 acres which it could lease, pocketing 12.5 cents of every net dollar earned. As former Gov. Keith Miller shouted with joy on the evening of the great leasing, "Tomorrow we will reach out to claim our birthright! We will rendezvous with our dreams!" As far as most Alaska officials were concerned, the oil companies could come in and drill every square yard of the state. Right now. *Now!* Every day of delay was costing plenty in royalties. It was also costing the state in another way: the royalties would come from net profits, and the delay in building the pipeline had raised the probable cost of the line by several billion dollars. This would have to be paid off before Alaska got another penny.

As the cost of waiting mounted, Alaska politicians got a bit hysterical and began writing all sorts of laws—which the oil companies have challenged in court—to guarantee that they would get at least a few hundred million dollars income every year—a modest sum, argued Gov. William A. Egan, that would in no way "diminish the opportunity for industry to make huge, huge profits, a billion dollars a year." In a sensible but rather pathetic moment, Governor Egan warned Alaskans that "we must still be mindful that the primary obligation of the companies involved is to the stockholders and board rooms in New York, Los Angeles and Houston. The sheer size of the enterprise in Alaska demands effective public control or we will have an economic state, larger and more powerful than the political state which contains it." . . .

The political and corporate allies had begun to fight among themselves because the conservationists were making them nervous, even frightened. Despite the friendliest possible cooperation from the Nixon Administration, things were not going smoothly for Alyeska Pipeline. The oil consortium had supposed that it would get such quick approval from the Interior Department that it would be in operation by 1972, but the oilmen had reckoned without the opposition of environmentalist groups who filed a lawsuit in 1970 and stopped the project dead in its frozen tracks.

Would the Alyeska companies pollute their domain as hideously as had the oil explorers at Naval Petroleum Reserve No. 4, just to the east of Prudhoe Bay? —a pollution still marked a quarter century later by disintegrating Quonset dormitories, squalid recreation shacks, rusting bulldozers, broken mobile cranes and hundreds of rusting oil drums: a vast garbage dump, laced together by miles of ruts through the tundra that will never heal. . . . There was no reason to think Prudhoe Bay oilmen would act any differently, for, as one confessed to *New York Times* writer Steven Roberts, "We like to think we're socially responsible, but in the long run our aim is to make money." Would there be endless leaks from the pipe? Would the forty-one-ship tanker fleet planned by the Alyeska consortium spill so much oil into the waters between the port of Valdez and Puget Sound as to ruin the annual $58 million fishing industry?

Under the National Environmental Policy Act, the Interior Department is required to answer such questions. In April 1970, responding to the environmentalists' lawsuits, U.S. District Court Judge George L. Hart, Jr., issued an injunction stopping construction of the pipeline until Interior came up with some answers.

Thereupon Interior threw together an environmental impact statement that was only 200 pages long and so ridiculously superficial that, under a barrage of hoots and jeers and catcalls from press and Congress, it was withdrawn and Interior settled down to a different form of attack: overkill. On March 20, 1972, a new statement was launched, this one running to 3,500 pages.

No sooner was it off press than Judge Hart, exhausted and drained of juices by being squeezed in the industry versus environmentalist vise ("I'm dead tired," he announced), ruled that this satisfied him and lifted his two-year-old ban on construction. Rogers Morton, who had succeeded Hickel at Interior, also announced his complete satisfaction, and said that he would issue a permit for building the pipeline as soon as he legally could.

Again, environmentalists fought back. Why not, they asked, hold public hearings on the question? Because, said Morton, public hearings would only add a "circus" atmosphere to the decision-making. However, though a public hearing was banned, Morton did give the public forty-five days to read, digest and submit written replies to Interior's 3,500-page environmental impact statement. For anyone coming cold to the debate, that would have been too brief a time in which to prepare rebuttal (made all the more difficult by Interior's "running out," so they said, of the statement and not getting a new supply for a couple of weeks), but for The Wilderness Society, Friends of the Earth and Environmental Defense Fund—which had kept right on top of the situation all along —it was plenty of time. They pulled together a counter argument running to

1,300 pages. Their rebuttal contained no mincing tea-party complaints but was heavy with scientific assessments. . . .

It's doubtful that Morton and his Interior gang gave this rebuttal the slightest attention, however, for on May 11 (only four days after his deadline for the filing of rebuttals) Morton announced that he had made up his mind and would give a go-ahead to the pipeline as soon as the courts got off his back. He didn't try to rebut the rebuttal; he simply ignored it, and Stewart Brandborg, executive director of The Wilderness Society, was hardly out of line when he concluded that Morton's "invitation for comments was a mere charade."

Indeed, the charade had been proved long before the rebuttal was submitted; it was proved at the moment when the Interior Department's own impact statement was released, for that contained even stronger evidence against the proposed trans-Alaska pipeline. Everywhere in these six volumes are chilling warnings. The mixture goes something like this (direct quotes are from Interior's own documents):

Every year Alaska has more than 1,000 earthquakes; most of these are slight, but the pipeline would cross three faults where two dozen significant earthquakes have been recorded in this century. "Any point along the southern two-thirds of the proposed pipeline route could be subjected to an earthquake of magnitude greater than 7.0 on the Richter scale . . ." and in some areas earthquakes of up to 8.5 magnitude should be anticipated. (The Alaskan earthquake of 1964, which cost $500 million in damage and caused a tidal wave that wiped out the old town of Valdez, had a magnitude of 8.5. The energy released by that earthquake was twice as great as the San Francisco quake of 1906.)

Aside from quakes, much of the ground along the pipeline route is highly unstable. Landslides could be commonplace, and they would cause pipeline leaks and ruptures. "In the event of a pipeline rupture, 14,000 barrels of oil could leak out during the time required for pump station shutdown and valve closure. After shutdown and valve closure, up to an additional 50,000 barrels of oil could drain from the pipeline at some localities." With smaller leaks, as much as 750 barrels of oil could be lost every day without being detected.

Since the pipeline would cross 350 streams, there would be major water pollution. As for land pollution, Atlantic Richfield admits that a spill of 25,000 barrels—a moderate spill by Alyeska standards—would cover 6.6 acres in winter, in level country (ARCO gives no estimate for hilly country in the summertime, when oil would run farther and faster). "There are no methods to remove oil from terrestrial surfaces without some destruction of vegetation." Some of the plant life along the pipeline route is found in no other part of the world. It could be wiped out.

Many miles of the pipe would be laid underground. Ditches to receive the pipe would be 6 feet wide and 7 feet deep; while the ditches lay open, they would be a trap for moose, caribou and bear, and "it is doubtful that any of the hoofed mammals or bears could escape without assistance."

Between Deadhorse and the Yukon River, a road 361 miles long would be built parallel to the pipeline; it would be laid on a base of gravel between 3 and 5 feet thick—requiring the excavation of about 21 million cubic yards of gravel, much of which would be scooped out of river beds, with great harm to fish life. The entire pipeline project would require quarrying about 67.5 million cubic yards of material, and this wouldn't count the 16 million cubic yards needed for developing the oil field itself. Where this stuff is dug, massive bleeding sores—not scars—would be left in the tundra. Many of the quarries would have to remain open because from time to time maintenance material would be required.

Biologists are afraid of what the sulfur dioxide emissions from the pump stations would do to the lichens, which are the primary forage of caribou; they are also afraid of the harmful effects to wildlife from the noise around the pump stations—which would be, at a distance of 600 feet, equivalent to a "noisy industrial area."

Basing an estimate on the experience of the worldwide tanker fleet, the Alyeska Pipeline Service Co.'s fleet would have an average of 1.69 collisions or groundings each year. From these, plus the illegal tank cleanings at sea that always occur, plus the accidental discharges in port and at sea that always occur, experts foresee a total of 613,000 barrels of oil washing around in the surf and gunking-up the beaches and ruining oyster beds and killing salmon. That's the equivalent of twelve major collisions a year.

The Prudhoe Bay oil field is expected eventually to cover about 880 square miles, and while that is only 0.15 per cent of Alaska's total land surface, it is quite enough—coupled with the pipeline and roadways feeding into it—to leave indelible evidence of man's presence: gouged, smeared, torn and built across so much of the terrain that "north of the Yukon River the proposed project would irreversibly and irretrievably affect wilderness values." From the road north would sprout other roads, and from them still others, until the Coke bottles and Schlitz cans cover the track of the caribou and man's spoor "irretrievably and irreversibly bisects a vast wilderness area."

Thus spake the government's own experts. And the Nixon Administration casually ignored them one and all.

That would have been that, except for the environmentalists. They appealed Hart's decision, and the U.S. Court of Appeals, on last February 8, sided with them, but indirectly. The court ignored the environmental questions and based its rulings solely on the Mineral Leasing Act of 1920, which limits rights of way across federal lands to 25 feet on either side of the pipe. So the Alaska pipeline would have only a 54-foot right of way (counting the 4-foot diameter of the pipe). The oilmen say this is an impossibly narrow corridor to work along. Some of their equipment is truly mammoth. But that's what the law says and that's what the court ruled, shrugging its beautiful shoulders and remarking, "We have no more power to grant their request [that is, the oil companies' request for a width waiver], of course, than we have the power to increase Congressional appropriations to needy recipients."

How the oilmen pulled their hair in rage. The very idea, interpreting the law exactly as it is written, when the Interior Department and other courts had been winking at the law for decades! On April 2, the U.S. Supreme Court said it would let the lower court's ruling stand, and thus the whole question was thrown back to Congress.

That is a terrible blow to the oil companies, for they know how slowly things move in that quicksand body. Some oilmen have urged President Nixon to declare a national emergency as one way to get around a drawn-out debate, but Secretary Morton says he doesn't think Nixon will respond to their prayers in that fashion. More than likely, he will simply cooperate tacitly with the oil companies as they increase the pressure on the public and Congress by withholding an ample supply of gasoline and heating fuel—a kind of coercive maneuver the companies have been using for several years. It is part of their high-pressure "energy crisis" propaganda campaign ($3 million spent on it via TV and the national press last year) to persuade us that if we would only let them drill and pipe anywhere they want, with no consideration for the environment, we wouldn't have trouble getting fuel.

The Congressional debate has veered sharply away from the simple question of the right-of-way width and into the much more important question of whether the trans-Alaska route is the correct one at any width. At present, the only seriously proposed alternative to a trans-Alaska pipeline is a trans-Canada pipeline, to be built down through the Mackenzie River Valley to Edmonton, and then on to the central United States.

Canadian officials much prefer this pipeline proposal. First of all—though this route would also have many environmental defects—it is much more comforting for them to contemplate than the specter of a tanker fleet spewing 600,000 barrels of oil onto their West Coast beaches each year. And, second, if the pipeline were built across Canada it could also be used to ship Canadian oil—which is the kind of thrifty piggyback that our less affluent neighbors to the north can certainly be forgiven for thinking about.

But the trans-Canada route is being advocated most loudly, and sometimes almost threateningly, by a group of Middle Western and Eastern members of Congress of both parties who are under tremendous pressure from constituents who have been getting shorted in the distribution of petroleum products. Any time the oil companies crimp back on fuel oil and gasoline supplies, the Midwest feels it the worst and the East Coast feels it next worst. . . .

The arguments for building the trans-Canada pipeline may not be the best in the world, but the arguments for building the trans-Alaska pipeline are often just plain stupid. Secretary Morton, for instance, says it's necessary for our "national security" to keep the oil totally in U.S. hands all the way to market —the implication being that Canada, our closest ally, can't be trusted in an emergency. Morton's argument disregards two obvious points: *(1)* in a war the trans-Alaska oil would have to dodge submarines half the way to the United States, whereas the trans-Canada oil would be routed so deeply through the boondocks all the way to market that saboteurs would get frostbite trying to find it; and *(2)* far from being an unreliable source of oil, Canada has usually tried to sell us more than our companies (preferring the bigger bargains in the Arab countries) have wanted to buy. In any event, the Department of Defense, apparently embarrassed by Morton's foolishness, has pointedly refused to endorse the national security argument for the trans-Alaska route.

The commercial arguments against the trans-Canada route are just as phony. The Alyeska Pipeline consortium keeps saying that the Canadian route just wouldn't work, that it would cost too much money, that it's a lousy idea, that it would take too long to build, etc. This is a perfect example of how corporate hotshots don't realize that just plain people are capable of reading trade magazines. Anyone with any curiosity about the problem has only to go to such a ready source as *Oil and Gas Journal,* for example, to find that a group of oil companies—in fact, some of the same companies that are in the Alyeska group and claiming the Canadian route is a bad idea—are saying out of the other side of their mouths that building a pipeline down through the Mackenzie Valley is perfectly feasible. More than feasible, they are saying it is the *only* way to bring natural gas out of the Prudhoe Bay fields. Moreover, they intend to start building a natural gas pipeline down through Canada by late summer and hope to have it completed within four years. This is, to repeat, a natural gas pipeline; but they expect to build an oil pipeline along the same route eventually.

So why not build it now? Short of beating an explanation out of Alyeska executives, one can only speculate. However, these are two fairly good guesses:

(1) The Canadian pipeline would make the source-to-market routing inflexible, whereas the trans-Alaska pipeline, by feeding into a tanker fleet, would give the oil companies a way to play with their commodity on the national and world markets.

At first the Alyeska oil companies were quite candid about their intent to sell some of the oil to Japan (some are still candid about it). In an interview with *National Journal* last March, Ronald H. Merett, economics and supply coordinator for B.P. Alaska Inc., said flatly that perhaps by 1980 there would be 400,000 or 500,000 barrels-a-day surplus (that's one-fourth the Alyeska production, at predicted peak) above what the West Coast of the United States could consume and if that were the case, it might be sold to Japan. Depending only on where the higher profits lay, he said, "you reach the point where it's a matter of indifference, from the oil companies' point of view, whether we sell it to Japan or the West Coast." (Japan has recently become a major partner with B.P. in the Mideast.)

When the same philosophy was expressed earlier by other oil company executives, conservationists and consumers raised hell at the idea that Alaska's wilderness would be raped not to lower petroleum prices in the United States but to add to Tokyo's smog. The criticism became so loud that some Alyeska executives began pretending they hadn't said they would sell to Japan except, maybe, on a swap basis: ship Alaskan oil to Japan and receive an equal amount of Japanese-owned Middle East oil, which the oil companies would then bring into the more profitable market on the East Coast. This shuffling of oil with Japan would give the companies an estimated 300 per cent markup over what they could earn if they carried their Alaskan oil directly to the West Coast. For one thing, by avoiding coastwise traffic they could use foreign-flag ships with their low-paid crews. (The Jones Act requires U.S.-flag vessels for coastwise commerce but not for foreign traffic.)

Another way of juggling the Alaskan oil on the high seas to achieve greater profits was discovered by Rep. Les Aspin last year. He uncovered a secret document showing that Amerada Hess (one of the Alyeska companies) wanted to build a pipeline across Costa Rica. Amerada Hess would ship some of its Alaskan oil through this pipeline, out the other end into another fleet of tankers which would carry it to Amerada refineries in the Virgin Islands (where Amerada recently expanded its refinery capacity from 50,000 barrels a day to 450,000) and thence to the higher-priced East Coast markets. All of this, too, could be carried in foreign-flag tankers. . . .

(2) Another likely reason why the Alyeska companies are pressing for the trans-Alaska route is that if the trans-Canada pipeline came first, the environmentalists would be in a strong position to argue against *ever* building across Alaska. The companies want to force the trans-Alaska pipeline now because once they spoil the virginity of the region in that way, it will be much less

difficult to persuade the public that doing it "just once more" somewhere else —either through another pipeline or lots and lots more drilling, wouldn't spoil the state's purity more than it had already been spoiled.

One thing is certain: the Alaska pipeline is just the beginning of the environmental despoilment the oilmen have in mind. There are at least ten promising sedimentary basins in Alaska that they want to get their drills into. As for the Continental Shelf around Alaska, the *Oil and Gas Journal* (February 28, 1972) describes it as "an untested but challenging province that some day should yield billions of barrels of oil." In the Arctic Islands, oil experts estimate, there is a reservoir with at least 5 billion barrels of recoverable oil, which would be worth, after all expenses, at least half a billion dollars at today's prices. Hickel, no doubt using estimates supplied by the oil companies, sees 100 billion barrels of oil coming out of the Arctic. But the International Petroleum Encyclopedia of 1972, an industry publication, is even more optimistic: ". . . crude oil potential of the Gulf of Alaska Tertiary province is 40 billion barrels, the Department of Interior disclosed in 1971 estimates. This compares with 125 billion barrels for the North Slope. Interior also says there are 120 trillion cubic feet of natural gas and 2.2 billion barrels of natural gas liquids possible there." . . .

Corporate Control

NATION REVIEW OF "*WEALTH AGAINST COMMONWEALTH*" WITH AUTHOR'S REPLY TO A *NATION* EDITORIAL (1894, 1899)

Wealth Against Commonwealth. By Henry Demarest Lloyd. Harper & Bros. 1894.

THIS BOOK IS a notable example of the rhetorical blunder of overstatement. It was clearly established in 1879, by the investigation of the committee of the New York Assembly known as the Hepburn committee, that agreements had been made between the Standard Oil Company and some of the trunk lines of railway which explicitly provided that the oil company should obtain transportation at less rates than any of its competitors. Other agreements of equally unjust and illegal character were disclosed by this investigation and by subsequent ones, and a temperate and judicial statement of the evidence would have constituted a most damaging indictment. But instead of this, we have over 500 octavo pages of the wildest rant. Much learning of the Standard Oil Company has made Mr. Lloyd mad. He raves more coherently at some times than at others; but he is never perfectly sane. Even in his lucid intervals it is evident that some deep disturbing thought is at work in his brain, and that the very mention of oil will bring on an explosion. He sees the emissaries of the Standard Company lurking behind every bush. He declares, and evidently believes, that the managers of this concern have seduced or imposed upon the Czar of Russia and have influenced the action of the British Parliament. They have nearly compassed the monopoly of the light-producing substances of this globe, and we doubt if Mr. Lloyd feels that the human race is altogether secure in the possession of sunlight.

In the consummation of this monopoly no arts have been too base, no methods too criminal, for the Standard Oil Company. Their iniquitous contracts with the railroads have been already referred to, but these are only a part of a gigantic scheme of oppression and extermination. It is a policy of "Thorough." No rival in the production of refined oil is to be permitted to exist. If tribute is paid, refiners who are not members of the company may be allowed to carry on business; but if they persist in asserting their independence, they are to be ruined. If they cannot be ruined by unfair freight charges, or by reducing prices, their employees are corrupted and seduced; and if all other measures fail, their factories are set on fire or blown up. In the pursuit of their infamous ends, the Standard Oil magnates have exhibited the most diabolical malignity and the most infernal persistency. Our Legislatures and our Congress are controlled or baffled, our judges are corrupted or imposed upon, our newspapers are bought. Occasionally some oil-producers or refiners have combined to oppose this frightful despotism, but these combinations have failed. When they have not been broken down by competition, they have been broken up by treachery, for the Standard Oil Company appears to have found that the leaders in these patriotic uprisings are not all of austere integrity.

If we examine the particulars of the case presented by Mr. Lloyd, we find a number of them to be supported by questionable evidence. It is in the first place a very suspicious circumstance that Mr. Lloyd never mentions the names of the individuals whose conduct he denounces. Some of them he enables us to identify by his insinuations, but this indirect method of attack arouses our distrust. We find ourselves wondering if Mr. Lloyd stands in fear of the penalties for libel, for it is hard to understand why, if he does not, he should have abstained from the use of a most formidable weapon. It is easy and it is idle to denounce a corporation; but if a wrongful act has been committed, it must have been committed by human beings, and to suppress their names is to make condemnation ineffective. In the second place, Mr. Lloyd calls witnesses without discrimination. Some of them are crack-brained, by his own admission. Some of them testify that they were bribed to commit arson and other crimes by the mysterious leaders of the Standard Oil Company. A dog would not be hung upon such evidence. Nor can Mr. Lloyd's citations of the testimony of reputable witnesses be allowed much weight, for he is so bitter in his advocacy that it would be grossly unfair to pass judgment upon his ex-parte statement. It would be like deciding a case after hearing only the address to the jury of the plaintiff's attorney.

Upon the whole, Mr. Lloyd's book is eminently calculated to arouse incredulity in the mind of any reader who understands the nature of evidence. Were we not satisfied from evidence *aliunde* that the managers of the Standard Oil Company had violated both law and justice in their attempts to suppress competition, we should be inclined to acquit them after reading this screed. It is quite beyond belief that these men should be capable of the height and depth of wickedness attributed to them, even if they possessed the superhuman powers with which they are credited. It is plain upon Mr. Lloyd's showing that their competitors would be no better than they if they had similar opportunities, and it is impossible to arouse sympathy for men whose complaint is that they were not allowed to make enormous profits, for it appears to have been the policy of the Standard Company to buy out its rivals at reasonable rates.

It naturally occurs to the reader, as he sees it maintained that the people are absolutely at the mercy of this great monopoly, that it will be difficult to devise a remedy. If the people cannot choose legislators and judges who are incorruptible, it seems that there is no resource left. Socialism, however, Mr. Lloyd avers, will cure our ills, and he draws a comparison between the horrors of the present competitive régime and the beauties of the future Altruria. We do not find Mr. Lloyd's ideal attractive. He appears to us to exhibit in his writing such indifference to truth, such incoherency of thought, such intemperance of speech, and such violence of passion, as to make him an undesirable leader. If reform can be had only through such reformers, it is better to endure our present ills. As to the Standard Oil Company, its history remains to be written, and the economic situation which it indicates remains to be described. No episode in economic history better deserves treatment by a competent investigator, and no situation more requires calm and dispassionate consideration.

"WEALTH VERSUS COMMONWEALTH."

To the Editor of The Nation:

Sir: In a recent editorial you say:

"There is a book called 'Wealth Against Commonwealth' which is directed against monopolies. It is filled with the most frightful accusations, and it has no doubt made a great impression on the public mind, but many of its charges are improbable, if not false, on their face, and none is established by sufficient evidence to sustain a verdict by a jury."

There are no "accusations" of mine in the book. It does not assume in the least to be a work of original research, nor to narrate things which I discovered. Except where its recital is of facts which are not in controversy, and some occurrences abroad, it is but a résumé of the official records, many of them court records.

You speak of a "verdict by a jury." The statements in the book—the book is mine, but the statements are not—are based specifically on the verdicts of juries in civil and criminal cases, the decisions of State and Federal courts, special tribunals like the Interstate Commerce Commission, and on the findings of State and national legislative investigations. The book has been before the public for five years, but it has not yet been shown that its résumé of the "verdicts" has been incorrectly given or has gone beyond the attested record. In every case I have reported the versions of the facts given by those concerned, as well as those versions which these official findings entitle all students to accept as the authorized versions. There are by actual count over 200 quotations from the arguments and facts urged by the defense.

Of course, there is a mathematical possibility, in the doctrine of chances, that all our judges and investigators, from United States Judge Baxter and the Judges of the Supreme Court of Ohio to the Honorable T. M. Cooley and his associates of the Interstate Commerce Commission, and the Hon. A. B. Hepburn and his committee of the New York Legislature of 1879, and the Hon. Shelby M. Cullom his fellow-members of the Senate special committee, and all the other members of all the other commissions and courts have been all wrong, and that not one of these "verdicts" which have been found by them after examination and cross-examination of witnesses under oath, is true, and that all the things done by men who, beginning penniless, have accumulated uncounted millions while they are yet in the prime of life, have been merely evangelical and "benevolent assimilation." If this be true, and these authorities fall, my book, I admit—but, under the circumstances, I admit it cheerfully—must fall with them, for it is built on them.

HENRY DEMAREST LLOYD.

WHY GASOLINE IS HIGH (1923)

E.C.S.

THE PRICE OF gasoline is high because our system of oil exploitation is wasteful and unjust. High prices are a consequence of private ownership of natural resources and the unrestricted right of individual capitalistic exploitation. High prices are not due to any particular personality, nor do they arise from any peculiar rapacity on the part of the Standard Oil companies. The whole problem is one of systems rather than persons. About 40 per cent of the ultimate selling price of gasoline, or *10 cents a gallon,* is due to the wastes and injustices of our method of exploitation.

Three prime factors in the production of crude oil and its products are responsible for this waste. These are:

1. Land royalties and bonuses.
2. Competitive leaseholds and competitive drilling.
3. Financial monopoly.

Our basic policy is that whoever owns the surface owns the oil underground. The landowner usually leases his land to an oil-exploitation company on a royalty basis, i.e., a stipulation to receive one-eighth or more of all the oil produced from his farm. The amount paid in the year 1919 in royalties and rents was $106,458,518, 11 per cent of a product valued at $931,793,423. In 1919 our production of crude oil was 377,719,000 barrels; in 1923 it will be over 600,000,000 barrels. Prices are about the same. Our contribution in royalty for 1923 will therefore be at least $1 a barrel on the approximately 150,000,000 barrels of gasoline to be manufactured. This amounts to about 2 1/2 cents per gallon of gasoline. In addition some $50,000,000 of royalty will be capitalized by those exploiting companies fortunate enough to own their oil lands in fee simple. This will equal about 1 cent more a gallon, or a total on account of royalties of 3 1/2 cents.

This is not all. There remains another imposition from the land system— land bonuses. Land which it is believed will prove highly prolific commands not only royalty and rent, but also a bonus or an initial consideration paid for the right to exploit under the standard form of lease. No one will dispute an average bonus cost of 15 cents per barrel, or on 600,000,000 barrels $90,000,000, which with interest and profits at 20 per cent equals $108,000,000, or almost two cents per gallon of gasoline.

The idea of private ownership, together with the further idea of the right of the producer to operate with unbridled initiative, has led to an oil-field development which is wasteful in the extreme: the system of competitive lease-holds and competitive drilling. Oil deposits recognize no property lines. Also, within certain limits of distance, oil is a drainable resource; your neighbor's well establishes lines of flowage to it, and, unless you retaliate, your oil is likely politely to cross your property line and be expelled from your neighbor's well. In short, it is a case of competitive drainage, with the devil taking the hindmost. Our land system does everything possible to aggravate this situation, and our laws do little or nothing to relieve it. The main source of return to the farmer is his fractional royalty of the oil produced. Naturally he is insistent on having the production from his farm reach a maximum. To safeguard his interest, there is generally written into the oil lease the commercial offset clause which compels the exploiter to drill a well opposite any commercially productive one on an adjacent farm. The result is that almost every oil field in the United States is tremendously over developed. The Mexia (Texas) oil field consists of about 1,000 productive acres. Up to August, 1922, some 540 productive wells had been drilled, an average of one to less than every two acres. One well to every six acres would have been the maximum the technical conditions would justify.

Of the 20,000 wells which will be drilled in this country during 1923 at least one in every five will be superfluous. These wells average in cost about $30,000, so that this waste will be about $120,000,000, which, capitalized for profits, amounts to $144,000,000, almost 2 1/2 cents per gallon of gasoline.

In addition, the cumulative effect of such development over a period of years must be reckoned with. These unnecessary wells require the same labor attendance, the same pumping powers, the same tubing, repairs, etc., as the necessary wells, and thus enhance operating costs for 1923 at least 5 cents per barrel on 600,000,000 barrels—$30,000,000, or 1/2 cent per gallon of gasoline.

No effective legislation has been passed to relieve this obviously wasteful condition. The maximum action has been the appointment of State railroad commissions which in time of extreme congestion can prohibit the drilling of a well until facilities are provided, but have no power to prescribe the proper spacing of the wells, which is the crux of the whole matter.

The vicious system of exploitation above described, producing as it does either a feast or a famine, has put an exceptionally large premium on financial strength. The investment banker, quick to realize his chance, has successfully grasped the opportunity, and the result is the Standard Oil companies. These companies are simply the product of the meeting of two systems: one, our land system; the other, our financial system. The Standard Oil companies feed on the chaos engendered by the land system and, due to their control of investment funds, prevent others from sharing the spoils. In this way the petroleum industry is nicely divided into two houses: the House of Have, the Standard Oil companies, well organized, with enormous banking reserves, unimpeachable financial connections, and a restrictive control over investment funds; and the House of Want, the independents, unorganized, with no financial reserves, with none or second-rate banking associates, and such associates dominated by the Standard banks.

The Standard turns this financial control to advantage in four principal ways: (a) purchase of flush production at low price, (b) manipulation of crude and refined inventories over long swings, (c) seasonal manipulation of refined oil inventories, (d) reduction in cost of raw material due to financial stability, loans, etc.

Under the land system described there is always overdrilling and over-development in a newly discovered oil pool. Transportation facilities and buyers are at a premium. The Standard companies furnish the facilities, purchase the oil—and get the premium. This is the root of the Standard control; it is the ever-ready buyer of raw material, at its price. The independents are never so situated.

Through its financial connections the Standard is in a position to direct its purchases of crude and refined oil with extreme finesse as regards the long price-swings. In 1914 the Prairie Oil and Gas Company purchased high-grade crude at from 40 to 80 cents per barrel and filled its tank farms with this cheap oil which it liquidated during the war at from $2.25 to $3.50 per barrel. The profit on this one turnover must have been close to $100,000,000. At the present time, with our stocks the greatest in history (about 400,000,000 barrels, almost all held by the Standard), oil has gone up 50 cents per barrel.

The oil business is highly seasonal; gasoline, the chief product, is much more easily sold in summer than in winter. Consequently, inadequately financed refiners sacrifice their product in the winter months. This the Standard willingly buys and stores. Inasmuch as there is regularly an increase in the stock of gasoline from autumn to spring of some 500,000,000 gallons, and inasmuch as the wholesale price is regularly four to five cents higher in summer than in winter, the profits can easily be realized.

The crude producer usually works on a shoe-string basis, and he requires a ready and reliable cash market for his oil, and often loans. These the Standard regularly affords. As a result of this service the Standard companies save up to 25 cents a barrel in their purchases of crude oil. When it is remembered that the Prairie Oil and Gas Company, which is only one of the Standard purchasers, buys about 100,000,000 barrels of oil per year, this profit can also be estimated. The aggregate of the various profits due to the Standard's financial control is probably not less than $100,000,000 a year or more than 1 1/2 cents per gallon on gasoline.

Taken together we have, then, on account of our system of oil exploitation, the following charges upon the consumer for every gallon of gasoline that he uses: 3 1/2 cents for royalties, 2 cents for land bonuses, 2 1/2 cents for drilling unnecessary wells, 1/2 cent for operating them, 1 1/2 cents for the Standard's financial control; a total of 10 cents.

Until we change our philosophy of exploitation, we can do little or nothing toward reducing the price of gasoline.

THE STANDARD OIL'S DEATH FACTORY (1924)

Mary Ross

ON FRIDAY Ernest Oelgert went "loony" at work. Someone was following him, he complained. Then he dodged about the Standard Oil plant at Elizabeth, N. J., shouting that three men were coming at him at once. They took him to the hospital in Elizabeth. He died there the next day, in convulsions.

Others who had worked beside him in what the men called the "loony-gas building" acted strangely. William McSweeney went home from work sick and so violent that his sister called a policeman. When the policeman came he had to get in three other men to put McSweeney in a strait-jacket. They say William Kresge lost twenty-two pounds in four weeks during which he had worked in the building. Walter Dymock, ill at home, got up at night and walked out a second-story window. A passerby found him and called an ambulance. On Sunday these men and one other, Herbert Fuson, were taken to New York to the Reconstruction Hospital, which specializes in the treatment of industrial diseases and accidents.

Dymock died on Monday in a violent delirium; McSweeney, who until a year ago had been a brigadier general in the army of the Irish Free State, died the next day; Kresge on Wednesday; Fuson, strait-jacketed also, on Thursday. The "loony-gas" story came back to the first page of the New York newspapers. Thirty-six other employees of the Elizabeth plant of the Standard Oil were placed under observation in hospitals, eight others in their homes. Some of them showed no symptoms, others had headaches, "mental disturbances," dreams or delirium.

With the deaths of the fourth and the fifth men came statements from the Standard Oil, one of whose executives had declared on the first day that "the men probably went insane because they worked too hard." The "loony-gas" was, in fact, no mystery, but lead tetra-ethyl; its manufacture, in a so-called research building, was the try-out of a new commercial undertaking on the part of the General Motors Chemical Company and the Standard Oil Company of

New Jersey, which together own the Ethyl Gasoline Company. The substance, known to chemists for more than half a century, and known as a deadly poison, is added to gasoline to keep engines from knocking. This ethyl gasoline, according to the Standard Oil Company, had, without waiting for fuller experimental tests, been put in use in 10,000 filling stations and garages.

From other sources came other bits of information. The discovery that lead tetra-ethyl would increase the power of gasoline and prevent the formation of carbon and knocking of the engine was made at the plant of the General Motors Chemical Company at Dayton, Ohio. It is claimed that gasoline in which a small amount of it is dissolved will give an 8 per cent increase in power with an increase in cost of only 6 per cent. Multiplying that gain by the billions of gallons of gasoline burned in the country's twelve million automobiles will give some idea of the profits at stake in the commercial exploitation of this discovery.

But lead tetra-ethyl is so poisonous that a little rubbed on a man's hand will lower his blood pressure, perhaps even make him unconscious, before he can cross the room to wash it off. Its poison is absorbed in this way through the skin, or inhaled through the lungs from fumes which escape from large retorts during the course of manufacture. These fumes, according to Dr. Gilman Thompson, who is consulting physician for the Standard Oil Company, cause a congestion of the brain which results in symptoms not unlike those of delirium tremens. The Standard Oil Company declares that no accidents have been reported from the use of the treated gasoline in which the lead compound is present in dilution, though Dr. Yandell Henderson, professor of applied physiology at Yale University, believes that handling this gasoline or breathing the exhaust from an engine in which it is burned constitutes an insidious menace to health, possibly even to life.

Two years ago the General Motors Company asked Dr. Henderson, who is an expert in this field, to give his opinion on the use of tetra-ethyl lead gas. He reported that lead thus volatilized attacked the brain and nerves rapidly, resulting in the most dangerous form of lead poisoning, with delirium, paralysis, and other severe symptoms characteristic of the poisoning, which may cause permanent damage to the body when they do not kill. He believed that the exhausts from automobiles using this fuel in heavy traffic might well poison pedestrians on the street; in a garage the results would be even more disastrous. The fumes are especially dangerous, as symptoms may not develop at once and serious harm may be done before the victim realizes his peril.

A year ago the companies interested in ethyl gasoline asked the Bureau of Mines to investigate it with a view to determining its toxicity and the effects of the exhaust fumes. At the time of the Elizabeth accidents, the results of that study had not yet been made public. Its conclusions indicate that the substance is not dangerous as a motor fuel, but no report has been made yet in regard to danger in its manufacture.

The companies had also asked the research staff at Harvard University to undertake another analysis, but that request was refused. They also asked a report from the recently established department of industrial hygiene at Columbia University. Work there has been carried on for several months but still is incomplete.

But the companies did not wait. Manufacture went on. Two workmen died at the Dayton plant. The Du Pont plant in Wilmington, which makes lead tetra-ethyl on a commercial scale, also killed some of its workers. Manufacture was started on August 1 at the Elizabeth plant on a small scale; it was planned to carry the work on in a research building for six months as a temporary expedient to develop a commercial technique which could guide the company in the building of a large permanent factory, probably in Chicago. The tragedy which closed its doors on October 25 involved the death or hospitalization of virtually every man who was then employed in the "loony-gas" plant, and efforts are being made to determine whether or not the suicide of a chemist who jumped to death from his boarding-house last September and the illness of others who quit during the fall are to be traced to the same poison.

Manufacture on a commercial scale, according to Dr. Gilman Thompson, consulting expert for the Standard Oil, involves "processes still more or less in a stage of development. . . . This has occasioned unforeseen accidents, which, as processes and apparatus are further perfected, should be avoidable in the future."

Work at the Du Pont plant has apparently suffered a somewhat similar development. Its president is quoted as saying:

> The Du Pont company, during the experimental period, experienced much trouble with the men becoming poisoned, *even to the extent of fatalities.* During the past year of production, when more than 100 men have been employed continuously, the difficulty has diminished steadily. In the past several months, under full production, only slight difficulties have been encountered. Experience has taught the necessary protection, both in plant and medical care.

An experience, however, bought dearly at the expense of those unfortunate enough to incur a "fatality"! And what, in human terms, are the present "slight difficulties"?

In the light of Mr. Du Pont's assurance that "workmen cumulatively poisoned by this material invariably indicate it in the incipient stages, before any harm is done, by a marked symptom," it is difficult to harmonize the collapse of the whole working force at Elizabeth on successive days with the statement of the Standard Oil that its men were protected by every safeguard of equipment and supervision. Investigations have been started by the prosecutor of Union County and the New Jersey State Department of Labor to determine whether or not proper ventilating devices, medical inspection, facilities for washing and for changing work-clothes, and similar measures were in force. Rumors of neglect must be sifted. The workmen who were poisoned and died were not scientists working open-eyed in the investigation of a dangerous substance; they were common laborers, hired at eighty-five cents an hour, to carry out a new method of commercial manufacture for the profit of the Standard Oil. When an accident involves the whole plant it is difficult to accept such an excuse as that offered in the case of the two deaths at Dayton, where it was said that "without desiring to attach any blame to the employees" it was "very difficult to get the men to make use of safety devices provided for their protection by the company."

In due time the legal machinery probably will grind out a decision placing the blame for the deaths of the five men. In due time, also, scientists will provide at least a majority opinion as to whether or not the new fuel, ethyl gasoline, is fit for use, humanly speaking. The health department of New York City and health officers in parts of New Jersey have barred its sale. The Standard Oil's original idea of having it tested scientifically before trouble had been reported was good, but any member of the general motor-using public will inquire why, with one adverse judgment and two other investigations still incomplete, the company rushed forward and put the suspicious substance on sale in those 10,000 filling stations of which the company itself speaks.

It is to be hoped that the Standard Oil's assertion that there are no reports of untoward incidents in the use of ethyl gasoline, with its fraction of one per cent of lead tetra-ethyl, means that none have occurred. The case of the nine or more men who have met death in its manufacture in the last few months, and of the several times that number who have suffered serious, perhaps permanent, disability, offers unfortunately no room for optimism. They were human material, bought in the labor market at eighty-five cents an hour, and scrapped in the feverish rush to try out and market a new product which promised tremendous financial returns. . . .

LA FOLLETTE AND STANDARD OIL (1924)

William Hard

. . . ROBERT LA FOLLETTE'S recommendations [as chairman of the Senate Committee on Manufactures] regarding the petroleum industry grew out of some fifteen hundred pages of testimony regarding conditions in the industry —testimony from producers, transporters, refiners, distributors. Mr. La Follette came to the conclusion that the petroleum industry is dominated and essentially controlled by the so-called "Standard" companies. In other words, he saw himself confronted by a "trust." He thereupon made eight recommendations, which can be analyzed down into five.

The first noteworthy thing about these five recommendations is that not one of them is to the effect that the Standard Oil Company of Indiana or any other Standard company or any company whatsoever in the petroleum industry should be smashed and made smaller. Not once in the course of these five recommendations does Mr. La Follette suggest that any existing unit in the petroleum industry should be artificially governmentally contracted. The necessary conclusion from this fact is that if the Standard Oil Company of Indiana can legitimately grow to be even larger than it is now it would encounter no opposition from Mr. La Follette as President.

Mr. La Follette, however, does suggest five courses of action for the Government to pursue for the purpose of establishing what he believes to be fairer and freer conditions in the petroleum industry.

The first is that all companies in the industry shall be obliged to install a uniform system of bookkeeping and shall be obliged to make reports to the Government showing their production, their storage, their costs, their prices, and other pertinent data, which the Government thereupon shall assemble and arrange in such a manner that at all times the full facts regarding the petroleum industry may be available to persons in the industry and the consuming public. This suggestion amounts to the proposition that petroleum companies shall send to the Government the sort of self-revealing data that all railroad companies now send to the Interstate Commerce Commission. It amounts to the proposition that petroleum is affected with a public interest and that petroleum companies should to a certain degree be obliged to behave as public utilities.

The second suggestion is that petroleum pipe-lines, engaged in pumping petroleum from place to place, shall be obliged to behave as common carriers and shall be obliged to have receiving stations and delivery stations wherever reasonably demanded. This suggestion amounts to the proposition that the present transportation law, which declares pipe-lines to be common carriers, shall be put into actual practical effective operation.

The third suggestion is that railroad freight rates upon petroleum products between certain points shall be sufficiently reduced to enable independent mid-continent petroleum companies to reach the Central and Eastern States in competition with the Standard companies.

The fourth suggestion is that exports of petroleum and of petroleum products from this country should be restricted in order to prevent the unduly rapid exhaustion of our domestic petroleum supply.

The fifth suggestion is that where oil companies have engaged in "price manipulations" and where they have engaged in restraint of trade through artificial divisions of marketing territory and where they have artificially limited production through alleged conspiracies based on the so-called "cracking process" patents, the Department of Justice should proceed against them.

This suggestion amounts to the proposition that the Sherman law, which is a law, even as the Volstead law is a law, should be enforced. . . .

After a study of Mr. La Follette's fifth suggestion . . . the Department of Justice has brought suit against the Standard Oil Company of Indiana and other petroleum companies to break up an alleged conspiracy limiting petroleum production through the so-called "cracking process" patents. The Department of Justice has also taken up the matter of marketing-territory divisions maintained by the so-called Standard companies and has begun to explore the possibility of an action which might break down the lines of those divisions. It finally has entered into a widespread inquiry, in collaboration with the chief legal officers of various State governments, regarding alleged price manipulations and conspiracies by numerous petroleum companies. . . .

La Follette [as a] . . . trust-buster . . . is not the enemy of the American idea in business. He is the candidate who gives most thought, whether with success or without success, to the progressive means by which the American idea in business can be continuously restored and maintained.

YOUR GASOLINE TANK (1931)

Lawrence M. Hughes

IN AN ADDRESS before the American Federation of Labor at Boston in October President Hoover suggested that the time has come to "reconsider" the anti-trust laws in the light of modern conditions. Speaking before the American Petroleum Institute at Chicago in November, Colonel William A. Donovan, former assistant attorney general, pointed out that "we may have reached a point where attempts will be made to modify the economic policy of the Sherman law and to substitute some form of government control." Colonel Donovan believed that in view of present chaotic conditions in the oil industry and the large supply of crude oil above ground, concerted efforts by producers to limit production and stabilize prices on a reasonable level of profit would not be in violation of the law.

Standard Oil became the "mother of trusts" primarily by its ability to control refining and transportation. The most significant trend in the industry today is toward control of markets. The dissolution of the old Standard Oil Company of New Jersey in 1911 introduced a period of vigorous competition in the industry. Independent concerns were able to combat the segregated members of the "Standard Oil group" on more nearly even terms. Coinciding as it did with the rapid extension in the use of the automobile, this new competition assumed the form largely of a fight for filling stations. A dozen large factions have grown tremendously in scope and power. Today most of the stations not already owned or controlled by one or another of these factions have been forced to become exclusive agents.

Thus the chain-store system has been extended in the oil industry on a wider scale than in any other. Not only are filling stations centrally controlled, but the products which they sell are controlled by the company from the time the oil issues from the earth until it is poured, as gasoline or lubricating oil, into your car. This might be described as the "internal" basis of monopoly. The "external" basis is the ability of a company to acquire or defeat competitors and to outwit the government and the public.

The dissolution created a number of intentionally unrelated regional Standard companies. Several of these have been forced to fight single-handed against stronger and semi-national companies whose growth has not been hampered by the anti-trust laws. Although certain members of the group sell in almost every country in the world, none, except Vacuum, a comparatively small member, sells throughout the United States. Vacuum, devoted primarily to lubricants, was immune from the regional restrictions. Mergers with independent companies have broadened the scope of some of them. Standard of New York has acquired General Petroleum and is selling along the length of the Pacific Coast, as well as in New York and New England. Subsidiaries of Standard of Indiana have enabled it to expand west to the Rockies and east to New England. Standard of New Jersey sells in Texas and Louisiana, as well as the East. But on the national marketing map there are still large gaps which none of these Standard Oil members alone has been able to fill.

Two independents, on the other hand, have already achieved fairly national distribution. The Texas Company and Shell Union (controlled by Royal Dutch-Shell) now have stations, owned or affiliated, in every State, and almost in every city of any size, in the country. The number of their filling stations is larger than that of any member of Standard Oil. Gulf, Cities Service, Sinclair, Tidewater Associated, Pure Oil, Continental, and Richfield—each has wide marketing territories. The freedom granted Shell here, coupled with the resources of its sponsors and the fact that it can undersell in many localities through the use of cheap Venezuelan oil, is particularly a thorn in the side of Standard Oil because Standard has such a large share of its business in British markets that it cannot raise a patriotic appeal here.

Royal Dutch-Shell today is the largest unit in the oil industry. With subsidiaries, it is perhaps two-thirds as large as all the members of the Standard Oil group combined. Gasoline, owing to the increased use of automobiles, now accounts for two-thirds of the industry's business, and more than three-fourths of the world's automobiles are in the United States. Regardless of success abroad, if Standard cannot defeat Shell here, it must fail. In order to defeat it Standard must have a unified chain of outlets.

And Standard is not beaten. Men responsible for the success of the original New Jersey company—notably John D. Rockefeller—are still large holders in the leading members of the group. Their methods still prevail. And these members—especially New Jersey, New York, Indiana, California, and Vacuum—still rank as large as or larger than their leading independent competitors. New Jersey's assets, for example, are two and one-half times as large as those of any other American oil company, twice as great as those of the older New Jersey company at the time of its dissolution. New York and Indiana each is larger than Texaco, Gulf, Shell Union, or the oil interests of Cities Service, and California compares favorably with them. Even Harry Sinclair's proposed $1,200,000,000 combination would fall half a billion dollars short of Standard of New Jersey. Because of their size and their close relationships, any large member of the Standard Oil group, conditions being opportune, might form a sound nucleus for monopoly.

Standard, frankly, would like to bring back the trust. But it wants no more $29,000,000 fines. By an expenditure of hundreds of millions of dollars for philanthropy and promotion, over a period of nineteen years, the group has brought itself back into the good graces of the government and the public. It wants to hold this esteem. Its efforts, therefore, to set aside the dissolution decree have been circumspect and entirely legitimate. A year or so ago New Jersey was permitted by the government to reacquire Anglo-American Petroleum as a subsidiary in the British Isles. A more important step in this direction was the announcement, last February, of plans for a merger of Socony and Vacuum as the General Petroleum Corporation. This proposal is now being fought by the Department of Justice. Decision on it will be made by the federal court at St. Louis, where the dissolution decree was rendered. Socony-Vacuum would not form a dominant company. It would market only about 9 per cent of the petroleum products sold in this country and would be in assets only about half as large as Standard of New Jersey. Favorable decision on the proposal, however, would set a significant precedent, and might set the wheels in motion for more important mergers among members of the family of Standard Oil. New Jersey, Indiana, and California might form a company with assets of nearly three and one-half billion dollars—virtually as large as all the Royal Dutch-Shell enterprises throughout the world. If all the members of Standard Oil were to recombine they would control half the assets of the world's twelve-billion-dollar oil industry.

Decision on the Socony-Vacuum plan, however, may take months, even years, and competition will not permit Standard Oil to be patient about it. Standard Oil is not lacking today in any of the qualities which could make it dominant, and it feels it must reach out for control in other directions. With the secrecy and almost with the speed with which the elder Rockefeller gained control of the oil-refining business of the country more than a half-century ago, the group is now setting out to control markets.

Vacuum has the most ambitious program. It is seeking to build up a chain of 122,000 filling stations by 1935, and it is now about a fifth of the way toward that goal. It is hardly too much to say that in this program Vacuum, smallest of the five Standard leaders, has been chosen for the role of marketing agent for the entire group.

But owing to the rush to build and acquire filling stations there are now three or four times as many as can profitably be operated. There are in fact some 315,000 stations. In more vivid terms, there are nearly as many filling stations as grocery stores and six times as many as there are drug-stores; there is one station for every eighty cars.

In its expansion program Vacuum, wisely, does not seek to add to this number. It is acquiring *existing* stations, not by outright purchase, but by obtaining, usually, 51 per cent control. This accomplishes the double advantage of control at about half cost (even so the program will involve an aggregate expenditure in excess of one billion dollars) and of keeping the operation in the hands of experienced local men. Vacuum, in fact, goes a step farther—it generally retains the name of the local company or operator. Thus, playing a silent part, it profits not only from the established identity and good-will of these stations in their local markets, but from efficiency and economy brought about by great resources and standardized methods. Moreover, in order to present itself as a local independent in all public contacts, each station usually carries several brands of gasoline. Under this guise, Vacuum may obtain a measure of control over the sale of competitors' products. And Vacuum, be it noted, is no longer merely a refiner and marketer of lubricants. It has introduced its own brand of gasoline, which will soon be sold nationally.

Despite its relatively small size, Vacuum is better qualified than any other member of Standard Oil to carry out such a project. For many years it has sold its lubricants not only in every State but in every city, town, and hamlet in the country. It has in the United States today some 75,000 outlets—"general stores," garages, and other places, as well as filling stations of its own and of other companies. The company boasts that every village large enough to support a post office has a Vacuum Oil dealer. Such is the framework on which the company can build.

If there were no other reason to suppose that in this project the company is acting largely for the other members of Standard Oil, there is the fact that, alone, Vacuum could not raise a billion dollars with which to finance it. Its entire assets are only a fifth of that amount, its entire annual sales not more than a third of it. Even New Jersey, eight and one-half times as large, could not hope to achieve this goal alone in six years. In its execution the plan shows evidence of coordinated effort on the part of all the major members of Standard Oil; in its inception it suggests the methods and personality of John D. Rockefeller.

The plan was formally launched early in 1929. Today some 25,000 of the stations already have been taken over. The number is steadily increasing. Because the operation of filling stations is not profitable and gasoline sales today, for the first time in many years, are not increasing, it is doubtful whether there will be more than 315,000 stations in the country by the end of 1935. When Vacuum has 122,000 it will have more than a third of the number. Actually its position will be much stronger. The stations being acquired represent in many respects the cream of the independents in the country. By 1935 Vacuum will probably be doing at least half of the gasoline business.

More important still, it can then be effective in coordinating and unifying all the scattered forces of Standard Oil, making it unnecessary for that company to seek repeal or modification of the anti-trust law or to attempt mergers in the face of them. A firm basis of monopoly will have been reestablished. That goal has not yet been reached. It will not be reached uncontested by Shell and other independents. Several of them are still strong enough to put serious obstacles in Standard Oil's path. Shell Union, for instance, has expanded rapidly in the past few years. Today, throughout the nation, it owns or controls some 35,000 stations.

Texaco reached nation-wide proportions even earlier. If it has not been expanding so rapidly as some of the others of late, it is still a factor in the fight. The other leaders are not idle. This year the aggressiveness of Cities Service and Sinclair has been especially notable. The presence of the Mellons in Gulf, of the Daweses in Pure Oil, of J. P. Morgan and Company in Continental, lends power and intensity to the struggle.

Of all the independents, however, Shell Union is the most to be reckoned with. Behind it are all the world-wide assets of Royal Dutch-Shell and forty years of growth and prosperity such as no oil group except Standard at the height of the trust has ever experienced. Behind it also is the sponsorship of the British government. For expansion in the United States Shell Union is now spending from $150,000,000 to $200,000,000 a year—pocketing temporary loss to intrench itself for ultimate gain. At its present rate of growth, it may have 75,000 stations by the end of 1935.

If both Vacuum and Shell Union were to achieve their objectives, the American gasoline market would then be divided between them. With the resources at their command it is not inconceivable that they could wipe out or absorb even the largest of the other factions.

Between Standard and Shell there might then ensue a battle to the death —a battle of price-cutting, "diversification," and "super-servicing" far more exaggerated than that in which they have long been engaged; and a battle from which the consumer would derive much temporary profit. Deterding admits that his interests are "always ready for a good fight." Standard has fought, too, on occasion; but with large competitors it would rather make agreements (in which the competitors, incidentally, have not usually had the upper hand). It goes without saying that neither Standard nor Shell can afford to "fight away" its profits.

There have in fact been recent evidences of willingness on the part of both, but particularly Shell, to cooperate. Standard of New Jersey and I. G. Farbenindustrie Aktiengesellschaft, the German chemical trust, control the hydrogenation process for extracting gasoline from coal, oil shale, and other minerals— a process which not only is said to return 105 barrels of refined from every 100 of crude, but which extends almost infinitely the oil resources of the nation. New Jersey has formed a company to license the process in this country. With other independents, Shell Union has taken stock in it. The control, however, remains in the hands of Standard Oil. Shell Union has been forced to participate because it dares not be left behind. It is not improbable that New Jersey may make as much from the licensing, over a long period of years, as it has ever made from the sale of oil.

With the other independents out of the way and Shell alone in Standard's path toward monopoly, it is logical that such agreements would be made. Controlling future refining through hydrogenation, and controlling a majority of the markets of the country, Standard could probably persuade Shell to the wisdom of such cooperation. The mere fact that they have long been enemies would not alter the supposition. In modern business, profits come first. Dividends must be paid. In order to continue them companies must be able and willing to adjust themselves to new situations as they arise. No one understands this better than those who guide the destinies of Standard Oil and Shell. There would be no necessity for merger or even for open agreements between them then. After all, such things are better done on the quiet. But *if* the Vacuum project goes through, *if* New Jersey can retain control of refining, Standard's control of the industry would follow. Monopoly would have closed its grip on the oil industry and on the public who must buy its products.

Now monopoly as such is not to be condemned. If such monopoly were established under close government supervision, then the development of closer relationship between production and consumption, the greater efficiency through elimination of waste in product and of duplication of facilities, the nation-wide uniformity of product and service would on the face of the matter be worthwhile to the public. The American Telephone and Telegraph Company as a virtual monopoly is doing a better job than its constituent companies could do separately. If the oil monopoly were built up openly, under close governmental and public supervision, it might even be a step toward government ownership and operation of this basic industry. If, however, the new Standard Oil trust were built up secretly, so that its existence or the extent of its control was unknown, it is probable that the increased efficiency would react only in favor of an "inside" few. Even the rank and file of the stockholders, collecting reasonable dividends regularly, need not be apprised of it. The effects of the monopoly would extend farther than the sale of oil products. Because of the immense profits and power which a few would enjoy, it might in time extend into every important phase of American life. . . .

CHAOS IN THE OIL INDUSTRY (1933)

George Ward Stocking

THE OIL INDUSTRY, under a self-imposed system of controlled production called proration, seemed until recently to be headed back toward prosperity. "The oil industry gives indication of being the first basic industry to emerge from the world depression." This was the optimistic message contained in the October report of the federal Oil Conservation Board, and for some time previous leaders of the industry had been giving public utterance to similar sentiments. What was the evidence? Mid-continent crude-oil prices at the end of the first half of 1932 were at more than twice the levels of a year previous; they were five times the lows of 1931. Consumption of crude oil during the first half of 1932 was more than 89 per cent of that for a similar period in 1929, when domestic consumption reached an all-time peak. It was more than 94 per cent of the 1931 figure. Gasoline consumption had shown an even better record; it set a new peak in 1931 despite the depression, and in the first six months of 1932 showed a decline of only 8 per cent compared with consumption during the same period of 1931. Of equal importance, the f. o. b. Gulf terminal price of sixty-five-octane gasoline advanced from slightly over three cents a gallon in the summer of 1931 to slightly less than six cents in the summer of 1932, an increase of approximately 75 per cent. What other major industry could boast a similar record?

Now, however, the oil industry has again been thrown into chaos. Proration orders of the Texas Railroad Commission have been held invalid, the Texas militia has been withdrawn from the East Texas field by order of the Supreme Court of the United States, "bootleg oil" has been produced in ever-increasing amounts, pipe-lines have been dynamited, and human lives threatened. The price of oil has responded promptly to these various influences; its upward trend has been sharply reversed; and leaders of the oil industry, formerly individualists of the most rugged sort, have been urging that the broader powers of federal and State governments be placed behind the industry's program of control.

Since Drake completed the first commercial petroleum well in this country in 1859 until the present time, oil production has been accompanied by waste on a spectacular scale. The waste has been widespread and notorious. It has rankled in the mind of the oil-field engineer and harassed the spirit of the conservationist. For many years, however, it did not disturb the equanimity of the business leaders of the industry, who were able to reap profits, frequently on a grand scale, because of the expanding demand for petroleum products. Despite the indifference of business men to the profligate manner in which our petroleum resources were being developed, a petroleum shortage during the war emergency accentuated the fears of the conservationists, gave rise to a general apprehension of petroleum shortage, quickened the activities of the State Department in protection of American oil interests abroad, and led eventually to the creation of the federal Oil Conservation Board. Immediately after its organization, the board began an investigation of the oil industry for the purpose of determining the extent of waste and means of checking it. The industry's response to this move, through the Report of the Committee of Eleven of the American Petroleum Institute, was a denial of waste, assurance of the ability of the industry to provide adequate supplies of petroleum during all time, and insistence that the industry only needed to be left alone.

That was in 1925. Since then the wail of the conservationist has been drowned by a flood of oil. The fear of shortage has gone down before the fact of surplus. Long before the present depression leaders in the oil business, untroubled by the record of waste in their industry, became seriously disturbed by accumulating oil stocks and declining prices. As the situation became more acute, the vision of the oil men was clarified. They saw what in the glaring light of rising prices had been hidden from view—waste in the production of oil. The truth began to be apparent during 1927. Accumulating stocks for more than half a dozen years had so weakened the oil price structure that it could not withstand the shock of the Oklahoma Greater Seminole field's peak daily output of 527,400 barrels. Between the discovery of the Seminole field a year earlier and August, 1927, prices of mid-continent 36°-gravity crude dropped from $2.29 per barrel to $1.28. The throes of Seminole foreran the birth of a conservation idea. It was christened proration. The child has grown large. Today its influence dominates oil production.

Uncontrolled production, we have been told recently, means the rapid infiltration of underground water and the premature drowning of oil pools. It means the wasteful dissipation of gas pressure, essential for maximum recovery. It means, through lower prices, the permanent destruction of thousands of "marginal" wells whose daily production, though individually small, accounts in the aggregate for about half our daily output. The predestined mission of proration is the elimination of these wastes. Such is its cloak of righteousness. Stripped of its disguise, it presents a different picture.

To bring the Seminole field under control and to restrict output to "market demand," a plan was put into operation involving the allocation of a daily "allowable" output to the various producers of the field. While Seminole was thus being subjected to a "rational" control, a proration program similar in purpose and character was being established in the Winkler field of West Texas. These initial voluntary efforts of the oil industry proved futile, however, in the face of a property system which placed a premium upon waste and which legalized robbery in the exploitation of an oil field. Since voluntary control was threatened with shipwreck upon the rugged rocks of individualism, an appeal was made to existing State conservation agencies to put the authority of law behind the industry's "conservation" program.

With the assistance of the Oklahoma Corporation Commission and the Texas Railroad Commission, machinery was eventually established whereby all the fields in these two States were subjected to a proration program under which a total allowable output for the State and for each of its pools was determined. This "allowable" was then allocated among the various pools and wells of the State on an "equitable" basis as determined by the producers of the pools. By 1931 a somewhat similar system had been established in the States of Oklahoma, California, and Kansas, which together with Texas produced approximately 86 per cent of the total domestic output. By means of specially devised cooperation among producers and with the assistance of the State militia in Oklahoma and Texas, despite the violent though temporary disturbance occasioned by the East Texas and Oklahoma fields in the summer of 1931, production was temporarily brought into balance with demand.

When the oil men have known what they wanted, the conservation agencies have given it to them. But there has sometimes been a conflict of interests. Operators fortunately situated within a particular field, realizing that the major advantages of curtailed output would be at their expense, have opposed proration. Likewise, refineries dependent upon the production of particular wells for their daily crude supply have found their interests running contrary to those of the larger companies. In general, small, independent producers in flush fields, whose profit possibilities may depend upon rapid development of their holdings, have been reluctant to accept the proration program. Where these conditions have existed, the conservation agencies have acted as umpires in harmonizing conflicting claims. A compromise figure having been agreed upon, it was customarily declared to be the precise and only amount of oil which could be produced without waste, and an order was issued prohibiting production in excess of this amount and allocating the allowable among the producing wells. In the late summer of 1932 independent East Texas producers, alleging that curtailment had been largely at their expense for the benefit of producers in other sections of the State, agitated for an increase in East Texas allowable and a decrease in the allowable of certain other pools of the State, in order that the balance between output and market demand might not be disturbed. Experts of the commission testified on this occasion that a decrease in production of certain pools could be effected only at the expense of physical waste. A few weeks later, however, when the seasonal peak of gasoline demand had passed and reduction in total State output was necessary to avoid price declines, these pools participated as a matter of course in a State-wide decrease in daily allowable of more than 127,000 barrels.

With the passing of time opposition to proration almost completely disappeared, save in the East Texas and Oklahoma City fields. Through threats of price cuts and promises of price advances recalcitrants have been temporarily whipped into line. Advancing prices, temporary though they proved, brought additional revenue into sorely straitened State treasuries, poured greater profits into the coffers of oil companies, and increased confidence in the hearts of the business leaders. Proration had accordingly come to be regarded as an act of statesmanship. More important, in the case of Champlin Refining Company *vs.* Corporation Commission of Oklahoma, the Supreme Court of the United States in a unanimous decision in May of 1932 placed the stamp of legality upon the program as applied in Oklahoma. As the masquerade of monopoly which the industry has staged has received such generous public applause, proration has now put on less modest garments. Not only is it called a measure of conservation, but it is said to afford a mechanism of escape from the economic depression which is so sorely troubling us.

Although the program has incidentally contributed to the elimination of waste in oil production, the chief wastes of the industry continue but little abated. In some instances, a controlled rate of production has doubtless resulted in a more efficient utilization of water pressure. On the other hand, in some instances, a controlled rate of production has no less certainly contributed toward a less efficient utilization of gas pressure. Because the property tract instead of the geological unit remains the basis of operation, and because individual profit rather than efficient production is still the object of oil operations, waste in this respect continues to bulk large. On October 31, 1930, the latest date for which data are available, 467,753,000 cubic feet of raw gas were being wasted directly, and an additional 595,562,000 cubic feet were being wasted after the gasoline content had been extracted, out of a total daily production of 2,045,828,000 cubic feet of gas incidental to oil production in Texas. For other States total figures are not available, but according to estimates of the Oklahoma Corporation Commission last year the Oklahoma City field alone was wasting about 203,000,000 cubic feet of residue gas daily. The annual fuel value of this gas, calculated from these combined figures, is equivalent to that of 18,868,000 tons of coal. Far more important is the fact that under a genuine conservation program, with a unified system of oil production, virtually all of this gas could be used for repressuring purposes, with a tremendous though indeterminable increase in oil recovery and a huge decline in the cost of producing oil. As daily output in the East Texas field was restricted from approximately 1,000,000 barrels of oil per day to approximately 310,000 barrels, the number of producing wells increased from 1,625 to 9,300, with an increase in developmental cost of more than $100,000,000. The only thing that can be said with certainty about a "conservation" program of this sort is that it has increased tremendously the cost of producing oil in this field.

As conservationists, the leaders of the industry have indeed been tilting at windmills. Behind a camouflage of conservation they have endeavored to carry through a program of price-fixing. In the language of the District Court of the United States for the Eastern District of Texas in a case involving the legality of the proration orders of the Texas Railroad Commission: "Under the thinly veiled pretense of going about to prevent physical waste, the commission has, in cooperation with persons interested in raising and maintaining prices of oil and its refined products, set on foot a plan which, seated in a desire to bring supply within the compass of demand, derives its impulse and spring from, and finds its scope and its extent in, the attempt to control the delicate adjustment of market supply and demand, in order to bring and keep oil prices up" (*sic*).

The increased purchasing power in the hands of the oil industry is secured at the expense of approximately twenty-five million users of automobiles in the United States. It represents a transfer of purchasing power from those who have little to those who have much. To the extent that it remains in the treasuries of the oil companies it may add chaos to confusion by contributing to the further expansion of an industry whose chief ailment is overexpansion. To the extent that it is paid out as dividends it will represent a concentration of purchasing power in the hands of a few at the expense of the many. It will thereby serve to aggravate a depression one of whose major causes, at any rate, has been maldistribution of purchasing power through oversaving. As a guide from the valley of depression to the plateau of prosperity, proration is apt to prove a chimera and a nightmare.

Despite this fact we seem to have launched irretrievably upon a program of regulation for the oil industry. In truth, the abandonment of proration in the light of the potentialities of East Texas might bring demoralization if not ruin to the industry. This field is the most stupendous in the history of oil production.

Because of its geographic extent and the widely disseminated character of the property holdings it is known as "the little man's paradise." With more than 9,000 wells in operation, it was estimated that two hours' open flow would yield 3,000,000 barrels of oil, approximately 50 per cent more than the daily consumption of the entire country. Later estimates indicate an even larger potential yield; but even if this rate were maintained, in less than one month East Texas alone could more than supply the annual American demand. Because of the large potential production of many wells and of the Texas marginal-well law, it has thus far proved impossible to frame proration orders which the courts will uphold. The withdrawal of the militia has further complicated the industry's attempt to restrict output. The threatened breakdown of proration in this field was responsible for the conference of the oil industry in Washington and its request for federal intervention. What the outcome will be is not yet clear. But despite the obvious shortcomings of the oil industry's program, what should be clear is that unrestricted competition in mining a migratory mineral whose ultimate recovery is dependent upon efficient utilization of gas and water pressure causes intolerable waste. Unrestricted competition, which carries with it the right to drill as many wells as the property-owner may deem expedient and to locate them wherever he wishes, not only greatly increases the cost of producing oil, but decreases ultimate recovery of a limited natural resources by perhaps 50 per cent. It leads inevitably to the confusion of surplus capacity and overproduction. In view of these facts, there seems to be no turning back. The way out lies straight ahead. What is needed is some sort of unified operation of oil fields, designated to eliminate needless duplication and to insure an efficient utilization of the pressure resources in oil recovery. A program which achieves this end must obviously carry with it adequate assurance that the consumer will be protected from unreasonably high prices for petroleum products. In no other industry is the challenge to social control so striking or the potentialities so rich. Here is a real opportunity for a new deal.

THE NRA OIL TRUST (1934)

Mauritz A. Hallgren

INDUSTRIAL SELF-DISCIPLINE, with all its usual monopolistic trappings, has been chosen as the method by which the Roosevelt Administration hopes to tame the petroleum industry. It was at first thought that this objective might be achieved by means of an elaborate price-fixing scheme to be administered by a public agency. Bad as this plan was, it at least had the merit of being subject to a mild but definite measure of social control. For various reasons, however, the proposal was abandoned, without the public hearings that had been promised by the Petroleum Administrator, and for it were substituted two voluntary agreements, in accordance with which the industry, or so it is contended, will discipline itself. The new arrangement has not only all the evils to be found in the original price-fixing scheme but several others for good measure. It provides for price-fixing by the industry itself, or rather by the dominant major companies, instead of by a public agency. It encourages centralization of control of the industry in the hands of relatively few companies. It slights the interest of the consuming public and affords no protection to small enterprises. Indeed, under this latest plan, which is now in operation, the major companies can in effect dictate the terms upon which independent gasoline distributors and others may do business. . . .

Since the price of oil and its products seemed to play such a prominent part in the petroleum war, some of the code-makers thought that price-fixing in some form should be provided for in the petroleum code. Secretary of the Interior Ickes, who was later to become the administrator of the code, favored price regulation in principle. General Hugh S. Johnson, the recovery administrator, was opposed to it, declaring that price control could only succeed when "both supply and demand were under control." . . . The industry itself was divided. One group, led by Wirt Franklin, president of the Independent Petroleum Association, was most emphatic in its advocacy of price regulation. This group, composed of officials of several of the major companies—though not those of first importance—including Standard Oil of California, Barnsdall, Consolidated, and the Independent Petroleum Association, and of a few marketing groups, such as the Illinois Petroleum Marketers' Association, finally captured control of the committee representing the American Petroleum Institute in the code negotiations. Among the companies that were opposed to price control as at first proposed were Standard of New Jersey, Standard of Indiana, Texas Company, Sun Oil, Skelly, Socony-Vacuum, and Royal Dutch Shell. Why these giants of the industry were disinclined to accept price-fixing is not altogether clear, though the suggestion has been made that they were not opposed to it in principle but objected to entering into any price-control arrangement over which the government had any direct authority, for fear of "slipping their heads into a government noose."

The outcome of the controversy was to place in the hands of the petroleum administrator sufficient authority to regulate prices at the refineries and filling stations for a trial period. . . . Administrator Ickes moved first to check the free flow of oil in the producing fields. His second step was to issue an order fixing prices for a trial period. . . . The schedule of prices and differentials contained in the order was worked out by the Planning and Coordination Committee, which was completely in the hands of the price-fixing faction of the industry.

The December 1 order was based on the most insubstantial of facts. Indeed, it can truthfully be said that it was not based on facts at all, but only on what the price-fixing advocates thought the traffic would bear. Except for statistics that might be buried in the books of individual companies, there were no facts available upon which even the most judicious and impartial Administrator could possibly base an equitable price for gasoline or crude oil. The cost of distributing gasoline in the retail market had, for example, never been broken down by cost experts for the industry as a whole. Although government agencies had made such studies in other fields, they had kept their hands off the retail gasoline cost structure. The industry has consistently balked any move to investigate its distribution costs. The major companies, as the Department of Commerce confessed in 1930, have gone so far as to refuse to allow any data to be published with respect to the proportion of their retail sales to the total volume of gasoline sales on the domestic market. Without even these rudimentary facts, how was it possible for the Planning and Coordination Committee or the Petroleum Administrator to arrive at the conclusion that a certain grade of gasoline must be sold at retail at a margin of five and one-half cents over the wholesale price in order to allow for costs and profit? Or that six and one-half cents would cover the costs of selling another grade of motor fuel?

The price-fixing order promptly aroused a storm of protest from many quarters, but especially from the surviving independent distributors. They contended that it would increase the cost of gasoline to the automobile owner an average of three cents throughout the country. In this they were supported not only by the Standard Statistics Company, a private agency in New York City, but also by the Consumers' Advisory Board of the NRA. Mrs. Mary H. Rumsey, chairman of the Consumers' Board, declared in a letter to Administrator Ickes that whereas the code had increased labor costs in the industry by only $125,000,000 annually, "the consumers' bill for petroleum products has been increased at a rate of over $500,000,000 annually." The independents asserted that they could profitably operate filling stations by selling gasoline at retail at a margin of no more than two and a half to three cents over the wholesale price. The larger companies, the independents declared, were insisting upon a margin of five and a half to six and a half cents in order to cover the cost of operating palatial filling stations in high-rent districts. They pointed to "the incredible waste and the insane duplication of marketing outlets," and added that "it would seem the petroleum industry has simply decided that the consumer must pay for all of this madness. . . .

The chief complaint of the independents, however, was that they could not hope to compete with the larger companies if they had to sell their goods at the same prices. The latter have a virtual monopoly on conveniently located filling station sites, and whereas there are many motorists who are willing to drive a few extra blocks to the "tankside" stations owned and operated by independent companies in order to buy gasoline a cent or two cheaper, few would go to that extra effort if they could get their motor fuel at the same price from stations situated on or close to the main traffic arteries. Moreover, the larger companies, out of their more abundant financial resources, can provide their customers with extra service "free of charge."

Administrator Ickes subsequently postponed the effective date of the price-fixing order. . . . That he took this step because of the protests of the independent companies and consumers' representatives is not borne out by the available facts. On the contrary, there is evidence to show that he was disturbed mainly by the reluctance of the giants of the industry to commit themselves publicly to the price-fixing scheme. Finally he issued an ultimatum . . . demanding that on a certain day and at a certain hour the industry place in his hands an agreement for a settlement of all its differences and problems. The major companies were by no means slow in responding to this plain-spoken invitation. Though they had carried on their warfare over a period of more than two generations, they managed miraculously to come to terms within a few days.

Their proposal, which the Administrator approved with a few unimportant modifications, consists of two agreements. The first provides for the organization of a pool, to be known as the National Petroleum Agency, which will "purchase, hold, and in an orderly way dispose of surplus gasoline which threatens the stability of the oil price structure, in an effort to bring the prices of gasoline into proper relationship with the present price of crude oil and to maintain and support such relationship." The second agreement provides for the establishment and maintenance of what is euphemistically called "marketing margins" for distributors, jobbers, and wholesalers of gasoline. The retail dealers' margins have been set at six cents a gallon for the better grades of gasoline and at three and three-fourths cents for gasoline below sixty-octane rating. Only the refiners are to be parties to this second agreement, and it is intended that they shall exercise a strict control over retail prices by means of standardized sales contracts. "The parties to this agreement shall use only such forms of contract in such transactions. Such contracts shall contain provisions controlling prices of products to ultimate consumers at retail."

It can hardly be argued that this is not bald and naked price-fixing. The industry is now in a position to pass on to the consuming public the entire cost of the palatial filling stations and all the other extravagant expenditures that have attended the development of unnecessary and uneconomic retail outlets. The independent distributor, whose costs are low, may no longer share the difference with the consumer, for when he buys his gasoline from the refiner he must agree to charge a certain retail price. Thus he is deprived of his only competitive advantage. Of course, a few refiners may refuse to sign the marketing agreement, but this is not likely to happen, since the pooling agreement gives the major companies plenty of power to compel recalcitrant refiners to come into the fold.

The price-fixing features alone are enough to condemn the present arrangement, but other objections to it can also be made. The authority to fix prices rests not with a public agency but with the industry itself; indeed, in the final analysis it rests with the financially more powerful companies. Authority to interpret other provisions of the dual agreement also rests with the industry. For example, the agreement "contemplates that orders and allocations, touching crude-oil production, imports, withdrawals from and additions to storage, and gasoline manufacture shall be such as to balance supply with consumer demand for petroleum products and to prevent the accumulation of supplies of crude oil or petroleum products in excess of desirable economic working levels." Who is to determine when supply and demand are balanced or what constitutes "desirable economic working levels"? It would seem essential from the standpoint of the public interest that this vast power to make decisions affecting not only the entire petroleum industry but every consumer of petroleum products should be placed in the hands of an impartial authority. Instead, Administrator Ickes has permitted the power to be exercised by the National Petroleum Agency, and more particularly by this association's board of governors, which is made up of persons financially interested in the decisions to be arrived at. More than that, the governors are to exercise their control mainly through pool purchases of "surplus" gasoline. By means of these purchases they will in effect be able to control the gasoline market. When the governors are not in session, five of their number may administer the pool's purchases and sales. In addition, "by a majority vote of the entire board of governors *or the vote of nine governors representing members of the association having in the aggregate more than 50 per cent in amount of participation in the association,* purchases may be suspended entirely until they are again authorized by a majority vote of the entire board of governors *and* the vote of nine governors representing such majority interest in amount." In other words, nine of the financially strongest companies have the power of life and death over the pool which is to "maintain and support proper relationships of gasoline prices." . . .

LIGHT ON THE OIL TRUST (1939)

The Nation

WE VENTURE TO SAY that as much could be learned about monopoly, its methods, its disguises, its phoenix-like ability to rise from the ashes of dissolution decrees, from an obscure bill now before the Senate Committee on the Judiciary as from the volumes of testimony piling up in the hearings of the Temporary National Economic Committee. The bill to which we refer, S 2181, was introduced by Senators Borah and Gillette. Its significance is not readily apparent, and it is unlikely that newspapers dependent on oil-company advertising will devote much space to explaining it. A bill "to prohibit interstate common-carrier pipe lines from transporting commodities in which such carriers have any interest" may seem of technical and minor importance. But it happens to strike at the heart of the new oil "trust" which has been growing up in place of the old trust, smashed by court order in 1911. For control of the pipe lines, the arteries through which oil pours from the great producing fields to the seaboards, is today's equivalent of the elder Rockefeller's secret alliance with the railroads. The enormous profits of the pipe lines—they earn from 24 to 400 per cent annually on net investment—have supplanted the rebates by which the creator of the Standard Oil trust milked and undermined his independent competitors.

The Borah-Gillette bill was introduced because oil interests succeeded in forcing a similar clause out of the Wheeler-Truman bill. The smell of oil has always been strong in the lobbies of Washington, and the oil lobby has always succeeded in the past and may succeed again in protecting monopoly control of pipe lines from Congressional attack. The first commercial oil pipe line of any importance was built in 1878 by independent western Pennsylvania oil producers in an attempt to escape the grip of the combination between the Pennsylvania Railroad and the Standard Oil Company, which was slowly forcing them out of business. Then as now control of transportation facilities meant control of the industry, and by 1883 Rockefeller succeeded in bringing this pipe line—the last hope the independents had to get their oil to market on fair terms—under his control. The pipe line assumed increasing importance in the minds of the oil monopolists as regulation of railroads made it more and more difficult to discriminate against the independent oil man. The anti-rebating provisions of the

Elkins Act of 1903 and the 1911 decision by the Supreme Court upholding the trust-busting decree against the old Standard Oil Company stimulated the construction of pipe lines. Control of the pipe line was used to squeeze out the independent as control of railroads serving the anthracite coal country was used against the independent mine owner.

The Hepburn Act in 1906 was an attempt to break up the coal-railroad combination. The original bill forbade a "common carrier" to convey commodities produced by a company owned by the carrier. In that form it would have applied to pipe lines as well as railroads. The oil lobby succeeded in changing the words "common carrier" to "railroad" before the bill was passed. Today the twenty interlocking major oil companies own 97 per cent of the oil pipe lines and determine the terms and rates on which oil is to be shipped to market.

Two figures tell what effect this has had on the independent oil producer. Twenty-five years ago the major companies produced no more than 20 per cent of their own crude oil. Today they produce 60 per cent. The combination that grew great on the supply of kerosene for lighting has now grown beyond anything the trustbusters dreamed of on the demand for gasoline to run the automobile and the airplane. In place of the trust we have interlocking financial controls and community of interest among twenty great companies taking 95 per cent of the crude oil produced in this country. The economic power of this combine overawes the agencies of law enforcement. The anti-trust laws could be used against the pipe-line monopoly. So could the anti-rebating provisions of the Interstate Commerce Act. Neither have been so used.

This is by no means merely an oil problem. It is also a railroad problem. And it is a coal problem. It is estimated that oil pipe lines drain half a billion dollars' worth of gross revenue from the railroads, enough to take most of them out of the red. But the economic power of the oil combine is great enough to muzzle the men who are responsible for the welfare of a 25-billion-dollar investment in railroads. The oil combine can threaten to divert freight unless the railroads behave. The combine's financiers can exert even more direct pressure. The Mellon and du Pont interests are but two examples of family concerns powerful in oil and also powerful enough as industrial freight customers of the railroads to swing the big stick over them. Du Pont is Phillips Petroleum. It is also General Motors. A similar situation exists in coal. Competing fuels have eaten up 50 per cent of the market for coal. Fuel oil is the chief competing fuel. Fuel oil constitutes 38 per cent of the oil industry's output but provides only 12 1/2 per cent of its revenue. There is reasonable ground for suspicion that sale of fuel oil is being subsidized at the expense of the gasoline consumer. Millions of dollars invested in coal and several hundred thousand mine families are affected. Why doesn't the coal industry fight? But our first- and third-largest bituminous coal companies are controlled by Mellon, and Mellon is also Gulf Oil. The second-largest coal company, now in bankruptcy, is controlled by Rockefeller-dominated trustees, and Rockefeller is Standard Oil. Oil can actually be shipped more cheaply by rail than by pipe line, but the pipe line is necessary to maintenance of monopoly controls. The consumer foots the bill. Railroad workers and investors, mine workers and mine owners, also pay in lost wages and lost investment. Could there be a more dramatic example of the economic wastes and pervasive power that flow from uncontrolled monopoly?

PIPE LINES AND PROFITS (1941)

I. F. Stone

THE HOPE THAT the Russo-Japanese pact does not mean Soviet abandonment of China is growing dimmer here, and this would be the psychological moment for the Administration to make Morgenthau and Jesse Jones stop piddling and fiddling over that $100,000,000 they promised the Chinese last fall. It would also be the psychological moment for an embargo on all oil shipments to Japan. The Chinese need a shot in the arm badly, and their continued resistance is as important to us in the East as Britain's is in the West. *Pravda*'s belly-crawling assurances yesterday to Hitler and its scarcely veiled invitation to the Japanese to help themselves to "vulnerable spots" in the East signal serious trouble ahead. I am informed in the Department of Commerce that our oil exports to Japan are still averaging about 400,000 barrels a week, and have been as high as 600,000 barrels. This includes crude oil for Japan's refineries, fuel oil for its navy, low-grade aviation gas, motor fuel for mechanized vehicles, and lubricating oils of all kinds. Since the oil companies are always asking for our intervention in their behalf in Latin America, since we helped them muscle in on the Near East fields after the last war, and since we may have to defend the Dutch East Indies, an embargo ought to apply to shipments from American oil-company properties anywhere—in the Dutch West Indies as well as the Dutch East Indies, on the Persian Gulf as well as the Gulf of Mexico. A government too flabby to keep its oil companies from fueling our enemies is too flabby to fight a successful war.

Rancid is the word for the contrast between the unwillingness of the oil companies to make this contribution to the security of their country and the many favors they continue to ask and receive here in the name of national defense. The State Department is making a fatted calf of Camacho in preparation for the return of our prodigal oil companies to Mexico. We have placed a Rockefeller in charge of promoting our Good Neighbor policy, and he has the help of a Chase National Bank executive in passing on Export-Import Bank loans to Latin America. Chase National, based on Standard Oil millions, is well known for neighborliness in Latin America, particularly in Cuba, where it financed a man named Machado. It and the oil dollar-a-year men could easily prove criticism unjust by exerting their influence to stop oil shipments to Japan. Some of them have been using their influence to obtain some extraordinary letters in behalf of their companies from Mr. Roosevelt, Mr. Stimson, and Mr. Knox. There is no good reason why this influence shouldn't work both ways.

So far the only embargo for which the oil trust's dollar-a-year men have been plugging is an embargo on Thurman Arnold. Thurman Arnold, like Senator O'Mahoney, derives ultimately from the oil state of Wyoming, and the oil companies aren't accustomed to back talk from that area. The Senator is so well house-broken that he didn't even mention the oil monopoly in the final report of his monopoly inquiry, a spectacle to make history gape. Arnold, though unpredictable, has backbone, and he started out last fall to use both the Sherman Act and the Elkins Act against the pipe lines. Control of transportation is as much the heart of the oil monopoly today as it was when Henry Demarest Lloyd wrote "Wealth Versus Commonwealth." The pipe lines are supposed to be common carriers; the oil monopoly has kept them private thoroughfares. The first move made by the oil companies was to obtain a report from the National Defense Commission, prepared by Leon Henderson, hinting that defense would be impaired if Arnold were permitted to demand divorcement of the pipe lines. The report said the companies would not build certain pipe lines badly needed for defense if he went ahead with this part of his anti-trust suit. When I asked where these pipe lines were to be built I was told that was a military secret. I then obtained possession of this military secret for 15 cents by buying a copy of the annual pipe-line number of the *Oil and Gas Journal,* which contained a map showing all existing pipe lines and the two proposed new ones referred to in the report.

One was to be built from Port St. Joe, Florida, to Chattanooga by Pure Oil (Dawes interests) and Gulf (Mellon). The other, from Baton Rouge to Portsmouth, was the competitive answer of Standard of New Jersey and Shell interests, which didn't propose to be put at a disadvantage in the Southeastern marketing area. The promoters of the first line ran into a snag and asked the legislature of Georgia for the right to acquire property by condemnation. The companies obtained a letter from the President saying this was needed for national defense, but on March 19 the legislature, though intensely pro-Roosevelt, refused the request, and the companies are now about to ask Congress for a law giving them the right of eminent domain in Georgia. The Cole committee, which since 1933 has spent about $500,000 investigating oil without ever doing much about it, was chosen as the oil-company forum. On January 24 Rear Admiral H. A. Stuart, director of naval petroleum reserves, had written Congressman John M. Coffee of Washington that the proposed pipe line was "a purely private enterprise" for the importation into the Southeast of "imported refined petroleum products, probably from Mexico, Venezuela, Colombia, etc. . . . and so far as I am aware would not be of any service to the navy." Admiral Stuart was forced to eat his words. On the witness stand before the Cole committee he was confronted with a letter from Secretary of the Navy Knox declaring that this pipe line was required for defense. Major Clifford V. Morgan, oil expert in the office of the Under Secretary of War, who also failed to see any connection between this pipe line and defense, was similarly confronted with a letter to the contrary from Secretary of War Stimson. The railroads and the brotherhoods claim that with 9,000 tank cars a day idle and a shortage of steel the defense argument really runs the other way. Congressman Lea elicited the information at the Cole committee's hearing that the Baton Rouge-Portsmouth line alone would require enough steel to build the 35,000-ton battleships.

Curiously enough, this is the moment at which the liberals on the ICC have finally prevailed upon their colleagues to exercise, for the first time, the power given them by Congress thirty-seven years ago to regulate pipe lines. An order has been issued reducing crude-oil pipe-line rates to an 8 percent return (they have been averaging 25 percent), and another order reduces the rate of two Midwestern gasoline pipe lines to a miserly 20 percent (they have been averaging

30 percent). No doubt the companies will use this as an additional argument for softening up the consent decree they are now negotiating behind the scenes with Thurman Arnold. Thus the ICC, like Providence, moves in mysterious ways. The joker is that very few independents can get to the pipe lines anyway. So long as we permit integrated companies to control the flow of oil from the well to the service-station pump, a reduction in the rates they charge themselves for the use of their own pipe lines merely forces them to put less in one pocket and more in another.

A PEOPLE'S WAR—OR MONOPOLY'S?
(1942)

I. F. Stone

I

IT IS PAINFUL to hear the slogan of a people's war raised by Cox of Georgia. "This bill"—for a Farm Rubber Agency—Cox told the House on Friday, "is in response to public demand for a broadening of the synthetic-rubber program. This is still a people's government, fighting a people's war." Those who have been watching the rubber program know that the first sentence in Cox's statement is literally true, though there is more wish than fulfilment in the second. Nowhere is the difference between a democratic and a monopolistic effort more clearly displayed than in the handling of rubber, and the President's decision to sign or veto the bill will reflect (1) his own comprehension of what a people's war really means and (2) the extent to which a people's war is possible in a monopoly-dominated America.

The bill was written by the five members of a subcommittee of the Senate Committee on Agriculture and Forestry—Senators Gillette, Norris, McNary, Wheeler, and Elmer Thomas. It represents the fruit of the investigation this subcommittee has been making since March 20 to discover how the war program can use farm products. Though it had only $5,000 to spend and has spent less than $2,000, and though its energetic counsel, Paul E. Hadlick, has had a staff consisting of one girl typist, it has taught us more about the problem of rubber and other synthetics than any other committee here. The bill written by this committee would set up a separate agency to arrange for the production of synthetic rubber from farm and forest products. And its purpose in establishing a separate agency, in the words of Senator Norris, is to see that the program is "carried out by men who are friends of it, and not those who have thrown cold water on it always in the past."

The truth is that our failure adequately to utilize all our sources of rubber does not differ fundamentally from our failure to achieve a total effort in steel, copper, aluminum, or magnesium. The difference is that opposition to the mishandling in those fields has come from labor unions, scattered small business men, and some independent engineers. In the case of rubber, the oil-rubber-chemical-alcohol combine has come up against a large and powerful segment of the property-owning classes themselves—the farmers. In that sense rubber from farm alcohol is, indeed, what the New York *Herald Tribune* recently called it, "political rubber." But what that organ intended as a sneer may be taken as an accolade, for here the processes of political democracy are at work to give us the rubber we need by the shortest, best, and cheapest route. If rubber from farm alcohol is "political rubber," then most of the rubber on order today in the $650,000,000 WPB-RFC program is "monopoly rubber," "Standard Oil rubber."

Few people yet realize that rubber from petroleum has never been manufactured on a commercial scale anywhere in the world, that the German Buna process which I. G. Farben never fully revealed to its subservient cartel partner, Standard Oil, is not a process for making rubber from oil. It is a process for making rubber from coal. The only process for making synthetic rubber which has been successfully used is the process for making it from grain alcohol, as the Russians are still doing and as the Poles did before their defeat. It was a shortage of grain, even more than a shortage of petroleum, which led the Germans to seek their rubber from coal gases. Standard Oil and its satellites and allies are now engaged in the difficult task of applying what they know of that German process to petroleum gases—the same gases we need for our aviation-gasoline program.

Ignorance, insincerity, and duplicity—it will be some time before we know the exact proportions of each—have mingled in the making of the present program. Although rubber from alcohol is an old story to chemists, the WPB was blanketed in official ignorance of its very existence until a few months ago when the Gillette subcommittee began its work. Under pressure from that committee it has now been decided to make 200,000 tons of our 800,000-ton program from alcohol, but the entire quota has been assigned to Union Carbide and Carbon, an ally of Standard Oil and part of the inner chemical ring. Union Carbide makes synthetic, not grain, alcohol and turns it into rubber by a variant of the oldest Russian method, a complicated four-step process long since improved in the Soviet Union. Today there are processes available in laboratories run by the Department of Agriculture and state colleges in Nebraska and Iowa which can produce butadiene—the raw material of Buna-type rubber—much more quickly and efficiently. The inventor of the Polish process is operating a pilot plant for a one-step process at the Publicker Alcohol Plant in Philadelphia, and the newer butylene-glycol process—an American discovery—skips the alcohol stage entirely.

Far more than rubber is involved in this struggle. The surpluses from our farms, the sulphite waste that flows from our pulp mills, the very husks of corn and hulls of oats contain countless wonders to which organic chemistry already holds the key. The alcohol, glycol, and furfural which chemists can derive from them are the materials from which we can draw fuels to replace our limited supplies of petroleum, plastics to replace our metals, and synthetics better than natural rubber. Here lies the solution of farm surpluses and the farm problem, but here also lies the death of the oil, rubber, chemical, and alcohol trusts. That's what all the shootin's for.

II

Today's announcement of the new policy on anti-trust prosecutions is an extraordinary climax to Thurman Arnold's revelations during the past week. Arnold had disclosed the way in which Standard Oil placed loyalty to its Nazi partner, I. G. Farben, above loyalty to the United States. He had shown that the development of synthetic rubber and many other important war materials in this country was stifled by Standard Oil on orders from Berlin. He had revealed, in the top ranks of Standard and its du Pont and Mellon allies, men who appear more interested in protecting their holdings abroad and their monopolies at home than in winning the war. These men and their henchmen are apparently so powerful that, after all these revelations, they can put the handcuffs on Thurman Arnold. The oil trust is calmly thumbing its nose at the American people.

It seems that the anti-trust laws, not the trusts, have been holding up the war effort. A War Production Board official tells me gravely that one War Department compilation showed that an anti-trust prosecution had lost the country 124 days and 23 evenings of the valuable time of one executive vice-president of an unnamed company. The international-cartel agreements on aluminum and synthetics and magnesium and dyestuffs will cost us precious lives and years. Yet here are the President and Attorney General Biddle and Secretary Stimson and Secretary Knox and the unwilling Arnold himself agreeing that prosecution of these and similar trust arrangements may be postponed for the duration because they take up so much of the time of important executives. The country would be better off if we lost all the time of some of these executives. If the officials of I. G. Farben had dared to act like some of the officials of Standard Oil, they would have been in a concentration camp a long time ago thanking their lucky stars that they hadn't been shot. Here we put up a sign outside their offices, "Do not disturb."

Inquiries into dyestuffs and magnesium are pending. Both are important in the war effort. Are they to be pinched off under the new policy? Either the Secretary of War or the Secretary of the Navy may veto the Attorney General, and the Attorney General can override their veto on a proposed prosecution only by appealing directly to the President. The Secretary of War and the Secretary of the Navy and the men around them were bred in the atmosphere and the service of big business and finance. Some among them have shown a capacity to rise above their background and training that commands confidence and earns gratitude. But these are the exceptions. Even with the best intentions a man cannot altogether shake loose from the habits and preconceptions of a lifetime. Their sympathies, their old friends, their dinner partners, often their own methods in business predispose them toward the very men Arnold has been attacking. If they had possessed this veto power six months ago, would Arnold have been allowed to continue the Standard Oil-I. G. Farben inquiry? I doubt it.

Had Standard Oil come forward after Pearl Harbor and offered to give up its foreign connections and place its patents at the disposal of the country, no one would object to a "let-bygones-be-bygones" attitude toward our anti-trust laws for the duration. But Standard did not do this. It threatened a libel suit when Nathan W. Robertson, one of *PM*'s Washington correspondents, revealed that Standard was refusing to pool its patents for butyl along with other synthetic-rubber formulas. It sought by underhanded means to keep its German connections even after we were in the war. Most important of all, Standard went right on stifling the development of war synthetics until Arnold got the goods on it and forced it into a consent decree. Who knows how many other cartel agreements hobbling this country's war effort are still in effect? Since the new anti-trust policy covers investigations as well as suits and prosecutions, War and Navy officials will often be faced with a choice between Arnold's suspicions and the assurances of their old friends and business associates. Is Arnold to be bound and gagged?

I asked a WPB official why the decision to suspend the anti-trust laws had not been made by Donald Nelson instead of by Stimson and Knox. He said Nelson didn't want the responsibility. It was felt that it would be wiser to leave the decision with the armed services, since the public regarded the War Production Board as dominated by business men. I suggested that the armed services when examined turned out to be as thoroughly dominated by big business men and corporation lawyers as the WPB. The answer very candidly was that the public didn't realize this. One of the sources of this new policy, for example, is a General Walter B. Pyron in Under Secretary of War Patterson's office. Pyron is liaison man between the War Department and the oil industry. He sits in on the meetings of the Petroleum War Industrial Council, a private, not a governmental, body. Suspension of the anti-trust laws for the duration was one of the main objectives of the council's meeting on March 3 and 4, and General Pyron carried the council's wishes to Patterson. The General was until recently vice-president of the Mellon Gulf Oil Company.

The oil trust which was so anxious to accommodate itself to Nazi business methods, and which now has its men in almost every important agency in Washington, is vitally concerned in bringing about a virtual suspension of the anti-trust laws. It wants to kill off the suit filed by Arnold against the trust in September of 1940. It has already disposed of his Elkins Act suit against its pipe lines with a consent decree so weak that the two attorneys who worked on the case for the government refused to sign it, and one of them resigned in disgust. More important than these suits are the protection of its secret world-wide agreements and connections and the precious patents it holds on the multifarious range of synthetic products which can now be made from petroleum. Oil is becoming a chemical industry, and Rockefeller and du Pont are merging their lordly empires. The consent decree on synthetic rubber leaves with them much of their power over the new synthetics, and the country remains dependent on their good faith and good-will. An Administration determined to let nothing stand in the way of victory would seize their patents under the War Powers Act and purge the government of their henchmen, instead of making them safe from the one weapon the people can use against them, the anti-trust laws.

"THE WELLHEAD WARRIORS" (1965)

Mel Wax

. . . NATURAL GAS supplies today one-third of the nation's total energy. The annual bill is about $1 billion for the consumer, who buys it from local utilities, who buy it from interstate pipe lines, who, in turn, buy it from producers.

Since 1954, the FPC has had the authority, buttressed by a crucial Supreme Court decision in the Phillips Petroleum case, to fix the producer's price at the wellhead of gas destined for interstate commerce. The producers fought hard to avoid this decision. They argued that Congress, when it passed the Natural Gas Act in 1938, never intended that the FPC should regulate producer prices —only pipe-line prices. They would settle for a compromise, if the FPC would agree to base price regulation on the "value" of the gas at the point of consumption rather than on the cost to the producer. Presumably, this would provide a freer market.

The stakes are fantastically high—billions and billions of dollars. A 1c per mcf (1,000 cubic feet) increase in the price of natural gas at the wellhead means a $130 million annual increase in the nation's natural gas bill for 35 million domestic and industrial customers. The FPC estimates that a mere 1c increase boosts the total value of the 276.2 trillion cubic feet of proven recoverable gas reserves in the ground by $15 billion.

It is not surprising, then, that the natural gas industry has launched a powerful, well-financed campaign to cut the FPC, and its regulatory powers, down to size, or, failing that, to persuade Congress it must pass legislation to nullify the Phillips decision.

President Johnson is from a gas-and-oil state; as a Senator he led the fight to prevent reappointment of consumer champion Leland Olds to the FPC, and he supported the depletion allowance crusade. The utilities are therefore cautiously optimistic, but it is an optimism tempered somewhat by the reality of a liberal, anti-monopoly Congress, plus a well-organized opposition to any new attacks on the FPC. . . .

Utility strategy is clear. The Independent Petroleum Association of America (IPAA) has kicked off a giant "informational" campaign intended to prod Congress into taking favorable action on new legislation that would nullify the Phillips decision, and to persuade consumers that utilities are really working on their side in seeking to be freed of the shackles of price regulation.

Legislation that would reverse the court's decision was introduced in the 89th Congress under the bipartisan auspices of Representatives Bruce Alger (R., Tex.) and John B. Williams (D., Miss.). What a *Washington Post* editorial writer described as "the wellhead warriors" have unveiled a three-point plan:

(1) Expose the "absurd methods" employed by the FPC to regulate producer prices of natural gas;

(2) Encourage Congressional investigations into FPC procedures;

(3) Invite "all industry organizations into the campaign against present regulation of natural gas."

The IPAA argues that the FPC, which failed to carry out the Supreme Court's mandate during the Eisenhower years, when utilities held a clear 4-1 majority on the commission, still has not determined a fair and legal way to fix prices. There is considerable justification for this contention. It was not until 1961, under Kennedy, that the FPC made any real effort to enforce the Court's ruling. Now, after lengthy hearings, it has finally received an examiner's recommendation in a key case involving area pricing at Texas' Permian Basin gas fields. The commission will make its ruling, and thereby set the standard, before Swidler's term expires in June.

Meanwhile, the FPC, imposing temporary controls, has since 1961 managed to hold the line on what had been a high-soaring price race, and meanwhile the companies have protested the restrictions. Said the authoritative *Oil and Gas Journal:*

> In ten years of experimenting, FPC has not yet come close to finding a legal and practical method of determining "just and reasonable" prices for gas at the wellhead. . . .

When the FPC sent the gas companies a questionnaire designed to help determine what a fair price at the wellhead would be, and to permit the natural gas companies to express their views, the slick public relations firm of Carl Byoir & Associates, Inc., launched a campaign for its client, Panhandle Eastern Pipeline Co. Soon the nation's business pages carried a picture of a pretty girl valiantly trying to support some 10 pounds of questionnaire forms. "Power industry spokesmen," read the caption, "say the questionnaire is a burden to business and that it will cost each company from $85,000 to $250,000 to fill in the answers."

Iowa Republican H. R. Gross rose in the House to demand that a rider be attached to the FPC appropriations bill, to prevent the commission from sending out cost questionnaires. FPC officials replied that they are charged by law with determining facts first, before trying to carry out their assignment of regulating prices. "We would really be subject to criticism if we tried to suck these figures out of our thumbs," said an FPC staffer.

IPAA general counsel Dan Jones wrote to members of Congress, saying: "The ten-year experiment by the FPC has involved a tremendous waste of public funds, unnecessary costs to the industry, and higher prices to the consumers of natural gas. We believe this situation warrants investigation by the Congress. . . ." At the same time, IPAA's public relations staff in Tulsa produced a pamphlet, "Regulating the Gas Producer—10 Years of Trial and Error," designed to convince consumers that they and the companies are on the same side.

In New Orleans last spring, a utility lobbyist urged his colleagues to campaign for repeal of federal regulation of natural gas "in terms even the dumbest Congressman can understand. . . ." This campaign apparently succeeded. Thirty-six Congressmen issued a manifesto demanding that the FPC's authority to regulate natural gas prices for producers be curtailed.

For seven years after the Phillips decision in 1954, the Eisenhower FPC, under Chairman Jerome K. Kuykendall, did nothing about regulating prices. In that time, scores of applications were received for producer price increases, and these automatically became effective, under bond, when the FPC failed to hold hearings. Even if the utilities have to rebate the excess charges, after hearings are ultimately held, it is a splendid way to get the use of millions in interest-free money.

In 1947, the average cost of natural gas at the wellhead was 5c per mcf. By 1953, just prior to the Phillips Petroleum decision, the price was 9.1c per mcf. In 1961, when Swidler's commission began enforcing the law, prices at the wellhead, which account for about half what the consumer must pay, skyrocketed to 16.3c per mcf.

Then the FPC began to hold long-delayed hearings on rate applications, and gas producers were ordered to refund $600 million in excess charges. The biggest single case involved the El Paso Natural Gas Company, which was told in late 1962 to return $79 million to customers in California, New Mexico and Arizona.

The David who slew that Goliath was William M. Bennett . . . who later became chief counsel for the California Public Utilities Commission and now is president of the commission. . . . Bennett has recently become chairman of the Washington-based National Committee for Fair Gas Prices, which will represent consumer interests in the coming fight with the natural gas producers. Unofficially, the United States Conference of Mayors, the American Municipal Association, and the AFL-CIO are backing the committee. Much of the bank roll is expected to come from the AFL-CIO.

California's Public Utilities Commission, under Governor Brown and Chairman Bennett, has been a consumer-minded, front-running agency, along with those of Wisconsin and New York. Regulatory bodies in New Jersey, Nevada, North Dakota, Washington and Rhode Island are represented on the new committee. Two oil states, Colorado and Wyoming, declined to join. Texas wasn't even invited.

California has, by far, the biggest stake in the battle. Ninety per cent of all California homes are heated by natural gas, and California industry depends on it as a fuel. In 1962, the latest year for which accurate figures are available, the state consumed 745 billion cubic feet, nearly three-quarters of it coming from out of state, at a cost of $266,850,000. That is more than 10 per cent of all natural gas moving in interstate commerce in the United States. No wonder Bennett and Brown are concerned about gas prices. . . .

The first positive steps toward determining how to fix prices were taken in 1960, when the FPC suggested setting prices on an area basis for each of the twenty-three gas-producing areas in the United States. Previously, the FPC had considered price regulation on an individual cost-of-service basis, the pattern normally followed for other utilities. Some producers welcomed the new approach, but when the Kennedy commission took over they changed their minds. Clearly, Swidler and his colleagues intended to be just as rough with area pricing as with a cost-of-service approach.

The FPC launched four extensive area investigations. FPC examiner Seymour Wenner issued the Permian Basin area report in September, recommending an area price of 16.5c per mcf, which is about where the price was in 1961. Producers still favor no regulation, but they would be willing to settle for 20c as an area price. The FPC is studying the examiner's report.

Bennett, incidentally, believes the pricing problem can be solved on an individual basis, by fixing wellhead prices for big producers. "Since so few companies control such a large share of the supply, if you regulate their prices, the others will fall in line."

Actually, there are some 30,000 independent natural gas companies and 5,000 members of the IPAA. But the ten largest sell 44 per cent of the natural gas, and the 100 largest account for 91.7 per cent. "Without control," said Swidler, "the principal competition between producers would be in a race to see which company could be the first to set new price peaks."

Twice in the past gas lobbyists have persuaded Congress to exempt them from FPC regulation by legislative fiat. The first time, in 1950, Harry Truman slapped them down with a veto. The second time, in 1956, Dwight Eisenhower was ready to sign the bill when it was disclosed that an oil lobbyist had offered a $2,500 bribe to the late Senator Francis Case (R., S.D.). He also vetoed. Now the well-heeled gas lobbyists are trying again. . . .

HOW TO MAKE A BILLION (1955)

Harvey O'Connor

ON THE THEORY that the more you take out of an oil well the less you have left, an ingenious tax theory has been evolved to assure the production of the biggest and most blatant crop of millionaires that the nation has seen since the "robber barons" flourished in the late nineteenth century.

The gimmick is "depletion allowance." The Treasury Department says it is the biggest of all loopholes in the tax laws, accounting for a loss of revenue of more than $500,000,000 a year on oil alone. The tall fortunes of the Texas tycoons—some estimated up to half-billion—garnered in the past twenty-five years come out of the deep holes of depletion allowance. In some cases Uncle Sam finds himself unable to pry a penny from the income of these nouveaux riches. If a well is a "dry hole," that is a deductible loss; if it produces, then 27 1/2 per cent can be deducted on gross income. When the accountants get through with the books, there is often little left for the Bureau of Internal Revenue to figure on.

So it is that Hugh Roy Cullen, Haroldson Lafayette Hunt, Clint Murchison, and Sid Richardson have been able to accumulate in a brief span of years what it took John D. Rockefeller half a lifetime of patient planning to pocket. Rockefeller was obliged to organize an oil empire the hard way; if the present-day Croesuses have enough holes drilled into Mother Earth, a rigged tax structure assures them opulence. If Lady Luck smiles, they come within an ace of being able to buy up the entire United States. The country's only safety from such fate is that nothing pays off like an oil well; Eastern railroads, international airlines, Babylonian hotels—these are desired more as a pride of pomp and power than a source of income.

The "Four Hundred" of Houston, and the flanking millionaires of Dallas, Fort Worth, Tulsa, and other Southwestern towns, are personal testimonials to the efficacy of depletion allowance. But the major oil companies—Esso's Humble, Socony's Magnolia, Gulf, Texaco—and a score of minor companies specializing in exploration and drilling owe their amazing profits to tax-deductible holes in the ground, sources of wealth whether they run rich with crude oil or "dry" with salt water. The smaller companies, unencumbered by the losses sustained by the majors in marketing, reveal the true delights of tax favoritism; Argo, Honolulu, Louisiana Land and Exploration, Midwest, Pacific Western, Texas Gulf Producing, Texas Pacific Coal and Oil regularly report net income ranging from 30 to 80 per cent of gross income. Add to these the unreported incomes of a hundred family or personal corporations, such as the Cullens' Quintana and the Murchisons' Delhi, and it is easy to see why the Texas crowd of "filthy rich"—so well celebrated in Edna Ferber's "Giant"—are elbowing polished Easterners out of Wall Street.

These men operate in a jungle of "wildcats." A wildcat is a well drilled in territory where oil has not been discovered. On the average, says the American Petroleum Institute, eight out of nine wildcats are "dusters"—dry holes. It sounds like an unpromising way to earn money.

Here is where the tax laws come in. If the man behind the wildcat is in the bracket where 90 per cent of his income would go into the federal treasury, then wildcatting is Open Sesame! He can hardly lose so long as he keeps on drilling. The money he spends drilling eight "dusters" is deductible from his gross income. The income from his ninth well, a producer, is pretty much velvet, for all the "intangible" expenses, such as the preliminary geological work, and all the labor, equipment, and fuel costs of drilling are deductible. On top of that he can deduct 27 1/2 per cent of his gross income on the well.

To illustrate: if the oil man is in the 90 per cent tax bracket and wells cost $100,000 apiece to drill, he will spend $900,000 on nine wells. The eight dry holes, however, will actually cost him only $10,000 apiece, Uncle Sam assuming the rest of the risk. The ninth well, the producer, may be a mint, opening up a new field where a hundred good wells can be drilled.

The theory of depletion allowance as applied to oil and some other minerals is quite unlike the depreciation allowed manufacturers. If a million-dollar plant has an expected life of twenty years, the owner may deduct $50,000 a year for depreciation. But depreciation is not calculated that way on an oil well. If a well in which $100,000 was invested produces $500,000 a year for ten years and then is exhausted, ordinary depreciation allowance would be $10,000 a year, but when it comes to oil, the tax laws do not base depreciation on the investment; instead, "depletion" is the key word, and the investor is allowed to deduct 27 1/2 per cent of his gross income each year. In ten years the owner could deduct $1,375,000 from his income tax on an investment of $100,000. That the deduction is allowed him on a natural resource he never created highlights this as the most extravagant of all gifts from the public purse to private operators.

"I know of no loophole in the laws so inequitable as the excessive depletion exemptions now enjoyed by oil and mining interests," said former President Truman. Senator Hubert Humphrey of Minnesota estimated that if depletion allowance had been dropped for ordinary depreciation, the entire tax increase on those earning less than $4,000 a year could have been avoided in the 1951 tax bill. In 1947 oil companies were able to deduct thirteen times more through depletion than they would have been allowed through the depreciation claimed by other industries. While most big industries are paying taxes at close to 70 per cent of their operating income, the oil industry is being tapped for about 25 per cent. The National Oil Marketers Association, feuding with the crude producers in 1953, estimated that the government could get a billion more in revenue by allowing "true" depletion instead of the flat figure of 27 1/2 per cent.

. . . The stocks of companies specializing in crude-oil production are the darlings of Wall Street. Financial consultants refer to oil stocks as "tax-sheltered investments," an observation that recently led the treasurer of Humble Oil and Refining, the biggest Texas producer, to complain that the stock tipsters were doing a "disservice" to the industry.

Some Wall Street firms operate various games based on depletion allowance. In one such the minimum ante is $50,000. If the wealthy gambler loses, he is out 10 cents on the dollar; if he wins, he can keep 27 1/2 cents for every dollar of gross oil income and also keep 10 per cent of the remainder, to give him 35 cents retained on his high-tax dollar instead of the dime he would have kept without benefit of oil's special indulgence. For the big oil companies there is little risk of losing the dime that the individual speculator might hazard. Armed with the best geophysical information and hundreds of millions of dollars for exploration, they make the greater part of their profits exactly on this kind of operation. Production is their big money-maker, and depletion allowance is the key.

Sensitive to criticism, they contend that these allowances are vital to the expanded oil production needed for national defense. Without them, wildcatting would slow down; there would be little incentive to drill in unexplored fields. The resulting scarcity of crude would drive up the price of gasoline, and the consumer would ultimately suffer. So runs the argument. Actually, however, drilling is being pushed so hard, thanks to depletion allowances, that we now have a "shut-in capacity" of two million barrels a day in excess of what the market can absorb. And the price of gasoline and fuel oil goes up anyway!

Depletion allowance is the deepest taproot of reaction in the United States. The hard-faced political primitives of Houston and Dallas, fortified by these easy millions, can guarantee that the Democratic Party, if it tries to be progressive, will be ruined. They can damn the middle-of-the-road Stevenson as a "creeping socialist" and split the solid South in two. They can do the same to Eisenhower, and are doing it, and can rejoice when the Republican Party is torn in twain. H. L. Hunt, barely noticing the expenditure, finances Facts Forum, the nation-wide radio and TV enterprise that equates moderation with communism.

Roy Cullen can take a flier with the Liberty radio network, where John T. Flynn painted the United Nations as the minion of Moscow. To fantastic hundred-thousand-acre ranches hidden away in western Texas and Mexico by these beneficiaries of depletion allowances come the leaders of native fascism in the United States Senate and House, for physical refreshment; in the deep pockets of these crude oil kings can be found financial refreshment not only for election campaigns but for the bizarre crusades that bedevil American politics.

The Widening Reach

WHAT WE SHOULD DO ABOUT MEXICO (1919)

John Kenneth Turner

NEITHER THE WICKEDNESS of Carranza nor the depravity of the Mexican nation but the policy of Wilson is the key to the Mexican situation. It is a policy, not of non-intervention, but of intervention. Military invasion is the most drastic form of intervention. The Wilson Administration has perpetrated two protracted invasions of Mexico, one lasting seven months and the other eleven months, as well as numerous invasions of shorter duration, each one legally an act of war. It has repeatedly threatened Mexico with force. Every diplomatic representation involving a threat is a form of intervention. Not to speak of aeroplanes, which have strangely flown hundreds of miles over Mexican territory, not once, but many times, American war vessels have been held in Mexican ports for long periods—are being kept in Mexican ports—in violation of international law and over repeated protests of the Mexican Government. . . .

Our interventionist policy has encouraged open and armed defiance of Mexican authority by American property-holders, as well as interventionist propaganda in the United States. In a communication denying that the oil companies seek intervention, published in *The Nation* of July 26, 1919, and signed "The Association of Oil Producers of Mexico," appears the following statement: "The oil companies seek only two things, which are recognition of their legal rights, and adequate protection for their men in the field. In both these contentions they have the support of the Department of State." This seems fairly innocent until one looks a little farther. We find an admission that the oil companies are supporting a rebel army on Mexican soil, and the following assertion is made: "Any money paid to Pelaez for the protection of property and to prevent destruction has been paid . . . with the full knowledge of the Foreign Offices of Great Britain and the United States." It is asserted that the payments to Pelaez began because of threats by Pelaez to destroy property, and the continuation of the payments is defended on the assumption that otherwise Pelaez would destroy property. But another object of the payments appears from these words: " 'King' Pelaez's troops are operating in the oil fields only, far from any railroad, for the reason that the Government is attempting to confiscate their oil values." That is to say, the oil men are employing a bandit army to defy the Mexican Government, as part of a scheme to prevent the application of Mexican laws to the Mexican oil industry. Confirming this well-known fact, Mr. LaGuardia, of New York, in a speech in the House of Representatives, July 10, 1919, said: "I call your attention to this small strip in red. . . . This is under the control of the Pelaez faction. . . . These forces protect the oil industries from being robbed by the Carranza faction. It is supported and paid for by the oil companies."

This armed defiance of the Mexican Government, to which American oil men make confession, is the result of a controversy with the Mexican Government over various purely internal questions, involving the imposition of taxes, the question of prior rights to the products of the sub-soil, and the question of the foreigner's privilege to appeal to his home government for intervention on behalf of what he considers to be his property rights. One of the assertions sent out officially by the National Association for the Protection of American Rights in Mexico and widely circulated in the press reads as follows: "No foreign corporation or individual can legally acquire or hold any mines, oil wells, land, or other real property in Mexico unless he renounces his citizenship." This statement, which purports to be based on a clause in Article 27 of the Mexican Constitution, is a typical example of interventionist falsehood. The Mexican Constitution does not require any foreigner to renounce his citizenship as a condition of acquiring Mexican property. It requires foreigners only to agree "to be considered Mexicans in respect to such property, and accordingly not to invoke the protection of their governments in respect to the same."

We require the same thing of foreigners in this country, although the requirement is not in the Constitution. The purpose of the clause is to compel aliens to seek the same fountains of justice as citizens; that is, the courts, which are open in Mexico the same as in the United States. A French wine manufacturer of California who feels that his property has been confiscated by the prohibition laws may seek justice in American courts, as any American may do. We do not permit him to continue making wine, while forcing American wine manufacturers out of business. Nor do we permit him to call the French navy to San Francisco harbor, there to train its guns on that port, while the French Foreign Office threatens war on behalf of French wine "rights" in the United States.

From the testimony of Messrs. Doheny, Beaty, and others before the investigating committee of the Senate we learn that the Association for the Protection of American Rights in Mexico was the outgrowth of a series of meetings held by oil men in New York, as a result of the decree of February 19, 1918. It was this decree that brought out the note of April 2, 1918, in which the Government of the United States called the attention of the Mexican Government "to the necessity which may arise to impel it to protect the property of its citizens in Mexico." In his testimony Mr. Doheny refers to "the dispute between the oil companies and the United States Government, on the one hand, and the Mexican Government, on the other." Other oil men mention the issue in similar terms. Finally Mr. Doheny testifies that the oil companies refused to comply with the decree of February 19, 1918, "with the consent and approval, and at the suggestion, of our own State Department." These statements would seem to suggest that the Wilson Administration was the determining factor in the launching of the oil corporations' rebellion against the Mexican Government.

Carranza is not making a serious effort to destroy Pelaez; for the attitude of the Government of the United States justifies a fear that such an effort would result in another invasion "to protect American lives and property." By our threat of force we have not only halted the economic program of the Mexican revolution, but have stopped its military operations against the bandits. American intervention is already here. It holds Carranza in a dilemma where there seems to be no choice except between defensive war and surrender to "the dignity and authority of the United States"—its authority to dictate Mexican oil legislation. . . .

MEXICO SHOWS THE WAY (1956)

Julian Halevy

. . . IT'S HIGHLY POSSIBLE that one or more Arab nations will decide to take over foreign-owned oil properties, and it's worthwhile at the moment to evaluate the accomplishments of *Petroleos Mexicanos* (Pemex), Mexico's government-owned oil company, during the eighteen years since President Cardenas reluctantly signed the order expropriating what is today the sixth largest oil industry outside the Soviet sphere.

In 1938, Lazaro Cardenas was trying to carry through his basic program of agrarian reform in the face of a dangerously anarchic domestic situation. To take over an industry for which Mexico lacked equipment, personnel and capital, and to risk international boycott and foreign intervention, seemed incredibly foolhardy; in fact, the decision to do so came as a complete surprise to the foreign-owned oil companies.

The expropriation was the culmination of a prolonged strike in the industry. It was precipitated by the refusal of the foreign oil companies to accept a decision of the arbitration boards and of the Mexican Supreme Court awarding more pay to the workers. After the expropriation decree, the companies (of which there were about a score), capitulated, but by then the oil was in the fire, and President Cardenas refused to backtrack. The government was launched on a stormy career as producer, refiner, exporter and distributor of oil.

What kind of job has Mexico done with the oil industry? U. S. oil-industry economists are inclined to take a dim view. The case against Pemex has been made as follows:

Since the government took over from private enterprise, production has fallen off drastically. In 1921, output of crude oil and natural gasoline reached a peak of 29 million (metric) tons per year; during the last three years, production has averaged about 13 million tons.

Income from exports of crude oil and products is far less than during the roaring twenties, when 500,000 barrels a day left Mexican ports. Current exports are edging up towards 100,000 barrels a day.

Refinery output fails to keep pace with domestic needs. For the last three years the country has been importing about 30,000 barrels per day of petroleum products at an annual cost of nearly seventy million dollars—a heavy charge on Mexico's vulnerable balance of payments.

Insufficient refinery capacity is only a symptom of Pemex's most serious problem: lack of investment capital. This dearth of funds manifests itself also in a crippled exploration program, antiquated and inadequate transportation and lack of equipment for the development of proved resources. All this in turn boils down to the simple economic fact that Pemex doesn't earn enough profits, either to plow back into the business or to attract outside investment.

Why doesn't Pemex make money? The answer lies in a price policy that eschews what private-enterprise economists would call reasonable profits and, in effect, subsidizes the Mexican economy at the expense of the oil industry. The price of leaded gasoline, including taxes, is less than 18 cents (U.S.) per gallon. Kerosene, major fuel in a country with little water power, no coal and exhausted forests, is 4 cents a gallon. Fuel oil has been supplied to the nationalized railways for many years at extremely low prices.

The net effect of this price policy is that the per-barrel return, in the form of direct profit on sales, is probably lower for Pemex than any other oil company in the world. Prices have been kept so low that when Pemex imported seventy million dollars' worth of petroleum products last year and distributed them through its regular marketing channels, the net loss to the company was twenty-one million dollars.

As long as Pemex maintains this unbusinesslike price policy, it will be unable to earn the capital necessary for expansion, and the gap between production and consumption (increasing about 9 per cent annually) will continue to expand. Instead of being a net earner, Pemex will be a net spender—a sad state of affairs for what was once a flourishing business.

This, in substance, is the case made by critics of nationalization, and it supports their contention that Mexico would have been far better off if foreign oil companies had kept control of the industry. Colonial nations, take heed!

The charges are met here with indignation. Almost to a man, the Mexican is loyal to what he feels is his industry, and underlying his attitude are the material evidences of another set of facts and figures:

It is true that production has dropped since the boom days of 1921. It is also true that it had dropped long before expropriation, from 200 million barrels in 1921 to less than thirty-five million in 1932. Nowhere else, not even in revolutionary Russia, did production ever decline so much so quickly.

The initial drop has been attributed to foreign business men reducing their investment in the face of union harassment. Far more significant, however, is the fact that in 1921 almost all the 200 million barrels came from the amazingly rich Golden Lane area on the gulf coast—an area which a few years later was producing mainly salt water because of over-exploitation. The fabulous Dos Bocas well in this region couldn't be controlled; it was permitted to spout 259,000 barrels a day onto the landscape until it exhausted itself.

Another factor contributing to the decline was lack of investment in exploration and development of reserves. During the pre-expropriation era (1901–1937), four major zones were discovered and development was confined to these established areas. But under Pemex's regime, concentrated exploration has resulted in the discovery of four new major producing areas, equivalent in potential to those already exploited. These new areas include almost a hundred oil fields, and reserves have climbed to 2,886 million barrels.

Despite lack of capital, boycotts and almost insuperable difficulties in securing personnel and equipment, production has risen since 1937 from forty-six million barrels to last year's ninety-one million. Drilling last year was highest in history, 639,414 meters, compared to the previous high of 538,000 meters in 1926.

As regards the drop in exports, part of the explanation lies in the development and industrialization of Mexico. During the twenties, almost all production was exported; last year the domestic market consumed sixty-five million barrels, leaving only twenty-five million for export. Other significant factors in export decline were a lack of tankers, limited market for Mexico's major surplus of heavy crudes and an international boycott against Mexico's oil during the years immediately following expropriation.

Necessity for imports of refined products is due less to lack of refinery capacity than to inadequate transportation facilities between population centers and refineries, which were originally located for the convenience of export-minded private companies without regard for domestic needs. Previous to 1938, all Mexican refineries were on the Gulf Coast with the exception of Atzcapotzalco, supplying Mexico City. This refinery, which in 1938 had a capacity of 14,000 barrels per day, now produces 100,000 barrels. Total refinery capacity, mostly developed since expropriation, is now 225,000 barrels per day.

Pemex has been concentrating a major part of its admittedly inadequate investment capital on coping with the problem of imports and dollar drain. New refineries have been built in strategic locations and pipe lines connect coastal refineries with industrial centers inland. A single lubricants refinery recently completed at Salamanca, in the state of Guanajato, is saving fifteen million dollars annually. Projects to be completed this year will cut forty million dollars from the annual bill for imports. Mexico's aim of oil autonomy is close to realization.

It is true that Mexico's task has been made infinitely more difficult by the low-price policy. No one is more aware of this than the Mexicans. It would have been very convenient for Pemex to raise its prices along with the 548 per cent rise in cost of living since 1939. That it did not indicates that values other than profits determine its policy. *Industrialization here depends on cheap oil.* There is inadequate water power and no coal. The impetus given industry and agriculture by eighteen years of subsidies from the government oil monopoly is incalculable. As a domestic fuel, kerosene is replacing charcoal and wood, natural resources almost exhausted in Mexico. *To aid a reforestation program, Pemex sells kerosene below cost.*

In 1937, the price of gasoline in Mexico City was 20 per cent higher than the average price in the United States. Today, the U.S. price is 80 per cent higher than the Mexican.

It's worth noting that as regards labor conditions in Mexico, the average wage in privately owned manufacturing industries during 1955 was about a dollar a day; in the oil industry it was over four dollars. This contrasts sharply with pre-expropriation wage scales, when oil worker salaries were equal to or lower than prevailing inadequate wages. Pemex has a program of worker benefits unique in Mexico. It includes free schooling, free medical care for workers and their families, pensions and a savings fund. Last year, the company spent five million dollars on medical care and schooling for the 35,000 oil workers and their families.

Finally, there is the question of direct taxes paid by the industry to the federal treasury. In terms of national gain, it is revealing to compare the figures for the periods before and after expropriation. From 1900 to 1937, private companies produced 1,895 million barrels of oil, mostly for export, on which federal taxes were paid amounting to 77 million pesos. From 1938 through 1955, Pemex produced 1,005 million barrels, mostly for national consumption, on which taxes were paid amounting to 5,000 million pesos.

It is this kind of responsibility to its workers, to the public and to the nation that makes Pemex popular here. Most Mexicans think that the government's expropriation of the oil industry is one of the best things that ever happened to the country. A return to private ownership is unthinkable.

The exploitation of Mexico by private companies before 1938 cannot be compared with modern investment procedures in the Middle East; nor can Arab rulers, taking a fifty-fifty split of fabulous profits, be compared with Mexico's progressive President Cardenas. Nevertheless, Arab leaders studying the history of Mexico's government-owned and operated oil industry might find something in it other than a warning.

MEXICO'S RUSH TO THE GUSHERS (1979)

Julia Preston

ONE SUNDAY in November last year, the head of PEMEX, Mexico's state oil monopoly, flabbergasted an international group of oilmen by announcing the discovery of yet another vast oilfield in the country's Southeast, this one steeping in 100 billion barrels of petroleum and 40 trillion feet of natural gas. Added to the astronomical 200 billion barrels of potential reserves proclaimed in September, these new figures, if taken at face value, would have made Mexico the happy holder of the largest oil reserves in the world. . . .

A few days later, however, the discomfited PEMEX director, Jorge Diaz Serrano, was forced to convene the press to clarify: only 7 percent of the petroleum at the new Chicontepec field could be recovered by current methods. It would take as many wells to develop the area—16,000—as PEMEX had drilled in its entire thirty-year history. In short, while the Chicontepec field would increase Mexico's potential reserves, the concrete prospects for use of the oil remained ambiguous.

This PEMEX fumble typifies the new Mexican oil industry that emerged after José Lopez Portillo became President in late 1976 and decided to turn Mexico into a major oil-exporting nation overnight. PEMEX has changed its policy from a notoriously conservative handling of Mexico's reserves to a broadly speculative one. It makes loose claims of huge, but unproven, "potential" reserves to lure national and foreign investors.

There is a concomitant eagerness of Americans to believe that Mexico's current oil bonanza is just an old-fashioned Texas-style gusher. From the viewpoint of the United States, a new petroleum supply that would reduce its reliance upon the Middle East seems to be opening up in the hemisphere, in a non-OPEC country which might be convinced to undercut the cartel. Oil profits could heal the Mexican economy as well, bankroll a swift economic development, open a wide market for American goods and create a haven for American investors and bankers. (Four-fifths of Mexico's many creditors are American banks; only two years ago they faced "near economic disintegration" there, as one Mexican banker put it recently.) Finally, new jobs south of the border would cut into illegal migration of Mexicans into the United States. At present more than five million unregistered Mexicans, about one-quarter of Mexico's working population, earn wages in the United States, drawing complaints from organized labor.

But Mexico's oil bonanza is not a simple gusher. Far from just stumbling on oil, the present Mexican Government was pushed by mainly American financial interests into exporting crude while in the throes of an economic crisis in 1976. Moving in great haste and without any clear public mandate, PEMEX began to publicize reserves it had previously kept secret and to massively accelerate exploration. . . .

In only two years Mexico's proven petroleum reserves have increased by 600 percent, to 40 billion barrels. At the end of 1978, PEMEX doubled its proven reserves in a single stroke. Recent revelations indicate that the eastern and southern coastal states float on a nearly continuous reservoir of petroleum that extends well into the Gulf of Mexico. Barely 10 percent of the country's known platforms have been drilled, with a dazzling success rate. By 1980, Mexico will double its crude production over 1976 to 2.25 million barrels per day, and increase exports twelve times. Though retaining about half for domestic use, at that time our neighbor will be in a position to supply up to 12 percent of the United States' daily import needs. . . .

In the drive to export, Lopez Portillo has dramatically reversed PEMEX's traditional policies. The state company, which was formed when the oil industry was nationalized in 1938, habitually de-emphasized exports, avoiding inflationary booms in foreign sales. It produced cheap petroleum for national demand, using equipment made in Mexico, creating jobs even at the expense of efficiency. PEMEX engineers, who salvaged the industry after foreigners bailed out in 1938, consistently reinvested earnings in refining and petrochemicals. Foreign private oil companies grumbled about this ornery self-reliance, pointing to PEMEX's low worker-productivity but the full Mexican control of the industry drew wide admiration from developing countries.

But now PEMEX plans to spend at least $15.2 billion in the next four years (more than three times its entire investment to date), double refining capacity and triple petrochemical output. As a result, the policy of domestic integration has been modified. Mexican-made equipment can't be turned out fast enough to meet accelerating needs, so PEMEX is now buying more than half its new equipment abroad, primarily in the United States—$3 billion worth by 1982. In late November, a firm in Houston, Texas, delivered two entire petrochemical plants to a refinery in the state of Chiapas, at the cost of $20 million. For the first time, PEMEX has booked a bundle of discreet contracts with private drilling firms for exploration. Though Mexican in name, these firms' licenses, equipment and financing are predominantly American. And since the push came at a time when money was scarce at home, Mexico has had to take out several huge loans in 1978, including two for $1 billion each that are mainly earmarked for PEMEX.

Such large-scale borrowing would have been impossible two years before. In late 1976, Mexico's credit had run dry; the peso had just been devalued by half; the foreign debt was $28 billion (one-third of the gross national product); $4 billion in capital had fled the country in several months and economic growth lagged behind the population increase. In December 1976, Mexico negotiated a special $1.2 billion credit line with the International Monetary Fund, after agreeing to a three-year austerity "adjustment program," in which everything from wages to the price of electricity became subject to I.M.F. scrutiny and approval. (A "recommendation" of the I.M.F.—in which the United States wields a controlling veto power—cannot, in practice, be turned down, because without this final approval, countries like Mexico can't obtain foreign loans.)

A confidential I.M.F. staff report, reflecting recent meetings with the Mexican Government, reveals that the fund generously exempted PEMEX from its otherwise stern insistence on spending cuts. In 1978, for example, the I.M.F. called for an additional reduction of 21 percent in the budget deficit projected by the Mexican Government, while giving state-owned companies wide leeway in spending "to allow for expansion in the investment programs of PEMEX." International banks have agreed that oil, in sufficiently large and accessible quantities, is excellent collateral. Thus, only two years after its fiscal crisis Mexico enjoys "greatly enhanced creditworthiness," to quote the I.M.F.; in December, the Inter-American Development Bank, to name one, made the largest loan in its history to Mexico.

PEMEX chief Diaz Serrano proclaimed in his latest report, "Either we use our oil now, immediately, with no more delays and no more infantile fears, or we will soon regret we failed to rise to the historical moment in which we live." The "infantile fears" are those of a growing number of Mexican critics who distrust a policy with profound economic consequences formulated under intense foreign pressure.

Another reason for unplugging the gusher was that Lopez Portillo urgently needed new political grease for the Mexican political machine. For three decades Mexico has run on the myth that modern Presidents bear the torch of the 1910 revolution, with its ideals of agrarian reform, national sovereignty and democratic rule. The myth has appeased the poor, confounded the rebellious and provided a legitimate public vocabulary for bureaucrats and wealthy entrepreneurs who privately command the advantage of Government favor through patronage and bossism. Now Lopez Portillo tacitly acknowledges the obsolescence of the myth. Eschewing hallowed catchwords, he talks like a technocrat. But at the same time he must quickly apply an emollient to ease the friction. He chose oil.

PEMEX's haste has made waste, however, and provided further ammunition for the Government's critics. In late 1977, for example, it announced a $1 billion pipeline to run natural gas from southern Mexico to the Texas border. At the asking price of $2.60 per thousand cubic feet, Diaz Serrano said the investment would pay for itself from sales within 200 days. The pipeline was assailed by left-nationalist political parties and "Old Guard" PEMEX veterans of the nationalization, who opposed hooking up to a single buyer who could command prices and drain reserves. Last January the negotiations were suspended when the Carter Administration said it would hold the import price to $1.75. With the pipeline already under way, PEMEX decided awkwardly to switch domestic industry to gas, which sells at 32 cents at home. One ruling party official called it "the sharpest blow to Lopez Portillo's public standing this term." Nor has PEMEX inspired confidence by repeatedly reminding Mexicans to hurry now, because their oil will be gone in forty years, or by figuring regularly in the national press as a major polluter of jungle waterways.

Furthermore, petroleum can only partially lubricate United States-Mexican relations. Although the United States will be the first foreigner to enjoy the oil bonanza (in 1977 it took four-fifths of Mexican petroleum exports), the two countries can never be completely friendly. The exchange is unequal between them. Mexico relies overwhelmingly on American capital, technology and tourism, and sells 70 percent of its exports here. We look to Mexico more casually, for cheap labor, primary goods and new consumers (Mexico is the third-largest buyer in the world for our products). We make the loans; Mexico obeys the rules when swamped in debt service. We export equipment to mechanize developing Mexican industries; Mexico exports displaced workers to us.

Mexico still harbors a lively tradition of anti-American nationalism. Though it has shown no intention of joining OPEC, neither will Mexico "scab" against OPEC for the United States, as Lopez Portillo said last September. A conspicuous United States push for a "special" relationship, such as is now proposed in State Department circles, might suit Lopez Portillo's immediate economic purposes, but it can only embarrass him before his constituency. By the same token, PEMEX is a wholly nationalized industry, and United States oil companies prefer to trade with corporations they can influence by owning shares. In sum, rather than as a major energy crutch, Mexico may better serve as what an American Embassy official in Mexico City called "a natural residual supply" for secondary supplies and stockpiling. . . .

Mexican officials project a 10 percent annual growth rate after 1980 on the basis of oil, but only an abrupt turnabout in present Government policy will deliver these dividends to those who need them. With the top 5 percent of its population receiving more than one-third of the national income while less than half the work force is fully employed, Mexico has the most polarized economy in Latin America. Huge private agribusinesses are subsidized while peasant farmers are abandoned to hunger. For lack of state support, millions of peasants in the last fifteen years have been driven off the land, and many end up working without papers in the United States.

Most projections agree that it will be a decade before petropeso investments begin to stem the northward movement of the jobless. But beyond this, pouring money into the present system will only hasten the concentration of wealth and the ousting of peasants. In leading the rush to abundance, Lopez Portillo has sought to make peace with a dominant neighbor and to stabilize and enrich Mexico, but not to change it. Without change, the oil bonanza can only further polarize the country. It is already polarizing politics, by withdrawing from nationalists one of their most prized institutions, the state oil industry. . . .

POINT 4—FOUR YEARS LATER (1953)

Paul A. Baran

PRESIDENT TRUMAN'S announcement, in his 1949 inaugural address, of a "bold new program" of American aid to underdeveloped countries was a shrewd political move. It was calculated not only to give a "Fair Deal" touch to the rapidly unfolding foreign policy of the cold war, making it more palatable to progressive opinion both in this country and in Western Europe, but also to conjure up for the American business community a new vision of prosperity, just as the postwar boom was apparently drawing to a close. These considerations, however, though important and urgent, were secondary. The main purpose of Point 4 was to counter Communist propaganda in backward countries with the prospect of economic and social development sponsored and generously aided by the United States.

The first objective was easily attained. Editorial writers and radio commentators were thrilled by the Administration's "imaginative" and "humanitarian" plan and talked and wrote about it so busily that they paid little attention to the State Department's flirtation with France, to American support of the French *guerre sale* in Indo-China, or to the rapid revival of fascism in West Germany and Japan. As a device for assuring prosperity, the proposal did not do so well. The recession of 1949 was short and mild, the international political scene was not conducive to much private investment abroad, and Wall Street accorded a rather sour reception to the idea of sinking large funds in underdeveloped countries. Nor was the chief purpose of Point 4 realized with any great success. Whatever propaganda value the program might have had was almost nullified by the magnetism of the victorious Chinese revolution and the United States' open alliance with the traditional colonial powers and native reactionary elements.

Under such circumstances not much enthusiasm for Point 4 was evinced by the policy-makers in Washington. The first Congressional appropriation for the newly established Technical Cooperation Administration did not exceed $34,000,000, and twenty-eight months later the London *Economist*—usually the State Department's most faithful friend on the other side of the Atlantic—noted that Mr. Truman's "bold new program" was "still being watered with little more than fine phrases and lavish promises." The situation was subsequently somewhat improved. For the fiscal year 1951–52 the Point 4 program got a larger appropriation, and for 1952–53 the amount, though about one-third less than the Administration requested, was still $137,000,000.

What is most important, however, is that this increased support for the Point 4 program is accompanied by a far-reaching "reinterpretation" of the nature and purpose of the entire undertaking. Indeed, altogether new wine is being poured into the old bottles, and it promises to be a much headier brew than that decanted in Mr. Truman's inaugural address. The first indication of what is to take the place of the President's noble promise to "supply the vitalizing force to stir the peoples of the world into triumphant action, not only against their human oppressors, but also against their ancient enemies—hunger, misery, and despair," was conveyed in a report of the International Development Advisory Board entitled "Partners in Progress." This report, prepared under the direction of Nelson Rockefeller, takes a "realistic view" of the United States' interest in underdeveloped countries and frankly places "first things first." "Since three-quarters of the imported materials included in the stock-pile program come from the underdeveloped areas," it declares, "it is to those countries that we must look for the bulk of any possible increase in these supplies." A great number of commodities are involved. "Aside from minerals, important expansions are contemplated to increase our supplies of rubber, petroleum, fats and oils, and some basic fibers."

This theme has been elaborated and solidified in another document called "Resources for Freedom," prepared by the President's Materials Policy Commission headed by William S. Paley. "The commission believes that the United States will find it increasingly worthwhile to turn abroad for more supplies of many basic materials, particularly minerals." Production of these materials must therefore be increased in the underdeveloped countries. And neither the Rockefeller nor the Paley report leaves any doubt about how this increase is to be obtained. "The production and distribution of goods and services is primarily a function of private enterprise, whether it involves food and manufactured goods to meet ever-growing civilian demand or whether it involves the production of strategic raw materials" ("Partners in Progress"). But although "private enterprise can and should continue to carry the major burden" ("Resources for Freedom"), it cannot be expected to carry it all. The government must step in and relieve private business of excessive responsibilities. Whenever outlays that are indispensable to the conduct of business are unattractive to private investors either because they would not be remunerative enough or would be too risky or too big, the government should pick up the check. In the words of *The Economist* (July 5, 1952) "a way has been found for the government to bear part of the burden in the name of national defense, which is the umbrella under which all those wanting subsidies now shelter from the storms of the free-enterprise system."

Spending on the Technical Cooperation Administration and on its Point 4 activities is thus given an altogether new significance. It is seen to be for the purpose of insuring a steady flow of strategic materials, smoothing the way for private enterprise, providing American corporations with free prospecting services of all kinds, saving them the "burden" of exploration, and financing undertakings that they find exceedingly useful but insufficiently profitable.

Once the principle of private profits but public losses is firmly established, the Rockefeller and Paley reports express profound solicitude for the health and happiness of the peoples inhabiting the underdeveloped countries. Indeed, as if to illustrate the astute observation of *The Economist* cited above, "Partners in Progress" proclaims that "an improvement in their living levels must be considered a vital part of our defense mobilization." Unless more food, more clothing, more medicine are supplied to the people in backward countries, the necessary expanded output of raw materials may be unattainable. It is needless to add that while appropriate investment in the nutrition and health of the natives of the "source countries" would be thus fully justified by "hard-headed self-interest," it is up to the government to provide what is required to support a reasonably efficient and contented labor force. As noted in "Partners in Progress," "the absenteeism on the Vitoria-Minas railroad was cut dramatically by effective malaria control. This has made it possible to reduce maintenance crews by one-third, which in turn has cut the cost of extracting and transporting iron ore and mica from the Rio Doce Valley."

Such expressions of concern for the welfare of the people only throw into sharper relief the nature of the entire program. While great pains are taken to prove that it is "vital" to the United States to obtain control of "the manganese and tungsten deposits of Latin America, Africa, and Asia, the chrome ores of Turkey and the Philippines, the timber stands of Chile and Brazil, the pulp-woods of Labrador" ("Partners in Progress"), little thought seems to have been given to the question whether such an arrangement would confer equally vital benefits on the people living in the backward areas.

It is undoubtedly true that exports of minerals and other raw materials could "provide the financial basis for a domestic development program" ("Resources for Freedom"), but the fact remains—though neither report mentions it—that none of the raw-materials-exporting regions have thus far been able to carry out any development program worthy of the name on such a "financial basis." The misery in the oil-rich and oil-exporting countries of the Near East is no less proverbial than the squalor, disease, and stagnation in cotton-rich and cotton-exporting Egypt, in sugar-rich and sugar-exporting Cuba, and in coffee-rich and coffee-exporting Brazil. The Paley report cites the prosperity of Venezuela as an example of the blessings that accrue to backward areas catering to the vital needs of the Standard Oil Company of New Jersey. But the less said about Venezuela the better. Harvey O'Connor's brilliant report on that country published in the July, 1951, issue of the *Monthly Review* reads like an account of conditions in India in the heyday of British domination:

> What has happened in Venezuela is a gold-plated disaster moving on noiseless oiled bearings toward tragedy. Its ancient, static, but self-sufficient economy has been tossed in the ash can. . . . When the oil runs out . . . the nation will be like an old tailors' chest filled with useless spangles. It was impoverished, disease-ridden, illiterate twenty-five years ago, and still is.

Nor is it by any means fortuitous that even large revenues derived from raw-material exports do not stimulate economic growth. In most under-developed countries all or the bulk of these revenues are collected by a small group of big proprietors who use them for luxurious living or deposit them as capital abroad. The share going to the corrupt governments supports a parasitic bureaucracy and an overgrown military establishment.

Such economic development as takes place is of necessity lopsided. The raw-materials-producing enterprises form islands of advanced technology in seas of general backwardness. In these islands cluster a relatively small number of native workers, business men, and lobbyists. Only there does growth take place, and it resembles that of a cancer rather than of healthy tissue. It assumes mainly the form of bigger and better hotels and night clubs, of residential construction for foreigners and privileged natives, and of some industrial and commercial establishments serving this small élite.

For the raw-materials wealth of the backward countries to provide a basis for their economic development, it would be necessary for the extraction and marketing of the raw materials to proceed within the framework of a well-considered plan of general economic growth. Only by using the proceeds of their general exportation for the harmonious development of industry and agriculture, only by advancing from a raw-materials economy to a technologically and economically balanced processing economy, can the underdeveloped countries attain a decent level of productivity and welfare. They are not likely to attain it by being Mr. Rockefeller's "partners in progress" or by supplying Mr. Paley with "resources for freedom." They are not likely to attain it by paying, as they currently do, over 17 per cent per annum for such capital as is invested in their economies by American corporations.

The scheme of creating a raw-materials base in backward regions and reserving the role of industrial center to the mother country is by no means new. It may "work" for a short time; it is bound in the longer run to lead to increased misery and colonial revolutions. . . .

VENEZUELA—SUICIDE BY OIL (1951)

Marcelle Michelin

ALMOST AT THE MOMENT that Prime Minister Mossadegh arrived in New York to plead Iran's case before the Security Council, an attempt to overthrow the military junta that governs Venezuela was suppressed with seven killed, ten wounded, and hundreds arrested. The American newspapers that announced the failure of the *putsch* also reported the State Department's anxiety lest any formula used to settle the Iran dispute might set a precedent for the settlement of some future dispute with Venezuela. Editorials in the same papers discussed "the explosive brew" upon which the army clique sits in Venezuela. Oil, of course, is the principal ingredient of this brew.

Foremost oil exporter and second-largest oil producer in the world after the United States, with seemingly inexhaustible subsoil riches of iron, copper, nickel, coal, asphalt, bauxite, gold, industrial diamonds, and asbestos, Venezuela, while flooded with American dollars, is paradoxically undergoing a major economic crisis. In fact, its economic well-being is threatened by the very petroleum production that finances two-thirds of its national budget and pays for more than five hundred million dollars' worth of annual imports from the United States. Venezuelan economists, foremost among them Arturo Uslar-Pietri, are warning that the nation is living on borrowed time and that unless it divorces its destiny from oil it will be committing economic suicide.

Since 1917, the first year of oil production, Venezuela has been deluged by a flood of easy money. But instead of transmuting the windfall into a permanent source of economic wealth, it has been flinging its unexpected riches to the winds. While oil for Western Hemisphere defense has gushed out of Lake

Maracaibo, Guárico, Monagas, and Anzoátequi, the American dollars received for it have evaporated in prodigal waste. Few of them have gone into projects to diversify the economy or into the construction of schools, housing, railroads, or highways into the interior.

Before the oil era Venezuela was a self-sufficient agricultural nation with a population of 2,000,000—cattle-raising Indios on the level plains, fisherfolk along the strip of coast, and warring Caciques in the Andes. The soil was poor, but living standards were low and primitive wants easily satisfied. Exports of coffee, cocoa, indigo, and hides, amounting to $20,000,000 annually, more than paid for the limited imports.

More than thirty years later, this land still produces food for only 2,000,000; but the population has more than doubled, and the national budget has been multiplied by twenty. Imports soared to $668,958,500 in 1949—mostly consumers' goods and luxury items. Venezuela is now a nation of modern cities, skyscrapers, and Cadillacs. Exports totaled $1,003,130,600 in 1949, but industries other than oil accounted for only $20,000,000 of this staggering sum. Thus it is painfully clear that once its wells run dry Venezuela will lose approximately 95 per cent of its annual income.

When a nation is suddenly rocketed into a fabulously high standard of living—even if this standard is by no means uniform—and its productive capacity fails to keep pace with its increasing demands, a dangerous imbalance is created. There is an illusion of well-being, a surface prosperity without foundations to sustain the future. Such a nation does not develop in a normal rhythm; it is pressured by an outer force into an expansion beyond its potential. Venezuela's whole economy is a parasite on oil, with its artificial prices, artificial markets, artificial purchasing power. Prices have soared beyond all reason. In December, 1950, forty-nine commodities were quoted in Caracas as being 76 per cent higher than in December, 1938, and thirty-seven commodities as being 104 per cent higher. Inflation is in full swing—witness the fact that the bolívar has been devaluated as much as 40 per cent.

From 1941 to 1945 the cost of imported items naturally exceeded that of native articles. But since 1946 the entire economy has been so dislocated that importing has become more remunerative than producing on the spot. Freighters arrive full and return almost empty. Because of rising costs national products like coffee, sugar, and textiles are no longer able to compete with foreign products either in Venezuela or on the world market. Many local industries must be subsidized by the government, with the result that the crippled economy leans more and more on petroleum dollars. And the more these dollars are wasted on imports, the less the land is cultivated, the less is manufactured, and the greater the paralysis of every activity but oil production.

Venezuela appears extravagantly wealthy. Caracas, the magnificent capital, has a pulse-quickening "get-rich-quick" atmosphere. But the Venezuelans to whom black gold has meant a better way of life are the fortunate minority of the cities and oil camps—landowners, business men, factory hands, government employees, corporation bureaucrats. The people of the pueblos and fishing villages go on laboriously wresting what sustenance they can from earth and water.

And petroleum has been a demoralizing factor even there. It has distorted the scale of values and bred instability, social inequality, and political unrest.

The "something for nothing" gambling spirit of the speculators and opportunists has infected even the peasants. The wholesale importation of foodstuffs is ruining agriculture—indigo has disappeared, coffee production has fallen off by two-thirds—and driving impoverished rural elements into the cities.

After the oil boom is over what will there be to fall back on? . . . A reserve of nine billion barrels—at 612,000,000 barrels a year—will last only fifteen or sixteen years. . . .

While the time is short, there is surely enough left for Venezuela to channel oil revenues into some permanent economic improvements—communication and transportation systems, power plants, irrigation projects, a revitalized agriculture, an expanded industrial base. President Gomez's shrewd 1918 oil law fully protected the country's rights while welcoming foreign exploitation. But he should have drawn up another law protecting Venezuela against itself and forcing it to anchor oil profits firmly in the Venezuelan earth. Venezuelans are the first to admit that they were totally unprepared for their overnight emergence as an oil-rich nation. Like lottery winners, they went on a spending spree, light-heartedly making the mistakes that led them into the financial morass in which they now flounder.

They are finally inaugurating a number of basic reforms. On June 30, 1949, an agrarian law was passed which is designed to put the nation back on a self-sustaining basis. . . . The foundations are being laid, also, for industrialization. For all these undertakings, Venezuela needs foreign capital and technicians. It may not solve its problems overnight, but it is at least making plans which if realized will enable it to survive the eventual exhaustion of its oil resources. . . .

LATIN AMERICA SLAMS THE DOOR (1971)

Penny Lernoux

. . . THROUGHOUT THE DECADE of the now moribund Alliance for Progress, the U.S. Government kept telling the Latins how generous American taxpayers were, but the fact of the matter is that more than 90 per cent of Alliance investment came from the Latins themselves. Most of the U.S. loans were tied to the purchase of American goods, and very few had any impact on the poverty-stricken millions the Alliance presumably was supposed to help. Far from eliminating the illiteracy, unemployment and sickness which confront more than one-third of the population, U.S. loans encouraged the formation of a small elite with sophisticated consumer tastes, and so impoverished state treasuries that since 1965 Latin America has been paying more to service its external debt than it receives in new loans. One-quarter of Mexico's income from foreign exchange this year will be used to pay interest on its $3.5 billion external debt, for example. There is little profit to be made from low-cost housing in contrast to the excellent returns shown for electric shavers and cake mixes, which explains why U.S. investment has concentrated on the manufacture of consumer goods in an area where 15 million people still live outside the money economy.

While Washington offices churned out PR releases praising the spirit of hemispheric cooperation under the Alliance, U.S. business representatives in Latin America were remitting $4 in profit for every $1 invested (Department of Commerce statistics). During the sixties alone foreign business sent $8.1 billion back to corporate headquarters. . . .

In Latin American eyes, today's Yankee imperialist is considerably more subtle and thus more dangerous than his grandfather who kept a private army to protect his oil interests in Mexico or set up banana dictatorships in Central America. The sins of the past, dating mainly from U.S. penetration in Latin America in the first decades of the century, have left a residue of distrust and dislike of the sort so brilliantly described by Colombia's Gabriel García Marquez in his best-selling *One Hundred Years of Solitude.* But even the most rabid gringo baiters recognize that García Marquez's Señor Brown and his terrifying slaughter of banana plantation workers are part of the past (in Colombia's case, the 1920s). What they worry about is Señor Brown's metamorphosis into a Spanish-speaking business administration graduate who manages to bend local law to his company's interests while charming the under secretary of foreign trade on the golf course. Bayonet tactics have been replaced by the smooth takeover of local industries, reasonable-sounding arguments supporting foreign investment, an intricate system of patent cartels and veiled threats. But if Señor Brown's descendants have changed their approach, so have Latin American governments, most of which employ economists and administrators trained in U.S. universities and/or corporations. While still groping for an indigenous political identity which is neither U.S.- nor Soviet-modeled, these countries have a fairly clear idea of economic priorities, and U.S. investment is not one of them.

The bell began to toll in 1968 when Peru's military junta, six days after seizing power, nationalized the International Petroleum Co. (IPC), a subsidiary of Standard Oil of New Jersey. The previous constitutional government of Fernando Belaunde Terry had tried to solve the problem of IPC but was handicapped, according to Belaunde's Finance Minister Manuel Ulloa, by harassment and threats from the U.S. Government and U.S. business. A month before his overthrow Belaunde made an agreement with IPC, which promised to cede its La Brea y Pariña oil fields to the government in return for the cancellation of a $144 million tax bill, new exploration rights and the expansion of its refinery at Talara on the coast of northern Peru. Described as a sellout by many Peruvians, the agreement served as a good excuse for the military to sack Belaunde. IPC's ownership of the La Brea y Pariña fields, whose 145-year history is obscured by a series of convoluted legal battles, has come to signify the worst sort of U.S. economic imperialism. The important point in the minds of most Peruvians was IPC's alleged history of buying influence in high government circles. The company's reputation may be judged by the response of the rest of the local U.S. business community which, when it came to the pinch, refused to support IPC publicly or privately. "IPC knows it has no future in

Peru. It would never be able to overcome years of ill feeling here," said a U.S. businessmen. "But it wants to make Peru an example before the world to show what happens if American property is expropriated." That principle was far more important than Standard Oil's $120 million investment, already amortized several times over. A good deal of shouting was heard in Washington and Lima about the Hickenlooper amendment, which forces the President to suspend aid and sugar quota benefits to any nation which expropriates U.S. property and does not take "appropriate steps" to provide just compensation within six months. But the example never was made primarily because the Nixon Administration, already involved in a nasty fishing war with Peru, Ecuador and Chile, allowed negotiations to drift into obscurity. . . .

The Venezuelans . . . are determined to reduce American influence on their economy. U.S. oil companies, which account for the major part of the $4.5 billion investment in Venezuela, recently were presented with a retroactive tax bill which hikes the Venezuelan Government's share of the profits to 79 per cent. The government also plans to nationalize the profitable gas industry and has begun moving in the direction of a new petroleum policy which will make the state-owned petroleum enterprise the majority shareholder in future oil operations. Once independent fiefdoms, the oil companies have been forced to accept increasingly tough government restrictions since the overthrow of dictator Marcos Pérez Jiménez in 1958. Today they are faced with the certainty that Venezuela's Center-Left congress will place a government padlock on all oil concessions which expire in 1983–84, these being the bulk of the companies' oil properties. Both houses passed the historic reversion law and President Caldera signed it in August. Under it, all property, including refineries, technical studies and administration buildings, as well as the land, revert to the state as the concessions expire. Meanwhile, the government will have the right to inspect and control installations to guarantee equipment is kept in good condition, and the companies will be forced to subscribe to a special maintenance fund which could total $1 billion. Described as "*de facto* nationalization" by the oil companies, the law substantially weakens their future bargaining position. The Venezuelans are well aware that without the refineries, pipelines and other essentials of an oil property, they would be forced to renegotiate concessions with the same companies on their terms. Under the new rules, the market will be open to all, and those who wish to come in will have to work through contracts which give the state 90 per cent of the profits and a say in management.

Despite threats and angry denunciations from such giants as Standard Oil of New Jersey and Shell, the Venezuelans hold the upper hand. Uncertain as the situation may appear to the oil companies, it is considerably less volatile than in the Middle East. Earlier expectations of massive development of atomic energy sources have not been realized, while world fuel needs have grown with a consequent increase in prices. Foreign oil companies no longer are in a position to dictate national policy in Venezuela or elsewhere because the petroleum producers, under the aegis of the Organization of Petroleum Exporting Countries (OPEC), have learned they, too, can form cartels to deal with the international giants. . . .

CRUDE OIL POLITICS (1947)

Keith Hutchison

IN 1943 E. L. DE GOLYER, the distinguished oil geologist, reported to the Department of the Interior that the center of gravity of world oil production was moving from the Gulf of Mexico-Caribbean area to the Persian Gulf. That shift will be rapidly accelerated by two pending deals which will make available to the worldwide marketing organizations of Standard Oil of New Jersey and Socony Vacuum immense quantities of Arabian and Iranian petroleum and so displace a large part of the Venezuelan production now sold by these companies in Europe. But even more important than the economic implications of these deals are their political consequences, for they suggest that the United States has become the senior member of the partnership which rules the oily destinies of the Middle East.

For a good many months negotiations have been in progress between Standard Oil of New Jersey and Socony Vacuum on the one hand and Standard Oil of California and the Texas Company, joint owners of a vast, rich, and rapidly developing concession in Saudi Arabia, on the other. While final details have still to be arranged, it appears that an agreement has been reached which will give the New Jersey concern a 30 per cent and Socony a 10 per cent interest in the Arabian-American Company—the subsidiary through which the California and Texas companies are exploiting the concession. The advantage to the sellers in this transaction is perhaps primarily financial; they are believed to have spent some $150,000,000 on development and will need at least as much more to build the projected pipe line across the Arabian desert to the Mediterranean. The practically unlimited resources of the two top Rockefeller concerns which are now joining them should insure against any financial difficulties in raising the required capital. In addition, the political reinforcement that the alliance provides probably proved an important consideration.

To Standard Oil of New Jersey and Socony the agreement offers a stake in what may turn out to be one of the most prolific oil fields of all time. Even more important, it assures them of a large supply of oil to feed to their distributing subsidiaries around the world. It is true that Standard of New Jersey owns a major share of Venezuelan oil, the chief source of supply for Europe at present. But rising demand in the Western Hemisphere, coupled with the possibility of lagging production in the United States, may mean that Caribbean supplies will be absorbed by nearer markets. Meanwhile the New Jersey company cannot draw on its fields in Austria, Hungary, and Rumania, which, for the time being at least, are under Soviet control, and Socony is handicapped by difficulties in the Netherlands East Indies that are retarding the reconstruction of its properties there. From Iraq, their only assured Middle Eastern supply until the new agreements become effective, the two companies are obtaining 10,000 barrels a day each—a drop in the bucket compared with average consumption outside the United States and Russia of some 2,400,000 barrels daily.

This unassuaged thirst for oil suggests at least a partial explanation for the second deal, which provides for the purchase by the same two American companies of a large but unspecified quantity of the Anglo-Iranian Company's production and for their participation in the construction of yet another trans-Arabian pipe line if terms can be arranged with the Arab rulers through whose territory it will pass. I say partial explanation, since it is possible that Anglo-Iranian pressed for a long-term contract of this kind as a quid pro quo for its approval of the Arabian-American deal.

Its bargaining power stemmed from the American desire to abrogate the "Red Line Agreement," which was signed in 1928 by all the participants in the Iraq Petroleum Company. These consist of the four following national groups —the Near East Development Company (controlled jointly by New Jersey and Socony), the D'Arcy Exploration Company (controlled by Anglo-Iranian), the Anglo-Saxon Petroleum Company (controlled by Royal Dutch-Shell), and the Compagnie Française des Pétroles (controlled by the French government). Each of these groups owns 23 3/4 per cent of Iraq Petroleum, the remaining 5 per cent being in the hands of a rather mysterious Armenian gentleman named Gulbenkian, who obtained the original Mosul concession from the Turks and has hung on to his interest like grim death.

These groups, joined together under political pressure for the exploitation of the northern Iraq oil deposits, decided that they had better make a pact to abstain from bidding against each other for new concessions. The upshot was the "Red Line Agreement," a long and detailed document which has never been published. In oil circles, however, it is well known that its central feature was an undertaking by the signatories that they would not enter separately into any crude-oil production arrangements within the territories of the old Turkish Empire. Also included, it is believed, were restrictions on competition in the sale of Middle Eastern oil.

Iran, by definition, was outside the Red Line territory, while Kuwait, the small British protectorate at the head of the Persian Gulf where Anglo-Iranian shares a rich concession with the Mellon family's Gulf Oil Company, was expressly excluded. Hence the prospective deal between Anglo-Iranian and the New Jersey and Socony companies does not violate the Red Line Agreement. But the case of the Saudi Arabian concession is very different. That is definitely within the Red Line area, and, in fact, the Iraq Petroleum Company, acting as agent for its shareholders, did attempt to secure it from King Ibn Saud. However, while it was cumbrously consulting its members, Standard of California and Texas nipped in and obtained the prize.

It has proved a prize indeed. Annual output from the handful of wells drilled has reached 27,000,000 barrels. Proved reserves total six billion barrels; probable reserves are immensely larger. And now Standard of New Jersey and Socony have cut themselves in on this wealth, leaving their fellow-signatories of the Red Line Agreement out in the cold. It is understood that the American companies take the view that the agreement lapsed when France was occupied by the Germans and became technically an enemy. The French government, on learning of this argument, which seems morally dubious even if it is legally sound, protested through its ambassadors in London and Washington. The Compagnie des Pétroles is reported to be starting a lawsuit in London with a view to establishing the currency of the Red Line Agreement. Probably it will be joined in this endeavor by Mr. Gulbenkian. Royal Dutch-Shell has not been heard from, but its interests would also appear to have been damaged by an arrangement which adds enormously to the crude supplies available to its chief rivals in the petroleum-distribution business. Anglo-Iranian, on the other hand, supports the American position; as we have seen, it will be compensated by a twenty-year purchase contract for its own output.

It badly needs such an arrangement, for Anglo-Iranian has never built up a really large sales organization of its own, and having more than doubled production in Iran during the war, it must now find additional outlets. Moreover, it is beginning to obtain an increasing flow of oil from the Kuwait field.

In the years before the war the effect of the Red Line Agreement was to slow up Middle Eastern oil development. Indeed, that may have been one of its purposes, for the big international oil concerns were all anxious lest too rapid an increase in supply should endanger a profitable price structure. But since the war's end, demand both in the United States and abroad has proved well beyond expert estimates, and barring a worldwide depression, increased Middle Eastern production should find an eager market. In any case a policy of checking development is no longer very feasible. The appetites of the Arab potentates have been whetted by news of the rapidly expanding royalty income of King Ibn Saud. They are urging concessionaires to get on with production and hinting that delay might induce them to deal with other oil-thirsty parties—Soviet Russia, for instance.

One group, alarmed by Middle Eastern developments and resentful of the encouragement given to them by the American government, consists of the independent producers of this country. They do not fear the entry of Arabian or Iranian oil into the United States, but they see it filling European needs and so depriving Venezuela and other lands bordering the Caribbean of one of their chief markets. The result, they suspect, will be to divert increasing amounts of Caribbean oil to American consumers and so intensify domestic competition. Undoubtedly the Navy and Interior departments hope that just this will occur. Although spokesmen for the independents insist that talk of declining American reserves is "propaganda," government experts feel that it is necessary to conserve domestic resources for both economic and strategic reasons. It is this difference which underlies the controversy over the Anglo-American Oil Agreement. The independents, charging that the agreement will facilitate both more government regulation and more foreign competition, have lobbied hard against its ratification by the Senate. The success they have scored appears to have been in vain. The private treaties which have been discussed in this article seem likely to achieve many of the objectives of the Anglo-American Oil Agreement, and they do not require the approval of the Senate.

Internationally, the consequences of the new Middle Eastern deals may well prove far-reaching. It is useless for the Foreign Office to assert that the agreement between Anglo-Iranian and the American companies is "purely commercial," or for the State Department to pretend that it has merely been "kept informed" about either this or the Arabian-American contract. It is all too obvious that deals of this nature impinge on high policy and equally obvious that the oil companies would not dare to go ahead with them unless sure of government support. And, it must not be forgotten, Anglo-Iranian is controlled by the British government.

The fact is that the United States has now been placed right in the center of the Middle Eastern picture. . . .

IF WE TAKE ARABIAN OIL (1944)

I. F. Stone

THE PROPOSED ARABIAN OIL DEAL brings us to the first great crossroads of post-war international policy. In one direction lies a new world order; in the other, a return to imperialism, with all it entails. To go into a colonial country and buy oil concessions by favors to desert sheiks, to embark on a long-range program for the exploitation of natural resources which belong to another people, is imperialism, however we choose to disguise it.

We are going into an area without representative government, a Biblical corner of the world whose people are likely in this generation to be inundated by modern ways. It is quite probable that, after awakening, they may resent, as the Mexican people resented, the transfer of the natural riches of their country to aliens, particularly aliens as arrogant and ruthless as our great oil companies have shown themselves to be in dealing with the weak, whether at home or abroad. One may be sure that these companies will do nothing to hasten the region's awakening, that they will link themselves with and support the most backward elements, political and religious, in Arab lands as they did in Latin American. The familiar imperialist headaches lie ahead of us if the Arabian oil deal goes through.

If we are to depend on Arabian oil, we must be prepared to defend the sea and air routes over which it must travel to the United States. The air routes across Africa, the sea lanes through the Mediterranean, will become national lifelines. We have a two-ocean navy; we shall need a three-ocean one. The Mediterranean, as well as the Atlantic and the Pacific, will become our concern. Any increase of British or French or Italian or Turkish or Russian naval or air power in the Mediterranean and Near Eastern areas will call for a comparable increase in our own. Arabian oil is supposed to be very cheap, and no doubt will continue to be so as long as Arab governments are willing to sell their resources cheaply, and Arab workmen will provide their labor at low wages. But what will the real cost of this oil be when we finish paying for the armament required to defend it?

If we have learned anything from this war, it is the precarious condition in which even the greatest of powers may find itself when dependent on distant sources of supply. We have seen how quickly and easily the American, British, and Dutch empires, with all their power and their supposedly impregnable fortresses, were cut off from their sources of rubber, tin, quinine, and many other raw materials, including the oil of the East Indies. We have seen that the possession of these raw materials was in some degree an obstacle to their national defense; Britain's oil and rubber interests, for example, successfully fought the establishment of synthetic sources of supply at home. For under capitalism these resources in lands which on the maps bear the same color as our own do not belong to you and me; these resources are in the hands of independent economic sovereigns whose profit and interest often run counter to those of the national sovereigns who defend them. Judging from the tenor of current discussion in Washington, I think all this needs to be spelled out again.

In peace time those who have the oil will be only too happy to sell it to us. In war time it will be sold to any power which controls access to it, whether its nationals were the pre-war owners or not. Military power will decide the question even before war has broken out, as the military power of Japan before Pearl Harbor provided the final argument for the sale to Japan of East Indian oil, nominally owned by the British, Dutch, and Americans. Economic interest will override national advantage; the Japanese had no trouble in buying scrap from us, though they were hardly in a position to seize Pittsburgh, as they were in a position to seize Borneo. It is true that in the "principles of proposed agreement" between the government and the oil companies it is said that "no sales of petroleum or other products will be made by the companies to any government or the nationals of any government when, in the opinion of the Department of State, such sales would militate against the interests of the United States." Let us not forget how easily these oil companies succeeded in deceiving the State Department, how willingly the State Department was deceived, how passionately it fought embargoes on the sale of our own domestic oil and scrap to Japan before the war.

The propaganda campaign which preceded this proposed Arabian oil deal is much like that which made it possible for Standard Oil interests after the First World War to muscle in on British oil preserves in Iraq. Now as then the aim has been (1) to spread fear that our oil resources are nearing exhaustion, and (2) to arouse suspicion of the British. Figures on oil resources need careful investigation; they seem to be adjusted upward or downward according to what the oil companies want at the moment. When it is proposed to begin the production of oil from coal, such Standard Oil experts as Per K. Frolich assure us that we have ample reserves of petroleum for this century anyway. When it is desired to embark on the financing of foreign oil resources, we are told that our oil is on the verge of exhaustion. In 1922, at the height of the last post-war scare, a committee of noted oil geologists assured us that we had only five billion barrels in reserve; proved reserves today, twenty-two years later, are twenty billion barrels.

"There is little enough oil left in the Western Hemisphere and in the United States in particular," Secretary Ickes recently wrote Senator Mead; ". . . our reserves in this country have a relatively short life expectancy of fourteen years." But the report made here by the Truman committee puts this estimate differently. It says that proved reserves are equal to but fourteen years' supply "based on current consumption," which is a horse of another color, for consumption today is at abnormal war-time levels. Let us compare these figures with those in the report of the National Resources Committee to the President in January, 1939. This report, on "energy resources and national policy," says that in 1938 we had fifteen billion barrels in reserve, or a twelve-year supply at the 1937 rate of consumption. So that we find ourselves today, in the midst of a great war, with five billion barrels more in reserve than we had then and a two-years-longer life expectancy, even at war-time rates of consumption. The final touch in this picture is supplied by a speech which Wallace E. Pratt, petroleum geologist of Standard Oil of New Jersey and its one "liberal" director, made before a Sigma Xi luncheon at Columbia University on December 6 last. Pratt said our petroleum reserves would probably last a hundred years; that recent scare stories were based on half-truths; that *proved* reserves were not necessarily a reflection of actual reserves; that the proved reserve has many times been low in our history; and that at least one-half of the prospective oil-producing territory of the United States has not been explored.

I believe the Arabian oil deal will serve to retard development of oil possibilities at home. I note that the big oil companies hope to couple it with "conservation" of resources in the United States—that is, restriction of domestic output and an international oil compact for restriction abroad. The National Resources Committee, in discussing the question of our future petroleum supply, dwelt on the role to be played by improved technology. The committee pointed out that from 1922 to 1936 the geologist had helped drillers add 10.8 billion barrels to reserves despite the production of 12.8 billion barrels during that period. It pointed out that from 1920 to the end of 1936 the chemist, by improved cracking processes, had conserved 8.5 billion barrels of crude oil, or an amount equal to three-fourths of total production from 1922 to 1936. It pointed out that today 65 to 85 per cent of the available oil still remains in the ground "after a field no longer yields oil by the older methods of production," and that this enormous margin of wastage is a challenge to the petroleum engineer. Finally, the committee reported that "the volume of the coal resources of the United States is such that they may be depended upon [by hydrogenation and other processes] to provide an adequate supply of motor fuel for many centuries after a shortage in crude petroleum arrives." Is money likely to be invested in the development of these possibilities so long as low-cost Arabian oil is available? Wouldn't we be better prepared against emergency if we developed these possibilities instead of becoming dependent on a distant and precarious source of supply?

The reserves of Arabia have been as exaggerated as the reserves of the United States have been understated. "Estimates by responsible authorities of the total reserves in Saudi Arabia," the Truman report says, "have varied from two and one-half billion barrels to twenty billion barrels, but most experts estimate it to be between two and one-half and three billion barrels." The figure used by most newspapers is twenty billion barrels. Coupled with this has been an alarmist and nationalistic exaggeration of the share we are supplying to the fuel requirements of United Nations in the war. The United States is currently producing about 70 per cent of all the petroleum used by the United Nations, and this is represented as a disproportionate sacrifice, though it would hardly seem so when equated with the greater sacrifice of men and resources by the Soviet Union and Great Britain. But the real reason we supply so much of the war's oil is because we control so much of the world's oil within and without our borders. Our share in the fueling of the war is almost exactly the same as our normal share in world petroleum production, which was 70.6 per cent in 1938, the last peace-time year. Two-fifths of the world's known reserves are within our own continental borders, and Americans control 57 1/2 per cent of the total world reserves. Under these circumstances, to picture the United States as a duped and plundered oil pauper is ludicrous. Just how much of the world's oil do we propose to hog! The oil scare hit the headlines in the wake of the tour of the five Senators to combat areas last summer. The Truman report is based, presumably, on their findings—actually, on their preconceptions. The best of the five, Mead and Brewster, proved themselves extraordinarily naïve, shallow, and credulous in discussing the Near Eastern oil situation. The worst, Chandler of Kentucky, a member of the "Beat Japan First" and anti-British blocs, had obviously an ax to grind. The whole drift of the Truman report is in the direction of an intense Anglo-American imperialist struggle for oil in the Near East. Its frame of reference is not a new world order in which basic resources may be developed for the benefit of all peoples. Its frame of reference is that we'd better hurry up and grab some oil before those wicked British take it away from us. It is not irrelevant to recall that before the war the Standard, Texas, and Gulf companies were allies of such great Nazi concerns as I. G. Farben against the Anglo-Dutch oil and rubber combinations. This kind of anti-British talk plays beautifully into German hands.

The kind of thinking the Senate has done in this field is indicated by the Truman report's discussion of the role government should play in the Arabian development. Government ownership of foreign oil concessions, the report says, "would presuppose a radical change in our economic system," while "partial government ownership . . . might discourage private enterprise." Did Britain become a socialist country when Churchill in 1913, under similar circumstances, insisted on obtaining for the British government majority control of the stock of the Anglo-Persian Oil Company?

ARAMCO'S SECRET REPORT ON PALESTINE (1948)

The Nation

THIS WEEK *The Nation* ASSOCIATES submitted to President Truman a memorandum pointing out how his Palestine policy has been undermined by the State Department working in close cooperation with the Middle Eastern oil companies. The basis of the memorandum is a document, never before published, which has been the subject of much rumor and speculation in Washington. This is the famous report written in Cairo last December by James Terry Duce, formerly a director of the Petroleum Administration and now vice-president of Aramco (Arabian-American Oil Company), to W. F. Moore, the president of the company. That report and the activities it describes have been major obstacles in the way of partition—in Palestine and the Arab states, in Washington, and at Lake Success. For Mr. Duce undertook, first, to assure the Arab rulers and political leaders through personal visits that they could count upon the active support of the oil companies and of the United States government experts in their opposition to the Jewish state, and, second, to kill partition by advising the State Department of its dangers and reporting the views and proposals of the Arab leaders.

When President Truman recognized Israel it looked as if the enemies of partition had been defeated. Events since then show that they have by no means given up. The State Department in the last few weeks has been trying to force the Jewish state to accept reduction in area—perhaps even to the dimensions of a "Vatican City"—in return for de jure recognition. This idea, which has been privately discussed by Americans at the U. N., stems from the Duce report. On December 10 in Cairo Azzam Pasha, secretary general of the Arab League, proposed such a solution to Mr. Duce, who with Azzam's permission passed it on to the State Department. The present intention of the department is to use the truce period, which expires on July 9, to negotiate a compromise more or less along these lines: at the very least Israel will be asked to relinquish the Negev and accept an enlarged Arab state under Abdullah, with an outlet to the sea presumably at Gaza and port rights at Haifa. These ceded areas and facilities would of course be actually subject to Great Britain, which controls Transjordan and its ruler.

Mr. Duce's report is a surprisingly naïve exposition of oil politics in the Middle East. It shows both the deference with which the oil-company executive approached the Arab leaders and his total ignorance of Jewish attitudes and intentions. One of his most "fruitful" experiences was the conversation with Azzam Pasha mentioned above, in the course of which the Arab leader suggested that a "compromise might be worked out which would satisfy the Arabs and still have some possibility of being acceptable to the Jews." The report says on this point:

> I remarked that, if so, it would be of extreme interest to get it before the proper people. He replied that he thought that the matter could be worked out on the basis of a Vatican State for the Jews which would have all the rights and privileges allotted to the Vatican by the present treaties. . . . I asked him where he thought this kind of state could be set up. He said, "Well, of course, the Arabs would like it as far away as possible," and jokingly mentioned Samoa and New Guinea and —as if an afterthought—"even the district around Tel Aviv." I asked him if I could carry his remark to the State Department and say it had been his. He replied that he had no substantial objection to my making such a report.

Mr. Duce was flattered to be received by Azzam Pasha. . . . They spent two hours alone and "had a very interesting discussion." The Arab League secretary complained that the United States government had "dragooned the various delegates to vote for the resolution of the General Assembly." Mr. Duce explained that Americans misunderstood the situation in the Middle East because they had been brought up on the Bible and thought of Palestine as the Jewish homeland; but he added that "a large proportion of the people who had dealt with the Middle Eastern situation and were experts on it for the United States government were opposed to partition because they thought that it would result in very serious events in the Middle Eastern area." He also told Azzam Pasha that the oil companies "had no political influence" and any attempt to bring direct pressure on the government would have injured the Arab case. The

Zionists, he said, "would have been quick to raise the question as to whether the United States was more interested in oil or in the blood of Jews."

Apparently Azzam Pasha fully understood that the cancellation of oil concessions would dry up a major source of dollar income, for Mr. Duce reports:

> I told him our company was anxious to go along with the development of the oil resources, that he had seen what had been done in Saudi Arabia during his visit recently, and that we wished to build a pipe line to the Mediterranean. I pointed out that the building of this pipe line would help all the countries along the way, and that financial benefits would be derived. . . . He said that he realized this; that he had supported us in the meetings of the League. He said there were great difficulties in controlling the populace, but that he hoped we would be permitted to continue to operate in safety; that he knew we were not pro-Zionist, and that it was in the interest of the Arab people to see us continue our operations.

Mr. Duce offered to do what he could "to assist Azzam Pasha in any contacts he might wish to have with the United States government unofficially," and the Arab leader replied that he "would call on me as he knew from experience that I was one of the people in the United States who could be trusted implicitly. . . . I asked him of what service I could be, and he asked me to tell the State Department people the truth about the matter in the Middle East."

In a conference with the head of the Misr Bank of Cairo, Hafifi Pasha, Mr. Duce hastened to explain his own and his company's attitude toward American policy:

> I told him . . . that I had advised my own government of the dangers which were inherent in partition and its support by . . . the United States; that I had wired my people when it had happened that I thought the United States had "set the woods on fire" and that our government was thus playing into the hands of destructive forces in the Middle East.

Mr. Duce then offered his own formula for winning American sympathy for the Arab cause, a formula which would present the "true story of the Middle East" in an attractive light. He suggested "historical romances, events in the Middle East which had a historic or a picturesque touch." He strongly urged that a "study be made of American publicity methods," and expressed the opinion that Mr. Truman had decided to support partition without fully understanding the consequences. He concluded with the remark that he "could see even more tragic consequences than the Arabs could see themselves," and that it was "the duty of all good people to work together to get this matter straightened out."

Mr. Duce met King Farouk's Chief of Cabinet, Ibrahim Abdelhadi Pasha, and told him that partition would produce anti-Semitism and bloodshed, with "tragic consequences for the Jews in many countries." To indicate further that he and Aramco, despite their alleged lack of interest in political affairs, were friendly to the Arab cause, Mr. Duce added: "I did not myself at all despair as to the ultimate solution of the Palestine problem; that the proposed two states in Palestine seemed to me politically and geographically impossible." He convinced Ibrahim Abdelhadi Pasha that if concessions were canceled, "the Arabs should bear in mind that they would hurt their friends and not their enemies, that a great many Zionists would be delighted if the Arabs took the opportunity to cancel the American and British oil concessions, as this would be a further weapon in Zionists' hands." The Egyptian official, who had shown considerable hostility at the start, replied that "he had been pleased to hear what I had to say and indicated that he would pass the information I had given him on to King Farouk. He told me, too, that after discussing the matter with me it was his opinion that the Arabs should give all facilities to us to continue our work."

In Cairo Mr. Duce also arranged to see Prince Feisal, Foreign Minister of Saudi Arabia and delegate to the United Nations. Before doing so he took pains to find out whether the visit of a man whose country had voted for partition would embarrass the Prince. To Mr. Duce's great relief Feisal "immediately set a date and time for me to appear at Shepheard's, where he was staying." Mr. Duce described his talk with Feisal in some detail:

> With him was Mardam Bey, the Syrian Prime Minister. Feisal began by telling me how much the Arab groups had appreciated my help in connection with their relations in Washington. He added, without any prompting on my part, that he knew that practically everybody in the oil companies was opposed to partition, but added that the companies themselves, as he well knew, were not concerned with political matters and had little influence in a case of this kind. I confirmed this fact to Prince Feisal. He turned then to Mardam Bey and told him how well pleased the Saudi Arabs were with their connection with the Arabian-American Oil Company, what good work we had done, and how fond they were of us. He then asked me how we were getting along with our affairs in Saudi Arabia. I told him that production had reached 300,000 barrels a day, and added that if we could get this Palestine matter settled and the pipe line built, greatly increased quantities of oil could be moved. I added, too, that probably the movement of these large quantities of oil would also result in the building of additional refining capacity in the north —much to the benefit of Syria and Lebanon. He said to me that he thought that the Syrians themselves should proceed to ratify the Syrian convention, as it was in the interests of all Arabs.

The reaction of Feisal should not have been a great surprise to Mr. Duce, for after all King Ibn Saud was receiving royalties from the oil companies at the rate of 21 cents a barrel—royalties which not only had saved the country from bankruptcy but were constantly replenishing the personal funds of the royal family. As was revealed by the special Senate committee investigating the national defense program, it was due to the influence of Aramco that the United States government, from 1940 to 1947, extended direct and indirect lend-lease and other assistance to Saudi Arabia in the amount of more than $99,000,000.

The Duce report informed the State Department that the Communists were active in the Middle East and insisted that the Russians were only waiting for the opportune moment to send an armed force into Palestine. At the same time, while admitting that he "had no contact with the Jewish side," Mr. Duce proceeded to tar the Jews with the Communist brush. He said:

> The significant fact is that the good Jews are leaving Palestine, and that Arabs are leaving Palestine to take refuge in other lands. The Palestine groups of Jews remaining are showing more radical tendencies. The red flag flies in Palestine along with the star of David, and it is generally recognized that Jewish Palestine will be organized as a communistic state.

Taken by itself the Duce report would be interesting only as a typical oil-company view of Middle Eastern affairs. As a document used by the State Department, its significance cannot be minimized. Oil dominates the department's policy in Palestine; colossal profits dominate the policy of Aramco. During the war, in return for government assistance, Aramco offered to make concessions in the price of oil to the navy. Instead, as the special Senate investigating committee reported, "the United States government was overcharged between $30,000,000 and $38,000,000 on sales made to the navy by Aramco and its affiliates between January 1, 1942, and June 30, 1947." It seems obvious that a company which gouged its government in time of war would have little hesitation about subverting public policy to increase its profits. But it is equally obvious that government officials who confuse the welfare of their country with the interests of the oil companies should be promptly cleared out of the State Department. They have done damage enough already.

WHAT NOW? (1958)

The Nation

. . . AMERICAN POLICY-MAKERS have refused to accept the proposition that there can never be any real stability in the Middle East until the Arab peoples are permitted to govern themselves. The regimes we have supported have been misbegotten, corrupt, dictatorial, semi-feudal and fantastically unpopular. But Mr. Dulles and his predecessors found them useful. They were "anti-Communist," they were "reasonable," and they did grant oil concessions. Over the years, the American stake in Middle Eastern oil has grown and, in the process, become closely allied with French, British, Dutch and other interests through a variety of cartel, consortium and joint-stock undertakings. From Mossadegh's action in nationalizing British oil interests in Iran in 1951 to the present time, the oil companies have been haunted by the fear of nationalization. Nationalization implies more than the local loss of profits and control; it threatens the structure of world-wide cartel pricing and marketing agreements. With the oil companies, "stability" has had a special and limited meaning. In their view, the more "popular" the regime, the greater the danger of nationalization. And the oil companies have exerted a great influence on American policy in the Middle East.

But—Mr. Dulles to the contrary—nationalization does not necessarily mean that a source of supply is "lost" to former customers. International shipping still uses the nationalized Suez Canal. The new regime in Iraq has announced that it will honor prior agreements, although these agreements will unquestionably be modified (they were, in fact, in process of modification before the coup). It should be plain as day that oil can never be obtained peacefully and efficiently without the cooperation not only of the Middle Eastern governments, but of the peoples as well. "Friendly" sheiks and emirs cannot guarantee continued delivery. Even before the present crisis, unnamed oil-company executives were quoted in the *Wall Street Journal* as saying that their Middle Eastern operations had a limited time expectancy—some said five, some ten years.

Ironically, Anglo-American oil operations have been a prime cause of revolutionary ferment in the Middle East. Arab nationalism has grown in more or less direct ratio to oil exports. Oil has been the key to nearly every coup since the 1920s. What could be more inflammatory than the contrast which oil has brought between opulent luxury and humiliating poverty? between oil-barren and oil-rich Arab states? While huge oil revenues have resulted in some economic progress, the lot of the people has not greatly improved. But of recent years, oil production has brought into being new middle-class elements with whom the nabobs have been unwilling to share wealth or power. These new elements were behind the coup in Iraq. And they can be the key to political stability; power must be more broadly based if oil revenues are to be effectively used to finance social and economic reforms or, for that matter, if the West is to retain an interest in Middle Eastern oil. For there is, as Aneurin Bevan has pointed out, something "arid and outmoded" about the logic of attempting to ensure stability and efficiency of oil production through the use of military force. . . .

IRAN'S FABULOUS OIL (1954)

A. Kessel

AN AGREEMENT settling the long-standing Iranian oil dispute has been initialed between the Iranian government and a consortium—cartel is not a very respectable word—of eight oil companies. Congratulatory notes have criss-crossed among the President of the United States, the Shah, Mr. Eden, and the various ambassadors, ministers, and oil company officials concerned, not to speak of Herbert Hoover, Jr., who seems to have been rewarded with something more concrete than congratulations. The New York *Times* called the agreement "a diplomatic victory for the West." The Iranians have been told that they are now embarked on a new era of national progress and prosperity. And the Shah and his ministers, renewing their "two years of treason" campaign against the former Mossadegh regime, are exhorting the Iranian parliament to ratify the agreement or else.

These widespread expressions of optimism are based on a number of misconceptions which have been sedulously propagated internationally ever since Iran nationalized its oil in 1949. For instance it has been widely publicized that Iran's general economy, as well as the government's revenues, are dependent upon the continued flow of black gold. This is a shockingly false picture. Let us examine the allegation in the light of four criteria: the oil industry's contribution to the national budget; its contribution to the national income; its contribution to employment; and, finally, its role in the life of the Iranian people.

The National Budget. The highest annual net money return to the Iranian government by the oil industry was in 1948–49 and amounted to $30,000,000. The national budget that year was approximately $300,000,000. Thus the oil revenue amounted to about 10 per cent of the national budget. It is true that since most of the oil revenue was in foreign exchange, its value was greater than the figures indicate. But by no stretch of the imagination can the revenue be calculated as forming the "major share" of the national budget.

The National Income. Iran is a large country (over 600,000 square miles), sparsely populated (about 18 to 20 millions), predominantly agricultural, and sadly lacking in statistics. Any estimate of its national income is bound to be hardly more than a reasonable guess. The latest such guess appears in the U. N. Statistical Year Book for 1952, which puts the figure at about $1,800,000,000 annually during recent years. Experts will affirm that the figure is more likely to be an under- than an over-estimate.

How much did the oil industry contribute to the national income? First, there are the cash revenues which accrue directly to the government; second, the wages and salaries earned by Iranians in the industry; third, the goods and services purchased by the industry in Iran. Even at the peak of its operation, the industry employed fewer than 100,000, mostly unskilled labor. Assuming an average income for these workers of $500 a year (an optimistic guess, about six times greater than the national average), this amounts to $50,000,000. The industry's purchases in Iran are limited, for its technical equipment, and the nontechnical goods and services for its non-Iranian employees, are purchased abroad. If we put the figure at $20,000,000 a year we are probably overestimating.

Let us recapitulate. Oil royalties at their peak amounted to $30,000,000; wages and salaries, $50,000,000; goods and services, $20,000,000. The oil industry's total contribution amounted to $100,000,000—or about 6 per cent of the annual national income of $1,800,000,000.

Shall we be generous and allow for a figure of 10 per cent?

Employment. Iran's male labor force can be estimated at 5,000,000 persons. The oil industry never employed more than 100,000, or about 2 per cent.

Oil Industry's Role. To the vast majority of the people of Iran the oil industry simply does not exist. They get nothing from it directly or indirectly. At least 85 per cent of the people live on a primitive agriculture; 20 per cent still lead a nomadic tribal existence. It has yet to be proven that the oil industry has raised the abysmally low standard of living of these Iranian masses by any substantial amount.

For two years, under Mossadegh's regime, the Abadan refineries were closed with no observable deterioration in the country's standard of living. If anything, conditions improved somewhat—employment was slightly higher, production was up a little, the trade balance was slightly more favorable. If it is true that when the new government took over after last year's pseudo-revolution the national coffers were empty, then this was not because the oil industry had been shut down. The main reasons lie in major shortcomings of the socio-economic organization of Iranian society which have no relation to the oil industry.

Why was there no settlement of the oil dispute during Mossadegh's regime? The public was given all sorts of reasons: the chauvinistic Iranians had lost their common sense; the stubborn playactor, Mossadegh, was unreasonable; the

Communists had taken over the country; the Iranian government was refusing to pay compensation to Anglo-Iranian. But there is another and more likely reason which never reached the headlines. The world oil cartel sets the world market price and wants to be able to continue doing so. Mossadegh's terms, in contrast, demanded independence of operation, including sales at prices outside the cartel's control. And it may be said in passing that Iran's production was potentially large enough and cheap enough to have posed a real threat to world prices under such conditions.

Some of the truth did leak out. The New York *Times* of August 26, 1953, wrote of the existing concern "for the world market price system for oil rather than with the question of compensation for Anglo-Iranian." And four days later the *Times* wrote: "If the Anglo-Iranian Company should regain control, the Iranian oil supplies might be channeled into world markets with a minimum of disturbance to prices. . . . Should no agreement be made with Anglo-Iranian, the reentry of Iranian oil in the international market could be serious. Another organization without adequate distribution outlets might drastically reduce prices in order to find a market. This would create chaos in world oil markets, for only a relatively few areas could compete in price with the low-cost production of Iran." On September 22, 1953, the *Times* referred to Iranian oil as "barred from world markets for more than two years by the successful British commercial blockade backed by world oil interests."

The inside story of the "popular revolt" which overthrew the Mossadegh regime in August last year will be known only after the various secret documents involved are made public. One may safely conjecture, however, that the story given to the press did not tell the whole truth. It may or may not be relevant, for instance, that the "revolution" broke out in Iran only a short time after Mossadegh had succeeded in selling $3,000,000 worth of oil to the Japanese, and the British had already lost their case in the Japanese courts trying to prevent the unloading of the oil.

The exact terms of the new agreement have not yet been divulged, but it is interesting to compare what we know of them to the terms of the old concession. The now defunct agreement with Anglo-Iranian was scheduled to remain in effect until 1993—approximately another forty years. The new agreement is for twenty-five years with provisions for three automatic renewals of five years each, *i.e.,* a total of forty years. Production, export, marketing, and all other operations are to be carried out by the consortium which, except for the presence of an Iranian member on the board, will be predominantly non-Iranian. Royalties to the Iranian government will be based on a fifty-fifty sharing of all marketing operations, an arrangement similar to that in Saudi Arabia, and one which American oil interests tried to induce Anglo-Iranian to offer to Iran at the time of nationalization.

It would appear then that the only real gain to the Iranian government in the new agreement is that the American oil companies assume responsibility for compensating Anglo-Iranian (*Time* estimated the amount involved as $600,000,000) in return for the privilege of sharing the profits.

What are the disadvantages to Iran? One is entitled to wonder, of course, how much the entrance of six powerful American oil companies into the Iranian domestic scene is going to affect the freedom of operation of the Iranian government. Apart from this, there is a more fundamental issue: the gains accruing to a society, especially an underdeveloped one, from the operation of any large industry are not confined to immediate cash returns. There are invaluable indirect factors, such as the creation of a skilled labor force, the growth of subsidiary service industries, the development of new industries related to the first, the creation of a sense of responsibility and managerial know-how on both the local and national level. During the forty years which Anglo-Iranian operated in Iran, such indirect gains to the Iranian economy were infinitesimal. The oil industry has been simply an isolated production island with a minimum number of contacts with the rest of the economy. There is no reason to suppose that the new consortium will act any differently from Anglo-Iranian. Indeed, from the point of view of a company operating solely for profit, there is no other way to act.

On the other hand the gains to Iran of continued independent operation of the nationalized industry in the form of increased self-reliance, a greater sense of political independence, and faster technological development under the pressure of necessity, would have far outweighed the loss in cash revenue. And had there existed no world oil cartel, there is every reason to believe that even the cash revenues would have proved as great as are now promised.

IRAQ'S EXPLOSIVE OIL (1958)

Charles F. Edmundson

THE MOST PERCEPTIVE REPORT on the State Department's reaction to the revolution in Iraq appeared on the front page of *The New York Times* of July 18. The headline read:

WEST TO KEEP OUT OF IRAQ
UNLESS OIL IS THREATENED

President Eisenhower's press secretary decried the story the same day, but the facts were clear. Two years ago, Secretary of State Dulles told a private meeting of oil-company executives in Washington that nationalization of oil properties abroad should be the signal for international intervention. We were now prepared to fulfill that pledge.

It was in August, 1956, that Secretary Dulles called a meeting of representatives of the major U.S. oil companies doing business abroad. The press was not informed and no records were to have been kept. But A. C. Ingraham, of the Socony Vacuum Oil Company of New York, kept a memorandum which became public when the Senate Anti-Trust Subcommittee subpoenaed Socony documents in another connection.

According to this document, which the State Department never repudiated, Secretary Dulles knew "the oil companies were interested in the nationalization issue and wanted to put forth his views." The nub of the memorandum is this:

> Therefore, he [Dulles] indicated, nationalization of this kind of an asset [oil properties] impressed with international interest goes far beyond the compensation of shareholders alone and should call for international intervention.

On the Senate floor, Senator Kefauver read the memorandum and inquired prophetically:

> Who is going to do the intervening? There is no indication that U.S. troops would not be used for this purpose. And what, may I ask, would Russia's reaction be to that?

It appears that Mr. Dulles' latest exercise in brinkmanship was spurred not only by Iraq's 250 million barrels of oil a year, but also by the fear that if Iraq could become master of its own oil, so could Saudi Arabia and Iran.

Title to exploit Middle East oil rests almost entirely in the hands of the American, British, French and Dutch companies which comprise the international oil cartel. And while Mr. Dulles is using the Army, Air Force, Navy and Marines to defend the cartel, the U.S. Department of Justice is prosecuting it for violating federal anti-trust laws. The Anti-Trust Division has been suing to break up the cartel since 1952. . . .

In essence, the Department of Justice charges this: that the oil companies pump crude oil from the fabulously productive Middle East wells at a cost of 20 to 30 cents a barrel—exclusive of profits, which are usually divided 50–50 with the producing country—and sell it at a collusive price varying over a period of years from $1.75 to $2.16 a barrel f.o.b. the Persian Gulf.

A reasonably bright high school student can take the published figures of the Iraq Petroleum Company and find that the crude oil pumped there brings a net of about $1.55 a barrel, to be split between the Government of Iraq and the participating companies. At a production rate of 250 million barrels a year, this gives the two sides some $400 million to divide.

Iraq accounts for somewhat less than a fifth of Middle East oil production, but the profit pattern is much the same throughout except for the recently arrived smaller companies, such as the Getty Oil Company and American Independent Oil. They have had to pay a stiff price for their concessions, and enjoy a considerably smaller profit margin.

Both at home and abroad, U. S. oil companies get the benefit of a 27 1/2 per cent annual allowance for the depletion of reserves. In the case of the oil companies producing abroad, income taxes which would be due the United States Government are drastically reduced by converting royalty payments into income taxes paid to the host country. Thus direct U. S. income taxes dwindle almost to nothing.

From 1953 to 1955, the biggest of the U.S. companies operating abroad—Arabian-American—paid no U. S. income taxes at all. In 1956, Aramco paid $200 million to the King of Saudi Arabia—which is approximately 700 times as much as the $282,000 which Aramco paid in income taxes to the United States.

Besides maintaining the vast military forces which help to secure oil company properties, the U. S. Government picks up the tab for any extraordinary operating expenses involved in keeping the Arab sheiks content. During the Second World War, when oil could not be sent to the West, King Ibn Saud's income dwindled. The U. S. Government was touched by this royal distress—touched for a total of $99 million.

To protect exorbitant profits, contrived in a manner which the Department of Justice says is illegal, Secretary Dulles is willing to risk war. To whip up public support for this policy, the press, except for a handful of newspapers, has encouraged the false notion that "Middle Eastern oil is vital to the defense of the Western World."

In World War II, Middle East oil was lost to the Allies as soon as Italy entered the conflict. And this was before the nuclear bomb, or even the old-fashioned "blockbuster," had been developed. No informed person anywhere believes that the West will have access to Middle East oil if and when World War III breaks out.

There is no lack of oil in the Western hemisphere to serve all the needs of the Western allies. New fields are being discovered all the way from Alaska to Tierra del Fuego. . . .

Senator Hennings of Missouri, a cautious middle-of-the-roader, estimates that the international oil cartel collects excessive profits adding up to $3 billion a year. Except for this profiteering in oil, he points out, the U.S. Government could reduce its foreign military and economic aid programs by hundreds of millions of dollars a year.

The writer was in the capital of Saudi Arabia a few years ago. An American-educated Arab official told him that he thought the oil companies and the Saudi Arabian Government both should materially reduce their "take" in order to make oil available to the underdeveloped nations at prices more nearly within their reach. He estimated that Saudi Arabian crude was being produced at a cost of no more than 25 cents a barrel. But the California-Texas and Standard-Vacuum refineries in Bombay were paying $2 a barrel, f.o.b. the oil field.

The principle at stake involves much more than the Arab nations. It is the right of *all* nations to reasonable access at equitable prices to the raw material resources of the world. It is a principle which the United States subscribed to in the Atlantic Charter and in the Declaration of the United Nations. But even if these documents did not exist, American, British, French and Dutch companies would have no moral right to stand astride the Middle East oil reserves. Here lie nearly 90 per cent of all known oil reserves outside the United States and Russia. To dole out this oil at "administered prices" so high as to call for action by the U.S. Department of Justice clearly constitutes an unjustifiable tax on the wealth of the whole world.

In 1954, while India was paying the oil companies and the oil-host countries a joint profit of about 700 per cent, the United States gave India $82.5 million in Point Four assistance. Indirectly, the American taxpayer was bearing the burden of the bloated profits of the oil companies and the fantastic extravagances of the petty kings and sheiks of Arabia. . . .

The British Government owns 54 per cent of all the vastly profitable British oil operations in the Middle East. At the present operating rate, this brings into the British Exchequer some $300 million a year from crude oil alone, and a large additional sum in profits after the crude is converted to gasoline, lubricants and other finished products. The remaining 46 per cent is owned by the stockholders of the British Petroleum Company. It is evident that both the British Government and the stockholders would lose if prices were brought down. (The French and Dutch holdings in Middle East oil are smaller, and their readjustment would be less painful.) But readjustment is needed for the sake of fairness to non-cartel countries and to fulfill the pledge of the Atlantic Charter and the Declaration of the United Nations. . . .

The oil cartel has fostered the impression that for Russia to share access to Middle Eastern oil would be a calamity. To judge from a United Nations study of the international oil industry, the advent of Russia as a major oil supplier might, on the contrary, lend some capitalistic flexibility to oil prices.

According to the U. N. study, the largest real oil-price competition in Europe occurred in Sweden from 1930 to 1933. This was forced upon the Western companies by *Naftsyndicat,* a subsidiary of the Russian oil monopoly. A study of oil prices by the Swedish Government, quoted in a U. S. Federal Trade Commission survey, reports that *Naftsyndicat,* which accounted for 27 per cent of the Scandinavian oil trade, "was the largest and most vigorous competitor."

Whether or not Russia gets a foothold in Middle Eastern oil, it may soon give the Anti-Trust Division an assist in Washington by challenging the cartel's monopoly prices. The Soviet Union has doubled its oil production in the five years ending in 1957, and expects to double it again by 1962.

As the Washington *Post* remarks editorially, "The severity of the (potential) oil crisis could be alleviated by more attention to alternate sources, more development of oil shales in this country and elsewhere, more sensible oil import and trade policies and the like." If this advice were followed, the knotty problem of what to do with Canadian and Venezuelan oil might be solved automatically. . . .

IRANIAN OIL WORKERS AND REVOLUTION (1979, 1980)

Kai Bird

IN THE WANING DAYS of the Pahlevi regime, just prior to the precipitous collapse of the Imperial army, hundreds of spontaneous revolutionary committees (komitehs) began to fill the power vacuum in the name of Ayatollah Ruhollah Khomeini. More than a year after the revolution, many of these relatively decentralized komitehs were still functioning in factories, schools, office buildings and villages across the country. None played a more significant role in the Iranian revolution, however, than the worker komitehs in the oil fields of Khuzistan. The decision of the oil workers to strike in defiance of martial law ultimately spelled the end of the Pahlevi dynasty. And despite the intense power struggle and political chaos endemic to post-revolutionary Iran, the oil worker komitehs have survived and retained control over the strategic oil fields. Worker control of this nature, of course, poses a highly disruptive precedent for some of the more conservative oil-producing states in the Middle East, a precedent which has already introduced a new element of unpredictability in the delicate workings of an international oil economy still dominated by the Western multinational oil companies.

Shah Mohammed Riza Pahlevi had been groomed for three decades to protect the flow of Iranian oil to the West from precisely this sort of internal challenge. For more than half a century Iran had been regarded as a pillar of the West's energy system. The Iranian oil fields, located in the southern province of Khuzistan, were the first to be developed in the Persian Gulf region. Production was brought on line in 1908 after an Australian mining speculator, William K. D'Arcy, obtained a sixty-year concession in 1901 that encompassed five-sixths of present-day Iran. Iranian oil was thus developed and controlled in all aspects until 1951 by the Anglo-Persian Oil Company, now known as British Petroleum.

By 1933 the British government owned 56 percent of the company's stock. Nationalist sentiments mounted during World War II and pressures escalated in the postwar period for nationalization. As Fred Halliday points out in his book, *Iran: Dictatorship and Development,* the oil company had profits of $613 million between 1915 and 1950, but Reza Shah received only $316 million in government royalties. Prices, of course, were determined by the global oil cartel outside the country and production levels for Iranian oil were determined exclusively by British Petroleum.

After his election as Prime Minister Mohammed Mossadeq tapped popular resentment against the British to nationalize oil in 1951. In response, British Petroleum initiated an international boycott of Iranian oil. Mossadeq was unable to market Iranian oil independently of the multinationals and as a result Iranian production plummeted for nearly four years.

The subsequent political crisis came to a head in 1953 when the Shah was briefly sent into exile—only to return in the wake of a successful coup d'état organized by the American Central Intelligence Agency. Mossadeq was imprisoned and negotiations were initiated to bring Iranian oil back onto the world market. The agreement in 1954 with the companies left the oil fields in government hands only in name. Actual control over price, output, and marketing reverted once again to the West. British Petroleum lost its exclusive control, however, to the American oil interests. Shell and five other American companies were given 54 percent in a new consortium, while British Petroleum's share was reduced to 40 percent. (A French oil company received 6 percent in the consortium.)

Production levels were determined by just two criteria: how much oil the multinationals wanted on the world market and how many billions of dollars the Shah needed to ply his military machine. By 1978, this alliance between the Shah and the multinationals squeezed some 5.5 million barrels per day out of the country's reserves. Iran was the source of some 10 percent of the United States' oil imports.

Today, the Iranian revolution has changed all that, and while the Western press has concerned itself with minor technical questions about the Iranians' capacity to produce significant oil for export without the benefit of expatriate engineers (the answer is an unequivocal yes), it has ignored the fact that the West will be dealing with an entirely new system. Across the negotiating table,

Western importers will still face a pinstripe executive from the National Iranian Oil Company, but behind that executive will stand the worker komiteh, exercising its collective will over the country's oil policies.

The oil industry is virtually controlled by dozens of independent worker komitehs which, though loyal to the central Government, are nevertheless participating in all the decisions related to the production and marketing of Iranian oil to the Western industrial world. Perhaps even more significant, the worker komitehs have unquestionably demonstrated that they can run the oil fields and refineries without their top-rank Iranian managers and without the expertise of some 800 foreign technicians. (The main Abadan refinery is still in operation producing refined oil for domestic use and the oil fields are producing more than 3 million barrels per day.)

The presence of these komitehs in nearly every phase of Iranian oil operations is responsible for a new national oil policy based on conservation, diversification of exports, a ban on exports to South Africa and Israel, the cancellation of expensive capital investments like the gas injection projects and a determination to eliminate the multinational middlemen in the marketing of their oil. Every aspect of the new policy has already had a direct impact on American, British, and other Western economies.

Since the revolution Teheran has, under pressure from the oil worker komitehs, sold a higher percentage of the oil on a government to government basis, thus by-passing the oil companies. For instance, as American imports of Iranian oil declined and then were embargoed after United States diplomats were taken hostage in Teheran, the Japanese seized the opportunity to negotiate relatively long-term government-to-government contracts for the same oil. In addition, the worker komitehs have encouraged Teheran to sell more oil on the spot market, where prices are well above the OPEC standards.

The political orientation of the worker komitehs in the oil fields has fluctuated considerably since the revolution. During the last few months of the Pahlevi regime, the underground komitehs in Abadan and Ahwaz, the two most important centers in the oil industry, contained a significant minority of secular leftists. Some of these elements were reportedly purged immediately after the revolution by conservative religious leaders. And komiteh elections later in the spring of 1979 led to the unseating of some of the more vocal political activists.

But on the whole, the demands made by the worker komitehs for the right to control conditions in their workplace and to participate in decisions with Teheran over production levels place them well to the left of the central government. Iranians with social democratic leanings look to the oil workers as an important counterweight to the conservative religious bloc. This is not to say that the oil workers opposed the creation of Khomeini's Islamic Republic. An overwhelming majority voted for it—with the expectation and hope that reactionary mullah elements would not be allowed to handle the reins of government. Most of the oil workers are devout, practicing Moslems but of the anti-clerical kind that believe that a religious movement which began with the uncompromising demand for the removal of the Shah will not end until the religion itself undergoes a radical reorientation.

"It is true," says Ahmed Moghadamizadeh, the elected speaker of the Abadan oil refinery central komiteh, "that many of us feel the revolution is moving too slowly. There are problems with some of the mullahs. . . . They are what we call Saffadi Shi'ia. We are followers of the reformist theology preached by the late Dr. Ali Shariati."

The radicalism of the oil workers is thus a reflection of ideological tensions *within* the religious camp. Secular critics no doubt exist, but any realistic hope of democratic and economic reforms, for the moment, lies in the religious realm. The masses of the Iranian people simply cannot be moved to any significant political action without using the language of religion.

Shi'ite Islam—as opposed to the Sunni brand of Islam practiced by most of Iran's Arab neighbors—contains two competing traditions, one radical and one fundamentalist and conservative. First, the Shi'ite sect's primary mandate has always been to struggle against illegitimate political authority on behalf of society's poor and powerless. But, second, the Shi'ites' independent hierarchy of clergy have been all too willing to seize temporal power for themselves. The term Saffadi Shi'ism (or state Shi'ism) is a reference to the Saffadi dynasty's 16th-century subjugation of the clergy to secular power. Reformist theologians, like the late Dr. Ali Shariati, charge that many corruptions of the religion, including the wearing of the chador for women, were introduced during the Saffadi dynasty.

Ayatollah Khomeini himself is reportedly torn between the two traditions, desiring on the one hand to construct an Islamic state premised on a rather undemocratic or mystical political consensus and on the other hand, still convinced that only an Islamic Republic can uplift Iran's impoverished millions. The contradictions between this Saffadi Shi'ism and the reformist, social egalitarian elements are sometimes quite bewildering. To begin with, it compels those revolutionaries who now command power in Teheran to deny the existence of class conflict. "In an Islamic Republic," says Hassan Bani Sadr, a Paris-trained economist and Khomeini aide still much admired by the oil workers, "there is no left and there is no right!"

The oil workers were initially immune, however, from the tensions that developed in Teheran among a number of competing factions in the Provisional Government of Premier Mehdi Bazargan. And they were also unaware that the Government had chosen to suppress—occasionally by force—labor unrest, peasant land grabs and ethnic minority demands for regional autonomy. The Government has repeatedly condemned attempts by worker komitehs in the automobile factories to shut out their managers. And, in several instances, the army has been used to expel peasants who had occupied their landlords' farms, chanting, "The land belongs to Allah, and Allah is the people!"

These indications of a rightward drift in the Provisional Revolutionary Government were initially unnoticed by the oil workers, isolated as they are in the southern oil fields along the Persian Gulf. The local worker komitehs professed unqualified support for former Prime Minister Mehdi Bazargan and his oil chief, lawyer Hassan Nazih. But, like many educated Iranians—practicing Moslems or otherwise—the oil workers universally expressed their marked preference for the late Ayatollah Mahmoud Taleghani, a radical religious leader based in Teheran who was imprisoned for many years with a group of Iranian Marxists. Taleghani, until his untimely death in mid-1979, was a strong advocate of the reformist theology popularized by Dr. Ali Shariati. "We give Khomeini due respect for so stubbornly refusing to compromise with the Shah," said a boilermaker in the Abadan refinery. "But after all, Dr. Shariati wrote this revolution. Khomeini only led it. And now that we have an Islamic Republic, Khomeini must rely on people like Taleghani if the revolution is to continue."

Expectations of substantial economic reform are extremely high among the oil workers of Abadan and Ahwaz. It is not surprising, therefore, that in the months immediately after the revolution, relations between the oil workers and Teheran could be tense. (Shortly before oil chief Hassan Nazih left for Geneva to attend the March 21, 1979 meeting of OPEC, he drafted a memorandum instructing a number of komitehs to disband. According to sources within the National Iranian Oil Company, Nazih was instructed to withdraw the memo by the Central Revolutionary Council.) The central komiteh of the Abadan refinery has been managing the unit's entire operations for nearly six months. The komitehs in Ahwaz have shut out the top six managers in the oil exploration and production departments. An engineer working in the sensitive production department in the Ahwaz fields told me, "We support Nazih so far because he has listened to our suggestions. He has not insisted on reinstatement of these discredited managers. He has agreed to scrap the expensive and wasteful gas injection projects, which were only needed when the Shah required us to produce at maximum capacity. And he has agreed not to produce more than 3.7 million to 4 million barrels per day. We believe anything above that level damages the reservoirs—and in any case, this country cannot efficiently spend oil revenues from more than 3 million barrels per day of exports. But if this Government ever began to squander our national treasure, I tell you, we'd strike the fields again."

It is unlikely, however, that the oil workers will ever become the cutting edge of a political movement. It should be remembered that they did not really come out against the Shah until October 3, 1978, nearly a month after the September 8 "Black Friday" massacre in Teheran. And even then, twelve of the twenty-nine-member central strike komiteh in Abadan voted against raising political demands. But the five-month-long strike has left its mark. The komitehs in the oil fields will remain, some as political "watchdog" organizations, but largely as highly politicized trade union vehicles.

Despite vast differences in pay and housing, both the worker and professional komitehs have agreed that substantial labor reforms are in order. The professionals—many of whom earn more than $25,000 a year—claim they are willing to take substantial pay cuts. Ahmed Moghadamizadeh, the speaker of the Abadan refinery komiteh, says that he believes the differences in wages should be narrowed to something like a minimum of $428 per month for a worker and a maximum of $2,142 for top management. (I talked to a 28-year-old welder in the Abadan refinery who, after six years on the job, earns about $180 per month. A 52-year-old boilermaker, by contrast, brings in $385 per month to support two wives and ten children. Some managers under the Pahlevi regime were earning more than $7,000 per month.)

The Government's reaction to these wage demands may become a political barometer of things to come. Slashing exorbitant wages is a popular and relatively painless solution. Allocating a larger portion of shrunken oil revenues among a strategic labor force already viewed as a worker aristocracy in the Iranian context may be politically difficult.

Even more sensitive are the public demands made by some of the worker komitehs for the right to supervise their own jobs. "We are not going to be slaves to these machines," says a young welder. "Labor in the West is forced to obey management and produce only for consumption, always more and more consumption. It is your God. But in an Islamic Republic, the community and not consumption is the main goal." The thirty-member central worker komiteh in the Abadan refinery has already voted to change the work rules, and a wage increase proposal is being drafted for presentation to the Government. The komiteh meets every other day inside the refinery—and it is not hard to believe that someday Iran's oil workers may be back on strike, this time for the economic reforms promised by what has to date been only a political revolution.

The Imperial Economy

WORLD OIL CARTEL (1952)

Barrow Lyons

WHAT CAN BE DONE in the public interest to control the great international cartels, some of which have more political and economic power than national governments? This baffling problem was brought into focus last week by the publication of the Federal Trade Commission's report on the petroleum industry.

The report vivisects the largest and most potent of all cartels. Despite the oil men's denial that a combine exists, no one can read the 378-page document without being convinced that for nearly a quarter-century the world's supply of "black gold" has been skillfully manipulated by a group of men exercising substantial control over production, prices, and distribution. The control has never been absolute. Every discovery of a new oil field created a problem. The United States' anti-trust laws made this country a difficult market to tame. But one by one the problems always yielded to the concerted action of the oil men; the report is studded with the agreements through which the new fields and the new companies were brought into line. In the United States the petroleum industry made "conservation" the shibboleth, and pro-rationing became the instrument for controlling production.

Detailed though the report is, there is one aspect of the oil cartel which it scarcely touches. This is the political power acquired by the cartel through its infiltration into national governments. When oil men occupy strategic diplomatic and administrative posts and are members of legislatures and control commissions, it is not surprising that government regulation of the industry proves ineffective. Sometimes, as in Britain, the cartel even enters into partnership with government, an arrangement which may be preferable since it is visible and above-board.

But the report does make clear the manner in which seven companies—five American, two foreign—acquired virtually exclusive rights to the major oil fields of the world outside of the United States, Russia, and Mexico. It traces the interlocking directorships and/or joint ownerships through which the cartel controls exploration, producing, transport, and marketing organizations in many parts of the world. It quotes certain basic agreements, obtained for the most part by the commission through subpoena, which show the world-enveloping pattern of the cartel and its guiding principles. The companies concerned say that all international agreements to control markets and production ended with the outbreak of World War II, but the report offers evidence to show that, whether or not the agreements were legally binding after the war began, the signatories continued to abide by them.

The seven companies named as dominating the world oil combine are Standard Oil of New Jersey, Standard Oil of California, Socony-Vacuum, Gulf Oil, and the Texas Company, all American; the Royal Dutch Shell group, controlled by British and Dutch interests; and Anglo-Iranian Oil, owned 55 per cent by the British government.

Suppressed for a year, the report was finally made public by the Senate Select Committee on Small Business. . . . Its findings have precipitated action against the major oil companies on several fronts. Hearings were scheduled . . . before a federal grand jury in Washington on government charges that twenty-one oil companies and six individuals have been in criminal conspiracy to control prices and production of crude oil and petroleum and to allocate markets throughout the world except in the U. S. S. R., its satellite countries, and Mexico. The Department of Justice, at the request of the Mutual Security Administration, has filed three civil suits in Federal District Court in New York to recover more than $67,000,000 from four American oil companies and six subsidiaries in alleged overcharges to the M. S. A. and its predecessor, the Economic Cooperation Administration, for oil delivered to Western European countries between May, 1949, and June, 1952. . . .

Spokesmen for the oil companies reacted to the court actions by charging that they were politically inspired. George V. Holton, chairman of the board of Socony-Vacuum, told the press that the M. S. A. suit "seems to be part of a deliberate program to make this and other oil companies engaged in international trade whipping boys during an election campaign. . . ." When the report was completed a year ago, the Petroleum Administration, which is dominated by the large oil companies, warned of dire consequences should it be released. This position was supported by some members of the State Department. The document was finally referred to Central Intelligence, which obligingly stamped it "secret." In succeeding months Clark Clifford and former Secretary of the Navy John L. Sullivan, acting in behalf of American oil interests, advised the President against releasing the report.

Meanwhile forces were gathering on the other side. Howard A. Cowden, president of the Consumers' Cooperative Association of Kansas City, Missouri, one of the largest farmer oil cooperatives in the country, was eager to get the report before the public—the cooperatives have always maintained that the oil cartel operates against the public interest as well as their own. The Missouri Farmers' Association, also in the oil business, was similarly interested. Cowden, representing the International Cooperative Petroleum Association, saw Prime Minister Mossadegh of Iran when he visited the United States early this year and discussed the possibility of having the Abadan refineries operated by cooperative groups from a dozen countries, including Britain and the United States. Mossadegh's initial response was favorable, but the State Department turned thumbs down on the idea. . . .

It is interesting that just as the American cooperative movement helped to bring about the present showdown with the oil cartel, so the Swedish cooperatives were largely responsible for an earlier inquiry. In 1945 the Swedish cooperatives, irked by the restrictive influence of the cartel, brought about the appointment of a parliamentary commission which announced its findings two years later. Many of these findings are incorporated in the F. T. C. report.

The Swedes established that as early as 1928 representatives of Standard Oil, Anglo-Iranian Oil, and Royal Dutch Shell signed a cartel agreement which was to serve as the basis for all succeeding compacts. Known variously as the "as is" or Achnacarry agreement, it provided for all the essential elements of monopoly—production and marketing quotas, prices, export quotas, and so on. Its terms were kept strictly secret by the oil companies. The "as is" document was supplemented by other agreements in 1930 and 1932. In 1934 a "Draft Memorandum of Principles" was drawn up which, though never formally signed, appears to have had the force of an international agreement. . . .

The Swedish inquiry brought some alleviation of the domestic oil situation; the international problem remained. In 1947 Thorsten Odhe, director of the International Cooperative Alliance, placed before the U. N. Economic and Social Council a series of proposals for international control of the oil industry—to implement Article VII of the Atlantic Charter and "to assure that all nations, large and small, can buy oil on an equal footing." Mr. Odhe declared:

> The salvation of the United Nations and the peace of the world can come only if the organization is able to face and handle the great economic empires, the real super-states of the modern world. No government has been able to control the oil combine in the general interest. We hope the United Nations can do so.

But the U. N. agency decided to postpone discussion of Mr. Odhe's proposals until 1949. In that year and in 1950 discussion was again postponed. In 1951 the item was deleted without the pretense of postponement. Each time the chief objectors to its consideration were the Americans and British, who between them control about 90 per cent of the world's oil resources outside the U. S. S. R.

THE "NATIONAL SECURITY" CARTEL (1974)

Stephen Nordlinger

As THE SHAH OF IRAN, nattily dressed in a brown plaid suit and camel's hair coat, flew off in early 1971 for his annual vacation at St. Moritz, he spoke triumphantly at the airport of new opportunities being opened by the power of the Arab nations to extract huge concessions from the international oil companies. By threats and an ample amount of wheeling and dealing, he had managed to best the wily old oil negotiators of the West in what now appears to have been a major step toward the first energy crisis in the peacetime history of the United States.

The shortages and the accompanying soaring prices for fuel that plague the American motorist and home owner can be traced in large part to those pivotal negotiations in Teheran more than three years ago. The Arab nations won an additional $10 billion for their oil, but much more important than that, they flexed their muscles and effectively cowed the companies.

Once the Arabs had proved their skill and strength at the bargaining table, they went on to achieve further concessions, most notably a share in the equity ownership of the companies. Then, after less than three years, the Arabs this past winter breached a five-year agreement made at Teheran by unilaterally quadrupling prices.

For this debacle, the oil companies must bear a large measure of responsibility. They had failed, in the face of mushrooming world demand, to build a production capacity sufficient to relieve the pressure on them at the negotiations. The defeat must also be attributed to the often ruthless behavior of the companies toward the Arab nations in years past. The Arabs, for the first time really sensing the full value of oil and the power of united action, were prepared to strike back.

But the heaviest blame for what transpired at Teheran must fall on the U.S. Government, which for more than twenty years had encouraged the companies to enter the waiting trap and then out of ignorance and fear undermined their bargaining position at the fateful negotiations. Teheran was the climax of a strategy in which the cause of national security, as defined by the State Department, dictated what masqueraded as a national energy policy.

In the name of national security, the government had espoused a policy that completely coincided with the short-term interests of the oil companies, but cost the American public multibillions in lost tax revenues and higher prices. The government fostered the growth of an international oil cartel that set prices and production levels and apportioned markets. Consequently, the oil companies were ill-prepared when the government failed to support them at the moment when they sought to present a united front to the Arabs— the decision again being made in the cause of national security, rather than according to a serious national energy policy, which in any case did not exist.

The maneuverings of the government and the industry have now been brought to light in days of testimony before the Senate Foreign Relations Subcommittee on Multinational Corporations, headed by Sen. Frank Church. . . .

The international oil crisis did not develop suddenly from the imposition of the oil embargo; it stems from actions by the oil companies that were subsequently condoned and even abetted by the government. These companies became a virtual supranational government and exercised powerful control, insofar as oil was concerned, over the foreign and domestic policies of the United States and the world. A close relationship developed between government officials, many enlisted straight from the oil business, and the industry itself.

A red boundary line, drawn with a pencil on July 31, 1928, has come to symbolize the power of the Seven Sisters, the seven international oil companies that over the decades have woven a tight fabric of joint, coordinated ventures. This line, which encircles Iraq as well as Saudi Arabia and other nations of the old Ottoman Empire, demarks the area in which four of these companies held sway by agreeing to curtail world crude output and limit competition in refining, marketing, and the securing of concessions.

In the early 1920s, the State Department proclaimed a so-called "open door policy" for oil exploration in the Middle East, so that American companies could secure equal rights with their British rivals in the mammoth reserves of Iraq. The companies insisted on this policy as an indispensable condition for their participation in the Middle East. However, the companies, sensing the advantages of cartel strength and fearing a possible oil glut, soon lost their enthusiasm for "open door" competition. The State Department, bowing to their new desires, abandoned a policy it had so strenuously pursued, and the Red Line Agreement came into being.

Also, in 1928, representatives of the three oil giants, Standard of New Jersey (now Exxon), Royal Dutch Shell and the Anglo-Iranian Oil Co. (now British Petroleum), gathered at an English castle, ostensibly to shoot grouse. From that meeting came a further agreement to restrict competition in the significant oil markets of the world. This agreement, precipitated by a price war in India, completed the chain of major company control from crude supply source through market distribution outlets for at least a decade and even during the dislocation of World War II. After the war, the seven companies continued their arrangements as rich new crude reserves developed in the Persian Gulf area, especially in Saudi Arabia and Kuwait.

According to testimony by David I. Haberman, an attorney in the Justice Department's antitrust division from 1953 to 1972, the companies expanded the number of interlocking, jointly owned production companies to unify control of concessions and crude output, and established a system of long-term mutual supply contracts that allowed exchanges among themselves without risk of competition from new companies.

The Federal Trade Commission in 1952 filed a 378-page report, "The International Petroleum Cartel," and the Justice Department announced a grand jury investigation that won banner headlines. But then the State Department, muttering "national security," moved in to protect the industry, and in effect took over the nation's antitrust policy. The Justice Department, by contrast, felt strongly that the country would be more secure if the cartel were broken up.

In a June 1952 memorandum . . . H. G. Morison, an Assistant Attorney General, advised Attorney General McGranery that, in the absence of competition, the Navy had bought oil during World War II at prices which bore no "relationship whatever to the low cost of producing oil" in the Middle East. While the United States was being charged $1.05 a barrel, the Arabian-American Oil Co. (Aramco) was making sales in Saudi Arabia to affiliated American companies and the Japanese at 70¢ and 84¢ a barrel. . . .

Despite manifold evidence of a cartel, President Truman was persuaded to pull the teeth of the Justice Department's case by reducing it from a criminal to a time-consuming civil action. The suit against Gulf, Exxon and Texaco was settled years later by consent decree; the cases against Mobil and Standard of California were dropped. According to a now declassified message sent by Dean Acheson to Morison at the Justice Department, the State Department feared that the criminal action would arouse a movement in the Middle East to nationalize the companies accused of conspiring, lead to a "decrease of political stability in the region," and discourage American companies from investing there.

Leonard J. Emmerglick, who left the Justice Department in 1954, apparently discouraged after working closely on the oil cartel case, testified that the decision to reduce the case to a civil action was taken by the National Security Council one Friday in the closing days of the Truman administration. That Sunday evening President Truman summoned Mr. Emmerglick to the living quarters of the White House and told him he had taken the potentially momentous action not on the advice of the Cabinet officers who attended the Security Council meeting but solely on the assurance of Gen. Omar Bradley that the national security called for the decision. However, documents now issued by the subcommittee indicate that the State Department determined the action. The consent decrees reached years later apparently had little effect on the activities of the companies.

Soon after scuttling the cartel case, the State Department, under John Foster Dulles, moved quickly to assure the domination by the major companies over the potentially lucrative Iranian crude supply by keeping the competition of independents out of the area. Again national security was cited, this time the threat of Soviet expansion. It was believed that the most reliable way to restore Iranian oil production after the collapse of the Anglo-Iranian Oil Co. following nationalization by Dr. Mohammed Mossadegh was to move in the major foreign and American companies.

A now declassified memorandum by Adrian S. Fisher, then legal adviser at State, said these companies lack "any particular desire" to produce this oil because of adequate supplies elsewhere, but the government's persuasion prevailed. The Justice Department finally went along with the Iranian decision, though its antitrust division strongly maintained that the agreement was totally inconsistent with the civil cartel case it was still pursuing in court. In the end, the State Department's decision killed any chance of making the cartel case stick, according to Senator Church. His subcommittee is seeking further documents which, investigators said, would link the entrance of the major companies into Iran to the termination of the criminal action. It is worth noting that, according to an internal Justice Department memorandum, the independent oil companies had wanted a 36 per cent share of the consortium, but the share was reduced to 5 per cent by the State Department. Despite the majors' professed reluctance to enter Iran, it turned out to be a "good investment," a former top official, Howard W. Page, testified.

There was some significant disagreement within the State Department itself over the handling of these crucial matters. The subcommittee has made public a memorandum written at the time by a key oil adviser, Richard Funkhouser, now serving with the Agency for International Development, which stated "that the ability to accommodate to changing situations in the Middle East is best developed under an environment of free competition rather than from efforts to 'hold the line,' which seldom succeed." Every encouragement, he said, should be given to independents to move Iranian oil.

Funkhouser quoted some oil executives and economists as believing that the Anglo-Iranian Oil Co. might never have been nationalized if there had been competitors in Iran. "There is a certain safety in numbers," he wrote, adding that a monopoly is "ideally easy to nationalize." Despite this advice, the government avoided any actions that would cause giant consortiums like Aramco or the one in Iran to relinquish parts of their concessions to competitors, and thus minimize the growing possibility of substantial takeovers by the Arab nations.

Out of this period that brought the collapse of the criminal action against the cartel and the granting of a concession in Iran to the major companies came the secret decision in 1950 to treat the royalties of the Arab nations as taxes, to be credited dollar for dollar against what the companies owed the U.S. Treasury. Once more, the justification was national security.

The corrupt regime of the late King Ibn Saud of Saudi Arabia, into whose purse went an enormous share of the oil revenues from Aramco, began demanding much more money in 1949 and 1950. Sharp increases in royalties, if treated merely as business expenses, would have been a severe blow to Aramco's profits. On the advice of the company and with the approval of Dean Acheson, the Saudis in 1950 changed the royalties to a so-called "income tax." The amount paid could then be deducted from U.S. taxes.

As a result of this Treasury Department tax ruling, the four companies that control Aramco—Exxon, Texaco, Standard of California and Mobil—which had paid $50 million in U.S. taxes in 1950, paid $6 million in 1951; and Saudi Arabia, which had received $66 million as royalties in 1950, got $110 million as taxes in 1951. Aramco lost nothing by this even swap and the Treasury Department lost a good deal. From then on, the American Government began losing close to $200 million a year in tax revenues from oil companies operating in the Middle East.

Testifying before the Church subcommittee, George C. McGee, a multi-millionaire oilman and at the time of the tax-credit decision the top man on Middle East affairs at the State Department, justified this new policy by what he described as the critical contest in the Middle East "between ourselves and the Soviets." The very corruption and ineptitude of such regimes as that of Ibn Saud made them especially vulnerable to a nationalization movement that would upset the stability of the area, the McGee argument went, and could be prevented only by a constant transfusion of American money.

The National Security Council made the decision in secret; there was no consultation with Congress. On this decision as well, McGee's adviser on petroleum matters, Funkhouser, said in a memorandum that the preferable route to political stability in the Middle East was not through tax favors but by reducing the size of the concessions held by individual companies, a move that would also promote competition. "Since many new American companies are interested in the area and financially strong enough to enter the field, continuation of oil properties in U.S. hands would be almost assured," Funkhouser said. "Middle East states prefer American companies to those of other nationalities."

In recalling the simultaneous decision by the company and the State Department to adopt the principle of the tax credit, McGee said that the solution was reached separately, although "our reasoning based on political grounds coincided with theirs." At that time Aramco was selling its entire production to Europe, but McGee said it was vital to the United States to have Saudi Arabian reserves owned by American companies "for a time of crisis."

The final chapter in the story of the symbiotic relationship of the major oil companies and the American Government began in the late 1950s and early 1960s. An excess production capacity prompted the companies unilaterally to cut the posted price of crude in the Middle East by 20¢ a barrel. This action precipitated the formation of the Arab cartel, the Organization of Petroleum Exporting Countries.

Alarmed by this development, John J. McCloy, former High Commissioner for Germany and then employed by the major oil companies, has disclosed to the Church subcommittee that he met secretly with President Kennedy to alert him to the danger posed by the Arab cartel. Subsequently he spoke to each and every Attorney General to apprise them, he said, of the unfolding situation. The companies sought nothing at the time from the government, because the ample spare production capacity available and the requests of the Arab nations for ever greater production put them in a strong position.

By the 1970s, however, the rapid rise in world demand for energy made the companies vulnerable. George T. Piercy, senior vice president of Exxon, admitted to the subcommittee that the industry had failed to anticipate this surge in demand, thus exposing it to pressure from the Arabs. In Libya, the new revolutionary regime of Col. Muammar el-Qaddafi won major concessions in 1970 from Occidental Petroleum, an independent that relied on Libyan crude.

The potential showdown feared by McCloy ten years earlier became a reality for the major companies as they approached the negotiations in Teheran in early 1971. McCloy stepped up his calls and visits to Washington. John N. Mitchell, the former Attorney General, said in a deposition for the subcommittee that McCloy, then representing twenty-three oil companies, met or talked to him four times in January 1971, as special agreements were prepared by the government and industry before the Teheran bargaining began.

At that time, two key State and Justice Department officials, James Akins and Dudley Chapman, went to New York and waited outside the door of McCloy's law office while the agreements were drawn up, thus indicating the continuing intimacy between government and the industry. According to testimony, the Justice Department secretly consented to the industry-sponsored agreements: one was to allow the major and independent companies to join in a united front to bargain with the Arabs for a new global contract without fear of antitrust prosecution; the other would permit a sharing of oil in the event any company was shut down by Libya.

Although the Justice Department granted the companies the right to bargain as a bloc, the State Department withdrew its support from the companies' desire to bargain with all the oil-producing countries at one time, including those in the Persian Gulf and Libya, so that there would be no leap-frogging price effect, with companies being picked off one by one.

At the request of the companies, John N. Irwin II, then Under Secretary of State, was sent on one day's notice to the Middle East to speak to some of the conservative nations. He had no time to prepare and, as he conceded to the subcommittee, he totally lacked any "real background" in the oil business. Quickly he submitted to the threats and astute maneuvering of the Shah of Iran and Arab leaders who convinced Irwin . . . that the negotiations with the Persian Gulf states and Libya must be separate. Without consulting the industry negotiators in Teheran, Irwin cabled back, according to his testimony, that the separate bargaining was necessary. His recommendation was routinely accepted by the State Department, and the industry, its position undercut, agreed to separate sessions in Teheran and later in Tripoli.

Justifying his recommendation, Irwin, true to the government's explanation for its past oil policy, told the subcommittee that his mission to the Middle East was to protect the national security, in this case against a threatened halt of production. There was no point, he suggested, in antagonizing the Arab nations. The message he brought to the Middle East—that the United States hoped that oil supplies would not be disrupted, that the companies must be cooperative and that the U.S. Government definitely would not become involved in the negotiations—strengthened the hand of the Arab negotiators. The entire Irwin mission, in fact, puzzled the Arabs, who probably expected the United States to take a tough stand. "I don't know what Mr. Irwin's visit was for," said Jamshid Amuzegar, the Iranian Foreign Minister, in an interview during the preliminary negotiations.

With the demand for oil exceeding production capacity, the Arabs were in a strong position at Teheran, yet the companies still held some cards. The Arabs needed oil revenues, on which they depended for 50 to 95 per cent of their incomes, and they relied heavily on the technical skills and other resources of the international companies. But in the wake of the Irwin mission, the companies struck the best deal they could get; it was supposed to last for five years. The agreement was hailed by the State Department as bringing "stability" to the Middle East, but within less than three years, it was torn up by the Arabs. Representatives of the industry, which had played its last trump, were summoned to "negotiation" in Vienna and the emboldened Arab nations unilaterally imposed new demands that sent the posted price of crude oil from $3.01 a barrel last October 1 to $11.65 in January, the present level. . . .

THE OIL WENT THATAWAY (1974)

Donald L. Barlett and James B. Steele

AFTER MONTHS OF escalating oil prices and sporadic product shortages, the Senate Permanent Subcommittee on Investigations in the week of January 21 finally assembled in a national forum to question the oil industry on the causes of the oil crisis. Fresh from holiday encounters with angry consumers back home, the Senators were quick to vent their constituents' frustration on the assembled oilmen. They grilled the executives on corporate profits, their companies' expansion abroad, their firms' relations with Arab rulers and other phases of their global operations. There were dramatic, news-making scenes, as when Sen. Henry Jackson placed a hurried telephone call to a Washington stockbroker to find out Exxon's 1973 dividend figures that a company executive could not provide. There were repeated photographs or television films of the executives seated uncomfortably under bright lights and submitting to a barrage of questions.

Since all of this made good theatre, the fact that the subcommittee was questioning the wrong corporate executives went unnoticed. The executives whose faces were flashed around the country that week were mostly officials of U.S. subsidiaries of the multinational oil companies. As such, they have played only a limited role in the corporate decisions that have led the nation into the present crisis. The men who should have been questioned by the Senators are the chief operating officers of Exxon Corporation or Gulf Oil Corporation, not officials of Exxon U.S.A. or Gulf U.S.A., as was the case with those two companies and the other majors summoned to the hearing.

The inability of the Senate subcommittee to make this distinction is not surprising. Most lawmakers, as well as most Americans, equate the names Exxon, Texaco, Mobil, Gulf and Standard Oil of California with the United States. All of those corporations were founded in the United States; their first operations were here; their international headquarters are here. Most of their stockholders are U.S. citizens. But in the last two decades in particular, these five multinational oil companies, which along with British Petroleum and Royal Dutch Shell comprise the so-called "Seven Sisters" of international oil, have undergone a fundamental change. And it is this change—more than the Arab oil embargo or the energy consuming habits of Americans—that is at the heart of the nation's current oil crisis.

For in this period, the United States became merely another customer of the American multinational oil companies which supply most of the free world's oil. The companies' annual reports to their stockholders and to the Securities and Exchange Commission display the pattern:

In the last ten years, the five largest multinational oil companies have sharply expanded their production, refining and marketing systems throughout Europe and Asia, and at the same time failed to build refineries and drill for oil at home.

¶Ten years ago, the petroleum sales of the five companies were about evenly divided between the United States and the rest of the world. By the end of 1972, these same five companies were selling nearly two barrels of oil in other countries for every barrel sold here.

¶The product sales of the five companies in the decade increased 119 per cent in the Eastern Hemisphere, where Western Europe and Japan are the leading markets, but only 46 per cent in the Western Hemisphere where the United States is the leading market.

¶The number of barrels of crude oil refined by the companies rose 32 per cent in the Western Hemisphere, compared to a 137 per cent jump in the Eastern Hemisphere.

The statistics on refining alone help explain why the United States today has a serious lack of oil. With demand running at upward of 18 million barrels daily, the nation has the capacity to refine only about 13 million. The shortage is made up by imports of refined products. Accordingly, in these months when most American refineries are straining to meet demand here, refineries across Europe are operating at a comfortable 80 to 85 per cent of capacity. Most European nations have a surplus refining capacity, and can accommodate unexpected spurts in demand because the American multinational oil companies have built many new refineries on the Continent in recent years.

All of this expansion in the Eastern Hemisphere was designed to take advantage of emerging new petroleum markets in Western Europe and Japan. For all the talk about the American greed for oil, the fact is that consumption has been rising much faster in Europe and Japan than in the United States. In the last twenty years, demand for crude oil has increased 110 per cent in the United States, 2,567 per cent in Japan and 1,597 per cent in West Germany. The latter increase is typical of the explosive growth in oil consumption across Europe.

Even the major oil companies now acknowledge that it has been more profitable for them to expand overseas rather than at home. When releasing their sharply higher earnings for 1973, several of the majors went out of their way to point out that most of their 1973 profits were earned in the Eastern Hemisphere. They made no mention, however, that those Eastern Hemisphere profits were made possible, at least in part, through an assortment of special tax allowances and benefits granted to no other business, and through a series of bookkeeping devices which enable multinational corporations to transfer income from one country to another, from one subsidiary to another.

This shift in their refining and marketing operations abroad helps explain why the companies have exaggerated the effect of the Arab oil embargo on the United States. The companies are far more dependent on Arab oil to supply their markets in Europe and Asia than in the United States. Of the 20 million barrels of oil produced daily by Arab nations before the embargo, roughly a million barrels were coming into the United States. The rest went to other nations in the free world—but carried by the ships of the multinational oil companies to be refined in their refineries and sold in their stations.

Gulf Oil Corp., for example, has 79 per cent of its worldwide reserves of crude oil in Kuwait alone. Texaco has 80 per cent of its worldwide reserves in Arab nations. Exxon has invested $4.8 billion in the Eastern Hemisphere, mostly in Arab states or in nations dependent on Arab oil.

The disparity between the interests of American consumers and American oil companies was aptly pointed out by the Washington correspondent of the London *Economist* on January 19:

> The public is having to learn quickly what the oil industry and the government have known for a long time but never talked much about. Not only is the United States not self-sufficient in oil, but the great oil companies, with their mostly American names, have interests and responsibilities that are not coterminous with American national or consumer interests.

There is nothing wrong about going abroad to make a profit. What has gone wrong is that public policy has encouraged the multinational companies to explore and refine oil abroad at the expense of exploring and building refineries at home. And now, when their failure to expand at home has caught up with them, the companies choose to blame the American consumer for the crisis.

The single most favorable program that has encouraged the multinational oil companies to drill for oil abroad rather than at home has been the system of foreign tax credits. In 1951, the oil companies managed to convince the Internal Revenue Service that royalties paid to Arab rulers for oil produced in their nations were really income taxes. Therefore, instead of being entered in their ledgers as cost items, the royalties were defined as taxes deductible dollar for dollar from the companies' U.S. taxes. Since the oil produced by the major companies in the Arab states has supplied markets in Western Europe and Asia, the American taxpayer in effect has helped subsidize the sale by the American oil industry of petroleum products around the globe.

Not only has the IRS ruling deprived the U.S. treasury of billions of dollars, it has also relieved the American multinational oil companies of a major expense of operating abroad. In 1971, the last year for which the IRS has statistics, the oil companies deducted a total of $1.5 billion in foreign taxes from their U.S. tax bill—much of it in payments to Middle Eastern rulers. It is a measure of how primitive our understanding is of this industry that Senator Jackson, at his January hearings, had to ask officials of the major oil companies to provide Congress with specific information on the amount of foreign taxes each has deducted from its U.S. income taxes in recent years.

But the fact that the Senate's so-called leading energy expert was forced to ask the oil companies for information he should have had at his fingertips is not unusual. There is no independent government agency to collect data on the oil industry or other suppliers of energy. There is not even a federal agency to verify the statistics the industry hands out. This places federal officials at the mercy of the oil industry for guidance in planning public programs or making decisions that affect virtually everyone.

Over the years, the oil industry has consistently been wrong or off target in many major predictions about its future. Nevertheless, those predictions formed the basis of public policy. The oil import program is a good example. Oilmen argued in the late 1950s that unless mandatory quotas were enacted to restrict the amount of low-cost foreign oil coming into the nation, the domestic producing industry would be destroyed, exploration would decline, and the nation would become more dependent on foreign oil. President Eisenhower imposed the controls in 1959. By last year, when President Nixon abolished the program, the domestic oil industry was in sharp decline, exploration for new wells had fallen off, and the nation was rapidly becoming more dependent on imported oil. Everything the industry warned would happen without the quota program happened with it.

In the last year, the industry has eagerly fed fears that the nation was running out of crude oil. Major oil companies ran color advertisements showing bulging reserves in the Middle East and dwindling reserves in the United States, thus creating the false impression that almost all of the world's major oil deposits are in Arab hands. In fact, a substantial amount of oil lies untapped in many parts of the world, including the United States. Middle East oil is so attractive to the companies because it can be produced there far cheaper than anywhere else. The oil rushes to the surface with incredible force, thus minimizing costs.

The industry itself once looked pessimistically on the Arabian peninsula because geologic reports indicated that there was little hope of finding oil there. It was not until petroleum was found on nearby Bahrain in 1930 that the oilmen seriously began exploring in Saudi Arabia. Today, the American people are told by the industry and the government that Saudi Arabia represents virtually the only hope of meeting this nation's long-range future oil needs.

There is no more conclusive argument for a major independent government capability to monitor the oil industry than the way the government has tried to manage the crisis since the start of the Arab embargo. Beginning in October, when a high official confidently predicted that there would be "homes without heat" this winter, the Administration has consistently overdramatized the extent of the shortage and helped create much of the panic seen today at the gas pump.

Before the embargo, the United States received less than 10 per cent of its oil from Arab states, but estimates repeatedly issued last fall by Administration aides predicted an oil shortage this winter ranging from 12 to 17 per cent. President Nixon himself contended that the Arab embargo had plunged the nation into a major energy crisis.

The danger of having no oil-planning policy has also been apparent in the bungling attempts of the Federal Energy Office (FEO) under William Simon to distribute the gasoline that is available. Stock levels show that, with demand down, there should be about enough gasoline available to meet demands this winter. But the FEO's faulty allocation formulas have given some states more gas than they need and short-changed others, mainly in the East.

During the winter, the Administration has continued to blame the Arab oil embargo for the shortage, but now, when it is increasingly obvious that there is no worldwide shortage of crude oil, the accusation is less and less persuasive. Europe, which is totally dependent on imported oil—the bulk of it being produced, transported, refined and marketed by the U.S. multinational firms—is experiencing no serious oil shortages today. Conservation measures such as driverless Sundays have been dropped or eased in almost all European countries. The wholesale price of many fuels has been dropping in recent weeks in European markets. The Kuwait Government recently rejected bids on state-owned oil because it felt the bids were too low. The implication of these developments is that oil is available, if someone will buy it.

For the Netherlands, which received roughly 2 million barrels of Arab oil daily before the embargo—or twice as much as the United States was receiving

—the multinational oil companies have successfully diverted supplies of non-Arab oil. The result is that the Dutch have plenty of oil and the Arab sanction against them has failed. But the multinational oil companies have not done the same thing for the United States, even though the United States received much less Arab oil than the Netherlands. Indeed, there has even been a decline in the amount of non-Arab oil coming into U.S. ports.

Non-Arab oil comes from Venezuela, Nigeria, Iran and Indonesia. Exactly where the decline has occurred is not clear, because the Administration has clamped a secrecy lid on the origins of oil imported into this country. For years, American taxpayers have given tax breaks to their oil companies to explore for foreign oil that might be required one day to meet the needs of the American market. The irony is that now, when such oil is needed, Americans are not getting it.

Speculation has risen that the oil companies are dissatisfied with the federal allocation program, which reportedly does not encourage some companies to import additional foreign oil. Whatever the cause, Congress and the Administration have been slow to grasp the fact that there is no worldwide shortage of oil and have failed to demand that the oil companies explain publicly why only the American consumer is cut short.

But even when such immediate problems as the embargo are resolved, the United States will still experience sporadic shortages of petroleum products in the period ahead. Refinery and storage capacity have not kept pace with a domestic demand that has been growing steadily at 4 to 5 per cent a year, while the major oil companies have expanded abroad to take advantage of emerging new petroleum markets that have been growing at rates up to 10 per cent a year. Some domestic shortages will thus be inevitable as the gap between demand and refining capacity continues to grow.

The oil crisis is a classic demonstration of multinational corporations in action. The major companies, most of them American, operate beyond the supervision or direction of the world's nations. Even the Arabs don't really know what happens to their oil once it leaves their shores. It is left to the companies to decide where to ship and refine it, what it will cost, which nations will get it and which ones won't. Right now, Americans seem to have come out on the short end of those decisions.

OPEC AND BIG OIL (1975)

Louis B. Schwartz

THE FORD ADMINISTRATION has come up with an amazing remedy for the "energy crisis." The cure advocated for the Arab-dictated extortionate price of petroleum is to raise prices still higher! It is proposed to tax imported crude at the rate of $3 per barrel, this to be added to the current international price of $11 with a pass-through of the new tax to the consumer. At the same time, it is proposed to drop price controls on domestic crude oil and gas. These steps, according to the President, will have the gratifying result that people will simply be forced to buy less gasoline and fuel oil. Accordingly, demand will decline, or at least "stabilize," and thus we shall have countered the cartel power of OPEC.

This Alice-in-Wonderland solution of the energy crisis is so divorced from economic reality that it must be regarded as disingenuous. The purpose of the proposal is not to restrict the use of oil, but to provide revenue to balance the politically attractive income tax cuts concurrently proposed. An additional purpose is to gratify all the interests in the United States that have for generations used the government to support artificially high prices for domestic oil, gas and competitive fuels. The recent quadrupling of the price of oil with no substantial "voluntary" curtailment of consumption, sufficiently demonstrates that oil consumption is relatively unresponsive to price change. Accordingly, further increases in price cannot be expected to cut demand significantly. They will, however, significantly contribute to inflation, and will cut the demand for other goods.

A real cut in demand for oil, and a real contribution to conservation, can be achieved only by rationing and, preferably for the long run, by tax or other legislation favoring the manufacture of small cars. A graduated tax based on horsepower would change car-buying habits in a manner that would not interfere seriously with travel, would reduce air pollution (in contrast to President Ford's proposal to relax clean-air standards) and would offset higher gas prices with increased miles per gallon. Along with this conservation effort should go a drive to break the OPEC cartel, thus reducing the price of imported, hence all, petroleum.

Real, as distinguished from phony, solutions of the oil crisis must respond to basic facts and rest on moral and economic principles. The central facts are that OPEC is controlling a price for crude oil that is approximately forty times the cost of production, that the multinational oil companies, which have been our "agents" to procure foreign oil and to negotiate with the sheiks, have failed us and that the U.S. Government's recent policy has been aimed at "collaboration" rather than "confrontation" with OPEC. Collaboration is Kissinger's program to bring the consumer states together with OPEC to "stabilize" the situation at current fantastic, cost-disregarding prices. Confrontation would aim at breaking the cartel, especially by concerting the U.S. buying power to make favorable bilateral deals with those suppliers who would reduce prices.

Prices should, in general, reflect costs. That is a principle of morals and economics. To the extent that prices reflect costs (including fair compensation to labor and a capital return sufficient to attract the necessary investment), a given expenditure of human effort will produce a maximum of human satisfaction. Putting it another way, price-cost parity allocates resources most efficiently. If oil that can be produced at 25¢ a barrel in the Middle East is sold at forty times that price, two misallocations follow: (1) The energy users, forced to divert enormous resources to pay this non-cost-justified price, will have less with which to buy meat, clothing, capital goods and services. The world is thus forced to forgo production for which it is ready to pay cost, in order to pay much more than cost for a monopolized resource; (2) the non-cost-justified rise in oil prices leads to an enormous and wasteful diversion of resources into finding alternatives to the monopolized resource. The difficult, expensive and dangerous development of nuclear energy, of oil production from the sea depths, of new means of extraction and transportation, absorb billions that would otherwise be spent for human needs other than fuel.

An even more dangerous misallocation of resources is occurring. The oil billions are being used to buy arms and the build-up of Arab military power will evoke a countervailing build-up of Israel's military power. Such a perversion of the world's productive resources and weapons of mutual destruction is, at a time when millions of human beings face death by starvation, not only reckless but disgusting. War is being brought closer to the Middle East, not merely war between the Arabs and the Israelis but war between their Big Power sponsors, and even war among the Arab states. In the chaos of expanding armaments each Arab state will see a deterioration of its relative military position vis-à-vis its neighbors, or much to be gained by putting to hideous use the new instruments being provided by the West (including Russia). The immorality of OPEC's extortion of monopoly prices for petroleum inheres therefore both in the excessive returns and in the use to which those returns are put.

This immoral and dangerous redistribution of wealth is the result of an agreement or conspiracy among the OPEC countries to limit production and to exact an arbitrary monopolistic price from the rest of the world. Cartel agreements of this type are illegal and even criminal under the laws of the Western nations when engaged in by private companies, for the reason, among others, that charging a monopoly price is equivalent to levying a tax on consumers. When interests inside or outside our country levy taxes upon us other than through our own political processes, the issue of "taxation without representation" arises. As in the case of the American Revolution, that issue can lead to violence. To say that the oil "belongs to them" is no answer to the charge of immoral and uneconomic exaction. Ownership, when dispersed among numerous proprietors, does not carry with it the power to exact prices above cost: competition among proprietors would usually divert trade to the low-cost producers. The power of OPEC nations to overcharge results from the agreement among them to consolidate their bargaining position, not from their individual "ownership."

OPEC is, of course, not the only cartel in the international oil market. The giant multinational oil firms functioned as a private cartel long before OPEC appeared on the scene. They collectively maintained the price of oil far above the cost of production, thus denying energy to some who could have paid a reasonable competitive price and misallocating resources toward production of more costly fuels. They maintained their united front not by an overt comprehensive cartel agreement, like OPEC, but by a complex network of interrelationships, including partnerships to develop new fields or markets, multiple contracts for exchange of oil and petroleum products among themselves and, above all, unspoken understandings—typical of oligopolies—not to challenge one another commercially but to "follow the leader" in pricing for particular markets. By this means, for example, Middle East oil was for decades sold in the Mediterranean on the basis of Gulf Coast prices, i.e., as if it had been produced at high cost in the United States and transported thousands instead of hundreds of miles. Moreover, there is little reason to doubt complaints of

OPEC members that the private cartel exploited their weak, unorganized suppliers as well as their weak, unorganized customers, exercising monopsony power on one side as well as monopoly power on the other.

There is small comfort for the rest of us in the "countervailing power" seemingly provided by the private oil cartelists confronting OPEC. The great multinational petroleum companies do not represent us. They certainly cannot be identified with any single national interest, e.g., of the United Kingdom, or the United States, or Holland or France. The obvious solution to tensions between superpowers . . . is a treaty of alliance, i.e., power sharing at the expense of the unorganized. It takes little imagination to envision the course of negotiations between OPEC and the cartelists. OPEC wants the highest price extractable from the industrial consumer nations. The oil companies' position is not inherently antagonistic to that desire, since any increase in the total revenues enlarges the companies' potential income (if the sheiks are not too greedy). Also, the value of the companies' reserves in the United States and elsewhere rises by breath-taking billions with each rise in the current price called for by the Saudis.

What will most preoccupy the companies is that the price increases be so handled as to avoid three undesirable responses: (1) A genuine rapid search for alternative energy sources which would reduce the demand for oil; (2) nationalization, excess profit taxation, or other adverse political responses in the "home" country; (3) any undermining of OPEC control, either through covert violation by a member, or by rapid development of non-OPEC oil fields, since an uncontrolled oil source would lead to price cutting and upset the balance of power among the oil companies in favor of whichever one found the new source. Arabia will be most understanding of the companies' apprehensions on each of these scores.

OPEC member countries have begun to buy or confiscate interests in the oil companies' transportation, refining and marketing operations—activities outside the boundaries of the producing country. The private organization is retained on a profitable basis to carry on the activities for the new owner. This progressive integration of the companies into the OPEC cartel tends to consolidate both the governmental and the private cartels. The main sources of supply become permanently tied to the main outlets to the market. The probability that a new refiner or marketer will come on the scene to serve consumers independently is reduced. The chance that a new oil discovery will find its way to consumers by a route other than through the cartelized marketers is slim. There is talk already that the consumer nations need to engage in a little "counternationalization" of Arab interest in non-Arab petroleum operations.

The grim picture is oversimplified—unavoidably so in a brief analysis. Company policies are not perfectly aligned, if for no other reason than that they are differentially dependent on OPEC oil. They are rivals for sources and markets as well as collaborators. Some of them are responsive to public opinion and to political pressures in the home country. But these moderating influences are inadequate to qualify the companies to represent the national interests of consumer countries. The underlying conflict of interests is too plain, and the history of the companies' commercial policies too dubious.

An American reaction to the situation was recently embodied in a bill, tentatively approved by a Subcommittee on Multinational Corporations of the Senate Committee on Foreign Relations. This "Foreign Oil Contracts Act of

1974" purportedly is intended to increase the political accountability of the international oil companies. It would require registration of all contracts for procurement of substantial quantities of crude or refined petroleum; forbid any "United States business entity" to enter into such contract without approval of the Federal Energy Administrator (but a contract is deemed approved if not disapproved within twenty days of registration); authorize the Administrator to inspect records of companies submitting contracts for approval; and make public all registered contracts, except to the extent that publication would "seriously interfere with the national interest in obtaining secure supplies" of petroleum products. In exercising his authority to approve, the Administrator would consider "any threat to the economic well-being of the United States or of other importing nations," the availability of other lower-priced oil, the tendency of the contract to concentrate access to any oil production "in the hands of one or a small number of corporations" and "the degree to which the Administrator was consulted during negotiation of the contract."

The bill is a travesty. It is confined to contracts and ignores structural integration, e.g., mergers and takeovers. It adopts a contract-by-contract approach instead of appraising the entire skein of relationships. It does not apply to contracts made prior to enactment. It does not authorize the Administrator to withdraw approval once given. It does not assure him a continuous flow of information on changing conditions that affect the desirability of the contract. Perhaps the most interesting feature is the hint that the Administrator should involve himself in *negotiating* the contracts. Considering that the Administrator is given only twenty days to pass upon registered contracts, it would be reassuring to believe that his agents would be scurrying about the world to influence contract formation. But that would be an illusion; the manpower would be lacking and the other participants in the negotiations would obstruct intrusions by outsiders. At best, a nominal participation by the Administrator would serve to justify swift formal approval of *faits accomplis*. The most revealing comment on this bill was its characterization by one "insider" as "a more feasible alternative to establishing a direct purchasing agency of the U.S. Government which would deal directly with OPEC nations and then allocate purchased oil among U.S. oil companies." The bill in short is a political gesture masquerading as effective governmental intervention—a triumph for the oil companies, for OPEC and for the highly placed officials in the government of the United States who favor "collaboration, not confrontation" with OPEC.

These forces find a governmental purchasing agency "less feasible" because it would expose and highlight the political confrontation between the importing governments and OPEC. But there is every reason for the industrialized democratic governments to press boldly for solutions grounded on economic justice and morality and to put away pseudo-solutions—including the one so often advanced these days, that we borrow back from the sheiks the billions which they are extorting from us.

The strangest and most frightening element in the whole situation is that the government of the United States seems committed, not merely to pseudo-solutions but actually to maintaining the monopolistic price levels dictated by OPEC. Secretary Kissinger, to the wrath of the French, the Japanese and others, is trying to organize a consumer nation "common front" which will, in negotiations with OPEC, settle for "stability" at or about current high prices. The sop to participating consumer nations would be some kind of insurance against Arab boycotts of individual nations, through an agreed sharing of supplies. The "gain" for the United States would be a putative (and wholly unreliable) enhancement of political influence with the sheiks, plus solidification of the U.S. world financial hegemony through the channeling of Arab billions back into U.S. investments and banks.

Behind these current manifestations of oil's power in Washington is a long, dark history of the betrayal of national interests by successive national governments. The people in government who are providing the current leaden life preserver are the ones who "promoted national security" with a suicidal national oil policy. That policy excluded oil imports in the decades when we could have had all we wanted at minimal cost, while stockpiling our own higher cost reserves for emergencies like the present; maintained a high price for domestic petroleum by encouraging state systems for manipulating production and prices in the interests of the least efficient producers; facilitated oligopolistic pricing in the domestic oil business; subsidized the oil barons through arbitrary tax credits, without requiring the exploration which those subsidies were supposed to finance; perpetuated a giant leak in the natural gas regulating system by allowing huge quantities of gas to escape federal regulation; and drove us into multibillion expenditures for high cost and dangerous alternate sources of energy, e.g., nuclear power. . . .

What, then, is it reasonable to expect of the American Government in the oil crisis? Very little. Its natural and traditional tendency is to make common cause with those who would exact the highest price for oil. But if the question is what should informed citizens demand in the way of a national oil policy, an answer is available.

A genuine attempt should be made to reduce needless petroleum consumption. This implies rationing and a shift to smaller cars.

A National Oil Resources Agency (NORA) should be created, and given exclusive right to import petroleum and to allocate imports among domestic refiners and marketers. The bargaining power of this consolidated buying agency, vis-à-vis OPEC and other suppliers, would be enormous. It might well be able to crack the cartel by playing members against one another.

NORA should be empowered to spend sums equivalent to the subsidies of the nuclear energy program or space exploration program to develop alternate energy supplies, e.g., from shale or geothermal sources. Investments like these would pay off in several ways. The threat would be efficacious in moderating the demands of OPEC and other suppliers. Low-cost additions to the energy supply would be fed into our energy system at cost, displacing higher cost oil. This contrasts with existing arrangements under which the oil companies themselves "diversify" into geothermal energy, for example, and market it at prices tied to the rigged international oil price. High-cost energy coming out of NORA's development program would be fed into our energy system at a calculated normalized price. The taxpayers would absorb the excess cost. That is surely preferable to the staggering increase in *all* petroleum prices which has been allowed to follow from the higher price of OPEC's oil, which is after all only a marginal part of America's total supply.

All oil company "secrets," at least in the international sphere, should by law be made accessible to NORA, which would exercise an inquisitorial power comparable to that of national bank examiners.

The Secretary of State should cease trying to organize a consumer nation cartel to engage in collective bargaining with the producer nation cartel on a basis that legitimates cartelization on both sides and freezes into the international trade system the current fantastic, cost-disregarding prices. A firm entente among the consumer nations is so unlikely, given their different situations and interests (political as well as economic), as to make doubtful the good faith of the attempt, which so far has served only to sidetrack a real solution. That solution lies, rather, in bilateral arrangements between particular suppliers and their customers. Iran or Venezuela may be willing to make concessions to country X that Libya would not consider. In this way, the solidarity of the cartel might begin to be undermined.

The OPEC nations are entitled to fair returns through conventional taxation and to royalties to the extent that each has legitimate property interests in the land. Some of them have, as underdeveloped states, moral claims upon us for constructive aid. They do not, any more than does the private cartel, have a right to dictate prices unrelated to costs, to bully us into supplying arms with which to threaten the peace of the world, to create a new crop of unearning billionaires, or to disrupt our fiscal and industrial order. A failure of nerve on the part of the Western democracies, an evasion of the challenge, can have only catastrophic consequences.

OPEC AT TWENTY (1980)

Joe Stork

OVER THE COURSE of two decades OPEC has developed from a gathering of frustrated oil officials, little known outside the industry and ignored within it, to what the Western media have consecrated as an assemblage with power rivaling that of the heads of the major industrial countries. Acclaimed by its friends as the champion of third world economic nationalism and reviled by the industrial consumers as the official scapegoat for the most serious economic crisis since the Great Depression, OPEC has become the most notorious acronym in the world, with the possible exception of CIA.

Both friend and foe, and to no little extent OPEC itself, have found it convenient to inflate OPEC's responsibility for the perceived shifts of power in the global struggle over the world's resources and product in this period. This twentieth anniversary calls for a more careful scrutiny of OPEC's accomplishments, to situate them within the movement of broader structural forces in the world economy, and to examine the explosive conjuncture of national struggles and economic demands of the formerly colonized world generally and the

Middle East in particular. The question is this: to what extent is OPEC, as an organization or as a constellation of its constituent regimes, responsible for the structural upheaval in the world economy? Alternatively, is it more a composite expression of broader forces, itself a constraining, modulating element, revising the agenda of the militant economic nationalists in search of a stable partnership, a global "social contract," with international capital?

This brief interpretation sees the emergence of OPEC and the various transformations wrought in its name as the consequence of contradictions inherent in the imperfect horizontal and vertical integration of the large oil firms, and in the colonial and neocolonial base of their control of low-cost crude in the Middle East. There are clearly demarcated years of transition in the evolution of the industry and the oil-producing regimes. The first we need to consider is the 1948–53 period, with the emergence of the Persian Gulf region as a major factor in world production and the consolidation of preeminent position by the American majors. The second period of transition is 1959–61, when the majors' pricing practices goaded the regimes to come together to form OPEC. The third transition was the 1969–71 period, when Libya's shift to the radical camp in OPEC set in motion a new, upward trend in crude oil prices. We are now living through a fourth transition period, resulting from the popular revolution in Iran and heading in still-uncharted directions.

Every phase in the development of the oil industry in the Middle East had its attendant challenge from the peoples of the region. In the post-World War II period this came preeminently from Iran under the leadership of Mohammed Mossadeq. The American firms, engaged in a subliminal struggle with their British counterparts for paramount control of the region's resources, took the important pre-emptive step to head off similar challenges among the Arab producers by instituting the so-called "profit-sharing" provision whereby the regimes would receive not a mere royalty per barrel exported but a nominal half-share of the companies' bonanza profits. Large amounts of cash for the conservative monarchs and sheiks whose continued rule was essential to the industry, together with the defeat of the Iranian challenge by 1953, brought a decade of unparalleled profitability for the companies and successfully insulated the oil regimes from nationalist currents.

The profit-sharing scheme also gave the producing regimes a stake in the official selling price on which their share was calculated. Oil revenues were meeting an increasingly larger share of total government revenues and national income. Development plans, military and civil service payrolls, and royal household budgets alike were threatened when the companies, without consultation or prior notification, unilaterally cut prices in February 1959 and again in August 1960. An advisor to the Saudi regime estimated that losses to the producers in those two years would total some $300 million.

These price cuts were the proximate cause for the formation of OPEC. A moving force was the then-Director General of Petroleum Affairs in the Saudi Ministry of Finance, Abdallah Tariki. Tariki, a commoner trained at the University of Texas, personified the intersection of nationalist politics and technocratic expertise that gave rise to the "oil consciousness" underlying OPEC's emergence. His dedication to educating the Saudi and Arab public in oil matters, to improving the terms of the concessions, and to achieving national control of resources set him apart from the venality and corruption that marked the Saudi regime as well as most of its neighbors. Following a visit to Baghdad by Tariki in August 1960, Iraq invited the oil officials of Kuwait, Iran, Venezuela and Saudi Arabia to meet in Baghdad from September 10–14.

Tariki's main support among the oil producers came from Perez Alfonzo of Venezuela. Venezuela's higher-cost crude was most threatened in the long term by the price-cutting trend. Tariki and Alfonzo had drafted before the meeting an "international oil compact," a schedule for production pro-rationing among the producing countries, as an essential ingredient in coping with the surplus production that was weakening the price structure. The first meeting established a framework for a permanent organization, declared a collective unwillingness to "remain indifferent with regard to the companies' attitude on prices," and expressed determination to stabilize prices "by other means," i.e., regulation of production.

The creation of OPEC, however significant it appears in retrospect, was incidental to the main forces at work in this transition period. The continuing trend toward greater production weakened prices where the market was competitive (chiefly Europe), resulting in a fall in the price per barrel of crude from around $1.85 in early 1960 to as low as $1.20 in 1969. The collision of this tendency, rooted in the specifics of the industry, with the economic nationalism of the producing states, led to OPEC, and was resolved in a way that exacerbated the problem. The demands of the producers for higher revenues could not be met by higher prices in this circumstance, but only by still higher rates of production, especially for the compliant regimes of Iran and Saudi Arabia.

OPEC's main achievement in this first decade of falling prices was to bar further reductions in their own revenue per barrel, and to reduce the inventive discounts and accounting rubrics used by the companies to secure profits by calling them something else. In 1963 the regimes received an average of 67 cents per barrel, compared with the companies' 82 cents; by 1969 this had shifted in favor of the regimes, 85 cents to 40 cents. The countries did pay a significant price for this financial accomplishment, though. First, they never secured the companies' recognition of OPEC as a collective bargaining agent, and acceded to company insistence on bilateral country-company negotiations. Second, the oil producers allowed the companies to determine the pace of negotiations, focusing interminable discussion on minor issues and ignoring larger ones altogether. Production scheduling was sabotaged within OPEC itself. Demands like participation in company management were not seriously pursued. And the major purpose of OPEC, to restore crude prices to the level of early 1959, was not accomplished at all in this decade.

One immediate reason for this rather lackluster performance in OPEC's first decade was the elimination of Tariki following the U.S.-supported palace coup in Saudi Arabia in October 1962 that brought Crown Prince Faisal to power. Tariki was removed from his influential position and permanently banished from the country. His replacement, Ahmad Zaki Yamani, came to play as important a role in OPEC as Tariki, but inflected it in a much different direction.

Yamani is far more typical than Tariki had been of the technocrats representing their respective countries in OPEC. Tariki was an articulate exponent of the economic nationalism then surging in the area. Yamani and his fellows saw their mission in terms of insulating oil matters from "the realm of ordinary politics." This approach was inculcated in the Western training the technocrats typically received. True, these technocrats had a much higher level of understanding of the industry they were dealing with than did the princes and courtiers who had "negotiated" the original concessions, and were thus able to strike more beneficial arrangements for the regimes in the financial domain. In the final analysis, though, they represented a modification in the evolution of the prevailing pattern, and not a radical challenge to it.

The class predilections of the technocrats who staff OPEC are subsidiary to the fact that OPEC is, after all, an association of regimes of varied political hues, and can be no more radical than the common political denomination of its components. The dominant states, Saudi Arabia and Iran, were both closely tied to the capitalist consuming countries and the oil companies, and to the United States in particular. Iraq was under severe pressure from the companies in the struggle over the nationalization of Iraqi reserves after 1960; the Shah and the Saudis were only too happy to expand their own production at Iraqi expense. Algeria's significance was limited due to its low production capacity and its exclusive ties to the French market.

The character of OPEC was thus effectively determined by those regimes that most owed their place to the companies and Western governments. Any threat to the companies was seen as a threat to themselves. Their strategic aim was to modulate the popular nationalist pressures underlying OPEC in order to establish a more equal "partnership" with the companies and make themselves more indispensable to the continued functioning of the system. For the dominant regimes, one important OPEC task was to pre-empt more radical associations. In the words of one source close to both the companies and the Saudi regime, "Oil has aroused certain emotions in the Middle East which must be satisfied, and this is OPEC's task."

The June War of 1967 marked a watershed in the intersection of the politics of oil and Palestine, a combination that grew more potent by the time of the next war in 1973. The decisive defeat in 1967 of the radical nationalist regimes in Egypt and Syria initiated a period of political ascendancy for Saudi Arabia and the oil-producing sheikdoms of the Gulf, enhancing the efficacy of the "protection money" with which they bankrolled the front-line states but entangling them in the conflicts and pressures surrounding the Arab nationalist struggles. At the same time a new polarization developed with the rise of the Palestinian resistance and revolutionary movements in Yemen and Oman. Most importantly, through its impact on Libya as a major oil producer, the 1967 war laid the groundwork for OPEC's transition in 1969–71.

Libya, an Italian colony through World War II, was then ruled by a weak monarch, Idris, beholden to Britain and the United States. It was, in the words of one high State Department official, "one of the most corrupt regimes in the world." Libya was to play the same kind of catalyzing role in the evolution of OPEC and the oil industry as Iran would play a decade later. Both Libya in 1969 and Iran in 1979 illustrate several features central to an analysis of OPEC. First, the achievements of OPEC as a group in both periods were precipitated by the respective political upheavals in Libya and Iran rather than through any concerted determination of OPEC. Second, these upheavals were closely related to the social and political impact of the oil industry in these two countries, and in particular to the avaricious character of the companies involved and the local ruling classes. Third, in each case the expansion of the oil industry and the growth of oil revenues was a response by international capital and its local adherents to the contradictions and tensions of the previous phase.

A sketch of the Libyan case will suffice. Exploration and development in Libya took on significant dimensions after the 1956 Suez crisis. The companies desired to diversify their Middle East operations into areas not susceptible to blockages of the Canal or the pipelines serving the eastern Mediterranean. Exports commenced in 1961, but production escalated sharply after the 1967 war closed the Canal and Palestinian forces had taken to sabotaging the Trans-Arabian Pipeline. On top of this, the British announced plans in 1968 to withdraw militarily from the Gulf. Libyan production zoomed by 49 percent in 1968, against 12 percent for the Middle East as a whole, and by another 23 percent in 1969. By early 1970 production reached 3.5 million barrels a day, just under the rate of long-established producer Saudi Arabia.

The political incentives to increased Libyan production were reinforced by its concession and pricing system. In contrast to the traditional concession patterns, where a closely held consortium of major companies controlled a country's reserves and production, Libya let out separate acreage blocks to various companies and consortia, including virtually all the majors but a number of smaller, independent American and European companies as well. For most of these, Libya represented their only stake in low-cost Middle East production. Moreover, the monarchy accepted its profit share based on the market price rather than the official posted price. A major like Exxon was impelled by its more substantial interests to the east to refrain from undercutting Saudi or Iranian production and paid Libya too according to the official price. The independents, though, with no such stake in the status quo, paid as little as 30 cents a barrel in taxes and contributed mightily to the continued price cutting in Europe.

By September 1, 1969, when the code "Palestine is ours" flashed among the lieutenants and captains taking part in the coup led by Colonel Muammar Qaddafi, Libyan production represented a substantial portion of crude supplies for several European countries, notably West Germany and Italy, and the only low-cost crude for a number of the smaller companies. For the industry as a whole, the pell-mell exploitation of the "Libyan Klondike" led to a far more serious vulnerability to interruption than the situation they sought to diversify from in the Gulf.

The new regime moved smartly to redress its paltry share of crude profits by tackling first the highly vulnerable independents with supply contracts to meet and no alternative sources. Any inclination of the majors to stand with the independents by making supplies available was offset by their satisfaction at seeing these corporate upstarts forced to pay at their level. The "conservation" cutbacks used by the Libyans to force agreement from the independents, combined with interruptions in pipeline deliveries to the eastern Mediterranean and galloping demand in the industrial countries, created temporary and localized shortages in the European markets. The price trend of a decade was reversed.

The resulting price increases buttressed Libyan demands for still higher revenues per barrel, and Libya's success was not lost on the rest of OPEC. The companies' long-standing argument that the market would not tolerate an increase was proven, at the least, outmoded. Qaddafi's militance proved infectious, and the regimes in Iran and Saudi Arabia could not demand less without undermining their admittedly thin nationalist credentials. OPEC's twenty-first regular meeting in December 1970 laid out demands for an increase in the tax rate from 50 to 55 percent, a hike in the posted price, an end to all remaining company discounts, new and more lucrative adjustments for quality and transportation differentials, and, taking the lesson of the last decade to heart, set a firm timetable for negotiations.

The majors did finally accede to these demands, but in a highly abrasive manner calculated to generate an atmosphere of crisis and confrontation totally unwarranted by their mutual interest in a higher price plateau. These negotiations of early 1971, OPEC's *first* successful effort at collective bargaining, demonstrated the value of suppressing political differences in pursuit of common financial goals, and ratified the new, upward trajectory for oil prices. Pressures built up quickly for further increases, and the inertia of the 1960s was reversed with a vengeance in the 1970s.

OPEC in and of itself was little more than a medium in this process, coordinating and tempering often radical popular demands in the turbulent transitionary societies that the oil-producing countries had become. In this time, as later, it could have done no less than it did. First, the slight shift in power represented by the outcome of these negotiations was cumulative and developed out of the contradictions in the world oil industry and the erosion of the monopoly power of the largest companies. Praise or blame for this rests not with OPEC but with the readiness of the more radical regimes to seize advantage of the unique and to some extent temporary conjuncture.

Second, the achievements in these negotiations were *strictly* financial in character and arbitrary in amount. The regimes raised their take of the market value of a barrel of oil, which sold then at a composite product price of $14 in Europe, from about $1 to $1.30. For the majors, the price structure was raised and strengthened, and the leverage of the independents in securing lower-cost crude and underselling in the market was sharply reduced. In short, their monopoly position was, if not restored, measurably strengthened. And this was accomplished in a manner where the blame could be laid at the feet of OPEC. The link between OPEC and the "energy crisis" in the United States, which was fomented by the oil companies in their concerted effort after 1968 to remove price controls on natural gas and raise prices for coal and uranium, was successfully forged in the media and the public consciousness.

Subsequent price hikes, though much more substantial, share these same features: they were largely precipitated by developments outside of OPEC's control—the 1973 war, convulsions in the world economy—and they were perfectly compatible with the interests of the major companies.

Given the symbolic importance of the October War and the embargo by the Arab oil-producing states (not OPEC) that accompanied it, several observations are in order. First, the increasing participation of the oil producers in the world market and its attendant regional political complexities has permanently altered their previous insulation from transcendant political crises such as the struggle for Palestine. The trajectory of Saudi ascendancy, so conducive to Western interests after 1967, could only intensify nationalist pressures in 1973 to implement an embargo. Second, the successful implementation of production cuts in the 1971 negotiations for financial ends reduced the plausibility of the argument that such tactics would not be useful for political purposes. Third, the essential function of the "oil weapon," once it was unsheathed in the waning days of the war, was as a class weapon, a device to reassert the hegemony of forces represented by Feisal and Sadat. As such, it is primarily a defensive weapon, to be brandished in the face of pressures from more militant regimes and political forces, such as the Palestinian movement.

OPEC's agenda in the '70s was not limited to the price question. From its very first meeting in Baghdad in September 1960, the matter of national control of resources and the local oil industry was enshrined in the demand for "participation." This was a term well suited to the political ambiguity that was OPEC: it could mean as much as nationalization, or as little as a pro-forma share in the management of the Western consortia. For Saudi Arabia's Yamani, it was a device for "appeasing patriotic sentiments."

On this question, even more than on prices, OPEC under Saudi and Iranian domination was primarily a force for undercutting rather than advancing the cause of national control. This was especially evident in Yamani's subversion of Iraq's struggle against the Western companies in the mid-1960s. Here, too, satisfaction of this demand was the cumulative result of the struggles of individual countries whose eventual success left OPEC's hierarchs little choice but to follow suit. The companies have been reduced in most instances to the status of "offtakers," or crude purchasers, but still have considerable operating responsibility as contractors in Saudi Arabia and the small Arab Gulf states as well as dominant positions in other stages of the industry.

One component essential to both administering prices and exercising national sovereignty is the control of production and its collective coordination in OPEC. This too was confirmed in OPEC's very first resolutions and was a key objective for Tariki and Perez. In this regard as in no other, Saudi resistance has been decisive until recently. For the whole argument for the indispensability of the giant companies was postulated in the end on their unfettered determination of how much crude would be produced and exported from each country. Their ability to play off one producer against another—against Iran under Mossadeq, against Iraq after Qassem—rested on this capacity to sow divisions among the producers by raising or lowering production and thus revenues. Nowhere was the substitution of Yamani for Tariki more profound in its impact on OPEC's evolution than on this question. The unwavering refusal of Yamani and the regime behind him to consider "production scheduling" under OPEC's aegis has been key to the preservation of Western oil interests in the Middle East. To this very day Yamani refuses to entertain the concept. After an OPEC meeting in March 1979, he testily responded to a reporter: "Sir, we refuse to talk about the level of production in Saudi Arabia with the OPEC member countries. It is not their affair. It is our own affair. And it has been our policy since the early 1960s to avoid any production program. Nothing has changed. We impose our ceiling. We raise or lower it—it is our affair."

This precious prerogative, Saudi ability to maneuver in this realm, is now confined within progressively narrowing parameters in which they must strive to balance off the collective weight of OPEC, the gluttonous needs of the West and the United States, and their own grossly exaggerated physical production capacity. The overthrow of the Pahlavi regime and the consequent sharp reduction in Iranian production over the period ahead has nearly eliminated the Saudi capacity to stabilize or lower prices. Moreover, a struggle has now ensued within the Saudi regime over appropriate production levels as dictated by revenue needs, global economic disquietude, and political responsibilities vis-à-vis the Palestinians and the separate Egyptian-Israeli peace.

This is the most important consequence of the Iranian revolution for OPEC's course in the years just ahead, and the salient feature of the current period of transition, which promises to be far more wrenching than those we have experienced to date. For the pace of local political disorders, the intractability of the global economic crisis, the intensity and velocity of the social contradictions in the oil-producing countries and in the industrial and poor countries as well presage a decade where OPEC may be no more than a relic of squandered opportunity.

A main structural feature of the period ahead is OPEC's more limited capacity to serve as "residual producer"—providing on call the oil the consuming world needs but cannot produce or secure from non-OPEC sources. At today's prices, and in light of the last decade's experience, the trend in OPEC is to limit production to meet proximate revenue needs and maximize long-term production capacity. According to OPEC, its ratio of proven reserves to production has fallen from 68.6 in 1960 to 41.2 in 1978. In the 1950s the OPEC countries added 100 billion barrels to their reserves, while cumulative production amounted to 12 billion barrels. In the 1960s, new reserves totaled 180 billion barrels; cumulative production was 33 billion barrels. Between 1971 and 1978 this relationship was drastically reversed: reserves added were only 28 billion barrels, while cumulative production reached 60 billion barrels.

One consequence of the transfer of majority ownership to the producing regimes has been more careful scrutiny of the producing companies' recovery techniques and other factors which affect the maximum productivity of a field. In many instances this has led to production restrictions and downward revision of capacity. The most startling instance of this has been Saudi Arabia: in 1972 Yamani was proposing, based on Aramco figures, production rates of over 20 million barrels a day by the mid-1980s. Today it is thought that Saudi capacity does not exceed 12 million barrels a day. Yamani himself alluded to this last year in commenting on the current Saudi production ceiling of 9.5 million barrels a day: "On paper we have a much greater capacity and a greater sustained capacity. But in reality we do not know exactly how much we are able to produce until we reach a certain level and then we start to face certain problems in the reservoir behavior."

These geological and technical constraints are more than matched by the political constraints deriving from the tremendous social tensions in the producing countries directly attributable to the influx of oil revenues, the heightened penetration of capitalist relations of exchange and production, and the consequent disruption of traditional patterns and identities. The prevailing social fabrics—which had accommodated until now the archaic and outmoded political forms congenial to Western control—are disintegrating under the impact of forces internal to but largely beyond the control of the separate OPEC states or of OPEC as a whole. The upheaval in Iran, the disquieting incidents in Mecca, the manifestations of great power interventions in the region all point to the perilously fragile character of the oil-producing regimes. In this era, will OPEC recede to a formal but marginal role as negotiating agent? Or can it be

re-forged by new regimes, with a new mandate, as an instrument for contributing to a new order?

TRILATERALISM GOES TO WORK (1977)

Kai Bird

PRESIDENT CARTER'S TRILATERAL APPROACH to foreign policy will
meet its first test in the Middle East. The volatile issues posed by the Arab-Israeli
conflict impose severe strains on the trilateral interdependence of America,
Europe and Japan because of their competition for stable energy supplies.
Carter's trilateral strategy—an outgrowth of his participation in David Rockefeller's Trilateral Commission—mandates a comprehensive peace settlement in
cooperation with a rising regional power, Saudi Arabia.

Two factors that have developed during the last year make a comprehensive
settlement a strong possibility: the willingness of new American leadership to
cooperate with a number of regional powers around the world, hoping in that
way to co-opt them into the international economic order; and the revival of
Arab unity by a convergence of conservative oil regimes (Saudi Arabia) and the
popular Pan-Arab moderates (Egypt and Syria). These two developments are
related, both having matured under the guise of the energy crisis.

The most brazen articulation of the Trilateral world view occurs in the
October 1975 issue of *Foreign Affairs,* "The United States and the Third World"
by Tom Farer. He observes first:

> There was a creaming off and co-optation of the natural elite of the working class
> [in America]. Some members were drawn off early by opening the channels to
> higher education. . . . Their followers were pacified in very small measure by
> vicarious participation in the structure of power and in very large measure by
> receipt of slightly increased shares of a very rapidly growing pie. There is no
> evidence that any existing wealth was redistributed.

Farer goes on to suggest, by analogy, that the managers of the three major
capitalist societies—America, Europe and Japan—can hope to co-opt and divide the Third World in the same way:

> For the most part, Third World elites are even less committed to human equality
> as a general condition of humanity than are we. They are talking about greater
> equality between states. And in their largely authoritarian systems, the state is they.
> . . . The central fact is that the overall number of people who have to be given a
> stake in the essential structures of the existing international economic system is
> relatively small.

Farer argues that a strategy of accommodation with a few Third World regional
powers can effectively diffuse the strident demands of the current North-South
negotiations. Saudi Arabia, Iran, Brazil, Venezuela, Mexico, Nigeria, India and

Indonesia are cited as the "cream" of the Third World—countries rich in natural resources and ruled by middle-class native elites who have for the most part broken all ties to their impoverished masses in the countryside. Farer points out that, though many of these native elites have suffered personal humiliation at the hand of Western colonialism, their immediate economic aspirations are quite compatible with the existing international economic system.

Thus, to stabilize the international order, the United States must apply balm to the personal sores induced by past colonial humiliations, allow the native elites of these regional powers a very small measure of "vicarious participation in the structures of power," and "slightly" increased shares of the world's economic growth.

It does not matter that the vast majority of humanity—and indeed, the majority of people even in these Third World regional powers—will have to remain outside the economic system. What is important is the marginal stabilization of that economic order, the buying of time for development of a wealthier system. Redistribution of present wealth and decentralized democracy have no place in such a system—and to the Trilateralist both ideals are deemed disruptive.

The assumption behind such a conciliatory approach to Third World elites is that the leadership which might supplant them could be much more substantively detrimental to basic American interests. Unlike the more conservative wing of the foreign policy establishment represented by Kissinger's crisis-management diplomacy, the liberals take a longer view. William Maynes expresses their concern in the July 1976 issue of *Foreign Affairs.* Maynes, a former secretary of the Carnegie Endowment for International Peace, was recently nominated to be Assistant Secretary for International Organizations at the State Department. He will probably play a leading role in U.S. relations with the United Nations and in the North-South dialogue. He writes:

> Like the moderate leadership in the American civil rights movement in the late 1960's, however, the moderate elements in the Third World have gone years without victories and urgently require some to prove that a moderate course can produce results. Otherwise, we can expect the extremists of international politics to take over.

The success or failure of this policy of co-optation of Third World elites will initially be determined by our relationship with the Arab oil producers— and Saudi Arabia in particular. Underlying Carter's energy policy is the assumption that Saudi Arabia can continue to be persuaded to produce oil at nearly three times the rate necessary to meet its external payments. The "special relationship" developed over the years between the Saudis and the Trilateral powers is mutually beneficial. Despite popular fears that they might whimsically cut off oil supplies, the Saudis are very much concerned that their oil diplomacy not lead to a radical disruption of the international economic order. Just as the United States needs time to develop alternative sources of energy, the conservative Saudi elite demand time to modernize their country gradually, without jeopardizing existing political structures.

It is not the price of oil as such but increased supply that is linked by the Saudis to a Middle East peace settlement. The goal of American diplomatic efforts in the Middle East is not to lower oil prices but to insure stable supplies. Christopher Makins, deputy director of the Trilateral Commission, told *The New York Times* (October 19, 1976) that the price of oil will in the long term depend on the cost of producing alternative fuels. By this measure, the world market price of standard crude set by OPEC is already underpriced.

Given the dependence of the Trilateral powers on oil and the concentration of world reserves in the Middle East, price is simply a function of the budget requirements of the oil producers. Saudi Arabia controls the entire system because it is the only OPEC country with a significant shut-in capacity. The Saudis have a potential production capacity of around 18 million barrels per day, but are currently producing only 8.5 million barrels per day. Without Saudi Arabia's 108 billion barrels of proven reserves, the world would run out of oil well before the forecast year of 2017. All other OPEC nations are producing at maximum capacity; some, like Kuwait, will soon begin a steady decline in their production capacity. Only Saudi Arabia has the political option to cut supplies indefinitely without cutting its national budget.

The Trilateral powers are more vulnerable currently than ever before to the oil weapon. United States oil imports have tripled since the 1973 oil embargo, while domestic crude production is down 12 percent. More than 42 percent of the oil consumed in the United States in 1976 was imported. Even more disturbing to the authors of "Operation Independence" is the shift toward greater reliance on Arab OPEC oil and away from non-Arab sources. Imports of Saudi oil increased 45 percent in 1975, while imports of Canadian oil actually declined 21 percent. Saudi crude alone accounted in 1976 for more than 23 percent of U.S. imports.

The Saudis are the only members of OPEC who can afford, or who want, to use their oil supplies as a political weapon. That was demonstrated at the December 1976 OPEC conference in Doha, when the Saudis decided to increase their production levels in the face of universal OPEC opposition. Most energy experts predict that Saudi Arabia alone must increase its production each year by at least a million barrels a day just to meet normal world demand. The Saudis were demonstrating from Doha that they would lift their 8.5 million-barrel ceiling—but only in return for a comprehensive peace settlement.

The Trilateral approach to international energy policy recognizes the intra-vulnerability of the three major industrial powers to a Saudi production cutback, and America's Trilateral allies are uneasily aware that their supplies of Saudi crude are directly contingent upon President Carter's willingness to impose a comprehensive peace settlement. Dr. Mason Willrich, director of the International Division of the Rockefeller Foundation, recently told an audience of energy experts at Princeton University: "In discussions we have had with our European and Japanese allies, they have emphasized that they want the United States committed to stable Saudi imports—for their own protection."

The major strategy, according to the Trilateralists, is to entangle the Saudis with the Americans and assure them a stake in the established economic order. Genuine co-optation of Saudi Arabia entails the creation of a credible regional power. No one in Washington's small foreign policy clique talks about it, but Saudi energy resources, military muscle and investments in Western industry will give it considerable influence in whatever "world order" emerges from the Trilateral vision. This influence already extends beyond the Arab world. All of black Africa today receives more foreign aid from Saudi Arabia alone than from the United States. (The Saudis allocate more than 13 percent of their gross national product to foreign assistance, compared to only .29 percent by the United States.)

Carter's policy of mutual entanglement with the oil regimes is thoroughly documented in Trilateral Commission reports: "Energy: A Strategy for International Action" and "Energy: The Imperative for a Trilateral Approach." These reports outline a policy of cooperation with the oil producers on questions of both energy and a Middle East peace settlement:

> The Trilateral countries have to recognize that the question of the supply of oil cannot be separated from the existence of political conflict in the Middle East. The prospect that a new crisis would bring a new reduction or cutoff of Arab oil and again drive the consuming nations apart highlights the need for an early settlement and for an agreed American-European-Japanese approach to it.

The report specifically rules out the possibility of military action against the oil producers and says "attempts to deny food or other supplies will court political disaster." America's special relationship with the oil producers, says another of the Trilateral reports on energy, "should accord to them a place in international economic councils commensurate with their increased economic status." This is a clear reference to "vicarious participation in the structure of power" spoken of by Tom Farer.

There are immediate and long-range costs to any policy that attempts to guarantee oil supplies from the Middle East, but the Trilateral reports boldly state what no politician has been willing to tell the American people:

> The building of petroleum-related industries such as refining and petrochemicals in the producing countries is natural and inevitable. The consuming countries should provide help, *even though the temporary effect will be to add to OPEC's bargaining power, create competition for their own industries, and aggravate their situation regarding the cost and supply of oil products.* (Italics added.)

Unknown to the American people—and without any real public debate— quiet alliances are being negotiated on their behalf to secure necessary natural resources, and oil in particular, that are controlled by the autocratic elites of a few regional Third World powers. These alliances will not even pretend to benefit the vast majority of mankind or answer the increasing tension posed by ever greater polarization between the rich and poor.

The bridge between the Trilateral powers and regional powers like Saudi Arabia is the multinational corporation. Aramco (the Arabian American Oil Co., representing Mobil, Exxon, Texaco and Standard Oil of California) is an appropriate conduit for Trilateral diplomacy. "In the energy field," says Dr. Willrich, "we have to forge an alliance between the federal government and the oil companies. Our long-term energy shortage problems are so serious that we ignore oil only to our own peril. . . . One of the major problems will be to persuade the American people that they are not being ripped off."

Aramco is a perfect tool for Trilateral policy makers to integrate the Saudis

into the international economic order. Aramco has created a company state in
Saudi Arabia over the last forty years—much as Delaware is a preserve of the
Du Pont Co. But Aramco has had the farsighted political good sense to forgo
confrontation tactics in its dealings with the Saudi elite. The company has never
humiliated the royal family and never blatantly usurped sovereignty, as did the
French and British colonialists in the Middle East. The company has made itself
indispensable to the production and marketing of oil, without openly transgress-
ing the strict boundaries of Saudi culture and religion. Aramco long ago recognized the royal family's right to regulate the pace of modernization—a decision
which allows the Saudi elite to manage gradually increasing demands for political participation.

In return, the Saudi monarchy has provided the company with long-
term security in a country of unusual political stability. Even while the Saudis negotiate 100 percent ownership of the oil fields, Aramco expresses un-
shaken confidence that its special relationship with Riyadh will continue for
many years.

James V. Knight, Aramco's vice president in Washington, D.C., recently
told *National Reports* (October 9, 1976), a Washington magazine on government
affairs and policy, "Rather than the so-called nationalization being a case of
'throw the rascals out,' you might say that Aramco is being strengthened all the
time. They [the four oil company partners] are going to continue to market the
oil."

Aramco is a strong structural factor conducive to Saudi cooperation
with the Trilateral powers. But the volatile nature of the Arab nationalist
movement could radically alter this "special relationship." Saudi relations
with the United States are more fragile than they appear; for one thing,
they are clouded by America's de facto alliance with Israel. The Saudis appear to need a comprehensive peace settlement just as desperately as does
Israel, but their hands are tied on the Palestinian issue. The Palestinians are
a direct internal political threat to the very existence of the Saudi monarchy, since yet another Arab defeat in confrontation with Israel could easily
galvanize a right-wing or Qaddafi-style *coup d'état.* Or conversely, the successful establishment of a leftist and secular state in Lebanon or Palestine-
Jordan threatens all conservative Arab regimes.

It is out of these fears that the Saudis have during the last year flexed
their economic muscle to alter the course of Arab politics. Late last year
they forced an abrupt end to the Lebanese civil war—first intervening to
prevent a complete victory over the Christians by a coalition of leftist Mus-
lim Lebanese and Palestinians, and then intervening again to save the PLO
from annihilation. And they have now forged a reconciliation among Egypt,
Syria and Jordan for the sole purpose of bringing a united Arab front—including a greatly emasculated and docile PLO—to the brink of a comprehensive peace settlement with Israel.

The assumption behind this flurry of Saudi diplomacy is that the United
States has the leverage and commitment to impose a moderate peace settlement
on Israel. The Saudis under King Khalid and Prince Fahd are doing what a
more cautious King Faisal would have forbidden—they are gambling. They
publicly demonstrate their willingness to increase oil production and their au-

thority over the PLO, and in return fully expect the Trilateralists to exercise their leverage on Israel.

The settlement they envision is probably very close to the kind of peace outlined in a 1975 Brookings Institution report ("Toward Peace in the Middle East"), signed by both Zbigniew Brzezinski and William Quandt, his Middle East aide at the National Security Council. The Brookings report endorses a Palestinian state or entity in the West Bank and Gaza, with perhaps nominal Arab or international sovereignty over the Old City of Jerusalem. The Saudis probably are counting on the creation of a right-wing autonomous Palestinian state in the West Bank and Gaza that excludes the Marxist elements in the PLO, and is perhaps loosely federated with the Hashemite Kingdom in Jordan.

A moderate, cooperative Saudi monarchy cannot indefinitely survive—much less continue to supply more than half of America's annually increased oil needs—without a comprehensive Middle East peace settlement. United States policy is similarly pinned to the survivability of Anwar Sadat and Hafez Assad, both Arab moderates who have recently demonstrated their ability to smother Palestinian autonomy. In the absence of a peace settlement that defuses the Palestinian nationalist movement, none of these regimes can expect to remain on a moderate course. Saudi Arabia will inexorably be maneuvered into politically motivated cutbacks in oil production. The Trilateralists can be expected to work very hard to impose a comprehensive peace settlement on Israel, and to co-opt Saudi Arabia into the established international economic system.

OPEC AND THE THIRD WORLD (1980)

Penny Lernoux

ONE OF THE MOST PUZZLING riddles for U.S. critics of the Organization of Petroleum Exporting Countries is why the oil-barren developing nations don't speak up. Here are the "NOPECs" on the edge of bankruptcy, facing an impossible oil import bill, and hardly a murmur to be heard from the Third World!

While the U.S. and European press worked itself into a froth of indignation over OPEC's recent "sock-it-to-'em" meeting in Caracas to set higher prices, there was no similar outburst from the NOPECs, whose precarious economic condition also figured on the agenda. Instead, the Third World was treated to the spectacle of the U.S. State Department and the U.S. Treasury carrying the banner for them. American officials repeatedly warned the oil cartel that higher prices in the volatile petroleum market would be the economic undoing of the poorer nations.

Explanations for the NOPECs' seemingly contradictory relations with

OPEC range from cowardice and awe of a successful Third World cartel to a shortsighted failure to see where their real interests lie. In fact, the NOPECs are perfectly aware of what is at stake, and therefore have limited their complaints to quiet—and effective—lobbying of friendly nations in OPEC, with the Central American countries taking their problems to Venezuela and the Moslem states going to Saudi Arabia. U.S. outbursts on the NOPECs' behalf are viewed by them as a cynical attempt to con OPEC into lowering prices for the benefit of First World consumers, who use 57 percent of the world's oil, compared with the NOPECs' consumption of only 13.8 percent. As an African diplomat observed, "We developing countries are paying for the First World's wasteful energy consumption and the oil companies' profits, which have pushed the price of oil beyond our reach."

Official U.S. breast-beating aside, OPEC has shown considerable concern for the NOPECs' plight. At the four-day meeting in Caracas, there was no disagreement about the continuation of a $5-billion-plus annual fund for aid to the non-oil-producing developing nations, in contrast to the heated and fruitless discussions over a unified price to be charged First World consumers.

Although such OPEC aid is frequently disdained in the industrialized world as a "mere pittance," it is considerably more generous than that provided by the First World. The OPEC countries earmark 2 percent of their gross national product for low-cost loans or outright gifts to the NOPECs in contrast to the industrialized countries, which contribute only 0.3 percent of their G.N.P., and most of that tied to First World products and technology. The latter's aid comes from renewable resources; OPEC funds do not.

The Venezuelans, Ecuadorians and Algerians want to institutionalize such lending through a $20 billion OPEC aid agency to enable the NOPECs to buy subsidized oil through donations or loans, depending on their economic situation. The proposal, which was made at Caracas, is now under study by OPEC's long-term strategy committee headed by Saudi Oil Minister Ahmad Zaki Yamani. The NOPECs "are absolutely right to complain to us about the lack of solidarity, not only in questions of money but also in more effective support and cooperation for their deteriorating economies," said Venezuela's Mines and Energy Minister Humberto Calderon. Venezuela has taken the lead in experimenting with a two-tiered pricing system to benefit the NOPECs, selling its crude to the oil-hungry Caribbean and Central American nations at $20 a barrel instead of $24. However, other OPEC nations are unlikely to follow suit as multi-tiered price systems are so complex that it would be impossible to detect whether the recipient of cheap OPEC oil is reselling or diverting it.

A more popular, behind-the-scenes development is government-to-government contracts, eliminating the giant oil company intermediaries and saving the NOPECs up to $10 a barrel. Thus, Brazil's state oil enterprise is buying 400,000 barrels a day from Iraq's oil company, and Colombia's state enterprise purchases 25,000 barrels a day from its Venezuelan counterpart. Altogether, such contracts have taken an estimated 35 percent of world oil exports out of the hands of the "Seven Sisters" (Exxon, Shell, Mobil, Texaco, British Petroleum, Standard Oil of California and Gulf).

Direct purchasing was one of six oil-related recommendations made at the meeting of nonaligned countries in Havana last September, but it also suits the strategy of a number of OPEC countries, such as Venezuela, which want to diversify their customers and lessen dependence on the Sisters. A declining dollar and the Carter Administration's freeze on Iranian bank deposits also have encouraged the Arab producers to intensify economic cooperation with the Latin American NOPECs, which offer alternative sources of supply, including food, and possibilities for investment. Arab delegations have visited most of the major Latin American countries, and Arab-Latin American banks have opened in Lima, Peru, and Caracas.

While most of these developments are motivated by commercial pragmatism, the identical view of the industrialized nations that NOPECs and OPEC hold also explains the developing countries' reluctance to attack the petroleum cartel publicly. Contrary to First World apologists who blame the world's economic ills on the bad guys in OPEC, studies by a variety of respected international institutions show that the source of world inflation and of NOPEC debt is the First World itself. In its annual report for 1978–79, for example, the General Agreement on Tariffs and Trade traces the resurgence of inflation not to petroleum price rises but to the failure of the industrialized countries to adopt strong and consistent anti-inflationary policies. GATT figures show that inflation had already begun climbing in Western Europe and the United States in mid-1978, six months before OPEC price increases and at a time when there was an oil glut on the world market.

Similarly, State and Treasury Department propaganda blaming oil price hikes for the NOPECs' $274 billion foreign debt is contradicted by the United Nations Conference on Trade and Development. UNCTAD's data show that the largest drain on these countries' economies is imports from the industrialized nations, high debt repayments to foreign banks and profit remittances by the subsidiaries of multinational corporations. Morgan Guaranty Trust also reports that the principal cause of the NOPECs' poor economic performance in 1978 was a 6 percent deterioration in their terms of trade with the First World, and not oil-price developments.

Higher oil prices may now push some NOPECs, such as Turkey, over the brink, but the OPEC nations are correct when they contend that they cannot be held responsible for the cumulative process that led those countries to this situation. Still, it's always easier to throw stones at sheiks than to put one's own house in order. The governments of the industrialized countries have not squarely faced the problem of short-term capital movements by the multinational corporations and banks, for example, although they are the principal source of the world's monetary instability and the underpinnings of the stateless and uncontrolled trillion-dollar Eurocurrency market. Nor do they want to admit that their own printing presses are the source of world liquidity and inflation. Between 1972 and 1977, total international monetary reserves grew by $240 billion, $177 billion of which were in dollars and Eurodollars. As the GATT, UNCTAD and Morgan Guaranty studies show, OPEC price rises barely kept pace with these inflationary increases.

"Energy Crisis"

THE ENERGY INDUSTRY'S
FRIGHT CAMPAIGN (1972)

Robert Sherrill

WHERE DID THE "ENERGY CRISIS" come from? To a large extent it came out of the hats of the oil and gas industry's propagandists. . . .

Always accompanying the ominous warnings one finds a commercial hand groping for the consumer's pocket. When the petroleum propagandists sound off, their object is quite obviously to panic us (and those feeble representatives of "us," Congress and the Federal Power Commission) into freeing the industry from any controls—production controls, environmental controls, price controls. . . .

The "energy shortage" as we know it today was detected in 1968. Something else interesting happened in that year: the U.S. Supreme Court ruled that the petroleum industry did not deserve a higher profit than had been allowed by the Federal Power Commission in the famous Permian Basin area rate case. Industry had argued that it deserved more money because its gas reserves were declining sharply. But the Court rejected this argument, noting: "There is . . . substantial evidence that additions to reserves have not been unsatisfactorily low, and that recent variations in the ratio of reserves to production are of quite limited significance." The Court noted further that each year new reserves exceeded production.

There is excellent circumstantial evidence, put together by Charles F. Wheatley, Jr., general manager and general counsel of the American Public Gas Association (a pro-consumer organization), that this Court ruling was seen by the oil and gas industry as an invitation to a life-or-death struggle over controls.

Industry was apparently determined to rid itself, once and for all, of the kind of government control which set wellhead gas rates on the basis of production costs plus fair return. If industry could get rid of those controls, then the price of oil and coal would also be allowed to soar—for their price levels were held back by the cheapness of gas.

And if the Supreme Court demanded a showing of shortage before it would go along with industry, then industry was prepared to juggle the record to show just that. Beginning in 1968, and for the first time in history, the industry claimed that it found less gas than it sold. It has been claiming the same thing for every year since. The basis for these claims is in industry's file cabinets, secret, not available to Congress or to the public. You just have to take industry's word for it.

Along with the official drop in the findings/production ratio, industry also began its drive to frighten the public through the popular press. Is it actually conceivable that those respectable executives would stoop to trickery for a buck? No less responsible a person than Hendrick S. Houthakker, professor of economics at Harvard and a former member of the Council of Economic Advisers, said, "I think frankly that the oil industry has been engaged in a scare campaign on this shortage question. I think they are making projections that are very debatable." And when George P. Shultz, now Secretary of the Treasury, testified before Congress in 1970 he exhibited such a rare degree of candor that oilmen have not forgiven him; he testified that in his opinion the oil and gas industry was perfectly capable of faking a crisis in order to manipulate government policy.

Industry's fright campaign can be easily documented by turning to that standard index of periodical literature, *Reader's Guide.* From March 1968 to February 1969 *Reader's Guide* lists not one magazine article on the topic of energy shortage. . . .

But in the twelve months following the Supreme Court decision, articles on the topic exploded into print, and they all appeared in magazines that can be counted on to give industry a helping hand: *Business Week, Nation's Business, U.S. News, Fortune* and *Forbes.* "LOOMING CRISIS IN NATURAL GAS," says one headline; already the crepe was being hung.

In the *next* twelve months the publicists really got the press's range, with no less than twenty-five articles: "SCROUNGING FOR FUEL," "IS THE CUPBOARD BARE?," etc. The barrage has continued during the last year and a half unabated. . . . *The New York Times,* the Washington *Star, The Washington Post* and the *Los Angeles Times* are among the important newspapers that have given extended coverage of the topic, for the most part in a vein that would not in any way frustrate the oil and gas industry's objectives.

A scare campaign, however, is not easily conducted. . . . On the one hand, they must convince the public that things are so bad it would be wise to leave matters with those who know best, Big Industry; but on the other hand, they must not frighten the public into advocating something radical.

In this episode, that public had to be convinced that, while fuel might not be *immediately* available, it *could* be produced if industry were encouraged to go get it. If the public became too alarmed, it might insist on trying what several *pro-publico* experts, among them former Federal Power Commissioners Lee White and Charles Ross, have suggested: some public ownership of the exploratory and distribution machinery of the oil-gas industry. When the propaganda juggernaut began back in 1969–70, industry apparently feared that it might be pushing too far too fast. It wanted real fright, but not a stampede. So the American Gas Association bought full-page ads, such as the following in October 22, 1970 *Wall Street Journal,* to quiet the flustered herd:

WHAT'S BEING DONE ABOUT GAS SUPPLY
Recent reports of natural gas shortages in various parts of the country have apparently led to speculation that we are running out of natural gas. Now this is simply not true.

What's happening is this: In certain areas, the demand for additional natural gas has outrun the *present* [their italics] ability to supply. Consequently, a number of utilities which have received requests for new large industrial loads have had to turn them down. These shortages are due partly to increased demands for natural gas —such as in the effort to fight air pollution—and partly to the fact that gas is now being consumed faster than new reserves are being developed.

This does *not* mean the country is running out of gas. (In fact, geologists estimate that proved and potential supplies are over 70 times our present annual consumption rate.)

Exactly one year later the American Gas Association was back again, placing ads in *Life* and other magazines, still with the obvious purpose of preventing outright hysteria. These ads assured Americans that there was no reason to lay in a supply of wood and peat, because, "There's no worry that your home will run short of gas. . . . We've been serving you for 100 years—and we don't intend to stop now." However, the gas patron was asked to bear one little burden: "It will take higher prices to keep the gas coming."

And higher prices the industry got. Within the past twelve months the Federal Power Commission has granted price increases that the American Public Gas Association estimates will cost the consumer as much as $4 billion. But industry, unsatisfied, kept up its ominous chatter. . . .

One finds such normally canny fellows as Ralph Lapp sometimes following the industrial crumbs into a trap, as he did in the recent *New York Times Magazine* article "We're Running Out of Gas," an expanded version of what he had previously written for *The New Republic.* As a plea for conservation, it was eloquent, but as a practical appraisal of the energy future in this country it was almost farcically pessimistic: not only will we be beggars in the world gas market by 1990, wrote Lapp, but within the foreseeable future there is no substitute fuel. Oil is also in short supply; coal is too dirty; imported liquefied gas is too expensive; the production of synthetic gas is too far in the future to offer hope; nuclear power is still beset with crippling problems. By the time he had completed his tale of woe, one felt the Arctic icecap descending upon us. "We have," he cried with his parting breath, "overcome nature."

Well, he's right: we *are* running out of gas, just as we are running out of all finite fuel materials—gas faster than most because it is more useful and popular than most. But beyond that, the only indisputable fact in the matter seems to be that, lacking objective data from sources other than industry, we cannot say how fast we are running out. And lacking more aggressive attempts to develop substitute fuels, we cannot say what could be made available. . . .

Although Lapp acknowledged that "huge amounts of undiscovered gas are thought to exist more than 15,000 feet below the earth's surface," he adds that "drilling that deep is prohibitively expensive."

Nonsense. Edward Leach, editor of *Pipeline & Gas Journal,* writing in the issue of October 1971, lays out what most gas producers know: drilling at the deeper levels, or offshore, is three to ten times more expensive than shallow onshore drilling, but the chance of finding gas at those levels and in those areas is nearly three times higher; the deep zones usually have "exceptionally large" volumes of gas, and deep-zone gas can be produced more cheaply because it is under greater pressure. All of which, wrote Leach, adds up to the fact that by drilling deeper "you are actually reducing the *basic unit* cost."

If we accept this man's know-how . . . then there is no reason to discount . . . the Potential Gas Committee's estimate that this part of the globe contains 1,178 trillion cubic feet of "potential" gas, or nearly four times the current known reserves. And inasmuch as deeper onshore drilling as well as offshore drilling returns a better cost-price ratio, there is no reason to accept higher prices, or at least much higher prices, without a fight.

. . . One reason we're running out of gas is that the industrial part of our economy has been slopping it up like hogs. "Roughly two-thirds of the gas sold since 1945 has been sold for industrial purposes and at prices designed to undercut the prices for coal and residual fuel oil," former FPC Commissioner Lawrence O'Connor pointed out recently. FPC Commissioner Rush Moody also pointed out recently that while residential and small consumers use only 21 per cent of the gas, they pay 46 per cent of the cost. Gas distributors have for a generation charged the housewife more per unit for the gas she uses to cook a pot roast than they charge Bethlehem Steel to cook an ingot, with the very predictable result that industry has fallen in love with this cheap fuel and has used it like mad wastrels.

. . . Getting the gas-gulping industries to return to coal would be not only an adequate answer but a sane answer. "Environmentalists will object," [Lapp] says, "to any move toward a substitution of coal or oil, with their high sulfur content and resultant air-pollution potential, for relatively clean-burning gas." There's no reason to talk that way. Why the assumption that coal must result in filth? Lapp is doubtless familiar with a generating process called MHD, used in West Germany, Japan and Russia; it reportedly results in far better combustion and thereby about one-third less stack effluents and two-thirds more power per pound of fuel than we are accustomed to getting from the ordinary method of burning coal. Built into the typical MHD power plant, also, is a recovery system that keeps just about all particulate matter out of the air. Two years ago the Office of Science and Technology estimated that development of MHD would save $11 billion in coal costs between 1985 and 2000.

So why don't we have MHD in this country? Why did the government this year budget a puny $3 million for developing MHD? One answer might be that the coal companies—which, since the inter-ties are almost total, means the oil and gas industry—do not want power plants that use $11 billion less of their product in a fifteen-year period.

And inasmuch as the American Gas Association acknowledges that "known minable reserves of coal in the United States could be converted to some 11,000,000,000,000,000 cubic feet of gas—enough to supply the nation's gas energy needs at current consumption rates for a full 500 years," one might also ask why it is that the most profitable industry in the world is spending only a measly $10 million annually out of its own pocket to develop that technique.

One might also wonder why, since our fuel supply is supposedly so precarious, the energy industry sells $1 billion worth of coal to other countries every year. And one can only marvel at the logic of the major U.S. oil companies, now engaged in despoiling other countries as they have their own, which pretend to be so concerned about our "crisis," when at the same time, in producing oil in Canada and Central and South America and Africa and the Middle East, they flare right in the field—burn as waste—a gas supply that totals a tenth of the world's annual production. But instead of addressing themselves straightforwardly to correcting such mistakes, the oil and gas industry continues its old buccaneering ways while the consumer is distracted by fright.

And the strategy is working well. Aside from the $4 billion gas price hike it got last year for "exploration incentives," the industry in recent months has used the shortage scare to: *(1)* obtain Interior Department approval for the cross-Alaska pipeline, so we (and Japan) will get that "desperately needed" oil, and despite the fact that the Interior crowd has conceded a pipeline across Canada would be less ecologically dangerous; *(2)* win approval for El Paso Natural Gas Company to import liquefied natural gas from Algeria at a cost that is bound to shove domestic prices much higher (the LNG, by the way, will be produced in Algeria with $350 million in loans directly from or guaranteed by the U.S. Government; and the construction and operation of El Paso's tankers will also be subsidized by the U.S. taxpayer); *(3)* get President Nixon and the State Department to help industry manipulate a deal for the purchase of Russian natural gas. Prior to Nixon's junket to Russia, a study of the proposal, prepared by Brown & Root of Texas, was quietly circulated in Washington for approval at top levels. Backstopping Nixon, and urging him to do industry's job with Russia, were the White House's petroleum adviser, Peter Flanigan, and Secretary of Commerce Peterson.

It shall not be supposed, however, that the Russian liquefied natural gas is all coming to this "energy-short" country. El Paso Natural Gas is cooking up its own deal with Russia to ship LNG to Japan as well as to U.S. West Coast ports.

Of course the public will also pay for all this. Flanigan has acknowledged that, as with El Paso in Algeria, "substantial government financial assistance would be appropriate." As for the tankers to carry the gas, Flanigan said that "gas consumers would pay for the U.S.-built ships over the life of the gas contract."

And the industry has accomplished another little thing while we were trembling: it convinced the FPC, which never takes too much convincing when industry talks, to set up a new mechanism by which gas prices can continue to go higher and higher on an *ad hoc* basis. This ruling would destroy the cost basis for pricing, established in 1954. The new proposal came out on April 6; it is politically so flammable that it probably won't go into effect until after the election. Putting their heads together, the Consumer Federation of America, the American Public Gas Association and the American Public Power Association figured that the new rate-making procedure will add "$500 billion or even as much as $1 trillion to consumers' bills over the life of the nation's gas reserves."

In an extraordinary letter to the FPC, Sen. Philip Hart intervened with his own extensive protest in predicting: "If the rule were adopted, the FPC would be abolishing regulation of wellhead prices for new gas. It would do so at a cost of billions of dollars to consumers from this year forward. . . . It does not provide for a rebate if later we learn that the natural gas shortage used as a defense of higher prices is more imagination than reality. . . . Worse, this rule binds all future Commissions to uphold the prices."

That is the crisis consumers had better pay attention to right now. . . .

THE PAD V CONSPIRACY (1979)

James Gannon

MOTORISTS WHO have suffered through the long gasoline lines of the 1970s can be forgiven a wistful look back to the 1950s and 1960s when gas was cheap and plentiful. It might have been even cheaper in the earlier days and more plentiful in this decade were it not for the manipulations of the oil companies.

That is the substance of an antitrust suit being quietly pursued by the attorneys general of California and five other states, in which they charge ten oil companies—Standard of California (Socal), Texaco, Union, Atlantic Richfield (Arco), Exxon, Getty, Gulf, Mobil, Phillips and Shell—with conspiracy to control the retail gasoline market.

The suit was initiated after it was learned that the gas shortage of 1973–74 originated in 1972—before the Arab oil boycott, which is usually blamed for the shortage. Last May a Federal District Court in Los Angeles released previously sealed information that traces price fixing and restraint of trade by the oil companies back more than a quarter of a century and highlights the hidden contribution of the oil companies to the product shortage of the 1970s.

"Control" is the operating concept. The indictment is a story of how the oil companies used their oligopolistic power to raise their own profits at the expense of the consuming public. The scope of the case brought by the states of California, Washington, Oregon and Arizona is limited to the Far West (PAD V in industry jargon—for Petroleum Allocation for Defense District Five), which they consider to be a market geographically separate from the rest of the country. But two Eastern states, Connecticut and Florida, have also joined the suit, giving it national implications.

The most revealing evidence comes from charts based on data compiled by the Lundberg Survey, an industry pricing service that takes price samples at more than 16,000 filling stations in about forty cities nationwide. Lundberg will sell its service to anyone, but the oil companies have always been its best customers—especially back in the 1960s when it was published weekly—because, in the words of Daniel Lundberg, who runs it, "Company reps were always driving around trying to find out what the competitors were doing; I could just do it cheaper."

After the 1973–74 gas shortage, a Georgia Tech marketing professor, Fred C. Allvine, bought the Lundberg service and used it for an attack on the oil companies. Allvine and James M. Patterson of Indiana University charged in a book called *Highway Robbery* (1974) that even before the Arab boycott the oil companies had contrived an artificial gasoline shortage to drive price-competitive independent marketers out of business. The book was underwritten by some of the independents . . . When the states became interested, they hired Allvine as a consultant, and he turned over his Lundberg data.

The states have refined the charts in Allvine and Patterson's book, which they call "unmanipulated, computer-generated plots" of the Lundberg Survey, and made them their Exhibit A. Prices for major company dealer stations and for independent retail outlets are averaged separately so that price patterns can be brought out. The patterns are virtually identical in twenty-one Western markets. San Francisco and Seattle, several hundred miles apart, show "an incredible coincidence [in] the two cities' pricing history." The twenty-one widely scattered cities, among them metropolitan Los Angeles and semirural Yakima, Wash., offer "thoroughly convincing evidence of the most tightly controlled, conspiratorially maintained market imaginable," the states charge.

The alleged conspiracy had two phases, reflecting changing circumstances in the world oil industry. The first spans two decades, from the 1950s to the early 1970s, when the seven biggest oil companies—Exxon, Mobil, Socal, Texaco, Gulf, British Petroleum and Royal Dutch/Shell—virtually dictated production, supply and marketing strategy for the entire world. Six of the multinational Big Seven are defendants. As far as the public knew, these and a few lesser companies were competitors. But according to the indictment, they had set up an intelligence network in PAD V to exchange market information—the kind of information Macy's would never tell Gimbel's.

The second phase of the conspiracy took place during the fourteen months prior to the Arab boycott of 1973–74. OPEC nations were beginning to take charge of production within their own boundaries. With foreign production profits slipping, the majors turned to domestic markets. But competition from independent dealers with no-frills service and cut-rate prices prevented total market control. The states accept Allvine's theory that the majors dealt with the situation by contriving an artificial shortage to cut off or limit supplies to the independents. . . .

. . . Sharing trade secrets is second nature to the oil companies. So when the majors put together an intelligence network in PAD V they were only doing locally what they long had been doing worldwide. Other companies found it in their interest to go along.

The companies built an inefficient retail system, at the heart of which were lessee-dealers who would buy gasoline for about 5 cents above wholesale, receiving in return delivery, advertising and credit cards. The dealers added their margin onto their cost to arrive at their retail price. The system left room for independent entrepreneurs. A sharp businessman could buy a major company's gasoline through brokers and beat the dealers with no-frills gas stations.

The majors were perfectly willing to sell, too. The more they sold, whether out the front door to dealers or out the back door to off-brand marketers or brokers, the more crude they could pump—and the more profits they could make. The system reached a peak of absurdity when the companies gave dealers price supports to meet competition.

When Korean War controls were lifted in 1953, the major companies took steps to assure an orderly market with relatively stable prices. In the West, where it was the biggest company, Socal became the pricing leader, or "reference" company. A Shell ex-employee is quoted in a pre-trial document as saying that Shell gasoline prices prior to the mid-1960s had no relation to the cost of production; price was a matter of "follow the leader," and the leader was Socal.

In the early 1950s, Socal established what the states called an "industry contact group" within its marketing division. It was staffed with employees whose job was to gather intelligence about competitors. They were ordered not to keep records or talk about their activities with fellow employees, and to use all available sources, including employees of rival firms, to collect information on competitors' activities. The main targets of their inquiries were retail prices and dealer subsidies. They would also discuss wholesale accounts to make sure commercial customers (cab or bus companies or government agencies) who wanted to buy one oil company's gasoline were not under contract to another. This was known in the oil business as respecting the other company's "paper." And the question asked was, "Do you have paper on this guy?" (Socal contends that the group comprised "marketing analysts and consultants" and that all questions about prices were asked by "clerks" solely for "verification.")

In 1957, assistant marketing vice president Theodore Wellman was named to head the group. . . . Individuals under him were generally assigned to specific marketing areas. . . . They would call or meet directly with their counterparts in other companies. Wellman himself communicated with Socal competitors at the executive level.

Agnar Nerheim, a key man under Wellman, had broader responsibilities. He collected inside information about dealer subsidies and discounts by independent refiners to their "off-brand" customers. . . . The dealers' main interest was in selling at prices that were competitive with the cut-rate independents in order to keep their sales volume up. The companies wanted to keep prices high; they would give supports reluctantly on an incremental basis, but when prices went too low to suit them, the supports would be stopped and the prices would shoot back up.

[Robert] Erhard [a Carter official] recalled telling Carter's dealers [later Exxon] that supports would end on a certain day at a certain hour, and noticing later that dealer allowances at the other companies would end at the same time. As the antitrust suit charges, the implication of "mutually agreed price restoration . . . is very strong."

The implications are even stronger in the charts based on the Lundberg Survey data. The charts show that during the period of gasoline oversupply, the prices charged by both major company dealers and independents in every Western city rose and fell in sawtooth patterns over six-week cycles. Price declines in each cycle were gradual, but "restorations" were instantaneous, "without any intermediate ascending prices," the states charge. Stock market analysts, economists and other experts consulted by lawyers for the states agreed that the near-identical price curves of the company dealers and the independents would not have occurred in a truly competitive market.

The notion of patterns is central to the states' argument, and the companies' defense attacks the accuracy of the charts on the ground that by plotting average prices they do not reflect the wide range of "diversity" among individual retail outlets. "The charts were never meant to show that everyone had the same price," said California's assistant attorney general Michael I. Spiegel. "They show patterns—intermediate prices on the way down, with restorations all at once. Even with price dispersion, that point is still valid."

Socal's "industry contact group" continued to meet through most of the 1960s, possibly until the Supreme Court ruled in 1969 that even infrequent meetings to discuss prices violated the Sherman Act. (Socal refers to the group as the "Wellman group," and says it broke up when Wellman retired in 1967.)

The states allege that informal high-level contacts among marketing executives went on as they always had—whether over martini lunches at the Petroleum Club or in informal meetings during oil conventions. They would discuss "problems," and few problems did not relate to prices. There were times when the Oil Information Committee of the Western Oil and Gas Association didn't bother to find neutral ground, but simply met in company board rooms. . . .

The most striking thing about the charts is the abrupt end of the sawtooth patterns in mid-August 1972, which coincides with the final termination of dealer allowances. This marks precisely the end of the old era of gasoline oversupply, and the beginning of the current period of product scarcity. And whatever OPEC or the Federal Government may have contributed since then, it demonstrates that the oil companies ushered in the new era.

Several major companies eliminated dealer supports on August 15, and by the end of the month these subsidies were virtually a thing of the past. The companies had set the dealers up in business, and now they knocked the props out from under them. Prices leveled off for several weeks, with the independents far enough below the dealers to take away volume. Then the oil companies dropped the other shoe.

In February 1973, the president of Arco warned of a coming "fuel crunch." Shortly thereafter, Arco was cutting back gasoline supplies to independents. By May it had implemented a "voluntary allocation" program—in reality, a system of company-conceived and company-administered gas rationing. Other companies did the same in what the states called "a coordinated plan by the major oil companies to end the surplus gasoline situation in order to dry up the independent marketers' supply."

The conditions for the alleged "fuel crunch" were created earlier, according to the states. Refinery utilization was as low as 85 percent of capacity in the second half of 1972 (92 percent is normal), even though PAD V was subjected to no import restrictions and the records of several crude storage facilities indicate no shortages of "feedstock" for the refineries.

The oil companies then used the "shortage" as an excuse to squeeze the independents. The Golden Eagle Oil Company, for example, could obtain from Phillips only 5.4 million gallons of gasoline in April 1973 compared with 8.9 million the previous month. Golden Eagle was lucky; Phillips cut off the independents in Phoenix altogether. Arco shut off the Goodrich Oil Company for two months in 1972, then created supply problems for nearly two years before canceling the contract. Mobil reduced supplies to the Southern Counties Oil Company in June 1973.

"Voluntary allocations" by the oil companies, under pressure from Congress, saved some of the independents, but it did not save price competition. The price curves on the charts show a relatively smooth and steady upward climb from 1973 to 1977. The majors had gained their objective: they controlled the market. The independents, under the discipline of short supply and allocations made mandatory by the Government, played ball with the majors at the expense of the consumers.

By the time the Arab boycott occurred in the fall of 1973, the majors' refineries were running at about 100 percent of capacity—well above normal. Gasoline supplies had already been reduced to a thin margin over demand, and the Arabs simply caught the oil companies with their inventories down. As the states' antitrust suit puts it: "There was never any shortage of any kind, but rather an artificial scarcity." . . .

The states are asking the court to end the oil companies' conspiracy and "restore competition" to the industry. . . .

HOW BIG OIL
TURNED OFF THE GAS (1979)

Fred J. Cook

THE GREAT "OIL CRISIS" of the summer of 1979 may well go down in history as one of the greatest frauds ever perpetrated on a helpless people. The truth is that there was no shortage of oil. This is verified by every responsible source. Indeed, solid statistics show that there was more oil available than there had been in 1978 when there were no gas lines, no murders of frustrated motorists—in a word, no "crisis."

President Carter's Sermon on the Mount on Sunday night, July 15, ignored the fraud. He insisted that the shortage was "real." To have admitted that it was not would have entailed an admission of the culpability of Big Oil and of President Carter's own recumbent Department of Energy.

The naïve may say to themselves, "Why, this cannot be." So let's begin by citing some sources: A Federal Trade Commission study concluded on May 30 that gasoline supplies were up from 4 to 8 percent (depending on the month in which the comparison was made) during the first four months of 1979 over the comparable period in 1978. U.S. Customs figures, independently verified by House of Representatives researchers, show that the "Iranian shortfall" so widely trumpeted to validate the "crisis" was a red herring, because imports of oil during the first five months of 1979 actually increased 10 percent over 1978. A world energy assessment by the Central Intelligence Agency shows that world oil production in the first quarter of 1979 was up despite the Iranian disruption; that U.S. imports through May showed a big increase over 1978 figures—and that American firms, in this very time of supposed crisis, were actually exporting more oil than they had in 1978.

Let's explore some of this data in greater depth before getting into the questions of how and why the nation was thrown into chaos with gas lines sometimes miles long; with truckers staging a nationwide protest against the high price and scarcity of diesel fuel; with some farmers plowing under crops because they could not get trucks to transport them.

When President Carter came down from the Mount, he thumped the table in the Oval Office and announced that he was not going to permit the importation of a single gallon of oil more than we had imported in 1977. What the public and practically all of the commentators didn't know was that we imported so much oil in 1977 that Big Oil suffered acute glut pains and couldn't get those damned prices up.

The American Petroleum Institute is the official spokesman for the industry. Its figures are accepted without question by the Department of Energy because they are the only figures the D.O.E. has. Other sources suspect that the Petroleum Institute's statistics often gild the lily for Big Oil, which is only to be expected. However, with this caveat, look at what the industry's own figures show: Total crude oil stocks in millions of barrels at year's end 1977 reached 339.859, a 19.1 percent increase over 1976. At year's end 1978, total stocks had dropped to 314.462, a decrease of 7.5 percent, bringing us into 1979 with a potentially short situation.

But, as in almost every facet of this story, things weren't what they seemed. In addition to the normal crude oil supplies, the Federal Government has established a Strategic Petroleum Reserve . . . stored in salt domes in Louisiana. . . .

If one includes the extra millions of barrels that were committed to this strategic reserve in 1978, the figures on the nation's total petroleum stocks, expressed in millions of barrels, read this way: 381.322 at end of 1978 compared with 347.689 at the end of that 1977 "glut" year. In other words, the nation came into 1979 with 9.7 percent more crude stocks on the market and in the reserve than it had had at the start of 1978, when the industry was moaning because it had so much oil it couldn't even get gasoline prices up to the permitted ceilings. It is enough to make one ask, "What the devil goes on here?" What went on is fairly obvious, though only the naïve would expect to get a straight answer from Dr. James R. Schlesinger's Department of Energy.

In January and February 1978, when I first began to poke my nose into the oil situation, I was intrigued and angered by the fact that No. 2 home-heating oil, which for at least half a century has been one of the cheapest products of the refineries, was selling at prices that made it more expensive than the more highly refined regular gasoline, once one discounted 12-cent-a-gallon state and Federal taxes on gasoline. My inquires brought the reply from industry sources and from the D.O.E. through my Congressman that there was virtually a price war on for gasoline because there was so much of it. Heating oil, however, had been decontrolled in the last days of the Ford Administration; the homeowner, anchored in place by his furnace, couldn't shop around—and so he was zapped.

Given this untidy situation, Big Oil drew down stocks during 1978 and by late fall had created a situation in which there began to be alarming talk of shortages. Shell Oil led the way, imposing drastic cuts on the delivery of gasoline to its retailers; Mobil, Citgo, the whole tribe fell into line behind the force play. Retail gasoline dealers roared their outrage; there was a nasty flareback of damaging publicity, and the big oil companies backed off for the moment, restoring deliveries to nearly normal.

Then, heaven sent, came the Iranian revolution, which closed down the oil fields. The myth of the "Iranian shortfall" was born. Actually, only 5 percent of our imported oil came from Iran, and this shortage was quickly offset by stepped-up production in Saudi Arabia, increased Alaskan supplies and lesser increases from other sources. C.I.A. figures show that free world production, expressed in thousands of barrels daily, rose to 46.515 in the first quarter of 1979 compared with 46.305 in 1978. Customs figures, as recorded by the Census Bureau, show that imports through May increased 10 percent over those for the first five weeks of 1978. Indeed, the imports for these first five months of 1979 almost matched the levels established in the glut year of 1977. The C.I.A. in-depth study echoed the Customs Service's findings. It showed imports in the first five months of 1979 outstripping those of 1978. During the first three months, imports averaged well over eight million barrels a day, and in April and May they were only slightly below that figure. By contrast, in 1978 imports reached the eight-million-barrel-a-day figure in only two of the first five months, and in the remaining months they trailed considerably behind the 1979 import figures.

The C.I.A. assessment revealed another curious fact. In this 1979 year of "crisis," American firms actually exported more oil in every one of the first five months than they had in either 1977 or 1978. Exports ranged from 329,000 barrels daily in January to 445,000 barrels daily in both April and May. Yet in lush 1977, exports had ranged from only 192,000 barrels daily to 288,000. The fact that we were actually exporting more oil in 1979 than we had in the two previous noncrisis years would seem to indicate manipulation of the market. This suspicion, shared by more than two-thirds of the American people, according to public opinion polls, is reinforced when one reads the Federal Trade Commission memo of May 30. Reporting on a study made by the commission's staff, the memo said: "The data indicates, among other things, that gasoline supplies in 1979 were up by 4–8 percent, depending on the time period, over 1978's. Net supply of gasoline in April was particularly plentiful compared to the previous April (up by 22.9 percent). Significantly, however, every time period—month, quarter, third—shows increased supplies and no indication of a shortage." Not only were supplies of gasoline more plentiful in 1979, but demand was down. According to figures from the Organization for Economic Cooperation and Development in Paris, U.S. oil consumption in the period from January to April 1979 was nearly 1 percent below the level of the same period in 1978.

Yet it was in late April and early May that the gasoline pumps in California suddenly went dry, beginning the drought that was to spread across the nation to New York, Washington, D.C., and cities in between. In a nation whose whole economy since World War II has been structured around networks of superhighways on which Federal and state governments have lavished billions of dollars, panic struck, accompanied by frustration and fury. The evidence establishes that none of this was necessary; it suggests that this was a "crisis" carefully orchestrated by Big Oil, aided and abetted by the complacent non-watchdog in the D.O.E. And even by President Carter himself—a President who has in his public pronouncements consistently followed the line set down by Big Oil.

Jack Anderson, the Washington columnist, has published excerpts from secret White House minutes indicating that President Carter deliberately cut back gasoline supplies to keep his pledge to other industrial nations that the United States would reduce oil consumption by 5 percent. At a May 7 meeting, just as motorists were queuing up for miles in California, Carter told his Cabinet: "Our priority will continue to be some heating, agriculture and emergency needs over highway driving. . . . There will be less gasoline, and it will cost more." . . .

Cost more! That is what this scenario is all about. The Carter Administration for months has backed every move that would make gasoline and other fuel products more costly, on the theory that higher prices would "force" conservation. For months, the Administration talked about $1-a-gallon gasoline. Privately, it was scripting an even more brutal program.

Jerry Ferrara, the outspoken executive director of the New Jersey Retail Gasoline Dealers Association, described in a television appearance on July 2 how he and his associates had "pounded on every door" in Washington seeking the adoption of a more sensible policy. He said he had met face to face with Dr. Schlesinger, and he added: "He [Schlesinger] said that if gasoline got up to $2 a gallon by 1981, the American people would have to conserve. And then he walked out of the room."

Virtually every tactic imaginable has been employed by the oil companies to generate the atmosphere of shortages and crisis that would open the floodgates of price. One of the most ingenious involved the stockpiling of crude and finished products on tankers dawdling at sea. Spokesmen for the maritime workers who man the tankers aver that big oil companies sent out word that their tankers were to steam at no more than 10 knots instead of the 16 to 17 they are capable of doing. "When tankers are reduced to 10 knots," one maritime spokesman says, "a voyage from Beaumont, Tex., to Boston that would usually take five days stretches out to nine. And when you have whole fleets of tankers out there, loaded with hundreds of thousands of gallons each, you are stockpiling a lot of stuff on the high seas." Not until the middle of June, another maritime spokesman says, did "one major oil company reverse its orders" and let its tankers steam at 16 to 17 knots.

The stall at sea has been matched by stalls in port. Turnaround time in port, which used to take from sixteen hours to one day, now frequently stretches to two or two and a half days. Sometimes refineries say they have no cargo ready to ship; at other times ships loaded with refined products come into port and find storage tanks so full that there is no way to unload. In one instance, a tanker loaded with regular and unleaded gas made the voyage from Beaumont to Florida, found no facility able to take its cargo—and went back to Beaumont with some 350,000 barrels of undelivered fuel. . . .

The stockpiling at sea and the delays in port are just a couple of the ploys that have helped to produce the oil panic of 1979. The oil industry, it would appear, had a couple of other even more important maneuvers up its sleeve. Justice Department antitrust lawyers have been trying to find out why it was that just at this time of supposed shortages, domestic crude oil production in the United States went into its steepest decline in seven years. In a preliminary and relatively unnoticed report, Justice Department attorneys concluded that, from December through April, the falloff in domestic drilling had cost the nation some eleven million barrels of gasoline. Since there are forty-two gallons to the barrel, that represents a lot of gasoline. This falloff in domestic production came at a time when oil company profits in the first quarter of 1979 were going through the roof. While the companies were demanding price decontrol as a prerequisite for increased domestic production, first quarter profits at Exxon were already up 37 percent; Gulf's were up 61 percent; and other majors like Standard Oil of Ohio were registering increases of more than 300 percent.

The drop in domestic drilling was accompanied by a second cutback, a reduction of refinery output. "That is where it all hangs out," one industry critic says. It does indeed. Refineries capable of operating at 91 to 92 percent of capacity (this is virtually full-out considering inevitable maintenance delays) dropped their runs in this season of our travail to a bare 84 percent. The American Petroleum Institute itself acknowledged that, in the second week of June, refineries were operating at only 84.1 percent of capacity. The following week, the runs were stepped up to 84.5 percent—still far below capacity at a time when, all reliable evidence shows, crude stocks were in plentiful supply, waiting to be processed.

The situation infuriated Representative Benjamin S. Rosenthal (D., N.Y.), chairman of the Subcommittee on Commerce, Consumer and Monetary Affairs of the powerful House Committee on Government Operations. It also upset Dr. Schlesinger, who confessed in June that he found the disparity between abundant crude oil stocks and low refinery runs "distressing" and "disturbing." He threatened action against oil companies that had poor refinery performance.

The sequel is perhaps best told in the words of Representative Rosenthal as recorded in the *Congressional Record* of June 29. The Congressman said:

> Following the hearing on June 14, Secretary of Energy Schlesinger admitted that we had more than adequate oil inventory stock and that he would undertake to use the Department of Energy's allocation authority to urge recalcitrant refiners in the direction of serving the consuming public. . . . On Thursday, June 24, Secretary Schlesinger reversed his stand, expressing fear that the U.S. multinational oil companies might retaliate by withholding oil from the United States. Thus, it becomes obvious that much of the blame for the current gasoline shortages must also be ascribed to deliberate actions by the oil companies and the Department of Energy. This "blackmail" threat by the U.S. multinational oil companies that ship crude oil to Europe instead of to the United States calls for a vigorous response by this Nation.

It would be difficult to find a clearer demonstration of the power of the oil forces that hold this nation in thrall, but what Representative Rosenthal called "this 'blackmail' threat" is not the only indication of the contempt in which Big Oil holds the Government and the people of the nation.

In November and December 1978, New Jersey's Commissioner of Energy, Joel R. Jacobson, conducted a series of hearings in which he tried to get the major oil companies to justify the prices they were charging for heating oil. The oil companies squirmed, dodged, protested they didn't have the information— and then defied him. "They say that's proprietary information to which we are not entitled," Jacobson said.

New York State's energy commissioner, James Larocca, ran into a similar stonewall, and now the oil companies are endeavoring to stonewall the Federal Government. Assistant Attorney General Barbara Allen Babcock described Big Oil's obstructionism to the Subcommittee on Energy and Power of the House of Representatives on June 29. Ms. Babcock explained that the Energy Information Administration of the D.O.E. had set up a Financial Reporting System in an effort to determine just what is happening and why. Congress had specifically authorized the E.I.A. to collect information from "major energy-producing companies" on company revenues, profits, cash flow, investments and other information, including "costs associated with exploration, development, production and other energy-related functions within each company."

The E.I.A., through its Financial Reporting System, finally drafted a fifty-page document which was sent to twenty-seven major energy-producing companies, directing them to file answers covering their 1977 operations by April 1, 1979. Instantly this information-collecting agency of D.O.E. ran into Big Oil's roadblock. Shell Oil went into Federal court in Delaware, seeking an injunction to keep the D.O.E. from doing what Congress had authorized it to do. Shell was joined in the action by Texaco, Phillips, Gulf, Mobil, Union, Continental and Coastal States Gas. There were two prongs to the companies' legal assault: first, they wanted the Federal court to issue an injunction preventing D.O.E. from collecting information; second, if D.O.E. should be permitted to collect data, the oil companies wanted them to be barred from disseminating it to anyone—to other Government agencies or even to Congress. "The plaintiff companies are particularly concerned that the Antitrust Division and the Federal Trade Commission be denied access to F.R.S. data because they believe it could lead to antitrust enforcement actions against them," Ms. Babcock testified.

A compromise of sorts was reached under which the oil companies agreed to fill out the D.O.E.'s questionnaires and D.O.E. agreed not to let any other agency see the information before August 1, when arguments for an injunction forbidding dissemination will be resumed in Federal court in Delaware. It would seem that an industry that has repeatedly avowed it has nothing to hide has gone to an irrational extreme to hide that "nothing."

The intransigence of Big Oil and its concern that its members might be hit with antitrust actions if the truth about its activities ever gets out are perfectly understandable to many average Americans whose pocketbooks have been riddled while oil company profits have escalated.

Fuel oil, first priced at 49.5 cents a gallon in late spring 1978, has jumped in a year to more than 70 cents, with the prospect that it will be priced at between 80 and 90 cents this coming winter. Regular gasoline, which as late as February was selling at 59.9 cents (only a few cents more than untaxed heating oil), now sells for from 89.9 to 91 cents. Unleaded and super-unleaded (the latter needed in many cars to avoid damaging knocks from low-octane unleaded) have zoomed in price at some stations to $1.45 or more.

This brutal escalation, which puts Dr. Schlesinger's $2 gasoline in our immediate future, has been achieved through the delightful collaboration between Dr. Schlesinger's D.O.E. and the oil industry. All during 1978, when the gas glut made it impossible to sell gasoline at ceiling prices, individual gas station owners were allowed to "bank" the differential on their records. Came 1979, the "shortage," zooming OPEC prices; and, with frustrated motorists on gas lines willing to pay anything, those deferred, spurious "banked" sums were tacked onto the already zooming prices. As usual, the consumer got zonked. The D.O.E. has now ended this banking system, but prices have already been driven to levels from which it is almost certain they will never come down. . . .

BIG OIL'S WASHINGTON SUBSIDIARY
(1979 and 1980)

Fred J. Cook

I

DESPITE JIMMY CARTER'S tough talk on the stump about a windfall profits tax, the American Petroleum Institute, the registered industry lobby for Big Oil, has infiltrated, and virtually runs, the Department of Energy. The pervasive influence of the oil industry on the department has two interrelated causes. High-level administrative positions are filled with corporate executive types, many of whom have direct ties to the oil industry; and the major work of the department is leased out, most of it through no-bid deals, to private consulting firms that, in turn, are consultants for the oil industry. This obvious conflict of interest, given the structure at the top, does not disturb the department, which has said time and again that it makes no effort to determine the private business ties of its hired advisers.

On April 29, 1977, the White House made public Carter's much-ballyhooed National Energy Plan, which Carter has upbraided Congress for not passing. Unmentioned at the time—and, indeed, virtually unrecognized until Daniel Guttman, a Washington lawyer and energy expert, called attention to it before a Senate subcommittee last October—was the fact that the basics of the plan were prepared by D.O.E. consultants who were also oil industry consultants.

A firm called Energy and Environmental Analysis received two contracts —one for $194,000, a second for $34,800—to work on the plan. Although the D.O.E. did not inquire into E.E.A.'s other associations, Guttman discovered by reading the firm's own brochures that its clients include Exxon, Shell Oil and Standard Oil of Ohio. A second consulting firm, Arthur D. Little, also worked on "the President's plan" and received $180,000 for its labors. The firm has worked for a number of coal producers and companies interested in nuclear and solar developments.

The inordinate amount of double-interest input into the President's National Energy Plan is just one example of the almost total penetration of the Energy Department by the oil interests. On November 15, the General Accounting Office issued a report bluntly stating that, in 1978, the department, which has 20,000 employees, spent 79 percent of its total budget, a whopping $8.5 billion, in 5,000 awards to private contractors who were to tell it what it was to do and how to do it. This was the worst record, the G.A.O. report said, compiled by any Federal agency. The G.A.O. report added:

> Each of the five organizations within the Department of Energy appears to be contracting with private firms to carry out some of its basic management functions. These contracts are written so that the contractors are required to perform activities such as program planning and development and establishing goals and priorities.

Some of these contracts also appear to provide contractors wide latitude for participation in the development of energy policy and offer the potential for allowing the
contractor to determine energy policy.

The footprints of the Rockefeller interests are all over this private-contract-
ing double-agent system that does so much to mold national energy policy. In
1974, the Federal Energy Administration, a predecessor of the D.O.E., entered
into a contract with a Parsippany, New Jersey, firm named R. Shriver Associates. The contract was issued at the insistence of David Rockefeller's Chase
Manhattan Bank. As the Department of Energy itself later explained: "Because
of their position in the banking world, Chase will only deal with the government
through a third party, and has so designated R. Shriver Associates."

The Shriver firm's task was to "prepare statistics of U.S. energy flows for
the International Energy Agency" and to monitor the agency's "policies and
procedures." In other words, it was given broad responsibility for compiling the
oil data on which national policy would be based. The Shriver relationship
continued into the Carter Administration. In 1977, it was hired to "document
the need for and the required characteristics of a National Gas Emergency
Management System." And when oil-industry divestiture was proposed by irate
Congressmen, the Shriver firm was given another contract to develop a "fact
sheet" for the use of the D.O.E.'s agencies.

This continued reliance on the consulting firm designated by Chase Manhattan had the effect of putting the department in the hands of the behemoths
of the oil industry. For as Guttman pointed out, previous Senate committee
findings showed that Chase board members included officers of Exxon and
Standard Oil of Ohio; that the Rockefeller family group, the largest single voting
interest in Chase, is among the top voting interests in Exxon, Mobil and Standard Oil of Indiana; and that Chase Manhattan itself is among the top voting
interests in Exxon, Mobil, Shell, SoCal, Standard of Indiana and Texaco. Quite
a package.

As a result of Chase's insistence on the employment of the Shriver firm,
one of its employees, a man named John Iannone, became an important figure
on the Washington energy scene. Although he was an outside consultant, Iannone was assigned office space at the Federal Energy Agency and became in
appearance, if not in actual fact, a member of the Government's energy establishment. His boss from April 1974 to July 1976 was Dr. Daniel B. Rathbun, who
was deputy assistant administrator for data. When Dr. Rathbun left Government employment to become a vice president of the American Petroleum Institute, Iannone followed him. Although Iannone had shed the Shriver mantle for
the cloak of the A.P.I., this did not alter his cozy relationship with his old
comrades in the D.O.E. He still had the run of the offices. Having once been
granted the cachet of a member of the establishment, he still carried a semi-
official aura about him, and had considerable influence with the Energy Department.

Senator Howard Metzenbaum first exposed Iannone's double-agent role
during hearings of the Senate Energy Committee in mid-1978. The testimony
showed that Iannone often was able to supply his A.P.I. superiors with D.O.E.
plans and papers before they became public. Such advance information, of
course, enabled the petroleum lobby to exert quiet pressure to get the rules

amended in the industry's interest before public-interest groups had any idea what was happening. Senator Metzenbaum charged that one change Iannone effected through his close ties with the D.O.E. raised the price of gasoline half a cent a gallon—and cost American consumers $600 million annually.

Iannone's most notable, though not most important, feat involved a letter that Senator Edward M. Kennedy had written to David J. Bardin, head of the Energy Department's Economic Regulatory Administration. Kennedy was inquiring about the allocation of oil to smaller refiners. Gerald Emmer, Bardin's assistant and one of Iannone's best contacts, gave the lobbyist a Xerox of Kennedy's letter; and investigation indicated that this copy wound up in A.P.I. files before Kennedy's original letter was delivered to Bardin. . . .

Disclosure of Iannone's years-long snooping led to demands for an investigation. Mark Green of Ralph Nader's Congress Watch obtained a copy of Iannone's own report to the petroleum institute, summarizing his successes in espionage and influence-wielding during the first three months of 1978. Green, Bardin and Representative John Dingell, chairman of the House Subcommittee on Energy and Power, all called on the D.O.E. to probe itself. The department's Inspector General undertook the task. A report of his investigation was issued April 23, 1979. Its first conclusion was that the American Petroleum Institute, as a result of Iannone's activities, "was able to obtain from D.O.E. staff copies of 23 draft rulemakings and internal D.O.E. memoranda and studies that had not been made formally available to the public in the latter half of 1977 and the first quarter of 1978."

Iannone himself had balked at testifying, and the American Petroleum Institute at first defied a subpoena to turn over its files. Iannone, by a series of legal actions, frustrated the Inspector General, but the institute finally agreed to make its documents available. These disclosed that it had set up a regular spy network, titled "Federal Agencies Department," and that three other agents—Henry Lum, Patricia Hammick and Susan Hodges—had cultivated contacts within the Department of Energy and flashed advance warnings. Iannone himself had supplied the petroleum institute with some 160 D.O.E. documents. The Inspector General concluded that Iannone, in his report to the A.P.I., had sometimes misrepresented or exaggerated his influence. Though this might be expected from an agent seeking to inflate his own importance, the investigation nevertheless substantiated Iannone's claim that he had modified a program of gasoline monitoring and decontrol known as Mogas so that it would yield larger profits for the oil industry. Iannone accomplished this by advocating that the base period for pricing be changed from November 1977 to June 1977. The theory was that, since gasoline prices are normally higher in summer, such a change would give the industry a higher base period with which to work. The D.O.E. Inspector General reported: "The documents received from API show that between August of 1977 and February of 1978, DOE did change the base month in its Mogas draft proposals from November to June." Iannone had claimed that he had been allowed to check the final Mogas rule making "for accuracy" before it was sent to the D.O.E.'s general counsel, and Bardin confirmed that he had ordered "the Mogas monitoring formula reviewed by API."

The snooping of Iannone and the subservience shown by the Energy Department to a lobby like the American Petroleum Institute in allowing it to "review" its regulations in advance could only take place in an agency riddled at the top by private interests. President Carter, the Trilateral Commission alumnus, has insisted from the moment he took office that fuel prices must go higher, ever and ever higher, and the high command of his Department of Energy has been loaded with corporate types whose thinking has been molded by their industry background. . . .

II

. . . The insatiable greed of the major oil companies—their determination to maximize profits at whatever cost to the American public—led them during the "gasoline crisis" of last summer to divert the oil they had bought under long-term contracts at the lowest prices from the American market to the sky-high spot market in Rotterdam.

Brian Ross, in a series on NBC's *Nightly News* in mid-October, backed mighty Exxon into a corner trying to explain the diversion of tankers from its Aruba refinery to Europe. First, Ed Hess, a vice president of Exxon, insisted such shipments were extremely "rare." He added that "for all intents and purposes in the recent past it [the oil shipments] all comes to the United States." Lloyd's of London told a different story. Its records showed that fifteen Exxon tankers left Aruba in the first part of this year, carrying more than three million barrels of various petroleum products to Europe. When Ross tried to question Hess about this discrepancy, Hess became suddenly unavailable. But A. K. Wolgast, manager of planning for Exxon International, pinch-hit and admitted the fifteen tanker shipments to Europe. Four tankerloads went to customers he refused to identify, apparently because they were spot-market shipments. Wolgast's rationale was that, since Exxon is an international company, it has customers in Europe, too, and it has to try to be "fair" to everybody.

Exxon was not alone in playing tunes on the spot market. *Energy User News* reported that Texaco had diverted 65,000 barrels a day from its Caribbean refineries to the spot market and that other Caribbean refineries—Bahamas Oil Refining Company, partly owned by Standard Oil of California, and Shell Curaçao NV—had played the same game.

All of this led Terence O'Rourke, energy adviser to President Carter's anti-inflation chief, Alfred Kahn, to prepare a devastating and exhaustively documented report on oil company machinations. Described as a confidential analysis for the White House, the report became public in late November. It accused "a handful" of major American companies of using their leverage on the world market to drive up prices. O'Rourke found, as had been charged, that U.S. companies diverted low-priced crude from the American to the spot market in Rotterdam. Then they cut off sales to smaller oil companies that traditionally had bought from them. This forced the smaller companies to pay spot-market prices, driving up those prices, driving up the price they had to charge on the American scene—and so building a higher price platform that would justify the majors in raising *their* prices, despite the fact that theirs was lower-priced crude.

It was a beautifully orchestrated merry-go-round—and the victims were the American people.

The effect, as O'Rourke correctly forecast, has been to lay the basis for further price rises. The ruthless manner in which major American companies manipulated the spot market did not go unnoticed in Saudi Arabia. The Saudis, the largest crude-oil suppliers and the most reasonable, had been selling their crude to the majors for considerably less than many other OPEC nations were charging. They had accused major American companies of just such an international spot-market rip-off before the last round of OPEC price increases, but no one had listened. The Saudis told Treasury Secretary G. William Miller that, unless Congress forced cutbacks in the huge oil company profits, OPEC would certainly try to get even. "They feel they've been taken advantage of by the oil companies," Miller said.

The Saudis followed up this warning by acting on their own even before OPEC leaders met in Venezuela on December 17, 1979. On December 13, Saudi Arabia, the United Arab Emirates, Qatar and Venezuela announced that they were raising oil prices $6 a barrel—a 33.3 percent increase for the Saudis, who furnish about 20 percent of our imported oil. This huge jump in crude-oil prices was expected to add at least 11 cents a gallon to gasoline and heating oil—that is, unless the Carter Administration takes some action to keep heating oil from tracking gasoline cent by cent. Then, on December 17—still before the OPEC oil ministers had begun their ultimately futile attempt to set a new benchmark price—several American majors seized upon the Saudi increases to jump up gas and heating-oil prices. Exxon and Chevron were the worst offenders, setting a 6-cent-a-gallon jump. Others raised prices 2 or 3 cents a gallon. All were reaping additional millions of dollars by charging higher prices on oil bought and refined months earlier at far cheaper rates. These increases are almost certain to be only a first step in what promises to be tremendous profits for the oil companies.

Meanwhile, landlords of 310,000 rent-controlled apartments in New York City were seeking $40-a-month rent hikes to cover the present jacked-up heating-oil prices. Through all of this, the American media continued to grumble about the "blackmail" being practiced by OPEC, while ignoring the clear evidence that OPEC's price piracy is the direct result of spot-market manipulations by the American majors and their oil cartel.

Those most cruelly victimized in this whole outrageous scam are American homeowners who heat with No. 2 fuel oil. Though gasoline had soared to an average of $1 or more a gallon before the latest price increase, heating oil, historically for a half-century one of the cheapest products of the refineries, has become almost as expensive. When, for example, I could buy Exxon regular gasoline for 95.1 cents a gallon, including 12 cents in state and Federal taxes, and I was paying 85.9 cents for heating oil that is untaxed in New Jersey, simple arithmetic tells me I was being robbed. . . .

The Dingell staff [of the House Subcommittee on Energy and Power, Rep. John D. Dingell, chairman] investigation gives the best insight into both parts of the problem. Having obtained the admission from the Department of Energy that it does not monitor prices but just trusts what the oil companies tell it because they are all honorable gentlemen together, the Dingell staff set out to discover how the home-heating oil prices are really set. After interviewing officials of major companies, the staff concluded: "Contrary to their recent testimony before Congressional committees, the major oil companies did no marginal cost analysis as the basis for their enormous price increases over the last year. Staff interviews of top officials of some of the major oil companies have revealed that most of the companies 'charge what the market will bear.' " ... The subcommittee memorandum added: "It is interesting to note, however, that what the major companies have done in most markets is to leapfrog each other on price, essentially ratcheting the price up, with each company following the market that has no relationship to cost increases."

This is the bleak and disgraceful record of what has happened since the Ford Administration, in its last bequest to Big Oil, decontrolled home-heating oil prices in June 1976. With the lid taken off, prices went from 19 cents a gallon then to today's "low price" of 88.9 cents. Yet, despite this graphic example of the rape of the American homeowner, all President Carter can do is call for more decontrol. He has already completely decontrolled "heavy oil," the especially gummy substance that can be brought up from the bottom of existing wells by the injection of steam. He has also signed a gradual decontrol order that will take the lid off all petroleum products by 1981. Had the president of Exxon himself sat in the White House, he couldn't have done much more for Big Oil.

It has been estimated that Jimmy Carter's full decontrol might add something like a trillion dollars to the revenues of the oil companies in the decade ahead. To make such a huge beneficence acceptable, Carter calls loudly for a "tough" windfall profits tax. The tax would smooth the way for everything, we are told. It would help pay some of the exorbitant home-heating costs of the poor, and it would provide the billions of dollars needed to find more oil and to develop synthetic fuels. . . .

Carter's rhetoric about a tough windfall tax blithely ignores what the Saudi Arabians know—that the *present* bloated oil company revenues are abundantly sufficient to finance oil explorations. The abysmal conduct of the oil industry in performing its function was spelled out in explicit detail by Daniel Guttman. . . . "Although it may surprise devotees of oil industry advertising," Guttman testified, "these corporations provide scandalously little support for R&D [research and development]. *Business Week*'s 1979 R&D survey, for example, shows that the oil industry continues to rest at the bottom of the industrial totem pole. In 1978, for example, the 'fuel' industry's (including Exxon, Gulf, Texaco, Shell, SoCal, Amoco and 14 other oil companies) R&D expenditures equaled 8.6 percent of profits. By comparison, the automotive industry spent 70.2 percent, the chemical industry spent 41.3 percent, the drug industry spent 48.4 percent, the 'electronics' industry spent 56.1 percent, and the leisure-time industry spent 48.1 percent. General Motors alone spent considerably more ($1.633 billion) than the twenty oil companies surveyed ($970 million). . . ."

MOBIL NEWS
THAT'S FIT TO PRINT (1979)

Robert Sherrill

ONE OF THE LONGEST-RUNNING propaganda acts in town belongs to
the Mobil Oil Corporation. . . .

Mobil spends more than $20 million a year through its propaganda office.
Most of this winds up paying for some of public television's cultural soap operas
and for idea ads (not product ads) strategically placed on the editorial pages of
the nation's major newspapers. The soap operas are the equivalent of an occupying army's distribution of candy and cigarettes. As Herman J. Schmidt, a top
Mobil official, once explained, "A reader sees a Mobil message, and associates
it with Big Oil. So he may be wary. But he also associates it with the company
that brings him *Upstairs, Downstairs,* so maybe he's a little more open-minded
and a little more receptive." Another Mobil P.R. official, Raymond D'Argenis,
was even more candid: "These programs," he said, "build enough acceptance
to allow us to get tough on substantive issues."

The public telly soap operas are for softening the general middle-class
populace, but the newspaper propaganda blitz is for conquering the so-called
opinion-shaping stratum. (Or so one is supposed to assume.) Planning of the
blitz began in 1969, after environmentalists and tax reformers had had an
especially good run of luck in arousing the public and Congress to consider
making Big Oil behave. That was the year, for example, that Congress reduced
the oil depletion allowance from 27 1/2 percent to 22 percent. It was also the
year of the spectacular Santa Barbara oil spill, after which Congress stiffened
the Outer Continental Shelf Lands Act of 1953 to make the oil companies liable
for cleaning up their messes.

While those pressures were building on the outside, internal corporate
changes that would make Mobil more willing to launch a counterattack were
also in motion. Rawleigh Warner, Jr., was elected chairman and chief executive
officer in 1969. Warner, a liberal Republican, . . . knew it was a waste of time
to continue buttering up conservatives, as the oil companies had always done.
After all, the conservatives were safely in pocket. He decided instead to subvert
the middle and the left with guile and lollipops. He chose as his emissary to "the
other side of the street," as he put it, a young Mobil labor relations lawyer by
the name of Herbert Schmertz, now a Mobil vice president. Schmertz's credentials were just the sort to give him safe-conduct into what Mobil would have
once called enemy territory. He had helped in John F. Kennedy's 1960 Presidential campaign, and he had been an advance man for Robert Kennedy's 1968
campaign (taking time off from Mobil to do it). Warner obviously does not
exaggerate when he says that one big reason Schmertz was promoted to become
Mobil's chief propagandist was his "ability to talk to the Democratic side of the
House and the Senate and to know some of those people—particularly some of

those people that we never, never would see before—the liberal element of the Democratic side."

Schmertz is usually credited with cooking up the newspaper ad crusade. But he admits it "was a confluence of people who came together on the idea. I'd say Rawleigh Warner, Bill Tavoulareas [Mobil president], myself, uh, couple of other people, perhaps, had the same feeling. I don't think any one person dragged anybody else. The top management here had the feeling that this is what they wanted to do."

But having decided that they wanted to spend millions propagandizing the American public in a new way, they could find no acceptable format. Just buying any old ad space wouldn't get the job done. They didn't want their stuff buried back among the truss ads and real estate blurbs. They wanted it framed and set apart and treated with journalistic reverence, and they wanted this to happen in the most prestigious newspapers.

And there was no way Mobil could make that scheme come true until, in 1970, *The New York Times* decided to open its Op-Ed (opposite-editorial) page to paid advertising. That was the hole through which Mobil launched its notorious propaganda blitz. Mark down October 19, 1970, as the date the *Times*'s editorial Maginot line fell forever to the corporate dollar. On that day Mobil's first Op-Ed "idea" ad appeared. Others would follow on an irregular basis through 1971, and beginning with January 13, 1972, a Mobil ad has appeared on the Op-Ed page every Thursday, in the lower right-hand corner of the page. Other corporations and organizations buy the same space from time to time—such as Johns-Manville, assuring the world that it is making asbestos fun to work with again; or the National Association of Railroads, telling us what a good job the trains are doing. But it is, despite such intruders, known as Mobil's corner. . . .

Coincidentally, the same ads that appear in the *Times* are also placed in other major newspapers. The *Boston Globe, The Wall Street Journal,* the *Washington Post,* the *Chicago Tribune* and the *Los Angeles Times* are the most important of these other outlets, but when an oil issue heats up in Congress, as the divestiture question did in 1976, Mobil will take out ads in more than 100 newspapers. None of these other appearances are nearly so important to Mobil's image, however, as the Op-Ed ads in the *Times.* . . .

Put in the crudest and most accurate way, as Michael Gerrard did for *Esquire* in a recent (excellent) survey of the Mobil propaganda machine, it comes down to this: "With sheer cash, Mobil has become a *Times* columnist." The nameless Mobil ad writer consumes, per appearance, more space than Reston or Wicker or Safire.

It's as though the *Times* were selling advertising space on the inside of its cranium. There is just so much skull and it can't be stretched. Similarly, the *Times* allots itself only so much space—two pages: the editorial and the Op-Ed pages—in which to express its opinions and to monitor the opinions of others. Any reduction in the control it maintains over those two pages is, practically speaking, a reduction in its self-allotted freedom of opinion. . . .

If it is baffling that a newspaper of the *Times*'s integrity sells a part of its skull like a billboard, it is doubly baffling when one considers the character of some of the corporations to which it sells the space. Mobil is very much to the point. Never mind the fact that Mobil has on occasion been accused by such organizations as the United Church of Christ of supporting the oppressive regimes of Rhodesia and South Africa; we'll pass over those escapades as mere matters of conscience. But Mobil has also, from time to time, been accused of criminal restraint of trade, of conspiring to raise prices by creating an artificial energy shortage, of conspiring with other large oil companies to monopolize the refining of petroleum products over the past generation. These accusations were based on the most painstakingly cautious and conservative Government investigations. Convictions, of course, have been another thing, American justice being rather reluctant to hurt the feelings of oil companies. Still, the accusations alone, not to mention the supporting evidence, are such that if Mobil were a man, his reputation would have been so damaged as to bar him from membership in some of the best clubs. One might think the *Times* would be more sensitive in choosing its editorial-page cronies. One might also think that by now the *Times* would be embarrassed sharing precious opinion pages with a corporation whose propaganda is so noticeably short on accuracy, candor or relevancy. In general, the Mobil ads fall into these categories:

Unintentional Comedy. In 1976, for example, the Senate was seriously considering legislation to break up the major oil companies' control of oil from well to refinery to retail pump. One of Mobil's ads attempted to show that the industry wasn't monopolized by seven or eight companies. Heck no, there were hundreds of oil companies competing like mad, said Mobil, and to prove the point, it filled the ad space with the names of many of them, under the heading "Meet some of our competitors."

It was a downright hilarious list of such "competitors" as By-Rite, E-Z-Serve, Gas Hut, Hy-Flash, Kickapoo, Miss Quick, Robin, Toot'N'Moo and Town Pump. "That's a lot of competition," wrote Mobil's ad man with a straight face. "So why is the Senate considering a bill to break up the oil industry? We'd suggest that you ask your Senator that one."

During the same period of panic over the divestiture legislation, Mobil worked up another ad quoting half a dozen allegedly objective experts on why divestiture would have all sorts of dire results. One they quoted was Prof. Neil H. Jacoby, a U.C.L.A. economist. The funny thing about using Jacoby as an "expert" forecaster is that Jacoby is the fellow who, only two years earlier, after OPEC had quadrupled its prices, came out with a book in which he predicted that OPEC "will cut the price of oil because it is in its economic interest to do so"—a happy eventuality that consumers are still awaiting.

Grotesque Distortions. For *The New York Times* of May 18, 1978, Mobil's clever ad man wrote: "When millions of Americans shivered during the harsh winter of 1977—many of them temporarily out of work because a natural gas shortage shut down their plants—some government officials pointed an accusing finger—at the petroleum industry, who else? The oil companies, it was suggested, were holding back production, waiting for prices to go up. And so the Interior Department ordered a comprehensive study.

"Well, the results of the investigation by the National Academy of Sciences have been announced by Interior Secretary Cecil D. Andrus. To the surprise of some in Washington but certainly not to ours, it 'found no evidence that there was any willfully withheld gas.' "

As an adequate summary of the quarrel, that does not even add up to a half-truth. The real sequence of events went like this: In an effort to blackmail the old Federal Power Commission into more and more price increases for natural gas, the industry began closing down wells in the early 1970s and crying "shortage." The F.P.C. staff found that 26 percent of offshore gas reserves committed to the interstate system in 1973 were not in production. Congressional investigations in 1975 found other evidence of industry blackmail of this sort. During the 1977–78 winter shortage, John F. O'Leary, the Deputy Secretary of Energy, said there was "no question" that some companies were withholding gas, awaiting higher prices.

Responding to these accusations, Andrus had ordered a study of the offshore natural gas situation almost as soon as he became Interior Secretary. The N.A.S. was asked to do the study. When it came out with its findings, they were not offered as final proof of anything. There were several reasons for this. In the first place, the study had concentrated on fields that had been long in production and were on the decline; the industry's newer, more promising fields were not investigated. Second, the fields that had been studied contained only 17 percent of the known offshore gas reserves, leaving the remaining 83 percent still in question. Secretary Andrus said the study did not settle the debate one way or another. You will, needless to say, find none of that in the Mobil Op-Ed ads. Nor will you find the Mobil ads mentioning one other significant part of the report, in which the science panel stated that the industry possessed woefully inaccurate records of its natural gas reserves.

Perhaps Mobil's greatest deception—it certainly is Mobil's most chronic deception—is its argument that the oil industry needs greater profits so that it can seek new sources of oil and gas and thereby guarantee that shortages will be avoided. Typical is the ad that appeared on February 19, 1976: "Without adequate profits, industry is hobbled in the search for new energy." Mobil pretends it is almost abusing its pocketbook to find more oil. In that same 1976 ad it claims that "for every dollar we earned in 1975, we spent nearly $2 in capital and exploration outlays."

A big spender for exploration? Not quite—or at least not by comparison. *Business Week* reported that in 1975 "Mobil's exploratory drilling in the U.S. was not only less than the others' [the other top-income majors] but also less venturesome. Though the company's total exploration and production expenditures were up 9.2 percent last year, most of the money was spent on production —exploration was actually down 17 percent. On average, reports *Oil and Gas Journal,* industry exploration budgets were up 19.1 percent. Mobil did not even rank in the top 10 when it came to wildcat wells, the biggest gambles of them all."

If Mobil wasn't using its enormous profits to look for more oil and gas, what was it using them for? Simple: it was investing heavily in diversification. In its *Times* ad of February 3, 1977, it boasted that "the right diet of investments . . . has filled us out. Made us a balanced, diversified energy company." That's a roundabout way of saying that Mobil has lost faith in the future of petroleum (not so dumb) and is moving closer to the lifeboats. Mobil has started spending its billions to make sure it will have a way to escape. It has bought Montgomery Ward. It has bought control of Container Corporation, the nation's leading maker of paperboard packaging. It has bought into the chemical industry so heavily—Mobil Chemical is the nation's largest manufacturer of disposable plastic products—that it grosses more than a billion dollars from that source each year. It has plunged heavily into real estate developments both in this country and abroad. More than 20 percent of Mobil's income is from nonoil industries—bought with excessive profits squeezed from an oil-consuming public led to believe the money would be spent on "exploration."

Although *Business Week* is certainly not a harsh critic of conglomerates, even it could not let this pass. "To the oil industry's critics," it wrote, "such diversification is self-indicting. Why, they ask, should the industry and its supporters continually call for higher prices and higher profits—supposedly to support greater efforts at finding oil and gas—when the companies are clearly spending more and more money in areas that have nothing to do with energy?"

Freedom. To read the Mobil ads, you would think that the corporation is the greatest champion of freedom since Patrick Henry. In 1974 Mobil wanted to run a bland commercial on all three television networks on the theme of offshore oil drilling. CBS and ABC turned Mobil down, fearing that they would have to supply equal time to opponents of offshore drilling. Thereupon Mobil used its Op-Ed ad space, on June 17, 1974, to argue that the networks' refusal was a violation of Mobil's free speech rights. With a roll of drums it concluded: "You know the principle at stake here. You've seen it in writing, more than once: 'Congress shall make no law . . . abridging the freedom of speech.' You've seen it in the First Amendment to the Constitution of the United States."

Mobil's ad claimed that the corporation only wanted to have a free and open discussion ("Any policy that restricts the flow of information or ideas is potentially harmful") and that it was dedicated to guaranteeing that the public heard both sides. But that didn't quite jibe with the *Times* ad itself. Here Mobil was giving its interpretation of what the First Amendment meant, but saying absolutely nothing about a prominent view opposed to that interpretation—namely that of the United States Supreme Court, which ruled the previous year that neither the Constitution nor Federal law requires broadcasters to sell commercial air time for statements on matters of public controversy. Significantly, the Court's foremost defender of free speech, Justice William O. Douglas, was counted in the 7-to-2 majority. Mobil chose to restrict the flow of that particular information.

The freedom Mobil promotes above all others is the freedom from Government regulation. . . . There is, of course, some irony in this. In the first place, the little old United States Government is too weak, incompetent and cowardly to regulate a corporation like Mobil, which has $32 billion annual sales, 200,000 employees and a handful of billion-dollar subsidiaries. What if the Government wanted to inspect Mobil's books to determine if it were obeying some required price guideline? Peter Behr of the *Baltimore Sun* put that question to Jack Meyer, assistant director of the Council on Wage and Price Stability for wage and price monitoring. Meyer is one of 135 employees in that agency. Said he: "If our job was to audit, the whole 135 of us could be sent to Mobil Oil and never be seen or heard from again."

The second irony arises from the fact that Government regulation made the major oil companies what they are today, filthy rich and apparently impregnable to competition. The Connally Hot Oil Act in the 1930s set up a Government mechanism by which the supply of oil would be restricted and its price artificially supported; cheap domestic oil was, in effect, outlawed. The Federal oil-import quota system established in the 1950s critically restricted the importation of foreign oil, which was then very cheap and would have been a blessing for the consumer. In a dozen other ways Government regulations have propped up, subsidized and shilled for the oil industry; yet the commonest theme in the Mobil Op-Ed ads is that "government intervention in the free-market mechanism for allocating economic resources is purely and simply counterproductive. The free market itself does it best." . . .

Has the high-priced "culture" and propaganda campaign resulted in more converts, more friends for Mobil? Not among the top bananas of Washington, it hasn't. President Carter told one consultant that of all the oil companies he has had to deal with, Mobil is the least responsive and the most irresponsible. . . .

Certainly Mobil has gained few friends among its corporate peers by pretending that support of a few soap operas and art shows has made it the greatest cultural patron of our era. For a corporation bringing in $32 billion a year, the $20 million in Mobil's arts and editorial budget is the exact equivalent of a gift of $20 from an individual earning $32,000 a year. Big deal. Mobil's generosity bubble was nicely punctured by Michael Gerrard, who reports that after "using known financial data to break the code to a survey by the Conference Board, I was astonished to learn that of the fifty companies that give away the most money, Mobil ranks *last* in gifts as a percent of pretax profits."

Is the Op-Ed propaganda persuasive with the public? It is highly unlikely that any reasonably intelligent person can fail to see through the patina of Mobil's enlightenment. . . . Mobil's ads preaching the doctrine of unlimited and unregulated economic growth as the best way of lifting up the poor ("To give everybody a share of the pie, the pie has to keep growing so it's big enough to go around") are poorly disguised arguments against conservation and environmental-protection laws.

If liberals can't see through Mobil's smarmy philosophy, *Fortune* magazine can. It observed: "The virtue Mobil perceives in being regarded as 'different' is that it can more readily sell its case to the traditional critics of the oil industry. When it gets down to fundamentals, however, Mobil has no message substantially different from that of the rest of the oil industry, or indeed from that of large corporate enterprise in general." . . .

But the question remains: Why does *The New York Times,* and why do the *Washington Post,* the *Los Angeles Times* and the other newspapers, allow their choicest spaces to be exploited for the sake of oil industry imagery? The publishers of those newspapers will tell you that it is for money, and they will rationalize their need for money in the most pathetic and the most pious fashion. An editor at the *Times* once asked publisher Arthur Sulzberger why they were selling the lower right-hand corner of the Op-Ed page to such questionable customers—in fact, why they were selling it at all. Sulzberger replied that the income from that corner paid for the rest of the page "where we can do what we want to do." I asked Edwin D. Gritz, who held several editorial-management positions with the *Washington Post* before becoming professor of journalism at American University, why the *Post* sold editorial page space to Mobil and his answer was much the same: "Look at it from the newspaperman's point of view, the publisher as well as the managing editor. If you're dedicated to a first-class paper you aren't going to louse up your Op-Ed page with a lot of ads. At the same time, you feel that you've got to pay for your groceries. And if you can sell discreetly an ad that does not either adulterate or minimize the editorial impact of those pages, do so, because that is a very valuable and high-priced space. You have to be realistic and realize that you can become a better newspaper if you have a better economic power base from which to fight your good fight."

The *Washington Post,* among the 500 largest corporations in America, with an income of $436,102,000 in 1977, can't afford to fight the good fight without selling a dozen inches or so of editorial space to Mobil each week? *The New York Times,* with an income of $509,520,000 in 1977, can't afford to pay for its own Op-Ed page? The Times-Mirror Company, with an income of more than $1 billion a year, must still pass the tin cup and share its premium space with Mobil?

No, that argument won't hold. There must be another reason. I think it is this: The real reason *The New York Times* willingly opens its precious Op-Ed page to Mobil gimmickry is that big corporations, whether they peddle oil or peddle papers, feel very comfortable with one another and see matters of protocol and decorum and business ethics pretty much the same way. . . .

Part IV
NUCLEAR POWER

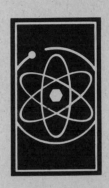

PREFACE

HIROSHIMA BROUGHT exhilaration and also some trepidation to the scientific community. Science had emerged from World War II as a basic national resource and scientists as men of influence if not power. If further military uses could be contained and an arms race forestalled, the atom would be a catalyst for world order. This was the hope and crusade of Leo Szilard and many of his colleagues. To some, the liberation of energy from the atom meant the ultimate liberation of mankind from scarcity. It might begin, physicist J.D. Bernal speculated, with some big projects in remote places "to tidy up the awkward parts of the world." But if a man-made world was to replace a natural one, then atomic energy and its necessary planning must be in public hands, reasoned mathematician Norbert Wiener.

Meanwhile, the postwar pressures mounted to weaken the wartime monopoly power of government which had developed atomic energy and let "free enterprise" produce electric power from this new source. To Leland Olds, former chairman of the Federal Power Commission, this move had to be exposed and resisted. It was part of a renewed drive by the utilities and their allies against the public power heritage. Their real intent was seen to constrain rather than develop new sources of energy.

McKinley Olson then takes us away from the early euphoria and plunges us squarely into the realities of nuclear power in Pennsylvania along the Susquehanna River, culminating in the accident at Three Mile Island in 1979. The remaining articles build the essential arguments for phasing out nuclear plants. They examine capital investment requirements and radioactive risks and the possible consequences for human liberty as well as life, given the conflicting role of the United States government as both promoter of nuclear power and protector of its citizenry.

"WE TURNED THE SWITCH" (1945)

Leo Szilard

ON MARCH 3, 1939, Dr. Walet Zinn and I, working on the seventh floor of the Pupin Building at Columbia University, completed a simple experiment to which we had been looking forward rather eagerly. Everything was ready, and all we had to do was to lean back, turn a switch, and watch the screen of a television tube. If flashes of light appeared on the screen, it would mean that neutrons were emitted in the fission of uranium, and that in turn would mean that the liberation of atomic energy was possible in our lifetime. We turned the switch, we saw the flashes, we watched them for about ten minutes—and then we switched everything off and went home. That night I knew that the world was headed for sorrow.

From March, 1939, until October of the same year work in the field of atomic energy was carried on by a handful of men who lacked many of the things they needed and most of all official recognition. From October, 1939, to the end of 1941 we still lacked many things, but we suffered from too much official recognition. Our increasing anxiety about what the Germans might be doing made our slow speed all the more intolerable. . . .

. . . Sometime during 1942 the army was brought into the picture, but the officers who were attached to us realized that they did not know what it was all about and did not make life difficult for us. Toward the end of 1942 and during the first half of 1943 all sorts of troubles developed, not all of them originating with the army. At that time it became evident to most of us that unless our organization could be changed quickly, we would have no bombs ready by the spring of 1944, when we expected the invasion of Europe to begin. We saw no way of bringing about a change without a major row, and we could not take the risk of losing thereby more time than we might gain. During 1943 and part of 1944 our greatest worry was the possibility that Germany would perfect an atomic bomb before the invasion of Europe. I myself was firmly convinced that the Germans were ahead of us in this work. Today I know that I was wrong and that when the war ended the Germans had not reached the point from which we started when our work began in earnest.

In 1945, when we ceased worrying about what the Germans might do to us, we began to worry about what the government of the United States might do to other countries. Discussion of the subject started in Chicago in March of this year. There were those among us who thought that we should not set the precedent of using atomic energy for the purposes of destruction. About sixty of us at Chicago took the view that Japan was essentially defeated and that it would be wrong to attack its cities with atomic bombs as if atomic bombs were simply another military weapon. Many atomic scientists at Oak Ridge took a similar view. The use of atomic bombs against Hiroshima and Nagasaki did not end but rather stimulated the discussion of this question.

For some four to six weeks after Hiroshima atomic scientists expressed no opinion on the political implications of the bomb, having been requested by the War Department to exercise the greatest possible reserve. Our response to this request does not mean that we were intimidated by the War Department. We kept silent because we all believed that Hiroshima was immediately followed by discussions between the United States, Great Britain, and Russia, as indeed it should have been, and we did not want to embarrass the President or the Secretary of State.

Then, early in October, in a visit to Washington, I happened to pick up a copy of the May-Johnson bill and brought it back with me to Chicago. We were somewhat alarmed when we read in the papers that hearings were held for one day before the House Military Affairs Committee and then closed down for good. Our alarm increased when on October 9 we discovered that the War Department's early requests to us to exercise discretion in our public utterances were not occasioned by any negotiations with other powers but by its desire to have the May-Johnson bill passed "without unnecessary discussions in Congress."

This caused the Atomic Scientists of Chicago to issue a manifesto calling for adequate hearings in Congress on the general issue involved before any bill on the domestic control of atomic energy should be passed. Our statement marked the beginning of the fight of the scientists against the May-Johnson bill. . . .

Feeling the need for a better understanding of what was happening in Washington, I went there and stayed six weeks. These are my conclusions: The most hopeful aspect of the situation in Washington is the fact that the problem of controlling atomic energy has so far not become a political problem, that is, the essential difference is not between Democrats and Republicans or between progressives and conservatives but rather between those who understand what atomic bombs may mean and those who do not understand it. The most important task would therefore seem to be somehow to impart to everyone a realization of the essentially non-terrestial nature of the atomic bomb.

I would like, therefore, to present tentatively the suggestion that the best way to put our foreign policy on a sound basis might consist in staging a demonstration of an atomic-bomb explosion for members of Congress, the President, and such other citizens as ought to witness it. Those of my friends who saw the tests in New Mexico on July 16 tell me how shaken they were by the experience. Most of them were ten miles or more away; if they had been nearer, the psychological effect would no doubt have been even greater. The risk which the statesmen would run individually by watching from a lesser distance appears to me small in comparison to the risk which we shall all incur collectively if we do not succeed in bringing home to them the non-terrestial nature of the phenomenon.

Naturally, I am not really worried about the future, except perhaps the next fifteen years. If we manage to get through the next fifteen years, alive, we shall probably emerge immune to atomic bombs. It seems to me that the greatest danger facing us at present is the possibility of a war which would arise more or less automatically out of an arms race in which the United States and Russia built up stockpiles of atomic bombs.

Is it possible to avert this danger? Let us assume that the United States and Russia agreed to have no stockpiles of atomic bombs and to permit no manufacture of atomic bombs on their territory. Let us, moreover, assume for the sake of argument that they both reserve the right to abrogate this arrangement at any time. Could Russia and the United States, under present-day conditions, make arrangements through which they could convince each other, as well as other nations, that secret violations of the agreement would be detected and would become known to the world? My answer to this question is emphatically Yes. Clearly the arrangements would have to include the right of inspection on the part of some international agency.

If Russia and the United States wanted to reassure each other concerning secret violations, they might go about it in the following way: After the agreement is ratified and becomes the law of the land, the President of the United States could call on all American engineers and scientists and ask them to pledge themselves to report to an international agency all violations committed on the territory of the United States. The Espionage Act would have to be modified so that it would no longer cover information of a scientific or technical nature, whether or not relating to national defense. All men classed as scientists or engineers would be invited to spend each year four weeks' vacation or six weeks' if you wish, abroad with their families as guests of the United Nations Organization. The Russian government would be expected to take similar action with respect to its own scientists and engineers.

No arrangement of this sort, of course, could rule out the possibility of war, and in case of war, sooner or later, atomic bombs would drop from the skies. Yet under such an arrangement war would break out only if one of the parties actually decided to start an arms race and risk a war. It would give us a respite which would be worth having, provided we know how to make use of it for building a permanent peace.

ATOMIC ISOLATIONISM (1945)

The Nation

THE DISCUSSION OF ATOMIC POWER has come down to earth. It is centered in the Johnson-May bill, which intrusts to the care of a nine-man commission the absolute control of the development of nuclear energy and related research activities. Since the commission would meet four times a year and be manned by dollar-a-year men, presumably with other business to attend to, the real authority is left in the hands of one full-time administrator. The possibilities of the abuse of this power are so great that Raymond Swing protested that "in the bill as now drawn control is vested in a way that might become a perfected fascist domination of our economic life. Certainly there is nothing in the bill to prevent it, there is everything to encourage it."

Just now the bill is being pushed with indecent haste through Senate and House. In the House Military Affairs Committee the hearings lasted only one day. With the exception of top administrators, not one of the important scientists who worked on the development of the bomb was called to testify. Apparently overawed by the War Department—which during a war gets into the habit of stepping out of the place assigned it in a free democracy—Representative May refused to reopen the hearings when urged to do so by Representative Helen Gahagan Douglas. But by the beginning of the week it was apparent that neither the general public nor the scientists were going to be stampeded into a decision that might determine the future destiny of our nation.

The Johnson-May bill sidesteps all the larger issues. There is no question of sharing the secret with others, of creating an international body to control the bomb, of consolidating a world organization to prevent a third world war, in which the bomb would be put to a fatal test. It discusses the issue of atomic power in such narrow terms of national security that we have very strong suspicions the bill came straight from the War Department to the desks of Senator Johnson and Representative May. For the War Department is apt to think in strategic categories that fail utterly to comprehend the world problem with which the achievement of nuclear fission has confronted us.

The argument behind the bill runs like this. The menace of atomic power is so great that its production must remain a closely guarded secret for as long as possible. The basic knowledge in the field of nuclear physics is of course widespread. But the specialized knowledge necessary to industrial production of bombs or power is still in our hands. It must remain there for as long as possible, and all research must be carefully controlled and directed so that when the secret is discovered by other nations we shall by that time be far ahead of them in perfecting the process, which now may be regarded as in a primitive state.

To this argument the plain man, with very little knowledge of nuclear physics but with a memory for events in the past year or two, asks how safe in fact shall he be against comparatively primitive missiles—say, bombs of the Hiroshima or Nagasaki variety—traveling at the speed of V-2's. For even primitive atomic bombs, it seems to him, can be classed as terminal weapons. It is here the military men are being either stupid or dishonest in speaking of counter-measures. It is perhaps for this reason that they are loath to have free testimony from the scientists who were responsible for the development of the bomb. Fortunately several groups of scientists have courageously spoken out, and it is vitally important that they and others be called to testify before the Committee on Military Affairs. The navy statement regarding countermeasures was at once challenged by the Atomic Scientists of Chicago. The main approach of the Johnson-May bill was called into question by a clear statement in favor of international control by Dr. Robert G. Wilson for the Association of Los Alamos Scientists. Dr. Wilson said:

> The fact that the atomic bomb represents such a concentrated form of destructive energy makes counter-measures against each of the large number of possible methods of delivery extremely difficult and uncertain. . . . One proposition is for this country to have more and bigger bombs than other countries. Merely having more bombs than other countries is not decisive if another country has enough bombs to demolish our cities and stores of weapons. The overwhelming advantage will lie with the aggressor, and our superiority might be lost in the first five minutes of a surprise attack.

The bill that is now being crowded through Congress with hysterical urgency provides a frail shield of national defense. Moreover, if the autocratic powers of the administrator are used as they may well be used, the free scientists of America are going to refuse to function within the strait-jacket into which they have been strapped. Most seriously of all, this measure, put forward as a domestic policy, actually represents the commitment of the United States to a particularly vicious form of isolationist foreign policy. We may pay lip service to the United Nations Organization, send our representatives to international conferences, but we hold in our own hand the power of life and death over the nations of the world. Such a policy would tend to emphasize rather than heal the rifts in international society today—particularly the rift between Russia and this country allied with Britain. The more firmly we insist upon unilateral control of the atomic bomb the more difficult it will be to persuade others that our faith in a world organization is genuine. . . .

EVERYBODY'S ATOM (1945)

J. D. Bernal

. . . THE PERFECTING OF THE ATOMIC BOMB is only the first impressive practical utilization of knowledge that appeared almost as startlingly as the bomb itself in the scientific world of fifty years ago. The discoveries of X-rays by Röntgen in 1895, followed by that of radio-activity by Becquerel, were totally unexpected; they broke up the complacent nineteenth-century, determinist, physical picture and started a major revolution in scientific thought. There followed the Rutherford theory of the atom with its heavy nucleus and attendant electron, which showed us a picture of matter very different from our old concrete imaginings; while the quantum theory of Planck and Bohr revealed modes of behavior of that matter even farther removed from common-sense experience. These ideas led to an almost unbroken sequence of discoveries—neutron, positron, meson—culminating just before the war with the splitting of the isotope of uranium which is the basis for the atomic bomb. The bomb itself is, therefore, the first large-scale, practical result of fifty years of intense, fundamental scientific activity.

What the effect of the use of atomic energy is likely to be on society, we can now only dimly see. Those who know most about it are prohibited by military secrecy from making any statement. I can write about it only because it is work in which I have at no time been involved. What is important now, however, is not an accurate presentation of the immediate, technical possibilities of the utilization of processes in atomic nuclei but rather an appreciation of the social effects which such utilization is bound to produce. The first obvious and incontestable fact is that we have here a concentration of energy of the order of a million times greater than any we have had before. That does not mean, of course, that we have as yet actually increased the available energy in this planet by any perceptible amount. The rarity of the original elements, the practical difficulties of extraction of the active isotopes, and the unavoidable inefficiency of the disintegration process may make the effective cost per energy unit for many years far greater than that of the more prosaic sources, coal and oil. We may feel reasonably sure, however, that the application of scientific analysis and practical ingenuity will overcome these difficulties in the course of a few years—if the effort which produced the atomic bomb is maintained at the same intensity.

Long before this time, however, there are obvious fields of utilization for costly but concentrated sources of energy. Such sources would obviously be at a premium in all remote parts of the world where the cost of transporting coal or oil is great and it is there that the use of atomic power will first be economic. It does not follow, however, that the best application of atomic energy is its transformation into mechanical power. Before this is achieved, we may be utilizing atomic energy for the production of extremely high temperatures and pressures: for a new metallurgy and ceramics, and in large-scale engineering as a super blasting agent. Already, in the availability of an enormous variety of radio-active elements in hitherto unthinkable quantities, we have means for the rapid increase of our chemical, biological, and medical knowledge.

Sooner or later, however, it will be possible to use atomic power economically to provide directly or indirectly for immediate human wants. In the crudest way, such energy could be used to pump water and make fertilizer, extending and intensifying agricultural exploitation. At the same time, by increasing the facility of transport, it can make agricultural products more rapidly available. This means, in effect, that the basic limitation of food supply, already being felt acutely in the world, can be removed. . . .

The development of the atomic bomb is a signal that another new frontier has opened, a frontier more illimitable than the physical frontier of mountain and prairie because it is not tied down to the geographical limitations of this globe but only to the capacities of human intelligence and human ability to cooperate. . . . With the unlimited possibilities of atomic energy, mutual suspicion and struggles for *lebensraum* can give way to a new, universal constructive effort full of excitement, uncertainty, hope, and promise. . . .

Perhaps as impressive as the atomic bomb itself is the feat of scientific organization and industrial production that made it possible in three years to go from what was a laboratory experiment involving hardly more than home-made apparatus and sub-microscopic quantities of substance, to a practical release of energy on a scale thousands of times greater than ever before achieved. Social discoveries are intrinsically more important than physical ones. A new way of doing things has an indefinite future not tied to any particular field of knowledge. The overriding need to avoid a fate similar to that we have inflicted on our enemy has shown what many scientists have long believed: that the potentials of modern science were not being realized for the simple reason that insufficient effort was being put into science. From now on this fact is as inescapable as the splitting of the atom itself. . . .

A mere increase of scientific activity, however, is not enough; it must be coordinated and directed to really worthy tasks. The objectives of science— "what needs to be done"—are set by the conditions of society. Sometimes perverse conditions, such as war, require superior methods of destruction, but normally the aim of science should be to enable individual men to realize their inherent possibilities, whether expressed in art, in science, or in simple human relations. The basic requirements of food, shelter, and work must first be met for the present population of the world and for its future increase. How such general directives can be translated into scientific research is a task for the scientists themselves. It needs to be organized—and organized on a world-wide basis. . . .

Even now we can see only a very small fraction of the possible applications of atomic energy. These applications must not be attacked in a haphazard way. Just as in war we had our priorities, so we must have them in peace. The jobs that atomic energy can do immediately are probably gigantic enterprises in remote places. Its use, therefore, must be concentrated where such action is likely to give the greatest human return, irrespective of national or individual interests. For example, even now the explosive force of the atom can be used to dig canals, to break open mountain chains, to melt ice barriers, and generally to tidy up the awkward parts of the world. . . .

TOO BIG FOR PRIVATE ENTERPRISE (1950)

Norbert Wiener

MODERN INDUSTRIAL LIFE depends on a continuous supply of power. At present rates of production, the oil furnished by our oil wells is expected to last a few centuries. Other sources of power, such as vegetation and water power, are certainly not adequate to provide for an indefinite future at our present rate of expenditure, and it appears that we have grossly overrated the possibility of using low-grade energy such as the tides.

The importance of atomic energy depends, then, on the time scale of which we are speaking. If we are speaking of decades, it is highly questionable whether we should gain anything from the exploitation of sources of atomic energy on a large scale. If we are talking of centuries, we must begin to think very seriously of the use of atomic energy; and if we are talking of millennia, there seems to be no hope for the continued existence of the human race on a civilized level without the efficient employment of atomic energy. If we can employ atomic energy at the full rate suggested by the conversion of matter into energy without any residual unused part, the now very questionable future of our human occupation of this world may well be a matter of many millions of years, and it becomes highly probable that the race's ultimate extinction will be the result of intrinsic biological factors rather than of scarcity.

Although atomic energy is plentiful when we obtain it, the investment in apparatus and materials necessary to bring us to the point of obtaining it is large. Cyclotrons do not come in pocket sizes, nor are they operated on household current. Thus we can see that the production of atomic energy cannot begin until we have at least moderately large-scale and expensive apparatus, and it must be production on a large scale indeed to be able to amortize the enormous preliminary expenses. We cannot escape the fact that atomic energy, if it is to pay off at all, is "big business." It is much too big business to be allowed to continue in the loose control of private hands. It is business of the order of magnitude of the state itself; and either the state must swallow it or it must swallow the state.

The form of the future exploitation of atomic energy begins to appear. It involves enormous generating plants, and it will not be cheap or even practicable unless we are prepared to make use of the overwhelming quantities of energy coming from these plants. This means that we shall be forced to provide for vast new uses of energy. Moreover, the energy which is produced will not be in suitable form for the propulsion of moderately sized vehicles or boats or implements. In order to convert it to these uses, we shall probably have to revise our entire concept of storage of energy, and either greatly perfect our existing storage batteries or manufacture synthetic fuels whose function it will be to act merely as safe and controllable carriers of energy. We shall then use the large new wells of power at our free disposition in order to revise our chemical and metallurgical industries from the ground up. It is highly possible, for example, that our now waning supply of metals will be augmented by the use of electrolytic processes so prodigal in energy and so dependent on low-grade ores that they are simply unthinkable at the present time. Again, we may hope for synthetic plastics which will make the maximum use of a number of cheap and plentiful materials, such as sand and limestone, together with some sort of carbon, and which will cut into many of the fields now domi...ated by wood and other cellulose products. They may even begin to compete much more seriously with the metals as materials of mechanical construction.

A large-scale use of energy is likely at some stage or other to change completely our system of agriculture. At present the engineer thinks of water as something which flows down hill into the ocean and thereby generates power. With large sources of atomic power available, the separation of sea water from its salt will be much more practicable than at present, and our rivers will be replaced by pipe channels in which the freshened sea water and such freshwater sources as are otherwise available will be pumped up hill; so that our agriculture will depend on universal irrigation. This will eliminate the large lacunae of practically unused country which still fill our maps and the eyes of travelers. This new country of the future which we will be forced to create by the logic of our new atomic and other inventions will be a man-made country, like Holland, and not a nature-made country, like the greater part of the United States and Russia at the present time.

The most completely man-made regions which we now know are the Dutch polders, reclaimed from the bottom of the Zuyder Zee. Recent magazine articles have made us familiar with the general economic patterns of the new Dutch lands. Land that comes easy may not seem to us to be subject to any great degree of material regulation, but land that is built from the bottom of the sea is no longer a raw material to be given to the first newcomer to exploit. Individualistic as the Dutch naturally are, they are not so individualistic that they are giving this rich polder land to any man in fee simple.

The land is rented and only to those superb farmers who are in a position to get the most out of it and at the same time conserve its value for future generations. When a country invests so large a part of its substance for the benefit of its ultimate future, it is not disposed to give up its rights in the future to the first passer-by. This is socialism, and it is a form of socialism which is inevitable when the very land that we live on and the very water that we drink are the product of the severe effort of the whole community.

Let it be noted that in the matter of tenure of land by fee simple, Los Alamos is on the same basis as the Dutch polders. No person is tolerated there if he has no function to fulfill, and there is no way in which one can buy one's way into the community permanently. On the other hand, the problem of personal freedom is probably more difficult, and less adequately adjusted, in these military camps than in the new lands of the Zuyder Zee.

The new centralized atmosphere of the age to come is likely to lead us in the direction of "big brotherism." This tendency must be countered by a continuous awareness of its dangerous possibilities. If we allow our politicians to identify "big brotherism" with a reasonable interest of the community in those things which the community has accomplished, we may be forced into fascism when the present laissez-faire methods have failed to outlive the age of oil and the age of coal. In the future we can no more conserve our liberties as squatters in areas of moral anarchy than we can be squatters on the highly developed land on which all of us will live. We shall enjoy our rights of freedom as explicit rights rather than merely as potential servitudes which no one has as yet taken the trouble to impose upon us.

BIG BUSINESS MOVES IN (1953)

Leland Olds

. . . THE ATOMIC ENERGY ACT, which became law in 1946, makes the Atomic Energy Commission responsible for the direction of the entire atomic-energy program. The commission owns the plants and raw materials; in fact, the government has the exclusive right to own not only fissionable material, that is, all material from which energy can be released by splitting atoms, but nuclear reactors, or plants for producing fissionable materials or atomic weapons. The act forbids the granting of private patents in certain parts of the atomic-energy field.

As the law stands today, new discoveries in the field of atomic development become public property. In a sense, then, atomic energy, as a vastly important new resource, is part of the public domain, like the public lands or the water power of streams, which are constitutionally under the jurisdiction of Congress. It represents a public investment some 400 times as great as the Louisiana Purchase. The vital question before the people today is how this new resource, with its tremendous possibilities for our civilization, can best be developed and utilized.

When Congress acted in 1946 to give the government a monopoly in the field, security reasons unquestionably carried great weight. So we find that the act itself contemplates a time when its terms will be reconsidered. In fact, Congress specifically directed the Atomic Energy Commission to advise the President and Congress when nuclear-power development had reached such a stage that supplemental legislation was necessary or desirable.

In December, 1952, as a basis for the coming review, the Joint Committee on Atomic Energy issued a document compiled by its staff containing some 400 pages of material culled from a wide range of addresses and reports. It includes no conclusions or recommendations, but material is summarized to suggest the current answers to such questions as: what is meant by atomic power? who is responsible for its development? why is there no atomic-power plant under construction today? who should own atomic-power plants and development facilities and why? how should atomic-power development be financed? what is the public interest in atomic-power development? what are its defense aspects? what is the effect of the patent situation on atomic-power development? what are the secrecy and safety problems? how might legislative changes affect atomic-power development? what is retarding it?

The Atomic Energy Commission is reported to be ready to recommend a revision of the law so as (1) to permit the licensing of American concerns to possess the quantities of uranium they would need to produce electric power; (2) to permit the licensing of such private firms to produce plutonium and other fissionable material as by-products in connection with their use of atomic energy to produce electric power; (3) to permit the government to make long-term contracts for the purchase of plutonium in order to assure private companies using uranium to make electric power a market for this by-product; and (4) to protect private patent rights of companies doing research and experimental work in developing electric power from the atom. The grave question that now arises is whether there is enough public understanding of the issues involved and of the significance of what is going forward to protect the public interest in this legislative proceeding. . . .

The gravity of the situation was emphasized by Oscar M. Ruebhausen, chairman of the New York Bar Association's committee on atomic energy, in an address to a meeting of the National Industrial Conference Board on atomic energy in industry in October, 1952. "There is today no substantial body of informed public opinion," he warned, "that can be drawn upon to formulate an atomic program for the future. There are, it is true, scattered throughout the country, both in government and out of it, groups of able men qualified to pass on atomic problems but *never in the history of our democracy have we been compelled to rely on so few to debate problems so vast.* There is a critical need for informed public thinking on these questions." (Italics mine.)

The critical need for informed public thinking is accentuated by the fact that a small group of very well-informed men, representing the private-power utilities and their industrial allies, knows exactly how it wants the Atomic Energy Act changed and is well organized to obtain these changes. Furthermore, it is mobilizing business behind its drive. One of the most articulate members of the group is Walker L. Cisler, president and general manager of the Detroit Edison Company, which together with the Dow Chemical Company has been working for some time under supervision of the Atomic Energy Commission on the generation of electricity with nuclear energy as fuel. Speaking at the American Management Association's recent conference, Mr. Cisler outlined his proposed amendments to the Atomic Energy Act. These would permit private enterprise (1) to build, own, and operate atomic-energy plants; (2) to use, sell, and distribute end-products, such as plutonium and radioactive isotopes, made in atomic-energy facilities; (3) to acquire, own, and dispose of source materials, such as uranium and thorium; (4) to obtain licenses from the Atomic Energy Commission, subject only to maintaining standards and conditions set up under the act; and (5) to obtain normal patent and trade-secret protection, subject only to full disclosure to the commission for its own use in protecting national security.

To get some idea of the significance of these proposals, we should look back six years to a day in July, 1947, when Mr. Cisler appeared in Washington before the House Interstate and Foreign Commerce Committee and asked virtual dismantlement of another important piece of federal legislation. At that time he wanted Congress to amend the Federal Power Act so that his company and a lot of other large power companies could engage in business across state lines without coming under Federal Power Commission regulation. He was, in effect, laying down the terms on which utilities were willing to give the people the advantages of modern power pooling, which he described as more economical use of power plants, greater reliability of service, and strengthening of the national security. The price the people must pay for these advantages was to grant the companies immunity from federal regulation.

So the amendments now proposed may be taken as the asking price of the private power industry for pushing work on the development of atomic power. If made the basis for changes in the law, they would have the effect of turning the atomic industry, lock, stock, and barrel, over to big business. Note particularly the narrow limitation proposed on the regulatory jurisdiction of the Atomic Energy Commission and the unlimited right to the monopoly privileges of patents.

During the past year, in increasing volume, the business chorus has been proclaiming this coming shift of atomic industry from government to private enterprise. A typical voice in the chorus is that of S. B. Roboff of Sylvania Electric Products. Addressing the National Industrial Conference Board's forum, Mr. Roboff forecast the day when so many privately owned reactors would be producing power, plutonium, and isotopes that it would be uneconomical for the government to build and operate reactors for the production, ultimately, of only one of these. He continued: "If to the general reactor program we added companies which are producing with private capital reactor materials, nuclear instruments, fuels, and other supplementary materials, the need for relying upon government sources for these materials would be removed and we would have, in effect, atomic energy on a private-enterprise basis."

Some three months later David E. Lilienthal, former chairman of the Tennessee Valley Authority and the Atomic Energy Commission, and now chairman of the Attapulgas Minerals and Chemicals Corporation, said . . . that "the production of fissionable material contributes a good place to start shifting atomic energy over to the competitive system by steps." After a transition period he foresaw the time when even the Atomic Energy Commission's famous Oak Ridge and Hanford plants could go out of public ownership. He summed up the attitude of business when he said that he did not want to see "our American competitive industrial system and our educational system as the first casualties of the atom."

Within the last few weeks the Atomic Industrial Forum, Inc., has made its bow. Walker L. Cisler, according to the *Electrical World,* is its "guiding spirit." This organization is designed to perform for the atomic-energy industry the same functions that the Edison Electric Institute performs for the electric-power industry. Clearly, a parallel organization to protect and promote the great consumer interest in atomic power is urgently called for.

But this is not the only evidence that the private-power monopoly is a jump ahead of consumers in the race to control atomic power. On April 11 the Atomic Energy Commission announced conclusion of an agreement under which two companies serving the utility industry will make a study aimed at industrial production of atomic power in the next few years. These companies are the Pioneer Service and Engineering Company, consultant to the electric utilities in all phases of the power business, and the Foster Wheeler Corporation of New

York, manufacturer of equipment for the power, oil-refining, and chemical industries. They are added to the four utility-industrial teams already at work. Under the agreement with the commission these companies, at their own expense, will make a one-year study to determine (1) the feasibility of their designing, building, and operating an atomic-power plant; (2) the economic and technical aspects of building such a plant in the next few years; and (3) whether the project will require any research and development beyond that already done by the government.

The two firms will also make recommendations to the Atomic Energy Commission on industry's role in undertaking and carrying out the power project. This will serve as the focus of industry's participation in the next stages of atomic-power development. But since the assignment involves matters of vital interest to the people, who have invested billions of dollars in the atomic program and are ultimate consumers of the power, the situation calls for a similar contract between the Atomic Energy Commission and an organization provided with sufficient funds to be able to represent all consumer groups in preparing the necessary studies, reports, and recommendations.

In this connection it should not be forgotten that publicly owned electric utilities in the United States, excluding those owned by the federal government, represent an investment of nearly two and a half billion dollars and supply some 3,700,000 customers with over forty billion kilowatt-hours per year. Including rural electric cooperatives, the people's investment in customer-owned power systems totals nearly five billion dollars and provides more than seven million customers with electric service. This great area of local autonomy in power supply cannot be overlooked in any move to revise national atomic-energy policy.

Last February the American Public Power Association, trade organization of the country's municipally owned electric systems, asked the Atomic Energy Commission for permission to participate in the atomic-power program on a basis of equality with privately owned systems. Subsequently . . . their Atomic Power Policy Committee, headed by Samuel B. Morris, general manager of the City of Los Angeles Department of Water and Power, clarified the association's position on the Atomic Energy Act in a letter to Chairman Dean of the commission. . . . The association considers the problem of government policy in the atomic-energy field "from the viewpoint of protecting the government's interest and of making available to the maximum number of people in the United States the benefits which may accrue from development of this new source of energy." To this end it endorses the provisions of the present Atomic Energy Act and urges that any amendments provide safeguards against monopolistic advantages for private groups.

The urgency of such organized effort to have the public represented in the forthcoming reappraisal of the law is apparent when *Barron's* weekly, authentic voice of Wall Street finance, headlines a front-page story in its March 2 issue: "Power for the Future: It Should Be Freed from the Legacy of the Past." The story deals with the announced intention of the Westinghouse Electric Corporation to build a multimillion-dollar atomic-energy equipment plant near Pittsburgh and with the company's statement that "this investment is an expression of our belief that private enterprise will become an increasingly important factor in the future development of nuclear energy."

Barron's hails this as representing "a new post-election high in corporate confidence in the free economy." The legacy from the past, from which the "power of the future" should be freed, is not the watering of capital stock or the manipulation of education and politics by the private-power industry, exposed by the Federal Trade Commission some twenty years ago. Rather, according to *Barron's,* it is "the old 'socializing' legislation looking toward extension of public power" and, more particularly, the so-called "preference clause," which is referred to as "probably the most arbitrary symbol of the clutch of the public-power philosophy upon the legislative mind." The "preference clause," granting public systems a prior claim on federal power, has been Congressional policy since the Reclamation Act of 1906. It appears in one form or another in the Federal Power Act, the Tennessee Valley Authority Act, the Bonneville Act, the Rural Electrification Act, and the Flood Control Act of 1944. It simply protects the people's own local electric systems in the right to obtain power from public resources, free from dependence on private monopoly as middleman.

Thus it becomes crystal clear that the alleged drive to eliminate federal monopoly and open the door to private monopoly in the development of atomic power is part of the larger private-power campaign against the federal power policy which has come down by unbroken evolution from the birth of the conservation movement in the days of President Theodore Roosevelt and his "great forester," Gifford Pinchot. It is a continuation of the battle that has been waged over the Tennessee Valley Authority, over legislative efforts to create Missouri and Columbia valley authorities, over appropriations for transmission lines to deliver government power to municipalities and rural electric cooperatives. It is perhaps a foretaste of a coming battle to save the great federal power developments from ex-President Hoover's proposed "going-out-of-business" sale. . . .

In the coming battle over the Atomic Energy Act we face the Muscle Shoals issue of the 1920's on a grander scale. In the Harding Administration they gave away Teapot Dome. But they never succeeded in giving away Muscle Shoals because Uncle George Norris, great Progressive Senator from Nebraska, stood in the way. The Muscle Shoals power plant in the Tennessee River, authorized for defense purposes during World War I, became the cornerstone of the Tennessee Valley Authority, which brought the country a new era of widespread use of electricity at low rates and influenced resources development in all parts of the world. . . . The private power industry does not intend to see atomic power, born of World War II, blossom into similar developments all over the United States.

But the power monopolies are not presenting the people with that clear-cut issue. They know that America is proud of the TVA and of what it has accomplished. In fact, only a few years ago they had Opinion Research, Inc., take a poll to find out whether their multimillion-dollar propaganda campaign against public power was successful. They were shocked to learn that 63 per cent of those polled favored the TVA. They found also that the same percentage thought it would be a good idea to have TVA's in other parts of the country. So the so-called Electric Companies' Advertising Program turned its guns on "creeping socialism."

The campaign against this bogyman reaches the people through every medium of advertising and public relations. It serves as groundwork for the campaign to turn over atomic energy to private companies. But here the propaganda is a baited hook. What private monopoly is offering the people is a quicker and cheaper voyage to the new promised land of atomic power. It charges that the present law means federal monopoly, that federal monopoly is holding back the development of commercially feasible atomic power and rendering the entire program more costly. It cites the automobile and television as examples of what can be accomplished by American ingenuity under the stimulus of the profit incentive and urges the virtual renunciation of the atom to "competitive private enterprise" as the key to progress.

Let us examine this line to see whether it does not reveal many of the characteristics of the proverbial goldbrick. The questions which we shall naturally want answered are: (1) Has development of the peaceful uses of atomic energy progressed at a reasonable rate under the existing Atomic Energy Act? (2) Does turning over the atomic business to private enterprise offer better prospects of progress? (3) Is there any reason why we should be rushed into making decisions which will profoundly affect our civilization for generations?

The simplest answer to the first question is that it is but a moment in man's technological history since the first atomic fire was lighted and controlled. In fact, it is only just over twenty years since the neutron, the bullet which splits the atom, was discovered and thirteen years since a start was made in using these bullets to produce atomic fission and chain reaction. Compared with the ages between the time when a mythical Prometheus brought man the gift of fire and the invention of the steam engine, the rate of atomic progress under government control has been phenomenal. In fact, had man waited for private enterprise to transform Einstein's great equation into useful atomic energy, a century would probably have been needed for the accomplishment of anything comparable to what has been done under government direction in the last decade. Remember that some fifty years elapsed between Faraday's discovery that rotating a wire loop through a magnetic field would produce electricity and the day when the first dynamo lighted an electric bulb.

Progress under the Atomic Energy Commission has by no means been limited to development of atomic weapons. Great forward steps have been taken in providing radioactive isotopes (particles) which are making revolutionary contributions in medicine, agriculture, and industry; the atomic-power program is well under way under the general direction of the Reactor Development Division set up by the commission in 1949.

Early in 1951 the A. E. C. announced that in cooperation with industrial concerns it was exploring the possibilities of their participation, on their own initiative and with their own resources, in developing the use of atomic energy for power purposes. A few months later it received four proposals from eight corporations working in pairs—the Monsanto Chemical Company and the Union Electric Company of Missouri, Detroit Edison and the Dow Chemical Company, Commonwealth Edison and the Public Service Company of Northern Illinois, and Pacific Gas and Electric and the Bechtel Corporation. (The Detroit Edison combination has since been joined by a number of other electric utilities.)

The Monsanto Chemical and Union Electric team came up with a proposal that the government build a pilot plant to produce power, with plutonium as a by-product; then private industry might build a full-scale plant at its own expense. Dow and Detroit Edison proposed a joint study to be followed by the building of a full-scale atomic-power plant without going through the pilot-plant stage. The Commonwealth Edison group proposed a public-private undertaking in which the government would build a reactor to produce power and plutonium, permitting private companies to build and own the generating equipment and sell electricity to the public.

Meanwhile Westinghouse and General Electric have been constructing reactor power plants for atomic-powered submarines. On March 31, the A. E. C. announced that the first of these experimental engines was in operation at its testing station in Arco, Idaho. These submarine plants may eventually produce power at somewhere between two and five cents per kilowatt-hour. This is high compared with five-to-eight-mill power in coal-fired steam electric stations, but a reactor power plant which Westinghouse is designing for a larger naval vessel will more nearly approximate the size of a utility steam plant and costs should come down.

Walter H. Zinn of the Argonne National Laboratory (A. E. C.) predicts that the country will have a central-station nuclear-fueled power plant operating four or five years after "we have definitely decided to construct and operate such a plant." He is already running an experimental "breeder reactor" which is providing enough power to light the small building in which it is housed. This is probably the world's first atomic-powered plant.

The latest authoritative word comes from Dr. W. L. Davidson, director of the commission's Office of Industrial Development. He says: "Nuclear electric power is already a fact, not mere fancy. In two separate reactor projects the A. E. C. has generated token amounts of electricity employing nuclear fuel as a source of heat."

Dr. Davidson points out, however, that the prime purpose behind these experimental reactors was something other than power, and that while there had been considerable research and development work on the general problem, no construction of major projects for the production of economic electric power had yet been authorized. He estimates that the cost of power from such a plant, if approved, would be about double the kilowatt-hour costs of power from conventional fuel plants, or about fifteen mills. He predicts that at least ten years will elapse before nuclear power will be generally competitive with power generated from coal, oil, or gas.

The time required for successful results is variously predicted as from three to ten years. Altogether, the conclusion seems warranted that pressure to amend the Atomic Energy Act is due to the fact that commercially feasible atomic power is so close to realization rather than to lack of progress under the Atomic Energy Commission.

This brings us to the second question: whether we can expect greater progress if development of atomic power is turned over to private enterprise. Here we are concerned with something very different from the development of an industry based on the invention of some new gadget or synthetic material. We are dealing with a great new energy resource that is vital to our whole way of life.

Samuel B. Morris, general manager of the Los Angeles Department of Water and Power and former dean of engineering at Stanford University, has given a simple answer to the contention that opening up atomic-power development to private enterprise would let in the fresh air of competition. Presenting the report of the Committee on Atomic Policy of the American Public Power Association, Mr. Morris said that the electric-utility industry is essentially a monopoly and not a field of dynamic private, competitive enterprise. To open the field of atomic power to private patents would, in effect, pile monopoly on monopoly. Citing the country's telephone colossus to illustrate his point, he suggested that the increasing rapidity of modern invention, by opening the way to a chain of patents, would foster a continuing monopoly in the vital field of atomic power. He stressed the fact that patents are not always a stimulus to production.

The energy-resources field offers many examples of the tendency to hold back rather than expedite development of competing products. In two cases the situation is strikingly parallel to the proposed use of atomic energy as a new industrial fuel—namely, the synthetic production of motor fuel and gas from coal and the extraction of oil from our vast shale deposits. In terms of both conservation and national security, bringing both processes to the point of commercial feasibility is probably as important as the application of atomic energy to production of electric power. But both products would be competitive with what the big oil companies have to sell, and private enterprise has shown no zest for their development.

The story of halting progress in the synthetic production of motor fuel and gas from coal is particularly revealing. Started years ago by the Bureau of Mines in cooperation with the University of Utah School of Mines, the undertaking was subsequently moved to Pittsburgh and finally wound up during the 1940's in the hands of Standard Oil of New Jersey and its close relative, Pittsburgh Consolidation Coal Company. To date these corporations have given no evidence of competitive drive to bring to fruition this contribution to our energy-resources economy. Meanwhile the Bureau of Mines has been making considerable progress in producing gasoline and diesel fuel from coal at its recently completed demonstration plant at Louisiana, Missouri. But as the "Bituminous Coal Annual" tersely puts it, the urging of the Bureau of Mines that private industry "proceed immediately on a large-scale basis with establishment of a synthetic-fuels industry . . . provoked a stiff debate with the National Petroleum Council on the economics of making oil from coal." And, significantly, the item for continuation of the bureau's work in this field has so far been cut from the 1954 federal budget.

Similarly, although the Bureau of Mines pilot plant at Rifle, Colorado, has brought the cost of producing gasoline from oil shales to within two cents of that for the regular petroleum product, there has been no rush on the part of private enterprise to take over and push the process to the point of commercial use. Yet in neither of these fields are there any of the legislative obstacles to a complete taking over by private enterprise that are criticized as holding back progress in development of atomic power. Moreover, the synthetic production of oil and gas is probably of more immediate public interest than the production of electricity by atomic energy. . . .

Furthermore, natural-gas markets in the Northeast are crying for more gas from the Southwest faster than the big pipe lines can expand their deliveries, and field prices, which a few years ago were around four and five cents per thousand cubic feet, are upward bound, with fifteen cents predicted within a year and twenty to twenty-five cents expected four years hence. These are prices at the beginning of the thousand-mile journey to the Northeast, with many costs still to be added before the consumer pays his bill. Testimony in the Federal Power Commission's natural-gas investigation suggests that perfection of the synthesis of gas from Appalachian coal would provide the Northeast with ample supplies at a price lower than future prices of Southwestern gas. But such development appears unlikely to be carried to the point of economic feasibility so long as the great oil companies have natural gas from their Southwestern reserves to unload at unregulated prices. . . . Altogether, experience suggests that private industry may well be more interested in delaying than in expediting the application of atomic energy to the field of power.

So we come to the final question: whether there is any urgent public need for a hasty decision on the atomic-energy issue. The answer seems to be that there is no hurry at all. All the agitation has been stirred up by a well-directed drive to get us to sell our atomic birthright for a mess of pottage for which we are not yet really hungry. It is more important for the country to be in control of atomic power when it finally arrives than to advance the date of arrival a few years by abdicating to private monopoly, assuming these to be the real alternatives.

Atomic power offers no quick road to lower electric rates. All present conceptions of what is practical would only substitute splitting atoms for burning coal, oil, or natural gas as the source of heat for standard steam-power plants. Spectacular reductions in cost of fuel would be counterbalanced by the necessity for increased investment in facilities for developing the heat and conveying it to the generator.

Professor Manson Benedict of the Massachusetts Institute of Technology, analyzing the possibilities of an atomic power plant in Boston, shows that if nuclear fuel were obtained at no cost at all, the allowable power-plant investment could not exceed $258 per kilowatt of capacity to be competitive with plants using conventional fuels. He compares this with the estimate of Dr. Donald Loughbridge, assistant director of the A. E. C.'s division of reactor development, that the cost of a nuclear plant, using present-day techniques, would be something like $500 or $600 per installed kilowatt, and concludes that "before nuclear fuels could compete with coal in Boston, it will be necessary to develop a successful breeding reactor and cut the cost of a nuclear power plant in half." A breeding reactor comes pretty close to perpetual motion in that it produces more nuclear fuel than it consumes in the process of producing heat, thus providing a much higher utilization of the uranium charge.

An unusually farsighted power company executive, Philip Sporn, president of American Gas and Electric Company, says that the chief thing hoped for from atomic power is that it will lower the cost of fuel in power production. But he hastens to add that the most optimistic assumption would be a reduction of perhaps 10 per cent in this part of the total cost of electricity. As the fuel cost of power in Boston is only about one-third of a cent, a 10 per cent saving would be negligible so far as the average consumer of electricity is concerned. Mr. Sporn considers atomic energy chiefly important as a supplement to coal in meeting the rapidly increasing demands for power. He calls attention to the estimate of the President's Materials Policy Commission that the country's electric-energy requirements will increase from just under 400,000,000 kilowatt-hours in 1950 to 1,400,000,000 kilowatt-hours in 1975, with coal's responsibility going up from about 90,000,000 to 300,000,000 tons.

There is, however, every indication that these requirements can be met without turning to a supplementary fuel. Although coal provides the country with an extraordinarily wide range of services, latest reports show that its market is actually falling off, that mechanization is counterbalancing increasing wages in maintaining relatively stable prices, and that the industry is today producing far less than its capacity. . . .

So we are driven to the conclusions (1) that great progress has been made in the peace-time uses of atomic fission under the present law; (2) that leadership in the development of synthetic energy resources has not come from the competitive urge of private enterprise but from the work of a federal agency; and (3) that there is no urgent reason why we should be rushed into a decision to revise the present set-up before we have developed public understanding of the wide range of contributions atomic energy may make to the future of our economy. . . .

THE HOT RIVER VALLEY (1974)

McKinley C. Olson

LIGHTNING FLASHED. The emergency warning system went off and a siren began to wail. One of the foremen yelled to his men, "Get the hell out of here." Workers on the night shift ran for their cars and trucks and pulled away from the construction site, racing at crazy speeds over the one-lane bridges and down the back-country roads.

This was in July 1971, about 7:00 in the evening in rural Pennsylvania. No one thought to alert the people who lived in the area. Farmers, their wives and children, watched bug-eyed from their porches as the vehicles flashed by.

It turned out to be a false alarm, touched off when lightning struck a power line, but the people around here will never forget that night. They live next door to the Peach Bottom nuclear power complex. In 1971 there was one atomic plant here; today there are three. Tomorrow there might be two more. And two more after that.

There have been other nervous moments. A year after that thunderstorm, toward the end of July, people in the neighboring county across the river from Peach Bottom were startled by the sound of a loud "woosh" in the night. One woman told the press it sounded like "the world's largest teakettle was leaving off steam." The power failed; frightened, people left their homes and made their way to phones to call the plant across the river. The atomic workers told the callers they had heard no noise, but the "wooshing" persisted for well over an hour. A few days later, the plant reported that lightning had struck again, hitting a transformer line and shutting down a large generator, which in turn gave off steam that made the sound.

Again, nothing of fatal consequence. But the people wonder if the plant was being evasive that night, even though they were told that residents on the plant side of the river, for some reason, didn't hear the "frightening noise."

These are samplings of the stories that are told along a secluded 26-mile stretch of the Susquehanna River in the southeast corner of Pennsylvania, 35 miles north of Baltimore, which could become the largest concentrated source of nuclear power in the world.

Philadelphia Electric Company has applied for a permit to build two more nuclear reactors across the river from the three existing reactors at its Peach Bottom complex, the newest two of which are among the largest in the world. The two proposed reactor stations would compare in size and output to these giants. And the utility already talks of building two additional atomic power plants a relatively short distance downstream from these.

The electricity generated by these nuclear plants is to serve the Philadelphia area, 65 miles to the north. That is a bone of contention for the residents of York and Lancaster counties, which face each other across the Susquehanna and share this nuclear development. They sense that they are being required to assume all the risks of nuclear power while being denied any of the benefits. Quite a few people here who derisively refer to York and Lancaster as The Nuclear Capital of the World, feel that they are already living with more than their fair share of nuclear power plants; they strongly oppose any more such neighbors. There is also a core of angry, outspoken activists who are against nuclear power plants in any contemporary form, shape, size or number.

Together, the merely uneasy and the bitterly opposed have joined forces in a local coalition to pit their meager resources against the nuclear establishment. These contestants, the sponsors of nuclear power and those who oppose it, are participating in what could well be a historic contest. . . .

I became actively interested in nuclear power in 1959 when, as a reporter and photographer for the York (Pa.) *Gazette and Daily,* I was assigned to cover the development of the first Peach Bottom plant. That was two years after the nation's first atomic plant had gone on line. Nuclear fission was already being hailed by its boosters as our coming energy source. By 1972, after years of funding and research, only thirty nuclear plants were operating in the country, producing only about 1 per cent of the power. This year, forty plants will deliver 4 per cent of the power. But this picture could change rapidly. Today, according to AEC figures forty-four plants are licensed to operate, fifty-four are being built and orders have been placed for another 109. By the year 2000, if current plans hold, more than 1,000 nuclear fission plants may be producing 30 to 60 per cent of the nation's energy.

Here at the start of my discussion it is important to differentiate between uranium or plutonium fission and nuclear *fusion*—still in embryo—which would combine hydrogen atoms from ordinary sea water at extremely high temperatures to produce unlimited energy in a controlled reaction. Nuclear fusion is considered safe by opponents of nuclear fission, who contend that a fusion reactor could not "run away" because it would not accumulate the dangerous radioactive wastes that characterize the fission process. The critics of nuclear power are speaking of power from fission. They contend that available sources of conventional power give us enough time to turn our backs on the atomic plants of today and the immediate tomorrow, and concentrate on developing other potential sources of power. Proponents of fission cite the alleged energy crisis as the prime reason why we must redouble our reliance on that approach to nuclear power.

Despite such fundamental disagreements, all reputable parties in the debate accept several basic premises. First, that a major fission power plant accident would be catastrophic in terms of death, disease and damage to property. Next, that the radioactive materials employed in the fission process are deadly. Plutonium-239, the most dangerous substance ever handled by man, is one of the by-products of today's reactors and will probably be the principal fuel of tomorrow's. A spoonful of plutonium dioxide particles, if dispersed in the air, is enough to kill millions of people. It also remains active for a long time, and must be contained with no leakage for thousands of years. Thus, even a short-term commitment to fission power means that we would saddle generations to come with its dangers.

The advocates of nuclear power along the Susquehanna are much the same as those elsewhere. They include the utilities that have invested in nuclear power or will do so; giant outfits such as Bechtel, Westinghouse, Gulf Atomic and General Electric which build the plants and supply the nuclear hardware; the Congressional Joint Committee on Atomic Energy and the ubiquitous Atomic Energy Commission (AEC), which has the conflicting roles of promoting the development of nuclear power and protecting the public from its hazards.

These groups form the nation's multibillion-dollar nuclear establishment. They employ a substantial number of people—the AEC alone has some 7,000 workers, a great many of whom have invested most if not the whole of long professional careers in the service of nuclear power. Thousands of well-salaried jobs and the comfort and welfare of many families depend today on the nuclear industry. In York and Lancaster counties, the most prominent targets of anti-nuclear attack are the Philadelphia Electric Company and the AEC.

The local foes of nuclear power include two small environmental groups (the one in York has some twenty-five members; its neighbor in Lancaster has around 100) and the Peach Bottom and Fulton Township government units which lie on either side of the river just above the Maryland line. Two other Pennsylvania environmental groups, larger and with more muscle, but with diversified interests, support the local protesters. All these in turn draw help and moral support from small but tenacious national environmental and scientific groups such as the Union of Concerned Scientists and the Committee for Nuclear Responsibility, both of which have membership lists bearing distinguished names.

The anti-nuclear people also have friends in the nation's capital, and the number there has been growing of late. Sen. Mike Gravel (D., Alas.) and Ralph Nader have been among the most outspoken critics of nuclear power in the capital. Back in Pennsylvania, former State Insurance Commissioner Herbert S. Denenberg, the consumer-orientated gadfly, entered the fray last summer with the pronouncement that "this is the most important issue ever to face the American public," and the cry that "it may be that nobody but God could write the insurance policy we need on nuclear plants." In addition, the city of Baltimore—which draws drinking water for some 2 million people from the Susquehanna River 9 miles below the Philadelphia Electric nuclear complex—the state of Maryland and the Chesapeake Bay Foundation (an environmental group) are all taking an active interest in the developments upstream.

The five nuclear plants in York County are on the west side of the river. Two are in the northern end, across the river and 5 miles south of Harrisburg, the state capital. The other three are bunched together in a nuclear power complex 26 miles downstream at Peach Bottom. Philadelphia Electric, which owns controlling interest in the three-plant complex, and operates it, has asked the AEC for a construction permit to build two more giant reactor plants—at a cost of $1.5 billion—in Lancaster County's Fulton Township, on a site directly across the river from the Peach Bottom complex. And Philadelphia Electric has notified authorities in Maryland that it thinks of building yet another pair of nuclear stations on the river in Cecil County, just below the state line.

The AEC controls the major checkpoints in the development of an atomic plant—issuing the original construction permit and later an operating permit (the AEC's final stamp of approval). The agency holds public hearings before awarding these permits. One recent study called these hearings "charades" because the AEC's "common set of interests" with the utilities and reactor manufacturers almost assures that citizen opposition to a nuclear plant will be defeated. Moreover, according to Steven Ebbin, director of the Environmental Policy Study Group at George Washington University, and Raphael Kasper, a nuclear engineer with the National Science Foundation, the issues are argued in technical and legalistic language that excludes the layman.

But the basic shortcoming of the AEC plant hearings is that they do not provide a forum for debating the issue of nuclear power as such. At most, they permit the AEC examiners to make sure the utility has lived up to the specifications established by the commission. Citizens concerned about the cumulative effects of low-level radiation discharges, the unsolved problems of storing radioactive waste for thousands of years, the danger of nuclear sabotage, theft or blackmail, are likely to derive little satisfaction from local AEC hearings, where the questions they want to raise are often dismissed as irrelevant to the purpose of that meeting.

In York, the anti-nuclear environmental group and its attorney have been trying, unsuccessfully, to keep Peach Bottom Units Two and Three—the two big new reactors—from operating. Petitions have also been filed by the York group and the Peach Bottom Township supervisors, opposing Philadelphia's application for a permit to build the two additional Fulton stations, which the environmental group and government bodies in Lancaster also oppose.

Philadelphia Electric wants to build these plants in Fulton Township because it already has rights-of-way and power lines there. Also, these large nuclear plants use a lot of water—Peach Bottom Units Two and Three will each take and discharge a billion gallons a day—and the Susquehanna, a mile and a half wide here, is one of the largest rivers east of the Mississippi. Furthermore, the site is only 65 miles from the utility's 1.2 million customers. And only 7,000 people live within a 5-mile radius of the nuclear complex at Peach Bottom, which accords with the AEC's policy of keeping atomic plants away from urban centers. Peach Bottom, however, is small rather than remote. It is less than 60 air miles from Washington, D.C., and about 30 per cent of the nation's 200 million people live within a 250-mile radius of this nuclear complex; 5 million of them within a 50-mile radius.

Upstream, near Harrisburg, Metropolitan Edison Company heads the consortium that is building two nuclear plants at Three Mile Island at a cost of $1 billion. Met Ed's first reactor, an 871-megawatt unit, was supposed to go on line this year, but there have been many delays. The second Met Ed unit, a 905-megawatt reactor, was scheduled to begin generating commercial power in 1976. The AEC says both plants are about 60 per cent completed.

Most of the local controversy is focused downstream, at Peach Bottom and Fulton. When I was last there, the only unit in operation was a small experimental, 40-megawatt high-temperature gas-cooled reactor, the one I began reporting on in 1959. It began to generate commercially in 1967 and has been running off and on ever since. Philadelphia Electric reports that it has been a successful prototype, but plans to retire the unit within a few years, since its output is too small to be commercially worthwhile. Its immediate neighbors dwarf their dome-shaped senior. These new twin, 1,065-megawatt General Electric boiling water reactors are as big as they come today. An AEC Peach Bottom report notes that "this total industrial complex . . . has . . . considerable visual impact . . . on the surrounding rural scene." The new reactors, turbines and generators are housed in smooth rectangular buildings. Freight cars standing next to the buildings seem borrowed from a child's toy railroad.

Thus far, Philadelphia Electric and the other utilities associated in the Peach Bottom project have spent about $750 million on the new plants. The final cost could be more than a billion dollars. Unit Two was supposed to go on line last year but has been plagued by generator and turbine trouble. It finally began generating this July. It is also possible that the utility may have to recool completely all the water it draws from the Susquehanna before returning it to the river. An initial AEC licensing board decision is asking for closed-circuit cooling for Peach Bottom Units Two and Three by January 1977. A final AEC ruling in favor of total cooling, to protect the ecology of the Susquehanna, would force Philadelphia Electric to close down its new reactors and, at the very least, build two additional cooling towers alongside the four already provided for partial cooling. Shutting down the plants and building the two towers would cost a minimum of $112 million, according to Philadelphia Electric.

Because of the AEC's current demand for closed-circuit cooling, Philadelphia Electric has incorporated this system into the design of the proposed Fulton reactor plants, which would feature two 1,160-megawatt high-temperature gas-cooled reactors—enormously larger versions of the prototype at Peach Bottom. Closed-circuit cooling, while it protects fish and other forms of marine life from the harmful effects of hot water, evaporates tremendous quantities of water, and that in turn could upset delicate ecological balances even in a body of water as large as Chesapeake Bay. Forty per cent of the bay's fresh-water input comes from the Susquehanna. The proposed Fulton reactors would evaporate some 28 million gallons of water a day. This loss and the evaporation from the five other nuclear plants on the river would approximate one-third of the Susquehanna's low water flow. A sharp reduction in the amount of fresh water emptying into the bay could ruin commercial fishing. Oysters, for one, thrive on the blend of fresh water and salt. Philadelphia Electric rather blithely brushes off this concern about the future of Chesapeake Bay, contending that if unexpected problems do arise, they can be handled without much trouble. The environmentalists and the anti-nuclear people are afraid that if the utility is found to be wrong it might be too late to repair the damage. This difference of opinion is typical of the nuclear controversy. The AEC and the nuclear industry display almost boundless confidence in their ability to solve all problems and contain all hazards should they arise. The anti-nuclear critics contend that the dangers inherent in the nuclear fission process are beyond the present ability of the engineers to contain. In the words of Dr. Henry W. Kendall, a high-energy physicist at M.I.T. and a leading spokesman for the Union of Concerned Scientists, the critics believe that the nuclear proponents should be required to "prove safety beyond all reasonable doubt, rather than for their opponents to prove the contrary." Legislation and suits calling for moratoriums on the operation, construction and export of nuclear-fission power plants until the safety issues have been resolved in the public interest have been introduced and filed by—among others—Ralph Nader, Sen. Mike Gravel and Friends of the Earth, an environmental group.

The pro-nuclear establishment, while conceding that there are grave dangers in the fission power cycle, argues that the ability of atomic power to provide our economy and way of life with the energy it needs to survive and prosper far outweigh the potential hazards. They also contend that it is efficient, clean and relatively cheap, once the heavy construction costs are absorbed. They cite the fact that reactors have been operated for the past seventeen years without a major mishap. Director-General Sigvard Elklund of the International Atomic Energy Agency, who says he "can't see how mankind can survive without more energy," which "nuclear power . . . only . . . [can provide] for the next ten years," contends that these seventeen years without a serious accident are the equivalent of more than 1,000 years of cumulative nuclear reactor experience. The atomic power advocates are fond of noting that fossil fuels are exhaustible, and contend that mining and burning coal, which they consider the only feasible alternative to nuclear power, are processes too damaging to the environment to be continued. Spokesmen for fission are quick to dismiss alternative sources of power such as solar and geothermal energy, which are free of the risks associated with atomic energy, on the grounds that they are impractical, prohibitively expensive, or beyond immediate reach. All these premises lead the pro-nuclear people to conclude that fission power is the only realistic means to bridge the immediate short-term energy gap and meet the increasing demands for power in the future. . . .

In its pristine form, the anti-nuclear objection is that fission power demands human and technical infallibility, not just for today and tomorrow but for thousands of years. Dr. Alvin Weinberg, former director of the AEC's Oak Ridge National Laboratory, admits that "once man has opted for nuclear power, he has committed himself to essentially perpetual surveillance of the apparatus of nuclear power."

Although most nuclear critics believe that it is impossible to build a "safe" nuclear power plant, they contend that even if it were, the whole nuclear cycle —power plants, fuel reprocessing centers, transportation, waste-storage facilities—is extremely vulnerable to the threat of accident, war, nuclear blackmail, sabotage and theft. Newspaper headlines and the everyday stuff of the six o'clock news testify to turbulent times. Russell W. Peterson, the former governor of Delaware and chairman of the President's Council on Environmental Quality, said recently that we should move our atomic plants out to sea, that being the only way he could imagine to guard them and population centers from "the potential of sabotage" in an age of growing terrorism.

The critics also believe that radioactive releases from normally functioning nuclear plants are much greater than the AEC and the nuclear industry admit; and that even the most minute emissions of radioactive materials, which all nuclear plants release, will in time increase the number of cancer, leukemia and heart disease victims by the thousands if not millions. The anti-nuclear crowd also contends that, some time, some place, a major reactor accident is bound to occur, and that when it does, enough radioactive poison will be released to kill and cripple many thousands of people, devastate cities and lay waste thousands of square miles of countryside. And, finally, that if we were to abandon atomic fission power and put all the time and research and development funds that it now commands into the development of other sources of energy, we could rather quickly provide society with safe alternatives.

Raymond L. Hovis . . . is an attorney in York who has been representing the York opponents of the Peach Bottom reactors, members of the York Committee for a Safe Environment, which is supported by the Central Pennsylvania Committee on Nuclear Power, and the Committee for Responsible Energy Sources of Philadelphia. A former member of the Pennsylvania House [and] a liberal Democrat . . . Hovis is determined to proceed cautiously and keep an open mind.

"I'm not totally opposed to atomic power," he said . . . , "but I'm afraid we're going to become a receptacle of nuclear power plants, now that they're talking about nine potential reactors within a 50-mile radius of the city of York (the county seat), if you include the two below the Maryland line in Cecil County." Within nine years, Hovis notes, Pennsylvania is supposed to have fourteen nuclear power plants in operation, most of them along the lower Susquehanna River. Only Illinois, slated for fifteen, would have more. "And no one has ever been asked to license five reactors 2 miles apart," Hovis said, referring to Philadelphia Electric's request to build the two Fulton plants in Lancaster County across the river from Peach Bottom. "As far as Peach Bottom goes, the only thing we can fight for now when it comes to the AEC and Philadelphia Electric is to try to force them to make the plants as safe as they can be under the circumstances."

Hovis said he was unsuccessful last summer when he appeared before a hearing of the AEC Safety and Licensing Board in York to protest the issuance of an operating permit for the new Peach Bottom plants. He tried to argue that atomic plants were proliferating in the York area at an alarming rate; that the AEC had refused to consider the cumulative effects of low-level radiation from the three Peach Bottom plants; that the agency had ignored the risks involved in transporting radioactive fuel and waste materials to and from the nuclear complex; and that the AEC had failed to compel Philadelphia Electric to produce a workable emergency evacuation plan in the event of a nuclear accident.

"The licensing board dismissed all these objections as irrelevant," Hovis said, and granted a conditional operating permit. He has appealed the decision to an AEC appeals board, and is prepared to take his case to court if the board rules against him.

Hovis shook his head ruefully as he thought of the time and work it takes to ready a case for the AEC. Pointing to a row of thick volumes pertaining to Peach Bottom alone, he said, "I had to go through 6 to 8 feet of reading material which the AEC handed me just to get started. I have at least $12,000 down in my time book, and I'm not finished yet." He knows that the chance of getting paid for his work, especially in full, is slight, but he has no intention of dropping the case. "I find it fascinating and very educational, in every way," Hovis said. Another anti-nuclear critic in York put it this way: "The problem is so immense that you go from anti-trust laws to windmills and hit everything in between."

All the winding paths of inquiry lead back to a beginning: How dangerous is nuclear power? And how much trust can we place in the hands of its champions?

From the very first, in the immediate postwar era, such people as Albert Einstein and David E. Lilienthal, the former head of the AEC, questioned the safety of atomic power. And, in 1946, an AEC safeguards panel told Lewis Strauss, then chairman of the AEC, that "the committee believes there is insufficient information available at this time to give assurance that the . . . reactor can be operated at this site without public hazard."

The reactor in question was the Fermi fast-breeder plant (a breeder reactor produces more fissionable fuel than it consumes) on Lake Erie not far from Detroit and Toledo. The critics charge that Strauss suppressed the go-slow recommendation, and a few months later the AEC allowed Fermi to build. Protests were lodged and the case went to the Supreme Court which decided for the AEC. The Fermi plant was built but its performance was marked by accidents and long breakdowns and it has since been shut down for good. The Fermi controversy aroused suspicions about atomic safety and the credibility of the AEC which persist to this day.

The next milestone in the nuclear power controversy came in 1953 when President Eisenhower unveiled his Atoms for Peace Program, implemented a year later by an amendment to the original Atomic Energy Act of 1946, an amendment which in essence invited private industry to share in the economic rewards of atomic power, which has been developed with public funds and workers. The 1954 amendment also made the AEC responsible both for promoting the development of nuclear power and protecting the public from it.

The private sector hesitated; it thought nuclear power would be too expensive to produce and sell. And nuclear power plant safety was an unknown factor: insurance companies were refusing to write policies.

The AEC's reply was a veiled warning that if industry refused to go nuclear, the government might set up its own atomic utility. Then the threat was sweetened: government subsidies would be available; the taxpayers would build demonstration reactors, and fuel would be supplied at attractive prices. The AEC also thought of a way to get around the insurance hurdle. The Brookhaven Laboratories were commissioned to delve into the hypothetical consequences of a nuclear plant accident. Its findings were presented to Congress in 1957 and they were staggering. A small runaway or exploding reactor could kill 3,400 people within 15 miles of the site; 43,000 people within a 45-mile radius could be injured. Property damage could reach the $7 billion mark, and radioactivity could contaminate an area the size of Maryland. Private insurance companies were unwilling to assume risks of this magnitude. But Congress, more daring, passed the Price-Anderson Act, a law which limited total liability in the event of a nuclear accident to $560 million, of which a utility would be liable for only $60 million. Taxpayers' money would cover the rest.

The critics were quick to point out that the gap between $7 billion in potential damages and $560 million in coverage meant that victims of such an accident might collect 8¢ on the dollar. But the American Nuclear Society hailed the measure as a "real vote of confidence" in atomic power, since even the limited risk that the insurance industry was willing to assume was the "greatest commitment they have ever made for a single hazard."

The AEC felt the Brookhaven report had served its purpose—to demonstrate that the government would have to underwrite the major portion of the nuclear insurance policy—and proposed that it be shelved and forgotten. But it continues to pop up at every debate on the basic premises of nuclear power. To compound the controversy surrounding the Price-Anderson Act, the AEC had its 1957 Brookhaven report updated in 1965. Using the larger reactors that had been developed since the first report, the second Brookhaven findings were indeed awesome: 45,000 deaths, 100,000 injuries, $18 billion to $280 billion in property damage, with fallout from this theoretical accident—equivalent to the release from several thousand Hiroshima-sized bombs—blanketing an area the size of Pennsylvania.

The AEC managed to keep this report secret until 1973, when Friends of the Earth got wind of it and filed a freedom-of-information suit. Reluctantly, the AEC made the report public.

That created another tempest. The findings were terrifying; even worse, the AEC had tried to conceal them. The commission replied that the Brookhaven reports of 1957 and 1965 were based on the "worst" that could happen, and the agency now awaits a new report from a study group headed by Dr. Norman Rasmussen, a nuclear physicist at M.I.T., which is avoiding the "worst case" approach and concentrating instead on the probability of a nuclear accident occurring and the likely consequences if one does. One finding which the Rasmussen report is supposed to make public is the prediction that the chance of an accident occurring for every 100 reactors is one in 10,000 per year or, one in a million a year for a community near any given atomic plant.

Ann Roosevelt, the legislative director and an energy specialist for Friends of the Earth, considers the forced disclosures of the 1965 report a major achievement. "The Price-Anderson Act was up in 1967," she told me in her Washington, D.C., office. "Hearings to renew the law were starting in 1965, the year the second Brookhaven report was completed. The utilities took one look at it and were horrified. They persuaded the AEC that its disclosure would cripple, perhaps even kill, the nuclear power business. So the AEC buried it, and kept it hidden, until we dug it up." Noting that Price-Anderson will be up for renewal again in 1977, Ms. Roosevelt said her group is preparing a determined challenge to the Act. The House has already voted for a ten-year extension. The matter is expected to come up soon in the Senate.

Some nuclear critics feel that even the catastrophic predictions of the Brookhaven reports understate the possible results of a major reactor accident. Dr. John W. Gofman claims that a runaway reactor could kill 5 million people and injure as many more. Gofman, a physician with a Ph.D. in nuclear-physical chemistry, does research work and teaches on the West Coast. He is the co-author with biophysicist Dr. Arthur R. Tamplin of the anti-nuclear book *Poisoned Power.*

Dr. Gofman is a spokesman for the Committee for Nuclear Responsibility, whose board includes the Nobel Laureates Linus Pauling, chemistry; Harold Urey, chemistry; James D. Watson, biology; George Wald, chemistry; as well as David R. Inglis, a nuclear physicist who was a member of the team that developed the first atom bomb, and the former senior physicist at the AEC's Argonne National Laboratory in Illinois, and Paul R. Ehrlich, the biologist from Stanford. Nevertheless, the champions of atomic power dismiss Dr. Gofman as a crank. The critics charge that the AEC's suppression of the updated Brookhaven report is a good example of why the agency cannot be trusted.

Another fear is that the AEC, in the manner of government regulatory agencies, may be identifying more with the industry it is supposed to supervise than with the public it is supposed to serve. Some people also feel the AEC has fallen prey to conceit. Ray Hovis, the York lawyer, put it this way: "People who work for the AEC and the utilities are the victims of their backgrounds. They've been working with nuclear power for so long, and have so much of their lives invested in it, that they have been sold on their own promotion. Nuclear power has been in existence for only thirty years, and these people . . . feel they know a hell of a lot more about it than anyone else."

Raymond Powell, a nuclear core physicist and the AEC licensing project manager for the Peach Bottom reactors, has spent his entire career in the atomic power field—a background "that is common for 75 per cent of the senior AEC people." Before joining the AEC, Powell worked in the private sector for AMF's Atomic Division in York.

Most of the people I've met in the nuclear establishment seem dedicated, capable and professional. Powell, whom I met with at AEC headquarters in Bethesda, Md., is that kind of man. He . . . has a deep faith in atomic power —seeming closer to certainty than mere confidence—that is characteristic of the nuclear industry. "This is the most regulated industry in the nation," Powell said. "If everyone met the kind of standards we impose, you'd hear no more about consumer complaints.

"We're very strict and rigid when it comes to basic specifications. And the whole nuclear process is one of continuous review—to upgrade all phases in the field as we go along. We have an environmental monitoring program. We're very conservative. You have to be," Powell insisted, "when you're talking about public safety." He pointed out that AEC staff recommendations at Peach Bottom "could cost Philadelphia Electric $2 million to $3 million if they have to shut down" to reduce the radioactive emissions from the new plants and build more cooling towers.

Powell readily conceded that "a lack of coolant is the most crucial point" of concern at a nuclear power plant, but insisted that every imaginable safeguard is employed to guard against it. He also said that radioactive emissions at Peach Bottom would be "as low *as practical,* using the current state of the art." (Emphasis added.) This would be only a fraction of the amount of natural background radiation in the area, Powell said, explaining that the AEC monitors radioactive discharges "at a point where the [smoke] stack ends, where it leaves the plant, where the plant loses control." This means that each plant is monitored individually. (Soil and milk tests are made to measure cumulative effects.) The anti-nuclear forces in York call this a meaningless standard, saying that the total amount of radioactivity released by all three nuclear plants at Peach Bottom is the relevant index. I tried to pin Powell down on this. He smiled politely, shrugged his shoulders, but declined to tell me what he thought would be the most valid yardstick. I later read an AEC instruction sheet which cautions its employees "never to disagree with established policy" at AEC safety policy hearings.

This attitude prompts people like Hovis to complain that "the whole trouble with the AEC—and the utilities—is that they say 'we'll meet whatever regulations exist.' But the AEC establishes the regulations. And you can't pin them down. It's like wrestling with an octopus waving arms of rules and regulations all around and in and out. When we talk about low-level radiation discharges, they tell us the emissions fall below the federal threshold for each plant. But this ignores the accumulated or total amount of radiation at Peach Bottom. It also ducks the validity of these federal standards. Whenever we raise the issue of future problems, we're assured that when the time comes they'll be taken care of. But what do you do, for instance, with a 'hot' nuclear plant? They're licensed for forty years. We've been told they'll get 'leaky' by then. They've never decommissioned a hot nuclear plant—and there's going to be hundreds of them around if this keeps up." Hovis showed me a thick AEC booklet on Peach Bottom which proposed an estimated $100 million figure to decontaminate completely a 1,100-megawatt nuclear plant.

Chauncey R. Kepford of York, who has a Ph.D. in chemistry, is one of the most active members of the local anti-nuclear group. He has channeled all his time and energy into his fight against nuclear fission, creating a whole new life style for himself in the process. He is very critical of the AEC public hearings: "We're strapped to the AEC's quasi-legal format, which means we can't stop these plants because the AEC in general is in the crazy position of being advocates of nuclear power, who assume it will be the normal means of power generation in the future. At most, all these guys are interested in is getting what they call 'proper technical regulation.' "

Kepford . . . moved to York several years ago to teach chemistry at the local Penn State extension campus. Before that he had worked as a radiation research chemist for a New England laboratory. While he was still teaching, Kepford came across a story in one of the local newspapers reporting that Met Ed Company had applied for a U.S. Corps of Army Engineers' permit to dump 50,000 picocuries of tritium (radioactive hydrogen) per liter of water into the Susquehanna River from the Three Mile Island atomic plants. Kepford thought this excessive, and he publicly questioned the Corps of Engineers and the utility about the proposed discharge. The amount was lowered from 50,000 to 500 picocuries. Curious, Kepford decided to look into the nuclear power issue.

"I started off by reading popular paperbacks on nuclear power," Kepford said. "But I was still kinda casual about it. Being a reference freak, I started checking up on the AEC and all the other government stuff. And what I found just blew my mind."

Kepford evolved into a full-time opponent of nuclear power. . . . [He] claims pressure from the nuclear establishment was applied to have him fired from Penn State. Protesting his dismissal, Kepford hired a lawyer, and a settlement was reached out of court. He said he has "enough money to keep going" while he pursues his fight against nuclear fission power. . . .

"The only real hope at Peach Bottom," Kepford contends, "is the courts. If the AEC appeals board turns us down, the next step is the Circuit Court of Appeals." He thinks the anti-nuclear position will receive a fair hearing in court. Justice William O. Douglas and the late Hugo Black, in their dissenting opinion in the Fermi atomic plant case, called the AEC's attitude "a light-hearted approach to the most awesome, the most deadly, the most dangerous process that man has ever conceived."

Dr. Gofman, discussing the AEC public hearing process, charges that "concerned citizens have been led, like lambs to the slaughter, into the promoters' arena. . . . But [this] is no technical controversy that can be resolved by a debate on the merits of specific gadgets in the nuclear power industry. What is really at issue is a moral question—the right of one generation of humans to take upon itself the arrogance of possibly compromising the earth as a habitable place for this and essentially all future generations."

I've attended AEC hearings. The utilities' representatives and the government people sit apart, but even so, I think it is difficult for a layman to distinguish between them—they all seem to be on the same pro-nuclear team. But those who work in the industry do not feel that way. I went to Philadelphia to talk to the key personnel in Philadelphia Electric Company's nuclear division. Jack L. Allen, a likable witty man, is the chief assistant mechanical engineer. He told me about Philadelphia Electric's four-year attempt to obtain an AEC construction permit for its proposed Limerick nuclear plant on the Schuylkill River near Pottstown. "We filed for a construction permit in February 1970 and haven't gotten it yet. It's the longest delay in AEC history." In its most recent annual report, the utility attributed the delay to "substantial changes in AEC regulations and prolonged public hearings." One after another, industry spokesmen, appearing at recent hearings on reactor safety conducted by the Joint Committee on Atomic Energy, complained that the new AEC standards for emergency core cooling systems are unnecessary, time-consuming and expensive.

"It's costing us $5 million a month to do nothing at Limerick," Allen said. "In the long run, the ratepayers will probably wind up paying for the delay. It's been two years since the AEC Advisory Committee on Reactor Safeguards hearing. We've satisfied every requirement, written and unwritten. We've asked the AEC five times for a variance to get moving at Limerick, because we can't turn a spadeful of dirt without a construction permit. But we've been having a real problem getting the AEC to schedule hearings for us." The solution, Allen says, "is to speed up the whole licensing procedure."

The Joint Committee would like to do that, too, but there are people even within the AEC, such as Oak Ridge safety director William B. Cottrell, who oppose shortening the procedure. It now takes seven-to-ten years from the time initial plans have been drawn to get an atomic plant operating. Allen showed me seven thick volumes on Peach Bottom, a project they have been working on for years. "We've answered 1,500 questions from the AEC on Peach Bottom alone," he said. Philadelphia Electric, the sixth largest private utility in the nation, is nevertheless determined to go nuclear. It has large interests in seven reactor plants. "We are planning for 70 per cent of our electric generation to come from nuclear plants by the mid-1980s," the utility said. This means "expenditures of $3.2 billion over the next five years, compared with $1.5 billion during the past five years." This is "more than a lot of money," Philadelphia Electric said. "It's an *enormous* [utility's emphasis] amount of money . . . that has to be raised in the financial market—at high rates of interest." Recently, in order to keep moving toward the nuclear future, Philadelphia Electric issued another mortgage bond issue, this one for $125 million.

A utility's profit is based on invested capital, and private utilities enjoy one of the highest industrial rates of return in the country. But even a mighty utility like Philadelphia Electric—with more than $95 million in profits for 1973, the last year for which complete figures were available—could take a back seat to those largely invisible sources of *"enormous* amount[s] of money . . . at high rates of interest." Some of the anti-nuclear critics believe that the real attraction of atomic power lies not in its ability to produce energy but in its ability to generate financial rewards for those who invest in it.

Trying to give me an idea of some of the costs involved, Philadelphia Electric engineer Robert Logue told me that Peach Bottom's $750 million figure included $40 million each for the two reactor cores, $180 million to fuel each of the two units for a year, and $15 million per reactor just to put in the fresh uranium fuel rods each year and take out the spent fuel and waste. "We're spending $1.5 million to $2 million a year just to monitor the temperature in the Susquehanna River."

Money. The nuclear industry has money on its side. Private money and government money. Money for attorneys, for consultants, for expert testimony. Money for laboratories, for salaries. There are no financial rewards worth mentioning, at least yet, in bucking the nuclear establishment. Experts who present anti-nuclear testimony at hearings consider themselves lucky if their expenses are paid. Sometimes they pick up a $50 fee. They labor out of conviction and are often stimulated by harassment, which at times has given the anti-nuclear crowd an air of martyrdom. Leo Goodman, who was the AFL-CIO's top energy expert and science adviser to the late Walter Reuther of the Auto Workers union before he was forced to retire, showed me a list he's compiled of "forty-three top scientists who," Goodman alleged, "have been fired or harassed because they either spoke out against nuclear power or questioned it."

I mention Goodman, and Chauncey Kepford in York because, right or wrong, they have the kind of intense passion that money can't buy, the kind of save-the-world religion that is said to move mountains. But money is also essential. "You'd have to have at least $50,000 to make a proper case against a utility in a nuclear power hearing," says Ray Hovis. "For studies and expert testimony—to really know what you're doing." He thinks the government should provide "seed money" for the opponents of nuclear power, to stimulate a debate which he feels would be in the public interest. Legal fees are no problem for Philadelphia Electric—its customers will pay them.

Hovis interrupted his discourse on legal expenses to exclaim, "God, it would be just unbelievable if these nuclear reactors ever blew up." There is no danger that an atomic power plant could ever explode like an atom bomb. Hovis was referring to the possibility of a loss-of-coolant accident.

Conventional steam-driven electric plants burn fossil fuels—sometimes as much as 100 tons an hour—to heat water in a boiler. In an atomic plant, the reactor takes the place of a boiler. The reactor core is a thick cylindrical steel containment vessel into which long, slender rods containing uranium fuel pellets are inserted and withdrawn to create and control the nuclear reaction. Reactors are also equipped with control rods, usually made of a special silver alloy, which can be inserted into the fuel core to modify or stop the reaction. Vast quantities of water are poured into a water-moderated reactor such as the giants at Peach Bottom, to promote the fission process as well as to cool it.

The reactor core is encased within walls of concrete and steel designed to withstand earthquake, flood or plane crashes.

The radioactive materials within the reactor must be covered at all times by water or cooled by gas to prevent the core from overheating and melting into a large radioactive mass that could not be cooled or contained.

The important word in the much discussed loss-of-coolant issue is "if"—*if* there's a sudden failure in the complex plumbing or steam supply piping systems; *if* all the many backup safety devices and systems prove inadequate or fail to function. What then?

Within an hour or so, a cloud of radioactivity would burst from the rent containment vessel, to be caught up and dispersed by the wind. Then, since nothing could contain this overheated radioactive fuel, it would melt together into a molten mass weighing several hundred thousand pounds and eat its way down through the reactor core and into the primary containment core and from there down into the earth. This is called the "China Syndrome," and no one is willing to guess exactly how far the molten mass would sink. In any case, a huge radioactive mass a couple of hundred feet down in the earth would take years to cool.

The barrier standing between us and such an accident is the emergency core cooling system, designed to pour emergency coolant into the core should the primary systems fail. This emergency system has never really been tested. According to the American Nuclear Society, a full-scale test would cost around $250 million—"prohibitively expensive" and "impractical," the society says—because a large part of the system would have to be destroyed for each test. Six out of six mini-scale tests of emergency core cooling systems sponsored by the AEC have failed. So all we have to go on is an earnest assurance from the AEC and the nuclear industry that the emergency system *will* work if and when the time comes.

Radioactive releases from a nuclear power plant are also of major concern. In the case of Peach Bottom, the AEC staff contends that there will be "significant" releases of radioactive iodine from the new plants and wants Philadelphia Electric to reduce them. The AEC licensing board, overruling the AEC staff, gave the utility a conditional operating permit for a specified time, during which the utility must monitor its radioactive discharges into the atmosphere, along with the effects of pouring heated water into the Susquehanna. If the AEC continues to find the iodine discharges excessive, it will probably recommend the installation of charcoal filters on the vent stacks. The agency will also require the utility to shut down the new plants and build more cooling towers if the ecology of the river appears to suffer under the present cooling system.

The AEC has reduced by 97 per cent its estimate of the number of millirems of iodine-131 that might injure a 2-year-old child. The thyroid gland has a special affinity for iodine, and a child's thyroid is considered especially vulnerable. Children are milk drinkers; thus a cow grazing on radioactive grass could pass the contamination on to a child. The nuclear critics contend that plants and animals consumed by man can concentrate massive quantities of radioactive substances. . . .

The nuclear industry is engaged in a determined public relations effort to convince the American public that nuclear fission is safe. Standard Rate and Data shows that it costs about $40,000 to put a full-page, four-color ad in *Time* —and the media have been laced with such nuclear promotion. The utilities have also been enclosing pro-nuclear material with their bills, a practice which it would cost the nuclear critics many thousands of dollars to duplicate. "We just about broke our treasury," says Ann Roosevelt of Friends of the Earth, "to run one full-page, black-and-white ad in the *San Francisco Chronicle*" at a cost of around $7,300. This ad has been quite effective. Reprinted as posters, it has found its way to doors and bulletin boards around the country.

Yet Ms. Roosevelt is confident that the foes of nuclear fission will win their fight. "We're doing something that has never been done before," she said, "in taking on a fully developed industry that's been protected by a mission-oriented Congress. Until a year ago, we could hardly get an anti-nuclear story in the newspapers because they were convinced that nuclear power was safe. We think it's a tremendous victory because the press is beginning to notice us." She showed me a much-quoted *New York Times* editorial of last year which said, in part, "Once so promising in the first enthusiasm of the atomic era, nuclear power generation is becoming something of a monster, with dangers to people and the environment so awesome as to raise serious doubts that this is indeed the best energy source of the future."

"Just look around," Ms. Roosevelt said. "Even the AEC banned the proposed reactors at Newbold Island, near Philadelphia and Trenton, because there were 'too many people' in the area. A RAND report in California called for a slowdown on nuclear fission. The Federation of American Scientists did too. Ralph Nader is against it. The Sierra Club reconsidered its policy on nuclear power and recently came out against it. Even Congress," Ms. Roosevelt said, "is beginning to wake up. It wasn't their fault. The Joint Committee on Atomic Power monopolized the field and Congress depended upon the committee for its information about nuclear power. This committee acts more like an executive committee than a legislative one. It has tremendous power. But no matter how much the Joint Committee says nuclear power is safe, the grass roots are growing. Congress is becoming aware of the problem. And I'm confident we're going to win." . . .

COMPLAINT FROM THE AEC (1974)

DEAR SIRS: At the same time the August 3rd issue of *The Nation* arrived, we also received copy of a news release from the insurance pools which provide liability insurance to the nuclear industry. The announcement from the insurance pools said:

The extraordinary safety record of the nuclear industry prompts additional premium refunds of $1,434,580 from the two American nuclear liability insurance pools. . . . Since the commencement of their operation in 1957, neither pool has ever received a claim arising from the operation of a nuclear reactor. They note that the good safety record of their insureds is without parallel in other industries. The safety record, they said, continues to confirm the effectiveness of the safety measures taken to protect the public. . . .

What a contrast to the tone of *The Nation*'s article "The Hot River Valley" by McKinley C. Olson.

The author says plutonium-239 is "the most dangerous substance ever handled by man." While we do not minimize the hazard potential of plutonium if improperly handled, it certainly is not "the most dangerous" substance. The article goes on to say that "A spoonful of plutonium dioxide particles, if dispersed in the air, is enough to kill millions of people." The impossibility of dispersing the plutonium so that it gets to millions of people is totally ignored. As is the fact that chlorine gas and many other hazardous and toxic substances in common use would also, if spread around, kill millions of people.

Mr. Olson goes on to report that the basic shortcomings of AEC plant hearings are that they do not provide a forum for debating the issue of nuclear power as such. The purpose of individual plant hearings is to address environmental and safety issues relative to a specific plant and a specific site.

There are other forums for debating the general issues of nuclear power. No mention is made of the months of public hearings on the general subjects of emergency cooling systems, radiation releases from nuclear plants and the nuclear fuel cycle. And the Congress has considered the nuclear power program since its inception, not only in the Congressional Joint Committee on Atomic Energy but also in the appropriations committees which must approve funding and in other committees as well.

Consider also the following statements. The article quotes an AEC licensing official as reporting, quite correctly, that radioactive discharges are monitored at the stack where they leave the plant. "This means that each plant is monitored individually. . . . The anti-nuclear forces in York call this a meaningless standard, saying that the total amount of radioactivity released by all three plants at Peach Bottom is the relevant index. . . ." We agree that the total amount of radioactivity released is what's important, and the way the total amount is kept at the lowest practical level is to control the releases from each plant. That is done by monitors at each plant. For purposes of release of radioactive effluents, the total amount released to the environment from all three plants must meet our regulations. There are not three limits at Peach Bottom; the total release from all three plants must adhere to the single limit.

Similarly, there is a statement, "They've never decommissioned a hot nuclear plant." That is untrue, and a single call to the AEC would have provided the author with information on the decommissioning of several reactors such as Hallam, Pathfinder, Elk River and Fermi I.

These are but a few examples of the incomplete and inaccurate reporting which characterizes this article. There are many others. They include the allegations of Dr. Sternglass which have been rebutted by reputable scientists and public health authorities in his own state. And contrary to Mr. Olson, the Reactor Safety Study headed by Prof. Norman Rasmussen *has* considered the "worst case" approach.

We at the AEC are attempting to provide information to the public upon which it can base its judgments on the role of nuclear power in helping to meet our energy needs. Some of the issues are controversial and they deserve a thorough airing. But they should be judged in an objective manner, which considers both the benefits and the risks. Regrettably, *The Nation*'s story fell far short of that mark.

JOHN A. HARRIS, DIRECTOR
Office of Information Services

DEAR SIRS: It is fatuous to cite citations from the insurance industry in behalf of atomic power. Both insurance pools and nuclear utilities are protected by Congress. A major nuclear accident, according to the most conservative estimates, would result in billions of dollars in property damages alone. The Price-Anderson Act limits the liability for a single nuclear accident to $560 million, of which all but $110 million is covered by taxpayer dollars. If nuclear power is as safe as its proponents claim, there would be no hesitation on the part of the nuclear utilities and the insurance companies to assume responsibility for total damages in the event of a nuclear accident. This, as a demonstration of monetary faith, would be a rebuttal to those such as Ralph Nader, who claims, "if there were no Price-Anderson, there would be no more nuclear power plants constructed."

Most of the points which the AEC letter of August 14 raises were also examined at some length in my article. I would, however, like to make a central point stronger: the basic shortcoming of *all* AEC bodies, boards and hearings is that they are populated for the most part by individuals who favor nuclear development, which means that life-and-death questions under the auspices of the AEC are more often debated in terms of *how* and *when* than of *if* and *should*. Here in the Midwest, David D. Comey, environmental director of the Chicago-based Businessmen for the Public Interest, and Myron Cherry, an environmental lawyer, have been demonstrating the precedent-making effectiveness of utilizing non-AEC governmental bodies to oppose or moderate the massive drive to increase both the size and number of atomic power plants.

And last, another word, please, about plutonium. A large atomic power plant operating at full capacity produces more than a couple hundred pounds (a conservative figure) of plutonium a year. The proposed breeder (plutonium) reactor of the immediate future would utilize a ton or more of plutonium in its operation. The reason reputable authorities are wont to say that plutonium is the most dangerous substance is twofold: its lethal capabilities and its extreme toxic longevity.

An ounce of plutonium could cause a worldwide epidemic of lung cancer. Plutonium, if exposed to air, ignites spontaneously; as it burns, it forms tiny particles of plutonium dioxide. An ounce of plutonium could form 10 trillion particles of plutonium dioxide, which could remain in the atmosphere with lethal implications for hundreds of thousands of years.

The AEC spokesman refers to the "impossibility of dispersing the plutonium." What makes him so sure?

MCKINLEY C. OLSON

THE UNACCEPTABLE RISK (1979)

McKinley C. Olson

TWO RELATED POINTS deserve to be made in the radioactive after-
math of the nuclear power plant accident on Three Mile Island in the Susquehanna River near Harrisburg. . . .

One is the fact that since the mid-1950s, it has been clear to many unbiased,
independent and knowledgeable people in this country . . . that it was folly to
pursue, or rely upon, nuclear fission power to produce electricity for widespread
consumption. The second is that the energy problems we face today can in large
measure be blamed upon our multibillion-dollar pursuit and development of
nuclear power.

In the first instance, we quickly learned that we were dealing with a
bewildering array of radioactive problems which ran through the entire length
and breadth of the nuclear fuel cycle, from the mining of uranium ore to the
containment and disposal of nuclear wastes to the decontamination of nuclear
power plants and other related radioactive facilities.

Next, it should have been clear that one self-serving segment of our society
was pushing the rest of us into the arms of a technology that could not tolerate,
nor contain, a major accident. And major accidents, in this world of human
error, faulty products, war, revolution, terrorism, earthquake and flood, are
bound to happen, especially when we continue to increase the probability that
a major nuclear accident will occur by increasing the number of nuclear power
plants in our society and, with them, the consequent increase in radioactive
shipments, storage facilities and the like.

Because the consequences of a major nuclear power accident would be so
devastating and disruptive, in every sense, the champions of nuclear power and
their sycophants have attempted to deal with their dilemma by maintaining that
the inevitable will never happen. As I write this, it still hasn't, but the accident
at Three Mile Island, the astounding fire in 1975 that crippled the emergency
safety systems at the Browns Ferry nuclear plant in Alabama and the partial
meltdown of the nuclear fuel core in 1966 at the Enrico Fermi plant near Detroit,
among others, should be indication enough to anyone with common sense, and
some shred of independence from the economic establishment, that we have
been flirting with nuclear catastrophe.

Instead of pursuing all the logical options that have been available to us
for years, among them conservation, energy efficiency, solar power, wind power,
geothermal power, oceanic heat, the use of coal, the tides, grain and wood
alcohol, wood itself, garbage, lumber and agricultural wastes, algae and the
process of photosynthesis, most of which we have largely ignored in spite of the
fact that their development would have been a boon to the economy in terms
of new jobs and industrial growth, we have allowed our Federal Government
—including the Congress and the courts—and a consortium of powerful public
utilities and giant private corporations, to squander precious years and billions

of dollars in the pursuit of a technology that, at best, will lay a 100,000-year curse in the form of plutonium waste upon this earth.

Also, it means that those places, such as Chicago, that are now harnessed to nuclear power have been tied to an economic albatross, for we can be fairly sure that a major nuclear power plant accident anywhere in this country will result in damages so ghastly as to arouse a clamor for the shutdown of nuclear plants everywhere, which, in turn, if we continue to rely upon nuclear power, would relegate a number of our regions and cities to the potential status of economic disaster areas.

There is a last lesson here: The nuclear power controversy, like the controversy over the war in Vietnam, teaches us that the Federal Government and our Federal employees must be constantly watched, and prodded, to insure that they serve the public interest rather than the interests of power, greed, ignorance and privilege.

Once again, authorities are attempting to minimize the dangers and awesome implications of their actions. As I write this, we are being told that the levels of radiation emanating from the Three Mile Island Nuclear Power Station are not alarming, even though it is an acknowledged fact that radiation, at any level, no matter how low, can cause genetic mutations; and even though we know that ionizing radiation is cumulative, and concentrated, in those who have been directly exposed to it, and, as it moves up through the human food chain causes cancer, leukemia and other cell-mutated diseases.

We are also being told that the situation at Three Mile Island is stable, whatever that means, and that there is no real danger that we will have to face up to the terrifying implications of a fuel core meltdown. And, if our brush with disaster does not turn out to be totally horrific, we will be asked to swallow their staggering contention that a near miss is as good as a mile.

In this, these defenders of the nuclear faith have been joined by the media and politicians who profess to be deeply troubled and concerned, but who conclude nevertheless that the nuclear fission power option is still a viable and rational answer to at least some of our energy needs.

This is the same chorus that has for the past twenty-five years been trying to lull our fears, and lead us into a catastrophic radioactive corner, even though, if we continue as we have, the shoe will surely fall. Who, then, will pick it up?

LETHAL SEEPAGE OF NUCLEAR WASTE (1977)

Robert Kaper

OIL SPILLS, exhaust fumes, asbestos fibers, Kepone: as the pace of worldwide industrialization increases, the list of environmental pollutants grows longer and longer. But while PCB and DDT make headlines, the most deadly pollutants on the list—the radioactive by-products released by the nuclear power industry—go almost unnoticed. There are two reasons: first, unlike the sludge that blackens beaches and the yellow smog that shrouds large cities, radioactive pollutants are invisible; second, their effects—cancer and birth defects—do not appear until years after contamination has taken place.

Whether noticed or not, large amounts of lethal radioactivity already have escaped into the air and water. And if the transition to nuclear energy continues, the rate of radioactive pollution is certain to increase. The Environmental Protection Agency, while cautioning that it lacks the hard data to make definite predictions of the health hazards from radioactive pollution, has concluded that its effect on public health will be "significant" and "particularly large" for certain kinds of radioactive substances.

For example, the EPA predicts that by the year 2000, if current standards are maintained, "planned releases" of radioactive substances will have accounted for approximately 14,000 "health effects" (cancer and birth defects). But as the agency itself points out, the projection is based on minimum estimates of future radiation release by only a portion of the nuclear industry. The estimates do not include the inevitable leakage from radioactive waste, contamination resulting from accidents and from radon gas, responsible for a type of cancer that is nearly 100 percent fatal, and radioactive dust released during uranium mining.

Many critics of nuclear energy consider the EPA estimates worthless. "The real risks are much greater," says a researcher for Critical Mass, a Ralph Nader organization that is studying the nuclear industry. "The problems involved in preventing radioactive waste from leaking into the environment are insurmountable."

The Energy Research and Development Administration (successor to the Atomic Energy Commission) is more optimistic than its critics. ERDA has consistently maintained that a federal repository for "permanent geologic storage of high-level wastes," the radioactive pieces of split uranium atoms resulting from nuclear fission, will someday be established. Yet after more than thirty years of producing the waste, ERDA still hasn't built the repository or even decided definitely where it is to be located.

The General Accounting Office estimates that by the end of the century the nuclear industry will have produced 265 million gallons of high-level liquid waste from the reprocessing of spent nuclear fuel. The concentration of radioactivity in such waste is so great that if it were pumped into holes drilled deep into the earth—as one disposal scheme proposed—it would melt the surrounding rock. The high-level waste so far produced has been stored temporarily in steel tanks which must be continuously cooled. Many of the tanks have sprung leaks and spilled hundreds of thousands of gallons of the deadly liquid into the ground.

In addition to high-level waste, the nuclear industry will have produced by the year 2000 more than a billion cubic feet of "low-level" waste—enough to pave a four-lane coast-to-coast highway a foot thick. In the past, low-level waste was defined as any radioactive waste that was not high-level. It could include anything from objects that were only suspected of being contaminated to dangerous, long-lasting substances like radium and plutonium. Recently, plutonium and other artificial elements have been placed in an intermediate category called transuranic waste. Studies by the EPA, the U.S. Geological Survey and the GAO have revealed serious deficiencies in low-level waste-disposal procedures which have resulted in contamination of streams and water tables.

Former Rep. Leo J. Ryan (D., Calif.), then head of the House Conservation, Energy, and Natural Resources Subcommittee, which recently investigated low-level waste disposal, said at the conclusion of the hearings, "We may have to face the realization that it just may not be possible to guarantee the containment of radioactive wastes over the ages until they are harmless to mankind."

Although leakage from nuclear wastes may be the main source of contamination, every phase of the nuclear fuel cycle—from the mining of uranium ore to the reprocessing of spent nuclear fuel—releases radioactivity into the environment. Pollution begins at the mines as dust and gas from the digging operations drift into the atmosphere. More dust and gas escape from the processing mills where the ore is crushed and chemically treated to extract the uranium. Wind and rain scatter radioactive particles from the tailings, waste rock, which are piled in the open outside the mills. Radon gas diffuses from them continuously.

Acid used to extract uranium from the ore is pumped into settling ponds to remove most, but not all, of the radioactive particles. What remains is diverted into nearby rivers. The still-secret enrichment process, which raises the percentage of U_{235}, the fissionable form of uranium in nuclear fuel, releases an unknown amount of radioactive aerosols and gases into the atmosphere. Here again, contaminated water from settling ponds is regularly discharged into nearby waterways.

Atomic power plants vent radioactive gas and steam and pump coolant water containing small amounts of radioactivity back into the rivers from which the water came. Spent fuel rods from the reactor are stored temporarily in cooling ponds near the plants, awaiting reprocessing. Because of technical problems, however, no commercial reprocessing plants are operating in the United States, so the highly radioactive fuel rods are rapidly filling up the available space.

Reprocessing is the step in the nuclear cycle that creates the most dangerous radioactive by-products. In this operation, the fuel rods are chopped up and dissolved in nitric acid to remove the still-usable uranium and the newly formed plutonium. What remains is the high-level waste mentioned earlier.

Nuclear Fuel Services, a subsidiary of Getty Oil, ran the only commercial fuel reprocessing plant in the country at West Valley, N.Y., near Buffalo until it decided to get out of the business. Redesigning the operation to meet new government safety standards imposed while the plant was temporarily shut down for expansion would have made further reprocessing unprofitable. The company left behind more than 600,000 gallons of high-level waste which it wants to turn over to the state of New York. An ERDA-contracted study has estimated that to dispose of it could cost as much as $540 million.

The same basic reprocessing operation also produces plutonium for nuclear weapons. The high-level waste thus created is stored in underground tanks at two facilities which operate under ERDA contracts—the Savannah River plant at Aiken, S.C., run by duPont, and the Hanford Works at Richland, Wash., run by a subsidiary of Atlantic Richfield Company.

Half of the tanks at the Savannah River plant have leaked at one time or another. Although secondary barriers have confined most of the leakage, several hundred gallons have seeped into the soil and contaminated the underlying ground water. The current ERDA contractor at Richland, Atlantic Richfield Hanford Co. (ARHCO) and its predecessors have had less success containing their leakage. Since the 1940s, eighteen of Hanford's tanks have spilled 430,000 gallons of high-level waste. From 1956 through 1958, 31 million gallons of partially decontaminated but still highly radioactive high-level waste were deliberately poured into the ground.

Regulations are tighter now but the waste is still getting away. In 1973, a Hanford leak that was undetected for forty-eight days spilled 115,000 gallons. Although weekly readings of the tank levels showed loss of fluid, the supervisor responsible said that he had been too busy to check further. An investigation by the AFC found that the absence of a "quality assurance" program had contributed to the delay in finding the leak. Yet the year before, the commission had approved a proposal from ARHCO to eliminate that program because of its expense. During a GAO investigation of the Hanford works in 1974, the AEC discovered thirty tanks that had not been monitored for at least two or three years—three of them not since 1949. The AEC said that it expected the leakage to get worse as the tanks got older.

Because it is so difficult to store high-level waste in liquid form, ERDA is testing ways to solidify it. Thus far, one method has had some success but can be used to solidify only acidic high-level wastes, less than 5 percent of the accumulated total. Although all high-level waste is originally acidic, that from the production of plutonium is neutralized so that it can be stored in tanks made of carbon steel instead of the more expensive stainless steel.

Since the neutralized waste can't be completely solidified, it must periodically be moved into new tanks as the old ones corrode and begin to leak. Unfortunately, engineers at Richland have been unable to figure out how to get the several hundred thousand tons of waste out of their tanks. The contents have partially crystallized and can no longer be pumped. Digging it out would scatter large amounts and create a severe radiation hazard. Pumping water back into the tanks to reliquefy the sludge would open up old leaks which have been plugged by the sediment. Cost estimates of either method range from $2 billion to $20 billion.

With all these difficulties and the fact that the Richland site is contaminated beyond redemption, ERDA has seriously considered paving the whole area and abandoning it. This would mean that, as the tanks corrode, the waste will eventually escape and seep into the ground.

Since constant maintenance is necessary to prevent overheating and control leakage, tank storage is at best only a temporary solution. Ideally, ERDA would like to isolate the waste in some heatproof and waterproof location deep underground. But where? For a while, the AEC planned to use a Kansas salt mine, but had to abandon the site when engineers discovered that oil prospectors had drilled a number of exploratory wells in the ground above the mine. Then in 1972, the AEC decided to store all new high-level waste for 100 years or so in a Retrievable Surface Storage Facility, until they could figure out what to do with it. Huge casks containing the waste were to have been shipped by rail from reprocessing plants in New York, South Carolina and Illinois to the storage site somewhere out West.

Commenting on this scheme in 1974, Dr. Frank Pittman, then director of the AEC's Division of Waste Management and Transportation, said: "There are available today proven methods for managing the high-level waste from the nuclear industry . . . the bugaboo of waste management cannot logically be used as a rationale for delays." A year later, with no explanation whatever, the commission dropped the whole idea. So, far from being a proven method, the Surface Storage Facility never left the drawing board.

ERDA officials testified before Congress last summer that they plan to store the waste underground, starting in 1985. However, since the agency has just this year begun a nationwide search for a suitable location, the 1985 date seems optimistic.

Although not nearly as dangerous as high-level wastes, low-level wastes may pose an even greater disposal problem because of their huge volume. For years, plutonium, uranium, radium and other dangerous low-level wastes were encased in concrete in ordinary steel drums and dumped into the ocean. One of the dump sites is less than 50 miles from San Francisco. From 1946 until the practice was stopped in 1970, the United States alone dumped more than 85,000 drums in the Atlantic and Pacific.

In 1975, an EPA survey team, using the research submarine *Alvin,* located some of the sites and inspected several of the drums. The pressure had crushed and broken open many of them, releasing the contents. One drum contained no concrete at all, only an inner coating of tar. The United States no longer dumps radioactive materials into the ocean, but other countries, including Great Britain, Belgium, the Netherlands and Switzerland, still do. The British package their wastes in steel drums containing asphalt. They make no attempt to prevent corrosion and eventual leakage, assuming that the ocean is big enough to dilute the escaping radioactivity to harmless levels.

Ocean dumping is regulated by an international treaty which controls the amount and type of materials disposed of and the locations. Unfortunately, Great Britain gets rid of even more of its radioactive wastes by piping it directly into the Irish Sea, a method that is completely unregulated. France does not bother with dumping at all but simply pumps its low-level liquid wastes into the North Sea.

Now that this country has stopped ocean dumping, most low-level wastes are buried in unlined trenches, like ordinary garbage. At present, there are six commercial and five federal burial sites. The commercial sites are licensed by the states in which they are located under an agreement with the Nuclear Regulatory Commission (NRC), the other half of the old AEC. In theory, the trenches are dug in areas where the geological conditions are such that the radioactive material will be confined in the trench. In practice, however, at least three federal sites and two commercial ones have been leaking radioactivity, in some cases into nearby streams. At a site operated by the Nuclear Engineering Company at Maxey Flats, Ky., state investigators found plutonium 800 feet from the trenches. The trenches are supposed to contain the substances until they become harmless—500,000 years for plutonium—yet in less than ten years some had escaped.

Although the NRC claims that all burial sites received a "favorable response" from the U.S. Geological Survey, representatives of that agency say they were not given "the necessary time to truly evaluate the sites." In some cases state authorities asked the USGS merely to review data supplied by the company applying for a license, the USGS's opinion being requested after the sites had been selected. A GAO investigation concluded that the sites were selected not for their ability to contain radioactivity but because they were on government land and close to customers.

Once the dump site is filled, the contractor's obligation ends and the responsibility for maintenance operations such as monitoring for leakage, guarding against theft, and pumping water out of trenches reverts to the state. Officials of the states in which the sites are located have gradually come to realize that because of the extremely long half-lives of plutonium and other buried substances, maintenance operations must continue virtually forever. To pay for this "perpetual care," some states are setting up trust funds, but none of them is large enough to handle major emergency measures or corrective actions that may sometimes be required. As usual, the action is being taken after the fact, after the dumping has been going on for years.

The government's dismal regulatory performance to date offers little hope that its "we'll-cross-that-bridge-when-we-come-to-it" attitude will change in the future. Policies and regulations dealing with nuclear pollution continue to be developed piecemeal and sporadically. The AEC first required "zero migration" of radioactivity from low-level trenches. When the trenches began to leak, the standard was relaxed so that existing conditions became acceptable.

This laissez-faire approach to regulation may be due in part to the composition of the NRC. According to a study released by Common Cause, 65 percent of the commission's top officials come from businesses having contracts with it. Allied Chemical, Gulf Oil, Union Carbide, ARCO, the Bechtel Corporation, General Electric and the other companies that operate the nuclear industry, are by their very nature as moneymaking enterprises inherently disposed to dump whatever they can't use into the nearest river. Every control imposed, every precaution taken, every filter installed takes another bite out of the profits.

The attitude of James Neel, president of Nuclear Engineering, is typical of the corporate viewpoint. In his testimony before the House panel on radioactive waste, Neel attempted to minimize the danger of the plutonium found leaking from his company's trenches by claiming that it could be "safely shielded with a mere piece of paper." An EPA official called the remark "completely irresponsible," adding, "only one type of radiation given off by plutonium can't penetrate paper and those parts of the body where it concentrates don't have even that little bit of protection."

Neel maintained that the amount of plutonium that escaped was below the permissible limits and would be highly diluted "by the time it does get into drinking water supplies." This excuse, which in one form or another invariably accompanies any discussions of radioactive contamination, ignores two crucial points. First, radioactivity is concentrated by living things as it moves up the food chain. Second, although the amounts discharged at each location may never exceed acceptable limits (except for occasional accidents), the radioactivity from the mines, mills, reprocessing plants, reactors and dumps all over the world will eventually add up to a significant amount. According to the latest ERDA figures, nineteen countries already have functioning atomic power plants and thirteen more are constructing them. Oil-rich Nigeria is currently negotiating with West Germany for its own nuclear facilities and Iran is doing the same with the United States.

Since there is no international control over radioactive discharge other than the ocean-dumping treaty, each of these countries can determine its own acceptable limits and enforce them as strictly or as loosely as it chooses. Unfortunately, the technical problems and great expense involved in preventing radioactive pollution create an overwhelming temptation to cut corners.

Exiled Russian physicist Zhores Medvedev recently reported that careless disposal procedures apparently caused a nuclear waste dump in the Soviet Union to blow up, killing hundreds of people. Three years ago, engineers at the Hanford works had to take special emergency measures when they discovered that a waste-disposal trench contained enough plutonium to "go critical." Citing this incident and others, a confidential ERDA study made public in September by Ralph Nader said that the government's treatment of radioactive wastes had been "marred in a sufficient number of instances to be a cause for concern" and that a "major radioactive waste problem already exists in the United States."

Yet, despite the unanswered questions and unavoidable dangers, the United States and the other industrialized nations of the world have already made a commitment to "go nuclear." Ten percent of the electricity generated in the United States now comes from atomic power; 13 percent is expected by 1985. The export of nuclear technology is too big a source of revenue for the countries engaged in it, Canada, France, West Germany, and the United States, to give up. Oil companies, hedging their bets against the day the reserves dry up, have invested heavily in the nuclear industry.

Barring any serious accidents such as the one in the Soviet Union, the conversion to clean, quiet nuclear power will, on the surface at least, appear to be a good thing: no more smoke from coal and oil boilers, no more rivers fouled from coal mine wastes, and no more oil spills. The only drawback will be a steady rise in the cancer rate. But by the time the increase is noticed, it may be too late to do anything about it. Cancer already kills 370,000 persons a year in the United States alone. It would take many thousands of additional deaths from nuclear pollution to make a significant difference in the statistics. By then, the world may be so dependent on nuclear power that a choice between it and a less deadly energy source will no longer be possible.

THE NUCLEAR INDUSTRY
FIGHTS BACK (1980)

Mark Hertsgaard

THERE IS NO DOUBT that the Three Mile Island accident shook America's nuclear industry—to the core. But it has now become obvious that, contrary to what many in the antinuclear movement believe, the blow was not fatal. In fact, the accident has made the massive conglomeration of corporate and financial capital of which the industry is composed more determined than ever that the United States go nuclear. The industry's executives are driven by more than just profit lust. At the industry's annual conference last November in San Francisco, it was clear that its officials perceive attacks against nuclear power as attacks against the American private enterprise system. Edward Teller, the father of the H-bomb, reminded his audience that "Much more is at stake than nuclear power or your own corporation. We are in a desperate struggle against whatever you wish to call them—no-growthers, environmentalists, elitists. They may well win the battle and, if they do, America is doomed and freedom is doomed."

Teller's rhetoric is only a spicier version of a view expounded by Leo Yochum, the number-three man at nuclear leader Westinghouse Power Systems Company. I interviewed Yochum during the darkest hours of the T.M.I. crisis. Just hours after radio broadcasts had confirmed the existence of an explosion-prone hydrogen bubble within the reactor core, the Westinghouse vice president reaffirmed his company's commitment to nuclear power. "I just don't understand this talk about nuclear being dead," he complained. "The market is going to return. After all, there is a nuclear imperative for this country."

Despite the T.M.I. humiliation, Yochum's viewpoint is shared by all sectors of the American nuclear colossus, from the utilities and uranium companies to Wall Street and the Big Four reactor manufacturing companies. Nuclear opponents must now battle an enemy whose basic ideological instincts for self-preservation have been aroused. To the industry, the nuclear conflict has escalated into a fundamental struggle over the future shape and viability of American capitalism. With that much at stake, to say nothing of the hundreds of millions of dollars in expected future profits, the nuclear industry is hardly ready to give up because a cooling pump malfunctioned at Three Mile Island. The fight over nuclear power is far, far from over.

The "nuclear power is dead" camp bases its confidence on two assumptions: that the nuclear corporations are not making any money, and that, after Three Mile Island, the public will not accept a major expansion of nuclear power. The first assumption is simplistic and not altogether true. The second is an overly optimistic reading of a public mood that could easily shift in the next few years.

It is true that nuclear power has not turned out to be the moneymaker prophesied back in the 1950s. Only Westinghouse of the Big Four reactor vendors claims any nuclear profits. But a decision to stay in the business is made by judging its future prospects, not by moaning about past losses that have been fully absorbed by now anyway. This rule is especially pertinent to the nuclear industry, where each of the Big Four has already made the basic investment in factories, testing laboratories and engineering teams. Under the circumstances, the "extra cost" of remaining in the business is considerably less than the potential profit.

Moreover, many nuclear executives say that even if they wanted to leave the business, they could not. The utilities, upon whom the Big Four depend for a large chunk of total corporate sales, have made it very clear that they plan to buy more nuclear plants in a few years. To abandon nuclear could cost a reactor manufacturer hundreds of millions of dollars in nonnuclear sales. An official of Babcock & Wilcox, the designer of the ill-fated Three Mile Island plant, stated, "There's no way we're going out. We depend on the utility business. We can't cut our own throats by leaving nuclear. Besides, we've still got plenty of work."

His last sentence refers to the immense backlog of nuclear plants that the Big Four are scheduled to deliver during the 1980s. More than 120 reactors are in the pipeline. That translates into more than $12 billion worth of business, and allows the companies to keep their engineering teams together while awaiting the domestic market's full-scale revival. As these plants come on line, they will gradually double what is by far the nuclear industry's most lucrative area of operations—the refueling and servicing of existing plants. There are seventy-two reactors currently operating in the United States, and General Electric and Westinghouse service another thirty-five abroad. The Big Four annually gross about $1 billion by tending to these plants. What is more, profit margins on such work are almost twice as high as for reactor sales.

Still another source of revenue is the overseas market. Fully 40 percent of General Electric's nuclear income is earned abroad. Westinghouse makes in excess of $25 million every year from the French, Japanese and other foreign companies who have bought its nuclear technology. As the rest of the world turns increasingly toward nuclear energy, the Big Four see a great potential for increasing nuclear exports, especially to energy-starved underdeveloped countries.

But the key question in ascertaining the nuclear industry's future prospects is: when will U.S. utilities start ordering significant numbers of nuclear power plants again? Industry officials expect orders to resume by 1983 at the latest, and sooner in the event of electricity brownouts or another oil embargo. The main reason behind the five-year slump of nuclear plant orders has been the United States' sagging demand for electricity. Following the 1974 oil crisis and recession, electricity demand fell to half its historic 7 percent growth rate. That left electric utilities with excess generating capacity, and caused them to defer scores of new power plants and drastically slash future construction plans. And it is not just nuclear sales that are off; coal-fired stations have been hit, too. Thus the orders slump is a result of a downturn in the utility business as a whole, not a repudiation of nuclear power per se.

In fact, the utilities like nuclear power very much. They plan to buy more of it as soon as they work off their overcapacity and the present regulatory uncertainty settles down. With the possible exception of Babcock & Wilcox, each of the Big Four is willing and able to wait a few years for the market's revival. After all, nuclear power makes up only a small proportion of their total corporate business. Being huge, diversified, wealthy multinational corporations, they can take their relatively minor nuclear losses for years if they so choose. As Gordon Hurlbert, the president of Westinghouse Power Systems Company, explains, "A year, two years, three, it really doesn't matter when it [the market revival] comes. I'm looking at nuclear power to pay my pension when I retire."

The optimism of executives like Hurlbert attests to their belief that nuclear power is integral to American capitalism. The industry offers two basic and powerful reasons why the United States cannot do without nuclear power. The first, the national security imperative, has been used to justify Government subsidies to the nuclear industry ever since the cold war. John Simpson, the man who ran Westinghouse's nuclear business for twenty-one years before his 1974 retirement, graphically articulated this viewpoint at the San Francisco conference: "You know, even if we killed hundreds of people a year, we'd still have to have nuclear. There's just no other way. The Russians could paralyze this country overnight by wrecking the Middle East oilfields. The United States just can't stand for that." Simpson makes the familiar argument that expansion of nuclear power will reduce U.S. vulnerability to another oil embargo or price explosion by cutting our imports of foreign oil.

The industry also asserts that nuclear power is necessary for a healthy economy. Without nuclear power, the economy will experience energy shortages. It will not grow enough to avoid an economic slowdown that, executives emphasize, would hit minorities, the poor and women first and hardest. In his keynote address to the San Francisco conference, Westinghouse chief executive Robert Kirby warned that the public "will have to choose . . . between nuclear energy and some though alternatives. Alternatives like inflation, higher unemployment, no economic growth and national insecurity."

Stripped of the solemn rhetoric, the industry's battle plan comes down to simple energy blackmail: no nukes, no jobs. A public opinion poll conducted by *CBS News* shortly after Three Mile Island indicates that Americans will probably give in to such a threat. Although the poll found that opposition to nuclear power had grown sharply in the last two years, it also showed that, when given a choice between further nuclear development and paying higher prices for foreign oil, Americans favored nuclear two to one.

. . . Recognizing that anything close to a repeat performance of the Harrisburg accident would probably finish nuclear power in the United States for good, the industry has committed well over $50 million to upgrade the safety of nuclear power plants. The new Institute for Nuclear Power Operations will improve the training of nuclear plant operators, which was sternly criticized by Congress, the Nuclear Regulatory Commission and the Kemeny Commission. The Nuclear Safety Analysis Center has also been established to maintain high technical standards within the industry.

These initiatives lay the groundwork for a public relations campaign designed to drum up mass support for an expanded nuclear power program. The Washington-based Committee on Energy Awareness (C.E.A.) that is running the campaign was established by the same ad hoc T.M.I. Response Committee of industry executives that set up the new safety centers. On November 8, 1979, the C.E.A. placed full-page ads in *The New York Times,* the *Los Angeles Times,* the *Washington Post,* the *Washington Star* and the *Boston Globe* that asked, "Where Will the Energy Come From?" A week later the same papers' readers were enlightened about "What Really Happened at Three Mile Island." . . .

The media campaign's main message is that nuclear power is safe and necessary. After all, even at Three Mile Island the safety systems worked and nobody was killed. And the industry is already studying and working to make nuclear power even safer for the future. . . . Since Three Mile Island, the official line shifted to "We need nuclear energy—like it or not." Babcock & Wilcox nuclear vice president John MacMillan expects that, when things start to get tough, "the antinuclear movement will be lost in the shuffle. The majority of middle-class Americans who depend on the growth of the economy for their jobs are going to make their voices known so strongly to the politicians that they'll have no choice but to go nuclear."

THE PRICE IS TOO HIGH (1979)

Richard Munson

TWENTY-FIVE YEARS AGO Atomic Energy Commission chairman Lewis Strauss predicted that nuclear power would be "too cheap to measure." Although admitting that Strauss may have been a bit optimistic, the nuclear industry continues to spend millions of dollars each year to convince consumers that nuclear energy saves them money. There is growing evidence that it does not.

Since 1974, utility executives have canceled orders for thirty-two reactors and deferred orders for 150 more. And some prominent Wall Street firms have advised their investors to beware of utilities planning nuclear power plants.

At the same time, Government forecasts of the nuclear potential have dropped dramatically. In the early 1970s, officials estimated that the United States would have 1,500 large reactors by the year 2000. Only a few years later, the projection was reduced to 400, and unofficial estimates now place the likely number below 300. (At present there are seventy licensed reactors; eighty-nine more are in construction and thirty-nine under review by the Nuclear Regulatory Commission.) The nuclear construction industry is in such a recession that, according to a trade journal, a new order is as rare as "the appearance of a comet." The recent near-disaster at the Three Mile Island nuclear facility in Pennsylvania has merely compounded the industry's financial woes.

Nuclear power has long been controversial on environmental and safety grounds. But as utility bills continue to climb, the controversy has become political. Meldrim Thomson, a strong advocate of reactors, was defeated last November when he ran for re-election as Governor of New Hampshire. Thomson's public support had dropped significantly after he approved a 17 percent utility rate hike in order to help finance the embattled Seabrook nuclear power plant.

Since 1957, when the first United States reactor began producing electricity at Shippingport, Pa., the economics of nuclear power have been mixed. One of the successful ventures, Northeast Utilities' Connecticut Yankee plant, cost only $189 per kilowatt of capacity and has operated at 73 percent of capacity for more than nine years. At the time, a standard coal plant similar in size to the Connecticut Yankee project produced energy at $150 per kilowatt.

There are, however, frightening cases of economic failure. For example, the construction cost of the Pilgrim nuclear plant near Plymouth Rock increased from $65 million in 1966 to $239 million in 1972—nearly four times the original estimate. These cost overruns resulted in upping the per kilowatt price from $98 to $360.

But comparing current successes and failures is not the crux of the nuclear debate; the real issue is whether nuclear power will become economical in the future. And, looking ahead, it is increasingly difficult to predict that it will. Since the Connecticut Yankee went on line in 1969, capital costs have increased six times, the price of the fuel has more than quadrupled, fuel enrichment costs have skyrocketed and, inasmuch as no satisfactory means of waste disposal has yet been found, that cost is still unknown.

To arrive at a true balance sheet for nuclear power, the hidden costs, those subsidized by the Government, must be included. Government subsidies have been, and remain, essential to the nuclear power industry. In 1952, David Lilienthal, the first chairman of the Atomic Energy Commission, outlined the risks associated with nuclear power and stated: "I wouldn't advise anybody who is responsible for private investment under present conditions to put his money or the money of those who rely on him into the development of power plants employing nuclear fission as a source of heat." The infant industry needed a cushion, and the Government obliged with a series of acts designed to encourage nuclear power development.

First, Congress approved the Price-Anderson legislation of 1957, relieving the nuclear industry of any liability problems arising from the risks of catastrophe associated with nuclear power generation. Second, the Government began pumping billions of dollars into nuclear research and development. Third, the Government subsidized, or permitted the industry to ignore, the costs of constructing fuel enrichment facilities, of regulation, of waste disposal and health costs associated with increased environmental radiation. A recent study by the Battelle Institute for the Department of Energy conservatively estimates that the industry has received at least $18 billion in Government subsidies. If this sum had been allocated equally over the cumulative output of nuclear plants since 1957, the cost per kilowatt-hour of nuclear electricity would have risen approximately 2 cents, a 95 percent increase. And even this estimate ignores the expenses of the Price-Anderson insurance legislation and of Federal uranium policies.

Disregarding the subsidies, nuclear proponents tend to focus only on the capital needed to build and fuel a nuclear reactor. But over the past few years, these costs alone have zoomed to the point that Donald Cook, chairman of American Electric Power, the largest utility in the United States, commented, "an erroneous conception of the economics of nuclear power" sent utilities "down the wrong road. The economics never materialized—and never will materialize."

Nuclear construction costs are increasing so rapidly that accurate estimates are difficult to make. In 1967, the A.E.C. predicted that reactors would cost $134 per kilowatt of generating capacity. By 1976, construction expenses increased to as much as $645 per kilowatt and current estimates are approximately $1,000 per kilowatt. One official of the Atomic Industrial Forum, a trade association, noted, "estimating capital costs for power plants is like shooting at a moving target."

According to Richard Morgan of the Environmental Action Foundation, "the dramatic increase in nuclear construction costs cannot be explained by inflation; since 1964, nuclear costs have increased more than ten times faster than the Consumer Price Index. Nor can rising costs in the construction industry be responsible; the cost of building an oil refinery has increased only one-tenth as fast as the cost of a nuclear reactor, and coal-fired plants have increased less than half as fast."

The only satisfactory explanation for these skyrocketing costs is that nuclear reactors are dangerous and complex. The utilities have often caused themselves expensive delays by not complying with Federal safety regulations. In 1973, for example, twenty-nine of the thirty completed reactors were held up because of unsafe equipment or plant design. Physicist Amory Lovins estimates that nuclear power requires a total investment of $3,000 per kilowatt of net, usable delivered electric power. In other words, the power for a single 100-watt bulb requires a $300 investment. Projected nuclear growth in the United States through the year 2000 could absorb more than one-fourth of the nation's entire net capital investment. Such extensive use of scarce capital is coming under increased attack.

Utilities also tend to ignore the costs on the opposite side of the construction process: the decommissioning of a nuclear plant. Some executives admit that dismantling a large reactor could cost $100 million; but even that may be optimistic. Elk River, a small experimental reactor in Minnesota, was dismantled for $6.9 million—almost $1 million more than it cost to build the plant. (Since Elk River was dismantled after only a few years, inflation was not a major factor.) The costs of decommissioning the contaminated plant at Three Mile Island over the next four or five years are as yet incalculable.

Not only are nuclear plants expensive to build and raze; they also produce far less electricity than was anticipated. On average, nuclear plants have delivered less than three-fourths of the electricity they were designed to produce. The power stations cannot run constantly at full capacity; they must close for at least a few weeks each year for maintenance, refueling or repairs. In addition, some plants are required to operate at reduced capacity for safety or environmental reasons.

Reactor manufacturers and the A.E.C. had promised utilities that nuclear plants would operate at 80 percent of capacity. A 1976 study by the Council on Economic Priorities found that on the average the plants have run at only 59 percent of capacity. In other words, the nation's nuclear plants have been out of service more than 40 percent of the time, about twice the outage rate planned for by the utilities. By contrast, coal-fired plants ran at 75 percent of capacity.

The champions of nuclear energy prefer to slide over high capital costs and low performance, and to emphasize instead the low fuel costs. And, indeed, in 1973 a pound of refined uranium oxide, or "yellow-cake," which sold for $7, could produce as much electricity as 2.5 tons of coal costing about $20 a ton.

But by 1978, the cost of a pound of yellowcake had reached $52. Despite considerable prospecting, no significant new uranium deposit has been discovered in the United States since 1965. Therefore, since mining companies must extract lower quality ores, the cost of yellowcake will continue to rise. At approximately $100 per pound, uranium fuel loses its once touted advantage over coal or oil.

There are, of course, overseas sources, but these are creating some of the conditions that now plague the petroleum market. In 1972, several uranium mining firms met secretly in Johannesburg, South Africa, to "discuss ways and means of assuring an adequate price for uranium." The group, dubbed "UPEC" by nuclear critics, held subsequent meetings in Paris, Toronto and Chicago.

The cost of the nuclear fuel cycle does not stop at the mines. For use in a reactor, the active fuel within yellowcake must be enriched from 1 to 3 percent. Enrichment, an energy-intensive and expensive technology, has more than doubled in price since 1973. The Government's three enrichment plants cost billions of dollars to build in the 1940s and 1950s and use more than 2 percent of the nation's total consumption of electricity.

Thus, to conserve uranium supplies and avoid expensive enrichment, nuclear proponents have pushed for recycling or reprocessing projects. In theory, reprocessing would recover 25 percent of a reactor's spent fuel. Unfortunately, the process has not worked, and the attempts to make it work are getting more expensive. In 1976, Nuclear Fuel Services abandoned its West Valley, N.Y., plant after learning that necessary alterations would cost approximately $600 million (twenty times the plant's original cost). In the same year, General Electric abandoned its Morris, Ill., reprocessing plant rather than spend the additional $100 million needed to make it work. The only current attempt to set up a commercial reprocessing plant is being made by Allied General Nuclear Services at Barnwell, S.C. It was to have been completed in 1974 at a cost of $100 million, but the estimate now is approximately $750 million. *The Wall Street Journal* labeled the Barnwell plant "one of the biggest white elephants of the nuclear age."

Along with reprocessing, the nuclear industry faces the technical and economic problems of radioactive wastes. To date, no acceptable method of long-term disposal has been devised and temporary Government storage facilities are inadequate. According to the Environmental Protection Agency, "even assuming the technical capability exists to insure total containment for the hazardous lifetime of the nuclear wastes, the cost of implementing the means to contain these wastes is enormous." As an example, the Department of Energy estimates that the price for safe disposal of 500,000 gallons of highly radioactive waste could come to more than half a billion dollars.

Not surprisingly, the rapidly inflated price of nuclear power construction, operation and fuel cycle is being translated into higher utility rates. The Environmental Action Foundation and the Critical Mass Energy Project have analyzed the rates of the 100 largest electric companies between 1973 and 1977 and have found that those firms with 5 percent or more of nuclear generating capacity increased their rates 27 percent more than did firms without reactors.

But despite the poor economic outlook, some utilities and manufacturers are strongly urging further nuclear development. This peculiar phenomenon can be explained by the peculiar nature of power company operations. As regulated monopolies, electric utilities are not subject to the normal pressures of competition. State regulatory commissions attempt to set rates that are designed to cover a utility's operating costs *plus* a profit on its investment comparable to the profits earned by competitive business with similar risks. The size of the profit depends on the size of the utility's investment; the larger the investment, the larger its profits. Thus, utilities have a built-in motive to overbuild their plants and to adopt expensive (capital-intensive) technologies like nuclear power.

Current regulatory measures also make it easier for utilities to finance expensive investment in nuclear energy. Until recently, investor-owned utilities, like all profit-making businesses, had to borrow money to finance new equipment. Some commissions, however, are allowing utilities to increase their rates in order to gain the necessary capital. A procedure called "construction work in progress" or C.W.I.P. allows utilities to include power facilities that are under construction in their rate bases. The result is an approximate 15 percent increase in electric rates and a further boost for utility profits.

In addition, Federal tax laws encourage a utility to go nuclear. Like other private businesses, utilities annually receive billions of dollars in tax breaks for investing in new equipment. But an obscure Federal tax code allows power companies to keep their tax savings rather than pass them on to consumers. The Environmental Action Foundation found that in 1976 utilities collected from their customers $2.1 billion in "phantom taxes" that they never paid to the Government. The more money a utility invests in construction, the more phantom taxes it can collect. And nuclear power plants are the most expensive investment a utility can make.

Fortunately, the alternatives to nuclear power are beginning to gain increased attention, even from economists. According to Denis Hayes of the Worldwatch Institute, "dollar for dollar, investments to increase energy efficiency save more than expenditures on new power plants will produce." Hayes believes that, without decreasing the standard of living, the United States can decrease its total energy consumption almost 50 percent by eliminating energy waste.

Current economic studies of price increases also show that coal-fired plants are competitive with nuclear reactors. In 1976, for example, the Congressional Research Service predicted that then-planned coal-fired and nuclear plants would produce electricity at approximately the same cost. After a thorough economic review in 1976, Harvard economist Irvin Bupp stated, "The only way you can conclude nuclear power will be cheaper eight to ten years from now is to make systematically optimistic assumptions about nuclear costs and be systematically pessimistic about coal." And after evaluating the operating records of existing nuclear plants, the Council on Economic Priorities predicted that, for most of the nation, new coal-fired plants would produce cheaper electricity than new reactors.

Solar energy is also becoming more attractive. Unlike fossil and nuclear fuels, sunlight cannot be exhausted, and since it can be used in decentralized facilities, the high costs of shipping conventional fuels and transmitting power could be eliminated (transmission and distribution today account for approximately 70 percent of the cost of providing electricity to the average residence in the United States).

In January 1978, the Department of Energy found that solar water and space heating was competitive with nuclear electricity and fuel oil in the four cities studied: Boston, Washington, Grand Junction, Colo., and Los Angeles. With the approval of solar tax credits, the study indicates that solar power is likely to be marginally competitive with natural gas.

The most exciting solar application is the photovoltaic cell that converts sunlight directly into electricity. Designed for the space program, the first solar cells were expensive—approximately $200 per peak watt in the late 1950s. Further research has brought the price down to $6 per peak watt. If a demand were created great enough to permit mass production, researchers believe the cost would drop even more dramatically. A recent United Nations report, for example, concludes that solar cells will become cheaper than nuclear power (approximately $1 per peak watt) if they receive a total investment of $1 billion —less than the cost of just one large nuclear plant.

The potential from other renewable sources is also significant. The Army Corps of Engineers recently estimated that adding turbines to existing small-scale dams would economically generate as much electricity as the United States currently receives from nuclear power. And as businesses and small entrepreneurs turn their attention to wind and biomass technologies, the price of solar energy will continue to drop.

According to a recent Federal task force, solar sources could produce up to 30 percent of total United States energy by the year 2000. This level is more than is now contributed by natural gas, more than by coal and nuclear power combined, and more than by our imported oil.

Citizens' groups around the country are beginning to master the complexities of energy economics. In addition to complaining about reactor safety, ratepayers are demanding that their state utility commissions investigate the wisdom of nuclear investments. The authority that utility commissions exercise over nuclear power varies according to state laws. Some of them control utility financing and could refuse the company permission to issue stocks and bonds for nuclear construction. Most commissions must also issue licenses before a utility can build any major new power facility. Before granting a license, the commissions must evaluate whether the plant is the most economical way to generate the needed electricity. In July 1978, the Wisconsin Public Service Commission, citing problems with uranium availability, waste disposal and decommissioning, ordered the utilities in the state to include no new reactors in their future plans. Also in 1978, the California Energy Commission canceled ╭ s for the Sun Desert nuclear reactor, noting that the needed energy could ╷ore cheaply "produced" through conservation and alternative sources.

Many consumer and environmental groups have effectively used economic arguments against nuclear power during hearings on a utility's proposed rate increase. In response to "unfavorable" commission decisions on rate hikes, Florida Power and Light, Detroit Edison, and Consumers Power in Jackson, Mich., canceled their nuclear projects. In 1976, the Wisconsin Public Service Commission granted the Madison Gas and Electric Company an $8 million rate increase only after the utility had agreed to drop plans for the Koshkonong nuclear plant. Also in 1976, the Seattle City Council overruled the municipal utility's plans for two nuclear plants, opting instead for conservation. One council member stated, "Conservation is the lowest-cost method of generating power, and can be accomplished through sensible management without affecting our standard of living."

Some citizens' groups have also successfully convinced their commissions to shift the financial risks associated with nuclear energy from consumers to stockholders. In 1976, for example, Safe Power for Maine gained a refund of $3 million in replacement power costs collected by Central Maine Power during a forced outage of the nuclear plant. The commission reasoned that the utility should collect damages from the manufacturer of the faulty equipment that caused the outage.

Despite its many environmental and social disadvantages, nuclear power has received public support because it was thought to be cheap. But a recent Harris poll shows that a 2-to-1 majority would oppose reactors if they believed nuclear power was more expensive than other sources. Clearly, more and more Americans will oppose nuclear power as cost increases and Government subsidies are added to their utility bills. The nuclear industry, already on shaky economic grounds, may not survive the challenge.

URANIUM RUSH
IN BLACK HILLS, S.D. (1979)

Bruce Johansen

WHEN IN 1871 CONGRESS put an end to treaty making with American Indians, the 371 treaties already signed left the first Americans with what appeared to be some of the least productive land that a rich continent had to offer. It was a time before sophisticated irrigation, and before dry-land farming techniques had been developed. Industrialization was only beginning to transform the cities of the Eastern seaboard and the demand for oil, gas and even coal was trivial by present-day standards. And, in 1871, Madame Curie had not yet isolated radium.

In a century, the circumstances of industrialization and technical change have made many of these treaty-guaranteed lands very valuable, not least because under their often barren surface lies a significant share of the country's remaining fossil fuel and its uranium resources.

The Indians' greatest mineral wealth is probably in uranium. According to a Federal Trade Commission report of October 1975, an estimated 16 percent of the United States' uranium reserves that are recoverable at present market prices are on reservation lands; this is about two-thirds of the uranium on land under the legal jurisdiction of the United States Government. There are almost 400 uranium leases on these lands, according to the F.T.C., and in recent years between 1 million and 2 million tons of uranium ore a year, about 20 percent of the national total, have been mined on reservation land.

Moreover, if to the uranium reserves on reservation land are added those estimated on land guaranteed to Indian nations by treaty, the Indians' share of uranium reserves within the United States rises to nearly 50 percent; the Council of Energy Resource Tribes places the figure at 75 percent to 80 percent. About two-thirds of the 150 million acres guaranteed to Indians by treaty has been alienated from them—by allotment, other means of sale, or by seizure without compensation. Some of these areas, notably the Black Hills of South Dakota, are now undergoing a uranium mining boom, though legal title to the land is still clouded.

Assertion of treaty claims to the Black Hills, as well as to other uranium-rich treaty lands, has begun to forge strong links in the West among groups supporting treaty rights and those opposing nuclear power and weapons development. Black Hills Indian activists have asked numerous anti-nuclear groups to help them "stop the poison at the source."

The conflict over the Black Hills goes back more than a century. Black Elk, a Lakota (Sioux) medicine man, was 11 years old during the summer of 1874 when, by his account (published in *Black Elk Speaks* by John Neihardt), an expedition under Gen. George Armstrong Custer invaded the *Paha Sapa* ("Hills that are Black"), the holy land of the Lakota, the name from which "Dakota" is derived. The Black Hills had been guaranteed to the Lakota "in perpetuity" by the Fort Laramie Treaty of 1868. Custer's expedition was on a geological mission; it was looking for gold. Custer found it, and in his wake several thousand gold seekers, ignoring the treaty, poured into the sacred Black Hills.

In the words of Black Elk, the Lakota and Cheyennes "painted their faces black"—went to war—to regain the Black Hills. The result was Custer's Last Stand, one of the best-remembered debacles in United States military history. The Hills never were ceded by treaty; as recently as July 1978, the tribal council of the Pine Ridge Sioux (the Government's name for the Oglala Lakota) rejected a $17.5 million Claims Commission offer for their land. As a result of that vote (and many before it) Mount Rushmore, among other tourist attractions, still stands on Lakota land.

In January 1977, another geological survey team emerged from the Hills—this time to announce the presence of uranium-bearing Precambrian rock formations near Nemo, southwest of Rapid City. The news ignited another rush for claims, which again ignored the question of title. Between February 15 and April 15, 1977, more than 1,200 location certificates were filed in the area, many of them by large companies such as Johns-Manville, American Copper & Nickel and Homestake Mining. Homestake had grown rich on the Custer strike—the profits from which later helped buy William Randolph Hearst a newspaper empire.

Other large companies had joined the uranium rush elsewhere in the Black Hills. The Tennessee Valley Authority, looking for fuel for the seventeen nuclear power plants for which it has licenses, acquired leases on 65,000 Black Hills acres and on 35,000 more acres just west of the Wyoming border. Since 1974, when the T.V.A. acquired these properties (including a processing mill), 6,000 test holes have been drilled and 5 million to 6 million tons of uranium identified—or about $500 million worth at the mine mouth. The Authority told local officials that it planned to begin mining and milling in the area by 1981. T.V.A. officials said that two mining methods were being considered: stripping and underground solution, whereby liquid-borne chemicals are injected into the ground to dissolve the uranium ore before it is drawn to the surface. Because the Black Hills are a watershed for much of western South Dakota, some concern has been expressed that solution mining could pollute the underground water on which ranchers and farmers rely. Despite protests, Union Carbide also announced uranium mining activities, planned to begin in late 1979 or early 1980. The form and size of these projects have not yet been made public.

The uranium rush in the Black Hills began at the same time that the American Indian Movement (A.I.M.) became the target of an F.B.I. campaign along COINTELPRO lines on and near the Pine Ridge Reservation. The climax of that harassment was the conviction in Fargo, N.D., Federal District Court of Leonard Peltier, an A.I.M. activist, for killing two F.B.I. agents. Many A.I.M. leaders suggested that mineral resources, and especially uranium, were the reason why so much attention had been paid to A.I.M. during the middle 1970s. Peltier wrote:

> In the late 19th century, land was stolen for economic reasons . . . we were left with what was believed to be worthless land. Still, we managed to live and defy the wish to exterminate us. Today, what was once called worthless land suddenly becomes valuable as the technology of white society advances. . . . [That society] would now like to push us off our reservations because beneath the barren land lie valuable mineral resources.

Though no proof has as yet come to light that the F.B.I.'s excessive attention to A.I.M. just when the uranium claims were being consolidated was part of an overall strategy, it is clear that—forced to defend themselves against largely fabricated criminal charges—A.I.M. members had little time to pursue treaty claims to the Black Hills and surrounding lands.

One thousand miles to the south, the Navajo Nation, which had signed a treaty in 1868, has also been facing increased uranium mining. About half the recoverable uranium within the United States lies within New Mexico—and about half of that is beneath the Navajo Nation. As in South Dakota, growing numbers of Navajos have come to oppose the mining, and to join forces with non-Indians who regard nuclear power plants and arms proliferation as a two-fold menace. Uranium had been mined on Navajo land since the late 1940s; the Indians dug the ore that started the United States' stockpile of nuclear weapons.

For thirty years after the first atomic explosions in New Mexico, uranium was mined much like any other mineral. More than 99 percent of the product of the mines was waste and left as tailings near mine sites after the uranium had been extracted. One of the mesalike waste piles grew to be a mile long and 70 feet high. On windy days, dust from the tailings blew into local communities, filling the air and settling on the water supplies. The Atomic Energy Commission assured worried local residents that the dust was harmless.

In February 1978, however, the Department of Energy released a Nuclear Waste Management Task Force report that said that people living near the tailings ran twice the risk of lung cancer as the general population. The *Navajo Times* carried reports of a Public Health Service study that asserted one in six uranium miners had died, or would die, prematurely of lung cancer. For some, the news came too late. Esther Keeswood, a member of the Coalition for Navajo Liberation from Shiprock, N.M., a reservation city near tailings piles, said the C.N.L. had documented the deaths of at least fifty residents (including uranium miners) from lung cancer and related diseases.

Kerr-McGee Company, the first corporation to mine uranium on the Navajo Nation lands (beginning in 1948) found the reservation location extremely lucrative—there were no taxes at the time, no health, safety or pollution regulations, and few other jobs for the many Navajos recently home from service in World War II. Labor was cheap.

The first uranium miners in the area, almost all of them Navajos, remember being sent into shallow tunnels within minutes after blasting. They loaded the radioactive ore into wheelbarrows and emerged from the mines spitting black mucus from the dust, and coughing so hard it gave many of them headaches, according to Tom Barry, energy writer for the *Navajo Times,* who interviewed the miners.

Such mining practices exposed the Navajos who worked for Kerr-McGee to between 100 and 1,000 times the limit now considered safe for exposure to radon gas. Officials for the Public Health Service have estimated these levels, but no one was monitoring the Navajo miners' health in the late 1940s.

It was only thirty years later, when an increasing number of deaths from lung cancer made it evident that Kerr-McGee had held life as cheaply as the workers' labor, that intense scrutiny of the first victims began. Today, as Navajo miners continue to die, children who play in water that has flowed over or through abandoned mines and tailings piles come home with burning sores.

Even if the tailings were to be buried—a staggering task—radioactive pollution could leak into the surrounding water table. A 1975 Environmental Protection Agency report found radioactive contamination of drinking water on a Navajo reservation in the Grants, N.M., area, near uranium mining and milling facilities. Doris Bunting of Citizens Against Nuclear Threats, a predominantly white group that has joined with C.N.L. and the National Indian Youth Council to oppose uranium mining, has supplied data indicating that radium-bearing sediments have spread into the Colorado River basin, from which water is drawn for much of the Southwest. Through the opposition to uranium mining in the area, among Indians and non-Indians alike, runs a deep concern for the long-term poisoning of land, air and water by low-level radiation. It has produced a demand from Indian and white groups for a moratorium on all uranium mining, exploration and milling until the issues of untreated radioactive tailings and other waste-disposal problems are faced and solved.

The threat of death which haunted the Navajos came at what company public relations specialists might have deemed an inappropriate time; the same rush for uranium that had filled the Black Hills with prospectors was coming to the Southwest, as arms stockpiling and the anticipated needs of nuclear plants drove up the demand, and the price, for the mineral. By late 1978, more than 700,000 acres of Indian land were under lease for uranium exploration and development in an area centering on Shiprock and Crownpoint, both in the Navajo Nation. Atlantic Richfield, Continental Oil, Exxon, Humble Oil, Homestake, Kerr-McGee, Mobil Oil, Pioneer Nuclear and United Nuclear were among the companies exploring, planning to mine, or already extracting ore.

The United States Geological Survey predicted that the water table at Crownpoint would drop 1,000 feet as a result of uranium mining, and that it would return to present levels thirty to fifty years after the mining ceased. Much of what water remained could be polluted by uranium residues, the report indicated. Local residents rose in anger, and found themselves neatly ambushed by the white man's law. The Indians owned the surface rights; the mineral rights in the area are owned by private companies such as the Santa Fe Railroad.

"If the water supply is depleted, then this [Crownpoint] will become a ghost town," said Joe Gmusea, a Navajo attorney. "The only people left will be the ones who come to work in the mines." John Redhouse, associate director of the Albuquerque-based National Indian Youth Council, said that the uranium boom is "an issue of spiritual and physical genocide."

The uranium boom has put the residents of Crownpoint into a position not unlike that faced by their ancestors who were driven up the sides of a mesa not far away, as cavalry troops circled below. The choice offered the Indians then, as now, was to assimilate—accommodate the white man's wishes—or starve.

The growing Indian opposition to uranium mining is an attempt to get off this modern-day mesa—and to do so by reaching out to others who are concerned more with the needs of future generations than with the immediate price tags of the international supermarket. The descendants of settlers and Indians of a century ago have been coming together in a regional alliance against what they see as a new invading force—the energy- and profit-hungry multinational corporations. With the growing energy development in the Rocky Mountains area (uranium included) has spread a recognition that parts of the region— including areas other than Indian reservations—are slated for devastation to provide power to the energy consumers of the East and West coasts, and profits to the companies that stoke that demand for energy.

Again, as a century ago, people who stand to lose their livelihoods to invaders are "painting their faces black." The historic twist is that, while a century ago Custer had Indian scouts, this time the Indians' allies are white.

Winoa La Duke of the International Indian Treaty Council may have been speaking for more people than Indians when, at an anti-nuclear demonstration near Grants, N.M., she said: "Indian people refuse to become the silent martyrs of the nuclear industry. We stand fighting in our homelands for a future free of the threat of genocide for our children."

NUCLEAR POWER AND
THE CONSTITUTION (1979)

John Shattuck

THERE ARE MANY FACETS to the growing national debate over atomic power, but probably none is more important than the impact nuclear development is beginning to have on civil liberties. Because the nuclear debate has centered around more visible and immediate issues of environment, health, safety and weaponry, civil libertarians skeptical about the constitutional dimension of these issues have generally stayed on the sidelines. Recent events may have changed that. Secrecy, official deception, violations of due process and political spying have emerged as major by-products of nuclear power.

One dramatic example is the nuclear Watergate that occurred when the Government systematically deceived the public for twenty-five years about the effects of nuclear testing on the health of soldiers and residents in Nevada and Utah in the early 1950s. They were told they were participating in a great public experiment and that fears of health hazards were "Communist-inspired scare stories." Documents disclosed in Congressional hearings last spring showed that the Eisenhower Administration followed a policy of deliberately misinforming the public about the dangers of low-level radiation. This was as serious an abuse of power as Watergate, and far more lethal.

Secrecy and official deception have also been spawned by commercial nuclear development. *The New York Times* reported earlier this year about a man in upstate New York who worked for the Nuclear Materials and Engineering Corporation, a subsidiary of Atlantic Richfield Company. The man had been asked to go into a crawl space in a silo holding 1,700 tons of high-grade uranium ore to see how the silo could be emptied. He incurred a huge overdose of low-level radiation, and six months later contracted massive cancer of the intestines, liver and spleen. After his death, two men claiming to be Federal agents came to his widow's house and demanded his employment records, saying they were classified. Meanwhile, the company refused to turn over to the widow many of her husband's medical files, asserting that they had been lost or misplaced. In short, responsible officials seemed to be going out of their way to cover up what may have been a typical case of low-level radiation poisoning.

We have also learned about another kind of secrecy in *The Progressive* case. The broadest and longest prior restraint in American history was in effect during much of 1979 against a magazine seeking to publish information obtained from public sources about the H-bomb. The Carter Administration's secrecy mania in this case proved to be even greater than the Nixon Administration's in the Pentagon Papers litigation. Government lawyers sought ratification by the courts of a new "born classified" theory intended to impose an official hammerlock on all information pertaining to nuclear weapons.

Next, we have learned about major due process violations in the licensing and operation of unsafe nuclear power plants:

§ The breakdown of procedural regulatory authority in the Three Mile Island crisis last March was epitomized by a comment of Nuclear Regulatory Commission chairman Joseph Hendrie recorded during one of the commission's closed meetings at the height of the crisis: "What's that amendment that protects freedom of the press? Whatever it is, I'm against it." In late July, the much-publicized Citizens' Advisory Panel, which President Carter set up after Three Mile Island, was disbanded after only one meeting because the panel was demanding too much information from the N.R.C.

§ An indication of the public's attitude toward procedural shortcuts in nuclear regulation was the $10-million jury verdict last March for the family of Karen Silkwood, a worker in an Oklahoma plutonium reprocessing plant who had sued the company for a wide variety of health and safety violations, and who died in an automobile accident that occurred under highly suspicious circumstances.

Finally, in recent months reports have surfaced about increasing political surveillance of opponents of nuclear power by nuclear power companies and local, state and Federal agencies.

One rather bizarre example of this last involved an apparent effort by Federal Bureau of Investigation agents to discredit a Congressional investigation of the Karen Silkwood case. Pete Stockton was a staff investigator for the Congressional Subcommittee on Energy and Environment, chaired by Representative John Dingell. The subcommittee had conducted an inquiry in 1976 into some of the allegations being made by the Silkwood family and supporters of their case. A year later, F.B.I. documents discovered in a pretrial hearing revealed that derogatory, unsubstantiated information about Stockton, Dingell, Silkwood and others had been recorded and disseminated by the F.B.I. One of the documents asserted that criticism of nuclear power through the Silkwood case was "Communist-inspired."

These recent disclosures can be put into perspective by posing a not-very-far-fetched hypothetical example. The manager of a plutonium plant receives a note from an organization claiming that it has stolen some highly lethal plutonium and is preparing to pulverize it over a heavily populated area unless the plant is permanently shut down. Many employees of the plant are known to have had access to the missing plutonium. At least one of them must have helped the outside group. The question is: how far should the police go to force a confession and obtain the missing plutonium before the group could carry out its threat?

Given the extraordinary nature of a terrorist threat involving plutonium, some would say that objections on civil liberties grounds to such investigative techniques as mass searches and even torture should fall by the wayside. In the wake of such an incident, political pressures would mount to develop a draconian security system to forestall a rash of nuclear terrorism. In fact, these pressures have long been building. During the Middle East war in 1973, for example, a secret order was given to all Federal guards on U.S. nuclear transport vehicles to shoot to kill any suspected saboteur.

On a more general level, security clearance systems are being created by the nuclear power industry in many parts of the country. The results of a study conducted last year by Ralph Nader showed the difference between the security programs of nuclear and nonnuclear power companies. Twenty-four nuclear utilities spent nearly $3 million to hire private detectives and investigatory agencies, while fifty-six nonnuclear power companies spent less than a total of $10,000 for these purposes. According to *The Atlanta Journal,* the Georgia Power Company poured more than $750,000 in 1976 into nuclear security measures. It was reported last year that this money was used to run an extensive political spying operation from an unmarked office in downtown Atlanta. The local Nader organization and the American Civil Liberties Union of Georgia were said to have been among the targets.

Paralleling these developments at the local level, the Federal Government is currently struggling to come to grips with the imperatives of nuclear security. In March 1977 the N.R.C. unveiled for public comment the first Government security clearance system ever to be proposed for an entire industry. The proposal, not yet finally approved, calls for intensive F.B.I.-type "full field investigations" to be used to probe the "character, associations and loyalty" of every person working in a nuclear power plant in the United States. These investigations would be patterned after inquiries now employed only at the highest level of the Government to screen people for access to the most sensitive classified information.

But the nuclear-industry program would be different from existing security investigations in several fundamental ways. These differences are clearly set forth in a 1975 report, "The Impact of Intensified Nuclear Safeguards on Civil Liberties," prepared by John H. Barton, an N.R.C. consultant and Stanford University Law School professor. First, the commission has made it clear that it wants to screen out people whose politics or associations are too controversial for nuclear employment—in other words, those who are disloyal to nuclear power. Such a program would thus go much further than existing security clearance procedures which screen out possible agents of a foreign government, and would intrude directly on constitutionally protected freedoms of speech and association. Second, the proposal would extend a relatively limited Government program to an entire private industry. Even then, it is not clear how far it would have to go—in fact, it would be illogical not to require the investigation and surveillance of anyone who transports nuclear materials, or who lives on a nuclear transportation route, or within the vicinity of a nuclear power plant.

The proposed system could lead to a massive invasion of privacy and First Amendment rights. The N.R.C. rule would permit Federal investigators to interview friends, neighbors, landlords, past employers and anyone else in the search for all manner of private information, including evidence of homosexuality "or other sexual perversion"; mental illness or treatment; "prior advocacy without subsequently established rejection of totalitarian, fascist, or Communist" beliefs; association with any organization that advocates the overthrow of the Government; and for anyone having immediate relatives living in "a nation whose interests may be inimical to those of the United States, or in satellites or occupied areas thereof."

When all the evidence about a person had been gathered, the N.R.C.'s standard for granting or denying a clearance is so vague that it would be very difficult to challenge a denial. The regulations say only that "[t]he decision to grant or deny special nuclear access is a comprehensive, common-sense judgment, made after consideration of all relevant information." There is no definition of "relevant information."

And this is not all—the N.R.C. recently asked Congress to amend the Freedom of Information Act to exempt any information about nuclear "safeguards." Apparently, it wants to put the entire nuclear industry under a blanket of secrecy so that working in a nuclear plant would be like working on the Central Intelligence Agency's *Glomar Explorer.*

This, then, is the dilemma that nuclear development poses for civil liberties: to effectively safeguard nuclear materials it may ultimately be necessary to alter our constitutional framework. The dilemma is dramatically highlighted in a draft of the Government's "Federal Response Plan for Peacetime Nuclear Emergencies," prepared in March 1976. What happens if there is a "peacetime nuclear emergency," like the meltdown of the reactor core at Three Mile Island, or the theft and detonation of some plutonium from the Barnwell plant in South Carolina? The Government assures us that:

> Planning efforts for responding to an emergency involving a serious dispersal of radioactive contamination or a nuclear detonation in peacetime will be directed not only toward physical survival, but also toward the preservation of the basic political, social and economic system and values of the affected area. Consequently, every effort will be made to:
> (*a*) Minimize, both in scope and duration, any restrictions, as required by circumstances, of the exercise of constitutional and other basic rights and liberties;
> (*b*) Preserve and/or reconstitute, as soon as possible, representative constitutional government.

Environmentalists have long called attention to nuclear pollution of the physical environment. But nuclear development may cause an even greater pollution of our legal and constitutional environment. Courts and legislatures and other legal institutions in the United States have sometimes restricted constitutional rights because of the apparent necessities of the times. For example, there were tremendous negative pressures on civil liberties during World War II, and the anti-Communist hysteria of the McCarthy era. But these pressures—dangerous as they were—were relatively short-lived because the historical factors that caused them were temporary. This may not be the case with nuclear development if it proceeds on a large scale, and that is why the impact of nuclear power on civil liberties is so profoundly disturbing.

Part V
ALTERNATIVES

PREFACE

THERE ARE A NUMBER of approaches to the problem of dwindling or of increasingly expensive energy resources. The most familiar route is to intensify the search for known fuels. In the case of fossil fuels, this may involve opening up new regions and mining or drilling deeper or more efficiently with improved techniques.

Alternatives may also mean, as suggested in the opening articles of this chapter, finding a new fuel source such as alcohol. Oil from shale remains a neglected potential, despite the extraordinarily abundant deposits, decades of government research and experimentation, and the long-claimed interest in such development by the petroleum industry. There have been warnings about an adverse environmental impact, but it may take a public yardstick experiment to appraise this. Oil from coal is also feasible. Such alternatives require tremendous capital investment and, judging by past performance, huge public subsidies. They will further the concentration of private economic control over energy. Equally troubling is the prospect of accelerated environmental degradation. "National emergency needs" may provide a convenient and not unfamiliar justification for overriding regional anxiety and opposition, once the industry concludes it is ready to launch such development.

More attractive to those concerned by the increasingly antidemocratic character of energy policy are the possibilities for shifting to simpler technologies which rely upon diverse, renewable sources such as grain, wind, water, and sunlight. The vision of windmills, small dams, and decentralized solar collectors weaken the claim as to the inevitability of mammoth, centralized power-generating stations with their high-cost and high-security technologies, all under the management of absentee owners. It is also hoped that these energy alternatives will enlist local business initiative and labor skill. Such steps could give renewed meaning to the ideal of community self-reliance while enhancing respect for the natural environment. The chapter offers several examples of such programs and of the research and political activities which seek to enlarge their number.

Emphasis upon expanding the energy supply can easily slight prior questions as to how energy is now used and how it might be better used. At stake here is not simply a definition of what constitutes waste and what kinds of conservation to promote, but what mechanisms now operate for making such judgments and for introducing the necessary constraints and incentives. It has been seen how the energy industry has sought to make itself the arbiter of all energy innovation and to integrate all such operations within its planning. The other corporations and financial institutions which dominate major sectors of the economy are equally insistent on their need and their right to decide on the direction of their capital investments. Such power is viewed as the heart of the workings of the economy. It is defined as freedom by those forces that hold it. What is the relation between such power and the needs of a public which sees its economic life increasingly battered and is beginning to experience energy not as a liberating force but as a trap? What recourse does it have?

HAVE WE FOUND
A NEW MOTOR FUEL? (1925)

John Collins

Is GASOLINE ABOUT to be supplanted as a motor fuel by a synthetic alcohol which can be sold more cheaply?

This is the dramatic possibility which seems not yet to have been glimpsed by the public in the discussion in trade and technical circles of a product lately put on the market in Germany. If the predictions in regard to this fuel are realized, it will mean a revolution in the oil industry with profound political and economic changes in its train.

One of the most disturbing economic phenomena in the United States is the rapid depletion of our petroleum supply. The Smithsonian Institution predicts the end of our reserves by 1927. The United States Geological Survey estimates that there remain underground in the United States and Alaska only 7,000 million barrels as compared with 53,000 million in the rest of the world.

To get the full significance of these figures in their relation to our economic future one must glance at world oil politics of the past few years. In the struggle for new petroleum sources abroad we have come off second best. All but a negligible portion of the 53,000 million barrels outside the United States now is under British control. It is not surprising, then, that the President's Oil Board has sent out during the past few weeks an emergency call for information on gasoline substitutes.

This quest for substitutes, while in progress in the United States since 1907, has been carried on with unusual vigor since the end of the war. Up to the present time nearly all experiments have been based on the idea of using ethyl alcohol. Potatoes, molasses, and beets have in turn been tried as sources. But costs of production have always been too high. Now from an unexpected source comes what appears to be a solution of the problem.

In the list of imports from Germany for the month of February there appeared opposite "Alcohol, methyl," the notation 62,971 gallons. For years this space had been blank. In our alcohol trading with Germany we had always been exporters. When in March the import figure reached 69,886 gallons with everything pointing to a progressive increase, it was evident that something revolutionary had occurred.

What had occurred was the discovery and commercialization by the German chemical cartel of "wood" alcohol made synthetically from water gas. As the process is understood here, a jet of steam is played on coal; the resulting liquid is placed under great pressure and passed over a catalyst. One yield is methyl alcohol. Another is "synthol," a substance said to be more efficient than tetraethyl lead as a gasoline power-increasing agent, with the additional advantage of being non-poisonous to handle.

The new process is a development of the idea by which the Germans, when blockaded by the Allied fleets during the war, plucked their fertilizers and explosives from the air. The most important thing about it is that it yields methyl alcohol, at a cost said to be a trifle under 18 cents per gallon. The cost of production by the wood-distillation process used by American manufacturers is about 70 cents.

Produced at such a low cost the new alcohol looms up as an actual possible successor to gasoline. According to Dr. Charles E. Lucke, head of the mechanical engineering department at Columbia, it could, if sold at 14 cents, drive 20-cent gasoline from the field. But this computation is based upon present automobile engine compression. Alcohol can be used under much higher compression than can gasoline and, says Dr. Lucke, in special engines the new German product might be competitive even on a basis of present costs. It should be noted that the present production cost of 18 cents per gallon is but the beginning of commercialization. Widening of markets and development of joint products would tend to reduce costs further. Moreover, another variable involved is the price of gasoline. As petroleum supplies dwindle the price of gasoline will, of course, tend to rise. In brief, in the new alcohol gasoline appears to have a competitor.

As a fuel, declares Dr. Lucke, the new alcohol should be superior to gasoline in every way. Being comparatively simple in chemical structure it burns completely, leaving no residue. Moreover, it presents a smaller fire hazard since it may be quenched with water.

"The principal difficulty involved in the transition from gasoline to alcohol will be distribution," says Dr. Lucke. To avoid touring difficulties the alcohol should be available all over the country at once. For this reason existing fuel-distributing agencies will probably have to be utilized. The best plan would be the introduction of the alcohol by degrees. It could be mixed with gasoline and the ratio gradually raised until the old fuel would be eliminated.

The immediate problem presented, however, is the acquisition of the process of production by someone in the United States. It may be true, as the Chemical Foundation claims, that the basic patents covering the secret were registered here in 1914 and have been reposing since the war in the collection seized from the Germans by the Alien Property Custodian. But it is generally admitted that these patents are too vaguely worded to be of any practical use to an American chemist.

To understand how American chemical manufacturers have attempted to cope with this problem it is necessary to review briefly their attitude toward the importation of the new alcohol. When details of the process arrived in this country it was generally conceded in chemical circles that this was a matter in which the tariff was impotent. The levy on alcohol imports is at present 12 cents per gallon. Under the flexible provision of the tariff act it may be raised to 18 cents. Such action in the face of the great disparity between costs, German and American, would have no appreciable effect save to boost the price unnecessarily to the consumer here.

Despite these circumstances, nearly all American chemical manufacturers rushed to Washington and demanded a tariff increase. What they may have in mind, it is whispered in chemical circles, is an embargo. The Government in a tariff inquiry may, if dumping is suspected, order the foreign producer to open his books. If the foreign producer balks, the usual procedure is the establishment of an embargo to be lifted eventually, perhaps by placing the commodity on an American valuation basis.

These tactics have prompted Dr. Marston T. Bogert, professor of chemistry at Columbia, to remark that the American chemical industry instead of devoting itself to laboratory research has been using the tariff to tax efficiency—a tax which the public pays. But in this particular case there have been some American chemical manufacturers who have not put all their eggs in the tariff basket. If one may place any credence in newspaper reports and trade gossip the Du Pont de Nemours Company has been negotiating directly with the Germans for the American rights. Simultaneously, according to the papers, the Du Pont Company has been erecting at Charleston, West Virginia, a plant to produce the new alcohol. . . .

To get the economic implications of this situation it is necessary to consider other news items, apparently unrelated, that have been appearing simultaneously with the alcohol reports. This group of items has centered about the tetra-ethyl lead or "loony gas" investigation. One report stated that the Ethyl Gasoline Corporation, manufacturers of tetra-ethyl lead, had voluntarily suspended business pending the report of a special inquiry into the harmfulness of their product. Another announced that the General Motors Corporation was about to introduce a special high-compression automobile engine.

E. I. Du Pont de Nemours, through ownership of 70 per cent of the stock, controls the General Motors Corporation. General Motors owns the Ethyl Gasoline Corporation jointly with the Standard Oil Company of New Jersey. One should not be surprised to see in the immediate future a new combination: Du Pont making the fuel alcohol, the Standard Oil Company distributing it, and General Motors controlling the high-compression engines in which to burn it. . . .

GASOHOL—
A 100-PROOF SOLUTION (1979)

Fred J. Cook

I

FOR THE LAST eight months, a 1964 Rambler Classic four-door sedan has been tooling around Washington, perking merrily along on alcohol, getting 20 miles to the gallon, and demonstrating to the blind and deaf Carter Administration that there *is* an alternative—that we do not have to be "a pitiful, helpless giant" caught forever in the toils of OPEC-Big Oil blackmail.

The alcohol-fueled old Rambler is the pet visual exhibit of Scott Skylar, for ten years an aide to Senator Jacob Javits specializing in energy problems, and now the Washington director of the National Council for Appropriate Technology. Skylar is one of a growing number of alternative-energy advocates. Theirs is largely a grass-roots movement that insists the Carter Administration's energy policy is as wrongheaded as it can be. . . .

Logic suggests that the Federal Government should have devoted its efforts to finding alternative sources of fuel, the only way to give OPEC and Big Oil the kind of competition on which the free enterprise system supposedly is based. But when Scott Skylar began asking questions four years ago, he found himself running into the stone wall that Big Oil had erected in the bureaucracy.

The experts in the Energy Research and Development Administration, which was later absorbed into the Department of Energy, parroted the lines furnished by the American Petroleum Institute, the industry's authorized apologist. Gasohol (a mixture of 90 percent gasoline and 10 percent alcohol) wouldn't work, they said, because alcohol doesn't have the B.T.U.s (British thermal units) that gasoline does, and so you would only be diluting your real energy source by using it.

"Everytime I suggested something, they had the answers why it wouldn't work," Skylar says. "They were the experts, and I figured they must be right. Some Nebraska gasohol advocates gave me some statistics that seemed to show that gasohol did work, that it gave even better mileage than pure gasoline, but when I went back to ERDA, they shot those figures down, too.

"Then a friend of mine in the Ford Motor Company told me about experiments that Volkswagen had run. I found Volkswagen had run literally hundreds of tests using different blends of gasoline and alcohol, and even pure alcohol. Their tests showed that alcohol really worked well. I went back to ERDA, and they gave me the old story about B.T.U.s—they never seemed to be able to think about anything but B.T.U.s—and they showed me some very inadequate data that had been furnished by the Petroleum Institute on tests that had been run on just seven cars. This made me mad."

Skylar did some further research, and he found that, while alcohol has only about two-thirds the B.T.U.s per gallon that gasoline does, it has "a much greater thermal efficiency. It is 1.4 times more efficient than gasoline in its direct conversion to power."

One great deterrent to the use of alcohol is its cost. It is not price competitive with gasoline even at today's inflated prices. Scott Skylar, for example, pays a gasohol dealer in Alexandria, Va., $1.20 a gallon for the alcohol he uses in his demonstration Rambler. But the reason alcohol prices today are so high is obvious; the availability of grain alcohol has been ignored. Modern alcohol is derived from petroleum, and either petroleum or natural gas is used to fuel the distilling process. Thus the Department of Energy can say truthfully, to a point, that the energy used to make alcohol costs far more than the energy produced is worth. But what happens when, instead of using the most costly substances in our economy, alcohol is made from the surplus corn or waste products of our farms and industry? And what happens when solar energy, not natural gas or petroleum, is used in the distilling process?

Lance Crombie, a Minnesota scientist turned farmer, has supplied some answers. Crombie is a former cancer researcher with a Ph.D. in microbiology. He is chairman of the Minnesota Heart Fund, an associate professor of pharmacology at the University of Minnesota and a member of the New York

Academy of Sciences. He also grows corn and wheat on his 600-acre farm in Webster, Minn.

When heating-oil prices jumped in the winter of 1976–77, Crombie found himself paying $450 just to heat his large brick house for the month of January. Such staggering monthly charges threatened to bankrupt him, and so he decided to put his scientific knowledge to use. The result, after some experimentation, was a cheap, homemade, solar-powered still. Crombie had 45,000 bushels of corn sitting in his bins that he could not market. The corn had cost him $2 a bushel to grow, and the going price was only $1.60. Instead of taking such a loss, Crombie decided to use his corn to make alcohol. Since he was using solar energy, not expensive fuels, Crombie came up with these results:

A bushel of corn produced 5 gallons of alcohol.

A mash called D.D.G.S. that resulted from the fermentation is ideal for feeding livestock, and Crombie could sell this mash for $2, just what it had cost him to grow the corn.

Costs of producing the 5 gallons of alcohol came to just 10 cents a gallon, and the alcohol could easily be sold for 50 cents a gallon. Deducting his total costs of $2.50, Crombie found he had a $2 profit on his five gallons. Crombie, however, wasn't interested in selling his alcohol. He wanted to use the fuel to run his car, his tractor, his other farm equipment—and to heat his home. His solar-powered still now accomplishes all of these objectives at minimal cost and inconvenience.

To heat his home, Crombie uses a 70 percent alcohol, 30 percent water solution (the water, he says, stretches the alcohol so that you end up consuming less alcohol than fuel oil for the same amount of heat). To use his mixture, Crombie increased the size of his furnace's fuel nozzle about 25 percent and adjusted the air valve to "tune in" the flame. When this was done, he found that his alcohol burned with a clean, hot, almost invisible yellow fire. A similar slight adjustment was needed to enlarge the main fuel jet in his car's carburetor—and Crombie was virtually free from his bondage to Big Oil.

Alcohol, Crombie insists, is the easiest fuel to produce and the least dangerous. It can be made from almost anything—waste paper, wood pulp, fruits, pumpkins, sugar cane, sugar beets—even from the refuse of canning and cheese plants and plain household garbage. Sugar beets, Crombie says, could provide an ideal energy source for a farmer who wants to produce his own fuel, and he estimates that 5 acres of sugar beets could be turned into a whole year's supply of alcohol.

There are other advantages. The biggest extra dividend from the national standpoint could be putting all our available farm land to work. Crombie points out that the Federal Government now pays farmers . . . [to limit] production so as not to glut the market. Crombie thinks all available acreage should be planted fence post to fence post; the surplus crops not needed for food should be turned into alcohol for energy, and then the Arabs and Big Oil wouldn't have a monopolistic field day at the national expense.

Does it sound too simple a solution to be valid? Well, Brazil for years now has been revamping its economy along the very lines that Crombie suggests— and has been doing so with phenomenal success. When the first OPEC energy crunch hit the Western industrialized world in 1973, Brazil, unlike the United States, turned quickly to the production of alcohol as an alternative fuel. Sugar cane, the manioc root and other tropical plants were fermented; alcohol was produced, and Brazil became the world leader in promoting this alternative to petroleum blackmail.

Brazil's National Alcohol Commission has approved some 170 projects and earmarked $800 million for biomass conversion and engine modification efforts. Last year, Brazil produced and consumed some 685 million gallons of ethyl alcohol as a gasoline substitute or supplement. Production is expected to reach 1 billion gallons annually in 1980 when gasoline pumps will be allowed to offer only two choices—gasohol or alcohol. By 1981, the president of the Brazilian Automotive Manufacturers' Association predicts, more than 16 percent of the 1 million cars annually manufactured will be equipped with engines to burn only alcohol.

Brazil's experience has demonstrated (as, indeed, have test projects in this country) that alcohol has several advantages over gasoline. It does leave a slight odor, especially when a car is idling, but it burns cooler, cleaner and more efficiently, giving virtually the same mileage as gasoline without spewing out lead or sulfur pollutants. Hydrocarbons are reduced to negligible levels.

It would seem that if Brazil could accomplish so much, the United States, with its vaunted scientific and technological expertise, should have been at least able to match the performance. Except that Big Oil stood in the way. As Scott Skylar found out, the ERDA and its successor, the Department of Energy, both had mind-sets against alternative energy sources. One simple fact illustrates how deep and pervasive was this oil-induced mental block: in President Carter's energy message of April 5, 1979, there is just one tepid sentence devoted to the possibilities of alcohol fuels. ("We can produce more gasohol, already being used to replace gasoline in several states.")

Dr. Schlesinger's D.O.E. did virtually nothing until the fall of 1977 when seventy-three Senators and Representatives—Senators Birch Bayh and Frank Church prominent among them—wrote Schlesinger and Agriculture Secretary Bob Bergland urging "a major national commitment" to the development of fuels from agricultural and forest products. Only then did the sluggish Federal bureaucracy begin to stir. The 1978 budget finally allotted a meager $5 million for "fuels from biomass" research. This figure was increased to $15.4 million in 1979, and an additional $3.9 million was appropriated for research on automotive engines using gasohol.

Senator Bayh got a bill passed by the last Congress to create a National Alcohol Fuels Commission, which he heads. He was also instrumental in the passage of a bill that waives the 4-cents-a-gallon Federal excise tax on alcohol fuels derived from agricultural or forest products. (Ten states have followed this lead by revoking state taxes on such fuels.)

Senator Church has sponsored a bill requiring the Energy Secretary to establish a program to replace gasoline with gasohol and mandating that 1 percent of all United States motor fuel production consist of gasohol by 1981. The mandated percentage would increase to 5 percent by 1985 and 10 percent by 1990. Critics have contended that Senator Church's program is too ambitious, that such goals cannot be met in the specified time frames. But one has to wonder, in light of the foot-dragging official record, whether the real reason is that Big Oil, which has been lobbying for decontrol and higher petroleum prices, does not *want* them to be met.

One thing is certain, progress is being made out in the Middle West and Southern farm belts. The State of Nebraska, which has pioneered in alcohol research, plans to build a 20-million-gallon-a-year alcohol plant to further the use of gasohol. A family farmer in South Dakota, using conventional methods, is distilling approximately 70 gallons a day at a cost of roughly 45 cents, a price that is reduced by revenue from the wet mash by-product sold as feed for livestock.

Farm cooperatives are spurring the use of gasohol. The Indiana Farm Bureau Co-op, which has its own facilities for producing alcohol, reported on March 1 that its sixty county associations had sold 1,237,519 gallons of gasohol in the first two months of this year. The Southwest Farmers Co-op in Selma, Ala., is also distilling its own alcohol. In Peoria, Ill., a commercial firm, Technical Industrial Products, which supplies many Midwestern outlets, plans to boost its alcohol producing capacity from 624,000 gallons a year to 11 million gallons. And a Bayh proposal encouraging farmers to grow energy crops on set-aside acreage without losing their Federal subsidies is now law.

Such are the signs of a rapidly growing grass-roots movement that may eventually prove too potent for even the lobbyists of Big Oil to squelch. If so, the Carter Administration and all its so-called energy experts will have been dragged kicking and screaming to acceptance of a policy like Brazil's that would reduce the nation's utter dependence on OPEC and would act as a deterrent on the inflationary pricing policies of OPEC's Big Oil cartel partners.

II

. . . Common sense says that there *has* to be an alternative to the nation's complete reliance on petroleum, and this common sense began to make its impact in this historic first week of May.

The Midwest farm belt was in revolt. Farmers who had sometimes had to sell wheat and corn at barely break-even prices, who had had to keep millions of acres out of production to stabilize even these prices, were flexing their political muscles. They were demanding that the Government sponsor programs that would convert their surplus crops into alcohol that could be used for energy.

The Washington Mall demonstration was staged to bring their point home to national leaders. It was made possible by a coalition of public interest groups that included Scott Skylar of the National Council for Appropriate Technology, aides to Ralph Nader and South Dakota farmers connected with American Agriculture Inc. The still they erected had two 30-foot-high continuous-fermentation columns and four large tanks that formed a distilling chain until alcohol was finally delivered into the last retaining tank. [A] demonstration model produced 2.5 gallons of alcohol from each bushel of corn, and it also produced methane gas and valuable feedstock by-products.

The demonstration's impact was felt on Friday, May 4, when Representative Richard Ottinger (D., N.Y.), chairman of a subcommittee of the House's Science and Technology Committee, opened the first of a series of hearings on energy developments.

Secretary of Agriculture Bob Bergland testified that making ethanol from grains "was not going to solve the energy crisis." His reasons: the grain production from the 400 million acres under cultivation fluctuates from year to year, depending on rainfall and other weather conditions. Yields in the 1970s varied from 70 bushels an acre to a record 101 bushels last year when conditions were ideal. "We cannot establish that we have a built-in surplus," he said, though he admitted he was happy that we have 1,200 million bushels of grain in reserve to draw on in case of bad yields. He also acknowledged that there are 11 million set-aside acres that farmers are being paid subsidies not to plant.

Bergland added that his department had talked to distillers about building new plants that would be needed for a full-scale alcohol-program and that there were two seemingly insurmountable obstacles: distillers would not invest the millions of dollars required to build the plants because they could not be guaranteed permanent supplies and because wheat and corn prices fluctuate wildly, affecting the possibilities of profit.

Ottinger, who had seen the demonstration on the mall and was apparently familiar with the work of Lance Crombie, the Minnesota farmer who uses a solar still to make alcohol that sells at from 50 to 60 cents a gallon, interrupted Bergland. Suppose the farmers of America utilized such technology to make their farms energy self-sufficient, wouldn't this make a considerable impact?

"One problem I have with the Government," he said, "is that they are always looking for something that will produce huge profits. Yet this farmer is doing it. If you add a little savings here and a little there, it all adds up."

Bergland conceded the point, but he held out only one hope for making a major national impact with alcohol. The nation, he said, has some 400 million acres of forests in which wood is rotting and going to waste. "We think cellulose conversion has a significant potential," he said.

Surprisingly, the long-resistant Department of Energy followed Bergland by weighing in with a hearty endorsement of a full-scale alcohol program. The witness was Alvin L. Alm, assistant secretary in charge of policy and evaluation. "We have concluded that there are a number of advantages and benefits to the country," he said. Alcohol, he declared, can extend our resources and reduce gasoline consumption.

"We have found that alcohol fuels can be produced with a positive gain as long as natural gas and petroleum are not used in the distilling process," he said. "We believe that further economies could be effected in technology."

Gasohol, even as it is, is price-competitive with unleaded premium gasoline and slightly more costly than regular. This alcohol is being produced by conventional methods to sell at between $1.20 and $1.50 a gallon, but Alm said it could be produced at "substantially cheaper prices." He estimated that if the nation used all its resources—grains and other agricultural products, coal and its massive tons of garbage—it might be possible by the 1990s to "extend the petroleum supply of the country by 80 percent, maybe more."

His testimony came as a surprise to Representative Dan Glickman, of Wichita, Kan., who said: "I think you have shown an incredible change of position in the last few weeks. I don't know whether you sincerely believe it or not, but I'm willing to accept it."

Alm assured the Congressman that he was absolutely sincere, and Glickman commented that his attitude seemed diametrically opposed to Bergland's. There seemed to be no coordination, Glickman said, in developing an alcohol fuel program, and he thought the national interest required a united effort by Agriculture, Energy, Treasury and Defense.

Ah, the national interest! That seems to have been largely overlooked in Big Oil's pursuit of bigger bucks, and never did the point become more obvious than in the testimony of two executives of Gulf Oil.

Gulf, it should be said, had exhibited unusual initiative for a petroleum company. For seven years at a research cost approximating $9 million, it had been conducting experiments to develop the very alcohol-conversion technology in which Congressman Ottinger's committee was interested.

The effort had been centered in Kansas City under the direction of Dr. George H. Emert. Dr. Emert had worked with a petrochemical plant, one not designed for fermentation and, therefore, far from maximally efficient. He had tested municipal solid wastes (garbage), agricultural wastes and pulp and paper wastes (these he had found ideal). His petrochemical plant, processing a ton of solid wastes a day, made 40 gallons of alcohol, but Dr. Emert's laboratory experiments indicated that an efficiently designed plant should yield 70 to 90 gallons a day from the same tonnage.

Dr. Emert and his staff of thirty researchers had mapped out for Gulf an ambitious schedule. This called for the construction of a 50-ton-per-day demonstration plant to be brought on stream sometime in 1980 or early 1981. Following that, Dr. Emert's schedule called for the construction of a full-scale commercial plant that would cost $112 million to build and would produce 50 million gallons of alcohol a year.

Enter now the witnesses from Gulf: George E. Huff, vice president for science and technology, and William P. Moyles, vice president for administration and development.

Huff testified about Emert's research and said Gulf would be able to bring a commercial plant into operation in 1983. Even allowing for four more years of inflation, Gulf estimated such a plant could sell alcohol for $1.45 a gallon, with a 15 percent profit after taxes.

Here Moyles took over. He said Gulf had made "a commercial decision" not to go ahead. Gulf has committed $2.5 billion to exploration for new natural gas and petroleum sources, Moyles said, and "we're trying to live within our cash flow." Thus, he indicated, the $112 million needed for Dr. Emert's plant on top of the $2.5 billion would be the straw that broke the camel's back. "It was just a question of where we were going to put our money," he said.

Representative Albert Gore jumped in.

"Is Gulf going ahead on its own?" he asked.

"*No, sir!*" Moyles declared emphatically.

Huff interjected that he thought the project feasible, that it can be done, that it should be done—but by someone else to whom Gulf would be willing to sell its technology.

"I find this fascinating," Gore said. "You have done all the research, and you have discovered, apparently to your horror, that it works."

In a continuing exchange with Gulf officials, Gore marveled that one wing of Gulf was enthusiastic about its alcohol project—and another wing wanted to sell it off. "I wonder if it might have occurred to you that the production of alcohol threatens your oil holdings?" he asked.

Moyles replied that it might be ten or fifteen years before the alcohol plant contributed to company earnings—this despite Huff's earlier testimony that such a plant would yield a 15 percent after-tax profit in 1983.

Gore commented that he thought "we're just plain crazy" and that "we're out of our minds" if we rely on the oil companies to develop alternate sources of energy to help solve our petroleum crisis. "This seems to me a classic example of what is wrong," he said.

Huff protested that Gulf *is* interested in developing alternate sources of energy. He said the company has committed $500 million to developing oil from shale and coal (but not $112 million for Dr. Emert's fermentation plant). Gore hopped on this alibi.

"But the big difference is that you can control the reserves without buying the material from farmers," he said. He pointed out that oil companies own 50 percent of the nation's coal reserves, and when Huff protested that the oil companies don't own the shale lands, the Federal Government does, Gore fired back:

"Yes, and the Federal Government owns all the offshore oil lands, too, but it's you and your Six Sisters who are developing them. What about the national interest? I say again I think we're crazy if we leave the nation's fuel future in the hands of the big oil companies." . . .

SHALE OIL (1965)

Roscoe Fleming

POWERFUL PRIVATE INTERESTS are again working hard to snatch control of the nation's largest potential oil resource—the shale deposits—from the people who own it. The purpose is twofold: first, to stifle immediate competition with the world oil cartel; second, to enable the latter to treat the shale as a private reserve, to be locked up for the industry's profit in the distant future.

The prize is a potential 2 *trillion* barrels of shale oil locked in a giant fossil lake that covers 16,000 square miles of western Colorado, and adjacent Wyoming and Utah. This is actually the world's largest known oil reserve, an energy resource almost as great as that of our coal deposits. About 72 per cent of the area containing an estimated 85 per cent of the oil is still owned by the public through the federal government. The rest, including some of the richest, is already in private hands.

The oil industry has blocked public research and development for decades, against the day when it hopes to take this enormous resource entirely out of public control. The industry's friends in Congress are right now seeking legislation to force the government to lease the public reserves, and to revive private claims that were canceled thirty-five years ago because claimants failed to follow them up as the law requires.

Only a small fraction of the total shale resource is recoverable by present techniques even under the most encouraging conditions, but the deposit is an indispensable ace in the hole for a nation whose material future will depend increasingly on liquid fuels.

Over much of the area the oil-bearing rock is 1,500 feet deep, striated horizontally with richer and leaner oil strata like the leaves of a book. Even the richest shale is 90 per cent rock, a tough, hard marlstone that doesn't break up easily. After breaking or pulverizing, it must be heated to drive off the hydrocarbons as vapor, which is then condensed by cooling.

The product is still not crude oil in the usual sense, but "kerogen," a mishmash of organics that resembles only the lowest-grade liquid crudes, and won't flow through a pipe line. It would therefore have to be refined on the spot, and the resulting gasoline and fuel oils would still have to be piped a thousand miles to any major markets.

Further, even the most elementary public conservation measures would insist that the developer not dump his spent shale ash to deface the mountains, and to blow "back east" on the winds. And the enterprise would have to bid for scarce Western water against prior users and usages, some of which at least would be rated as more in the public interest than the production of shale oil.

For another consideration, the government gets 12.5 per cent royalties on mineral production from dry lands, and 16.5 per cent from offshore minerals. Shale-oil production probably could not stand paying such royalties on top of its other handicaps. But would the public in turn stand for granting it concessions free of royalties?

One member of an advisory committee to Interior Secretary Stewart Udall said that it would cost $100 million to build even a modest refinery of 50,000 barrels daily capacity. No wonder the committee member most outspoken in the public interest, Harvard economist John Kenneth Galbraith, has said that the oil industry's real purpose is not to develop the resource, but to "alienate the land." . . .

On February 26, the Denver *Post* quoted Rep. Wayne Aspinall of Colorado, chairman of the House Interior and Insular Affairs Committee, as saying that his committee may call members of the advisory commission to "answer some searching questions," not about the topic itself, but about "the personal ideology of members of the commission. . . . We may have to go outside the report to find out what prompted them to take their positions. . . . The report and the operation in which it was prepared remind me of my boyhood days on the farm where we used to get some guineas, quail and other strange fowl into our back yard and it always took time to get them to live with the chickens." The *Post* reported that Mr. Aspinall took particular exception to the views of Galbraith. . . . For half a century Coloradoans have been assured that their state possesses one of the nation's great mineral treasures and that a big shale industry is just around the corner—only to see this glittering prospect maddeningly move into the future like a mirage into the desert. They want something *now,* and their politicians encourage them to believe that shale development can be instantly achieved as from a cake mix, and that they can have this cake and eat it too.

But now Udall, unpopularly clear-eyed, comments that the advisory report, although split several ways, does indicate that a shale-oil industry is "at least a decade away." That same old decade with which they've been put off for decades!

Actually, Resources for the Future (whose director, Dr. Joseph L. Fisher, was chairman of the advisory committee) commented years ago that the oil industry's only interest in shale is as insurance for the far future, when the now-plentiful well deposits are exhausted. However, Colorado's two Senators and its Republican Governor continue to insist that delay is outrage, and demand that the deposits be turned over to private industry for quick development.

The same oil industry that is now coyly willing to relieve the taxpayer of his burden of shale reserves has previously opposed even federal research, let alone development. After Hitler's submarines sank so many oil tankers, Congress enacted a crash program for turning coal and shale into liquid fuels. The Bureau of Mines, in charge, opened a shale mine at Rifle, Colo., and built an experimental continuous-flow retort (previously, shale oil had been refined only in batches, a tedious and inefficient process). Everyone agrees that the bureau did a fine job. It devised methods by which it could lay down broken-up shale at the retort for 30¢ a ton, and lowered the total immediate cost of producing liquid from shale to somewhere near the cost from petroleum.

But then came the election of Eisenhower and the ascendancy of the oil industry to a place of potency through its advisory committee to the Department of Interior. Interior Secretary Douglas McKay, the industry's great and good friend, got Congress to abolish the coal and shale programs. The industry's leaders ostensibly feared competition from the government, something most unlikely under any conceivable administration.

Revival of the program in any form was stymied until recently, when a group of the large oil companies with oil-shale acreage financed a research program at Rifle under direction of the Colorado School of Mines Research Foundation. The school's president, Dr. Orlo E. Childs, was a member of the advisory committee named by Udall. This program is still too young to have produced results.

Union Oil Co., a have-not so far as major reserves either here or abroad are concerned, but possessor or lessee of several thousand acres of shale lands, built a $5 million experimental refinery near Rifle in the late 1950s. But after three years' operation it was shut down without any announcement of plans for commercial development.

There is one more entrant. The Oil Shale Corp. of Los Angeles bought U.S. rights to the so-called Aspergren process of Sweden, and commissioned the University of Denver to conduct small-scale recovery experiments with it. This process involves heating steel or ceramic balls and mixing them with the pulverized shale. The heat drives off most of the hydrocarbons as vapor which can then be recondensed, while the spent shale retains enough fuel value to provide the heat. But as with other processes, there is no announcement that this ingenious device is useful on a commercial scale. Apparently methods rapid and cheap enough for commercial exploitation have yet to be developed.

Why doesn't the industry experiment on its own lands, which are ample for commercial development? Galbraith answers that its reluctance to do so again shows a desire to dominate, rather than to develop. Besides, this resource will grow more valuable with time, so the industry may prefer to save its own holdings until later.

In one respect the oil-shale people do have a case: The government subsidizes other petroleum interests far more heavily than the shale companies. Well producers enjoy a "depletion allowance" free from taxes of 27.5 per cent of their gross income, not to exceed 50 per cent of net. This was granted them early in the Hoover administration, ostensibly to compensate for the wasting nature of their resource. In practice, it means hundreds of millions of extra dollars yearly for the industry. But developers of shale get only 15 per cent, so that the rival producers of petroleum are almost twice as heavily favored. The shale people contend that they should have the 27.5 per cent allowance also, and that it should be reckoned against the higher value of kerogen, their equivalent of crude oil, rather than against the much smaller value of shale rock in place.

Of course, reduction of the oil-depletion allowance would better serve the public interest, since it would increase government revenue, but with Congressmen from oil-producing states always alert to spring to arms, this is unlikely. So if there is any concession, it will be toward a larger depletion allowance for shale production.

SYNTHETIC ALL THE WAY (1954)

Harry Levine

STANDING IDLE on desolate coal fields near Louisiana, Missouri, is a vast conglomeration of giant retorts, furnaces, shafts, and conveyor belts. This once-powerful industrial plant, which cost $50,000,000 to build, has been quietly rusting away since March, 1953. Part of it was completed only eight months before the closing of the plant and was never used.

Built by the United States government to demonstrate the manufacture of synthetic fuel, the plant has just been leased to the Hercules Powder Company for six years for slightly above $2,000,000. Under the terms of the lease the company will retain an option to buy. Meanwhile it will not have to pay property taxes. At the time it was shut down the Louisiana plant was converting soft coal into synthetic liquid fuel at a cost within pennies of the cost of natural crude oil—and producing 100 barrels a day. It was the only large-scale demonstration plant of the kind in the country.

Late in 1952, just before the end of the Truman Administration, Oscar Chapman, then Secretary of the Interior, called in a dozen or so Senators to his office—among them Lister Hill, Wayne Morse, and Paul Douglas. After showing them performance charts of Louisiana, Chapman offered them some parting advice. "Keep an eye on this plant," he said. "As soon as the Republicans take over, they'll probably close it down. Then, after everything is quiet, it will be given away to industry." Chapman clearly foresaw the government give-away program with which we have now become all too familiar.

Louisiana was no small gift. Consider our present oil demands. We produce only 6,500,000 barrels of domestic oil daily, but we consume 7,500,000. The difference must be imported. In recent years this has become increasingly expensive. Last year Eugene Ayres, vice-president of the Gulf Research and Development Company and a widely recognized authority on the subject, told a power conference in Chicago: "The rest of the world is increasing its oil consumption more rapidly than we are. The most obvious explanation is that the rest of the world has a far greater margin for technological improvement and for potential demand than we have." From this Ayres concluded: "Imports should soon cost more because of competitive bidding from the rest of the world."

Then he added: "At first glance the picture of the future as drawn may seem rather dismal for the United States. But it happens that the United States is blessed with exceptional abundance of oil-shale and coal. Eventually the whole world must depend upon supplemental [synthetic] fuel sources, and about half the oil-shale and coal of the world is in the United States. If we feel we must do any worrying about the future we should concentrate our attention on the few decades of transition, starting before 1970, when we shall have less natural petroleum and the rest of the world more."

If Ayres's analysis was correct—and officials of the Interior Department believe it was—what was behind the decision to close the Louisiana plant and turn it over to private industry? Undoubtedly the biggest factor was pressure from the oil industry, specifically the National Petroleum Council. One official at the Bureau of Mines said to this writer: "We were going along fine with synthetic-fuel research until the Democrats started talking about large-scale production. That got the oil people all excited about the 'government going into the oil business,' and they have been breathing hot down our necks ever since."

The Administration's stated reasons for disposing of Louisiana are these: First, as announced by Secretary McKay on January 13, "the Interior Department will encourage private industry to assume primary responsibility as soon as any project reaches an advanced developmental stage." Second, "the cost of producing synthetic fuels from coal by known processes is discouragingly high" —to quote a Bureau of Mines statement. Third, according to a spokesman for the Interior Department, "we have learned everything we needed to know at Louisiana. There was no point in keeping it open any more."

How sound are these reasons? When Secretary McKay says private industry should be encouraged to assume "primary responsibility" he either has his tongue in his cheek or is being academic. At this stage the oil companies have no interest in coal, and the hard-pressed coal industry, already on a three-day week, certainly lacks the funds necessary for large-scale research. After spending $500,000 on a two-and-one-half-year study of production of oil from coal, the National Petroleum Council reached the conclusion that the process was "definitely uneconomical under present conditions." The lowest wholesale cost of gasoline made synthetically from coal, the council asserted, would be 29 cents a gallon.

Of course the oil men have an ax to grind, but one is surprised to find the Bureau of Mines in its program statement on synthetic liquid fuels published February, 1954, adopting the same figure—a complete turnabout from its previous estimates.

In February, 1948, the bureau hired the Bechtel Corporation, an engineering firm, to conduct a survey and, using Bechtel's figures, worked out an estimate of 13 to 15 cents a gallon—with the sale of by-products thrown in to bring the cost down. This was only a few pennies away from the prevailing wholesale price of commercial gasoline, 12 cents a gallon. The oil industry objected and promptly made estimates of its own—coming up with a cost of 40 cents a gallon, not figuring revenue from by-products.

The Bureau of Mines then went out and hired Ebasco Services, a highly respected New York engineering firm. Ebasco started from scratch. Late in 1950 it handed in a report that considered everything, right down to the cost of housing for workers if a commercial plant were built and to methods of obtaining private financing. The Ebasco report concluded that the cost of producing high-test gasoline from coal would be some 17 cents a gallon.

Ironically, no one has issued a report on the real cost of producing natural crude oil. At present federal law gives oil-well owners a 27 1/2 per cent tax exemption on gross profits, because of the expendable nature of oil, but this exemption cannot be applied to the cost of synthetic oil. "If we were honest with our bookkeeping—that is, if the 27 1/2 per cent exemption were granted to everyone—any number of kinds of synthetic oil could sell for as little as or less than natural crude," one scientist at the Bureau of Mines told this writer.

The government's third and last contention, that it has already learned at Louisiana everything it needed to know, is the shakiest. Dr. Henry H. Storch, chief of the synthetic-fuels division of the Interior Department, said to this writer a few weeks ago: "I still feel it would be desirable to keep Louisiana in a standby condition. Within six months or a year we will have to go back to a large-scale plant to demonstrate our latest findings." And last March, when J. J. Forbes, director of the Bureau of Mines, and Dr. Lewis McCabe, chief of the fuels and explosives division, appeared before the House subcommittee on appropriations, Dr. McCabe said: "What we would like to do is put the plant at Louisiana on a standby basis and let it stay there until such time as the new process would come in on a bigger scale." Dr. Forbes added: "They have only started and have made the first runs to get some basic information." Their testimony hardly indicates that the Bureau of Mines has learned everything it needs to know at Louisiana.

THE SYNFUEL GIVEAWAY (1979)

John Tirman

IN THE EARLY nineteenth century, the brilliant social theorist Henri de Saint-Simon prophesied that the emerging industrial societies would (and should) be administered by the *industriels*—engineers, technicians and businessmen—at the expense of the revolutionary impulses of democracy and equality then current in Europe. The new class, he argued, "shall henceforth do consciously, and with better directed and more useful effort, what they have hitherto done unconsciously, slowly, indecisively, and too ineffectually." The

Frenchman maintained that the egalitarian demands popularized by Rousseau would be effortlessly turned aside by the increased productivity and material prosperity the technocrats would achieve.

The Ninety-Sixth Congress now seems intent upon advancing Saint-Simon's vision by a giant leap. Out of its frustration with the difficulties of legislating a coherent, effective energy policy, the Democratic leadership has pushed through bills designed by President Carter and former Secretary of Energy James Schlesinger that will authorize a handful of *industriels* to guide America's energy future. This new vehicle of technocracy is called the Energy Mobilization Board (E.M.B.), and it is designed to hasten the development of synthetic fuels.

The E.M.B./synthetic fuels offensive was launched by the President in his July 15 "national malaise" speech, and has largely been accepted by Congress. In that July address Carter promised the "most massive peacetime commitment of funds in our nation's history," a total of $88 billion over ten years, to develop synfuels. The Carter proposal sailed through the Senate with an additional $14 billion added to it—$7.3 billion in immediate funding. The Iranian crisis provided the impetus, and the House, which authorized only $3 billion months ago, is expected to share the new sense of urgency when the two bills are discussed in conference. Carter's ambitious program, he said at the time, necessitated an Energy Mobilization Board "to make absolutely certain that nothing stands in the way of achieving our goals."

The creation of the E.M.B. is plainly directed at the obstructionist tactics employed with some success by opponents of large energy projects. Oil and utility executives have long complained that environmentalists have prevented new refineries and generating plants from being built, and have delayed plans for nuclear plants, offshore drilling and liquefied natural gas terminals. Businessmen contend that years wasted on environmental impact studies, court battles and work stoppages have sent costs soaring and have retarded domestic energy production. Ecofreaks have blocked coal fields from being stripped, oil from being processed, pipelines from being built—and they have been aided and abetted by weak-kneed regulators and reams of red tape. As Senator Henry Jackson puts it: "We have created an institutional crisis. . . . Everyone has the power to delay decisions on energy projects, and too many decision makers are unwilling to decide." The E.M.B. will change all that. . . .

The bill targets agencies (like the Environmental Protection Agency and local zoning boards) and laws (like Federal and state clean air statutes) that were enacted to insure orderly development, environmental protection and public participation. The four-member E.M.B. is empowered to assign priority status to dozens of nonnuclear energy projects, to override Federal, state and local procedural law in order to expedite the decision-making process, and to act on its own if the governing agencies miss deadlines established by the E.M.B. Several Congressmen wanted stronger language that would authorize the E.M.B. to overturn substantive law as well, to throw out pollution laws and land-use ordinances as the E.M.B. saw fit. The House endorsed that authority as embodied in the Commerce Committee bill promoted by Representative John Dingell. Carter supported the Dingell bill, all the while claiming that the Administration would request that the substantive-law waiver be eliminated from the final House-Senate conference version. Because of Carter's equivocation, the final compromise may include the power to vitiate substantive Federal laws. Environmental critics rightly complain that the difference between "substantive" and "procedural" law is often obscure; as one Senate staffer puts it: "In our laws, the procedure is the substance." Critics also charge that a "grandfathering" clause, requiring a complicated series of executive orders, will effectively prevent states and localities from halting ongoing projects that are creating unanticipated problems.

Exactly how the E.M.B. is likely to work can be predicted from past experience in analogous situations. The Trans-Alaskan Pipeline required special Congressional action in 1973 to circumvent further environmental and right-of-way challenges that had delayed its construction. Now, with a glut of crude oil from Prudhoe Bay resting in California, it is apparent that many of the objections that were silenced at the time were correct: the pipeline should have been built to the Midwest, where most of the oil is supposed to go. Charles Cicchetti, now a member of the Wisconsin Public Services Commission, suggested in a study of the pipeline that the oil companies involved wanted to build it to the Alaskan port of Valdez in hopes of selling Alaskan crude to the Japanese. A fuller debate at the time might have averted the current fiasco. Another case: in 1970 a New York corporate lawyer set up a company, Maine Clean Fuels, and applied for a permit to build an oil refinery and terminal on Sears Island in pristine Penobscot Bay, Maine. After months of public hearings and debate, the state's Environmental Improvement Commission voted to deny the permit. *Maine Times* editor John Cole offers this assessment of the case: "The primary lesson learned . . . was the recognition that governing bodies must first design and produce the legal tools for allowing and channeling public participation. Without the Site Location Law . . . the Maine debate over the issue would quite likely have been useless." If there had been an E.M.B. in 1970–71, however, the "procedural" protection of public debate could have been sidestepped and the ill-considered project approved.

The E.M.B. itself is likely to become an unwieldy bureaucracy; it typically takes years for new Federal bodies to hit their stride and work effectively. And the board's actions will not foreclose lengthy court battles. By raising serious constitutional questions of federalism, it may even provoke more litigation, as Senator Abraham Ribicoff has suggested, simply adding to the burdens of energy deployment.

But the technology the board is designed to expedite is also likely to be costly, wasteful, environmentally harmful and burdensome in its own right. Its chief beneficiaries will be the oil companies, not the people.

There's nothing really new about synthetic fuels. The Nazis flew their planes with oil from coal near the end of World War II, and shale oil was being produced before Colonel Drake ushered in the petroleum age at Titusville, Pennsylvania, in 1859. But the cost of synthetics development has been prohibitive. Small pilot projects have been launched in recent years by oil companies and the Government to improve the technology and test the feasibility of producing large quantities. In fiscal 1979, the Department of Energy's outlay for synfuels was $350 million, most of it going to the oil companies—Exxon, Gulf, Mobil and others. But even with the tax subsidies and America's need to curtail OPEC imports, the oil giants have been unwilling to press synfuel development because of its high costs. The most optimistic estimates peg synfuel at $30 per barrel, about 50 percent higher than Saudi crude.

Even some conservative economists and oilmen have been cautious in their endorsement of the plan, although they will play along if their own risk is minimized. John Sawhill, one of Nixon's energy czars and now a Deputy Secretary of Energy, offers the conventional wisdom: "The success of the synfuel program will require some incentives to private industry, either in the form of price guarantees or subsidized loans." The national commitment to synfuels, financed by the windfall profits tax is, he says, "synonymous with energy independence."

The commitment to synfuels certainly means healthy profits for the major oil companies owning vast coal deposits that will operate the plants. The Carter program guarantees them a market and a rate of return that a "free market" would not. The irony of this scam should not be overlooked: the oil companies, bursting with excess profits from OPEC price hikes and fuel decontrol, will have the windfall taxes on those profits returned to them to produce synthetic oil for guaranteed prices. And, of course, their coal reserves will be more valuable as well.

In an industry notorious for oligopoly, the synfuel program will compound the effects of market concentration. A confidential Federal Trade Commission report . . . notes that there is "evidence to suggest that the oil companies have sought the capability to control the pace of synfuel development." Energy conglomerates that produce and market competing fuels "can bring this technology to commercialization at the rate at which total profits are maximized. A firm in this position has an incentive to use its market power to discourage potential competitors."

Moreover, the synfuel advocates, with their claims of production levels and technical competence, are playing loose with the truth. The process by which synthetic fuels are produced is itself energy-intensive. Three times more energy is required to produce a barrel of synthetic oil than in conventional drilling. That means that the *net* energy produced is lower than claimed. The evidence that large-scale coal liquefaction is even feasible is somewhat in doubt. Last year, Dr. L. E. Swabb of Exxon observed that "assuming coal liquefaction is viable, commercial plants could come on stream in the late 1990s. . . . We are not satisfied with what we have now." And then there is the question of coal production: the President's synfuel target will require an additional 230 million tons of coal per year, 25 percent more than Carter's ambitious goal in the National Energy Plan, which even two years ago was widely regarded as being unreachable.

Even more troubling than this gift to the oil barons, though, are the frightening implications for the environment and the colossal cost of the program. The likely ecological effects are awesome. All synfuel production requires massive amounts of water, which is already in short supply in the Western region most often mentioned for plant siting. Large quantities of ash waste are produced and must be disposed of. And the fuel itself burns dirty. A study conducted for the Council on Environmental Quality by a group of prominent scientists warns that widespread use of synfuels would hasten an already worrisome trend toward dangerously high levels of carbon dioxide in the atmosphere, which creates the infamous "greenhouse" effect—the gradual warming of the earth's atmosphere. Although the multiple pollution problems of synfuels were pressed upon Carter by a coalition of environmental activists during his Camp David summiteering, he has disregarded their admonitions.

The economics of synfuels are equally burdensome. The Rand Corporation, evaluating the likely cost ecalation based on past Government performance with public projects and weapons procurement, anticipates cost overruns of around 300 percent, perhaps as high as 500 percent. That could raise the synfuel project to $400 billion over the next decade. As *The Wall Street Journal* commented, "Aside from the question of ending up with an inefficient, obsolete technology after a crash effort, there is the matter of diverting capital resources from the rest of the economy." Couple that with the President's hope to build another 100 or so nuclear power plants at more than a billion dollars each, and we will have a severe capital shortage in the coming decade that can only exacerbate our current economic woes.

Although our Washington decision makers are reluctant to admit it, alternatives to imported oil *and* synfuels *and* nuclear power do exist. . . . The most thrifty and efficient tools available are conservation and solar technologies. Carter usually mentions conservation only as a voluntary measure, and his much-trumpeted solar energy initiatives amount to a tiny fraction of that promised for nukes and synfuel. Yet with conservation alone, a 20 percent reduction in total energy demand (currently 38 million barrels per day of oil equivalent)—considered to be relatively easy with technical alterations in existing equipment—would reduce consumption by an equivalent of more than 7 million barrels per day, *more than all the oil we import from OPEC.* . . .

GEOTHERMAL ENERGY (1977)

Sheldon Bierman and Gaillard T. Hunt

WHATEVER HAPPENED TO the Geothermal Energy Research, Development, and Demonstration Act of 1974? It passed by a vote of 404 to 3 in the House and by voice vote in the Senate. But somewhere in the short trip from the Capitol to the headquarters of the Energy Research and Development Agency (ERDA) at the foot of the Hill, the law lost some of its steam. What was to be a great geyser of public investment in a new energy source became a trickle of tepid water.

Geologists believe that American geothermal resources can be economically developed, with present techniques, to produce the energy of about ten nuclear or ten large coal-fired plants. This equals 100 million barrels of oil per year, equivalent to two weeks of our foreign oil imports. Japan, Iceland, Mexico,

New Zealand and other countries are already producing geothermal energy on a large scale. America has lagged behind.

The 1974 Act had wide sponsorship; when it came up for hearings optimism abounded. Dr. Dixie Lee Ray, then chairman of the AEC, spoke enthusiastically of the University of California's plans, through its Lawrence Berkeley Laboratory, to build demonstration plants; it was spending $1 million on this project in 1975. Dr. Ray said, "We believe that such systems represent a very large potential resource in the United States." Other witnesses agreed, and some scientists who hoped for breakthroughs to new techniques speculated that geothermal energy might eventually become a resource equal to oil. Even allowing for boosterism, it was clear that everyone concerned agreed geothermal energy should be developed.

So the Act passed, strengthening the earlier authority of the AEC in the geothermal area, and specifically mandating that the government build plants to produce electricity from geothermal energy. But Frank Zarb, then assistant director for Natural Resources, Energy, and Science at the Office of Management and Budget, and John Sawhill, FEA administrator, came up to the Hill to put the Nixon administration's hex on any suggestion that the government might be elbowing in, even marginally, on private profits. Their main worry was the demonstration plants. Zarb said, "We do not believe that demonstration projects should be initiated now in the relative infancy of the program. Also we should recognize the possibility that private industry could step in and fund some or all of the demonstration projects." Sawhill added, "Clearly demonstration plants must be built and operated. . . . The question is really who should build the plants and when?" But the Act's sponsor, Rep. Mike McCormack (D., Wash.), was determined on this point. "Since any demonstration program is available to anyone in private industry, it would strike me that the earlier the demonstration program is completed, the more incentive there is for private industry to become involved. I just want to make the point that I differ with you on the inference drawn in your statement."

So when the Act passed there was no confusion about Congress's will: the AEC, or ERDA as it would soon become, was to lead the way by actually getting into the geothermal business. Government would take the risks, drill holes, install pipes and turbines, and sell the electricity to a power system. There could be no faster way to find out what the technical problems were and how to solve them, or to show the power companies and others that they could get profitable electricity from the heat in the earth.

Now, three years later, there are still no demonstration plants. "It's clear that the specifics of the Act have not been carried out," says Dr. Thomas Ratchford, one of the experts who drafted the Act, who is now at the American Association for the Advancement of Science. There are four or five types of geothermal energy resource: steam, hot dry rock, gases under pressure and hot water, either clean or briny. There were supposed to be, says Ratchford, "one or two plants for each; so by the end of the demonstration period—what was that, five years?—we should have six or eight plants on line of 1 to 10 megawatts each."

But now there are only a couple of ERDA demonstration plants under construction: one at Raft River in Idaho, and one in the Imperial Valley of California. There is no plant in northern Nevada; Lawrence Berkeley Laboratory had plans for one there but they were scotched.

The full explanation for this delay would probably require a book, and it isn't clear what the title would be. Part of the text might be called "Welfare for Industry—How the Technical Fraternity in Government Looks After Its Brethren in Industry." Another part might be "Cutting Them Off at OMB—How to Ambush Public Power Legislation." There seem to be no real villains, and certainly there are no heroes. In fact all the characters think alike: they don't believe government should take risks or lose money, or even make money, and above all they don't believe government should get in the way of what private industry might want to do—some day.

The Nixon men, enthusiastically voted down by Congress, simply went back to OMB and ERDA and imposed their view. No one in the Carter administration has suggested a change. The present OMB official working on ERDA has said that the agency definitely will not be moving into the type of exploration "traditionally associated with the private sector." In his view ERDA should not build plants unless their success under commercial management is a good bet.

It is not hard to restrain ERDA; it believes in "working with industry," not in leading it. The Definition Report of ERDA's Geothermal Research, Development and Demonstration program says its goal is "to work with industry to provide the nation with an acceptable option. . . ." This approach requires the agency to avoid the risks inherent in the large-scale demonstration plants it was supposed to build.

In place of the development of the geothermal lodes on federal lands ERDA has turned to subsidizing a limited number of private projects. The federal government has leased out more than 1.5 million acres of known geothermal resource areas (KGRAs) from the public lands in the Western states. The prime tracts have often gone to those that least want to see geothermal competition, the large oil companies. They will hold them on long-term renewable leases, either as speculations or as hedges against competition. The leases do not obligate the companies to drill, nor even require that they turn over their data to ERDA scientists if they do drill. ERDA prefers to leave this voluntary. In southern Utah, the agency has proposed to buy some data from private drilling, but on terms heavily benefiting the firms that get the contracts.

North central Nevada is the classic case. In 1973, under the AEC, the Lawrence Berkeley Laboratory began prospecting there for geothermal resources on some 88,000 acres of public land that was withdrawn from leasing for two years. There are hot springs in the area, so the geologists began delicate measurements of ground temperature, magnetic and electrical phenomena, microseismic activity, and so on. ERDA recalls in a recent review that "At the initiation of this program in 1973 the objective was to find a site for a 10 megawatt demonstration power plant in the north central Nevada portion of the Basin and Range province. . . . In 1973 the project was reoriented. A demonstration plant was no longer a specific objective. . . ." In short, just as Congress was calling for demonstration plants, ERDA and OMB were "reorienting" away from them.

The Lawrence Berkeley geologists decided there was something large and hot in the area: they reported, "data suggest the presence of a capped hot-water reservoir area north-northwest of Leach Hot Springs," Grass Valley, Nevada. It is "evident that, from existing data, Grass Valley offers a more promising geothermal potential than does [nearby] Buffalo Valley." So in February 1976 ERDA convened a review panel, whose geologist members perforce agreed "that a well coordinated drilling program is in order . . ." involving several holes up to 300 meters to probe for the best place for a 1,000-meter hole to confirm what they thought was there: a large and hot body of potential value to the hungry power grids of California and the Pacific Northwest.

But the oil industry, represented on the panel by men from Chevron (Standard Oil Company of California) and its affiliate, AMAX, had not been idle. The review panel quickly became an unannounced advisory meeting on the propriety of federal drilling and lease exploration. The head of ERDA's program for assessing geothermal reservoirs, Dr. John W. Salisbury, outlined industry's opposition to withdrawals of public land from leasing. He then stressed that ERDA's mission, as he saw it, is to "foster industry," by which standard the Lawrence Berkeley program was a "negative factor," since it was raising the value of the public lands. Salisbury said that, "within the economical, political and philosophical context of the ERDA program as it should be, this northern Nevada project is kind of an embarrassment, frankly. Since it is our purpose to foster the geothermal industry we are not going to continue to pursue this program."

So in the summer of 1977 Buffalo and Grass Valleys baked in the Nevada sun, free of geothermal prospectors, test wells and the scientists from the University of California. The 88,000 acres that were withdrawn from leasing have been thrown open again, and large tracts in the region have been snapped up by companies such as Chevron. This shuts out public development for five years, and longer if they want. The R.J. Reynolds Industries subsidiary, Aminoil USA, took the leases in Grass Valley itself, and has no plans to drill. Chevron is unlikely to want to drill in that area because it is already drilling for geothermal energy in Beowawe, Nev., a few miles to the east.

Thus the dread threat of public competition, even in an unproven and experimental area, has been driven off the geothermal lodes of northern Nevada by the very ERDA scientists and managers who were supposed to stir up a little development. ERDA has not asked, in federal geothermal leases for Grass Valley or Buffalo Valley, for any provisions that would require lessees to consult with Lawrence Berkeley personnel or to disclose drilling results. Some of these scientists regret keenly the lost chance to confirm their three years or so of observations, but they will say nothing for attribution. They know their disappointment is only part of the frustration of the Geothermal Energy Research, Development, and Demonstration Act of 1974; that the crisis in energy applies only to the public and not to the settled ways of doing business between the government and the big oil companies. . . .

INDUSTRY HIDES
FROM THE SUN (1977)

Harvey Wasserman

Now, in houses with a south aspect, the sun's rays penetrate into the porticoes in winter, but in summer the path is right over our heads and above the roof so that there is shade. If, then, this is the best arrangement, we should build the south side loftier to get the winter sun, and the north side lower to keep out the cold winds.

—XENOPHON, *Memorabilia Socratia*

IN 1952, HARRY TRUMAN'S Materials Policy Commission on Resources for Freedom reported that by 1975 there would be a market for 13 million solar-heated houses in the United States. But cheap oil, gas and coal—and Dwight Eisenhower's 1954 "Atoms for Peace" speech at the United Nations—nipped the solar industry in the bud.

Now the oil and gas crisis—the "Sputnik" of solar energy—has it going again. At the end of December 1975, a major study by the Energy Research and Development Administration (ERDA) reported that "solar heating can now compete economically" with electric heat in New York and at least a dozen other Northern cities ranging in frigidity from Boston to Bismarck. "The technology is maturing quite rapidly," says Robert L. Hirsch, an ERDA solar research administrator. "Costs are coming down quite nicely."

According to the ERDA report, half the 866,000 single-family houses built in 1975 were equipped with electric heat, and the guess is that the same ratio held for 1976. The report said that every one of those houses could have been profitably fitted with solar heating features. In states like New York, where electricity costs are high, solar heating would pay for itself in ten years or less. Small wonder, then, that the Arthur D. Little think-tank recently reported that the solar industry could be in the billion-dollar-per-year class as early as 1980.

The ERDA report was just further confirmation of what a growing legion of natural energy researchers as well as environmentalists have been arguing for some time—that solar energy could rapidly supply a large share of America's energy needs, could in fact be the answer to the ever-growing problems of polluting, nonrenewable fossil and nuclear power.

Solar energy and its wind, tidal and geothermal companions have been more or less relegated to sideshow status by the major energy corporations. In a well-planned and richly funded campaign, we've been treated over the last year or two to a long series of ads, speeches and pamphlets "proving" that, although the major corporations are doing their very best to develop natural energy technology, it just isn't "realistic."

The fact of the matter is, however, that the future of solar energy depends on politics, not on technological breakthroughs. "The basic groundwork has been laid and proven," says Fran Koster, a natural energy educator and organizer of a massive "Toward Tomorrow" fair at the University of Massachusetts last summer. "There is a lot of sophisticated work now in progress, and the future success is obvious. These are essentially very simple technologies, and when the implementation money finally does come, you're going to see some very amazing changes in the way energy is produced in this country."

Koster's optimism is shared by a large number of researchers and developers in the field, who recently received what amounts to their Magna Carta from a young energy researcher named Amory Lovins, whose major study on natural energy was published last November in *Foreign Affairs*. In a long, detailed analysis, Lovins demonstrated that a tough program of conservation, combined with rapid development of renewable energy technologies, could bring a total phase-out of not only nuclear but also fossil-generating facilities in the United States by the third decade of the next century.

Lovins's plan, however, has as much to do with the localization of installations as with the further development of windmills and solar panels. "We really need no big plants of any kind," he told me in a telephone interview. "We could be running the country with no central power stations. Electricity costs twice as much in many cases to deliver as it does to generate, and pretty soon people are going to realize that generating power with nuclear reactors is like cutting butter with a chain saw."

Lovins's model is based on small-scale generation at the source of demand, with a drastic reduction in the emphasis on electrical use. "We already have an excess of electrical capacity in many places," he says. "And we also know that a generator next door is considerably more reliable than one miles away."

He sees a vast network of solar systems, windmills and the like—all locally controlled and maintained—as the basic premise of the natural energy argument. Hydroelectric power is still quite arguably the cheapest form of electrical generation, and its proponents claim its potential has been downgraded in the push to nuclear power. Wood has entered the picture as well, and detailed studies now available point to the world's vast remaining forests as a potential energy source of major importance. The forests in question are not, of course, virgin or wilderness stands, but those in places like New England and large areas of the West that have already been logged and are now in desperate need of thinning and other care. New breeds of fast-growing, high-bulk trees can be raised profitably for energy use.

Even garbage has become a factor. St. Louis now operates a $70-million trash-fired generating facility that disposes of the city's solid wastes while producing power and paying for itself by sorting and selling the recyclable materials. Other more exotic ways of distilling garbage into gas now also appear to be approaching cost-competitive status.

What it comes down to is an essentially unexplored energy frontier with limitless potential but an uncertain schedule, a schedule dependent, essentially, on the winds of politics. "There's no doubt what we can do," says Lovins, "but it may take several years to clear away institutional barriers." That last is a massive underestimate of the opposition.

Those institutional barriers amount to little less than the entire nuclear, fossil-fuel and utilities industries. In most cases, these powerful corporations are in an either/or position on natural energy—either it stays small, or they lose their huge investments. The utilities, for example, would find it difficult to collect bills on independently owned solar generating panels, and although both G.E. and Westinghouse are conducting solar research on grants from ERDA, there is an uneasy feeling among independent researchers and nuclear opponents that they may be more interested in protecting their multibillion-dollar stake in atomic power than in revolutionizing energy generation. As Sen. Gaylord Nelson recently told *The Christian Science Monitor,* "The suspicion is almost unavoidable that the giant firms, because of their large investments in nuclear technology, hope that solar energy will not gain rapidly."

"I have no doubt," adds Prof. William Heronemous, "that the major utilities have played a role in sabotaging natural energy development. They certainly have a lot to lose." Heronemous is a University of Massachusetts engineer, and one of the world's leading experts on wind energy. His own plans for massive wind generators off the Atlantic coast have fallen on deaf ears at ERDA, but a small-scale windmill of his design recently received some federal money after Heronemous and his co-workers had spent years scraping together bits and pieces of financing to keep the project alive.

Like others in the field, Heronemous is reluctant to level charges of direct sabotage against anyone. But until now government money for solar research —even in the face of the energy crisis—has been scarce. The final Ford administration's allocation of $250 million to $300 million is an improvement over previous years, but still a drop in the bucket when compared to federal money devoted to the atom. A change may come now that Carter is in office, but so far ERDA has been staffed more by holdovers from the old Atomic Energy Commission than by solar pioneers. "There's not so much a conspiracy as a strongly held ERDA view that natural energy is not where it's at," says Lovins. "The nuclear business is very complicated, and people aren't giving time to other things. You don't need to impute conspiratorial bad faith to get the same results."

Others are less kind. Large grants to G.E. and Westinghouse for solar energy products have annoyed the opponents of nuclear power who feel the money should have gone to independent researchers without such a clear stake in competing technologies. At the same time, the National Aeronautics and Space Administration's Plum Brooke windmill project at Sandusky, Ohio, has done little to encourage confidence in the government's enthusiasm for a solar solution. The multimillion-dollar 100-kilowatt machine was brought on line in October 1975, but has been plagued with malfunctions. Among other things, critics charge that the designers of the 100-foot windmill ignored the advice of their own consultants and repeated many of the mistakes encountered in earlier projects.

One of the grislier clashes between nuclear and natural energy has come in New Hampshire, where state workers have inexplicably taken to destroying hydro-electric facilities that were supposedly being put into mothballs. While New Hampshire's archconservative Gov. Meldrim Thomson pushed hard for a controversial $2 billion, 2,300-megawatt nuclear facility at the coastal town of Seabrook, his government has mysteriously allowed some twenty hydroelectric facilities to sit idle, including the Lochmere dam at the town of Tilton. Thomson had assured local authorities that work on the 800-kilowatt facility would be limited to a canal there, but James B. Walker, a local businessman, later charged that "when work started, one of the first things done was to smash out the turbines and dynamite the inlet structure in the powerhouse." President of a local conservation society, Walker wrote in a public letter that "there is a formerly large, but presently untapped reservoir of energy in New Hampshire," and wondered what could possibly be the "rationale behind the apparent ongoing action in abandoning hydropower in New Hampshire."

Similar charges have been leveled in other states, where it is said that hydro facilities have been abandoned and many coal- and oil-fired plants allowed to fall into disarray, while state authorities argue for nuclear expansion. An essential part of Lovins's analysis is his contention that existing sources of power could easily tide the country over until massive application of solar technologies were made ready. But the validity of that assertion depends obviously on the present and potential capacity of current facilities, and it is here that some of the bitterest battles may be fought. In that context, the New Hampshire situation, and others like it, are alarming, to say the least.

But another, perhaps key factor in the economics of the question has until recently been given scant attention by the environmentalists. It is the factor of jobs. For some time now, the construction trades unions and their colleagues on the AFL-CIO labor councils have been the shock troops of the nuclear industry, serving as its most visible and vocal supporters. Nuclear construction, they claim, means jobs.

True enough, nuclear projects result in several thousand high-paying positions for a period of five to ten years. There has been up to 50 percent unemployment among the construction trades for the past few years, and for them nuclear construction is powerfully attractive. But, at least in the abstract, the jobs argument has become increasingly the property of natural energy proponents. "You couldn't find a worse way to spend money with long-term jobs in mind than nuclear construction," says Koster. "Almost every study I've seen indicates that energy is on the bottom of the list of job-producing industries, and the nukes are lowest on the energy list."

Atomic construction is heavily capital-intensive, which means that it soaks up large quantities of expensive building material and equipment for plants which, when completed, will use relatively little labor. It takes, after all, fewer than 200 workers to operate a 2,300-megawatt nuclear power plant.

Renewable energy, on the other hand, involves costs of 50 percent or more on the labor side. Indeed, a recent draft legislative report on "Energy and Employment in New York State" argued that the conservation industry alone would provide three times as many jobs per dollar as fossil or nuclear energy plants. Wood and wind energy would produce jobs at rates of one and a half to six times that of conventional sources, and the statistics in other renewable energy fields are comparable.

The argument has gained some force among unions such as the woodworking trades, the United Auto Workers, which pioneered anti-nuclear interventions on health grounds, and the United Mine Workers, who have an obvious economic stake in the slowdown of nuclear power. The job appeal also attracted the support of Ed Sadlowski, the maverick steelworker.

But the argument doesn't weigh much with unions whose jobs are on the line today. "Essentially our position is that nuclear power is here," says Tony

Mazzocchi of the Oil, Chemical and Atomic Workers Union (OCAW). Mazzocchi's union has been highly critical of both the nuclear industry and the government on issues of health and safety. But Mazzocchi's position is still "that solar energy will not create jobs for people who are distressed at the moment. It's a question of the guys that are going to build that plant—jobs for whom, and where. It's one thing to be against nuclear power because it's dangerous; it's another thing to talk on the jobs issue. Because for the anti-nuke people, the jobs issue is a losing line."

What loses about that line, of course, is not that natural energy sources and conservation won't create jobs, but that the jobs aren't available right now, and when they become available may not be the highly skilled, high-paying union jobs provided by heavy nuclear construction. The Oregon experience with bottle recycling has proven that conservation can and does create *more* jobs—but that the jobs are largely unskilled and, quite often, nonunion. A similar situation exists in the housing trades, which would be the ones most likely to benefit from the growth of a solar panel industry, and it would probably be true throughout much of the nascent natural energy field. Thus to a large extent the labor hostility is aroused not so much by the threat to present jobs as by fears about *what kind* of jobs, and what type of unions—if any—natural energy will promote.

Organized labor in Europe, Japan and Australia is far more sharply divided on the nuclear question. Railroad unions in Australia have balked at handling even raw uranium for fear of promoting worldwide nuclear proliferation, while in Japan electrical unions that stand to benefit directly from nuclear construction have been opposed to it.

So far, however, the pro-solar forces here have had to content themselves with lining up whatever union support they can get while pushing the point that some of the pro-nuclear unions are as tightly bound to the economic investments of the nuclear industry as are the executives themselves. It is here that the bothersome conflict between environmentalists and organized labor has been most damaging, and it is here also, unfortunately, that the long-range future of solar energy may be decided. Without substantial labor support, the financing needed to bring large-scale applications of renewable energy technologies on line are hard to envision. And it could well be that an appeal to the unskilled, unorganized and "invisible" working population may ultimately be the one with the most force.

For, despite the battle of conflicting interests, the solar industry is growing fast. It is now possible to order solar heating and cooling hardware, solar water heaters, solar swimming pool heaters, windmills and other natural energy apparatus from any of a hundred separate companies. A partial catalogue of those in the business reads like this: Solaron, Sunenergy, Sunearth, Suntek, Sun Wind, Sunworks, Northwind, Windworks, Earthwind, Kedco, Electro, Heliotrope, Helion, Solector, Sunsave, Solar Survival, Daystar, Total Environmental Action and so on. Henry Marvin, ERDA solar director, likens the market to the days before Henry Ford, "where you had a car that cost whatever the entrepreneur who just made it could get for it."

But indications are that the industry is a good deal further along than that. It is now possible to build solar features into a new house for as little as $3,000 to $6,000, depending on what percentage of the heating you want to cover.

Prices are higher for fitting houses already standing, but as fossil and nuclear fuel prices soar, the pay-back period shrinks from the ten-year rule of thumb.

At the same time, basic advances seem to be making natural technology cheaper by the day. A recent University of Delaware breakthrough in the development of solar cells designed to generate electricity is expected to drop the cost of the cells by at least 26 percent, and to put the project a full two years ahead of schedule. What makes that figure remarkable is that the projections were made just two years ago. "We expect to be five years ahead by the early 1980s," says Dr. Alan Barnett, director for the university's Institute of Energy Conversion. "We're talking seriously about a 'per acre' and 'square mile' technology. And once you've deployed the stuff, it'll stay there and keep producing forever."

The innovation at Delaware involves cadmium and copper sulfide cells, but parallel work is also being done in silicone-based cells. Developers in both fields quote cost figures for cell production in the 1980s that would make their use competitive with nuclear energy, although they also caution that the ability to mass-produce the cells may be limited for some time.

Professor Heronemous, however, expresses no such reservations. "If this were war," he says, "we'd have these things out in a year." An outspoken critic of nuclear power, Heronemous claims that 20 percent or more of the East's energy needs could be met by large-scale windmills off the Atlantic Coast by the year 2000. Meanwhile, he is working on small-scale machines. "We're shooting for a production-line version of wind-powered electric heaters to sell for less than $9,000. There are very few who think we can do it, but we're hoping to see 9 million in operation in the next twenty years."

The chief technological hurdle to natural energy generation is storage, for the batteries currently available make holding electricity over cloudy or windless stretches prohibitively expensive. But ultimately politics will decide how far and how fast renewable sources become available. The bulk of new information on natural energy shows clearly that it has arrived. How fast it is incorporated into society depends on such "nontechnological" factors as ERDA budgets, who the recipients of future research and development grants are to be and, ultimately, the willingness of the government and the public to practice conservation while the gaps in solar technology are being filled.

Here will be the true test of the Carter administration's energy policy. If the government is willing to crack down on energy wastage and to allocate the needed billions—not just millions—to get the solar industry moving as fast as it should move, nuclear power could very quickly take its place alongside the Edsel in the Hall of Obsolete Technologies.

It would be naïve, however, to wait for such changes from on high. In the long run the advancement of solar technology will depend on the ability of the environmental side to make a case for it as an efficient, job-producing energy source that is cheap and available to everyone.

When the movement attains the necessary critical mass, we will see windmills, solar panels and their attendant armies of tradespeople swarming all over the unpolluted landscape.

Part VI
AFTERWORD

PREFACE

ONE CONCLUDING CHAPTER will not unlock all the puzzles or make whole the various elements of an energy policy appropriate for a democratic society and a peaceful world. What it does introduce are some underlying propositions for thinking about energy and the related issues of technological innovation, industrial planning, and democratic control. The chapter is the shortest in this book, not because of any lack of suitable articles, but because of a concern to remain within the limits of one moderately priced and manageable volume. It is also assumed that the wealth of materials introduced thus far will have stimulated the reader to extract many of the larger problems and principles relevant to American energy history and prospects.

Energy policy should be determined by the kind of society Americans seek, not the other way around. While there is every reason for using such resources wisely, the country has neither a shortage of energy nor of the intelligence to make it available. The need is for the political will to support its purposes.

Thoroughgoing democratic values require an economy committed to the just development and distribution of energy for people everywhere. Economic justice must extend to the energy rights of the succeeding generations who will have to live in the environment we bequeath them. Safeguarding the natural heritage from deterioration is therefore a precondition for an energy bill of rights. Economic democracy also requires that energy decisions affecting people's lives be accountable to them. Mechanisms must be found for bringing energy policies directly into the political process and for expanding citizen participation in debate and control.

Present energy practices run counter to such objectives. Corporate and governmental action has given highest priority to resources which are the most expensive, the most limited, or the most dangerous. Basic information has been guarded as proprietary or secret. Socially desirable technologies have received minimum encouragement or have been withheld when they threaten private planning. Absentee owners have been indifferent to the needs and the will of local communities when introducing or shifting energy installations at home and abroad. Public government has been neutralized or captured. (Noting the number of private contractors working for the oil industry while also serving the Energy Department, one public interest lawyer testified in 1979 that were there a truth-in-government law, "the agency would be listed on the stock exchange rather than in the government organizational manual.") An artificial energy crisis has been used to convince the American people that its national interest is in the Persian Gulf and that military force is needed to keep producing regions in line. Energy has been abandoned to the profit manipulations of global corporations who also take responsibility for imports. Treating fossil fuels as commodities has been harmful to American development; treating solar prospects in the same fashion could be fatal.

Public ownership and democratic planning of basic energy resources are starting points for reversing these patterns. There is everything to be learned about how to plan democratically. While there is no ready model to adopt, there are relevant experiences worth careful review. Some come from the American public power tradition. The nation should encourage experiments at every level of the political economy.

When evaluating energy alternatives, we must ask which provide the most widespread and satisfying employment; which are most in harmony with the realities of total energy availability; which least distort the overall demand on the nation's capital investment; which entail least violence to nature; which are most likely to respect the rights of other people to use energy and to encourage international cooperation in the sharing; which are most likely to foster a garrison state; and which are most likely to maximize community self-reliance. By such tests nuclear energy and many of the proposed high-technology synthetic fuels appear to come out poorly in contrast to renewable possibilities for meeting the balanced needs of the economy.

If conservation is to be more than landscaping of the present system of production, end use planning must be introduced whereby the community develops the power to limit energy-devouring production while encouraging socially needed goods and services. The arguments for the rebuilding of mass transportation and the rethinking of agribusiness are persuasive because they link energy concerns, full employment objectives, and more satisfying daily life. Such planning ultimately involves democratically set priorities and controls over capital investment.

Global cooperation and global planning must be introduced for dealing with world resource allocation and environmental protection. The continuing struggles over the law of the sea suggest how difficult a task that is. Unfortunately the United States lost a major opportunity to advance such an ideal when it was content to have American-based corporations dominate oil. Now that the producers are in the ascendancy, it becomes a little awkward for the United States to advance the principle that energy resources ought to be the monopoly of no people. Meanwhile, it keeps a discreet silence about the administered prices of the industrial goods its corporations sell abroad and at home. It would also be in the national interest to encourage non-OPEC regions of the world to develop their own energy resources. Instead the United States and the world-lending agencies have resisted extending the financial help needed and thus have furthered dependency upon the existing oil corporations and now also upon OPEC.

The giant corporation is not going to wither away because of talk about democratic planning. Independent information about its power over the present energy system and about alternatives must become widespread to counter the pervasive corporate defenses. There must be popular organization to fight for public purposes and control. Active public participation is imperative if planning is to be democratic. "More government" provides no automatic solution to the problem of irresponsible power. Even a program as visionary as the TVA could become "just another power company" willing to buy strip-mine coal on the cheap and to push nuclear construction while neglecting the more difficult task of sustaining the grass-roots ideal. Wherever possible community and regional energy projects with which the people can identify must be developed. One recalls the efforts of community organizer Danilo Dolci to have poor peasants in Sicily take responsibility for the building of a desperately needed dam which had been promised to them by their rulers for many years. To Dolci the result when the dam opened was "democratic water" which would give its builders confidence in their own efforts and courage for the next community venture. It would also weaken the foundations of the old order which had promoted this dependency.

Five articles have been selected for this afterword, not because each offers a distinct model or because together they form a unified picture, but because each wrestles with troubling and overlapping ideas that touch on economic survival, the limits of intelligence, the nature of politics and the content of our lives. (One genuine regret is that space limitations ultimately forced the dropping of many less grandly conceived but equally illuminating pieces rooted in a local experience or an individual life.)

We begin with Herbert Hoover in 1920, a decade before he was to confront the Great Depression from the White House. He is perplexed by some of the same evidence of human and physical waste and of energy needs that now move socialist Michael Harrington more than fifty years later. His unhesitating answer as an engineer lies in "some broadvisioned national guidance" to replace the present haphazard development. Engineering and national planning could make the difference. As a democratic socialist Harrington is angered by the inequitable distribution of wealth and power which so plainly emerges in the energy crisis of 1973–74. Where government has intervened it has been largely on the side of privilege. The planning he seeks requires structural changes to allow public determination of the sources and uses of energy.

Economist E.F. Schumacher is not reassured because planning may be in the hands of responsible engineers or compassionate socialists. With Gandhi he is wary of dreams of alternative systems "so perfect that no one will need to be good." His search is for a scale of technology attuned to human interest in feeling competent and creative. J. Bronowski sees no need for the scientist to apologize, even in the ruins of Nagasaki. The spirit of science has humanized our values. He is optimistic that if its imagination and critical demands can be nourished within each of us, the resulting democracy of the intellect will lead to moral and humane explorations of our political problems. To Emile Capouya, however, the restoration of a politics sensitive to daily experience and direct control of the citizen requires nothing short of a thoroughgoing revolution.

NATIONALIZED POWER (1920)

Herbert Hoover

THE TIME HAS ARRIVED in our national development when we must have a definite national program in the development of our great engineering problems. Our rail and water transport, our water supplies for irrigation, our reclamation, the provision of future fuel resources, the development and distribution of electrical power, all cry out for some broad-visioned national guidance. We must create a national engineering sense of provision for the nation as a whole. . . . It is our duty as citizens to give voice to these critical matters of national policy which our daily contact with this, the fundamentally constructive profession, illuminates to us. Just as our medical associations voice the necessity of safeguards to national health; as the bar associations, of safeguards to our judiciary, so the engineers should exert themselves in our national engineering policies. We have none; but we need some, or the next generation will face a lower instead of a higher standard of living than ours.

The development of our transportation, fuel, power, and water under private initiative has been one of the stimuli that has created the greatness of our people. It has been easy to compass when the problems were more local and filled with speculative profits. There, however, arises a time when this haphazard development must be coordinated in order to secure its best results to the nation as a whole. This system has given us a 50 per cent result; if we are to have 100 per cent we must have a national conception and national guidance. This last 50 per cent involves problems beyond individual initiative alone. Not only is individual initiative insufficient because the problems involve political, financial, interstate matters beyond corporate ability, but we have, with practically unanimous consent of the country, adopted a policy of the limitation of profits in the operation of public transportation and power and some other utilities, and, through the pressure of public opinion we are rapidly coming to a limitation of profit in the development of other large sections of national resources which tend to become natural monopolies. While the limitation of these profits makes for public good, on the other hand they also militate against individualistic development of national resources and necessitate the cooperation of the community as a whole to secure initiative for wider development in the national sense.

Certain of our national resources have always been in national ownership, such as waterways. Certain others, such as reclamation, irrigation, distribution of water for power, are rapidly coming under government control. In others, such as timber, coal, and oil, the possible exhaustion brings their conservation or provision for the nation's future into national concern. In our railway problem, national action has until recently been directed wholly to limitation of profits. Latterly, it has undertaken to regulate wages and give some small recognition to the necessity of equipment. But microscopic attention has been given to the greater problem of how to get more transportation, to get it so organized as to secure real economic operation in its broad sense.

We have a long list of such problems. . . . During the past year the American Institute of Mining Engineers undertook to look into the economic situation of this industry as a national whole. It was demonstrated to be the worst functioning industry in the country. Owing to seasonal and other irregularities of demand, the average term of employment in the bituminous industry is less than 190 days per annum. If this industry could be operated a normal work year, 125,000 men could be turned to other production. It is an industry in which 30 per cent more capital is invested than would otherwise be necessary. The cost of coal to the consumer and the risks to the operator are greatly increased, and, above all, it presents a great human problem fraught with all the terrible misery and strikes and justified discontent that flow from intermittent employment.

I am not proposing any nationalization of the coal mines; far from it. What is required is that we should realize that with our necessary social view of prohibition of combination there remains a national problem beyond the solution of any individual coal operator or any group of operators. It must have national guidance and national plan for its solution, a cooperation of great consumers, railways, operators and miners—but what individual operator can do this?

In respect to our coal supplies again, if we would look forward to the next generation, we have a problem of conservation of immense importance. In this connection, it has been ably proposed by our members that the national Government should cooperate in investigating the possibilities of the establishment of a great electrical trunk line throughout the great power-consuming districts of the Northeast, and that we should feed into this great power-road, power generated at the mines and available water sources, drawing from it at every town and city. The consummation of this project means cheaper power to all consumers. It means a great economy in consumption of coal. It means more regularity in output. It thus means greater ability to compete in world manufacture. It means great relief to the railways from expansion. It means an increased standard of living and a decreased cost of living to a very large section of our population. We have again such a problem in providing adequate power resources upon the Pacific Coast, where today hundreds of thousands of acres of fertile land are practically non-producing for lack of pumping power.

Of other problems akin to this, we are confronted throughout the West with the fact that a large portion of our average low water supply is already under engagement for irrigation and power. The time has come when that expansion of the land available for cultivation, or into more intensive cultivation, is a factor of mountain storage of water to increase our stream flows in the low season. We have thus a storage problem on a scale we have not hitherto dreamed of, and, again, it is a problem involving cooperation in financial, economic, distribution, navigation, interstate questions, in which individual initiative must have the assistance of the community.

Another series of such problems lies in our oil supplies. If we are to have a mercantile marine and to maintain our navy on a basis of equivalent efficiency with foreign navies, if we are to maintain the development of the gas engine—the greatest lift in our standard of living and saving of labor in fifty years—we are confronted with the necessity of securing additional oil supplies from outside our own boundaries. Our own supplies, so far as now known, do not represent twenty-five years at our present rate of consumption. The Institute many months ago was the first to give warning to the Federal Government of the gradual absorption of all of the oil sources of the world by other great Powers, and that within a short time we should be dependent upon the good will of these Powers for our necessary oil supplies. No private individual can compete with foreign governments in the measures that they are adopting to hog the resources of the world. This problem again is an engineering problem that requires more than private initiative.

A problem of even more pressing importance than these is the whole question of transportation. At the present moment, our inability to move the commodities which we create is stifling production. It is increasing the cost of distribution and has placed a tax on the American people in decreased production and increased cost of distribution greater than all the taxes imposed by the war.

We have today in Minneapolis ample proof of the frightful cost imposed upon the farmer, consumer, and public. There is a premium over freight cost from ten to twenty cents a bushel for wheat at the mill door compared to wheat in the elevator a few hundred miles away, solely because cars are not available. Either the farmer is losing the amount, or the consumer paying it. Furthermore, to carry the picture further, the railways, in an endeavor to remedy this, are diverting cars from the lumber industry. Already certain mills are partially closed; men are thrown out of employment in the mills and in the building trades. Is this not a price in human misery and national efficiency that warrants some national concern? It is a problem that does not lie alone in expansion of railway facilities. It lies also in the proper expansion of waterways and their coordination with the railway transportation of the country. We have been dabbling in the improvement of water transportation of the United States for a hundred years, and, so far as I know, never yet have we considered it as a problem requiring complete coordination of the entire transport problem for the whole country. We have spent enough money improving useless creeks to have made several competent waterways. Every congressional district in the United States has angled for appropriations for carrying mud from one hole to another as their proper participation in the national plunder. They have never considered that the taxes taken from the people as a whole should be devoted to those points that will benefit the people as a whole.

One result of the policy pursued has been that our waterways have been so badly handled that they have not been able even to compete with the railways, and today, with an enormous increase in railway rates, we find ourselves utterly unable to handle the great bulk commodities of the country at the possible lower charge over our waterways. The opening of the St. Lawrence to ocean-going vessels means five cents a bushel to every farmer in ten States. Likewise, of no less importance are our internal waterways.

These projects have a simple result in the engineer's mind: they make greater production possible with less human effort; they increase the standard of life; they provide for our children. All of these problems are much akin, and the time has come when they need some illumination, guidance, cooperation in their solution from the Federal Government. Nor do I mean a vast extension of federal bureaucracy in federal ownership. If, in the first instance, through an agency of the central Government, we could have an adequate study and preparation of plan and method made of these problems, for engineering development over the next fifty years, viewed solely in their national aspects, we would have taken the first step toward the adequate provision of an increasing standard of living and a lower cost of living for our descendants.

The second step is to determine that our Government will be a government of cooperation, limiting profits surely, but holding to individual initiative as the single hope of human development. In order that we shall have some central point in the Federal Government where these problems may be adequately considered, from which they can be ventilated for the verdict of public opinion, where the business brains of the country can be called into conference and cooperation with the Government, and therefore with the people, the engineers of the United States have proposed time and again that a Cabinet department should be established in Washington, either new or to replace the Interior Department, to which should be assigned the whole question of public works. You are familiar enough with the advantages of such a department from an everyday administration point of view, and enormous saving to the Government from the duplication or competition of the six or seven departments now engaged in engineering construction work of this character, but on this occasion I wish to call your attention to the fact that such a department has become an essential from the point of view of proper consideration and presentation to the American people of these broader national engineering problems, upon which the next generation must depend if our country is to march forward.

SAY WHAT YOU MEAN— SOCIALISM (1974)

Michael Harrington

. . . THERE IS NOW SOME HOPE that America will finally grow up and join all the other advanced industrial democracies in which discussion of socialism is a commonplace.

I noticed this hopeful tendency during the height of the energy consciousness last winter. . . . For a few brief months the disastrous consequences of the normal state of affairs in the United States—that the government follows the priorities of the corporations, with expensive, anti-social results—were writ large on the very surface of everyday experience.

To be sure, people tried to forget the energy crisis the minute the waiting lines vanished from the gas pump. As soon as the OPEC embargo was over, the nation tried to pretend that the winter of its oil discontent had never happened. The difficulty is that the issue will not go away. Assuming the most reassuring of projections—that everyone can get plenty of gas at the corner station (which is not at all certain for even the immediate future)—$50 billion will flow from the affluent West to the OPEC powers this year, a fact which establishment organs like *The Economist* of London understand will change the whole world market. There are possibilities of both recession and further inflation in that incredible transfer of funds, and the $9 billion loss imposed upon the Third World as a result of higher energy prices this year is certain to exacerbate the danger of famine.

. . . The United States will continue to be reminded of the perverseness of its economic system, not by clever Socialist insights but by brutal economic and social facts. In that context, is there a serious political possibility that American liberalism might be forced (as British liberalism was in the early part of the century) to consider basic alternatives to the fundamental structure of this society? And if so, how is that promising development to be encouraged?

Before turning to that specific political issue, let me be a bit more precise about the late capitalist system in America by making a very summary analysis of the energy crisis, which has been forcing some people to think about the issue. Our plight is not primarily the result of the Yom Kippur war and the OPEC boycott that followed upon it. It stems, rather, from the federal socialization of private, corporate goals in the oil industry. In 1950, as part of the anti-Communist strategy in the Middle East, the National Security Council and the Treasury Department secretly decided to allow the American companies to deduct 100 per cent of the taxes they paid to oil-producing powers from their American taxes. This was better than twice the deduction that a normal corporation received; it meant that the industry and the oil-rich governments could raise taxes per barrel and send the bill to the American taxpayer; it laid the basis for a collusive relationship—at first utterly dominated by the companies; now much less so—between the OPEC nations and the oil giants.

Second, President Eisenhower climaxed a generation of oil *dirigisme* in 1959 by imposing oil import quotas. In the name of national defense, we effectively "drained America first" at a cost to consumers—in higher prices for protected American crude—of as much as $4 billion a year. Third, Eisenhower initiated a federal highway program, the most momentous social measure of his administration, which helped destroy the railroads, mass transit, the orderly and planned development of urban space and which reinforced the evils of poverty and racism in the isolated central city. The nation was thus made dependent on the increasingly expensive and decreasingly efficient private car and is still paying in the neighborhood of $5 billion of federal subsidies a year for this destructive inanity. Finally, a whole series of special deductions—for depletion, intangible drilling costs, etc.—were worth billions and turned the profit and loss statements of the big oil companies into exercises in creative writing.

All the outrages which are so plainly visible in the energy crisis are . . . to be found throughout the rest of society. The internal revenue core is a labyrinth of special privileges, providing about $80 billion in tax savings, mainly for the rich, per year; all industry is dependent upon governmental management of the level of effective demand in the economy, a project which is almost always carried out by giving corporations carrots, but which rarely takes to them with a stick; and so on. This is the picture of a capitalist—or corporate collectivist —society, with a governmentally planned economy maximizing the interests of wealthy individuals and big companies.

The result is an incredible maldistribution of wealth. In 1974, so Nixon's Council of Economic Advisers told us this year, the lowest 20 per cent of American families received 5.4 per cent of the national income; the top 5 per cent got 15.9 per cent. That was a slight rise at the bottom (0.3 per cent) and a slight decrease at the top (1.6 per cent) but even that token redistribution falsifies the reality, because the figures omit the imputed rental value of owner-occupied homes and capital gains. A more accurate and shocking computation is the analysis of the distribution of wealth included in the government's recently published Social Indicators. Though the figures date from 1962, there is not the slightest reason to think that there has been any substantial improvement. We are told that the bottom fifth of America owns 0.2 per cent of the wealth, while the top fifth owns 76 per cent. That means that the top fifth possesses three times as much as the other four-fifths!

I have cited these figures and made my summary comments on the energy crisis to stress two propositions: the federal intervention into the economy is ordinarily anti-social because it follows corporate priorities; this intervention results in a continual and probably increasing maldistribution of wealth. On both counts, there are reasons to believe that something is radically wrong with the system itself. It is true, as Marx pointed out, that modes of production do not simply produce goods and services but also perpetuate themselves and their social relationships. That was bad enough when it took place in a relatively *laissez-faire* economy of the 19th century (the model of capitalism in *Das Kapital* is roughly the same one to be found in *The Wealth of Nations*); it is much more intolerable when such oligarchic results are carefully promoted by the power and technology of the democratic state.

. . . The consequences for the liberal approach to reform are serious. For the long-range tendency of the system is anti-liberal and that means that after every surge of social creativity—say the New Deal of the 1930s or the Great Society of the 1960s—the forces of the old order flow into and dominate the new institutions and turn them to their own purposes. Thus Richard Nixon, the one-time free marketeer, is now a Keynesian President who has used wage and price controls (to benefit the rich), run the highest peacetime deficits in our history, and in general employed liberal techniques for conservative ends. The serious pursuit of liberal aims requires that one go beyond liberalism.

. . . It is particularly important to probe the resistance, not simply of American society or of its corporate rulers, but of liberalism itself to a philosophy of structural change—i.e., toward what everyone else in the world rightly calls socialism. Putting aside for a moment the obvious anti-Socialists (businessmen, big and small, and all those under their ideological influence), I call attention to a paradox: if one examines the official positions of Americans for Democratic Action, or the New Democratic Coalition's statement of principles in 1972, they are seen to be Socialist in all respects save one—they do not mention socialism. They are for the redistribution of wealth, for government intervention on behalf of the poor, minorities and working people, and for the extension of public ownership. Why is it, if these liberal organizations urge essentially social democratic programs, that they have so steadfastly refused any social democratic identification? And, much more to the point, does the use of the term "Socialist" make any difference at all? Why bother with 19th-century nomenclature if the late-20th-century substance is satisfactory?

First of all, why do the best of liberals advocate Socialist programs which do not speak their own name? The obvious and compelling answer is politics. In America, with the exception of a few unusual constituencies, the Socialist label is a hindrance in mainstream electoral politics. Socialism is associated in the popular mind with totalitarianism, foreign ideology, atheism. These associations are not true, but unfortunately truth, particularly complicated truth, is no defense in a political struggle. Therefore, the extremely difficult question which must be answered before one can seriously propose to introduce the idea of socialism into American life is, why should any candidate take the risk? If it is possible to campaign for Socialist ideas, as long as they are not so described, why bother with the idea of socialism?

American business supplies the beginnings of an answer. It has taken the idea of socialism with dead seriousness over the past three-quarters of a century, investing considerable time and money to repulse an ideology which never achieved more than 6 per cent of the Presidential vote. Why did the corporations bother so much about the label? In part because businessmen, for all their pride in their pragmatism, are among the most dogmatic ideologues to be found in the nation. Even as sophisticated, informed and empirical a paper as *The Wall Street Journal* becomes in its editorials absolutely metaphysical in its devotion to the free-market panacea. The Committee for Economic Development is much more shrewd and worldly than the National Association of Manufacturers—that is the difference between the *haute* and *petite bourgeoisie*—but I suspect that even the magnates of the CED dream of those marvelous supply-and-demand curves intersecting in a Newtonian, frictionless space to assure the most efficient allocation of resources and happiness. In short, one reason for the anti-socialism of big business is sincerity.

But there is another, more cynical, reason. Anti-socialism is an extremely effective weapon for opposing liberal reform and that has been its realistic political function for generations. Norman Thomas used to tell of the Chicago ward boss in the 1930s who gathered his precinct workers together. "Do you remember," he said, "that we told you last year that Social Security is socialistic and we are against it?" They did. "Well we're for it now. It isn't socialistic any more." In the 1970s that ward boss metamorphosed into Richard Nixon, the Keynesian, the proponent of a guaranteed annual income, the advocate of a form—the cheapest, most private-sector-oriented form, to be sure, but a form, nevertheless—of national health insurance, and so on. Policies which he would have denounced as "socialistic" when he came to Congress in the mid-1940s were now part of dynamic free enterprise.

The point is that as long as the anti-Socialist prejudice is widespread it is an effective barrier to incremental reform. It is not an accident that the Tennessee Valley Authority has never been imitated, though, despite its environmental sins, it is an obvious success. All of that fantasy so expensively and assiduously promoted by the business-owned and -operated power companies—all that anti-socialism—had its effect. Indeed, Sen. Adlai Stevenson's proposed federal gas and oil corporation, based on the TVA model, was introduced with the specific disclaimer that its sponsor remained absolutely loyal to the American economic system (which really means, to the American economic myth).

American anti-socialism also helps create self-fulfilling prophecies which are extremely useful to the conservative cause. If the public is persuaded that the private sector, with its managed desires, its built-in obsolescence, its enormous, unpaid social costs, is the realm of freedom, then politicians will see to it that the public sector is as underfinanced and shoddy as possible. Which, of course, then proves that the public sector is bad, the private sector good. So, when there is a desperate need to expand the public sector—as there is now in the energy industry—we may be sure that the nation will not act, or that, at best, it will act in a timid fashion calculated to give the edge, and even the control, of the public undertaking to the private sector.

So liberals have a very real interest in making the rational discussion of socialism possible in the mainstream of the society; for until that is done liberal reform will be crippled and even blocked. Second, if it is true, . . . that this society is being forced willy-nilly to structural change, the persistence of anti-socialism in the major parties will guarantee that the nation will either not respond to the challenge or will do so on terms dictated by the corporate ideologies. Only those structural changes will be allowed which are certified as non- or anti-Socialist, as in the case of Nixon's use of "Left" techniques for Right purposes. Thus, even though a liberal organization can propose (though not enact) many of the individual components of a Socialist program, the basic animating spirit which must accompany each of those components—that there must be a fundamental change in the distribution of wealth, in the mode of economic decision making and in the very character of our dominant corporate institutions: in short, a wholesale democratization of economic power—will be lacking.

In sum, it is a bitter fact of late-20th-century life that Socialist ideas without the idea of socialism can be, have been, and will be used for reactionary purposes. As the energy crisis, the specter of famine in the poor parts of the globe and all the other basic, structural issues rush in upon us, it is of utmost importance that there be a response as powerful and integrated as the problems that provoke it. That could mean employing Left techniques for Right purposes; but it could, and should mean, socialism.

But how, then, can this last possibility be made political in the America of the mid-1970s?

First of all, one cannot begin by either converting or defeating incumbent liberal politicians. The same reason applies in both cases: in the absence of a mass Socialist consciousness in the electorate (or more precisely, given an anti-Soviet consciousness), practical politicians will not make themselves vulnerable by proclaiming themselves Socialist, and insurgents flying the Socialist banner will not defeat them. The most that a Socialist campaign will achieve under such circumstances is to give aid and comfort to the conservative opponents. Thus the crucial issue at this point is, how can we change the circumstances that limit our options so severely?

. . . I do not for a moment urge a nonelectoral approach to the building of Socialist consciousness—to community organization, or mass education, as counterposed to political campaign involvement. The first way in which the intolerable circumstances can be changed is for Socialists to participate alongside liberals in their common struggle for immediate reform. That is easy enough, particularly since so many liberal demands are . . . quite Socialist in content. In the course of that joint effort, what Socialists must stress is the necessity that an idea of socialism should animate and radicalize all those Socialist ideas.

. . . We must move toward the socialization of energy in the United States. First of all, there must be a coordinated national plan with regard to both the sources and the uses of energy. We cannot go on destructively and irresponsibly proliferating energy needs according to private priorities. That has already brought us a transportation system which has been disastrous for urban life, the poor, the minorities and the environment, to name but a few of the victims. And having allowed ourselves to get into this dangerous and shameful plight because the government acted as the effective agent of the oil companies, we cannot turn to those malefactors and subsidize their control of alternative energy technologies. What energy will be produced and how used must be publicly and democratically decided.

It is no easy task. Socialists, who are particularly aware of events in this area, do not view nationalization as a sovereign and simple remedy. They know from the European experience that nationalized industries often behave exactly

like their private counterparts. Even in America, the Tennessee Valley Authority, which has provided such irrefutable proof of the efficiency and worth of
public enterprise, has also demonstrated a lack of concern for the environment
by encouraging strip mining. The mere transfer of ownership title from a private
to a public corporation can be a technique of reaction, as Bismarck was among
the first to prove. What is needed in the area of energy—and in so many other
spheres of American and world life—is not alone a formal change in ownership
but a substantial change in decision making as well. And that is not quickly
accomplished.

If one could nationalize the entire energy industry at a single stroke, the
most likely effect would be to confer governmental power on the very private
executives who have produced the present miserable situation. The more prudent course is to take three first steps in an ongoing battle to win actual
democratic control:

¶Establish in the executive a national energy planning mechanism whose
proposals would be subject to debate and vote in the Congress.

¶Create a national gas and oil corporation to act as a yardstick and to
develop new sources of energy (shale, coal, gasification and liquefaction, etc.)
for permanent public ownership by the people.

¶Pass a law providing for public (consumer and employee) representatives
on the boards of directors of all major American oil companies for the purpose
of bringing into the open all information with regard to pricing, profits and new
technology.

The allocation of food throughout the United States and the world cannot
be left to agribusiness and multi-billion-dollar export corporations. There
should be a national food plan, charged with expanding production and captur-
ing surpluses in order to turn them over to an international anti-famine authority and to use them within the United States to drive down prices. All family
farmers and genuine cooperatives should be guaranteed a rising standard of
living to be provided, not by subsidies to curtail production and raise prices but
by direct federal expenditure after the greatest possible food yield is achieved.
Agribusiness should be subject to the same kind of controls that are put on the
energy corporations, and the United States should explore the desirability of
nationalizing at least one of the major export concerns.

In this area, as in so many others, the nation cannot arrogantly assume that
it can, or should, continue to consume an enormously disproportionate share
of the world's resources. It is an outrage that even as children starve in Bangladesh and Chad, millions of Americans are suffering from overweight. Barbara Ward has estimated that during the past ten years, one-third of the world's
increased demand for food came not from population increases but from stuffing
by the affluent. The people of the United States use as much fertilizer on their
ornamental gardens as India employs to produce food—and our pets consume
a high percentage of the globe's fish protein.

Third, the assumption that the corporate infrastructure of American society is sound and should be allowed to make basic allocation decisions within a
system provided, and paid for, by the government and the people is clearly false.
In a federally subsidized environment, oil corporations, auto companies, food
giants and the rest of big industry made disastrous choices and were handsomely
rewarded by the public for the harm they did the nation.

All major corporations should be required to have public representatives on the board of directors and to make their fundamental choices in the full light of day. This should specifically include provision for democratic employee participation in decision making at every level, from the shop floor to the board room. Where companies are already primarily wards of the state—the defense corporations, the railroads—they should be taken over and managed by the state. In all cases where either public ownership or board membership is indicated, stringent requirements should be set up for the personnel who will represent the people's interest. Specifically, the commissions which monitor such operations must exclude present or former managers or major stockholders in the industry.

The power of those managers and major stockholders should be permanently abridged by the passage of tax laws which strike at wealth itself. The idea that the accident of birth confers upon a Nelson Rockefeller dominion over hundreds of millions of dollars in assets and billions in economic power is an affront to democratic values. In the "robber baron" period of American enterprise there was at least a semblance of truth in the proposition that entrepreneurs who risked their fortunes should be allowed to benefit from their investments. But in a society in which the internally generated profits of industry provide most "risk" capital and in which the government more and more assumes the responsibility for the economic direction of the society, it is preposterous to allow wealth to pass on from generation to generation. The federal tax code is one of the most important instruments for structurally altering the concentration of economic and political power.

These new policies for energy, food and the corporations are obviously only the beginning of a program which can lead America, and the world, out of the impasse in which both now find themselves. . . .

NIGHT THOUGHTS ABOUT PROGRESS (1974)

E. F. Schumacher

. . . NINETEENTH-CENTURY TECHNOLOGY led the economists to the idea of economies of scale—the bigger the better. There was truth in this idea and it worked. But we have come a long way since then, and in the second half of the 20th century it is not difficult to see that things can become too big—that there are diminishing returns in the economies of scale—and bigness puts people off. Nor is it difficult to see that we now have a science and the *possibility* of technology to make things small again. Today it is true to say that "the economies of scale" was a 19th-century truth which, because of the advance of science and of technological skills, has become—if not all along the line, certainly over wide fields of application—a 20th-century myth.

. . . Most people have not discovered this yet, but that is only because myths are powerful and tend to blind people to new truth. Having tried this particular new truth—albeit, initially, only in the context of the developing countries—I have found that it works. There is no reason at all why we should submit to so-called trends, when they make our lives miserable and destroy our self-respect and when they destroy living nature around us and exhaust the earth's nonrenewable resources.

What we need are design studies for mini-plants. An example is a study which the Intermediate Technology Development Group in London has recently brought to a successful conclusion. . . . I had encountered numerous situations in developing countries where farmers could not get their eggs to market because they could not get hold of egg trays, or, in fact, any packaging material. The smallest unit to produce egg trays, it emerged on investigation, would cost something in the region of £250,000 and turn out a million egg trays a month. The people who needed the egg trays had neither that kind of money nor that size requirement. They could do nothing, then, except go on relying on imports, which had proved unreliable and for which they lacked foreign exchange. The raw material needed for the production of egg trays is waste paper, of which they had a plentiful supply and which they exported at throw-away prices.

Although the manufacturers of the existing production units claimed that anything smaller than their smallest would be hopelessly uneconomic, a small unit—a "mini-plant"—was designed, by going back to "first principles." It was successfully manufactured and is now on sale, costing 2 or 3 per cent of the smallest unit hitherto available and with a capacity of the same order. Far from being uneconomic, the small unit eliminates the need for large and complex business organization, heavy long-distance transport, concentrated raw material and energy supplies. Socially speaking, fifty small units will, of course, have an effect very different from that of one large unit. Production, hitherto reserved to those already rich and powerful, becomes accessible again to "the small man" in a small place, outside the big city.

The example of the egg-packing-material unit is by no means unique. At the same time, I must emphasize that the number of available examples is still small—not because the opportunities are limited but because the work has not been done. In general, people would rather talk about the problems of our time than do something about them. The doing . . . will have to include—as perhaps its most important component—systematic design work to make things small again, to bring them back to human scale.

The implications of a technology moving ever more rapidly in the direction of giantism, complexity and violence are becoming so clear that no great gifts of prophecy are needed to understand where they are taking us. In human terms, giantism leads to frustration all round; it entails a degree of specialization that destroys work satisfaction and produces fragmentary men, too specialized to be wise. In social terms, it means exclusion: an ever increasing proportion of mankind finds itself excluded from the productive process, except in the role of technological gap fillers, whether on the factory floor or in some vast, "open-style" office. The frustration and exclusion disrupt all traditional life patterns and engender widespread irresponsibility, which may well be the most important factor behind the so-called population explosion. In ecological terms, it means damage: the tolerance margins of nature are, it seems, very well adjusted to the "human scale," but—as we can observe only too frequently—they cannot cope with giantism and the violence of super-technology. In resources terms, it means exhaustion. Gigantic industrial concentrations, operating gigantic machines whose primary object is to "save" human labor, have to rely exclusively on highly concentrated resources; this means that naturally concentrated resources, like high-grade ores and the best fossil fuels, are used with the greatest profligacy, while the artificial "concentration" of resources further increases the need for high-grade fuels.

We should now give some real thought to the possibility of reforming our technology in the directions of smallness, simplicity and nonviolence. Striving for nonviolence would mean to try to work with the gentle and incredibly efficient methods of nature instead of bludgeoning nature and forcing one's way through her. Biological processes are normally far less violent than mechanical ones; prevention is nonviolent as compared with cure; recycling is nonviolent as compared with so-called "disposal." Giantism, of course, is of the very nature of violence: it violates all the laws of harmony and balance. We can also say that mass production is violent, whereas production by the masses may be nonviolent. It can easily be seen that smallness—that is, fitting the human scale; simplicity—that is, fitting the fundamentally simple requirements and interests of man; and nonviolence—that is, fitting the *modus operandi* of living nature around us—that these three belong closely together and are really three different aspects of the same thing. It is the opposite of hubris, of the cocksureness of narrow specialists, for whom nobody could be more incomprehensible than Sir Isaac Newton when he said:

> I do not know what I may appear to the world, but to myself I seem to have been only a boy playing on the seashore, and diverting myself in now and then finding a smoother pebble or a prettier shell than ordinary, whilst the great ocean of truth lay all undiscovered before me.

There is nothing more dangerous than the ruthless application of fragmentary knowledge, yet ruthlessness is written all over our present-day technology. If we pride ourselves on the progress made in science and technology since the days of Newton, we should be all the more confident that we can design a survival technology which will amplify life instead of leading straight into ecological disaster. The battle of the future will be between two groups of innovators, whom we might name "the people of the forward stampede" on the one side, and "the homecomers" on the other. The former always talk about "breakthroughs"—a breakthrough a day keeps the crisis at bay—and these breakthroughs almost invariably imply more violence, more inescapable subjugation of man under the requirements of "the system." The latter are concerned with bringing things back to human scale, to real human requirements, and to the organic harmonies of nature.

Agriculture is a vivid example. A great deal of agricultural R&D is going on under various auspices all over the world; it is almost exclusively in the direction of larger scale, greater complexity and more violence. "Organic" agriculture, based on the proper recycling of organic materials, decentralization, diversification and other "natural" principles, receives virtually no official attention, let alone support. Yet it can be said that agricultural systems which utterly and completely depend on the chemical and pharmaceutical industries, which in turn utterly and completely depend on the free availability of nonrenewable materials such as oil, leave much to be desired—particularly if they cannot guarantee the long-term health of soil, plants, animals and men. In Britain an organization called the "Soil Association" has been exploring these problems for twenty-five years—and never received any official support. It is in touch with farmers in many countries who farm productively and profitably without depending on significant inputs from the chemical industry.

Technological talents will have a new direction in which to work, and of course they will have to work with the fullness of modern knowledge and ability. The "homecomers" will require more creativity than "the people of the forward stampede." It takes a touch of genius and a lot of courage to move toward simplicity. One would not expect, therefore, that more than a small fraction of the current R&D will be switched into the new direction; but that small fraction is the price we must pay if we wish to survive. And it needs to be done everywhere—in government, in industry, in agriculture and in academic institutions.

SCIENCE AND HUMAN VALUES (1956)

J. Bronowski

. . . ON AN EVENING some time in 1945 each of us in his own way learned that his imagination had been dwarfed. We looked up and saw the power of which we had been proud loom over us like the ruins of Nagasaki.

The power of science for good and for evil has troubled other minds than ours. We are not here fumbling with a new dilemma; our subject and our fears are as old as the tool-making civilizations. Men have been killed with weapons before now: what happened at Nagasaki was only more massive (for 40,000 were killed there by a flash which lasted seconds) and more ironical (for the bomb exploded over the main Christian community in Japan). Nothing happened eleven years ago except that we changed the scale of our indifference to man; and conscience, in revenge, for an instant became immediate to us. Before this immediacy fades in a sequence of televised atomic tests, let us acknowledge our subject for what it is: civilization face to face with its own implications. The implications are both the industrial slum which Nagasaki was before it was bombed, and the ashy desolation which the bomb made of the slum. And civilization asks of both ruins, *Is You Is Or Is You Ain't Ma Baby?*

The man whom I imagine to be asking this question, wryly with a sense of shame, is not a scientist; he is civilized man. It is of course more usual for each member of civilization to take flight from its consequences by protesting that others have failed him. Those whose education and perhaps tastes have confined them to the humanities protest that the scientists alone are to blame, for plainly no mandarin ever made a bomb or an industry. The scientists say, with equal contempt, that the Greek scholars and the earnest explorers of cave paintings do well to wash their hands of blame; but what in fact are they doing to help direct the society whose ills grow more often from inaction than from error?

There is no comfort in such bickering. When Shelley pictured science as a modern Prometheus who would wake the world to a wonderful dream of Godwin, he was alas too simple. But it is as pointless to read what has happened since as a nightmare. Dream or nightmare, we have to live our experience as it is, and we have to live it awake. We live in a world which is penetrated through and through by science, and which is both whole and real. We cannot turn it into a game simply by taking sides.

And this make-believe game might cost us what we value most: the human content of our lives. The scholar who disdains science may speak in fun, but his fun is not quite a laughing matter. To think of science as a set of special tricks, to see the scientist as the manipulator of outlandish skills—this is the root of the poison mandrake which flourishes rank in the comic strips. There is no more threatening and no more degrading doctrine than the fancy that somehow we may shelve the responsibility for making the decisions of our society by passing it to a few scientists armored with a special magic. This is another dream, the dream of H. G. Wells, in which the tall elegant engineers rule, with perfect benevolence, a humanity which has no business except to be happy. To H. G. Wells this was a dream of heaven—a modern version of the idle, harp-resounding heaven of other childhood pieties. But in fact it is the picture of a slave society, and should make us shiver whenever we hear a man of sensibility dismiss science as someone else's concern. The world today is made, it is powered, by science; and for any man to abdicate an interest in science is to walk with open eyes towards slavery.

Has science fastened upon our society a monstrous gift of destruction which we can neither undo nor master, and which, like a clockwork automaton in a nightmare, is set to break our necks? Is science an automaton, and has it lamed our sense of values?

These questions are not answered by holding a Sunday symposium of moralists. They are not even answered by the painstaking neutralism of the textbooks on scientific method. We must begin from a study of what scientists do when they are neither posed for photographs on the steps of space-ships nor bumbling professorially in the cartoons. But we must get to the *heart* of what they do; we must lay bare the conditions which make it possible for them to work at all.

When we do so we find, leaf by leaf, the organic values which I have been unfolding. And we find that they are not at odds with the values by which alone mankind can survive. On the contrary, like the other creative activities which grew from the Renaissance, science has humanized our values. Men have asked for freedom, justice and respect precisely as the scientific spirit has spread among them. The dilemma of today is not that human values cannot control a mechanical science. It is the other way about: the scientific spirit is more human than the machinery of governments. We have not let either the tolerance or the empiricism of science enter the parochial rules by which we still try to prescribe the behavior of nations. Our conduct as states clings to a code of self-interest which science, like humanity, has long left behind.

The body of technical science burdens and threatens us because we are trying to employ the body without the spirit; we are trying to buy the corpse of science. We are hag-ridden by the power of nature, which we should command, because we think its command needs less devotion and understanding than its discovery. And because we know how gunpowder works, we sigh for the days before atomic bombs. But massacre is not prevented by sticking to gunpowder; the Thirty Years' War is proof of that. Massacre is prevented by the scientist's ethic, and the poet's, and every creator's: that the end for which we work exists and is judged only by the means which we use to reach it. This is the human sum of the values of science. It is the basis of a society which scrupulously seeks knowledge to match and govern its power. But it is not the scientist who can govern society; his duty is to teach it the implications and the values in his work. Sir Thomas More said in 1516 that the single-minded man must not govern but teach; and went to the scaffold for neglecting his own counsel.

The exploration of the artist is no less truthful and strenuous than that of the scientist. If science seems to carry conviction and recognition more immediately, this is because here the critics are also those who work at the matter. There is not, as in the arts, a gap between the functions (and therefore between the fashions) of those who *comment* and those who *do*. Nevertheless, the great artist works as devotedly to uncover the implications of his vision as does the great scientist. They grow, they haunt his thought, and their most inspired flash is the end of a lifetime of silent exploration. Turn to the three versions of *Faust* at which Goethe worked year in and year out. Or watch Shakespeare at work. Early in this essay I quoted from *Romeo and Juliet* the image of death as a bee that stings other people, but that comes to Juliet to drink her sweetness—

> *Death that hath suckt the honey*
> *of thy breath.*

More than ten years later Shakespeare came back to the image and unexpectedly made it concrete, a metaphor made into a person in the drama. The drama is *Antony and Cleopatra;* the scene is the high tower; and to it death comes in person, as an asp hidden among figs. The image of the asp carries, of course, many undertones; and most moving among these is Cleopatra's fancy that this death, which should sting, has come to her to suck the sweetness. Cleopatra is speaking, bitterly, tenderly, about the asp:

> *Peace, peace:*
> *Dost thou not see my Baby at my breast,*
> *That suckes the Nurse asleepe.*

The man who wrote these words still carried in his ear the echo from Juliet's tomb, and what he added to it was the span of his life's work.

Whether our work is art or science or the daily work of society, it is only the form in which we explore our experience which is different; the need to explore remains the same. This is why, at bottom, the society of scientists is more important than their discoveries. What science has to teach us here is not its techniques but its spirit: the irresistible need to explore. Perhaps the techniques of science may be practiced for a time without its spirit, in secret establishments, as the Egyptians practiced their priestcraft. But the inspiration of science for four hundred years has been opposite to this. It has created the values of our intellectual life and, with the arts, has taught them to our civilization. Science has nothing to be ashamed of even in the ruins of Nagasaki. The shame is theirs who appeal to other values than the human and imaginative values which science has evolved. The shame is ours if we do not make science part of our world, intellectually as much as physically, so that we may at last hold these halves of the world together by the same values. For it is the lesson of science that the concept is more profound than its laws, and the act of judging more critical than the judgment. In a book that I wrote about poetry I said,

> *Poetry does not move us to be just*
> *or unjust, in itself. It moves us to*
> *thoughts in whose light justice and*
> *injustice are seen in fearful sharpness*
> *of outline.*

What is true of poetry is true of all creative thought. And what I said then of one value is true of all human values. The values by which we are to survive are not rules for just and unjust conduct, but are those deeper illuminations in whose light justice and injustice, good and evil, means and ends are seen in fearful sharpness of outline.

THE HUMAN MATRIX (1958)

Emile Capouya

THE PRESIDENT OF the United States poses for the camera beside the nose of a guided missile. The President smiles, the missile cone remains impassive. Nothing strange in that. Presidents are flesh and blood, and they often smile. Atomic warheads, of course, simply go off with a bang. It is all quite natural, yet no less embarrassing for being so. If we Americans respond to the President's smile with a sheepish grin, it is because we are embarrassed by the aptness of the tableau. It is a gross symbol for what we all know—that our misdirected technology has worked us into a corner.

Since the beginning of the industrial revolution, our technical advances have had increasingly awkward consequences. Of course, now that we have weapons capable of obliterating man and all his works, the problem posed by a blind technology looks particularly acute. But it is far from new, and it has always been serious. Long before we were offered the final insult of extinction, we were forced to learn how unpleasant life could be (in spite of flush toilets, chemical fertilizers and the internal-combustion engine) when its tempo was made to follow the rhythms of machine production. We even had reason to suspect that the machine had made the ideal of democracy irrelevant—technologically obsolete. We knew something was wrong.

But knowing that something is wrong with our control of science is not the same as an accurate diagnosis, let alone a cure. And, given our climate of thought, an accurate diagnosis is hard to come by. The trouble is that scientific technology is in fact the great mover and shaker in the modern world; it goes against the bias of the age to state the problem in any terms other than those suggested by our preoccupation with the nature and role of science.

Even our political rivalry with the Soviet Union is seen from this point of view. The Russians demonstrate that they are better than we are at rocketry; the practical men who govern us conclude that we must exaggerate the technical bias of our educational system; a cheer goes up from engineering faculties across the nation; an answering clamor is raised by professors in the humanities. The whole comedy revolves around science. Even the opposition has to suggest that traditional liberal education will make us more, not less, fit to beat the Russians at colonizing the fixed stars.

The best of the joke is that, when they are not speaking for their respective trade unions, humanists and technicians, philosophers and scientists, stretch out imploring hands to one another, looking for comfort in their metaphysical distress. It is true that on the issue of education the claims made by both factions are tinged with a certain vulgar *arrivisme;* it sometimes looks as if the sciences and the humanities, in the persons of their professors, are lobbying for dear life, concerned not so much with the shape of the future as with insuring that the future, whatever its shape, has a place for them. But when the campaign is over, the harsh things said in the heat of battle are forgotten. Then Hans Reichenbach warns his fellow philosophers that they must bone up on science or else get left. Then Robert Oppenheimer begs his fellow scientists to break out of their stultifying specialties, and pursue science in a more philosophic spirit. It would seem that the philosopher and the scientist are doomed to wander in search of each other in the conceptual labyrinth that both have created in the modern world.

But what if they should meet in the maze, and join hands, and look deep into each other's eyes—what kind of enlightenment could we expect? Why do we think it important for scientist and humanist to know each other and know each other's trades? Why do we assume that if they cannot understand each other's shoptalk they cannot understand anything? We never used to make that assumption about artisans, craftsmen, or even men who followed a profession. The smith knew that you waxed your thread before sewing with it. The cobbler suspected that hot iron was easier to work than cold. For the rest, it had taken each of them seven years to learn his own trade, and neither thought it necessary, desirable, or even practicable, to learn the other's mystery. Yet they never felt that they could not meet as men and brothers; they did meet, on the level of politics, religion and art, the fundamental concerns of men. If, nowadays, the professor of Romance languages and the professor of theoretical physics feel mutually isolated and alienated, it must be that politics, religion and art are not what they ought to be.

But these are the domain of wisdom, as a trade or specialty is the domain of skill. Politics—the life of the citizen, or the life of common action; religion —the sanction for action, or the life of common values; art—the gratuitous aesthetic, or the life of communion and self-recognition: these are the manlike activities. All others are instrumental and illiberal, and there is no use in making a mystique of them. Trades and professions begin as a compound of tinkering and drudgery, and civilization does not reside in them. Politics, religion and art are the human, the civil, matrix. And if the virtue has gone out of that sphere, if politics, religion and art are dead, our first concern must be to revivify them.

Politics is dead because its present-day goals respond to no significant need, and because its direction is not in the hands of the people whom, by courtesy, we call citizens. Our politics is concerned, on the internal level, with administering the division of profits produced by our industrial machine, according to a system that is not just, humanly useful, or otherwise edifying. Externally, it carries on a dangerous rivalry with other great industrial complexes. In the formation and execution of the policies that make up our politics, the citizen has no voice, no function. The two great vote-gathering machines, the Republican and Democratic parties, harvest the suffrages of the qualified voters most efficiently; nevertheless the parade of consultation is a farce because, by and large, no serious issues are allowed to emerge. We may debate in public which branch of our armed forces is to bear the chief responsibility and get the largest share of power and glory in the struggle with the Russians. But we are not vouchsafed the privilege of debating whether or not to fight the Russians at all; and yet that issue might make more sense to the voter than any other.

Breathing life into politics will take two things: defining goals that are useful and (if I may be forgiven the word) elevating, and facilitating the citizen's active participation in his own destiny. We know the arguments against the practicability of mass democracy, or Utopian communities, or phalansteries, or, for that matter, the town meeting. Nevertheless, we simply cannot afford to leave the situation as it is, a nexus of patronage and intimidation on every level from ward to nation. There are good, practical reasons for not meddling with that corrupt system, but they appeal only to those who are satisfied with a shadowplay in place of a living politics.

Religion, the moral springs of action, our codified ethos, is dead because it is a rubber-stamp for our dead politics. Perhaps religion, by its nature, must always be after the fact. Perhaps it must always be the rationalization of our actions rather than the inspiration therefor. But it might be worth a little effort to find out if that sad conclusion is necessarily so. We all suspect that a great upheaval would occur if the holy texts were ever taken seriously by those who profess the faith; maybe the first step would be for the preachers to take themselves seriously, instead of acting as unpaid and unregarded apologists for the status quo.

Art, of course, is a matter of nerve-tone and muscle-tone, a matter of energy, exuberance, élan. A living art never yet coiffed a dead politics and a dead religion. Before the life of communion and self-recognition can become meaningful, we must live the life of common action on a manlike level, and in the light of values worthy of being entertained by men.

What we have been talking about amounts to revolution, a new deal all round. It is unfortunate that the very notion of radical change is in such discredit today, when we are in a state of crisis that calls for nothing less. Our unwillingness to contemplate the necessity of revolution is a sad legacy of the thirties, and the fiasco in which the doctrinaire and self-satisfied program of the Marxists ended. To design a revolution worthy of the name would be to take up the responsibility for carrying on Western civilization—a responsibility that our leaders have abdicated. The possibility of an atomic war, the encroachment of mindless industrialism, the emergence of the super-state with its rites, tests and penalties—any of these may put a period to all speculation about liberty and all practical concern for it. Our manhood demands that we begin at once to think seriously about the direction that a humanly useful revolution should take.

Index

sion, 177–81; distribution system, 182–85; divestiture legislation, 296; early years, 130–31, 161–64; encroachment on national oil reserves, 138–43; energy crisis role, 273–300; exploratory drilling, 164–67, 247, 249–50, 293, 297; foreign policy influence, 199–201, 211, 215–16, 222–26, 230; and geothermal development, 389; government subsidies, 379–80, 406; independents, 166, 171, 173, 175, 179, 182, 183, 184, 185, 186, 218, 261, 262; and national interest, 376; New Deal, 181–86; nuclear investments, 345, 358; permanent interests, 146; political influence of, 288–93, 399; post–World War I, 164–71, 178; and private utilities, 119, 121, 123, 142; profits, 139, 144, 147, 177, 285; propaganda and lobbying, 133, 159, 173, 186, 214, 220, 273–77, 294–300; railroads and, 161, 171, 185–86; regulation of, 143, 145, 163, 164, 170–71, 180, 254–55, 273, 298–99; research and development, 293; resistance to pollution control, 276; safety record, 167–70; and synfuel development, 319–20, 368, 371, 373, 381–82, 384–85; tax breaks, 196–98, 231, 244–45, 249, 258; and World War I, 128–30, 177; in World War II, 128–30, 187–92, 226, 239. *See also* international oil cartel; oil crisis; oil exports; oil imports; oil monopoly; oil prices; oil production; oil refining and refineries; pipelines
oil monopoly: vs. agriculture, 190; and anti-trust laws, 171, 191–92, 278–82; basis of, 166–67, 172–76; and chemical industry, 190, 192; control of markets, 172–76, 182, 254, 279–82; control of pipelines, 185–88; growth of, 161–64, 172–76; Latin American exploitation, 199–201, 205–7, 211–15; mergers and takeovers, 255; price-fixing, 171, 180, 181, 182, 278–82, 291–93; proration policy, 176–81; railroads and, 185–86; World War II, 187–92. *See also* Congress; international oil cartel; multinational corporations; oil industry; Standard Oil companies
oil pipelines, *see* pipelines
oil policy, *see* energy policy; names of presidential administrations
oil prices: Arab stake in, 258; cartel cuts, 246, 258–59; in Depression, 177; Libyan, 261; Mexican, 202, 203; multinational policies, 171, 180, 181, 182, 253–54, 278–82, 291–93; New Deal controls, 181–85; in 1920's, 178; and oil consumption, 252; OPEC policies, 235, 241, 246, 252–53, 254, 262, 270, 272, 292, 296; and resource allocation, 252–53; spot-market, 235, 291–92; World War II, 243
oil production: cartel-controlled, 241; from coal, 41, 220, 221, 367; crude, 164–67, 172, 177, 186, 283, 286; excess capacity, 245; for home heating, 283, 286, 287, 292–93; non-Arab, 251; offshore, 253; and oil prices, 259; OPEC policies, 253, 259, 260, 263–64, 279; pollution from, 144, 148–52; proration, 177–81; Saudi policy, 263–64, 267, 269–70, 283; from shale, 176, 256, 319, 367, 377–80, 384; waste, 164–67, 177–81, 276–77. See also Arab oil; oil exploration; oil industry; oil refining and refineries; names of countries
oil refining and refineries, 145, 162, 172, 174; American, 247, 248; Asian, 247; in energy crisis, 281, 285, 286, 291; European, 247, 248; hydrogenation process, 176; Iran, 236–37, 238; Mexican, 201–2, 203, 205; and price-fixing, 184; and proration, 179; for shale oil, 378, 379. *See also* oil industry; oil production; names of countries
oil resources, *see* American oil and gas resources; Arab oil; names of countries

Oil Shale Corporation of Los Angeles, 379
oil shortage, *see* energy crisis; oil crisis
oil spills, 147–52
oil tankers, 148–52, 277, 291; for Alaskan oil, 156, 158, 160; diverted to Europe, 291; Liberian, 150; stockpiling supplies on, 285
oil workers: Iranian, 233–38; Mexican, 203–4
Oklahoma, 95, 178–79
Oklahoma Corporation Commission, 178, 179, 180
Old Ben Coal Company, 45
Olds, Leland, 193, 303, 312–21, 422
O'Leary, John F., 297
Olin Aluminum, 81
Oman, 260
Olmsted, Frederick Law, xvii
Olson, McKinley C., 303, 321–39, 422
One Hundred Years of Solitude (Marquez), 214
OPEC, *see* Organization of Petroleum Exporting Countries
Opinion Research, Inc., 316
Oppenheimer, J. Robert, 418
Oregon, 110; bottle recycling, 394; electricity rates, 77; (oil) antitrust suit, 278–82; public power systems, 69, 82, 88. *See also* Pacific Northwest
Oregon Reclamation Congress, 90–91
Organization for Economic Cooperation and Development, 284
Organization of Petroleum Exporting Countries (OPEC), 215, 237, 370, 371, 384, 400, 405; agenda in the 1970's, 263; and Arab nationalist struggles, 260–62; Caracas meeting (1980), 271; Doha conference (1976), 267; and the energy crisis, 262, 281; fair returns for, 257; formation of, 245, 258–59; future of, 264–65; history of, 257–65; and international oil cartel, 251–57, 258–65; Kissinger-Ford policies, 252, 255–56; Libya and, 260–62; and Mexican oil, 205, 207; 1971 agreements, 241, 245–46; participation demands, 263; political character of, 260; price policies, 235, 241, 246, 252–53, 254, 262, 270, 272, 292, 296; production policies, 253, 259, 260, 263–64, 279; reserves, 264; Third World and, 270–72; world economy role, 258. *See also* Arab oil; Middle East politics; oil diplomacy; names of countries
O'Rourke, Terence, 291–92
Osborn, Elburt, 31, 32
Ottinger, Richard, 374, 375
Ottoman Empire, 242
Outer Continental Shelf Lands Act (1953), 294

P & P Coal Company, 45
Pacific Gas and Electric, 101, 122, 123, 317; and Elk Hills oil field, 142
Pacific Northwest, 81–92, 93; fishing and lumbering industries, 85, 92; fuel shortage, 89; geothermal energy for, 389; organized labor, 91; postwar planning for, 84–92; public utility districts, 81–84, 91, 93; in World War II, 81–85, 87. *See also* West Coast; names of states
Pacific Power and Light Company, 91
Pacific Western Oil, 197
Packard, David, 142
Page, Howard W., 244
Pahlavi, Mohammad Reza, 277, 233–38, 241, 246. *See also* Iran
Palestine and Palestinians, 130, 132, 222–26, 260, 262, 263, 269, 270; pipeline sabotage, 261; as threat to

ABOUT THE EDITOR AND CONTRIBUTORS

ROBERT ENGLER, editor of *America's Energy,* professor of political science at the City University of New York, author of the influential *The Politics of Oil* and *The Brotherhood of Oil.*

HARRIETTE SIMPSON ARNOW, author of *The Dollmaker* and other novels and social histories of the Cumberland pioneers.

GEORGE L. BAKER, staff writer for a West Coast chain of newspapers.

PAUL A. BARAN, economist, author of *The Political Economy of Growth* and, with Paul M. Sweezy, of *Monopoly Capital.*

DONALD L. BARLETT & JAMES B. STEELE: Pulitzer Prize winning investigative team from the *Philadelphia Inquirer,* authors of *Empire: The Life, Legend and Madness of Howard Hughes.*

J. D. BERNAL, British physicist, author of *The Social Function of Science* and *Science in History.*

WENDELL BERRY, poet and novelist, author of *The Broken Ground* and *The Unsettling of America.*

SHELDON BIERMAN, attorney, co-author of *Innovation and Monopoly: Geothermal Energy in the West.*

KAI BIRD, journalist with extensive experience in the Middle East, associate editor of *The Nation* and co-author of *Bangladesh: The Unfinished Revolution.*

THOMAS BROM, consultant for the Community Ownership Organizing Project, Oakland, California.

J. BRONOWSKI, mathematician, and literary and scientific writer, author of *William Blake: A Man Without a Mask* and *Science and Human Values.*

JAMES M. CAIN, journalist and novelist, author of *The Postman Always Rings Twice.*

EMILE CAPOUYA, former literary editor of *The Nation*, senior editor at several publishing houses, and teacher.

BRUCE CATTON, contributing editor of *The Nation* and author of *The War Lords of Washington.*

HARRY M. CAUDILL, Kentucky attorney, author of *Night Comes to the Cumberlands* and *The Watches of the Night.*

STUART CHASE, economist, author of *The Tragedy of Waste* and *Rich Land, Poor Land.*

GORDON R. CLAPP, long-time executive and then board chairman of the Tennessee Valley Authority, author of *TVA: An Approach to the Development of a Region.*

MCALISTER COLEMAN, labor journalist, author of *Men and Coal.*

JOHN COLLINS, writer, business and technical journals.

FRED J. COOK, journalist and regular contributor to *The Nation,* author of *The Warfare State* and *The Nightmare Decade.*

MORRIS LLEWELLYN COOKE, engineer and power expert, directed Giant Power Survey for Pennsylvania Governor Gifford Pinchot, first head of the Rural Electrification Administration.

EDWARD COWAN, correspondent, *The New York Times,* author of *Oil and Water: The Torrey Canyon Disaster.*

CHARLES F. EDMUNDSON, journalist, associate editor of *Fortune* magazine.

ROSCOE FLEMING, columnist for the *Denver Post* and other publications.

L. THOMAS GALLOWAY, attorney for the Center for Law and Social Policy, has focused on coal mine safety and health.

JAMES GANNON, television news writer, producer NBC News *Weekend* and *Prime Time Sunday.*

JULIAN HALEVY, novelist and correspondent who has covered Mexico.

WALTON HAMILTON, economist and law professor, author of *The Politics of Industry* and co-author of *The Case of Bituminous Coal.*

WILLIAM HARD, Washington correspondent for *The Nation.*

MICHAEL HARRINGTON, political scientist and chairman of the Democratic Socialist Organizing Committee, author of *The Other America* and *Toward a Democratic Left.*

MARK HERTSGAARD, with the Institute of Policy Studies in Washington, where he does research on the nuclear power industry.

ERNEST F. HOLLINGS, United States Senator from South Carolina, chairman of the Senate National Ocean Policy Study and sponsor of the Coastal Zone Management Act.

HERBERT HOOVER, mining engineer, Secretary of Commerce, 1921–1928 and President of the United States, 1929–1932.

GAILLARD HUNT, Washington attorney, with the United States Department of Energy at its founding.

KEITH HUTCHISON, former *Nation* editor, author, *The Decline and Fall of British Capitalism.*

BRUCE JOHANSEN, journalist, co-author, *Wasi'chu: The Continuing Indian Wars.*

ROBERT KAPER, a Washington-based freelance writer.

A. KESSEL, Iranian engineer, formerly employed by the Anglo-Iranian Oil Company, and research assistant, University of Chicago, specializing in underdeveloped areas.

JUDSON KING, reformer, advocate of public power, director of National Popular Government League, and author of *The Conservation Fight: From Theodore Roosevelt to the Tennessee Valley Authority.*

ERNEST KIRSCHTEN, editor of editorial page of *St. Louis Star-Times.*

FIORELLO H. LA GUARDIA, Congressman from New York for ten years and mayor of New York City, 1934–1945.

PENNY LERNOUX, Latin-American correspondent for *The Nation* and Copley News Service, author of *Cry of the People.*

IRVING LIKE, Long Island attorney, represents communities and citizen groups before regulatory agencies and in court, challenging electric rate increases, offshore drilling, and nuclear power development.

DUANE LOCKARD, from a family of coal miners, a political scientist and author of *The Perverted Priorities of American Politics.*

BARROW LYONS, formerly economist for Securities and Exchange Commission.

J. DAVITT McATEER, attorney for the Center for Law and Social Policy, staff of the United Mine Workers during reform period, author of *Coal Mine Health and Safety.*

MARK McKEON, a freelance writer who lives in St. Joseph, Minnesota.

CAREY McWILLIAMS, editor *The Nation,* 1951–1976, author of *Ill Fares the Land* and of *The Education of Carey McWilliams.*

LEE METCALF, United States Senator from Montana, long-time critic of private utilities and corporate power, co-author of *Overcharge.*

MARCELLE MICHELIN has lived in Venezuela, been Paris correspondent for France-Amerique (New York), and has published several works of fiction.

RICHARD MUNSON, coordinator for Solar Lobby and the Center for Renewable Resources.

GEORGE W. NORRIS, United States Senator from Nebraska, champion of public hydroelectric development which culminated in the TVA, author of *Fighting Liberal* (autobiography).

HARVEY O'CONNOR, journalist and labor editor, author of *The Empire of Oil* and *World Crisis in Oil.*

LELAND OLDS, authority on electric power development and natural gas regulation, served ten years as member and then chairman of the Federal Power Commission.

McKINLEY OLSON, a Chicago-based editor-writer-photographer, former editor and editorial writer for the *York* (Pa.) *Gazette and Daily.*

JULIA PRESTON, writer on Latin American affairs, who is currently doing a study of the destruction of Indian cultures in modern Peru.

STEPHEN (H.S.) RAUSHENBUSH, economist, activist critic of the power industry, author of *Power Control* and *The Power Fight.*

WALLACE I. ROBERTS, reporter on the *Providence Journal-Bulletin.*

WILLIAM H. RODGERS, JR., law professor, author of *Brown-Out: The Power Crisis in America* and *Corporate Country.*

MARY ROSS, associate editor of *Survey,* who devoted special attention to the subject of public health.

E. F. SCHUMACHER, economist and founder of the Intermediate Technology Department Group in London, author of *Small Is Beautiful: Economics as if People Mattered* and *A Guide for the Perplexed.*

LOUIS B. SCHWARTZ, professor of law and economics, formerly with the Antitrust Division of the U.S. Department of Justice, author of *Free Enterprise* and *Economic Organization.*

CURTIS SELTZER, scholar and journalist who has followed the coal industry, is currently doing a study of the mine worker reform movement.

JOHN SHATTUCK, a legislative director of the American Civil Liberties Union and the head of its Washington office.

ROBERT SHERRILL, White House correspondent for *The Nation,* author of *Gothic Politics in the Deep South* and *Why They Call It Politics: A Guide to America's Government.*

GEORGE SOULE, economist, former director of the National Bureau of Economic Research, editor of *The New Republic,* and author of *A Planned Society* and *Planning, U.S.A.*

GEORGE W. STOCKING, economist, author of *The Oil Industry and The Competitive System,* and co-author of *Monopoly and Free Enterprise.*

I. F. STONE, former Washington co-editor of *The Nation,* founder and editor of I. F. Stone's *Weekly,* and author of *Business as Usual* and *The Haunted Fifties.*

JOE STORK, editor of MEREP, journal of Middle East Research and Education Project, and author of *Middle East Oil and the Energy Crisis.*

RAYMOND GRAM SWING, journalist and radio commentator, author of *Forerunners of American Fascism.*

LEO SZILARD, physicist, active in atomic research and development, co-author of Franck report urging that atom bomb not be used against Japan, and active in postwar movement to control military use.

JOHN TIRMAN, political and economic researcher, specializing in energy for a national magazine.

JAMES PETER WARBASSE, surgeon and first president of the Cooperative League of America, author of *Cooperative Democracy.*

COLSTON E. WARNE, economist and president of Consumers Union.

HARVEY WASSERMAN, anti-nuclear activist, author of *Harvey Wasserman's History of the United States* and *Energy War: Reports from the Front.*

JACK WAUGH, reporter, *Christian Science Monitor,* covering the Southwest.

MEL WAX, urban affairs writer for the *San Francisco Chronicle,* and later public affairs director of educational TV station KQED in San Francisco.

NORBERT WIENER, mathematician, author of *Cybernetics: Or Control and Communication in the Animal and the Machine* and *The Human Use of Human Beings: Cybernetics and Society.*